Principles of Business Forecasting

Keith Ord
Georgetown University

Robert Fildes
Lancaster University

 SOUTH-WESTERN
CENGAGE Learning™

Australia · Brazil · Canada · Mexico · Singapore · Spain · United Kingdom · United States

Principles of Business Forecasting

Keith Ord, Robert Fildes

Senior Vice President, LRS/Acquisitions & Solutions Planning: Jack W. Calhoun

Editorial Director, Business & Economics: Erin Joyner

Editor-in-Chief: Joe Sabatino

Sr. Acquisitions Editor: Charles McCormick, Jr.

Developmental Editor: Kendra Brown

Marketing Coordinator: Eileen Corcoran

Sr. Content Project Manager: Martha Conway

Media Editor: Chris Valentine

Manufacturing Planner: Ron Montgomery

Sr. Marketing Communications Manager: Libby Shipp

Production Service: MPS Ltd.

Sr. Art Director: Stacy Shirley

Internal Designer: Mike Stratton

Cover Designer: Lou Ann Thesing

Cover Image: iStock Photo

Sr. Rights Acquisitions Specialist: Deanna Ettinger

Permissions Researcher: Jillian Santos, PreMedia Global

For product information and technology assistance, contact us at **Cengage Learning Customer & Sales Support, 1-800-354-9706**

For permission to use material from this text or product, submit all requests online at **www.cengage.com/permissions** Further permissions questions can be emailed to **permissionrequest@cengage.com**

Microsoft® Office Excel® is a registered trademark of Microsoft Corporation in the U.S. and/or other countries. All rights reserved.

Microsoft Office Excel screenshots are © 2012 Microsoft Corporation. All rights reserved.

SPSS® is a registered trademark of IBM. © Copyright IBM Corporation 1994, 2012.

SAS screenshots are Copyright © 2011 SAS Institute Inc., SAS Campus Drive, Cary, North Carolina 27513, USA. All rights reserved.

The names of all products mentioned herein, including @Risk, Minitab, EViews, ForecastPro, and OxMetrics, are used for identification purposes only and may be trademarks or registered trademarks of their respective owners. South-Western disclaims any affiliation, association, connection with, sponsorship, or endorsement by such owners.

Library of Congress Control Number: **2011933702**
ISBN-13: 978-0-324-31127-3
ISBN-10: 0-324-31127-3

South-Western
5191 Natorp Boulevard
Mason, OH 45040
USA

Cengage Learning products are represented in Canada by Nelson Education, Ltd.

For your course and learning solutions, visit **www.cengage.com** Purchase any of our products at your local college store or at our preferred online store **www.cengagebrain.com**

Printed in the United States of America
1 2 3 4 5 6 7 16 15 14 13 12

About the Authors

Keith Ord is Sebes Fellow and Professor of Operations and Information Management at the McDonough School of Business at Georgetown University. He received his Ph.D. in theoretical statistics from the University of London and held faculty positions at the Universities of Bristol and Warwick before moving to the Pennsylvania State University in 1980 and then to Georgetown University in 1999. His research interests include time series and forecasting, spatial modeling, and the statistical modeling of business processes. He is a coauthor of *Forecasting with Exponential Smoothing: The State Space Approach* (2008), and he also coauthored Kendall's *Advanced Theory of Statistics*. He is a past editor and current associate editor of the *International Journal of Forecasting* and also serves on the editorial boards of several other journals. Keith is a Fellow of the American Statistical Association and of the International Institute of Forecasters.

Robert Fildes is Distinguished Professor of Management Science in the Management School, Lancaster University, and Director of the Lancaster Centre for Forecasting. He has a mathematics degree from Oxford and a Ph.D. in statistics from the University of California. He was cofounder of the *Journal of Forecasting* in 1981 and of the *International Journal of Forecasting (IJF)* in 1985. From 1988 through 1997, he was editor-in-chief of the *IJF* and remains an associate editor. He was president of the International Institute of Forecasters between 2000 and 2004. His research interests are concerned with the comparative evaluation of different forecasting methods, the implementation of improved forecasting procedures in organizations, and the design of forecasting systems. In 1976, he wrote one of the earliest business forecasting textbooks. Although the book is long out of print, many of its core ideas have survived the test of time, to surface again here in a more modern disguise. Robert is a Fellow of the International Institute of Forecasters and of the Operational Research Society.

Brief Contents

The Appendices are located on the textbook companion site. **Students:** *Visit* **www.cengagebrain.com** *and search using ISBN 9780324311273.*

Contents

Note: Topics marked with an "*" are advanced and may be omitted as needed for introductory courses.

*The Appendices are located on the textbook companion site. **Students:** Visit **www.cengagebrain.com** and search using ISBN 9780324311273.*

Preface

Business forecasting is art woven into science and principle teamed with pragmatism. Virtually every manager has to make plans or decisions that depend on forecasts. Research over the past 50 years shows that taking an analytical approach, rather than just relying on informal intuition, leads to more accurate forecasts and more effective plans and decisions. However, forecasting is often the poor relation of more theoretical statistical material in regression and time series analysis. Despite our backgrounds as statisticians and management scientists, we believe that this approach is misguided and think that a student leaving business school should know how to produce a reasonable forecast and how to evaluate the forecasts of others.

Forecasting is important: Every day we are confronted with forecasts ranging from predictions of the weather to prognostications of stock prices and the state of the economy. Our motivation in writing this book is to provide business and management students with the tools and the insights to make effective forecasts. But we also aim to assist practitioners and managers who need guidance on how to improve their performance within their line of work.

Focus of the Book

What makes this book unique is its emphasis on incorporating the latest research findings to help practicing forecasters carry out their job and to enable students to prepare for a managerial or analytical career. The book not only provides an introduction to both standard and advanced approaches to forecasting, but also presents general principles that underlie forecasting practice. In turn, we show how good practice can be established within a systematic framework for the forecasting enterprise. The book builds unashamedly on Scott Armstrong's reference book, *Principles of Forecasting* (2001), although our focus here is on putting these principles to work to produce forecasts.

As a starting point, we recognize that there can never be just one approach to forecasting that meets all needs, but that we must invest in "horses for courses."[1] To achieve that goal, we consider a series of steps summarized by the mnemonic **PHIVE** (pronounced "five" or "pea-hive," according to taste). The letters stand for the five stages of forecasting that must be incorporated into the forecasting task:

> **P**urpose
>
> **H**orizon
>
> **I**nformation
>
> **V**alue
>
> **E**valuation.

Chapter 1 elaborates on these concepts.

In short, good forecasting is a challenge. This observation means that the reader must engage in working on real data with all its aberrations. Wherever possible, we have used information from actual governmental or business sources, so that it is possible to go

---

[1] For U.S. readers, this British racing term means that certain horses run better on certain courses. In the context of this book, it means that certain forecasting approaches are better for certain purposes.

back to the source and update the database. Not only does this activity make forecasting more realistic, but we also get to see how well our forecasts did with the new *out-of-sample* data.

As technology improves, databases expand exponentially and most forecasting activities become unthinkable without a computer and well-designed software. Good programs are continuously evolving and tend to focus on different aspects of the forecasting enterprise (e.g., sales or macroeconomics). Accordingly, we have used a variety of software in the book, so that the user can link the methodology to his or her available resources. Our only caveat is to recommend strongly that you, the reader, have effective forecasting software available!

At the end of each chapter, we list a set of principles that the forecaster should keep in mind. Some of these—such as "Check the data for outliers"—may seem obvious, but if they are overlooked, the result may be a forecasting disaster. Just as the driver of an automobile must pay simultaneous attention to multiple indicators, the effective forecaster must internalize these principles in everyday practice.

No book can include all aspects of forecasting and answer every question. Nevertheless, we have tried to provide resources that enable the most comprehensive coverage possible. We include end-of-chapter *Exercises* that lead the reader from the classroom toward the role of practicing forecaster. We also include *Discussion Questions* throughout each chapter and *Minicases* at the end of most chapters, aimed to stimulate thinking beyond the narrow confines of the technical issues. Three online appendices provide, respectively, a summary of basic statistical methods, a glossary of technical terms, and a description of available forecasting software.

In the end, the successful forecaster has to engage with all the complexities of real data in an organizational setting. We hope that this book meets the challenge of providing a set of operational principles that helps the user in that quest.

Structure of the Book

Introduction (Chapters 1 and 2) Chapter 1 provides an overview of forecasting, including a variety of situations in which both time series and cross-sectional data can help the forecaster's understanding; then Chapter 2 introduces the basic statistical tools that are needed in later chapters. The remainder of the book falls into three parts.

Extrapolative Methods (Chapters 3–6) The focus of these chapters is on using a single time series to forecast in the short to medium term—so-called *extrapolative methods*. In Chapter 3, we consider regular (nonseasonal) time series and introduce *exponential smoothing* methods for series with and without a trend. This is perhaps the "industry-standard" approach to forecasting for many important applications. We then extend the discussion in Chapter 4 to include seasonal series, particularly the so-called Holt–Winters methods, but also give attention to seasonal adjustment procedures that are important for macroeconomic series.

The discussion in Chapters 3 and 4 is limited to forecasting *methods*, which can provide useful point forecasts but do not produce measures of uncertainty. Thus, in Chapter 5 we consider the class of *state-space models*, which provides a natural framework for exponential smoothing and allows the creation of prediction intervals. State-space models are closely linked to the *AutoRegressive Integrated Moving Average* (ARIMA) models developed by George Box and Gwilym Jenkins, two of the famous names in forecasting, so Chapter 6 explores this connection and develops prediction intervals with the use of these models. However, just as point forecasts change, so do the related measures of uncertainty; hence, in Chapter 6 we also consider models for changing uncertainty (*ARCH/GARCH* models), which are widely used in financial analysis.

Statistical Model Building (Chapters 7–9) Business forecasting involves both the analysis of time series and the use of cross-sectional databases (e.g., the decisions by banks and companies to extend credit to new customers). We begin these developments by considering simple *linear regression* in Chapter 7, where we examine the use of a single predictor variable to assist in explaining the variations in the dependent variable to be forecast. This discussion leads naturally to the topic of *multiple regression*—the use of two or more predictor variables—in Chapter 8.

Model development and checking are the themes of Chapter 9. Although it sometimes appears that regression modeling is just a matter of downloading the database and running a suitable statistical program, genuine applications involve the careful selection of variables and database building. Even when those phases are complete, the resulting model must be checked to ensure that the final form satisfies—or at least approximates—the underlying statistical assumptions. These models also need to produce forecasts that are more accurate than those provided by simpler extrapolative alternatives.

Advanced Methods and Forecasting Practice (Chapters 10–13) The material in these chapters forms an essential knowledge base for the modern forecaster but might be beyond a first course in forecasting. As the forecasting literature expands, new methods emerge and solutions to new problems are developed. Thus, Chapter 10 covers more advanced techniques, such as *classification* and *regression trees, logistic regression, neural networks*, and *vector autoregressive* models. These topics have seen considerable theoretical development in the last few years and have clear implications for improved practice.

Forecasting practice often relies heavily on subjective judgments by experts—and nonexperts—in the field. In Chapter 11, we consider different approaches to *judgmental forecasting* and discuss when judgmental inputs can add value. The choice to use either judgmental or quantitative forecasting methods is a false dichotomy, because the correct answer is often to use both in combination to capitalize on their respective strengths.

Procedures for comparing forecasting methods—often a "hot topic" for an organization—are fraught with difficulties, so in the two final chapters we focus attention on forecasting in practice. The first section of Chapter 12 considers the core question of how forecasts and forecasting methods should be evaluated. The second section examines how forecasts are prepared in organizations through a software-based *forecasting support system*. We consider what characterizes an effective support system and how such systems and the methods they contain should be evaluated. We also cover three important application areas in more detail: operations, marketing, and modeling that is focused on individual customer behavior.

Because the purpose of forecasting is to aid planning, and the reason for planning is to ensure that "things don't just happen," the best models in the world will not help if the forecaster and the user are not communicating properly. Accordingly, Chapter 13 examines the construction of a forecasting system within an organization, concentrating on the interaction between the forecaster and the user of the forecasts. Unfortunately, forecasts are rarely as accurate as their users would like, so this final chapter also considers the risks of inaccurate forecasts and how organizations can try to cope with the remaining uncertainties.

Use of the Book

Although Chapter 2 includes a brief summary of basic statistical methods, this text assumes that most readers have taken a first course in applied statistics or have an equivalent background. In our experience, many students have an interest in forecasting beyond the formulas and routines that sometimes form the core of statistical or econometrics courses. However, occasionally we have been forced to include material that is more demanding mathematically and/or statistically. We have designated those sections, as well as more advanced exercises, with an asterisk (*). Thus, we anticipate that the book might appeal to three broad groups of readers:

MBA Students and Advanced Undergraduates in Business Chapters 1–4 and 7–9 would form the core of the course, supported by Chapters 5 and 6 or by Chapters 11 and 13, depending on whether the course was more technically or organizationally focused.

Master's Degree Programs in Applied Statistics, Management Science, and Operations Chapters 1–10 and 12 would be the principal components of a course for students in these programs, with the expectation that much of Chapters 2 and 7 could be omitted.

Forecasting Practitioners The modern forecaster who wishes to be on top of the latest ideas should ultimately become familiar with all the material in the book, although we would expect him or her to chart a course like one of those just outlined and then build on that knowledge with experience. However, some forecasters have a more limited developmental agenda that is focused on their particular organizational responsibilities. For an operations forecaster, Chapters 1–4 should be supplemented by Chapter 7, Chapter 11, and the sections of Chapter 12 that discuss evaluation and operations. Marketing forecasters also need to develop their skills in regression (Chapters 8 and 9), as well as the sections of Chapter 12 that consider marketing models. Chapter 13 offers guidance that any practicing forecaster should find interesting and important.

Learning and Teaching Resources

The textbook companion site provides resources for both students and instructors.

Students: In addition to the end-of-book appendices, access the following resources by going to *www.cengagebrain.com* and searching ISBN 9780324311273.

- **Excel Data Sets and Supplemental Excel Macros:** A critical element in every good forecasting text is the provision of data sets for readers to test out their developing skills. The companion website includes all the data sets used in the book, both in the examples and the exercises. In addition to the data sets, a set of Excel macros is available to carry out the exponential smoothing methods that are discussed in Chapters 3 and 4. This is for two good reasons: First, exponential smoothing software often is not available (or if it is, it is not well designed) in standard statistical packages and second, despite the apparent simplicity of such software, a number of hazards confront the student who must carry out the calculations in Excel alone. But we are the first to admit that these macros are not the equivalent of a professional forecasting package such as ForecastPro. A macro for nonlinear trend curves is also available online.

Instructors: Access the following textbook resources by going to *login.cengage.com*, logging in with your faculty account username and password, and using ISBN 9780324311273 to search for and to add these resources to your account "Bookshelf." In addition to the Excel data sets and macros just described, the following materials are available:

- **Solutions Manual:** The Solutions Manual includes solutions to all the exercises. Instructors are encouraged to be selective in the content they make available to students.

- **Microsoft PowerPoint Slides:** Outline PowerPoint lecture slides are available for each chapter and help to clarify content and guide student note-taking.

Online Forecasting Resources

These days, the Web provides many resources that support every activity humans contemplate. Forecasting is no exception. We list here a few of the resources a practicing forecaster would wish to consider:

- Two key academic publications that an ambitious reader might need to consult (e.g., in writing a dissertation) are the *International Journal of Forecasting* (*IJF*) and the *Journal of Forecasting*. Occasionally, survey articles in these journals are written at a level accessible to all readers. Most of the remaining articles published are technical in nature.
- International Institute of Forecasters (*www.forecasters.org*): The IIF is a nonprofit organization and the publisher of the *IJF*. The Institute organizes an annual symposium that attracts a worldwide group of participants. The Institute also sponsors occasional professional workshops in various topics.
- *Foresight: The International Journal of Applied Forecasting*: This journal, published by the IIF, aims to provide practicing forecasters with easy-to-read material on important topics that summarize the latest research ideas.
- Website on forecasting principles (*http://forecastingprinciples.com*), also available via *www.forecasters.org*: This site aims to cover most, if not all, aspects of forecasting, offering advice to both researchers and practitioners. Sponsored by the IIF, and based on the material in Armstrong (2001) which has been regularly updated, the site contains much that is useful, from a method selection "tree" to a dictionary. We have drawn heavily on the content of the book and the site in preparing this text.
- Software resources (see online Appendix C): Good software for forecasting is essential, but there is no perfect package. We discuss some of the best known alternatives in this appendix.
- Institute of Business Forecasting and Planning (IBF) (*www.ibf.org*): The IBF is a for-profit organization that organizes professional conferences and publishes the *Journal of Business Forecasting*. The primary focus of the site, which also offers a job search facility, is on forecasting for supply chain organizations.
- Applied Forecasting (*www.appliedforecasting.com*): This site provides a compendium of current news and the latest research in forecasting.
- Principal data resources: These are listed in Chapter 1.

Customized Learning Solutions

Choose content from Cengage Learning's extensive library of texts and collections, add or create your own original work, and create customized media and technology that fits your course needs. The Cengage Learning Custom Solutions editorial team will work with you through each step, allowing you to concentrate on the most important thing—your students. Learn more about all our services at *www.cengage.com/custom* or contact your local Cengage Learning sales representative for more information.

Acknowledgments

In the preparation of this book, we have benefited from comments from forecasting colleagues around the world. Particular thanks are due to Geoff Allen (University of Massachusetts, Amherst), Paul Goodwin (University of Bath), Herman Stekler (George Washington University), and Peg Young (U.S. Department of Transportation). Thanks are also due to colleagues at Lancaster: Steven Finlay, Tao Huang, Nikos Kourentzes, and Nicos Pavlidis. The Excel macros were developed by MSc students Sachin Rastogi and Young Ho Seo. Likewise, at Georgetown, we acknowledge the contributions of Bob Thomas (who provided the case study in Chapter 10), Gabriel Morales Becker, Alex Cope, Michael Granat, Michelle Kim, Sam King, Hannah Liu, and Jay Schulze, as well as the students who contributed the minicase studies described in Chapter 8. Moreover, the book would not have been conceived and developed without the research that has been stimulated by the founding of the International Institute of Forecasters and the publication of the *Journal of Forecasting* and the *International Journal of Forecasting*.

We would also like to thank all of the instructors who provided valuable feedback on early versions of the manuscript including:

Christopher S. Decker, University of Nebraska–Omaha
John R. Grandzol, Bloomsburg University
Joshua Kerr, California State University–East Bay
Kenneth D. Lawrence, New Jersey Institute of Technology
Peter Schuhmann, UNC–Wilmington
William J. (Joey) Smith, University of West Georgia
Fallaw Sowell, Carnegie Mellon University
Herman Stekler, George Washington University
Houston H. Stokes, University of Illinois–Chicago
Thomas Traynor, Wright State University
Raja Velu, Syracuse University
William W.S. Wei, Temple University

We also wish to acknowledge the support we have drawn from our families. For RF, it has consisted of ignoring almost all aspects of the project but putting up with the odd complaint and providing occasional cups of tea. For KO, both tea and coffee were provided, along with a willingness to accept even more clutter than usual. As with most projects, there was considerable optimism from all parties as to the completion date; hopefully, the revenue projections won't prove as inaccurate!

The following title was an indispensable reference for us throughout the writing process: Armstrong, J. S. (ed.). (2001), *Principles of Forecasting: A Handbook for Researchers and Practitioners*, Boston and Dordrecht: Kluwer.

Finally, we want to thank the members of our South-Western publishing team for their assistance throughout the development and production of the text: Charles McCormick (Sr. Acquisitions Editor), who has guided this project from its earliest days, Kendra Brown (Developmental Editor), Martha Conway (Sr. Content Project Manager), Chris Valentine (Media Editor), Diane Bowdler (Developmental Editor), Laura Ansara Sr. Developmental Editor), Eileen Corcoran (Marketing Coordinator), and Lynn Lustberg of Macmillan Publishing Solutions.

Keith Ord

Robert Fildes

CHAPTER 1

Forecasting, the Why and the How

*One cannot divine nor **forecast** the conditions that will make happiness; one only stumbles upon them by chance, in a lucky hour, at the world's end somewhere, and hold fast to the days, as to fortune or fame.*

—Willa Sibert Cather, American author and winner of the Pulitzer Prize
(*http://thinkexist.com/quotes/*)

Introduction

Many of us follow familiar rituals after climbing out of bed in the morning. One of these activities is to check the weather forecast. Between sips of coffee, we may scan the newspaper, listen to the TV or radio, or check an online weather service. At the simplest level, we obtain a short summary, such as, "Cloudy early in downtown Washington, some sun in the afternoon, with a high of 76°F (24°C) expected." There might also be a travelers' warning for those proposing to visit Mexico in the next couple of days, with a hurricane force 6 expected to hit land south of Cancún. More detail is often forthcoming and may include such information as

- A summary of expected temperatures at intervals during the day.
- The probability of precipitation or of the storm.
- Summary forecasts for the next few days.

Meteorologists provide a reasonable degree of detail in their forecasts for up to 7–10 days ahead, after which broader assessments, such as "above or below average temperatures," are about as much as can be usefully provided. If we are concerned about the weather several months ahead, we rely on long-term average values for the time of year.

What does the weather report have to do with business forecasting? In fact, weather is an important factor affecting the sales of many products, such as swimsuits, fresh fruit, and barbecue food. In addition, it affects holiday and business travel.

The example also raises the most basic question of what we mean by a forecast:

> ### Forecast
>
> A prediction or estimate of an actual outcome expected at a future time period or for another situation.

Here we have two types of outcome: the expected temperatures over the course of the day and a predicted event, a hurricane. In this book, we will be concerned with predicting both types of outcome. When we are told the forecast, we understand it to mean the most likely outcome (e.g., that the hurricane occurs or that the temperature will reach 76°F). Sometimes, forecasts include estimated probabilities that the outcome will happen, such as "There is a 70 percent chance of rain this evening." In the United States such probability weather forecasts are common, whereas they are absent in Britain. The other key feature of this weather forecast is that it is precise: It tells us where and when these events are expected to happen. So this simple example serves to illustrate a number of basic features of any forecasting problem.

We now explore these features of forecasting in more detail, asking why, what, and how, as well as providing a number of examples of different forecasting issues.

Discussion Question *What other forecasts are regularly included in the daily newspapers, such as the* Wall Street Journal, *the* New York Times, *or the* Times of London?

1.1   Why Forecast?

Why do we check the weather forecast? Partly, we may do so out of idle curiosity, but the activity also serves to guide our planning for the days ahead. The planning activity may include such decisions as what to wear, whether to carry (and maybe lose) an umbrella, or whether to go ahead with a scheduled outdoor activity or travel plan. The forecast helps us plan, and planning, in turn, may improve our quality of life, compared with just rushing out the door. If we examine the elements of this simple vignette, we arrive at the following motivation for forecasting:

> ### Forecasting and Planning
>
> The purpose of forecasting is to inform the process of planning.
>
> The purpose of planning is to develop a course of action so that things don't "just happen" based on a no-change forecast.

Before embarking on a forecasting exercise, we should always consider the reasons for generating the forecast, how it fits with possible plans, and the kind of forecast we therefore need. Using the mnemonic PHIVE, we may identify five components in any exercise:

- *P*urpose
- *H*orizon
- *I*nformation
- *V*alue
- *E*valuation.

1.1.1 Purpose

What do we hope to achieve by generating the forecast? What plans depend on the results of the forecasting exercise? The meteorologist provides information to a broad range of individuals and organizations, and they are all interested for their own reasons. For some organizations such as the weather service, it suffices to know that there is a demand for their forecasting services.

1.1.2 Horizon

How far ahead do we wish to forecast? We refer to this period as the *forecasting horizon*: how far we wish to see ahead. In turn, the horizon depends on our purpose in forecasting. The methods we employ for short-term forecasting will consider only the factors that change rapidly, whereas longer term forecasts need to take into account a larger number of factors that may change during the time frame of interest. We also refer to the *forecast origin*, the point in time from which the forecasts start, usually corresponding to the time of the latest available information. As we know, weather forecasts are quite accurate up to 7–10 days ahead, but they tend to be more like long-term seasonal averages beyond that time frame. The horizon often affects the accuracy and usefulness of a forecast.

1.1.3 Information

What do we know that may help us in forecasting, and when will we know it? Detailed information is useful only if it is available in a timely fashion. Tomorrow's financial reports may provide an excellent explanation of today's events, but they are of no use in forecasting stock prices today. Likewise, information is of value only if it has an impact on the forecasting procedure we seek to implement. The weather forecast was for downtown Washington, but if we were planning an outing to the nearby coast, the city forecast would give us only limited help. Thus, we tailor the level of detail in the forecast to satisfy our planning needs. Population changes may have a major effect upon sales ten years from now, but such changes take place at a relatively slow rate and would be irrelevant to forecasting sales in the next three months.

What do we know and when will we know it? A large-scale forecasting model may take into account a broad range of key factors, but if we have to wait several months for the data to become available, the forecasts may be too dated to be useful. Thus, a forecaster often relies upon leading indicators, such as closing levels of a major stock index or a survey of consumer sentiment, to signal changes in short-term economic conditions. These factors do not provide a cause-and-effect description of what is happening, but they may well yield a timely assessment of potential changes.

The distinction between forecasting and explanation is often somewhat blurred. On the one hand, we may consider so-called pure forecasts that use only currently available information. On the other hand, a detailed description of a process (e.g., a macroeconomic model of the economy or a model of the world's climate) may enable us to answer what-if questions based upon the understanding that the detailed description provides. Such models typically require more information than pure forecasting exercises. When seeking to answer what-if questions, it is entirely reasonable to use data that are available only after the fact, because they provide an indication of the likely effects of certain policy decisions. They may also provide an explanation of the forecast errors we have made. In this book, we focus primarily upon pure forecasts, although the methods discussed in later chapters are useful in both contexts.

1.1.4   Value

How valuable is the forecast? What would you pay to have perfect knowledge of a future event? For example, a weather forecast is useful to an individual in that she is better able to decide on appropriate clothing. However, most of us would not pay very much for such information, and we do not need to know exactly how much rain will fall.

In contrast, the agricultural sector is very interested in using weather forecasts to plan irrigation and the planting of crops, and it is willing to pay for more accurate location-specific forecasts. In a different context, consider a company with thousands of product lines. Although the value of forecasts for any single line may be modest, an effective forecasting system for the complete range of products is very valuable in making production and inventory decisions.

1.1.5   Evaluation

How do we know whether a particular forecasting exercise was effective? The obvious answer is that we should compare past results with the forecasts that were made, possibly comparing several different forecasting methods as we proceed. We examine several such criteria in Chapter 2, all of which are based upon the differences between forecasts and actual values. A statement about checking forecast performance might seem almost too obvious to be worth making, yet the evidence suggests that some companies never go back to check their forecasting performance. For example, an informal survey conducted by the software company Business Forecasting Systems produced the results shown in Table 1.1. Respondents who used statistical forecasts were asked how they did so:

> As a Baseline: Use the statistical forecast as a baseline and then make judgmental adjustments
>
> or
>
> As a Reference: Use the statistical forecast as a reference, or "sanity check," on some other principal forecast.

Respondents were then asked whether they regularly checked the performance of the forecasts. The *percentages* in each category who said yes are given in Table 1.1. The survey was small and relied upon self-reporting, but the figures are striking nevertheless. The baseline group is making adjustments to the statistical forecasts, yet nearly half of them are not checking to see whether those adjustments improve forecast performance. Nearly one-third

TABLE 1.1 PERCENTAGES OF RESPONDENTS WHO REGULARLY MONITOR FORECASTING PERFORMANCE

| Use Made of Statistical Forecast | Percentages of Respondents Who Checked | | | |
| | Adjusted/Principal Forecast | | Statistical Forecast | |
	Yes	No	Yes	No
As a baseline	91	9	57	43
As a reference	71	29	29	71

Source: Trends Business Forecasting Systems Newsletter, February, 2010.

of the reference group do not even check their principal forecasts, and more than two-thirds fail to check the statistical forecasts.

If you don't check from time to time, how do you know whether your approach is any good? Making effective forecasts is as much an art as it is a science, but asking about PHIVE before you start the exercise will help avoid expensive mistakes.

Monitoring Forecast Errors

Always check on forecast performance. Checking helps you avoid repeating mistakes and leads to improved results.

EXAMPLE 1.1 ■ PHIVE in Action

Some years ago, a state agency asked one of the authors (JKO) to develop a short-term forecasting system for state tax revenues. The author used simple extrapolative models (the details don't matter at this stage) to accomplish the job. The *purpose* was to provide the state legislators with a revenue-forecasting model that they could use to compare with the forecasts generated by the executive branch (the governor's office). Because all state representatives are up for reelection every two years, the *horizon* was two years. The monthly state revenues were published typically within a month of the end of the collection period; because these figures are a matter of public record, the necessary *information* was freely available. Some additional information, such as upcoming changes in tax rates, was also provided. The *value* of the study lay in the provision of an independent forecasting system for the legislature to serve as a check on the executive's budgetary proposals.

As happens all too often with forecasting systems, no follow-up study was performed to *evaluate* performance. However, several years later, I was pleasantly surprised to learn that the system was still in use and that the outputs compared quite favorably with the forecasts from the state econometric model sponsored by the governor's office. A firm of consultants provided the econometric model for, I believe, around $100,000 per year (compared with a one-time payment of $10,000 for the short-term model). Doubtless, the econometric model is also used for other purposes, and the fees are probably well spent. ■

Discussion Question *There was a two-year cycle in the tax revenues data. Why might this be?*

1.2   What and Why Do Organizations Forecast?

Organizations—large and small, public, government, or private sector—have numerous forecasting needs. To plan their operations, they need to estimate the demand they expect for their products and services. They also need to know how their actions—for example, their marketing plans, including promotions and prices—will affect demand and in turn affect revenues and costs. Figure 1.1 captures some of the complexities that organizations face. Fortunately, many of the variables can, for the most part, be ignored. In the short term, such features as the technology (used by the organization or its customers), legislation, and social trends can be regarded as fixed. Operational and tactical (medium-term) decisions depend primarily on demand (as it is affected by competition) and the finance needed to support the organization. In the longer term, where the organization's strategy is updated, the variables in the outer box come into play; for example, social and demographic trends can change a market dramatically. In Europe, an aging population requires a different set of services (e.g., health) than a younger market. In the United States, shifts in consumer tastes relating to the changing composition of the population with regard to ethnic origin and geography also affect consumption patterns.

Discussion Question   *What might a nuclear electricity supplier or a water company need to forecast with regard to its key assets? Why?*

Discussion Question   *A state or national government provides unemployment benefits for a period of six months following a layoff (or leaving school). It continues for a further six months if the applicant attends a job training program. What variables would the government need to forecast for its annual planning?*

Each of these discussion questions points up the critical linkage between forecasting and planning: If the organization or the person does not act on the forecast, then it has no value beyond mere curiosity. These issues are pursued further in the end-of-chapter minicases.

FIGURE 1.1   AN ORGANIZATION'S FORECASTING NEEDS

© Cengage Learning 2013.

Examples of Forecasting Problems

Forecasting involves using currently available data to make statements about likely future developments. Such data often arise as a time series:

> ### Time Series
>
> A set of comparable observations ordered in time. The values may refer to either a point in time ("the current value of the Dow Jones Index is just above 12,000") or an aggregate over a period of time ("total sales for the last month were 350 units").

We usually assume that the observations are equally spaced in time. On occasion, this assumption is incorrect, but we may make some adjustment to the data so that it is a closer approximation. For example, the months of the year differ in length, but we usually treat them as equally spaced. If the time series refers to data such as sales, we may use average sales per day during the month or average sales per trading day (allowing for possible closures on Sundays and public holidays). The revised time series then conforms more closely to the assumption of equal spacing.

An interesting example of such adjustments occurs with stock market data. The New York Stock Exchange (NYSE) is generally open for trading Monday through Friday, 9:30 a.m. to 4 p.m. The NYSE is closed on weekends and public holidays. Nevertheless, it is often possible to ignore the breaks in trading and to treat time series relating to the price of a stock or the trading volume (e.g., the number of shares traded per hour) as being recorded at regular equal intervals.

In the rest of this book, we typically assume that observations are recorded at equally spaced times and effectively ignore the distinction between data either recorded at a point in time or aggregated across time. Such a step poses no problems for the formal development of the forecasting methods, but it needs to be taken into account in applications.

We now examine a few series in detail. Note that we always start out with plots of the data, whether time series or cross sectional. It would be difficult to overemphasize the importance of this first step in any forecasting study. Beyond the initial benefit of identifying unusual observations (whether data entry errors or genuinely strange values), such plots serve to identify patterns in the data and to suggest possible approaches to forecasting.

1.3.1   Retail Sales

Figure 1.2 shows the level of retail sales and food services in the United States over the period from January 1992 to December 2009 (see *US_retail_sales.xlsx*). The data refer to current dollars, so no allowance has been made for the effects of inflation. The series shows more or less steady growth, which is due to a combination of real growth in the economy and inflation. The inflationary elements could be removed by using a price index and *deflating* the current values to obtain real growth figures, but for the present we will examine the series in current dollars.

The second feature that is evident is a regular within-year fluctuation, which we refer to as a *seasonal pattern*. Here, it reflects high sales in December and a drop-off in January. We also observe that the fluctuations are increasing over time, indicating a proportional effect (up or down by a given percentage) rather than a fluctuation by an absolute amount.

The one diagram imparts a lot of information, and it is reasonable to ask whether the different parts of the total information package can be filtered out, rather than trying to read

FIGURE 1.2   U.S. MONTHLY RETAIL SALES AND FOOD SERVICES

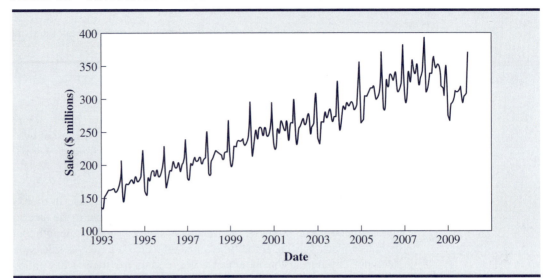

Source: U.S. Census Bureau via EconStats, *www.econstats.com/retsal/retsal_m1.htm.* Data shown is from file US_retail_sales.xlsx.

everything from one diagram. The answer is that we can do that by identifying a separate seasonal component and then adjusting the original series by those seasonal factors to produce a seasonally adjusted series. The advantages of doing so are that we can examine not only underlying trends without being distracted by seasonal fluctuations but also the seasonal pattern to look for changes over time. This process of *decomposition* is particularly important for macroeconomic series, and most U.S. and UK government series are published in seasonally adjusted form.

1.3.2 Seasonal Patterns for Retail Sales

We will discuss the process of seasonal adjustment more rigorously in Chapter 4, but for purposes of the present discussion we use a set of seasonal factors published by the U.S. Census Bureau.

The seasonal patterns are shown in Figure 1.3. The December peak and subsequent drop for January and February are clearly evident. Looking more closely, we see that the seasonal pattern is fairly stable, but the magnitude of the peaks and troughs has diminished over time. When we use the seasonal factors to remove these effects, we arrive at the deseasonalized series shown in Figure 1.4. This plot shows a fairly steady upward trend until nearly the end of 2007, when the recession began. [The National Bureau of Economic Research (NBER) officially dated the start of the recession as December 2007.]

Discussion Question *Looking ahead two years from the present, how would you expect the series to behave?*

One other feature of the data worth noting is that the latter part of the series seems more volatile than the earlier part, as shown in Figure 1.5. Whether this change is due to inflation or changes in consumer habits would require that we examine the series after adjusting for inflation. We leave this examination as an exercise in Minicase 1.4.

FIGURE 1.3 SEASONAL FACTORS FOR U.S. MONTHLY TOTAL SALES FOR RETAIL SALES AND FOOD SERVICES

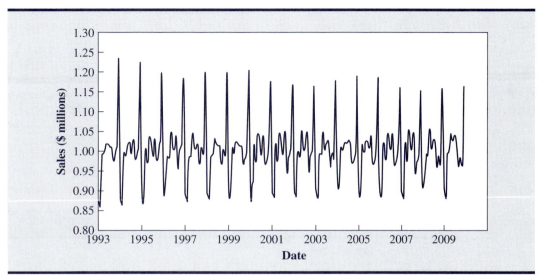

Source: U.S. Census Bureau via EconStats, www.econstats.com/retsal/retsal_m1.htm.
Data: US_retail_sales.xlsx.

FIGURE 1.4 SEASONALLY ADJUSTED SERIES FOR U.S. MONTHLY TOTAL SALES FOR RETAIL AND FOOD SERVICES

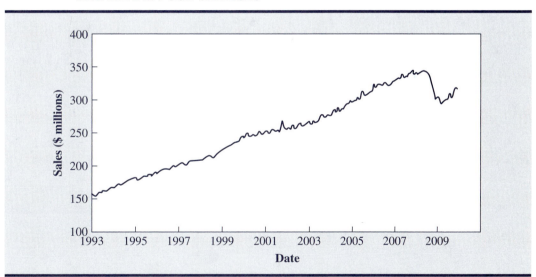

Source: U.S. Census Bureau via EconStats, www.econstats.com/retsal/retsal_m1.htm.
Data: US_retail_sales.xlsx.

The information contained in these various time series enables the forecaster to make statements about the potential December sales peak in conjunction with the likely change relative to the previous year. Such forecasts feed into decisions on overall inventory and staffing levels, as well as financial requirements.

How else could we make use of this information? One possibility is to look at the changes in the level of sales over time. Better yet, because the retail industry talks about

FIGURE 1.5   MONTH-TO-MONTH CHANGES IN RETAIL SALES

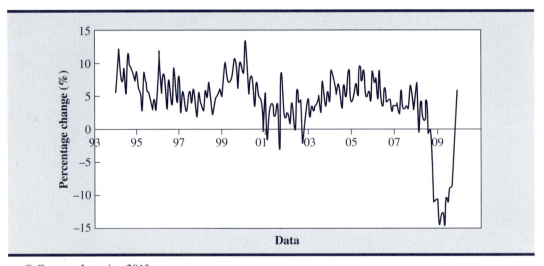

© Cengage Learning 2013.

FIGURE 1.6   YEAR-OVER-YEAR PERCENTAGE CHANGE IN U.S. MONTHLY RETAIL
                  SALES AND FOOD SERVICE

© Cengage Learning 2013.

percentage changes for a given month, j, from one year to the next, we can transform the data as follows:

$$\% \text{ change over year } t = \frac{100\,[(\text{Sales in year } t, \text{ month } j) - (\text{Sales in year } t{-}1, \text{ month } j)]}{[\text{Sales in year } t{-}1, \text{ month } j]}$$

That is, we look at the percentage change for this month compared with that for the same month last year.

The resulting plot is shown in Figure 1.6. We can see the periods of relative growth and stagnation. Note particularly the slowdown in the economy during 2001–2002 and the sharp decline starting at the end of December 2007.

FIGURE 1.7   SERIOUS INJURIES AND DEATHS ON UK ROADS
(January 1975–December 1984)

Source: Harvey and Durbin (1986). Data shown is from file Road_accidents.xlsx.

1.3.3 UK Road Accidents

As an example of a series displaying both seasonal and other effects, we consider a time series on injuries caused by road accidents in the United Kingdom over the period from January 1975 to December 1984, examined in detail by Harvey and Durbin (1986). The series is shown in Figure 1.7. The seasonal peak in December is quite evident, although the pattern breaks up somewhat in the later years. The other feature worthy of note is the step-change decline in early 1983, which was when the wearing of seat belts became mandatory. Analysis of the series provides a way to determine the effectiveness of the seat belt legislation, as we shall see in Minicase 9.2 in Chapter 9.

1.3.4 Airline Travel

A major issue in time series analysis is how to deal with unusual observations or shifts in the general level. The data on road accidents represent a series in which a change was anticipated; by contrast, an event might be totally unexpected, as with the tragic events in the United States on September 11, 2001. Figure 1.8 shows the number of revenue passenger miles traveled domestically in the United States, by month, from January 2000 to December 2009. The impact of that day upon air travel is clearly seen; September 2001 is marked on the diagram.

Discussion Question   *How would you estimate the effect of 9/11 upon the airline industry with respect to losses in revenue passenger miles?*

1.3.5 Sports Forecasting: Soccer (AKA Football!)

Sports forecasting is big business. In many countries, betting on the outcome of a game is legal, be it American football, soccer, or tennis. In fact, gamblers go a stage further: They can and do bet on the detailed developments in a game. In soccer, this type of betting can include the number of players cautioned; in tennis, the number of games played in the longest set. Here again, the data are different. Although the outcome (win, draw, or lose in soccer) is recorded over time, the observations are not observed at regular intervals.

Figure 1.9 shows a time series graph of the data as they fall into these three categories; they are also labeled so as to distinguish between a home game and an away game. What

FIGURE 1.8 MONTHLY U.S DOMESTIC AIR PASSENGER MILES (BILLIONS)
(*January 2000–December 2009*)

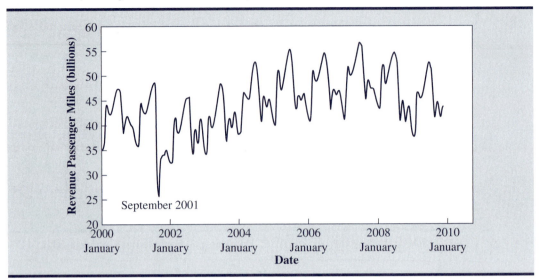

Source: Bureau of Transportation Statistics, U.S. Department of Transportation. Data shown is from file Revenue_miles.xlsx.

FIGURE 1.9 THE RECORD OF ITALIAN SOCCER CLUB FLORENCE (FIORENTINA) DURING THE 2004–2005 SEASON

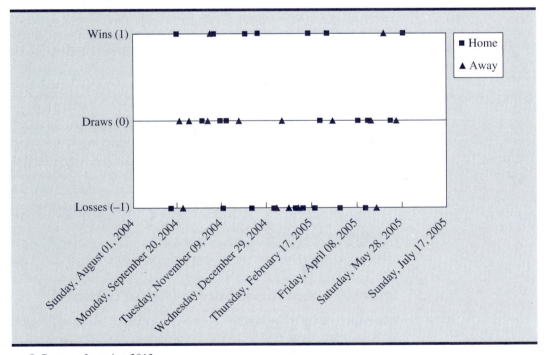

© Cengage Learning 2013.

makes this example different from the earlier ones is that the aim here is to forecast the outcome of an event: win, draw, or lose in our example. Sports betting companies use data on events in each minute of the game to predict the outcomes. Their aim is to help set the appropriate betting odds to ensure that they make a profit (Vaughan Williams, 2005). They use the regression methods of Chapters 7–10 to carry out the modeling and forecasting.

Discussion Question *What conclusions can you draw from Figure 1.9 about the strength of the Fiorentina team: Overall? Over time? Home and away?*

1.3.6 Sports Forecasting: A Cross-sectional Example— Baseball Salaries

Sports management also relies on forecasting. The manager's decisions on whom to sign, whom to release, and even whom to play all depend on forecasts of performance. Usually, such forecasts are made intuitively on the basis of the manager's experience. However, in one now famous example, Billy Beane, general manager of the Oakland Athletics baseball team, used statistical methods to identify players who were undervalued (see Lewis, 2003, for a nontechnical description of Beane's management ideas and the 2011 film). In thinking about the problem of trading players, one relevant relationship is what determines their current salary. Figure 1.10 shows the relationship between salary and the years played in the major leagues. The data here are cross sectional: All observations on players and their salaries were made over the same (relatively short) period. Critically, the time the data were recorded should be irrelevant to interpreting the relationship.

> **Cross-sectional data**
>
> Measurements on multiple units (here, players) recorded over a single time period for one or more variables (salaries, years in the major leagues).

Of course, many other variables affect salary, not the least of which are the player's previous season's performance and personal characteristics, such as age. In developing an understanding of whether a player is undervalued, these factors all have to be taken into account. We discuss this question in more detail in Chapter 7.

FIGURE 1.10   SCATTERPLOT OF BASEBALL PLAYERS' SALARIES AGAINST THE NUMBER OF YEARS PLAYED IN THE MAJOR LEAGUES

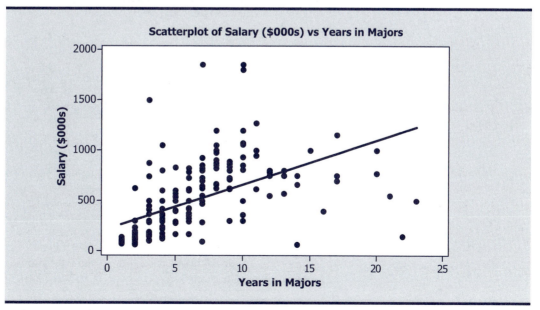

Source: We wish to acknowledge StatLib of the Department of Statistics at Carnegie Mellon University. Data shown is from file Baseball.xlsx.

1.3.7 **Stochastic Processes**

Observations may occur over time without forming a time series as we have defined it. For example, consider the flow of customers into and out of a supermarket. An individual customer arrives at a certain time (arrival time), spends some time selecting items for purchase (processing time), then waits in line (waiting time) before being served at the checkout (service time). If we examine the number of arrivals per unit of time or the number of customers served in a given time, we can define a time series by using successive counts. However, from the perspective of the individual customer, the elapsed waiting and service times are important. These individual times form, not a time series, but rather outputs from a random (or *stochastic*) process. Such processes are beyond the scope of this book; for details see, for example, Winston and Albright (2011).

1.4 How to Forecast

In Section 1.2, we used PHIVE to explain why we should generate forecasts. The next question is how? The how question depends heavily on the components of PHIVE. When we seek to establish a forecasting system, we first need to provide answers to the following questions:

- Do we have the necessary data to enable the use of statistical methods, or will the forecasting process be essentially judgmental? We leave the use of judgmental adjustments to statistical forecasts for later discussion (Chapters 11 and 13).
- If the process is based upon judgment, is the forecaster working alone or is a group involved?
- If the process is statistical, is the analysis to be based upon a single series or are explanatory variables to be included in the study?

The responses to these questions lead to a range of possible approaches, many of which are described in later chapters. The sequence of choices and the available methodologies are summarized briefly in Figure 1.11. A much more detailed discussion of the choice of

FIGURE 1.11   A SIMPLIFIED METHODOLOGY TREE FOR FORECASTING

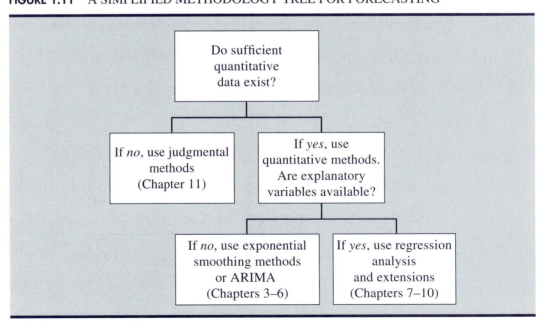

© Cengage Learning 2013.

forecasting procedures is deferred to Chapter 13, because we must first develop an understanding of each principal approach.

Forecasting Step by Step

On the basis of our preliminary discussion of PHIVE, we can identify seven major steps in the forecasting process:

1. Define the forecasting and planning problem, and decide the value of better forecasts.
2. Determine the resources to be devoted to providing the forecasts.
3. Collect relevant data, whether from a survey, from company records, or from information generated by other agencies (e.g., government figures).
4. Conduct an initial analysis of the data.
5. Select an appropriate forecasting method.
6. Generate forecasts.
7. Validate the forecasting exercise by checking forecasts against actual outcomes.

Ideally, we could use these seven steps as a checklist and work our way through them. Life is not quite that simple, however. For example, we used PHIVE to discuss step 1 in Section 1.1. Although we may be comfortable with our initial definition of the problem, we may have to revisit our understanding. Step 2 is also important: The resources assigned to the forecasting exercise should be commensurate with the potential added value of improved forecasts. If there is little value in achieving improved forecast accuracy, there's no point in using scarce resources for that purpose. By contrast, if the problem is such that small improvements in accuracy have a large payoff, spending substantial sums is worthwhile. Step 3 determines whether the forecasting task is feasible: The relevant data may not be available (either at all or in a timely fashion), so we would have to go back to the drawing board.

Once we have completed steps 1–3, we need to carry out an initial analysis of the data. We describe these steps in detail in Chapter 2, but it is worth noting that the analysis serves two purposes: cleaning the data and understanding the data. *Cleaning the data* involves looking for unusual observations and perhaps correcting data-recording errors; identifying factors that need to be taken into account, such as seasonal patterns or public holidays; and making sure that the data are comparable to each other and represent the phenomenon of interest. For example, shipments to wholesalers do not truly represent sales if they are made on a sale-or-return basis. The second component, *understanding the data*, enables the choice of forecasting method as well as providing insights about the potential reliability of the resulting forecasts. As in other endeavors, the KISS principle is valuable (keep it simple, statistician).

Once our iterations through steps 1–4 are complete, we can move on to method selection, using the refinements of Figure 1.11. Only at this stage are we in a position to generate the forecasts. Much of the remainder of this book is concerned with the technical aspects of steps 5 and 6. The final step, which must not be overlooked, is to validate the forecasting process by comparing actual outcomes with forecasts. At the developmental stage, this can be done by means of a so-called *hold-out sample*, in which we split the available data into two parts and then use only the first part (the *estimation sample*) to calibrate the forecasting method. Once everything is set, we use the second part (the hold-out sample) to check the performance of the forecast. When the forecasting system is up and running, periodic checks on performance are essential. Overall, the seven steps should be seen as an integrated process that operates more smoothly as the forecaster gains practical experience; that integration is the subject of the final chapter of the book.

> Whenever possible, the development of a forecasting method should include the partition of the data into an *estimation sample* (used to estimate the parameters, etc.) and a *hold-out sample* (used to test the performance of the proposed forecasting method).
>   Once the method is selected, the entire sample should be used for future forecasting purposes.

1.6   Computer Packages for Forecasting

Almost all statistical packages include routines for regression analyses and for time series analysis. The basic procedures for regression are relatively standard, although the quality of the procedures for testing the adequacy of alternative models with the use of diagnostic statistics varies considerably. Computer software for time series analysis is even more variable. Some packages include only the most basic forecasting procedures, and the methods provided vary enormously. In the course of this book, the reader will observe that we have used a number of general-purpose software programs: Excel (graphs and macros only), Minitab, SAS, and SPSS. We have also used some specialized programs, notably EViews (for econometric modeling), Forecast Pro (for forecasting), and PCGive (for both econometrics and forecasting). Each program has its merits, but none provides coverage of all the topics we discuss. A brief summary of the capabilities of the major forecasting packages is provided in Appendix C, located on the textbook companion site.

1.7   Data Sources

Thanks to the Internet, finding and downloading data are now relatively painless tasks. The data sets used in this book are all available on the website for the book*, and they are all contained in Excel 2007 (.xlsx) files. These files may be read directly by any of the programs we have used.

All U.S. government departments have publicly available websites from which data may be downloaded; for example, two major agencies that supply economic data are the Census Bureau (*www.census.gov*) and the Bureau of Labor Statistics (*www.bls.gov*). In the United Kingdom, the UK National Statistics site provides similar data (*www.statistics.gov.uk/hub/index.html*). Also, all major companies have websites from which data on their overall operations can be obtained, although these data are not always packaged in a ready-to-download format.

Numerous specialist databases that provide downloadable data series are also available. Some are free, and others require either a personal or an institutional subscription. The following are several such sources of particular interest:

- EconStats (*www.econstats.com/index.htm*) contains a large amount of economic and financial data on the United States and on several other countries, including the United Kingdom, China, and Japan.
- Data.gov.uk (*http://Data.gov.uk/*) offers easy-to-access government statistical series for the United Kingdom.
- Intute (*http://intute.ac.uk/*) provides an extensive database of web resources for education and research.
- Econdata (*http://econdata.net/*) contains regional socioeconomic data for the United States.
- The Forecasting Principles website (*www.forecastingprinciples.com*) provides a variety of links to other sources and data sets.

The Rest of the Book

The overall plan of the book broadly follows the different branches of the methodology tree shown in Figure 1.11. After a brief review of basic statistics and a discussion of accuracy measures in Chapter 2, we go on to examine extrapolative methods for single time series in Chapters 3 and 4. These methods are introduced in a pragmatic way as "good ideas" in those chapters; the statistical underpinnings of the methods are then developed in Chapters 5 and 6. In Chapters 7–9, we develop models that may be used for either cross-sectional or time series data but that involve the inclusion of explanatory variables. Chapter 10 describes a variety of more advanced techniques, which have become an integral part of forecasting practice in recent years, while in Chapter 11 we turn for some light relief to judgmental methods for forecasting; such methods are perhaps overused in modern industry, but they do have a substantial role to play and it is important to understand how they interface with statistical procedures and how they are best carried out. Chapter 12 discusses how all the methods so far presented can be applied in a variety of contexts—forecasting is not a topic to be examined in a vacuum. Finally, in Chapter 13, we examine forecasting in practice and try to provide signposts to guide the forecaster to successful applications of the tools of her trade.

Summary

In this chapter, we have discussed the reasons organizations have for forecasting, as well as its role in both operational and strategic planning. The why and what of forecasting have been analyzed in detail by using PHIVE: the purpose that underlies the forecasting activity, the forecast horizon, the information available, the value of the forecasting exercise, and the need to evaluate forecasts. We then examined several series that showed different data patterns, including seasonal patterns, and we explored the idea of seasonal decomposition. Other issues discussed were the examination of cross-sectional data for forecasting and the impact of unexpected events. Finally, as an introduction to the remainder of the book, we briefly explored the how of forecasting, which depends on the aims of the forecasting activity and the data available.

Minicases

Minicase 1.1 Inventory Planning

The Nuts'n'Bolts hardware store stocks some high-value items and a large number of relatively low-value components. Inventory is reviewed weekly, and orders are placed with suppliers when inventory levels indicate that current levels are "too low." Most suppliers deliver the low-value items within two weeks; some of the high-value items may take four weeks for delivery. How would you develop a forecasting system to predict the sales of such items at the individual (SKU = stock-keeping unit) level? How would you use such forecasts to plan future purchases?

Use PHIVE to go through the necessary steps. For purposes of the discussion, assume that that any historical data you might need can be made available.

Minicase 1.2 Long-Term Growth

You work for a consulting firm that is bidding on a contract to forecast the growth prospects of an electronics company over the next five years. The company has developed a specialized computer chip that is used in highly sensitive medical equipment and does not anticipate creating any new product lines, although periodic improvements to the chip are anticipated.

Write a short proposal describing how you would develop such forecasts, using PHIVE as a guide. For purposes of the assignment, assume that that any historical data you might need can be made available, but describe carefully the nature of the data needed.

Minicase 1.3 Sales Forecasting

A company sells many hundreds of clothing products by mail order and through the Internet. The firm also offers the customer four different purchase schemes, from pay on purchase through payment over different periods (of 6 and 12 months). The final plan allows a postponement of any payment for 12 months.

The firm has to ensure a supply of its advertised products to meet forecast demand. Inventory policy has consequences for the distribution network because the products need to be stocked and then shipped. The retailer also has to decide which customers to target through mailings to stimulate further purchases.

What variables would the company need to forecast? What strategic financial decisions may need to be linked to the various customer purchase plans? Use the PHIVE framework to guide your thinking.

Minicase 1.4 Adjusting for Inflation

The data file for U.S. retail sales (*US_retail_sales.xlsx*) also contains monthly data for the Consumer Price Index (CPI). Create a series called "real prices" by dividing sales by the *CPI;* then replicate Figures 1.2, 1.4, and 1.5 for this series. Compare your results with the three figures provided in the text, commenting on major differences. (Use the same seasonal adjustment factors.)

References

Harvey, A. C., and Durbin, J. (1986). The effects of seat belt legislation on British road casualties: A case study in structural time series modelling. *Journal of the Royal Statistical Society*, series A, 149, 187–227.

Lewis, M. (2003). *Moneyball: The Art of Winning an Unfair Game.* New York: Norton.

Vaughan Williams, L. (2005). *Information Efficiency in Financial and Betting Markets.* Cambridge, UK: Cambridge University Press.

Winston, W., and Albright, S. C. (2011). *Practical Management Science*, 2nd ed. Pacific Grove, CA: Duxbury.

CHAPTER 2

Basic Tools for Forecasting

DDD: Draw the doggone diagram!

— In memory of the late David Hildebrand, who stated the matter rather more forcibly!

Introduction

In most of the chapters in this book, we assume that some kind of database is available from which to build numerical forecasts. In some situations, the data may be already available (e.g., government figures for macroeconomic forecasting); in other cases, the data may be collected directly (e.g., sales figures or purchasing behavior from scanning records). Such data may be incomplete or subject to error, they may not relate directly to the key variables of interest, and they may not be available in a timely fashion. Nevertheless, they are all we have, and we must learn to understand and respect them if not to love them. Indeed, such is the basis of any good relationship!

At a conceptual level, we need to understand how the data are compiled and how they relate to the forecasting issues we seek to address. We must establish from the outset that the data are appropriate for the *purpose* (the *P* in *PHIVE*) we have in mind, as noted in Chapter 1. Otherwise, we are only living up to the old adage "Garbage in, garbage out." We will not keep repeating this message in chapter after chapter, but the *PHIVE* issues must always be examined before embarking on a forecasting project. We must then examine the data to understand their structure and main features and to summarize the available information (the *I* in *PHIVE*).

In Section 2.1, we examine the types of data that arise in practice, and then we turn to graphical summaries in Sections 2.2 and 2.3. Section 2.4 describes the basic numerical summaries that are useful, and we then move on to measures of association in Section 2.5. Sometimes the original form of the data is not appropriate, and some kind of transformation or modification is needed. This topic is the focus of Section 2.6. The steps described in all these sections are essentially those of preliminary data analysis, although similar procedures will be undertaken later in the context of model diagnostics.

Methods for the generation of forecasts are the focus of later chapters, but in this chapter we consider the evaluation of outputs from the forecasting process. Thus, in Section 2.7, we examine measures of forecasting accuracy and the evaluation of forecasting performance (the *E* in *PHIVE*), after which we turn to prediction intervals in Section 2.8. These capture the uncertainty in our forecasts. The chapter ends with a discussion of some underlying principles.

 ## Types of Data

A database may be thought of as a table with multiple dimensions, as the following examples illustrate:

- *A survey of prospective voters in an upcoming election:* The measured variables might include voting intentions, party affiliation, age, gender, and address.
- *A portfolio of stocks:* For each company, we would record contact information, market capitalization, opening and closing stock prices, dividend payments over suitable periods, and news announcements.
- *The economy of the United States:* The factors of interest would certainly include gross domestic product (*GDP*), consumer expenditures, capital investment, government revenues and expenditures, and imports and exports.

You are undoubtedly able to add to the list.

A survey of voters refers to *cross-sectional data* in that what matters is the inherent variation across respondents. For practical purposes, we view the data as being collected in the same (short) time period. Of course, voters may change their minds at a later stage, and such shifts of opinion are a major source of discrepancies between opinion polls and election outcomes.

The closing price for a particular stock or fund, recorded daily over several months or even years, represents an example of *time series data*. We are interested in the movement of the price over time. The same applies if we track the movements over time of aggregate macroeconomic variables such as *GDP*; it is their development over time that is important.

Types of data

Cross-sectional data are measurements on multiple units, recorded in a single time period.

A *time series* is a set of comparable measurements recorded on a single variable over multiple time periods.

Panel data are cross-sectional measurements that are repeated over time, such as monthly expenditures for a sample of consumers.

From these examples, we see that a database may be cross-sectional, or time dependent, or both. (Consider tracking voting intentions over time or looking at consumer expenditures for different regions of a country.) Although forecasting practice often involves multiple series, such as the sales of different product lines, the methods we examine have the common theme of using past data to predict future outcomes. Thus, our primary focus in the first part of the book is on the use of time series data. For convenience, we begin our development of these ideas in the context of a single time series, even though applications may involve a large number of such series.

As methods of data capture have become more sophisticated (e.g., scanners in supermarkets), it has become possible to develop databases that relate to individuals, be they consumers or students. Forecasting may then involve the use of cross-sectional data to predict individual preferences or to evaluate a new customer based upon individuals with similar demographic characteristics.

By way of example, consider the data shown in Tables 2.1, 2.2, and 2.3. Table 2.1 shows the weekly sales of a consumer product in a certain market area; the product is produced by a major U.S. manufacturer. This data set will be examined in greater detail in Chapter 3. The data are genuine, but we have labeled the product WFJ Sales to preserve confidentiality. Table 2.2 shows the annual numbers of domestic passengers at Washington Dulles International Airport for the years 1963–2007. Clearly, both data sets are time series, but the sales figures are fairly stable (at least after the first 12 weeks or so) whereas the passenger series shows a strong upward movement. Table 2.3, appearing later in the chapter, involves cross-sectional data on company financial success.

2.1.1   Use of Large Databases

A manager responsible for a large number of product lines may well claim that "the forecasting can all be done by computer, so there is no need to waste time on model building or detailed examinations of individual series." This assertion is half right. The computer can indeed remove most of the drudgery from the forecasting exercise; see, for example, the forecasting methods described in Chapter 3. However, a computer is like a sheepdog: Properly trained, it can deliver a sound flock of forecasts; poorly trained, it can create mayhem. Even if the task in question involves thousands of series to be forecast, there is no substitute for understanding the general structure of the data so that we can identify appropriate forecasting procedures. The manager can then focus on the products that are providing unusual results.

TABLE 2.1   VALUE OF WEEKLY SALES OF PRODUCT WFJ SALES ($)

Week	Sales	Week	Sales	Week	Sales
1	23,056	22	33,631	43	32,187
2	24,817	23	32,900	44	30,322
3	24,300	24	34,426	45	34,588
4	23,242	25	33,777	46	38,879
5	22,862	26	34,849	47	37,166
6	22,863	27	30,986	48	37,111
7	23,391	28	33,321	49	39,021
8	22,469	29	34,003	50	40,737
9	22,241	30	35,417	51	42,358
10	24,367	31	33,822	52	51,914
11	29,457	32	32,723	53	35,404
12	31,294	33	34,925	54	30,555
13	38,713	34	33,460	55	30,421
14	35,749	35	30,999	56	30,972
15	39,768	36	31,286	57	32,336
16	32,419	37	35,030	58	28,194
17	37,503	38	34,260	59	29,203
18	31,474	39	35,001	60	28,155
19	35,625	40	36,040	61	28,404
20	33,159	41	36,056	62	34,128
21	34,306	42	31,397		

Week 1 is first week of January. Data shown is from file WFJ_sales.xlsx.

TABLE 2.2   WASHINGTON DULLES INTERNATIONAL AIRPORT, DOMESTIC
PASSENGERS, 1963–2007 (000s)

Year	Passengers	Year	Passengers	Year	Passengers
1963	641	1978	2,518	1993	8,501
1964	728	1979	2,858	1994	8,947
1965	920	1980	2,086	1995	9,653
1966	1,079	1981	1,889	1996	10,095
1967	1,427	1982	2,248	1997	10,697
1968	1,602	1983	2,651	1998	12,445
1969	1,928	1984	3,136	1999	16,055
1970	1,869	1985	4,538	2000	15,873
1971	1,881	1986	8,394	2001	14,021
1972	1,992	1987	9,980	2002	13,146
1973	2,083	1988	8,650	2003	12,928
1974	2,004	1989	9,224	2004	18,213
1975	2,000	1990	9,043	2005	22,129
1976	2,251	1991	9,406	2006	17,787
1977	2,267	1992	9,408	2007	18,792

Source: U.S. Department of Transportation, Bureau of Transport Statistics. Data shown is from file Dulles.xlsx.

To build an effective forecasting system, therefore, we need to understand the kind of data we are handling. That does not mean examining every series in detail, or even at all, but rather looking at a sample of series in order to establish a framework for effective forecasting. Thus, we need to understand when and how to use forecasting methods, how to interpret the results, and how to recognize their limitations.

 ## 2.2   Time Series Plots

Our aim in the next several sections is not to provide detailed technical presentations on the construction of the various plots; rather, we indicate their application in the current context. Guidelines for producing these plots and other analyses appear on the book's website for Excel, EViews, Forecast Pro, Minitab, SAS, and SPSS. Also, you are encouraged to make use of the tutorials provided by these programs, as well as their Help commands. The plots in this chapter are generated by Minitab, unless stated otherwise.

The time series plot for WFJ Sales is shown in Figure 2.1. As its name suggests, a time series plot shows the variable of interest on the vertical axis and time on the horizontal axis. Several features are immediately apparent. Sales are low for the first 12 weeks and then remain stable until week 46, when there is an increase over the Thanksgiving-to-Christmas period and then a peak in the last week of the year. Sales in the next year are lower than for the final weeks of the previous year, but higher than for the corresponding period a year before. We should not make too much of data for one product over little more than a year, but inspection of the plot has revealed a number of interesting patterns that we might check out for similar products. If these patterns were found to persist across a number of product lines, we would need to take them into account in production planning. For example, the company might initiate extra shifts or overtime to cover peak periods and might plan to replenish inventories during slack times.

FIGURE 2.1   TIME SERIES PLOT OF WEEKLY WFJ SALES

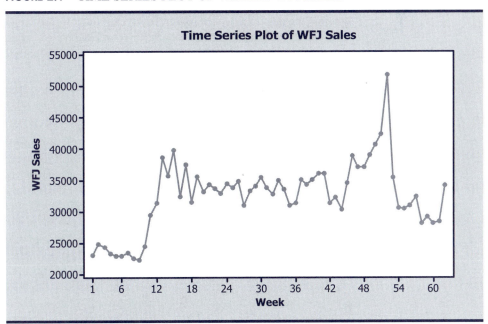

Data: WFJ_sales.xlsx.

FIGURE 2.2   TIME SERIES PLOT OF DOMESTIC PASSENGERS AT DULLES, 1963–2007

Data: Dulles.xlsx.

The second time plot, in Figure 2.2, presents the data on airline passengers in Table 2.2. The figure shows steady growth from 1962 to 1979 (the airport opened in 1962), then a pause followed by rapid growth in the late eighties. A further pause in the early nineties was followed by a long period of growth, with peaks in 1999 and 2005, and then short-term declines. A detailed explanation of these changes lies outside the present discussion; more detailed explanations would require us to examine airport expansion plans, overall levels of passenger demand, the traffic at other airports in the area, and so on. The key point is that a time series plot can tell us a lot about the phenomenon under study and often suggests suitable approaches to forecasting.

2.2.1 Seasonal Plots

Figure 2.1 has some elements of a seasonal pattern (the end-of-year peak) but with just one year of data from which to identify seasonal behavior. Clearly, Figure 2.2 has no seasonal pattern, because the figures represent complete years. However, seasonal variations are often very important for planning purposes, and it is desirable to have a graphical procedure that allows us to explore whether seasonal patterns exist. For monthly data, for example, we may plot the variable of interest against the months and generate a separate, but overlaid, plot for a succession of years. In Figure 2.3A, we provide such a plot for airline revenue passenger miles (*RPM*). *RPM* measures the total number of revenue-generating miles flown by passengers of U.S. airlines, measured in billions of miles. To avoid cluttering the diagram, we use only five years of data, for 2000–2004; a multicolored diagram that could be created online is more informative and can readily accommodate more years without confusion.

In Figure 2.3A, the line for each year lies above those for earlier years, with only rare exceptions. This configuration indicates the steady growth in airline traffic over the period

FIGURE 2.3 SEASONAL PLOTS FOR AIRLINE REVENUE PASSENGER MILES
FOR 2000–2004
A: Scatterplot by Month, with Years Overlaid, of RPM vs. Month
B: Time Series Plot of RPM, with Each Year Identified as a Subgroup

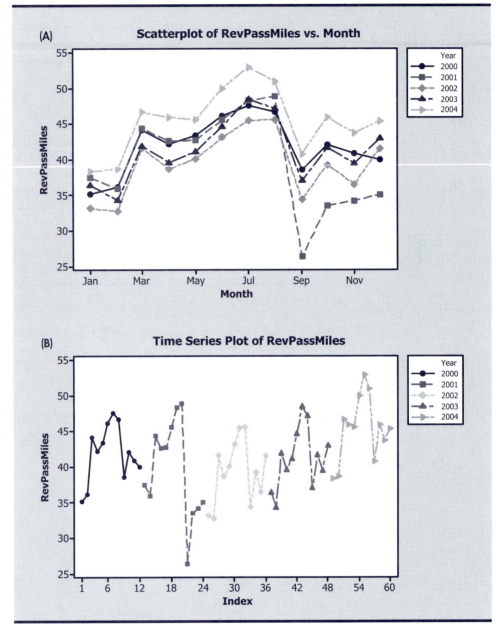

Data shown is from file Revenue_miles.xlsx.

shown. Figure 2.3B also shows the trend and the seasonal peaks and allows easy comparison of successive seasonal cycles. There is a major seasonal peak in the summer, as well as a lesser peak in March–April depending on the timing of Easter. These plots of the data provide considerable insight into the variations in demand for air travel. "Draw the doggone diagram" (DDD) is indeed wise counsel!

2.3 Scatterplots

The time series plots displayed so far show the evolution of a single series over time. As we saw with the seasonal plot, we can show multiple series on the same chart, although some care is required to make the axes sufficiently similar. An alternative is to plot the variable of interest against one or more potential explanatory variables, to see how far knowledge of the explanatory variable(s) might improve the forecasts of the variable of interest. Such scatterplots are valuable for both cross-sectional and time series data.

In Figure 2.4, we show a cross-sectional scatterplot for data taken from *BusinessWeek* in 2004 that apply to 100 "Hot Growth Companies." The companies were selected on the basis of their performance over the previous three years in respect of sales growth, earnings growth, and the return on invested capital, all taken as three-year averages. The data are given in Table 2.3. In the diagram, we plot the price–earnings (*P/E*) ratio against the return on capital (*ROC*) in order to determine whether variations in *ROC* are a major determinant of the company's P/E ratio. Although, clearly, some relationship exists between the two variables, it is also clear that the stock prices reflect a much more complex evaluation of a company's performance than simply looking at the recent return on capital.

In its report, *BusinessWeek* ranked the 100 companies, and we may check how far these two factors went into the ranking by looking at the relevant scatterplots, shown in Figure 2.5. The plots exhibit a strong relationship between *ROC* and rank, but a much weaker one between the P/E ratio and rank. Such a finding is hardly surprising: The *BusinessWeek* ranking gave 50 percent weight to a company's *ROC* ranking, along with 25 percent each for sales growth and profits growth.

We often have multiple variables of interest and want to look for relationships among them. Rather than generate a series of scatterplots, we may combine them into a *matrix*

FIGURE 2.4   SCATTERPLOT OF P/E RATIO VS. RETURN ON CAPITAL
FOR 100 HOT GROWTH COMPANIES

Data shown is from file Growth_companies.xlsx.

TABLE 2.3   LISTING OF RANK, P/E RATIO VS. RETURN ON CAPITAL FOR 100 HOT GROWTH COMPANIES

Rank	Return on Capital	P/E Ratio	Rank	Return on Capital	P/E Ratio	Rank	Return on Capital	P/E Ratio
1	51.5	37	35	19.6	17	68	15.5	14
2	68.5	53	36	16.7	11	69	12.6	17
3	35.3	71	37	13.1	41	70	7.6	24
4	28.7	21	38	17.8	43	71	7.5	43
5	28.2	26	39	17.7	28	72	13.4	28
6	29.8	14	40	14.5	52	73	7.4	14
7	24.4	36	41	15.2	22	74	15.6	26
8	27.4	38	42	8.9	*	75	11.5	25
9	32.3	24	43	14.7	31	76	10.0	31
10	35.1	37	44	12.0	19	77	8.6	15
11	32.5	26	45	10.9	19	78	14.0	31
12	15.9	36	46	14.8	22	79	12.9	20
13	18.5	47	47	15.9	11	80	10.4	16
14	15.0	22	48	12.9	38	81	12.2	19
15	22.3	13	49	21.8	21	82	9.3	32
16	17.2	26	50	12.1	30	83	12.6	21
17	21.2	24	51	8.5	25	84	12.5	26
18	13.5	19	52	18.6	25	85	13.0	39
19	30.3	48	53	12.1	22	86	15.8	32
20	21.2	27	54	15.1	21	87	14.4	28
21	14.1	50	55	17.9	15	88	10.6	16
22	26.7	55	56	9.0	25	89	12.2	31
23	16.1	23	57	11.0	29	90	11.4	13
24	20.3	33	58	18.1	24	91	11.7	6
25	21.2	15	59	6.3	30	92	12.3	37
26	18.3	14	60	15.1	23	93	12.3	29
27	30.6	22	61	15.9	22	94	14.5	20
28	16.6	34	62	15.8	19	95	13.0	28
29	15.7	7	63	18.9	23	96	14.0	23
30	13.4	42	64	12.7	18	97	10.6	30
31	28.2	18	65	15.1	28	98	11.0	21
32	11.2	45	66	8.7	29	99	10.4	31
33	17.3	26	67	15.1	25	100	11.1	29
34	19.9	27						

*P/E ratio not recorded

Source: BusinessWeek, June 7, 2004, pp. 104–109. *Data:* Growth_companies.xlsx.

plot, which is just a two-way array of plots of each variable against each of the others. The matrix plot for P/E ratio, *ROC*, and rank is shown in Figure 2.6. The three plots in the upper right are those shown in Figures 2.4 and 2.5. The plots in the bottom left are these same three plots, but with the *x*- and *y*-axes reversed. The matrix plot provides a condensed summary of the relationships among multiple variables and is a useful screening device for relevant variables in the early stages of a forecasting exercise.

For the data shown, the relationship between the P/E ratio and the *ROC* appears to be weaker than we might expect. The reason lies in the set of data used. We are looking at

FIGURE 2.5   A: SCATTERPLOT OF RETURN ON CAPITAL VS. RANK.
B: SCATTERPLOT OF P/E RATIO VS. RANK

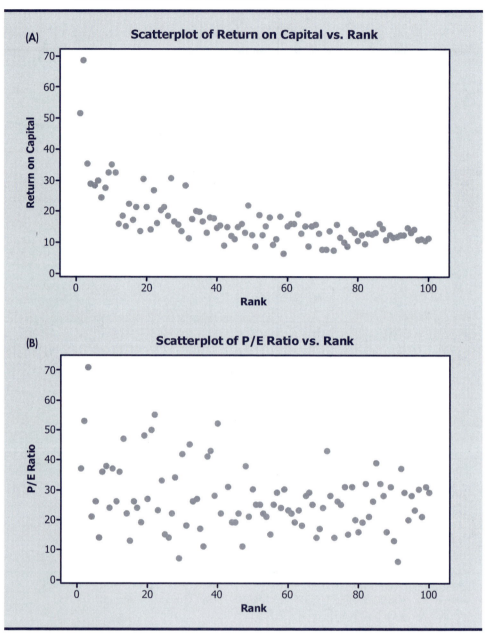

Data: Growth_companies.xlsx.

the records of 100 companies selected for their recent strong performance, so these companies have strong financial foundations. A random sample of *all* companies would show greater variations in performance but a stronger overall relationship. A fundamental, but often overlooked, feature of any statistical study—especially any forecasting study—is that the sample data must be relevant for the task in hand. The data set in Table 2.3 is useful if we are trying to evaluate a possible investment in a growth company, but much less so if we are trying to understand overall market valuations.

FIGURE 2.6   MATRIX PLOT FOR P/E RATIO, ROC, AND RANK FOR 100 HOT
GROWTH COMPANIES

Data: Growth_companies.xlsx.

2.4 Summarizing the Data

Graphical summaries provide invaluable insights. Time plots and scatterplots should always be used in the early stages of a forecasting study to aid understanding. Furthermore, as we will see in later chapters, such diagrams also play an invaluable role in providing diagnostics for further model development. Even when we have a large number of items to forecast, plots for a sample from the whole set of series provide useful guidance and insights.

At the same time, we must recognize that, although graphical methods provide qualitative insights, we often need some kind of numerical summary, such as the average level of sales over time or the variability in P/E ratios across companies. These measures are also valuable for diagnostic purposes, when we seek to summarize forecasting errors, as in Section 2.7.

2.4.1 Notational Conventions

At this stage, we need to elaborate upon some notational conventions because we will use the following framework throughout the remainder of the book:

1. *Random variables and observations:* When we speak of an *observation*, it is something we have already recorded, a specific number or category. By contrast, when we talk about *future observations*, uncertainty exists. For example, for tomorrow's closing price of the Dow Jones Index, we face a range of possibilities that can be described by a probability distribution. Such a variable, with both a set of possible values and an associated probability distribution, is known as a *random variable*. Texts with a more theoretical orientation often use uppercase letters to denote random variables and lowercase letters for observations that have already been recorded. By contrast,

books that are more applied often make no distinction but rely upon the context to make the difference clear. We will follow the second course of action and generally use the same notation for both existing observations and random variables.

2. *Variables and parameters:* As just noted, *variables* are entities that we can observe, such as sales or incomes. By contrast, *parameters* contribute to the description of an underlying process (e.g., a population mean) and are typically not observable. We distinguish these concepts by using the Roman alphabet for variables (sample values), but Greek letters for parameters (population values). Thus, the variable we wish to forecast will always be denoted by Y and, where appropriate, the sample mean and standard deviation by $\bar{Y}$ and S. The corresponding population mean and standard deviation will be denoted by μ (mu) and σ (sigma), respectively.

3. *Probability distributions:* The concept of a probability distribution can be somewhat elusive in a time series context. Consider the daily closing prices for a stock such as IBM. There is only one IBM, and only one closing price each day. Nevertheless, we could define a probability distribution for future closing prices, known as a *predictive* (or *prediction*) *distribution*. That is, probabilities are associated with the set of possible prices. Such a "population" is conceptual in that the values are not attached to real items and only one actual value will ever be recorded.

2.4.2   Measures of Average

By far the most important measure of average is the *arithmetic mean*, often known simply as the mean or the average.

Arithmetic Mean

Given a set of n values $Y_1, Y_2, \ldots, Y_n$, the arithmetic mean is

$$\bar{Y} = \frac{Y_1 + Y_2 + \cdots + Y_n}{n} = \frac{1}{n} \sum_{i=1}^{i=n} Y_i. \tag{2.1}$$

That is, the sum of the observations is divided by the number of values included.

When the range of the summation is clear from the context, such as the index going from 1 to n in the formula, we often write the summation sign without including the limits.

An alternative measure of average is given by the *median,* defined as follows:

Median and Order Statistics

Given a set of n values $Y_1, Y_2, \ldots, Y_n$, we place these values in ascending order to define the *order statistics*, written as $Y_{(1)} \leq Y_{(2)} \leq \cdots \leq Y_{(n)}$. Then

If n is odd, $n = 2m + 1$ and the *median* is $Y_{(m+1)}$.

If n is even, $n = 2m$ and the *median* is $\frac{1}{2}[Y_{(m)} + Y_{(m+1)}]$. The median is the "middle" value.

EXAMPLE 2.1 ■ Calculation of the mean and median

Suppose the sales of a popular book over a seven-week period are as follows:

Week	1	2	3	4	5	6	7
Sales (000s)	15	10	12	16	9	8	14

The mean is $\bar{Y} = \dfrac{(15 + 10 + 12 + 16 + 9 + 8 + 14)}{7} = 12$.

The *order statistics* are 8, 9, 10, 12, 14, 15, 16.

Hence, the median is the fourth value in the sequence, which also happens to be 12. If data for week 8 now become available (sales = 16), then the mean becomes 12.5 and the median is ½[12 + 14] = 13. However, suppose that sales for week 8 had been 116, because of a sudden surge in popularity. Then the mean becomes 25, yet the median remains at 13. In general, the mean is sensitive to extreme observations but the median is not.

Which value represents the "true" average? The question cannot be answered as framed. The median provides a better view of weekly sales over the first eight weeks, but we are more interested in the numbers actually sold. The forecaster has the unenviable task of trying to decide whether future sales will continue at the giddy level of 100,000+ or whether they will revert to the earlier, more modest level. The wise forecaster would enquire into the reasons for the sudden jump, such as a rare large order or a major publicity event. ■

Discussion Question *How would you describe housing prices in an area if you were (a) planning to buy a home in the area and (b) seeking to forecast revenues from the local property tax.*

2.4.3 Measures of Variation

A safe investment is an investment whose value does not fluctuate much over time. Similarly, inventory planning is much more straightforward if sales are virtually the same each period. Implicit in both of these statements is the idea that we use some measure of variability to evaluate risk, whether of losing money or of running out of stock. Three measures of variability are in common use: the *range*, the *mean absolute deviation*, and the *standard deviation*. The standard deviation is derived from the *variance*, which we also define here.

Range

The *range* denotes the difference between the largest and smallest values in the sample:
$$Range = Y_{(n)} - Y_{(1)}.$$

The *deviations* are defined as the differences between each observation and the mean written as $d = Y - \bar{Y}$. By construction, the mean of the deviations is zero; so, to compute a measure of variability, we use either the absolute values or the squared values. The absolute values are indicated by vertical lines on either side of the variable, such as $|d|$ for the absolute value of the deviation d.

If we use the squares, our units of measurement become squared also. For example, revenues (in \$) become $(\$)^2$, so we reverse the operation after computing the average by taking the square root. These various measures are defined as follows, in terms of the deviations:

Measures of Dispersion

The *mean absolute deviation* is the average of the deviations about the mean, irrespective of the sign:
$$MAD = \frac{\sum |d_i|}{n}. \qquad (2.2)$$

The *variance* is an average of the squared deviations about the mean:
$$S^2 = \frac{\sum d_i^2}{(n-1)}. \qquad (2.3)$$

Standard Deviation—a Measure of Dispersion

The *standard deviation* is the square root of the variance:

$$S = \sqrt{S^2} = \sqrt{\frac{\sum d_i^2}{(n-1)}}. \tag{2.4}$$

EXAMPLE 2.2 ■ Calculation of measures of variation

Consider the values for the seven weeks of book sales, given in Example 2.1. From the order statistics, we immediately see that the range is

$$Range = 16 - 8 = 8.$$

However, if week 8 is entered with sales = 116, the range shoots up to $116 - 8 = 108$. This simple example illustrates both the strength and the weakness of the range: It is very easy to compute, but it is severely affected by extreme values. The vulnerability of the range to extreme values makes it unsuitable for most purposes in forecasting.

The deviations for the seven weeks are as follows:

Week	1	2	3	4	5	6	7	Sums
Sales (000s)	15	10	12	16	9	8	14	84
Deviation	+3	−2	0	+4	−3	−4	+2	0
$|d|$	3	2	0	4	3	4	2	18
d^2	9	4	0	16	9	16	4	58

From the table, we have $MAD = 18/7 = 2.57$, $S^2 = 58/6 = 9.67$ and $S = 3.11$. ■

Why do we use $(n-1)$ rather than n in the denominator of the variance? The reason is that, because we are using the deviations, if we had only one observation, its deviation would necessarily be zero. In other words, we have no information about the variability in the data. Likewise, in our sample of seven, if we know six of the deviations, we can work out the value of the seventh observation from the fact that they must sum to zero. In effect, by subtracting the mean from each observation, we have "lost" an observation. In statistical parlance, this is known as *losing a degree of freedom* (*DF*), and we say that the variance is computed under the assumption that there are $(n-1)$ degrees of freedom, which we abbreviate to $(n-1)$ DF. In later chapters, we sometimes lose several DF, and the definitions of variability will change accordingly. This adjustment has the benefit of making the sample variance an unbiased estimator of the population variance. (See Appendix A, Section A3, located on the textbook companion site.)

Note: S gives greater weight to the more extreme observations by squaring them, and it may be shown that $S > MAD$ whenever MAD is greater than zero.

Discussion Question   *Why don't we use $(n-1)$ in the MAD?*

2.4.4 Assessing Variability

The statement that book sales have a standard deviation of 3.11 (thousand, remember) conveys little about the inherent variability in the data from week to week, unless, like any penniless author, we live and breathe details about the sales of that particular book. To produce a more standard frame of reference, we use *standardized scores*. Given a sample mean $\bar{Y}$ and sample standard deviation S, we define the standardized scores for the observations, also known as Z-scores, as

$$Z_i = \frac{Y_i - \bar{Y}}{S}.$$

$$1.5 = \frac{X - 52.0338}{43.60541}$$

Each deviation is divided by the standard deviation. It follows that the Z-scores have zero mean and a standard deviation equal to 1.0. Following our simple example, we obtain the following table:

Week	1	2	3	4	5	6	7
Sales (000s)	15	10	12	16	9	8	14
Deviation	+3	−2	0	+4	−3	−4	+2
Z-score	0.96	−0.64	0	1.29	−0.96	−1.29	0.64

The Z-scores still do not provide much information until we provide a frame of reference. In this book, we typically use Z-scores to examine forecast errors and proceed in three steps:

1. Check that the observed distribution of the errors is approximately normal. (For details, see on-line Appendix A, Section A5 or a statistical text such as Anderson *et al.*, 2011).
2. If the assumption is satisfied, relate the Z-score to the normal distribution [tables are available in any statistics textbook (see Anderson et al., 2011) or use the Excel function =NORMDIST (value, 0, 1, 1), which calculates the cumulative probability of Z-score <value from a normal distribution with mean 0 and variance 1]:

   - The probability that $|Z| > 1$ is about 0.32 (or about 3 in 10).
   - The probability that $|Z| > 2$ is about 0.046 (about 5 in 100).
   - The probability that $|Z| > 3$ is about 0.0027 (about 3 in 1000).

   Most software packages include similar functions.
3. Create a time series plot of the residuals (and/or Z-scores), when appropriate, to determine whether any observations appear to be extreme.

At this stage, we do not pursue the systematic use of Z-scores, except to recognize that whenever you see a Z-score whose absolute value is greater than 3, the observation is atypical, because the probability of such an occurrence is less than 3 in 1000 (if the distribution is approximately normal). Often, such large values signify that something unusual has happened, and we refer to these kinds of observations as *outliers*. In cross-sectional studies, it is sometimes admissible to just delete such observations (e.g., a report of a 280-year-old man is undoubtedly a recording error). In time series forecasting, we wish to retain the complete sequence of values and must investigate more closely, often finding special circumstances (e.g., a strike, bad weather, a special sales promotion) for which we had not allowed. Outliers indicate the need for further exploration, not routine rejection. We defer the detailed treatment of outliers to Chapter 9.

2.4.5 An Example: Hot Growth Companies

The default summary outputs for Minitab and Excel for the data in Table 2.3 on "Hot Growth Companies" are shown in Figure 2.7. The output from other programs may have a somewhat different format, but the summary measures included are similar and most programs allow

FIGURE 2.7 DESCRIPTIVE STATISTICS FOR HOT GROWTH COMPANIES

Descriptive Statistics: Return on Capital, P-E Ratio

Variable	N	N*	Mean	SE Mean	StDev	Variance	Minimum	Q1
Return on Capital	100	0	17.028	0.900	8.998	80.961	6.300	12.100
P-E Ratio	99	1	27.06	1.12	11.11	123.36	6.00	20.00

Variable	Median	Q3	Maximum	Range
Return on Capital	14.900	18.575	68.500	62.200
P-E Ratio	25.00	31.00	71.00	65.00

(A) Minitab

(B) Growth_companies.xlsx

Data: Growth_companies.xlsx.

TABLE 2.4 Z-SCORES FOR HOT GROWTH COMPANIES

Rank	Return on Capital	P/E Ratio	Z-ROC	Z-PE
1	51.5	37	**3.83**	0.89
2	68.5	53	**5.72**	2.33
3	35.3	71	2.03	**3.95**
4	28.7	21	1.30	−0.55
5	28.2	26	1.24	−0.10
6	29.8	14	1.42	−1.18
7	24.4	36	0.82	0.80
94	14.5	20	−0.28	−0.64
95	13.0	28	−0.45	0.08
96	14.0	23	−0.34	−0.37
97	10.6	30	−0.71	0.26
98	11.0	21	−0.67	−0.55
99	10.4	31	−0.74	0.35
100	11.1	29	−0.66	0.17

© Cengage Learning 2013.

a variety of options. Excel typically produces too many decimal places; for ease of comparison, our output has been edited to produce a reasonable number of decimal places. Note that the count of observations is one fewer for the *P/E* ratio because we had a missing value. The missing value was a true outlier given that the company had negative earnings.

Given the mean and standard deviation, we proceed to compute the Z-scores, shown in Table 2.4. We list the top seven companies because the interesting features are associated with the top few on the list; those ranked 94–100 are provided for comparison. In Table 2.4, the Z-scores whose absolute values are greater than 3 are in bold type; none of the remaining companies had any Z-scores outside ±3. From the table, it is clear that the first two companies on the list have an *ROC* much greater than the rest, whereas the third has a P/E ratio that is much larger. Numbers 94–100 have negative Z-scores for *ROC* and typically small scores for their P/E ratios. That is, they do not look so good, although this is only with reference to the illustrious company they are keeping. Across all public companies, these 100 would show impressive figures that yielded positive Z-scores.

2.5 Correlation

In the previous section, we produced numerical summaries to complement the graphical analysis of Section 2.2. We now develop a statistic that performs a similar function for the scatterplots of Section 2.3: the *correlation coefficient*. Before defining the coefficient, we examine Figure 2.8; in each case, the horizontal axis may be interpreted as time. The six plots suggest the following:

$Y1$ increases with time and is perfectly related to time.

$Y2$ decreases with time and is perfectly related to time.

$Y3$ tends to increase with time but is not perfectly related to time.

$Y4$ tends to decrease with time, but the relationship is weaker than that for $Y3$.

$Y5$ shows virtually no relationship with time.

$Y6$ is perfectly related to time, but the relationship is not linear.

FIGURE 2.8   PLOTS OF HYPOTHETICAL DATA AGAINST TIME

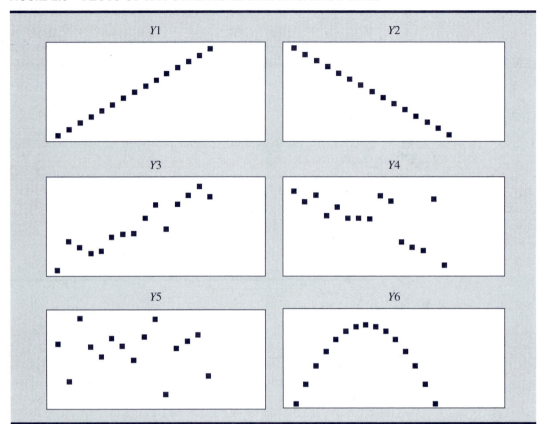

© Cengage Learning 2013.

Our measure should reflect these differences but not be affected by changes in the origin or changes of scale. The origins and scales of the variables are deliberately omitted from the diagrams because they do not affect the degree of association between the two variables. The most commonly used measure that satisfies these criteria is the *(Pearson) product moment correlation coefficient*, which we simply refer to as *the* correlation. We use the letter r to denote the sample coefficient and the Greek letter ρ (rho) to denote the corresponding population quantity. Our definition refers to the sample quantity; the population definition follows on replacing the sample components by their corresponding population parameters.

The Correlation Coefficient

The sample *correlation* between X and Y is defined as

$$r = \frac{\sum_{i=1}^{n}(X_i - \bar{X})(Y_i - \bar{Y})}{\sqrt{\sum_{i=1}^{n}(X_i - \bar{X})^2 \sum_{i=1}^{n}(Y_i - \bar{Y})^2}}. \tag{2.5}$$

The numerator represents the sum of cross products of the deviations, and the denominator terms are sums of squares of the two sets of deviations.

When we divide denominator by $(n-1)$, the two terms inside the square-root sign become the sample variances of X and Y, respectively; Thus, upon taking the square root, the denominator represents the product of the two standard deviations S_X and S_Y. The numerator divided by $(n-1)$ is known as the sample *covariance* between X and Y, denoted by S_{XY}. Thus, the correlation may be written as

$$r = \frac{S_{XY}}{S_X S_Y}. \qquad (2.6)$$

It may be shown that, for $Y1$ in Figure 2.8, $r = 1$, the maximum value possible. Similarly, $Y2$ has $r = -1$, the minimum possible. The other correlations are, 0.93, –0.66, –0.09, and 0, for $Y3$, $Y4$, $Y5$, and $Y6$, respectively. In general, we see that the *absolute* value of r declines as the relationship gets weaker. At first sight, the result for $Y6$ appears odd: There is a clear relationship with X, but the correlation is zero. The reason for this is that r measures *linear* association, but the relationship with X is *quadratic* rather than linear. A good example is the relationship between total revenue and price: Charge too much or too little, and total revenue is low.

Discussion Question *How would you measure the relationship between Y6 and time?*

EXAMPLE 2.3 ■ Calculation of the correlation

Based on the data from Example 2.1, the detailed calculations for the correlation between sales and time are shown in the table that follows. A spreadsheet could readily be set up in this format for direct calculations, but all standard software packages have a correlation function.

Week, X	1	2	3	4	5	6	7	Sums
Sales (000s), Y	15	10	12	16	9	8	14	
$X - \bar{X}$	−3	−2	−1	0	1	2	3	0
$Y - \bar{Y}$	+3	−2	0	+4	−3	−4	+2	0
$(X - \bar{X})^2$	9	4	1	0	1	4	9	28
$(Y - \bar{Y})^2$	9	4	0	16	9	16	4	58
$(X - \bar{X})(Y - \bar{Y})$	−9	4	0	0	−3	−8	6	−10

Thus, $S_{XY} = -10/6$, $S_X = \sqrt{28/6}$, and $S_Y = \sqrt{58/6}$, so $r = -0.248$. ■

The example shows a weak negative correlation for sales with time; that is, sales may be declining slightly over time.

EXAMPLE 2.4 ■ Correlation for Hot Growth Companies

For the data given in Table 2.3, the correlations among rank, *ROC*, and P/E ratio are as follows:

Variables	Correlation
Rank and ROC	–0.647
Rank and P/E ratio	–0.267
ROC and P/E ratio	0.306

As expected, there is a strong negative correlation between the rank and the *ROC*, because 50 percent of the weight for the ranking is based upon *ROC*. (A high *ROC* relates to a small number for the rank.) The correlation between the P/E ratio and the rank is also negative but weaker (no direct weighting). Finally, we see a modest positive correlation between the *ROC* and the P/E ratio. We may compare these numbers with the plots in Figure 2.5 to gain some insight into their interpretation.

2.6 Transformations

We now examine the annual figures for the number of passengers on domestic flights out of Dulles airport. The descriptive statistics are as follows:

Descriptive Statistics: Passengers

Variable	N	Mean	SE Mean	StDev	Minimum	Q1	Median	Q3	Maximum
Passengers	45	7111	892	5987	641	1996	4538	10396	22129

Dulles, we have a problem! What does the average of 7111 mean? Such levels were typical of the mideighties, but the "average" in a strongly trending series like this one has no meaning. Certainly, using either the mean or the median to forecast the next year's traffic would make no sense.

How should we deal with a series that reveals a strong trend? Everyday conversation provides a clue. We talk of the return on an investment, an increase over the previous year of a variable in sales, or the percentage change in *GDP*. This approach is partly a matter of convenience; some ideas are more readily communicated using (percentage) changes rather than raw figures. Thus, we may regard 3 percent growth in *GDP* as reasonable, 1 percent as anemic, and 10 percent as unsustainable. The same information conveyed in currency terms would be hard to comprehend.

From the forecasting perspective, there are two further reasons for considering such alternatives:

- Because we are examining changes, the forecast relates directly back to the previously observed value; such forecasts are unlikely to be wildly off target.
- Mean levels calculated in terms of absolute changes or percentage changes are often more stable and more meaningful than averages computed from the original series.

We now explore these ideas in greater detail.

2.6.1 Differences and Growth Rates

The change in the absolute level of a series from one period to the next is known as the *(first) difference*[1] of the series and is written as

$$DY_t = Y_t - Y_{t-1}. \tag{2.7}$$

At time t, the previous value Y_{t-1} is already known. If the forecast for the difference is written as $\hat{D}_t$, the forecast for period t becomes

$$F_t = Y_{t-1} + \hat{D}_t. \tag{2.8}$$

---

[1]Some texts use the Greek capital letter Δ (delta) and others use ∇ (an inverted delta, or "del"), but the use of *D* seems a better mnemonic device for "difference."

That is, the complete forecast is the previous level plus the forecast of the change. Similarly, the rate of growth over time is written as[2]

$$GY_t = 100 \frac{(Y_t - Y_{t-1})}{Y_{t-1}}. \tag{2.9}$$

Expression (2.9) also defines the one-period return on an investment, given the opening price of Y_{t-1}. Once the growth rate, denoted by $\hat{G}_t$, has been predicted, the forecast for the next time period is

$$F_t = Y_{t-1}\left[1 + \frac{\hat{G}_t}{100}\right]. \tag{2.10}$$

The time plots for *DY* and *GY* for the Dulles passengers' series are shown in Figure 2.9A and 2.9B. Both series show a fairly stable level over time, so the mean becomes a useful summary again, although *GY* is trending slightly downward, indicating a slowing in percentage growth.

Another feature of Figure 2.9A is that the variability in *DY* is much greater at the end of the series than it is at the beginning. By contrast, the *GY* series has more consistent fluctuations. We could claim that *GY* has a stable variance over time, a claim that would be hard to make for *DY*. Which should we use? In part, the choice will depend upon the purpose behind the forecasting exercise, but an often reasonable guideline is a commonsense one: Do you naturally think of changes in the time series in absolute terms or in relative (i.e., percentage) terms? If the answer is "absolute," use *DY*; if it is "relative," use *GY*. In this case, both transformed series show some unusual values, so further investigation is warranted. Out of interest, we note that Dulles airport underwent a significant expansion in 1984.

The summary statistics for *DY* and *GY* are as follows:

Descriptive Statistics: Difference, Growth Rate

Variable	N	N*	Mean	SE Mean	StDev	Minimum	Q1	Median	Q3	Maximum
Difference	44	1	413	232	1536	−4342	−74	221	552	5285
Growth rate	44	1	9.41	2.83	18.78	−26.99	−1.53	5.93	18.21	84.95

These figures also reflect the considerable fluctuations that appear in each series.

2.6.2   The Log Transform

George Orwell's classic novel *1984* contains, a scene in which the chocolate ration is reduced by 50 percent and then increased by 50 percent. The main character, Winston, complains that he does not have as much chocolate as before, but he is sharply rebuked for his remarks. However, Winston is right:

$$\left(1 - \frac{50}{100}\right)\left(1 + \frac{50}{100}\right) = 0.75.$$

So Winston has 25 percent less chocolate than before. To avoid this asymmetry, we may use the logarithmic (or log) transform, usually with the *natural logarithm* defined on the base

---

[2]The use of *G* to describe the growth rate is nonstandard; we use it here for the same reason as before: It is a convenient mnemonic device.

FIGURE 2.9   A: TIME SERIES PLOT FOR THE FIRST DIFFERENCES OF THE DULLES
PASSENGERS SERIES (*DY*)
B: TIME SERIES PLOT FOR THE GROWTH RATES FOR THE DULLES
PASSENGERS SERIES (*GY*)

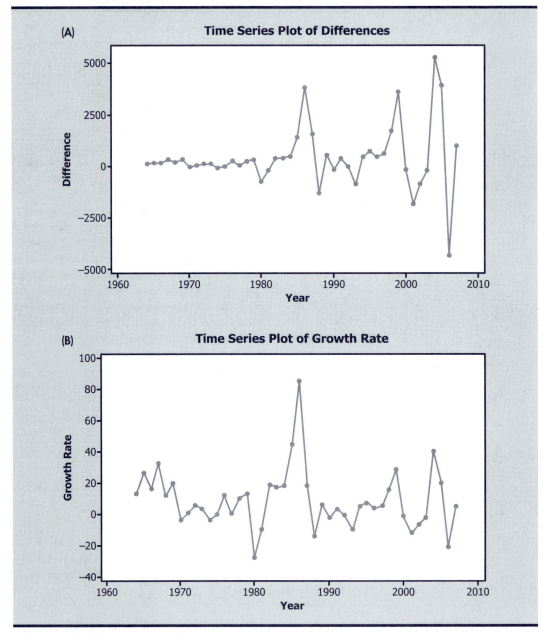

Data: Dulles.xlsx.

$e = 2.71828. \ldots$ The log transform may be written as $L_t = \ln(Y_t)$, and any software
package has a function such as ln to compute the natural logarithm. To convert back to
the original units, we use an inverse function (or reverse transformation) called exp, so we
have $Y_t = \exp(L_t)$. The (first) difference in logarithms represents the logarithm of the ratio:

$$\mathrm{DL}_t = \ln(Y_t/Y_{t-1}) = \ln(Y_t) - \ln(Y_{t-1}). \tag{2.11}$$

FIGURE 2.10   TIME SERIES PLOT FOR THE FIRST DIFFERENCE OF LOGARITHMS FOR
THE DULLES PASSENGERS' SERIES (DL_Pass)

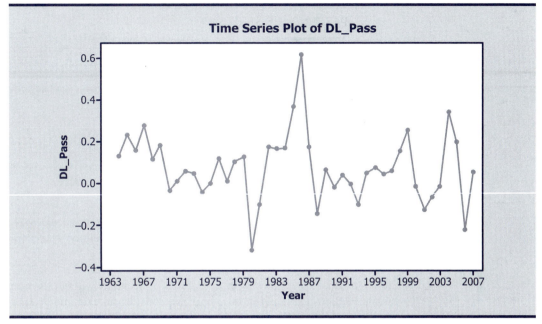

Data: Dulles.xlsx.

The primary purpose of the log transform is to convert exponential (or proportional) growth into linear growth. The transform often has the secondary benefit of stabilizing the variance, as did the use of growth rates. Indeed, the log and growth rate transforms tend to produce similar results, as can be seen by comparing the plot of the log differences for the Dulles passengers' series in Figure 2.10 with Figure 2.9B.

If we generate a forecast of the log difference, say, DL_t, then the forecast for the original series requires that we reverse the log transform by using the exponential function, usually written as exp. Given the previous value, Y_{t-1}, the forecast for period t becomes

$$\hat{Y}_t = Y_{t-1} \exp(\widehat{DL}_t) \tag{2.12}$$

EXAMPLE 2.5 ■ Calculation of forecast using log differences

The actual number of passengers using Dulles International Airport in 2007 was 18,792 (in thousands). To make a forecast for 2008, we might use the last value for the log difference, which is 0.05496. Then equation (2.12) yields

$$\hat{Y}_t = 18792 \exp(0.05496) = 18792*1.0565 = 19854.$$

When x is small, $\exp(x) \approx 1 + x$, which explains why the growth rate and log transform analyses often produce similar results.   ■

2.7   How to Measure Forecasting Accuracy

A key question in any forecasting endeavor is how to measure performance. Performance measures are of particular value when we come to select a forecasting procedure, because we may compare alternatives and choose the method with the best track record. Then, once the method is being used on a regular basis, we need similar measures to tell us

TABLE 2.5   DAILY HIGH TEMPERATURE FORECASTS FOR AT REAGAN
NATIONAL AIRPORT, WASHINGTON, DC (*December 17–22, 2003*)

	Forecasts (days ahead)					Actual Temperature (°F)
Date	**1**	**2**	**3**	**4**	**5**	
December 17, 2003	42	40	42	44	48	50
December 18, 2003	36	38	42	50	54	38
December 19, 2003	38	40	52	54	52	37
December 20, 2003	44	52	56	54	48	40
December 21, 2003	52	58	56	48	48	44
December 22, 2003	58	56	44	48	50	57

Source: Washington Post. Data shown is from file DC_weather.xlsx.

whether the forecasts are maintaining their historical level of accuracy. If a particular set of forecasts is not performing adequately, managerial intervention is needed to get things back on track.

The generation of forecasts and the selection of a preferred method occupy a major portion of the book. Therefore, to discuss issues of accuracy without the need to develop forecasting methods explicitly at this stage, we consider an example taken from meteorology. Weather forecasts that appear in the media are not directed at a particular audience, and there is no reason to suppose that forecasts of temperature would have any inherent bias. However, we would expect that such forecasts (and this is typically true of all forecasts) would become less accurate as the forecast horizon increases (in this case, the number of days ahead).

We consider a set of local forecasts for daily high temperatures, extracted from the *Washington Post* for the period from December 17, 2003, to January 5, 2004. The forecasts are generated by *Accuweather,* a weather-forecasting organization. The forecasts appear for 1–5 days ahead, so the initial data could be summarized as shown in Table 2.5 (first few days only). However, this form of presentation is not useful for the evaluation of the forecasts, because, for example, the four-day forecast made on December 17 refers to conditions to be observed on December 21. To match forecasts to actual outcomes, we must slide the columns down, as shown in Table 2.6. We may now compare forecasts in the same row.

In a general sense, it is useful to refer to a forecast for period t as F_t when the time origin of the forecast is not an issue. However, when timing matters, we need to report both the period being forecast and the number of periods ahead of time that the forecast was made. The notation[3] must reflect this information. Accordingly, we will use $F_t(h)$ to denote the forecast for period t, made h periods ahead. Thus, $F_{14}(1)$ refers to the one-step-ahead forecast made for period 14 at period 13, $F_{14}(2)$ to the two-step-ahead forecast made for period 14 at time 12, and so on. These values will be eventually compared with the observed value in period 14, Y_{14}. The general format for calculating the errors is shown in Table 2.7. When there is no risk of confusion, we will use F_t to represent $F_t(1)$.

2.7.1   Measures of Forecasting Accuracy

Now that we have a set of forecasts and actual values with which to compare them, how should the comparisons be made? In principle, the criteria used should reflect the decision maker's loss function (e.g., minimize cost, achieve a certain level of customer service), but

---

[3]The notation for forecasts is not standard. Some texts use F_{t+h} to denote forecasts h steps ahead for Y_{t+h}. Although this notation is simpler than ours and appears to work well when expressed algebraically, as it is here, the notation F_{13+2} (*not* equal to F_{15}!) is potentially confusing and $F_{15}(2)$ is clearer.

TABLE 2.6   TEMPERATURE FORECASTS FOR WASHINGTON, DC

Date	\multicolumn{5}{c}{Forecast Lead Time (days ahead)}	Actual Temperature (°F)
	1	**2**	**3**	**4**	**5**	
December 17, 2003						50
December 18, 2003	42					38
December 19, 2003	36	40				37
December 20, 2003	38	38	42			40
December 21, 2003	44	40	42	44		44
December 22, 2003	52	52	52	50	48	57
December 23, 2003	58	58	56	54	54	62
December 24, 2003	54	56	56	54	52	56
December 25, 2003	45	44	44	48	48	43
December 26, 2003	47	46	49	48	48	44
December 27, 2003	54	52	54	54	50	54
December 28, 2003	54	55	54	50	54	52
December 29, 2003	60	59	58	54	54	60
December 30, 2003	55	53	49	49	51	54
December 31, 2003	53	50	55	53	48	49
January 1, 2004	52	52	56	57	50	55
January 2, 2004	54	54	45	52	48	50
January 3, 2004	69	64	64	62	60	68
January 4, 2004	64	64	62	60	56	72
January 5, 2004	62	58	54	54	51	49

Data: DC_weather.xlsx.

TABLE 2.7   STRUCTURE OF FORECASTS FOR 1, 2, 3, . . . PERIODS AHEAD

Period	\multicolumn{4}{c}{Forecast Lead Time (days ahead)}	Actual
	1	**2**	**3**	**. . .**	
t	$F_t(1)$	$F_t(2)$	$F_t(3)$	. . .	Y_t
$t+1$	$F_{t+1}(1)$	$F_{t+1}(2)$	$F_{t+1}(3)$	. . .	Y_{t+1}
$t+2$	$F_{t+2}(1)$	$F_{t+2}(2)$	$F_{t+2}(3)$	. . .	Y_{t+2}

such information may not be available or the forecasts might be used for multiple purposes. We must then develop general-purpose criteria that can be used in a variety of circumstances. A natural approach is to look at the differences between the observed values and the forecasts and to use their average as a performance measure. Suppose that we start from *forecast origin t* so that the forecasts are made successively (one-step-ahead) for periods $t+1, t+2, \ldots, t+m$, there being m such forecasts in all. Then the one-step-ahead forecast error at time $t+i$ may be denoted by

$$e_{t+i} = Y_{t+i} - F_{t+i}.$$

A possible indicator is the mean of the errors:

The *MEAN ERROR* (*ME*) is given by

$$ME = \sum_{i=1}^{m} (Y_{t+i} - F_{t+i})/m = \sum_{i=1}^{m} e_{t+i}/m. \tag{2.13}$$

The mean error is a useful way of detecting bias in a forecast; that is, *ME* will be large and positive (negative) when the actual value is consistently greater (less) than the forecast. When the variable of interest is strictly positive, such as the number of employees or sales revenues, a percentage measure is often more useful; that is, we express the error as a percentage of the actual value and then take an average.

The *MEAN PERCENTAGE ERROR* (*MPE*) is

$$MPE = \frac{100}{m} \sum_{i=1}^{m} \frac{(Y_{t+i} - F_{t+i})}{Y_{t+i}} = \frac{100}{m} \sum_{i=1}^{m} \frac{e_{t+i}}{Y_{t+i}}. \tag{2.14}$$

Note that *ME* is a useful measure for the temperature data, but *MPE* is not because the temperature can fall below zero. More importantly, temperature does not have a natural origin, so the *MPE* would give different (and equally meaningless) results, depending on whether we used the Fahrenheit or Celsius scale.

EXAMPLE 2.6 ■ Calculation of *ME* and *MPE* (*Electricity.xlsx*)

The calculations of *ME* and *MPE* are illustrated in Table 2.8, in which the data represent the monthly electricity consumption (in KWH, kilowatt hours) in a Washington, DC, household; the column of forecasts represents the consumption in the corresponding month in the previous year. Consumption is low in the winter and high in the summer because the home uses gas heating and electric air-conditioning.

As noted, the *ME* and *MPE* are useful measures of bias. From Table 2.8, we see that the household generally reduced its consumption over the year, so the forecasts tended to be too high. In passing, we note that the year-over-year change is given by comparing the totals for the two years—13,190 and 11,270 KWH, respectively. Such a comparison indicates a 14.6 percent drop. The 18.7 percent average given by the *MPE* reflects month-by-month forecasting performance, not the change in the yearly totals.

A limitation of these measures is that they do not reflect variability. Positive and negative errors could virtually cancel each other out, yet substantial forecasting errors could remain. To see this effect, suppose we used the average monthly figure for the first year to predict the usage in the second year. The average is 1099 KWH, a figure that seriously underestimates summer consumption and overestimates the rest of the year. Yet the *ME* would be unchanged. The *MPE* expands to –37.2, because the errors are larger in the months with low consumption. Such changes are largely illusory. For example, a forecast value of 800 KWH per month is clearly not very useful, yet it reduces the *MPE* to –0.1 (since the monthly average consumption turns out to be 800 KWH).

From this discussion, we evidently also need measures that account for the magnitude of the errors regardless of their signs.   ■

TABLE 2.8   ANALYSIS OF FORECASTING ACCURACY FOR ELECTRICITY CONSUMPTION IN A WASHINGTON, DC, HOUSEHOLD

(A) One Year Ahead Monthly Forecast = Actual Value for that Month in the Previous Year

Period	Actual	Forecast	Errors	Absolute Errors	Percentage Errors	Absolute Percentage Errors	Squared Errors
Jan.	790	820	−30	30	−3.8	3.8	900
Feb.	810	790	20	20	2.5	2.5	400
Mar.	680	720	−40	40	−5.9	5.9	1,600
Apr.	500	640	−140	140	−28.0	28.0	19,600
May	520	780	−260	260	−50.0	50.0	67,600
Jun.	810	980	−170	170	−21.0	21.0	28,900
Jul.	1,120	1,550	−430	430	−38.4	38.4	184,900
Aug.	1,840	1,850	−10	10	−0.5	0.5	100
Sep.	1,600	1,880	−280	280	−17.5	17.5	78,400
Oct.	1,250	1,600	−350	350	−28.0	28.0	122,500
Nov.	740	890	−150	150	−20.3	20.3	22,500
Dec.	610	690	−80	80	−13.1	13.1	6,400

ME = −160.0   MPE = −18.7   Mean Actual = 939.2

MAE = 163.3   MAPE = 19.1   Mean Forecast = 1099.2

MSE = 44,483.3   RMSE = 210.9

(B) One Month Ahead Monthly Forecast = Previous Month's Actual

Period	Actual	Forecast	Errors	Absolute Errors	Percentage Errors	Absolute Percentage Errors	Squared Errors
Jan.	790	690	100	100	12.7	12.7	10,000
Feb.	810	790	20	20	2.5	2.5	400
Mar.	680	810	−130	130	−19.1	19.1	16,900
Apr.	500	680	−180	180	−36.0	36.0	32,400
May	520	500	20	20	3.8	3.8	400
Jun.	810	520	290	290	35.8	35.8	84,100
Jul.	1,120	810	310	310	27.7	27.7	96,100
Aug.	1,840	1,120	720	720	39.1	39.1	518,400
Sep.	1,600	1,840	−240	240	−15.0	15.0	57,600
Oct.	1,250	1,600	−350	350	−28.0	28.0	122,500
Nov.	740	1,250	−510	510	−68.9	68.9	260,100
Dec.	610	740	−130	130	−21.3	21.3	16,900

ME = −6.7   MPE = −5.6

MAE = 250.0   MAPE = 25.8

MSE = 101,316.7 RMSE = 318.3

Data shown is from file Electricity.xlsx.

2.7.2 Measures of Absolute Error

The simplest way to gauge the variability in forecasting performance is to examine the *absolute error*, defined as the value of the error regardless of its sign and expressed as

$$|e_i| = |Y_i - F_i|. \tag{2.15}$$

Thus, if we generate a forecast of $F = 100$, the absolute error is 20 whenever the actual value turns out to be either 80 or 120. As before, we may consider various averages, based upon the absolute errors. Those in common use are summarized in the box that follows.

The *MASE* is a new measure introduced by Hyndman and Koehler (2006). The *MASE* is the ratio of the *MAE* for the current set of forecasts to the *MAE* for forecasts made with the use of the random walk, whose forecast specifies the most recent observation as the forecast for the next period. It should be noted that our definition differs from that of Hyndman and Koehler, as it covers only a single period. When *MASE* is greater than 1, we may conclude that the random-walk forecasts are superior for 1 period ahead. When *MASE* is less than 1, the method under consideration is superior to the random walk.

Theil's U is a long-established criterion that is widely used in econometrics; its structure is similar to that of MASE, using squares in place of absolute values.

One-step Ahead Error Measures starting at Forecast Origin t

Mean absolute error:

$$MAE = \sum_{i=1}^{m} |Y_{t+i} - F_{t+i}|/m = \sum_{i=1}^{m} |e_{t+i}|/m \tag{2.16}$$

Mean absolute percentage error:

$$MAPE = \frac{100}{m} \sum_{i=1}^{m} \frac{|Y_{t+i} - F_{t+i}|}{Y_{t+i}} = \frac{100}{m} \sum_{i=1}^{m} \frac{|e_{t+i}|}{Y_{t+i}} \tag{2.17}$$

Mean square error:

$$MSE = \sum_{i=1}^{m} (Y_{t+i} - F_{t+i})^2/m = \sum_{i=1}^{m} e_{t+i}^2/m \tag{2.18}$$

Root-mean-square error:

$$RMSE = \sqrt{MSE} \tag{2.19}$$

Mean absolute scaled error:

$$MASE = \frac{\sum_{i=1}^{m} |Y_{t+i} - F_{t+i}|}{\sum_{i=1}^{m} |Y_{t+i} - Y_{t+i-1}|} \tag{2.20}$$

Theil's U:

$$U = \frac{\left\{\sum_{i=1}^{m} [Y_{t+i} - F_{t+i}]^2\right\}^{1/2}}{\left\{\sum_{i=1}^{m} [Y_{t+i} - Y_{t+i-1}]^2\right\}^{1/2}} \tag{2.21}$$

The following comments are in order:

1. *MAPE* should be used only when $Y > 0$; *MASE* and U are not so restricted.
2. The *RMSE* is used because the *MSE* involves squared errors so that the *MSE* is measured in dollars squared. Taking the square root to obtain the *RMSE* restores the original units of dollars and makes interpretation more straightforward.

3. The *RMSE* gives greater weight to large (absolute) errors. It can be shown that *RMSE* ≥ *MAE* for any set of *m* forecasts; recall the discussion in Section 2.4.3.

4. The measure using absolute values always equals or exceeds the absolute value of the measure based on the errors, so *MAE* ≥ *ME* and *MAPE* ≥ *MPE*. Values that are close in magnitude suggest a systematic bias in the forecasts.

5. *MAPE*, *MASE*, and *U* are scale free and so can be used to make comparisons across multiple series. The other measures are scale dependent and cannot be used to make such comparisons without an additional scaling.

6. All these measures may be defined for more than one period ahead simply by replacing the one-step-ahead forecasts by their *h*-step-ahead counterparts.

EXAMPLE 2.7 ■ Calculation of absolute error measures

Recall the absolute error measures computed in Table 2.8 for the electricity forecasts. The individual terms are shown in the various columns, and *MAE*, *MAPE*, and *MSE* are then evaluated as the column averages. *RMSE* follows directly from equation (2.18)—that is, by taking the square root of *MSE*. Part (B) of Table 2.8 gives the error measures for the random-walk (one month ahead) forecasts, so *MASE* is given by the ratio of the forecast *MAE* in part (A) of the table to the *MAE* of the random-walk forecasts. Relative to the random-walk methods, the forecasts based upon the same month in the previous year provide a 35 percent [= 100 * (250.0 − 163.3)/250.0] reduction in the mean absolute error.

Table 2.9 provides a comparison of the three sets of forecasts for electricity consumption:

- Last year's value for the same month, as given in Table 2.8
- Monthly average for the previous year (= 1099 for all 12 months)
- Forecast set at 800 for all 12 months.

From the table, we see that the forecasts based upon last year's figures are clearly more accurate. Indeed, some local utilities use these forecasts to estimate customers' bills when no meter readings are available. The *ME* and *MPE* values indicate that the forecasts were somewhat biased. Did the household deliberately try to conserve energy? Perhaps, but the lower figures in the summer suggest that the second year had a cooler summer; this is not something that could be reliably forecast at the beginning of January.   ■

EXAMPLE 2.8 ■ Comparison of weather-forecasting errors

We may now use the measures we have examined to assess the performance of the various forecasts presented in Table 2.6. The results are given in Table 2.10; the *MPE* and the *MAPE* are not reported, because they are not sensible measures in this case. As is to be expected, the *MAE* and *RMSE* generally increase as the forecast horizon is extended; forecasts become less accurate as we get farther away from the event.

TABLE 2.9   COMPARISON OF FORECASTS FOR ELECTRICITY DATA

Forecasting Method	Error Measure						
	ME	MPE	MAE	MAPE	RMSE	MASE	U
Last year's values	−160	−18.7	163	19.1	211	0.65	0.66
Monthly average	−160	−37.2	396	51.5	440	1.58	1.38
All *F* = 800	139	0.1	299	28.8	433	1.20	1.36
Random walk	−6.7	−5.6	250	25.8	318	1.00	1.00

Data: Electricity.xlsx.

TABLE 2.10   SUMMARY OF FORECAST ERRORS FOR WEATHER DATA
(Values Computed over December 22 to January 5)

	Steps Ahead				
Measure	1	2	3	4	5
ME	−0.53	0.53	1.13	1.73	3.53
MAE	3.47	3.20	3.80	4.67	5.27
RMSE	4.75	4.07	4.64	5.49	6.43
MASE	0.42	0.30	0.35	0.40	0.69
U	0.47	0.32	0.35	0.40	0.61

Data: DC_weather.xlsx.

Theoretically, the *RMSE* for forecasts should increase as the lead time increases. However, we note that this condition may be violated in practice when a small number of observations is used to estimate the summary measures, as is illustrated in the table for lags 1 and 2. Overall, the expert weather forecasts are clearly superior to those produced by a random walk (as measured by *MASE* and *U*).   ■

2.8   Prediction Intervals

Thus far, our discussion has centered upon *point forecasts*—that is, future observations for which we report a single forecast value. For many purposes, managers seem to feel comfortable with a single figure. However, such confidence in a single number is often misplaced.

Consider, for example, the generation of weekly sales forecasts. Our method might generate a forecast of 600 units for next week. The manager who plans for the sale of *exactly* 600 units and never considers the possibility of selling more or fewer units is naïve and will probably become an ex-manager fairly quickly! Why? Because the demand for most products is inherently variable! Some weeks will see sales below the forecast level, and some will see more. When sales fall short of the point forecast, the business will incur holding costs for unsold inventory or may have to destroy perishable stock. When sales exceed the point forecasts, not only will the business lose sales, but disappointed customers may go elsewhere in the future. The best choice of inventory level will depend upon the relative costs of lost sales and excess inventory, which are determined by the statistical distribution of possible sales—that is, *predictive (prediction) distribution*. The selection of the best inventory level in this case is known as the *newsvendor problem*, because it was originally formulated in the context of selling newspapers. Our purpose here is not to dwell upon the details, which may be found in most management science texts, such as Winston and Albright (2001), but rather to emphasize the fundamental role that the predictive distribution plays in such cases. If we know the (relative) magnitudes of the costs of lost sales and of excess inventory, we may define an overall cost function and then select the level of inventory to minimize cost. (See Exercise 2.13 for further details.)

Sometimes these costs are difficult to assess, and the manager will prefer to guarantee a certain level of service. For example, suppose that we wish to meet demand 95 percent of the time. We then need to add a *safety stock* to the point forecast to ensure that the probability of a stock-out is no more than 5 percent. There are two principal approaches to this issue:

1. Assume that the predictive distribution for demand follows the normal law (although such an assumption is at best an approximation and needs to be checked; see on-line Appendix A).
2. Use an empirical error distribution based upon the errors already observed. There are several ways to perform this analysis, and we now discuss this approach further.

2.8.1   Using the Normal Distribution

If we assume that the standard deviation (*SD*) of the distribution is known and the distribution is normal, we may use the upper 95 percent point of the standard normal distribution.[4] [This value is 1.645, from Table A.1 in Appendix A; alternatively, we may use the Excel function Norminv.] So the appropriate stock level is

$$Mean + 1.645 * (SD). \tag{2.22}$$

The mean in this case is the point forecast. Thus, if the point forecast is 600, with an associated SD of 25, the manager would stock 600 + 1.645 * 25, or 641 units to achieve the desired level of customer service.

Expression (2.22) is an example of a *one-sided prediction interval*: The probability is 0.95 that demand will be equal to or less than 641, under the assumption that our forecasting method is appropriate for the sales of that particular product. Typically, the SD is unknown and must be estimated from the sample that was used to generate the point forecast. In other words, we use the sample *RMSE* to estimate the SD.

In many forecasting applications, employing two-sided prediction intervals is more common. Putting these ingredients together, we define the two-sided $100(1 - \alpha)$ percent prediction interval as

$$Forecast \pm z_{\alpha/2} * (RMSE). \tag{2.23}$$

Here, $z_{\alpha/2}$ denotes the upper $100(1 - \alpha/2)$ percentage point of the normal distribution. At this point, although we are using the sample value of *RMSE* to estimate the SD, we are not making any allowance for this fact. In Chapter 6, we define prediction intervals more precisely.

2.8.2   Empirical Prediction Intervals

We first form the empirical distribution, derived from the observed errors. In Table 2.11, we consider the $n = 15$ observed errors for the weather forecast data and proceed as follows:

1. Rank the values from smallest to largest.
2. Assign the percentage value $100(i - 0.5)/n$ to the *i*th smallest observation; in this case, the percentage values are 100/30, 300/30, and so on.
3. Form the prediction interval by selecting an appropriate pair of percentage points. In the example, 80 percent intervals would be a natural choice using the second-smallest and second-largest observed errors.

The empirical prediction distribution is then defined by adding the appropriate error for the chosen percentage point to the point forecast.

---

[4]The normal distribution is by far the most widely used distribution in the construction of prediction intervals. Hence, it is critical to check that the forecast errors are approximately normally distributed. (See Appendix A for details on testing for normality.)

TABLE 2.11   COMPARISON OF 80 PERCENT PREDICTION INTERVALS FOR
WEATHER DATA

	Percentile	1-Day	2-Day	3-Day	4-Day	5-Day
	3.3	−13	−9	−6	−5	−5
	10.0	−4	−4	−5	−5	−4
	16.7	−4	−3	−5	−4	−2
	23.3	−3	−2	−2	−4	−2
	30.0	−2	−1	−1	−2	1
	36.7	−2	−1	−1	−2	2
	43.3	−1	0	0	0	3
	50.0	−1	1	0	2	4
	56.7	0	1	2	2	4
	63.3	0	2	4	5	5
	70.0	2	3	5	6	6
	76.7	3	4	5	6	8
	83.3	4	4	5	7	8
	90.0	5	5	6	8	9
	96.7	8	8	10	12	16
Intervals (80%)						
Empirical	Lower	−4	−4	−5	−5	−4
	Upper	5	5	6	8	9
Normal	Lower	−6.1	−5.2	−5.9	−7.0	−8.2
	Upper	6.1	5.2	5.9	7.0	8.2

© Cengage Learning 2013.

EXAMPLE 2.9 ■ Evaluation of prediction intervals

Table 2.11 shows the ordered error terms based upon the forecasts made one to five days
ahead. Then, each of the normal ($z = 1.282$ for an 80% interval) and empirical approaches
is used to create the 80 prediction intervals. The normal intervals use the *RMSE* figure given
in Table 2.10, and the empirical intervals use the second-smallest and second-largest values to provide the 80 percent coverage. In this example, the normal intervals are slightly
wider, but that is very much the result of the large error on the last day. By construction, the
normal intervals are symmetric whereas the empirical intervals need not be.   ■

2.8.3 Prediction Intervals: Summary

The principal reason for constructing prediction intervals is to provide an indication of the
reliability of the point forecasts. The limits so derived are sometimes expressed as *optimistic*
and *pessimistic* forecasts. Such nomenclature is useful as a way of presenting the concept
to others, but a precise formulation of the limits should be used, rather than a vague assessment of extreme outcomes.

In Example 2.9, we may observe that the extreme changes in the weather at the end of the
sample period led to greater inaccuracies in forecasting and a considerable increase in the

RMSE. In turn, such events contribute to much wider intervals, particularly with small samples. Finally, note that prediction intervals may be used for retrospective analysis as here, but their primary purpose is to provide assessments of uncertainty for future events. A detailed discussion of prediction intervals must await the formal development of forecasting models. The reader who wishes to preview these discussions should consult Sections 5.2 and 6.7.

2.9   Basic Principles

This book, like most other texts on business forecasting, tends to devote most of its space to discussions of forecasting methods and underlying statistical models. However, if the groundwork is not properly laid, the best methods in the world cannot save the forecaster from the effects of poor data selection and inadequate preparation. The volume edited by Scott Armstrong (2001) is particularly valuable in suggesting key principles that underlie good forecasting practice. We make extensive use of this source, among others, in formulating our own sets of principles at the end of each chapter.

[2.1] Ensure that the data match the forecasting situation.   Once the underlying purpose of the forecasting exercise has been specified, the ideal data set can be identified. However, the ideal may not be available for many reasons. For example, macroeconomic data are published with a lag that may be of several months' duration and, even then, may be published only as a preliminary estimate. The forecaster needs to examine the available data with respect to the end use to which the forecasts will be put and to make sure that a match exists.

[2.2] Clean the data.   Data may be omitted, wrongly recorded, or affected by changing definitions. Adjustments should be made where necessary, but a record of such changes should be kept and made available to users of the forecasts. Data cleaning can be very time consuming, although the plots and numerical summaries described in this chapter will go a long way toward identifying data errors. Failure to clean the data can lead to the familiar situation of "Garbage in, garbage out."

[2.3] Use transformations as required by the nature of the data.   We examined differences, growth rates, and log transforms in Section 2.6. The forecaster needs to consider whether the original measurements provide the most appropriate framework for generating forecasts or whether some form of transformation is desirable. The basic pattern of no growth (use original data), linear growth (use differences), or relative growth (use growth rates or log differences) will often provide adequate guidance. This issue will be revisited periodically in later chapters.

[2.4] Use graphical representations of the data.   As we have seen in Sections 2.2 and 2.3, plotting the data can provide a variety of insights and may also suggest suitable transformations or adjustments. Graphical analysis should always be the first step in developing forecasting procedures, even if applied to only a small sample from a larger set of series.

[2.5] Adjust for unsystematic past events (e.g., outliers).   Data may be affected by the weather, political upheavals, supply shortages, or other events. Such factors need to be taken into account when clear reasons can be identified for the unusual observations. The forecaster should resist the temptation to give the data a "face-lift" by overadjusting for every minor event.

[2.6] Adjust for systematic events (e.g., seasonal effects).   Systematic events such as weekends, public holidays, and seasonal patterns can affect the observed process and must be taken into account. We will discuss these adjustments in Chapter 9.

[2.7] Use error measures that adjust for scale in the data when comparing across series. When you compare forecasts for a single series, scale-dependent measures such as the *MAE* or *RMSE* are useful. However, when you compare across different series, you should use scale-free measures, such as the *MAPE* (if appropriate), or relative error measures, such as the *MASE*.

[2.8] Use multiple measures of performance based upon the observed forecast errors. If forecasters are able to use different measures to compare performance, they can better assess performance relative to their particular needs. Multiple measures allow users to focus on those attributes of a forecasting procedure which they deem most relevant and also to check on the robustness of their conclusions. For example, one user may value simplicity and be willing to accept somewhat reduced accuracy to keep things simple. Another may wish to avoid large errors, in which case the *RMSE* becomes most relevant, because it depends upon squared errors. A third may avoid the *RMSE* purely because it gives such weight to large errors.

Summary

In this chapter, we have described the basic tools of data analysis. In particular, we examined the following topics:

- Scatterplots and time series plots for preliminary analysis of the data (Sections 2.2 and 2.3).
- Basic summary statistics for individual variables (Section 2.4).
- Correlation as a measure of association for cross-sectional data (Section 2.5).
- Transformations of the data (Section 2.6).
- Measures of forecasting accuracy as noted previously this is inconsistent. A full stop only at the end (Section 2.7).
- Prediction intervals as a measure of the uncertainty related to point forecasts (Section 2.8).

Finally, in Section 2.9, we briefly examined some of the underlying principles that should be kept in mind when starting out on a forecasting exercise.

Exercises

Time series data in books do not necessarily reflect the latest figures. When it is appropriate, readers are encouraged to go to the original sources quoted in the text and download the latest figures. Readers may then use the extended data sets to redo the exercises, and the two sets of results may be compared.

2.1   The average monthly temperatures for Boulder, Colorado, from January 1991 to September 2008 are given in *Boulder.xlsx* (*Source:* U.S. Department of Commerce, National Oceanic and Atmospheric Administration). Plot the time series, and create a seasonal plot for the last four years of the series. Comment on your results.

2.2   The following table contains data on railroad passenger injuries in the United States (*Rail_safety.xlsx*) from 1991 to 2007. "Injuries" represents the number of persons injured in the given year, "train-miles" denotes the millions of miles traveled by trains, and the final column is the ratio that defines the number of injuries per 100 million miles traveled.
   a. Create a scatterplot for injuries against train-miles.
   b. Plot each of the three time series.
   c. Does the level of injuries appear to be changing over time? If so, in what way?

Year	Injuries	Train-Miles	Injuries per Train-Mile
1990	473	72	657
1991	382	74	516
1992	411	74	555
1993	559	75	745
1994	497	75	663
1995	573	76	754
1996	513	77	666
1997	601	78	770
1998	535	78	683
1999	481	82	584
2000	658	84	781
2001	746	88	850
2002	877	90	979
2003	726	89	812
2004	679	89	760
2005	935	90	1,040
2006	761	92	828
2007	938	95	990

Source: U.S. Department of Transportation, Federal Railroad Administration

2.3 An investor has a portfolio consisting of holdings in nine stocks (*Returns.xlsx*). The end-of-year returns over the previous year are, in increasing order,

$$-5.0, -3.7, 0.9, 4.8, 6.2, 8.9, 11.2, 18.6, 25.4.$$

  a. Compute the summary statistics (mean, median, *MAD*, and *S*).
  b. Just before the close of business in the last trading session of the year, the company that had reported the 5.0 percent drop declares bankruptcy, so the return becomes –100 percent. Recompute the results, and comment on your findings.
  c. Are simple summary statistics relevant to this investor? How would you modify the calculations, if at all?

2.4 For the temperature data (*Boulder.xlsx*) in Exercise 2.1, compute the summary statistics (mean, median, *MAD*, and *S*) overall and for each month. Comment on your results. Does it make sense to compute summary statistics across all values, rather than month by month? Explain why or why not.

2.5 Compute the summary statistics (mean, median, *MAD*, and *S*) for each of the variables listed in Exercise 2.2 (*Rail_safety.xlsx*). Are these numbers a sensible summary of safety conditions? Explain why or why not.

2.6 Calculate the correlation between the monthly values of electricity consumption (*Electricity.xlsx*) for year 1 (listed as forecasts in the table) and year 2 (actual) in Table 2.8. Interpret the result.

2.7 Compute the correlations for the "Hot Growth Companies" in Table 2.3 (*Growth_companies.xlsx*) for each pair of variables rank, P/E ratio, and return, using the first 50 and second 50 values separately. Compare these results with those given in Example 2.4. Explain the differences.

2.8 The quarterly sales figures and percentage growth figures for Netflix are given in *Netflix.xlsx* and in the table that follows. Produce a time series plot for each of these variables.
   a. Are the mean and median useful in this case? Explain why or why not.
   b. Calculate the growth rate for each quarter relative to the same quarter in the previous year; that is, for quarter 1 of 2001, we have 100(17.06 – 5.17)/5.17 = 230. After allowing for the start-up phase of the company, do sales show signs of leveling off?

Year	Quarter	Quarterly Sales	Growth—Absolute	Growth—Percent
2000	1	5.17	*	*
2000	2	7.15	1.97	38.1
2000	3	10.18	3.04	42.5
2000	4	13.39	3.21	31.5
2001	1	17.06	3.67	27.4
2001	2	18.36	1.30	7.6
2001	3	18.88	0.52	2.8
2001	4	21.62	2.74	14.5
2002	1	30.53	8.91	41.2
2002	2	36.36	5.83	19.1
2002	3	40.73	4.37	12.0
2002	4	45.19	4.46	10.9
2003	1	55.67	10.48	23.2
2003	2	63.19	7.52	13.5
2003	3	72.20	9.02	14.3
2003	4	81.19	8.99	12.4
2004	1	99.82	18.63	22.9
2004	2	119.71	19.89	19.9
2004	3	140.41	20.70	17.3
2004	4	140.66	0.25	0.2
2005	1	152.45	11.79	8.4
2005	2	164.03	11.58	7.6
2005	3	172.74	8.71	5.3
2005	4	193.00	20.26	11.7
2006	1	224.13	31.13	16.1
2006	2	239.35	15.22	6.8
2006	3	255.95	16.60	6.9
2006	4	277.23	21.28	8.3
2007	1	305.32	28.09	10.1
2007	2	303.69	−1.63	−0.5
2007	3	293.97	−9.72	−3.2
2007	4	302.36	8.39	2.9

Source: Netflix Annual Reports

2.9 Use the data in *Boulder.xlsx*, sheet Data(2), to generate forecasts 12 months ahead; that is, the forecast corresponds to the value for the same month in the previous year. Compute the *ME, MAE, RMSE,* and *MASE* for these forecasts. Repeat the analysis, this time using the monthly averages calculated in Exercise 2.4.
   a. Which set of forecasts appears to work better?
   b. Is the comparison fair? (*Hint:* What do you know and when do you know it?)
   c. What conclusions would you draw about the choice between the two methods?

2.10 The average temperatures (in °F) on the day (January 20) of the president's inauguration (*Inauguration.xlsx*) are shown in the following table:

a. Summarize the data numerically and graphically.
b. Create a 95 percent prediction interval for the inauguration of President Obama in 2009.
c. The actual value was 35°. Does that come as a surprise, given the width of the interval?

Year	1937	1941	1945	1949	1953	1957	1961	1965	1969
Temperature	33	29	36	38	48	44	22	37	35
Year	1973	1977	1981	1985	1989	1993	1997	2001	2005
Temperature	42	27	55	7	52	40	34	36	35

Source: Washington Post, November 12, 2008

2.11 Compute 95 percent prediction intervals for the 12-month forecasts for temperature (*Boulder.xlsx*) generated in Exercise 2.10, using (a) the normal distribution with the estimated *RMSE* and (b) the empirical distribution with all the observed errors. Find the percentage of the observations that lies outside the limits in each case. Are these figures close to 95 percent?

2.12 Use the data in Table 2.8 (*Electricity.xlsx*) to generate forecasts for electricity consumption for the household in year 3, based on the end of year 2 as the forecast origin. Use the normal distribution to generate 90 percent prediction intervals for these forecasts.

2.13 Following the discussion in Section 2.8 on inventory management, construct a cost function, assuming that the cost of lost sales is C times that of the cost of holding unsold stock. Past records show that the prediction distribution for future sales is

$$P(\text{Sales} = x) = \frac{1}{21}, \quad x = 90, 91, \ldots, 109, 110$$

$$P(\text{Sales} = x) = 0, \quad \text{otherwise}$$

Find the optimal inventory level, in the sense of minimizing overall cost, when $C = 1$ and when $C = 3$. What should the safety stock be to guarantee a service level of 90 percent?

Minicases

Minicase 2.1 Baseball Salaries

As part of a project with the Graphics Section of the American Statistical Association, Dr. Lorraine Denby compiled data on baseball salaries. We focus on the data that relate only to pitchers and their salaries for the 1986 season. The data are included in the file *Baseball.xlsx*, and we wish to acknowledge StatLib of the Department of Statistics at Carnegie Mellon University for allowing us access to these data.

1. Summarize the data on salaries, using the measures discussed in Section 2.4.
2. The data file also includes information on the number of years a player has spent in the major leagues, his career earned run average (*ERA*), the number of innings he has pitched, and his career wins and losses. Generate scatterplots of these variables with salary, and examine their correlations.
3. Older players often accept short-term lower paid contracts toward the end of their playing careers. To allow for this feature of the data, eliminate players with 12 or more years of experience from the data set and rerun the analysis.

Summarize your conclusions.

Minicase 2.2 Whither Walmart?

As Walmart has grown, so has its stock proved to be a solid investment in both good times and bad. To determine whether a future investment in the stock is worthwhile, we need to consider the plans the company has for future growth. The annual reports provide a considerable amount of information (see *http://walmartstores.com/investors/*).

One aspect of Walmart's future strategy is its investment in different types of retail outlets, known as Walmart stores, Superstores, and Sam's Club. As the name suggests, the Superstore may be thought of as an upgrade of the Walmart store, being generally larger in size and carrying a wider range of merchandise. The Sam's Clubs are more oriented toward bulk purchasing. The spreadsheet *Walmart.xlsx* provides annual data on the numbers of each type of store in the United States on March 31, the end of the fiscal year, for the period 1995–2008:

Another feature of interest to the potential investor is the growth in sales over time. The spreadsheet also provides quarterly sales figures for the period from the first quarter of 2003 through the fourth quarter of 2007.

The spreadsheet *Walmart.xlsx* is reproduced here for convenience:

Year	Wal-Mart Stores	Super Stores	Sam's Club	Year	Quarter	Sales ($ billion)
1995	2176	154	453	2003	3	62.6
1996	2218	255	470	2003	4	62.5
1997	1960	344	436	2004	1	74.5
1998	1921	441	443	2004	2	64.8
1999	1860	564	451	2004	3	69.7
2000	1801	721	463	2004	4	68.5
2001	1736	888	475	2005	1	82.2
2002	1647	1066	500	2005	2	70.0
2003	1568	1258	525	2005	3	75.9
2004	1478	1471	538	2005	4	74.6
2005	1353	1713	551	2006	1	88.4
2006	1209	1980	567	2006	2	78.8
2007	1075	2256	579	2006	3	84.5
2008	971	2447	591	2006	4	83.5
				2007	1	98.1
Note: Financial year ends on January 31				2007	2	85.4
				2007	3	92.0
				2007	4	90.9
				2008	1	106.3

Source: Walmart annual reports, 1994–2008

1. Summarize the changes in types of store over the period. What does your summary say about Walmart's plans for the future?

2. Compute the growth in sales over time. Is there any evidence that the rate of growth is slowing or increasing?

Minicase 2.3 Economic Recessions

The following data summarize the length (in months) of each recession in the period 1929–2008, as determined by the National Bureau of Economic Research (NBER):

Onset	Duration	End	Gap
August 1929	43	February 1933	50
May 1937	13	May 1938	80
February 1945	8	September 1945	37
November 1948	11	September 1949	45
July 1953	10	April 1954	39
August 1957	8	March 1958	24
April 1960	10	January 1961	106
December 1969	11	October 1970	36
November 1973	16	February 1975	58
January 1980	6	June 1980	12
July 1981	16	October 1982	92
July 1990	8	February 1991	120
March 2001	8	October 2001	73
December 2007	19	June 2009	

Source: National Bureau of Economic Research. Data shown is from file Recessions.xlsx.

Note that the NBER defines the end of a recession as the time at which the national economy shows an upturn. It does not mean that the economy has recovered to its previous level of activity.

    a. Calculate the average length of a recession, and provide a 95 percent confidence interval for this quantity. Interpret the result.

    b. Calculate the average time between recessions (*Gap*), and provide a 95 percent confidence interval for this quantity. Interpret the result.

    c. Is there any correlation between the length of a recession and the period of growth immediately preceding it, referred to as "Gap" in the table?

    d. Is there any correlation between the length of a recession and the period of growth immediately following a recession?

    e. Comment on your findings.

References

Anderson, D. R., Sweeney, D. J., and Williams, T. A. (2011), *Statistics for Business and Economics*, 11th ed. Mason, OH: South-Western.

Armstrong, J. S. (2001). *Principles of Forecasting: A Handbook for Researchers and Practitioners*. Boston and Dordrecht: Kluwer.

Hyndman, R. J., and Koehler, A. B. (2006). Another look at measures of forecast accuracy. *International Journal of Forecasting, 22,* 679–688.

Winston, W., and Albright, S. C. (2001). *Practical Management Science*, 2nd ed. Pacific Grove, CA: Duxbury.

CHAPTER 3

Forecasting Trends: Exponential Smoothing

CONTENTS

What's past is prologue.

—Shakespeare, *The Tempest*

Introduction

Forecasts may be based upon subjective judgmental assessments, numerical procedures, or some combination of the two. Judgmental procedures are valuable when we have no track record on which to base our forecasts or when circumstances appear to have undergone fundamental changes. However, such forecasts are often time consuming to generate and may be subject to a variety of conscious or unconscious biases. Often, we find that even simple analyses of available data can perform as well as judgmental procedures and that they may be much quicker and less expensive to produce. Careful subjective adjustments to quantitative forecasts may ultimately be the best combination, but we first need to develop an effective arsenal of quantitative methods. Accordingly, we will now focus on quantitative methods and defer consideration of judgmental methods to Chapter 11.

We begin in Section 3.1 by drawing a distinction between *methods* and *models*, a distinction that is often ignored but that has important implications for how we approach a forecasting task. Section 3.2 then provides a general overview of extrapolation methods before we move on in Section 3.3 to the use of different weighted means as forecasts. Our aim is to balance the following potentially conflicting directives:

- Use all the data.
- Pay more attention to the recent past.

Or, to restate, "All data are important, but recent data are even more important." These ideas lead directly to the use of time-dependent averages—notably, simple moving averages and exponentially weighted moving averages (or exponential smoothing, as it is usually called).

When there are clear trends in the data, a simple averaging procedure cannot capture the trend and therefore will not work. As a consequence, we must extend our methods to incorporate such systematic movements, the subject of Section 3.4. Sections 3.5 and 3.6 consider damped smoothing methods and various other approaches to forecasting trends. Section 3.7 provides prediction intervals for one-step-ahead forecasts, relying implicitly upon models we will develop fully in Chapter 5. Section 3.8 considers transformations of series to improve the underlying assumptions. Finally, in Section 3.9 we explore some of the principles that underlie the use of simple extrapolation methods.

Software

Good software should provide for the automatic operation of a variety of exponential smoothing methods and ways to select from among them. We summarize some of the alternatives in Appendix C, located on the textbook companion site. At this stage, we merely note that the level of support for exponential smoothing methods varies considerably across different software providers. For example, Excel includes only simple exponential smoothing, and even then its application is far from automatic. To achieve some consistency in the numerical results obtained from these methods, we present two Excel macros to carry out the estimation procedures. These macros are available on the book's website, which provides detailed instructions for users. A brief summary is included in Appendix 3A at the end of this chapter.

3.1   Method or Model?

The development of various quantitative approaches to forecasting occupies the next eight chapters, as we move steadily from heuristic forecasting methods to procedures that rely upon careful modeling of the process being studied. One of the pleasant discoveries we make along the way is that various heuristic forecasting methods often match up to specific statistical models of the data, even though this property was not known at the time the methods were first proposed. As in other areas of research, we often proceed by discovering what works and then we try to figure out why. This chapter concentrates on what works, and we emphasize the distinction in our terminology in the text box below, even though the difference between the two terms (method and model) is sometimes ignored in discussions of forecasting.

Method or Model

A *forecast function* is an equation for calculating the forecasts over the forecast horizon.

A *forecasting method* is a (numerical) procedure for generating a forecast. It involves the direct use of a forecast function. When such methods are not based upon an underlying statistical model, they are termed *heuristic*.

A *statistical (forecasting) model* is a statistical description of the data-generating process from which a forecasting method may be derived. Forecasts are made using a forecast function derived from the model. A statistical model is a necessary foundation for the construction of prediction intervals.

3.1.1 A Forecasting Model

We might formulate a simple trend model for a time series as

$$Y_t = \beta_0 + \beta_1 t + \varepsilon_t, \tag{3.1}$$

where Y_t denotes the time series being studied; β_0 and β_1 are the level and slope (or trend) *parameters*, respectively; and ε_t denotes a random error term corresponding to the part of the series that cannot be described by the linear trend. If we make appropriate assumptions about the nature of the error term, we can estimate the unknown parameters β_0 and β_1. The resulting estimates are typically written as b_0 and b_1. Thus, the forecasting *model* gives rise to a forecast *function*, whose estimated version may be written as

$$F_t = b_0 + b_1 t, \tag{3.2}$$

where F_t denotes a forecast for time period t, b_0 is the (estimated) *intercept* that represents the value at time zero, and b_1 is the (estimated) *slope* (or trend), which represents the increase in forecast values from one period to the next.

Equation (3.2) is the forecast function, and the statistical model given by equation (3.1) enables the construction of prediction intervals. If we were to proceed directly to employ equation (3.2) for forecasting without such a model, we would indeed have a forecasting method, but one that suffered from two drawbacks:

1. It lacks a formal basis for choosing values for the parameters, although various ad hoc procedures could be developed.
2. There is no way to assess the uncertainty inherent in the forecasts.

Of course, if you choose a poor statistical model, you will get poor forecasts and poor assessments of uncertainty—maybe not always, but on average.

In this chapter, we focus primarily on methods. These methods will be underpinned by the statistical models we later introduce in Chapter 5. On the basis of these models, we are able to consider prediction intervals, which we do in Section 3.8.

3.2 Extrapolation Methods

Extrapolative methods of forecasting focus on a single time series to identify past patterns in the historical data. These patterns are then extrapolated to map out the likely future path of the series. The overall structure is shown in Figure 3.1.

Figure 3.1 is to be interpreted as follows: We denote the particular series of interest (e.g., weekly sales) by Y. We have recorded the observations $Y_1, Y_2, \ldots, Y_t$ over t *weeks*, which represent all the data currently available. Our interest lies in forecasting sales over the next h weeks, known as the *forecasting horizon*; that is, we are interested in providing forecasts for future sales, denoted by $Y_{t+1}, Y_{t+2}, \ldots, Y_{t+h}$.

Although we use the same notation to describe past, present, and future, there is a key difference: The past and present values are already observed, whereas the future Ys represent random variables; that is, we cannot write down their values, but we can describe them in terms of a set of possible values and the associated probabilities. This concept is illustrated in Figure 3.2, which shows a time series observed for periods 1–12, but to be forecast for periods 13–20, typically with increasing uncertainty in the forecast as the horizon increases.

The (point) forecasts for future sales are all made at time t ($= 12$ here), known as the *forecast origin*, so the first forecast (for period 13) will be made one step ahead, the second (for period 14) two steps ahead, and so on. When the results for period 13 are known, that period becomes the new forecast origin and we can compute a new forecast for period 14, which will then be only one step ahead. We need to distinguish these different forecasts, as illustrated in Table 3.1. Suppose that the initial forecast origin is week 12 and we wish to make forecasts in week 12 for weeks 13, 14, and 15. Then in week 13 we would make a new set of forecasts for weeks 14 and 15; finally, in week 14 we would make a forecast for week 15. A quick look at the table indicates that we are considering six forecasts, all of which are based upon different information or relate to different time periods. As introduced in Chapter 2 (Section 2.7.1 and Table 2.7), the notation $F_{14}(2)$ refers to the forecast for Y_{14} made two weeks earlier in week 12. The subscript always indicates which time period is being forecast, and the term in parentheses records how far ahead the forecast is made (the forecast horizon). When no ambiguity arises, we will use F_{t+1} to represent the one-step-ahead forecast $F_{t+1}(1)$ so that $F_{13} = F_{13}(1)$ and so on.

This notation may seem a bit elaborate, but it is important to know both the forecast origin and for how many periods ahead the forecast is being made. That is, the term "forecast for period 15" is ambiguous until we know when the forecast was made, and it would be impossible to evaluate the forecast's accuracy without that information.

FIGURE 3.1   GENERAL FRAMEWORK FOR FORECASTING WITH A SINGLE SERIES

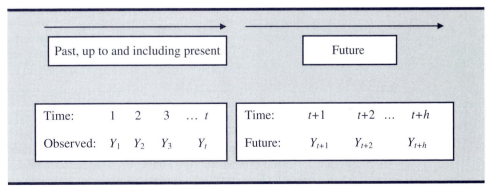

FIGURE 3.2   PLOT OF ACTUAL SALES FOR PERIODS 1–12 AND A RANGE OF
POSSIBLE VALUES FOR PERIODS 13–20

© Cengage Learning 2013.

TABLE 3.1   NOTATION FOR FORECASTS MADE AT DIFFERENT FORECAST
ORIGINS AND FOR VARYING FORECAST HORIZONS

Forecast Origin	12	13	14
Forecast for period 13	$F_{13}(1)$		
Forecast for period 14	$F_{14}(2)$	$F_{14}(1)$	
Forecast for period 15	$F_{15}(3)$	$F_{15}(2)$	$F_{15}(1)$

© Cengage Learning 2013.

3.2.1   Extrapolation of the Mean Value

Figure 3.3 (previously shown as Figure 2.1) shows the weekly sales figures for 62 weeks of a product line for a major U.S. manufacturer, which we continue to refer to as WFJ Sales. The series starts at the beginning of the calendar year, picks up after 12 weeks or so, and then stabilizes until a surge in the last few weeks of the year, before dropping back at the beginning of the next year (but at a higher level than a year earlier).

Suppose we traveled back in time and we were back at midyear (week 26) and wished to forecast sales for the next few weeks. A naïve approach would be to take the average of the 26 weeks to date, which we write as

$$\bar{Y}(26) = \sum_{i=1}^{26} Y_i/26 = 30102.$$

The bar denotes the operation of taking the mean over the 26 observations. Inspection of Figure 3.4, which shows the first 26 weeks of the series and the mean level, suggests that such a value would be too low a forecast. Somehow, we need to give less weight to the first part of the series and focus on the more recent values.

FIGURE 3.3   TIME SERIES PLOT OF WEEKLY SALES FOR WFJ

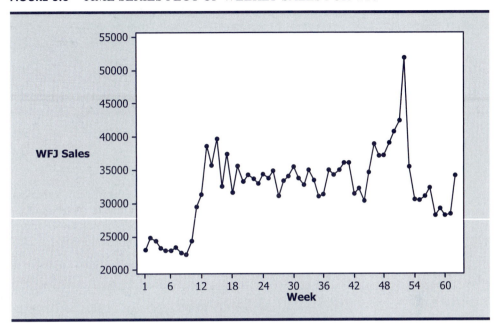

Data shown is from file WFJ_sales.xlsx. © Cengage Learning 2013.

FIGURE 3.4   TIME SERIES PLOT FOR WEEKLY SALES FOR WFJ FOR THE FIRST
26 WEEKS, COMPARED WITH THE AVERAGE

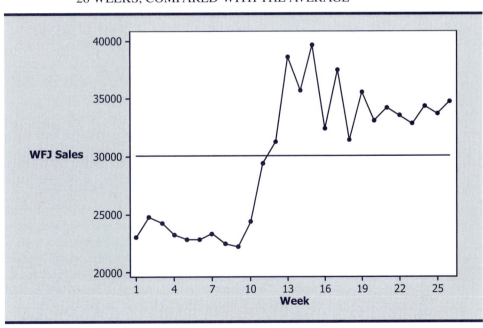

Data shown is from file WFJ_sales.xlsx. © Cengage Learning 2013.

Locally Constant Forecasts

A series is locally constant if the mean level changes gradually over time but there is no reason to expect a systematic increase or decrease in the future. The forecast function is

$$F_t(h) = \text{constant};$$

that is, the plot showing future forecasts is a horizontal line. When a new observation becomes available, the constant is updated.

3.2.2 Use of Moving Averages

One way to proceed is to use an average of the last few values in the series. In general, we may use the last K terms of the series and update each time to include only the K values. We refer to the result as a moving average, which contains K terms, the most recent of which is observation t (the most recent available observation):

Moving Average

The *moving average* of order K evaluated at time t is denoted by $MA(t|K)$:

$$MA(t|K) = \frac{Y_t + Y_{t-1} + \cdots + Y_{t-K+1}}{K}$$

We then forecast the time series at time $(t+1)$, using the formula

$$F_{t+1} = MA(t|K).$$

Suppose now that we decide to use a three-week moving average, or $K = 3$. The first such average would be $MA(3|3) = [23056 + 24817 + 24300]/3 = 24058$, as shown in Table 3.2. When a new observation becomes available, the new moving average is $MA(4|3) = [24817 + 24300 + 23242]/3 = 24120$, and so on. Each time, we drop the oldest observation and enter the new one; a slightly quicker way of doing the calculation is to write

$$\textit{New average} = MA(t+1|K) = \textit{Old average} + \frac{[\textit{New value} - \textit{Oldest value}]}{K} \quad (3.3)$$

$$= MA(t|K) + \frac{Y_{t+1} - Y_{t+1-K}}{K}.$$

A variation of this updating mechanism will feature prominently in later developments. But now, how should we choose K? A simple comparison provides an insight. Table 3.2 summarizes the calculations for $K = 3$ and for $K = 7$, which we respectively refer to as MA(3) and MA(7), and the two averages and the original series are plotted in Figure 3.5. The first forecast that we can calculate for MA(3) is for week 4, which uses the first three observations. This forecast corresponds to the one-step-ahead forecast for week 4 made in week 3. The first forecast for MA(7) is for period 8.

From Figure 3.5, we see that the three-term moving average adapts more quickly to movements in the series, but the seven-term average produces a greater degree of smoothing. To decide which method is preferable, we need to evaluate suitable measures of forecast performance, as discussed in Chapter 2. However, before we do so, we introduce another form of adaptive average.

TABLE 3.2 CALCULATION OF MOVING AVERAGES FOR WFJ SALES

Week	WFJ Sales	MA (3)	MA (7)
1	23,056		
2	24,817		
3	24,300		
4	23,242	24058	
5	22,862	24120	
6	22,863	23468	
7	23,391	22989	
8	22,469	23039	23504
9	22,241	22908	23421
10	24,367	22701	23053
11	29,457	23026	23062
12	31,294	25355	23950
13	38,713	28372	25154
14	35,749	33155	27419
15	39,768	35252	29184
16	32,419	38077	31656
17	37,503	35979	33110
18	31,474	36563	34986
19	35,625	33799	35274
20	33,159	34867	35893
21	34,306	33419	35100
22	33,631	34363	34893
23	32,900	33698	34017
24	34,426	33612	34085
25	33,777	33652	33646
26	34,849	33701	33975

Data shown is from file WFJ_sales_MA.xlsx. © Cengage Learning 2013.

FIGURE 3.5 WFJ SALES FOR FIRST 26 WEEKS, WITH MOVING AVERAGES OF LENGTHS 3 AND 7

3.3 Simple Exponential Smoothing

The simple moving average introduced in the previous section suffers from two drawbacks. First, the averaging process seems rather capricious in that an observation is given full weight one period and none the next, when it reaches the Kth, or "oldest," position. Second, if we use a large number of terms, we have to keep all the past values until they are finally removed from the average. This second objection is now of minor importance in practice, although it used to be critical when computer storage was much more limited or when forecasts had to be updated by hand. Ultimately, any method should be judged by its performance in forecasting, although it would be nice to have a technique that adjusted more smoothly over time. Exactly such a method was introduced by Robert G. Brown (often referred to as the father of exponential smoothing), whose 1959 and 1963 books on forecasting are justly recognized as classics.

When a new observation is recorded, the new sample mean of the available data may be expressed as

$$New\ mean = Old\ mean + \frac{(Difference\ between\ new\ observation\ and\ old\ mean)}{New\ sample\ size\ (= old\ sample\ size\ +\ 1)}.$$

We can see from this expression that we need only record the previous mean and the latest value, a useful feature when updating anything from sales reports to batting averages. However, as the series length increases, the mean becomes increasingly unresponsive to fluctuations in recent values because each observation has weight equal to 1/(sample size). The update of the simple MA, given in equation (3.3), avoided this problem and maintained a constant coefficient ($1/K$), but at the cost of dumping the oldest observation completely. The aim is to construct some kind of average that describes the recent behavior of the series, but in a way that adjusts smoothly over time. We refer to such an average as the *local (mean) level*. If we use too many observations, the estimated level may be out of date, whereas if we use too few, the estimate may be inaccurate and jump around a lot. So, instead of discussing the issue in terms of a moving average, we refer to the local level at time t as L_t and resolve these two conflicting elements by using an updating relationship of the form

$$L_{t+1} = L_t + \alpha(Y_{t+1} - L_t). \tag{3.4}$$

That is,

New local level = Old local level + α* (Difference between new observation and old local level).

Exponential Smoothing

The basic equation for *exponential smoothing* is

$$L_{t+1} = L_t + \alpha(Y_{t+1} - L_t).$$

The process involves comparing the latest observation with the previous weighted average and making a proportional adjustment, governed by the coefficient α, known as the *smoothing constant*. By convention. we constrain the coefficient to the range $0 < \alpha < 1$ so that only a part of the difference between the old level and the new observation is used in the updating. Inspection of equation (3.4) indicates that this form of average provides a constant weight (α) to the latest observation. Further, the updates require only the latest observation and the previous local level. The average in equation (3.4) is known as an *exponentially weighted moving average* (EWMA), and we now explain the origin of that name. If we start with the expression for period ($t + 1$) and substitute into it the comparable expression for time t, we obtain

$$L_{t+1} = (1 - \alpha)L_t + \alpha Y_{t+1} = (1 - \alpha)[(1 - \alpha)L_{t-1} + \alpha Y_t] + \alpha Y_{t+1}$$
$$= (1 - \alpha)^2 L_{t-1} + \alpha[(1 - \alpha)Y_t + Y_{t+1}].$$

Continuing to substitute the earlier smoothed means, we eventually arrive back at the start of the series with the expression

$$L_{t+1} = (1 - \alpha)^{t+1}L_0 + \alpha[Y_{t+1} + (1 - \alpha)Y_t + (1 - \alpha)^2 Y_{t-1} + \cdots + (1 - \alpha)^t Y_1].$$

$$(3.5)$$

The right-hand side contains a weighted average of the observations, and the weights $\{\alpha, \alpha(1 - \alpha), \alpha(1 - \alpha)^2, \ldots\}$ decay steadily over time. If the weights are plotted against time and a smooth curve is drawn through the values, that curve is exponential—hence the name "exponentially weighted moving average." The decay is slower for small values of α, so we can control the rate of decay by choosing α appropriately. Figure 3.6 illustrates the decay rates for $\alpha = 0.5$ and $\alpha = 0.2$. At $\alpha = 0.5$, over 99 percent of the weight falls on the first seven observations whereas the comparable figure for $\alpha = 0.2$ is only 79 percent. As α gets smaller, so does this percentage. Thus, just as we could choose K to control the rate of adjustment of the simple moving average, we may select α to achieve similar adjustments for the EWMA.

Caution: Equation (3.5) depends on a starting value L_0. When t and α are both small, the weight attached to the starting value may be high, as seen in the following table (in these circumstances, it is recommended that more sophisticated software be used that enables an optimal value for the starting level):

α	t	Weight on Starting Value
0.50	10	0.001
	30	0.000
0.20	10	0.107
	30	0.001
0.05	10	0.599
	30	0.215

FIGURE 3.6   WEIGHTS ON DIFFERENT LAGS IN AN EXPONENTIALLY WEIGHTED MOVING AVERAGE

3.3.1   Forecasting with the EWMA, or Simple Exponential Smoothing

The next step is to convert these averages into forecasts. When we use the EWMA for forecasting, we refer to the method as *simple* (or *single*) *exponential smoothing* (SES).[1] The underlying logic of this process is that, although we believe that the process will fluctuate, we have no evidence to suggest that it is likely to go up, go down, or stay the same. In such circumstances, the average level for future observations is best forecast by our current estimate of the local level. Thus, forecasts made at time t for all future time periods will be the same; that is,

$$F_{t+1}(1) = F_{t+2}(2) = \cdots = F_{t+h}(h) = L_t. \tag{3.6}$$

At first sight, this equation may seem rather strange, but think of the case of stock prices. The latest price is assumed to capture all the relevant information about the value of the stock, so the current price is the best forecast for all future periods until new information comes along. We must recognize that, as the lead time increases, the forecasts will usually become less accurate.

Equation (3.4) may now be written in the terms of the forecasts as

$$F_{t+1}(1) = F_t(1) + \alpha[Y_t - F_t(1)]. \tag{3.7}$$

That is, the new one-step-ahead forecast is the previous forecast, partially adjusted by the amount the previous forecast was in error. Because this equation considers only the one-step-ahead forecasts, it may also be written as

$$F_{t+1} = F_t + \alpha(Y_t - F_t). \tag{3.8}$$

To set up the calculations that are implicit in the equation, we need to specify the value for α, as well as a starting value $F_1 = L_0$. We have already discussed the effects of different α values. Earlier literature recommended a choice in the range $0.1 < \alpha < 0.3$ to allow the EWMA to change relatively slowly, and values from that range often work well for series such as sales figures. However, relying on an arbitrary preset smoothing parameter is not advisable. Most computer programs now provide efficient estimates of the smoothing constant, based upon minimizing the mean squared error for the estimation sample (or, equivalently, the *RMSE*):

$$MSE = \frac{\sum_{i=1}^{t}(Y_i - F_i)^2}{t}. \tag{3.9}$$

MSE is computed with the use of the first t values, which constitute the *estimation*, or *fitting*, sample. Forecasts may then be generated for time periods $t + 1, t + 2$.

Choosing the Smoothing Parameter

When forecasting with exponential smoothing,
- use optimum smoothing parameters, not preset values.

EXAMPLE 3.1 ■ Basic SES calculations

A short series of hypothetical sales data is given in Table 3.3. The first observation is used as the forecast for period 2, and the smoothing constant is set at $\alpha = 0.3$. Thus, from equation (3.7), we have, for $t = 2$,

$$F_3(1) = F_2(1) + \alpha[Y_2 - F_2(1)]$$
$$= 5.00 + 0.3*(6.00 - 5.00) = 5.30$$

---

[1]The term "SES" is perhaps unfortunate, because the term "smoothing" tends to be overused in time series analysis. Nonetheless, "SES" is in common usage.

TABLE 3.3   ILLUSTRATION OF SPREADSHEET CALCULATIONS FOR SES

Time	Sales	Forecast	Error	Error^2	Absolute Error	Absolute Percentage Error
1	5					
2	6	5.00	1.00	1.00	1.00	16.67
3	7	5.30	1.70	2.89	1.70	24.29
4	8	5.81	2.19	4.80	2.19	27.38
5	7	6.47	0.53	0.28	0.53	7.61
6	6	6.63	−0.63	0.39	0.63	10.45
7	5	6.44	−1.44	2.07	1.44	28.78
8	6	6.01	−0.01	0.00	0.01	0.12
9	7	6.01	0.99	0.99	0.99	14.21
10	8	6.30	1.70	2.88	1.70	21.21
11	7	6.81	0.19	0.04	0.19	2.68
12	6	6.87	−0.87	0.75	0.87	14.48
13		6.61				
		Means	**0.44**	**1.51**	**1.02**	**15.12**
			RMSE = 1.23			

© Cengage Learning 2013.

The forecasts are computed successively in the same way. The forecast errors, their squares, their absolute values, and their absolute values as a percentage of the observed series are shown in succeeding columns. The last row of the table gives the mean error, the *MSE*, the *MAE*, and the *MAPE*, calculated over observations 3 through 12. The calculations may be checked by using the Excel macro *SES.xlsm*, available on the book's website.   ■

Discussion Question   *If you had to make a subjective choice for the value of the smoothing constant, what value would you choose for (a) a product with long-term steady sales and (b) a stock price index?*

3.3.2   An Excel Macro for SES

The Excel macro *SES.xlsm* uses Solver to select the best value for α by minimizing the *MSE*; the macro is available on the book's website. The macro allows the user to partition the data series into estimation and hold-out samples and computes summary statistics for each subsample. The mean absolute error (*MAE*) or the mean absolute percentage error (*MAPE*) could be used in place of the *MSE*. The estimated value of α is typically similar in all three cases, unless we are dealing with a very short series or one that contains some unusual observations, which we will refer to as outliers.

Starting Values   We must still resolve the choice of starting values. Two principal options are commonly used: (1) to use the first observation as F_1, or (2) to use an average of a number of initial observations; recommendations vary from the first 3 or 4 up to 6 or 12 or even the mean of the whole sample. Gardner (1985) provides a good review of the options but states, "There appears to be no empirical evidence favoring any particular method." With such variations, it is evident that different software programs will produce different forecasts; further, some packages are very coy about the methods they employ. The macro allows the choice of the first observation only or an average of the first four observations.

When either the sample size or α is large, the choice of starting value is relatively unimportant and the different approaches yield similar results. When both the sample size and α are small, more sophisticated methods should be used.[2]

Caution: All major forecasting packages include fitting routines for SES, although the particular algorithms employed vary, so the results may differ somewhat from those shown in this book.

We now explore the effects of changing α for forecasts of WFJ Sales. The macro was used in each case to generate the results.

EXAMPLE 3.2 ■ SES forecasts for WFJ Sales (*WFJ_sales.xlsx*)

We used the first 26 observations of the WFJ Sales series as the estimation sample. The one-step-ahead *MSE* (taken over observations 6 to 26) is minimized[3] when $\alpha = 0.729$. Table 3.4 shows the first ten one-step-ahead forecasts for WFJ sales, from period 26 as origin, using SES with $\alpha = 0.2$ and 0.5, as well as 0.729, for comparison purposes. Thus, the first out-of-sample forecast is available at period 27, and the one-step-ahead forecasts are listed for weeks 27–36. The starting value was based upon an average of the first four observations in each case. The three sets of forecasts correspond to the following:

- SES(0.2): Simple exponential smoothing with $\alpha = 0.2$.
- SES(0.5): Simple exponential smoothing with $\alpha = 0.5$.
- SES(opt): Simple exponential smoothing with $\alpha = 0.729$.

To illustrate the nature of the calculations, consider time period 28 for $\alpha = 0.2$. From equation (3.7), we have

$$F_{28}(1) = 33884 + 0.2(30986 - 33884)$$
$$= 33304$$

Similarly, for $t = 29$, we find that $F_{29}(1) = 33308$. ■

TABLE 3.4 ACTUAL AND ONE-STEP-AHEAD FORECASTS FOR WFJ SALES
(For periods 27–36, starting from period 26 as origin and using SES.xlsm)

Period	WFJ Sales	SES (0.2)	SES (0.5)	SES (opt)
27	30986	33884	33842	33858
28	33321	33304	34346	34580
29	34003	33308	32666	31963
30	35417	33447	32993	32952
31	33822	33841	33498	33717
32	32723	33837	34458	34955
33	34925	33614	34140	34130
34	33460	33876	33432	33105
35	30999	33793	34178	34431
36	31286	33234	33819	33723

© Cengage Learning 2013.

[2]In Section 5.1, we discuss fitting a complete model to estimate both the smoothing parameter and the starting value.
[3]The observations over which the *MSE* is minimized also varies with the software employed. We prefer not to include the values used for start-up, but practice varies.

FIGURE 3.7 SES FORECASTS FOR WFJ SALES: THE EFFECTS OF DIFFERENT
SMOOTHING CONSTANTS

© Cengage Learning 2013.

Figure 3.7 shows the one-step-ahead forecasts for weeks 27–36. The forecasts for SES(0.2) are smoother than those for SES(0.5) and SES(opt), which adapt more quickly to the latest observation.

3.3.3 The Use of Hold-Out Samples

Recall that in Example 3.2 we partitioned the original series into two parts. That partition provides a framework for an examination of the relative performance of alternative methods. For this purpose, we use the accuracy measures developed in Section 2.7.

When we split the series into two parts, we refer to the first part as the *estimation* sample, used to estimate the starting values and the smoothing parameters. This sample typically contains the first 75–80 percent of the observations, although the forecaster may choose to use a smaller percentage for longer series. The parameters are commonly estimated by minimizing the mean squared error (*MSE*), although the mean absolute error (*MAE*) and mean absolute percentage error (*MAPE*) are also used.

The *hold-out* sample represents the last 20–25 percent of the observations and is used to check forecasting performance. No matter how many parameters are estimated with the estimation sample, each method under consideration can be evaluated with the use of the "new" observations contained in the hold-out sample. Thus, the hold-out sample provides a level playing field for such comparisons.

In-Sample and Out-of-Sample (Hold-out) Error Measures

Measures of performance based upon the estimation sample are referred to as *in-sample*; measures based upon the *hold-out sample* are referred to as *out-of-sample*.

Some programs allow repeated estimation and evaluation of the forecast error by advancing the estimation sample one observation at a time and repeating the error calculations, a process known as using a *rolling origin*. For example, if the hold-out sample comprised 12 observations, we would have an initial set of forecast errors at horizons 1, 2, . . . , 12. We then advance one period and generate forecasts 1, 2, . . . , 11 steps ahead, using the last 11 values. This operation is repeated with the last 10, 9, . . . , 1 observations, to produce 12 one-step-ahead forecasts, 11 two-step-ahead forecasts, and so on, thereby providing a more complete assessment of forecast performance. The use of a rolling origin provides a more reliable assessment of performance (Fildes, 1992). For further discussion of forecasting accuracy measures, see Tashman (2000). In addition, a rolling origin reflects practical applications because an organization typically adds the latest observations to the database and reruns the analysis.

EXAMPLE 3.3 ■ Comparison of one-step-ahead forecasts

To examine the forecasting performance of the various methods discussed to date, we carried out the experiment described next, using the series WFJ Sales. Following recommended practice, we used an out-of-sample evaluation. In other words, we fit the first part of the series to the data and then examined the performance of the forecasting method by seeing how well it worked on later observations. In this example, we used a hold-out sample of more than 50 percent of the observations because our primary focus was on evaluating forecasting methods; a larger hold-out sample provides a better basis for comparisons. We compared five methods:

1. MA(3): A moving average of three terms
2. MA(8): A moving average of eight terms
3. SES(0.2): Simple exponential smoothing with $\alpha = 0.2$
4. SES(0.5): Simple exponential smoothing with $\alpha = 0.5$
5. SES(opt): Simple exponential smoothing with $\alpha = 0.729$

For each of the SES sets of forecasts, we used the first four terms to generate the starting value, as in the previous example. We then generated the one-step-ahead forecasts for 36 time periods (periods 27–62), starting at forecast origin $t = 26$. Only method 5 requires any parameter estimation, and we felt that an estimation sample of 26 would suffice. The summary results appear in the Table 3.5. The best performance on each criterion is shown in bold. In this case, the best-fitting optimal SES scheme performs best on all counts. However, it may well happen that the different criteria lead to different conclusions. ■

3.3.4 Some General Comments

On average, SES tends to outperform MA, as observed in an empirical comparison of their performance in the M3 forecasting competition, as reported by Makridakis and Hibon (2000) and in various other studies. In addition, as we shall see in Chapter 5, SES corresponds

TABLE 3.5 SUMMARY ERROR MEASURES FOR ONE-STEP-AHEAD FORECASTS OF WFJ SALES DATA (*Hold-out sample, periods 27–62*)

Method	MAE	RMSE	MAPE
Number of Observations	**36**	**36**	**36**
MA(3)	3067	4320	8.9
MA(8)	3749	4865	11.0
SES(0.2)	3389	4342	9.9
SES(0.5)	2832	3980	8.2
SES(opt)	**2561**	**3915**	**7.3**

Data: WFJ_sales.xlsx. © Cengage Learning 2013.

TABLE 3.6 EFFECTS OF FITTING BY MINIMIZATION OF RMSE, MAE, OR MAPE

Estimation Criterion	RMSE		MAE		MAPE	
Sample	Estimation	Hold-Out	Estimation	Hold-Out	Estimation	Hold-Out
Error Measure						
RMSE	3200	3915	3217	3921	3217	3921
MAE	2288	2561	2247	2624	2247	2624
MAPE	7.0	7.3	6.9	7.5	6.9	7.5
Value of α	0.729		0.660		0.660	

Data: WFJ_sales.xlsx. © Cengage Learning 2013.

to an intuitively appealing underlying statistical model of the data, whereas MA does not. Given the inferior properties and overall performance of moving-average–based procedures, we do not recommend their direct use for forecasting. However, moving averages have other uses, particularly in the area of seasonal adjustment, as we shall see in Chapter 4 (Sections 4.3–4.5).

One final question refers to the choice of fitting procedure. We could minimize the *MSE* (or, equivalently, the *RMSE*) or instead choose to minimize the *MAPE* or the *MAE*. To examine the effects of such a choice, we again use the WFJ series. The data through period 26 were used for estimation of the smoothing constant by each method in turn. Different options for the starting values (the first observation and the first four observations) for the level produced essentially identical forecasts for periods 27–62. Only the results for the starting value based upon the average of the first four observations are given in Table 3.6.

In this example, the choice of fitting method produces only marginal differences in the results,[4] a phenomenon that tends to happen, provided that adequate data are available for estimation. Indeed, the macro produced identical values for the smoothing constant when *MAE* and *MAPE* were used; these two criteria produce similar results whenever the typical percentage error is small. Finally, we note that the out-of-sample error measures tend to be somewhat higher than those calculated for the estimation sample. This outcome should not come as a surprise, because the smoothing constant was chosen to minimize the appropriate criterion within the estimation sample, not the hold-out sample.

3.4 Linear Exponential Smoothing

Table 3.7 shows the quarterly revenues (sales) for Netflix for the period from the first quarter of 2000—through the fourth quarter of 2003. (A longer series is considered in Minicase 3.1 at the end of the chapter.) For such a rapidly increasing series, it is natural to think about incorporating a trend line into our forecasting method. Figure 3.8 shows two such possibilities: Plot (A) shows a linear trend, and plot (B) shows a quadratic trend.[5]

The quadratic seems to provide an excellent fit, but we must be wary of such global models—that is, models which assume a never-changing trend into the far future. Indeed, the road to chapter 11 bankruptcy proceedings is littered with the remains of companies,

---

[4]The calculations were made with Excel Solver, using the macro *SES.xlsm*, available on the book's website.
[5]The calculations involved in creating these trend lines do not concern us here. A detailed explanation is given in Chapter 8 (Section 8.2).

TABLE 3.7   QUARTERLY REVENUE (SALES) FOR NETFLIX
(*Q1 2000–Q4 2003 ($ Million)*)

Year	Quarter	Quarterly Sales	Year	Quarter	Quarterly Sales
2000	1	5.17	2002	1	30.53
2000	2	7.15	2002	2	36.36
2000	3	10.18	2002	3	40.73
2000	4	13.39	2002	4	45.19
2001	1	17.06	2003	1	55.67
2001	2	18.36	2003	2	63.19
2001	3	18.88	2003	3	72.20
2001	4	21.62	2003	4	81.19

Data shown is from file Netflix_1.xlsx. © Cengage Learning 2013.

which believed that such optimistic growth patterns would persist. A successful start-up company will often show dramatic growth in the early years, but the growth moderates as the company and its markets mature and competitors emerge. The Netflix record is impressive, but investors should not get too carried away: The trend is likely to change over time. Accordingly, we introduce methods with a local trend estimate in the next section.

> ## Locally Linear Forecasts
>
> A time series is said to have a local linear trend if the mean level at any point in time is expected to increase (or decrease) linearly over time. The forecast function has the general form
>
> $$F_t(h) = \text{Intercept} + h*\text{Trend};$$
>
> that is, the plot showing future forecasts is a straight line. When a new observation is recorded, estimates of the intercept and trend are updated.

3.4.1   Basic Structure for LES

Global trend models assume that the trend remains constant over the whole time series. Because we are reluctant to rely upon the continuation of global patterns, we now develop tools that project trends more locally, just as we looked at local levels earlier. To understand the approach, we begin with the components of a straight line: the intercept (or starting level at time zero) and the trend (or slope), which we denote by L and T, respectively. To produce forecasts that are sensitive to recent changes in the series, we now define the following variables:

L_t = level of series at time t

T_t = trend (slope) of series at time t.

The level and trend measured at time t represent our current state of knowledge about these quantities. Thus, when we seek to forecast h periods ahead. we may construct a trend line that starts at level L_t and has trend T_t. That is, the forecast function for one-step-ahead is

$$F_{t+1}(1) = F_{t+1} = (\text{level at time } t) + (\text{trend at time } t) = L_t + T_t.$$

More generally, the forecast h steps ahead is

$$F_{t+h}(h) = (\text{level at time } t) + h*(\text{trend at time } t) \tag{3.10}$$
$$= L_t + hT_t.$$

Recall that, for SES, the trend is zero, so the forecast reduces to $F_{t+h}(h) = L_t$.

FIGURE 3.8   LINEAR (A) AND QUADRATIC (B) TREND LINES FOR NETFLIX SALES

Data: Netflix_1.xlsx. © Cengage Learning 2013.

3.4.2 Updating Relationships

We now consider updating the level and the trend, using equations like those we used for SES in Section 3.3. We define the observed error (e_t) as the difference between the newly observed value of the series and its previous one-step-ahead forecast:

$$e_t = Y_t - F_t = Y_t - (L_{t-1} + T_{t-1}).$$

Given the latest observation Y_t, we update the expressions for the level and the trend by making partial adjustments that depend upon the error:

$$L_t = L_{t-1} + T_{t-1} + \alpha e_t \qquad (3.11)$$
$$T_t = T_{t-1} + \alpha\beta e_t.$$

These equations may be explained as follows:

- The new level is the old level (adjusted for the increase produced by the trend) plus a partial adjustment (with weight α) for the most recent error.
- The new trend is the old trend plus a partial adjustment (with weight $\alpha\beta$) for the error.

Equations (3.11) are known as the *error correction form* of the updating equations. As may be checked by substitution, the update of the trend can also be expressed as

$$T_t = T_{t-1} + \beta(L_t - L_{t-1} - T_{t-1}). \qquad (3.12)$$

In this form, it is apparent that a second round of smoothing is applied to estimate the trend, leading some authors to describe the method as *double exponential smoothing*. Because the forecast function (3.10) defines a straight line, we prefer the name *linear exponential smoothing* (*LES*). The method is also known as *Holt's method*, after one of its originators (Holt, 2004). If we set the trend equal to zero at all times, we are back at simple exponential smoothing; in that case, T_t vanishes and the equation for L_t reduces to equation (3.7) on identifying L_t as F_{t+1}.

3.4.3   Starting Values

To set this forecasting procedure in motion, we need starting values for the level and trend, as well as values for the two smoothing constants α and β. The smoothing constants may be specified by the user, and conventional wisdom decrees using $0.05 < \alpha < 0.3$ and $0.05 < \beta < 0.15$. These guidelines are not always appropriate, however; it is better to view them as suggesting initial values in a procedure for selecting optimal coefficients by minimizing the *MSE* over some initial sample, as we did for SES. The performance of the resulting forecasting equations should be checked out of sample, as in Example 3.4.

As with SES, different programs use a variety of procedures to set starting values (Gardner, 1985). The macro *LES.xlsm* is available on the book's website and is described briefly in Appendix 3A at the end of the chapter.[6] The macro uses the starting values

$$T_3 = \frac{(Y_3 - Y_1)}{2} \quad \text{for the trend}$$

and

$$L_3 = \frac{(Y_1 + Y_2 + Y_3)}{3} + \frac{(Y_3 - Y_1)}{2} \quad \text{for the level.}$$

These values correspond to fitting a straight line to the first three observations. Once the initial values are set, equations (3.11) are used to update the level and trend as each new observation becomes available.

Caution: All major forecasting packages include fitting routines for LES, although the particular algorithms employed vary, so the results may differ somewhat from those shown in this book.

---

[6]Note that different starting values for estimating the parameter may lead to different final values. Try several values to ensure that a global minimum has been reached.

TABLE 3.8 LES CALCULATIONS FOR HYPOTHETICAL SALES DATA
Alpha = 0.3, Beta = 0.1

Period	Sales	Level	Trend	Forecast	Error	Error^2	|Error|	APE
1	5							
2	7							
3	9							
4	10	9.00	2.00	11.00	−1.00	1.00	1.00	10.00
5	11	10.70	1.97	12.67	−1.67	2.79	1.67	15.18
6	12	12.17	1.92	14.09	−2.09	4.36	2.09	17.41
7	16	13.46	1.86	15.32	0.68	0.46	0.68	4.25
8	17	15.52	1.88	17.40	−0.40	0.16	0.40	2.36
9	20	17.28	1.87	19.15	0.85	0.73	0.85	4.27
10	17	19.40	1.89	21.29	−4.29	18.44	4.29	25.26
11	21	20.01	1.76	21.77	−0.77	0.59	0.77	3.66
12	22	21.54	1.74	23.28	−1.28	1.63	1.28	5.80
13		22.89	1.70	24.59				

ME	RMSE	MAE	MAPE
−1.12	1.91	1.50	9.77

Data shown is from file Example 3_5.xlsx. Averages taken over Periods 5–12.
© Cengage Learning 2013.

EXAMPLE 3.4 ■ Spreadsheet for LES calculations

A short series of hypothetical sales data is given in Table 3.8. The smoothing constants are set at $\alpha = 0.3$, $\beta = 0.1$, and the calculations were performed by the macro. Thus, the first three observations were used to set initial values for the level and trend, and the forecast error measures were then computed with the use of observations 5–12. These values are genuine forecasts because no estimation is involved. The entries corresponding to time period 13 represent the one-step-ahead forecast and its components. The forecast errors and their squares, absolute values, and absolute percentage errors (*APEs*) are shown in succeeding columns. The last two rows of the table give the *ME, RMSE, MAE,* and *MAPE,* calculated over periods 5–12. ■

EXAMPLE 3.5 ■ Linear exponential smoothing for WFJ Sales

We now consider the use of LES for the WFJ Sales data given in Table 3.4. We consider the three fitting criteria in turn: *MSE, MAE,* and *MAPE,* again using *LES.xlsm.* Table 3.9 shows the results for each criterion. As expected, the values of the error measures in the estimation sample are systematically less than those for the hold-out forecasts.

This table shows a number of interesting features:

- The *RMSE* and *MAPE* fitting criteria produce almost identical results in this case, and the overall differences among all three criteria are slight.
- The hold-out sample produces somewhat higher values for the error measures, as would be expected.
- The estimates of β are always zero, suggesting a constant trend.

Too much should not be made of a single example, but three important conclusions can be drawn for general application:

1. Retain an adequate number of observations for out-of-sample testing. If you have sufficient data, retain at least 10–12 observations for this purpose.
2. Different fitting criteria tend to produce similar results.

Finally, a comparison of Tables 3.7 and 3.9 indicates that there is no benefit to using LES in this case; SES does just as well, confirming our initial impression that the series did not show any marked trend, after the initial period when sales were lower. ■

TABLE 3.9   ESTIMATION SAMPLE (ES) AND HOLD-OUT (HO) SAMPLE RESULTS
FOR WFJ SALES

Error Measure	Fitting Criterion					
	RMSE		MAE		MAPE	
	Estimation Sample	Hold-Out	Estimation Sample	Hold-Out	Estimation Sample	Hold-Out
RMSE	3129	4033	3147	4079	3129	4034
MAE	2333	2694	2325	2752	2333	2695
MAPE	7.36	7.91	7.38	8.13	7.36	7.92
Value of α	0.70		0.62		0.70	
Value of β	0.00		0.00		0.00	

Data: WFJ_sales.xlsx. © Cengage Learning 2013.

EXAMPLE 3.6 ■ Forecasting Netflix sales with LES

The sales figures for Netflix shown in Table 3.7 exhibit a very strong trend, and we would
expect LES to perform much better than SES in this case. The series was fitted to observations 1–16 with the use of the macro *LES.xlsm*. The error measures are calculated from the
fitted values for observations 5–16 in each case; a hold-out sample was not used because
we have a short series and are interested in the quality of the fit in this example, rather than
in forecast performance. From Figure 3.9A, we see that the SES forecast always under-
shoots the next value of the series because it fails to allow for the upward trend.   ■

Discussion Question   *How would you choose among SES, LES, or a fitted straight line
for use with a given series?*

FIGURE 3.9   NETFLIX SALES AND ONE-STEP-AHEAD FORECASTS FOR
OBSERVATIONS 1–16 FROM (A) SINGLE EXPONENTIAL
SMOOTHING AND (B) LINEAR EXPONENTIAL SMOOTHING

(A) Single Exponential Smoothing

FIGURE 3.9 (CONTINUED)

(B) Linear Exponential Smoothing

Data: Netflix_1.xlsx. © Cengage Learning 2013.

The results are summarized in Table 3.10. LES is clearly much superior to SES, as we would expect. The choice of fitting method makes very little difference in this case. However, we observe that α is set at its upper level of 1.0, indicating that even LES may have problems. Again, if we step back from the technical details and look at the plot of the data in Figure 3.8, we see that the growth is exponential rather than linear. In Section 3.8, we examine the use of transformations as a way of dealing with this question.

TABLE 3.10   SUMMARY MEASURES FOR SES AND LES FOR NETFLIX SALES

Method (fitting criterion)	SES (All)	LES (RMSE)	LES (MAE/MAPE)
RMSE	6.29	2.80	2.80
MAE	5.46	1.90	1.90
MAPE	14.47	5.98	5.97
α	1.00	1.00	1.00
β		0.49	0.55

Calculated over first quarter 2001 through fourth quarter 2003. © Cengage Learning 2013.

Exponential Smoothing with a Damped Trend

As we saw earlier, the growth rate for Netflix slowed as the company matured. This phenomenon is quite common in time series for sales where a product line matures and sales may then decline unless the product is upgraded in some way. Indeed, such a product life cycle is a standard expectation in marketing. We can accommodate these kinds of life-cycle effects by modifying the updating equations for the level and trend. We anticipate that, in the absence of random errors, the level should flatten out unless the process encounters some new stimulus. In turn, this expectation means that the trend should approach zero. Intuitively, we look for a means of forecasting that damps down the trend component as the forecast horizon is extended. In other words, we assume that the series will level out over time. We achieve this representation in our model by introducing a damping factor so that equations (3.11) become

$$L_t = L_{t-1} + \phi T_{t-1} + \alpha e_t$$
$$T_t = \phi T_{t-1} + \alpha \beta e_t. \tag{3.13}$$

In equations (3.13), we have inserted a *damping factor* ϕ with a value between 0 and 1 in front of every occurrence of the trend term T_{t-1}. We select ϕ to be positive but less than 1 so that the effect is to shift the trend term toward zero, or to dampen it. If we compute the forecast function for h steps ahead, we obtain

$$F_{t+h}(h) = L_t + (\phi + \phi^2 + \cdots + \phi^h)T_t. \tag{3.14}$$

This forecast levels out over time, approaching the limiting value $L_t + T_t/(1 - \phi)$ because the damping factor is less than 1. This limiting value contrasts sharply with LES, where $\phi = 1$ and the forecast keeps increasing because $F_{t+h}(h) = L_t + hT_t$.

   The damped trend model was introduced by Gardner and McKenzie (1985) and has proved surprisingly effective (Makridakis and Hibon, 2000).

EXAMPLE 3.7 ■ Forecasting Netflix sales with the damped trend method

We took the damping factor to be $\phi = 0.95$ and repeated the forecasting exercise under damped LES, with the same fitting procedures as before. The results are summarized in Table 3.11. The forecasts are marginally inferior to those from LES without damping; indeed, the optimal value for $\phi = 1.00$, but if we believe that company expansion is slowing, then the damped form may be preferable for future use.   ■

TABLE 3.11   ONE-STEP-AHEAD FITTED VALUES AND FORECASTS FOR NETFLIX SALES UNDER THE DAMPED TREND METHOD ($\phi = 0.95$)

Period	Netflix Sales	Forecast	
1	5.17		
2	7.15		
3	10.18		
4	13.39	12.51	**RMSE** = 2.85
5	17.06	16.36	
6	18.36	20.37	**MAE** = 1.95
7	18.88	20.42	
8	21.62	19.99	**MAPE** = 6.04
9	30.53	23.66	
10	36.36	36.56	$\alpha = 1.00$
11	40.73	42.15	$\beta = 0.59$
12	45.19	45.57	$\phi = 0.95$
13	55.67	49.70	
14	63.19	63.60	
15	72.20	70.71	
16	81.19	80.45	

Data: Netflix_1.xlsx. © Cengage Learning 2013.

FIGURE 3.10   POSSIBLE TREND PATTERNS

No Trend

Damped Trend

Additive Trend

Multiplicative Trend

© Cengage Learning 2013.

3.5.1 Choice of Method

The different forms of exponential smoothing apply to certain types of time series. Figure 3.10 shows a categorization of series by the form of the trend (no trend, additive trend, damped trend, multiplicative trend). In choosing a method, the aim is to match it with the type of data. Often, however, the form of the series is unknown. By implication in our earlier discussion, we have recommended choosing the method that performs best on the hold-out sample, using one or more of the criteria discussed. When the series is too short to allow for a hold-out sample of reasonable size, we use the measures defined for the estimation sample, as well as our understanding of the time series itself. This approach is developed in Chapter 5.

3.6 Other Approaches to Trend Forecasting

Several other methods of trend forecasting are worthy of a brief mention. For a more comprehensive review of recent developments, see the excellent review article by Gardner (2006).

3.6.1 Brown's Method of Double Exponential Smoothing (DES)

As noted earlier, Robert Brown was the original developer of exponential smoothing methods and his books (1959, 1963) have become classics. His initial derivation of exponential smoothing was based on minimizing the weighted sum of squared errors, where the past squared errors are discounted by α, α^2, etc. For a local linear trend, his method reduces to the use of LES with $\alpha = \beta$. Unless data are very limited, there is no particular benefit to imposing this restriction, and we do not consider it further. However, the discounted least squares approach is particularly useful when complex nonlinear functions are involved and updating equations are not readily available.

3.6.2 SES with (Constant) Drift

If we set $\beta = 0$, the updated equations (3.11) become

$$L_t = L_{t-1} + T + \alpha e_t$$
$$T_t = T_{t-1} = T.$$

This version may be referred to as *SES with drift*, because the level increases by a fixed amount each period. Although the method is just a special case of LES, the simpler structure makes it easier to derive an optimal value for T by using the estimation sample, rather than the start-up values we have considered hitherto. This scheme (sometimes called the *Theta Method:* Assimakopoulos and Nikolopoulos, 2000) is often surprisingly effective, as shown by Hyndman and Billah (2003), who compared it to other methods using the data of the M3 competition (Makridakis and Hibon, 2000).

3.6.3 Tracking Signals

Trigg and Leach (1967) introduced the concept of a tracking signal, whereby not only the level and trend, but also the smoothing parameters, are updated each time. For example, for SES, we would use the updated value for α given by

$$\alpha_t = \frac{|E_{t-1}|}{M_{t-1}}, \tag{3.15}$$

where E_t and M_t are smoothed values of the error and the absolute error, respectively. That is,

$$\begin{aligned} E_t &= \delta e_t + (1 - \delta)E_{t-1} \\ M_t &= \delta |e_t| + (1 - \delta)M_{t-1}. \end{aligned} \tag{3.16}$$

Typically, a value of δ in the range 0.1–0.2 is used. If a string of positive errors occurs, the value of α_t increases to speed up the adjustment process; the reverse occurs for negative errors. Initial values are set to zero.

Over the years, there has been considerable debate over the benefits of tracking signals; for example, Gardner (1985) found no real evidence that forecasts based upon tracking signals provided any improvements. A generally preferred approach is to update the parameter estimate regularly, which is no longer much of a computational problem even for large numbers of series. Rather, Fildes et al. (1998) found that regular updating produced more consistent gains over all forecast horizons. From the practical viewpoint, a forecasting system may incorporate data on a weekly or monthly basis and then the forecasting analysis should be rerun at regular intervals to find revised parameters. That way, updating is straightforward and should not be a problem with modern forecasting systems.

3.6.4 Linear Moving Averages

In Section 3.2, we considered a simple moving average as an alternative to SES, albeit not a recommended approach. We could also look at the successive differences in the series $Y_t - Y_{t-1}$ and take a moving average of these values to estimate the trend. The net effect is to estimate the trend by $\dfrac{Y_t - Y_{t-K}}{K}$ for a K-term moving average. Again, exponential smoothing for a trend via LES usually provides better forecasts.

Prediction Intervals

Our discussion thus far has been purely in terms of point forecasts, yet in Chapter 2 (Section 2.9) we stressed the importance of interval forecasts. At this stage, we restrict attention to the construction of prediction intervals for one-step-ahead forecasts. Intervals for forecasts made two or more periods ahead require the specification of an underlying statistical model, so we defer that discussion to Chapter 5. Indeed, the intervals for one-step-ahead forecasting also imply an underlying model, but we can bypass that requirement for now by using the approximate interval given in Section 2.9, based upon the normal distribution:

$$\text{Forecast} \pm z_{\alpha/2}*(RMSE).$$

In other words, the outcome is expected to lie within the range

$$[\text{Forecast} - z_{\alpha/2}*(RMSE), \text{Forecast} + z_{\alpha/2}*(RMSE)], 100(1 - \alpha)\% \text{ of the time.}$$

We may also construct a prediction interval empirically, using the alternative approach given in Section 2.9; the interpretation is the same, but the interval need not be symmetric.

EXAMPLE 3.8 ■ Prediction interval for Netflix
From Table 3.11, the point forecast for the next period (2003.4) was 80.45 with $RMSE = 2.85$. The resulting (approximate) 95 percent prediction interval is

$$80.45 \pm 1.96 * 2.85 = 80.45 \pm 5.59 = (74.86, 86.04).$$

The actual outcome is expected to lie in the range 74.86–86.04 approximately 95 percent of the time. As the forecasting horizon increases, the intervals get progressively wider, as we shall see in Chapter 5 (Section 5.2). ■

EXAMPLE 3.9 ■ Prediction interval for WFJ Sales
The first 52 observations of the series are used as the estimation sample, which provides 50 observed error terms. To obtain comparability between the normal and empirical intervals, we use confidence levels of 90, 94, and 98 percent, meaning that we use the pairs (3, 48), (2, 49), and (1, 50) of the 50 ranked error terms, as shown in Table 3.12A. The half-widths of the prediction intervals (Table 3.12B) show that the distribution may be somewhat more heavy tailed than the normal distribution. Finally, the two sets of 90 percent one-step-ahead prediction intervals for periods 53–62 are shown in Table 3.12C, along with the actual values of the series. These ten observations occur around the year's end,

TABLE 3.12 ONE-STEP-AHEAD PREDICTION INTERVALS FOR WFJ SALES SERIES

(A) Smallest and largest observed errors

	Smallest Five		Largest Five	
Rank	Value		Rank	Value
1	−6575		46	3750
2	−5259		47	3874
3	−4605		48	5091
4	−3657		49	5512
5	−2682		50	8035

(Continued)

TABLE 3.12 (CONTINUED)

(B) Half-width of 90 percent prediction interval

Level	90	94	98
Normal	5070	5794	7169
Empirical	4848	5386	7305

(C) Normal and empirical prediction intervals for observations 53–62

Period	WFJ Sales	Point Forecast	90% Normal PI Lower	90% Normal PI Upper	90% Empirical PI Lower	90% Empirical PI Upper
53	35404*	49852	44782	54922	45247	54942
54	30555*	38390	33320	43459	33785	43480
55	30421	32174	27104	37244	27569	37265
56	30972	30783	25713	35853	26179	35874
57	32336	30933	25863	36003	26329	36024
58	28194	32046	26976	37116	27442	37137
59	29203	28990	23920	34060	24386	34081
60	28155	29159	24089	34229	24554	34250
61	28404	28363	23293	33432	23758	33453
62	34128*	28396	23326	33465	23791	33486

*Values show actual observations falling outside the intervals given by the two methods.

Data: WFJ_Sales.xlsx. © Cengage Learning 2013.

when the volume of sales changes dramatically, so it comes as no surprise that the two sets of prediction intervals cover only seven out of ten actual values. ∎

Discussion Question   *Suppose a revised forecasting method describes the WFJ Sales data for periods 1–52 pretty well. But four actual observations fall outside the normal prediction interval for periods 53–62. What possible explanations are there for this occurrence?*

3.8   The Use of Transformations

The forecasts derived from the LES method require that the series be locally linear. Intuitively, if the trend for the last few time periods in the series appears to be close to a straight line, the LES method should work well. However, in many cases this assumption is not realistic. For example, suppose we are trying to forecast the *GDP* of a country that has experienced growth of around 5 percent per year in recent years. Then, ignoring statistical variation for the moment, we might describe such growth by the expression

$$Y_t = (1.05)^t Y_0 \quad \text{or} \quad Y_t = 1.05 Y_{t-1}.$$

When plotted, this function is an exponential curve, which increases at an increasing rate in monetary terms. Any linear approximation will undershoot the true function sooner or later, (This observation was first made hundreds of years ago by Malthus regarding linear growth in the world's food supply and exponential population growth, leading to starvation.) For very short-term forecasts, undershooting may not matter, but it becomes serious as the forecasting horizon increases. More complex nonlinear patterns may also exist; for example, many products have a sales history of growth, then stability, then a decline as they are superseded by new (and presumably improved) items. Such series can be forecast in two ways:

1. Transform the series so that the trend becomes linear.
2. Convert the series to growth over time, forecast the growth rate, and then convert back to the original series.

We now examine each approach in turn.

3.8.1   The Log Transform

We defined the logarithmic transformation in Chapter 2 (Section 2.6.2). For the exponential growth equation just given, the log transform yields

$$\ln Y_t = \ln(1.05) + \ln Y_{t-1}.$$

If we now write $Z_t = \ln Y_t$, the reverse transformation is

$$Y_t = \exp(Z_t) = \exp[\ln(1.05) + \ln Y_{t-1}]$$
$$= 1.05\, Y_{t-1}.$$

Of course, the growth rate is rarely constant. (If it were, we would estimate it by means of the averaging methods of Chapter 2.) Instead, where the log-transform produces a linear trend, we can apply LES. We must then transform back to the original series to obtain the forecasts of interest.

Typically, the effect of the log transform process is to improve forecasting performance for exponential growth curves.

EXAMPLE 3.10 ■ Forecasting Netflix sales data with the log transform

We applied LES to the transformed series, using *LES.xlsm*. We applied the same procedures for setting starting values and estimating the parameters as before. The summary statistics are presented in Table 3.13. The table gives the results of estimating the parameters by minimizing the *MSE* of (a) the transformed values and (b) the original values. The summary values are computed after transforming back to the original units; otherwise comparisons between methods are not feasible. Also, we are interested in forecasting the original series, not the transformed values.

The comparative results in Table 3.13 indicate that the log transform does somewhat worse in this case. However, we must stress that these comparisons are based upon a small sample for a single series and that no general conclusions should be drawn. The only solid

TABLE 3.13   SUMMARY MEASURES FOR LES FOR NETFLIX SALES, USING A LOG TRANSFORM*

	Fitted with MSE of Log Series	Fitted with MSE of Original Series
RMSE	3.66	2.80
MAE	2.93	1.90
MAPE	8.57	5.98
Value of α	1	1
Value of β	0.97	0.49

*Error measures refer to the original units of the observations.
Data: Netflix_1.xlsx. © Cengage Learning 2013.

conclusion that can be drawn is the intuitively obvious one that SES should not be used for strongly trending series; whether to use LES on the original or transformed series or to use SES on growth rates remains a question for further examination in any particular study. ■

3.8.2 Use of Growth Rates

We begin by defining the growth rate. Assuming that the variable has a natural origin, we see that the growth rate from one time period to the next is

$$G_t = 100 * \frac{Y_t - Y_{t-1}}{Y_{t-1}}. \tag{3.17}$$

The growth rate, is approximately equal to $\ln Y_t - \ln Y_{t-1}$, as indicated in Exercise 3.16.

Note that growth, by this definition, can be negative. For example, the period-by-period returns on an investment are defined exactly as in equation (3.17). After we compute the single-period growth rates, we use SES to predict the growth for the next period, which we denote by $g_{t+1}(1) = g_{t+1}$, following our usual convention. The one-step-ahead forecast for the original series is given by

$$F_{t+1}(1) = F_{t+1} = Y_t * \left[1 + \frac{g_{t+1}}{100} \right]. \tag{3.18}$$

In other words, we unscramble the growth forecast to determine the forecast for the original series.

EXAMPLE 3.11 ■ Forecasting Netflix sales data by means of the growth rate
The quarterly sales (in $ million) for Netflix are shown for the first quarter of 2000 through the fourth quarter of 2003 in Table 3.14. The growth rates for one quarter over the immediately preceding quarter are then computed with equation (3.17). The growth rates are plotted in Figure 3.11, which clearly reveals the instability in the early growth phase. The one-step-ahead forecasts of the growth rate are generated by using the first value to define the initial forecast, F_1. Given that we have only 16 observations, we selected the optimal

TABLE 3.14   GROWTH RATE ANALYSIS OF NETFLIX QUARTERLY SALES, 2000–2003

Year	Quarter	Quarterly Sales	Growth Percentage	Growth Forecast	Sales Forecast	
2000	1	5.17				
2000	2	7.15	38.1	38.1		
2000	3	10.18	42.5	38.1	9.9	**RMSE = 4.66**
2000	4	13.39	31.5	41.9	14.1	
2001	1	17.06	27.4	33.0	19.0	**MAE = 3.91**
2001	2	18.36	7.6	28.2	22.7	
2001	3	18.88	2.8	10.5	23.5	**MAPE = 12.08**
2001	4	21.62	14.5	3.9	20.9	
2002	1	30.53	41.2	13.0	22.5	$\alpha = 0.86$
2002	2	36.36	19.1	37.2	34.5	
2002	3	40.73	12.0	21.7	49.9	
2002	4	45.19	10.9	13.4	49.6	
2003	1	55.67	23.2	11.3	51.2	
2003	2	63.19	13.5	21.5	62.0	
2003	3	72.20	14.3	14.6	76.8	
2003	4	81.19	12.4	14.3	82.8	

Quarterly revenue (sales) in $ million; growth in %. *Data:* Netflix_1.xlsx.
© Cengage Learning 2013.

FIGURE 3.11   NETFLIX GROWTH RATES (*First quarter 2000–Fourth quarter 2003*)

© Cengage Learning 2013.

value for α by minimizing the *MSE* over all the data points; the optimal value for α obtained from SES is 0.86. The one-step-ahead sales forecasts (strictly fitted values because we used the entire series to estimate the smoothing constant) are then given in the last column of Table 3.14, generated from equation (3.18).

The growth rate is highly variable, as is clear from Table 3.14, and the optimal value for α varies considerably with the time span of the data chosen. Short series often lead to unstable estimates. The calculation of the various error measures, as in Table 3.5, is left as Exercise 3.6. The forecasts are not the best, but the evaluation of growth rates seems intuitively more reasonable than trying to forecast rapidly growing dollar amounts with SES. In particular, we can look for a slowdown in growth as a company matures. Minicase 3.1 at the end of the chapter uses more recent data to examine the growth of Netflix. ■

3.8.3   **The Box–Cox Transformations**

The logarithmic transformation is appealing because it reflects proportional rather than absolute change. For many series in business and economics, the notion of proportional, or percentage, change is a natural framework; we often encounter statements, such as "We expect *GDP* to grow by 2.5 percent next year," leading to exponential growth. However, proportional change may project future growth patterns in excess of reasonable expectations. An examination of Table 3.14 shows that the growth rate for Netflix moderated over time, and the extended series given in Table 3.20 (Minicase 3.1) shows an even more marked slowdown.

How can we allow for the "irrational exuberance" sometimes shown by exponential growth but where the logarithmic transformation fails to induce linearity? We have already discussed a modification of LES to allow for a damped trend; this modification can be applied after the log transform when appropriate. A second possibility is to select a transformation that is more moderate than the logarithmic form.

Instead of restricting the choice to the original units or the logarithmic transform, Box and Cox (1964) suggested using a power transformation, of which the square root and the cube root are the most obvious cases. On occasion, such transformations may have a natural interpretation, as when one is considering the volume of a sphere; the cube root is proportional to the radius of the sphere. It is difficult, however, to find any examples in

TABLE 3.15   VALUES OF TRANSFORMED NETFLIX DATA

Year	Quarter	Period	Quarterly Sales	Logarithm of sales	Square Root of Sales	Cube Root of Sales
2000	1	1	5.17	1.64	2.27	1.73
2000	2	2	7.15	1.97	2.67	1.93
2000	3	3	10.18	2.32	3.19	2.17
2000	4	4	13.39	2.59	3.66	2.37
2001	1	5	17.06	2.84	4.13	2.57
2001	2	6	18.36	2.91	4.28	2.64
2001	3	7	18.88	2.94	4.34	2.66
2001	4	8	21.62	3.07	4.65	2.79
2002	1	9	30.53	3.42	5.53	3.12
2002	2	10	36.36	3.59	6.03	3.31
2002	3	11	40.73	3.71	6.38	3.44
2002	4	12	45.19	3.81	6.72	3.56
2003	1	13	55.67	4.02	7.46	3.82
2003	2	14	63.19	4.15	7.95	3.98
2003	3	15	72.20	4.28	8.50	4.16
2003	4	16	81.19	4.40	9.01	4.33

Data: Netflix_1.xlsx. © Cengage Learning 2013.

business or economics in which such transformations have intuitive appeal. Nevertheless, from a purely empirical perspective, these transforms may provide better forecasts.

Given the original series Y_t we define the Box–Cox transform[7] as

$$Z_t = Y_t^c. \tag{3.19}$$

The parameter c is usually restricted to the range $-1 \le c \le 1$. where $c = 1$ corresponds to the original series and $c = -1$ represents the reciprocal. (Think of miles per gallon versus gallons per mile.) We will use only the square and cube root in our examples; in general, the choice among different values for c may be made by comparing the *MSEs* for the various options after transforming back to the original units. This reverse transformation is $Y_t = Z_t^{1/c}$.

The transformed data values are shown in Table 3.15, and the values are plotted in Figure 3.12. From the plots, we can see that the log transform overcorrects, exhibiting a slight curvature or flattening out. By contrast, the square- and cube-root plots suggest straight-line trends.

EXAMPLE 3.12 ■ Forecasting Netflix sales by means of the Box–Cox transform

We considered the square- and cube-root transformations for the Netflix series. The results given in Table 3.16 relate to fitting by minimizing the *MSE* for the transformed series. When the *MSE* for the original data is used to estimate the parameters, the forecasting results are similar and are omitted.

When we compare the results in Tables 3.10 and 3.16, we see that the square-root transformation seems to provide the best performance with *RMSE*, but the margin of superiority is very slight and the estimated parameter values ($\alpha = 1$, $\beta = 0$) give cause for concern. The problem arises because the level is not smoothed at all ($\alpha = 1$), while the trend is not updated at all from its initial value, $\beta = 0$. We must stress again the very limited amount of data used in the analysis.   ■

[7]Box and Cox (1964) used the slightly more complex form $Z_t = [Y_t^c - 1]/c$, which has numerical advantages when one is seeking an optimal value for c. For our purposes, the simpler form in equation (3.19) suffices.

FIGURE 3.12   PLOTS OF TRANSFORMED NETFLIX DATA

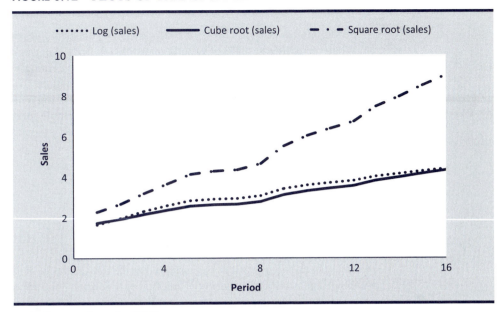

© Cengage Learning 2013.

TABLE 3.16   LES SUMMARY MEASURES FOR NETFLIX SALES, USING THE
BOX–COX TRANSFORM

Transform	c	α	β	RMSE	MAE	MAPE
Cube root	0.333	1.00	0.11	2.50	2.00	6.93
Square root	0.500	1.00	0.00	2.37	1.91	6.30

© Cengage Learning 2013.

Discussion Question *Suppose you carry out an extensive analysis and conclude that the best forecasting model involves a Box–Cox transform with c = ⅓. Would you feel comfortable using this transform and reporting the results to management? Why or why not?*

When to Transform

- Do not use complex transforms unless they are supported by both theory and data.
- Always compare transformed methods with a benchmark by transforming the forecasts back to the data series of interest.

 ## Model Selection

In the course of this chapter, we have outlined a considerable number of forecasting methods, and more are to come in the next chapter when we discuss seasonality. For any particular forecasting task, one approach may naturally suggest itself in preference to another. For example, it is always reasonable to ask and answer the following questions:

- Does the series display a trend? Do we expect the trend to continue into the future? If so, then
    ✓ Use a method that includes a trend.

- Do the observations tend to be more (or less) variable over time? If so, then
  ✓ Transform the data to obtain roughly constant variability.

In addition, we need to check for conformity with the principles outlined in the next section. When there are a number of equally plausible methods, we usually rely on comparing their out-of-sample forecasting performance. When we are dealing with a large number of series, it is usually feasible to examine the preceding questions for a (possibly small) sample of all the series. We may overcome such obstacles by using a common estimation sample to fit each method and then generating a set of out-of-sample forecasts that can be compared with values in the hold-out sample. We then choose the method that corresponds to the best value of the selected criterion (*RMSE, MAE, MAPE,* etc.), calculated over the sample of time series. We return to the issue of method selection in Chapter 5 (Section 5.3), in which the analysis is reinforced by the development of underlying models.

Principles for Extrapolative Models

To avoid undue repetition, we assume that the data series being forecast is appropriate for the problem at hand in terms of relevance, timeliness, and reporting accuracy. These assumptions are by no means trivial, but we have discussed them in the previous chapters and they remain critical to any forecasting exercise. We should always recall the maxim "Garbage in, garbage out." If the data do not satisfy the aforementioned criteria, further analysis may be useless. As before, Armstrong (2001) is a valuable resource, and many of the principles quoted reflect his ideas. A few principles are repeated from Chapter 2 because they are an integral part of the forecasting approach described in the current chapter.

[3.1] Plot the series. Data plotting should be the first step in any analysis. If a large number of series is involved, plot a selection of them. Such plots will often serve to identify data-recording errors, missing values, and unusual events.

[3.2] Clean the data. Data plots and simple screening procedures (checks for outliers) provide the basis for making adjustments for anomalous values. Make sure that the adjustments are for valid data-recording reasons, and keep a record of all such changes.

[3.3] Use transformations as required by expectations about the process. Such transformations may involve a conversion current to real-dollar values, a logarithmic transformation to reflect proportional growth, or a switch to growth rates to account for trends. The intelligent use of knowledge related to the phenomenon being studied helps to avoid "crazy" forecasts.

[3.4] Select simple methods, unless convincing empirical evidence calls for greater complexity. The set of exponential smoothing methods described in this chapter relies upon only the past history of the series in question. Such extrapolative methods often suffice in the short to medium term, unless measurements on key explanatory variables are available.

[3.5] Evaluate alternative methods, preferably using out-of-sample data. Methods that use more parameters or that are based on a more complicated nonlinear transform often fit better within the estimation sample, but this advantage may be illusory. Out-of-sample testing provides an even playing field for comparing the performance of different methods. Note that the estimation sample can be used to make such comparisons, provided that due care is taken (see Chapter 5).

[3.6] Update the estimates frequently. Regular updating of the parameter estimates is found to improve forecasting performance because it helps to take into account any changes in the behavior of the series. Once the database has been established and updated with the most recent information, updating the parameter estimates is straightforward.

Summary

Extrapolative forecasts are useful in the short to medium term whenever the recent behavior of the series under study is sufficient to provide a framework for forecasting. When a series does not display marked changes in level over time, simple exponential smoothing (SES), as described in Section 3.3, usually suffices. However, many series do contain systematic trends, and in such circumstances linear exponential smoothing (LES) should be considered, as described in Section 3.4. A series may display nonlinear behavior, either in the growth pattern or because of some kind of life cycle, as is the case for the sales of many products. In Section 3.5, we explored the use of damped trend methods to handle these issues. Other extrapolative methods were reviewed briefly in Section 3.6. The construction of one-step-ahead prediction intervals was examined in Section 3.7. Section 3.8 looked at different transformations. We have introduced quite a number of different variants of exponential smoothing in this chapter so in Section 3.9 we discussed model selection – how to choose between them. Finally, some basic principles for forecasting with extrapolative methods were summarized in Section 3.9.

Exercises

3.1 Table 3.17 shows the growth rate in the U.S. gross domestic product (*GDP*).
   a. Use three- and seven-term moving averages to generate one-step-ahead forecasts for 1981 to the end of the series. Graph the results, and comment on the differences between the two moving averages.
   b. Compare the performance of the two procedures by calculating the *RMSE* and *MAE*. Why is the *MAPE* inappropriate in this case?

3.2 Table 3.18 shows the annual percentage change in the consumer price index (*CPI*) for 1991–2007.
   a. Use three- and seven-term moving averages to generate one-step-ahead forecasts for 1998 to the end of the series.
   b. Compare the performance of the two procedures by calculating the *RMSE* and *MAE*.
   c. Calculate the *MASE* for the one-step-ahead forecasts. Why is the *MAPE* inappropriate in this case?

3.3 Use the data in Table 3.17 to generate forecasts for *GDP* growth by simple exponential smoothing (SES).
   a. With the observed value for 1963 as the starting value, compute the one-step-ahead forecasts for 1981–2007, using each of $\alpha = 0.2, 0.5$, and 0.8 in turn.
   b. Compare the forecasting performance for the given values of α by calculating the *RMSE* and *MAE* over the period 1981–2007.
   c. How does this method compare with the moving-average procedures used in Exercise 3.1? (Be careful to make comparisons over the same time periods.)

3.4 Rework the analysis in Exercise 3.3, using the optimal value of α. (Use the macro *SES.xlsm* or other suitable software.)

3.5 Use the data in Table 3.18 to generate forecasts for changes in the *CPI* by means of simple exponential smoothing (SES).
   a. Use the observed value for 1991 as the starting value, and compute the one-step-ahead forecasts for subsequent years for $\alpha = 0.2, 0.5$, and 0.8 in turn.
   b. Compare the performance for the given values of α by calculating the *RMSE* and *MAE* over the period 1998–2007.
   c. How does this method compare with the moving-average procedures used in Exercise 3.2? (Be careful to make comparisons over the same time periods.)

TABLE 3.17   PERCENTAGE CHANGE IN U.S. GROSS DOMESTIC PRODUCT, ADJUSTED FOR INFLATION

Year	GDP Growth	Year	GDP Growth
1963	4.4	1986	3.5
1964	5.8	1987	3.4
1965	6.4	1988	4.1
1966	6.5	1989	3.5
1967	2.5	1990	1.9
1968	4.8	1991	−0.2
1969	3.1	1992	3.3
1970	0.2	1993	2.7
1971	3.4	1994	4.0
1972	5.3	1995	2.5
1973	5.8	1996	3.7
1974	−0.5	1997	4.5
1975	−0.2	1998	4.2
1976	5.3	1999	4.5
1977	4.6	2000	3.8
1978	5.6	2001	0.8
1979	3.2	2002	1.9
1980	−0.2	2003	3.0
1981	2.5	2004	4.4
1982	−1.9	2005	2.9
1983	4.5	2006	2.8
1984	7.2	2007	2.0
1985	4.5		

Source: Bureau of Economic Analysis, U.S. Department of Commerce. Data shown is from file GDP_change.xlsx.

TABLE 3.18   PERCENTAGE CHANGE IN THE CONSUMER PRICE INDEX, DECEMBER TO DECEMBER

Year	Percentage Increase	Year	Percentage Increase
1991	3.1	2000	3.4
1992	2.9	2001	1.6
1993	2.7	2002	2.4
1994	2.7	2003	1.9
1995	2.5	2004	3.3
1996	3.3	2005	3.4
1997	1.7	2006	2.5
1998	1.6	2007	4.1
1999	2.7		

Source: Bureau of Labor Statistics, U.S. Department of Labor. Data shown is from file CPI_change.xlsx.

TABLE 3.19   FREE ON BOARD (FOB) SPOT PRICE OF SAUDI ARABIAN LIGHT
OIL (IN U.S. DOLLARS PER BARREL)

Year	Spot Price ($/barrel)	Year	Spot Price ($/barrel)
1989	13.15	1998	15.50
1990	18.40	1999	10.03
1991	24.00	2000	23.45
1992	15.90	2001	20.90
1993	16.80	2002	18.90
1994	12.40	2003	27.39
1995	16.63	2004	27.08
1996	18.20	2005	34.05
1997	22.98	2006	55.01

Source: U.S. Department of Energy, Energy Information Administration.
Data shown is from file SA_oil_spot.xlsx.

3.6   Rework the analysis in Exercise 3.5, using the optimal value of α. (Use the macro *SES.xlsm*
or other suitable software.)

3.7   Table 3.19 gives the spot price of Saudi Arabian Light Oil (in U.S. dollars per barrel). The
prices are quoted for early January in each year.
  a.   Use the observed value for 1989 as the starting value, and compute the one-step-ahead
  forecasts for subsequent years for each of $\alpha = 0.2, 0.5$, and 0.8 in turn.
  b.   With the same starting value, find the optimal level for α, using the data for the period
  1990–2003 as the estimation sample. Use *SES.xlsm* or other suitable software.
  c.   Generate the forecasts for 2004–2006.
  d.   Compute the out-of-sample *RMSE*, *MAE*, and *MAPE* for each case, and contrast the
  results.

3.8   Repeat the analysis in Exercise 3.7, using linear exponential smoothing. (Use *LES.xlsm* or
other suitable software.) Compare the forecasting performance of the two methods.

3.9   Repeat the analysis in Exercise 3.8, using 1989–2004 and then 1989–2005 as the estimation samples. Generate the 95 percent prediction intervals for the one-step-ahead forecasts
in each case, using the normal approximation. Do the prediction intervals include the
observed values? Interpret your results.

3.10   Compute the estimation error measures for SES and LES for the Netflix series given in
Table 3.7 (*Netflix.xlsx*). Compare the results. Use different time ranges for the estimation
sample, and note how the optimal value of α varies.

3.11   Use LES to forecast the number of domestic passengers at Dulles airport for 2004–2007
(see Table 2.12, *Dulles.xlsx*), with the years 1963–2003 as the estimation sample. Then use
the complete data set to make forecasts for 2008–2012.

3.12   Dulles Airport was greatly expanded in the mid-eighties, producing a significant increase in
the number of passengers. Rerun the analyses of Exercise 3.11, using the years 1986–2003
as the estimation sample. Compare your results with those for the complete sample. What
conclusions do you draw from the comparison?

3.13   Rerun the analyses of Exercise 3.10 for the damped trend and log transform versions of
LES, and compare the results of the four methods, using *RMSE*, *MAE*, and *MAPE*.

3.14   Rerun the analyses of Exercise 3.12 for the damped trend and log transform versions of
LES, and compare the results of the four methods, using *RMSE*, *MAE*, and *MAPE*.

3.15   Use the observed errors from the estimation sample in Exercise 3.12 to generate empirical
90 percent prediction intervals for the one-step-ahead forecasts for 2004–2007.

3.16* Show that $\ln(Y_t/Y_{t-1}) \doteq \dfrac{Y_t - Y_{t-1}}{Y_{t-1}}$ and, hence, that the log transform and growth rate methods often produce similar results. (*Hint:* $\ln(1 + x) \doteq x$ for small x.)

3.17* Demonstrate that equation (3.12) may be rewritten as the second equation in equations (3.11) by substituting the expression for the level at time t.

3.18* Repeat the analysis for the data on oil prices in Table 3.19, using the Box–Cox transform with $c = 0.333$ and $c = 0.50$. Compare the results with the original forecasts ($c = 1.0$).

Minicases

Minicase 3.1 The Growth of Netflix

Home entertainment has become a major element of the modern economy. Whereas 25 years ago television was the primary form of in-home entertainment, the VCR and then the DVD player have become widely owned alternatives to a night at the movies. In addition, PCs are increasingly used for movie watching.

In response to these technological developments, a variety of organizations now provide movie rentals. At first these services were restricted to videotape rentals, but now they focus almost exclusively on DVD rentals and sales. Many such business units, including some national chains, are conventional bricks-and-mortar stores.

Netflix initiated a different business plan. Subscribers sign up for a given number of movies and provide Netflix with a list of movies they would like to view. Once one DVD is returned, the next one on the list is mailed to the subscriber. Moreover, because technology does not stand still, Netflix is extending its business to include online rentals. The Netflix annual report for 2009 indicates that, as of the end of 2009, the company had over 12 million subscribers and annual total rental revenues in excess of $1.6 billion.

As a market analyst, you would like to know how the company is faring in the marketplace and whether it is likely to continue to grow at the same rate. Table 3.20 is an extension of Table 3.14 and provides the following quarterly data over the period from quarter 1 of 2000 to quarter 4 of 2009:

- S = quarterly revenue (or sales, $ million)
- G = sales growth rate over previous quarter (percent)
- N = number of subscribers at end of quarter (000s) [not available for 2009]

To assess the company's prospects, carry out the following analyses and comment on the results:

1. Develop forecasting methods for each of the series S, G, and N, using data through quarter 4 of 2008. Then use your results to generate forecasts for 2009 and 2010.
2. What other factors would you wish to take into account before making forecasts one quarter ahead? Eight quarters ahead?

Minicase 3.2 The Evolution of Walmart

Consider the data on Walmart stores given in Chapter 2 (Table 2.11) and available in *Walmart.xlsx*. In Minicase 2.2, we used basic statistical tools to examine the changing

TABLE 3.20   NETFLIX SALES DATA FOR THE PERIOD FROM QUARTER 1, 2000–QUARTER 4, 2009

Year	Quarter	Quarterly Revenues	Growth – percentage	Subscribers at End of Period (000s)
2000	1	5.17	*	
2000	2	7.15	38.1	
2000	3	10.18	42.5	
2000	4	13.39	31.5	
2001	1	17.06	27.4	
2001	2	18.36	7.6	
2001	3	18.88	2.8	
2001	4	21.62	14.5	
2002	1	30.53	41.2	
2002	2	36.36	19.1	
2002	3	40.73	12.0	
2002	4	45.19	10.9	
2003	1	55.67	23.2	1052
2003	2	63.19	13.5	1147
2003	3	72.20	14.3	1291
2003	4	81.19	12.4	1487
2004	1	99.82	22.9	1932
2004	2	119.71	19.9	2093
2004	3	140.41	17.3	2229
2004	4	140.66	0.2	2610
2005	1	152.45	8.4	3018
2005	2	164.03	7.6	3196
2005	3	172.74	5.3	3592
2005	4	193.00	11.7	4179
2006	1	224.13	16.1	4866
2006	2	239.35	6.8	5169
2006	3	255.95	6.9	5662
2006	4	277.23	8.3	6316
2007	1	305.32	10.1	6797
2007	2	303.69	−0.5	6742
2007	3	293.97	−3.2	7028
2007	4	302.36	2.9	7479
2008	1	326.18	7.9	8243
2008	2	337.61	3.5	8411
2008	3	341.27	1.1	8672
2008	4	359.94	5.5	9390
2009	1	394.1	9.5	*
2009	2	408.59	3.7	*
2009	3	423.12	3.6	*
2009	4	444.19	5.0	12268

Source: Annual reports available on *http://ir.netflix.com*. Data shown is from file Netflix_2.xlsx.

composition of store types and the company's growth. The objective now is to use exponential smoothing methods to generate the following forecasts:

1. Store composition for the next three years.
2. Sales for the next eight quarters.

In each case, plot the fitted and observed values of the series and identify any possible shortcomings in your forecasts. What steps, if any, might be taken to improve the forecasts *without collecting any new data*?

Minicase 3.3 Volatility in the Dow Jones Index

The efficient markets hypothesis (EMH) in finance embodies the notion that financial markets process new information rapidly in order that the best forecast of a stock's price in the next (short) time period be the current price. The EMH is also known as the random-walk hypothesis because any movement from the present state is essentially unpredictable. The errors (or stock returns, which in this context are given by $e_t = Y_t - Y_{t-1}$) are so defined because the last period's closing price is the current forecast. The EMH corresponds to the assumption that the successive errors are independent and unpredictable from publicly available information. There is a vast literature on the EMH in its various forms (see, for example, *http://en.wikipedia.org/wiki/Efficient-market_hypothesis*), and our purpose is not to discuss the ideas in any detail. Rather, we note that, in forecasting terms, the EMH translates into the use of SES with $\alpha = 1$, essentially of no real value to the stock trader.

Despite many efforts to the contrary, it is essentially impossible for any purely statistical forecasting method to beat the random walk for any long period of time. Insider information can, of course, be of considerable value, but those forecasters tend not to be at liberty (to talk about their methods). Nevertheless, some interesting questions can be answered that relate to *volatility*. Toward that end, we can examine the pattern of the forecast errors to determine whether the inherent variability in those forecasts varies over time. When variability is high, considerable opportunities exist for traders to buy or sell options (Hull, 2002). Conversely, when variability is very low, there is little room in the market for such contracts.

We may examine the absolute values of the one-step-ahead errors $|e_t| = |Y_t - Y_{t-1}|$. The spreadsheet *DowJones.xlsx* provides daily closing prices for the period 2001–2005, along with the values of the returns and their absolute values.

1. Examine the validity of the EMH for this series.
2. Use the SES to develop a forecasting method for the absolute values of the returns. Is volatility predictable, at least to some extent?

References

Armstrong, J. S., ed. (2001). *Principles of Forecasting: A Handbook for Researchers and Practitioners*. Boston and Dordrecht: Kluwer.

Assimakopoulos, V. & Nikolopoulos, K. (2000). The theta model: a decomposition approach to forecasting. *International Journal of Forecasting*, 16, 521–530.

Box, G. E. P., & Cox, D. R. (1964). An analysis of transformations. *Journal of the Royal Statistical Society, series B*, 26, 211–252.

Brown, R. G. (1959). *Statistical Forecasting for Inventory Control*. New York: McGraw-Hill.

Brown, R. G. (1963). *Smoothing, Forecasting and Prediction of Discrete Time Series*. Englewood Cliffs, NJ: Prentice-Hall.

Fildes, R. (1992). The evaluation of extrapolative forecasting methods. *International Journal of Forecasting*, 8, 81–98.

Fildes, R., Hibon, M., Makridakis, S., & Meade, N. (1998). Generalising about univariate forecasting methods: Further empirical evidence. *International Journal of Forecasting*, 14, 339–358.

Gardner, E. S., Jr. (1985). Exponential smoothing: The state of the art. *Journal of Forecasting*, 4, 1–28.

Gardner, E. S., Jr. (2006). Exponential smoothing: The state of the art—Part II. *International Journal of Forecasting*, 22, 637–677.

Gardner, E. S., Jr., and McKenzie, E. (1985). Forecasting trends in time series. *Management Science*, 31, 1237–1246.

Holt, C. C. (2004). Forecasting seasonals and trends by exponentially weighted moving averages. *International Journal of Forecasting*, 20, 5–10. Reprint of Office of Naval Research Memorandum 52/1957, Carnegie Institute of Technology.

Hull, J. C. (2002). *Fundamentals of Futures and Options Markets,* 4th ed. Upper Saddle River, NJ: Prentice-Hall.

Hyndman, R. J., & Billah, B. (2003). Unmasking the theta method. *International Journal of Forecasting*, 19, 287–290.

Makridakis, S., & Hibon, M. (2000). The M3-competition: Results, conclusions and implications. *International Journal of Forecasting*, 16, 451–476.

Tashman, J. (2000). Out-of-sample tests of forecasting accuracy: an analysis and review. *International Journal of Forecasting*, 16, 437–450.

Trigg, D. W., & Leach, D. H. (1967). Exponential smoothing with an adaptive response rate. *Operational Research Quarterly*, 18, 53–59.

Appendix 3A Excel Macros

This appendix provides a brief summary of the capabilities of the SES and LES macros used in this chapter. Full descriptions, along with the Excel files, are available on the book's website.

Simple Exponential Smoothing (SES.xlsm)

1. The initial value for the level may be either the first observation or the average of the first four observations.
2. The smoothing parameter may be estimated by minimizing the *RMSE, MAE*, or *MAPE*. The solution is obtained numerically with Solver.
3. The user may specify the estimation and hold-out samples.
4. One-step-ahead forecasts are generated for the hold-out sample.

Linear Exponential Smoothing (LES.xlsm)

1. The starting values for the level and the trend use the values defined in Section 3.4.3.
2. The smoothing parameter may be estimated by minimizing the *RMSE*. The solution is obtained numerically with Solver.
3. The user may specify the estimation and hold-out samples.
4. One-step-ahead forecasts are generated for the hold-out sample.
5. Four options are available:
   a. LES for the original series
   b. LES with a logarithmic transformation
   c. Damped LES
   d. LES with a Box–Cox transform.

CHAPTER 4

Seasonal Series: Forecasting and Decomposition

Every season has its peaks and valleys. What you have to try to do is eliminate the Grand Canyon.

—Andy van Slyke, professional baseball player

Introduction

In the previous chapter, we examined forecasting methods for time series that contain trends. However, there are often other elements in a series that must be taken into account. In particular, the data frequently exhibit a seasonal pattern, such as sales of ice cream being higher in the summer. The term *seasonal* indicates a pattern that occurs within a *known* time frame. For example, the gross domestic product (*GDP*) is measured quarterly, so that the seasonal pattern relates to the calendar year and has a periodicity of 4. Likewise, unemployment is reported monthly, so that the seasonal pattern is again related to the calendar year, but now with a periodicity of 12. In both cases, seasonal effects arise because of the weather, so there may be lost production in the winter because of poor working and road conditions; in addition, the mix of economic activities varies as the result of more or less predictable changes, including holidays. From our perspective, it is important to emphasize that the period (such as a year) is known and that the patterns within a period (such as a year) tend to be similar from one period (or year) to the next.

However, we will use the term *seasonal* more widely in this book, to refer to any pattern that occurs within a known fixed time frame. Thus, days of the week are an important seasonal effect for retail sales, because certain days (e.g., Saturdays) are known to produce higher levels of sales, whereas midweek sales tend to be lower. A further example is provided by the 24 hours within a day, which reveal a regular pattern for electricity consumption. In both these cases, seasonal effects exist in the annual cycle as well, so there are multiple seasonalities. The key feature in all these examples is that the time period(s) involved is (are) of *known* and *fixed* duration.

Why do we need to concern ourselves with seasonal effects? As always, forecasts underpin planning. A retailer needs to make inventory decisions and to plan deployment of the work force, whereas a utility company needs to plan for capacity that will meet peak demand, and to set lower prices for off-peak demand because the marginal cost of off-peak production is very low.

In Section 4.1, we examine the components of a time series, including trend and seasonality. Then, in Section 4.2, we look at forecasting for purely seasonal patterns—that is, for series that exhibit no trend. Series such as the average monthly temperature in a given location exhibit very little trend relative to seasonal changes (global warming notwithstanding), and such purely seasonal series represent a simpler place from which to start our investigations. This starting point provides a natural progression to series that exhibit both trends and seasonal components, and we use a decomposition approach in Sections 4.3 and 4.4 to develop forecasts for such series. This approach leads to the creation of deseasonalized series—that is, series whose values have been adjusted to remove the effects of seasonal changes. Such methods are widely used in the presentation of macroeconomic data; indeed, many series produced by the United States and other governments are published only in a seasonally adjusted form. The most popular approach to the creation of such series is known as the Census X-12 method, developed by the U.S. Bureau of the Census and described briefly in Section 4.5.

Most economic and business series display both trend and seasonal elements that evolve over time, and Sections 4.6 and 4.7 develop forecasting methods for such series. As with the exponential smoothing methods described in Chapter 3, we assume that a time series can be represented by a set of components. We then develop a forecast for each component and produce a forecast for the series that is a combination of all these elements. These methods are generally employed for monthly and quarterly series. Weekly series are often treated rather differently, as there may be very few years' worth of data to estimate so many (weekly) components; this issue is examined in Section 4.8. Prediction intervals for seasonal forecasts are developed in Section 4.9. The chapter concludes with a discussion of underlying principles in Section 4.10 and the chapter summary.

4.1 # Components of a Time Series

We have introduced the trend and seasonal components of a time series, but there are also other components that are less regular. For example, the economy goes through business cycles of expansion and contraction; such cycles have tended to average around four years in the United States, but vary between two and ten years in duration. The duration of business cycles is not known in advance, nor is it stable from one cycle to the next. Some commentators have suggested that the business cycle is related to the four-year cycle of U.S. presidential elections, presumably on the grounds that a strong economy begets reelection! Similar suggestions apply in the United Kingdom and elsewhere. Even if successive administrations strive to induce such cycles, there is no guarantee that they will be of any predetermined length. One particularly well-established cycle occurs in the number of observed sunspots, with a mean time between peaks of around 10.7 years. The essential point is that such variations are of random duration (though with a predictable mean). We reserve the term *cyclical* for such patterns.

> ## Seasonal and Cyclical Time Series
>
> A time series is said to have a **seasonal** component if it displays a recurrent pattern with a fixed and known duration.
> A time series is said to have a **cyclical** component if it displays somewhat regular fluctuations around the trend but those fluctuations have a periodicity of variable and unknown duration.

In addition to the trend and the seasonal and cyclical components, the series will contain a random error component, which, as before, represents the variations not accounted for by the other components. In common with most introductions to forecasting, we will absorb the cyclical component into the trend term and concentrate upon just three components: *trend* (T), *seasonal* (S), and *error* (E). Because our current focus is upon short- to medium-term forecasts, this simplification rarely causes any problems in practice. The combination of these components is illustrated in Figure 4.1. In the example, the trend is an

FIGURE 4.1   THE COMPONENTS OF A TIME SERIES

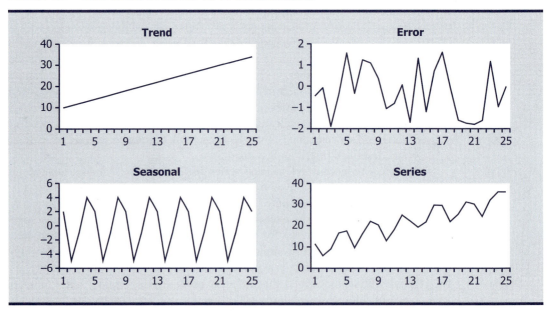

upward-sloping straight line and the seasonal pattern corresponds to quarterly data (of periodicity 4). The error terms do not display any regular pattern. The three components are added together to provide the plot of the complete series (series A in Figure 4.1). In any forecasting exercise, we cannot observe the separate components and must find a way to create such elements from the observed (composite) series.

Algebraically, the three components are combined by addition to create the time series (Y):

$$Y = T + S + E. \tag{4.1}$$

Equation (4.1) is known as the *(purely) additive* model for a series. Other models are possible, of which the two best known are the *(purely) multiplicative* model,

$$Y = TSE, \tag{4.2}$$

and the *mixed additive–multiplicative* model,

$$Y = TS + E. \tag{4.3}$$

Whenever the trend and the seasonal component are multiplied together, larger levels in the series will tend to exhibit larger peaks and troughs. In addition, when the error term is also multiplicative, the magnitude of the forecast errors will tend to rise and fall with the level of the series.

Before we consider forecasts derived from these equations, we examine forecasting for purely seasonal patterns—that is, series devoid of any trend. Although this situation is uncommon for business series over periods of a year or more, for short-term forecasts (e.g., retail sales over the next month of a product in a store) such models are often more than adequate. In addition, the approach aids in understanding the methods that examine both trend and seasonality and is useful if we wish to decompose the series into deseasonalized and seasonal components. It is then possible to generate forecasts for the deseasonalized series by using the methods of Chapter 3 and to combine those values with forecasts for the purely seasonal component.

Forecasting Purely Seasonal Series

Notwithstanding the longer term effects, if any, of global warming, data relating to different aspects of the weather reflect our natural understanding of a strong seasonal pattern with little or no trend. Some other purely seasonal series are specially created, such as the seasonal index for U.S. retail sales shown earlier in Figure 1.3. Cyclical components may also exist, but these are sufficiently long term that they may often be safely ignored when examining data that cover only a few years.

EXAMPLE 4.1 ■ Temperatures in Boulder, Colorado

Figure 4.2 is a time plot of monthly average temperatures for Boulder, Colorado, over the period 1991–2007. The data are available in the file *Boulder.xlsx*. The seasonal pattern is very clear. Nevertheless, we may also use the seasonal plot, introduced in Chapter 2, as a useful way to detect seasonal patterns when trends also exist. In the present context, we plot temperature against the month of the year, so that there are 12 points on the x-axis; a separate but overlaid plot is then constructed for each year. The results for temperature data for the period 1991–95 are shown in Figure 4.3; only four years of data were used to avoid cluttering up a black-and-white graph. The strong seasonal pattern is clear, and the extensive overlapping indicates the absence of any marked trend. An alternative seasonal plot is obtained if we plot temperature against time but color-code each year separately. This version of a seasonal plot is examined in Exercise 4.1.   ■

FIGURE 4.2 MONTHLY AVERAGE TEMPERATURES (IN DEGREES FAHRENHEIT) IN BOULDER, COLORADO, 1991–2007

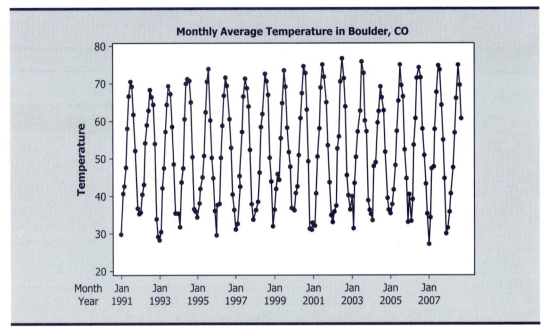

Source: Earth System Research Laboratory, Physical Sciences Division, National Oceanic and Atmospheric Administration (*www.cdc.noaa.gov/Boulder/Boulder.mm.html*). Data shown is from file Boulder.xlsx.

FIGURE 4.3 SEASONAL PLOT OF AVERAGE TEMPERATURE (IN DEGREES FAHRENHEIT) IN BOULDER, COLORADO (*1991–95, Plotted against month, partitioned by year*)

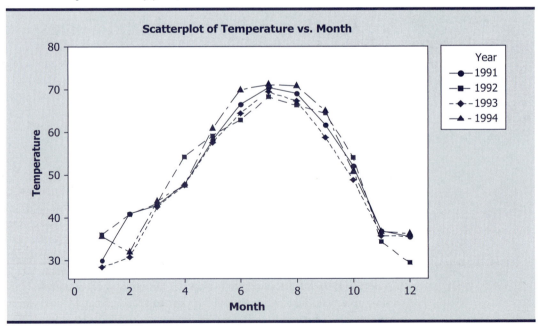

Source: Earth System Research Laboratory, Physical Sciences Division, National Oceanic and Atmospheric Administration (*www.cdc.noaa.gov/Boulder/Boulder.mm.html*). *Data:* Boulder.xlsx.

TABLE 4.1   ACTUAL AND FORECAST VALUES FOR MONTHLY TEMPERATURES IN BOULDER, COLORADO FOR 2006

	JAN	FEB	MAR	APR	MAY	JUN	JUL	AUG	SEP	OCT	NOV	DEC
Average	34.1	36.2	42.5	48.6	57.8	65.6	72.4	70.1	62.8	51.7	39.9	34.7
Actual	40.7	33.7	39.4	53.9	61.0	71.6	74.4	71.6	58.4	51.0	43.4	35.3
Error	6.6	−2.5	−3.1	5.3	3.2	6.0	2.0	1.5	−4.4	−0.7	3.5	0.6
Abs error	6.6	2.5	3.1	5.3	3.2	6.0	2.0	1.5	4.4	0.7	3.5	0.6
Sq. error	43.5	6.5	9.7	27.7	9.9	35.7	4.0	2.4	19.8	0.5	12.5	0.3

Data: Boulder.xlsx. © Cengage Learning 2013.

Suppose we wish to forecast monthly average temperatures 12 months ahead for the year 2006, which constitutes the hold-out sample. The simplest approach would be to take an average for each month over the period 1991–2005 and use that as the forecast. The results are shown in Table 4.1. Over the hold-out period, the mean absolute error (*MAE*) is 3.29 degrees and the root-mean-square error is 3.79 degrees.

If we now consider forecasts for 2007, we could recompute the monthly averages. At the other extreme, we could ignore all the past history and use only the values for the most recent year if we felt that the temperature patterns were changing rapidly. Both options seem rather extreme, given the discussions about smoothing in the previous chapter, so instead we adopt a seasonal smoothing procedure.

4.2.1   Purely Seasonal Exponential Smoothing

A seasonal version of simple exponential smoothing (SES) may be written as

*New forecast for a given "month" = Old forecast for that "month" + smoothing constant * forecast error.*

We use "months" within a "year" to denote the seasonal structure, but in keeping with our earlier comments, the same general idea applies to any purely seasonal series. Algebraically, if we use *m* to denote the number of periods (months) in a year, the relationship becomes

$$F_{t+m}(m) = F_t(m) + \gamma[Y_t - F_t(m)]. \qquad (4.4)$$

The smoothing parameter (γ) represents the rate of adjustment to the latest error. In words, this expression states that the "forecast for period $t + m$ made m steps earlier, denoted by $F_{t+m}(m)$, is given by the m-step-ahead forecast [made at time $t - m$] for period t, adjusted by the error observed for that earlier forecast." The error term in this situation is $e_t = Y_t - F_t(m)$, so equation (4.4) may be rewritten as $F_{t+m}(m) = F_t(m) + \gamma e_t$. For example, the forecast for July 2011 equals the July 2010 forecast plus a partial error adjustment (based upon the difference between the observed values for July 2010 and its forecast a year earlier on the basis of the data available up to and including July 2009). Because we are focusing purely on the seasonal effects, we do not use data for any months other than previous July values. This prevents the July 2011 forecast from changing (once the July 2010 value has been observed and the forecast updated), despite our having observed August and subsequent values. Another way of looking at this situation is to think in terms of 12 separate series (one for each month) that are updated independently of each other. We update each series as soon as that monthly value is recorded, but we do not use the updated forecast until the next year.

We use equation (4.4) to forecast the temperature data 12 months ahead for the period January 2006 through September 2008. For the start-up values, we used the monthly data for 1991 and then estimated the smoothing constant γ by minimizing the root-mean-squared

TABLE 4.2   SUMMARY RESULTS FOR FORECASTING AVERAGE
TEMPERATURES IN BOULDER, CO (*January 2006–September 2008*)

Gamma	ME	MSE	MAE	RMSE
Fitted				
gamma = 0.177	0.33	10.85	2.56	3.29
Forecasts				
Smoothed ($\gamma = 0.177$)	0.18	10.86	2.68	3.30
1 (naïve)	−0.42	21.51	3.27	4.64
0 (no change)	1.05	18.13	3.38	4.26

The first row represents the results for the estimation sample, and the remaining rows are the results for the different forecasting methods.

© Cengage Learning 2013.

error (*RMSE*) over the 156 observations for the years 1993–2005. Minimization of the mean absolute errors (*MAE*) produced similar results. The spreadsheet *SES_12 months* provides the basis for completing these calculations. In this example, the mean absolute percentage error (*MAPE*) is not sensible, because the variable is not ratio-scaled, as it has no natural origin; consider how the *MAPE* changes if we switch from the Fahrenheit scale to Celsius!

The results are summarized in Table 4.2. For comparative purposes, we included the forecasting performance of the naïve "same as last year" approach (corresponding to $\gamma = 1$) and the "nothing changes" approach, or arithmetic mean forecasts (with $\gamma = 0$). The results show the better performance of the monthly SES scheme.

4.3   Forecasting Using a Seasonal Decomposition

Most of the series we are likely to encounter contain both trend and seasonal components. Because we observe only the aggregate series and not the components, one approach to forecasting is to decompose the time series into its trend, seasonal, and error components. We could remove the seasonal component and forecast the deseasonalized, or seasonally adjusted, version of the series, using the methods of Chapter 3. We may also forecast the seasonal components and then recombine the two to forecast the overall series.

Our primary interest is in forecasting, and we will approach the topic from that direction, although decomposition methods are often used in the analysis of macroeconomic series, with particular interest in removing seasonal effects. Over many years, the U.S. Census Bureau has supported decomposition software, the current version of which is known as Census X-12. This program is applied to most major economic series, such as *GDP*, some of which are published only in seasonally adjusted form. We present a brief description of Census X-12 in Section 4.5 and a reference to access downloadable versions. Our present focus is upon the fundamental ideas underlying seasonal adjustment. The basic steps in the process are as follows:

1. Generate estimates of the trend by averaging out the seasonal component.
2. Estimate the seasonal component by removing the trend from the series.
3. Create a deseasonalized series.
4. Forecast the trend and the seasonal pattern separately.
5. Recombine the trend forecast with the seasonal component to produce a forecast for the original series.

Decomposition

Pure Decomposition. Use all n data points to estimate the fitted value at each time t (**two-sided** decomposition).
Forecasting Decomposition. Use only the data up to and including time t to predict the value at time $t + 1$ (**one-sided** decomposition).

There are two basic versions of seasonal adjustment. The first version is based upon the purely additive model, originally specified is equation (4.1) as

$$Y_t = T_t + S_t + E_t, \tag{4.5}$$

where T denotes the trend term, S designates the seasonal component, and E is the random error (often referred to as the *irregular component* in this context); we have added time subscripts in equation (4.5) for later use. Likewise, the mixed additive–multiplicative scheme given in equation (4.3) is represented by

$$Y_t = T_t S_t + E_t. \tag{4.6}$$

A key element in this approach is the use of moving averages, introduced in Section 3.2.2:

Moving Average

A (simple) *moving average* of order K, denoted by $MA(K)$, is the average of K successive terms in a time series, taken over successive sets of K, so that the first average is $(Y_1 + Y_2 + \cdots + Y_K)/K$, the second is $(Y_2 + Y_3 + \cdots + Y_{K+1})/K$, and so on.

The moving average is used to produce an average that is free of seasonal effects. That is, we might average over four consecutive quarters ($K = 4$) or 12 consecutive months ($K = 12$). This average provides an estimate[1] of the trend term, T_t. We use past values of the series to estimate the trend so that, for example, in a quarterly series $K = 4$ and the first trend estimate is $T_5 = (Y_1 + Y_2 + \cdots + Y_4)/4$. We then compute the detrended series Y_t^{DT} as

$$Y_t^{DT} = Y_t - T_t = S_t + E_t. \tag{4.7}$$

We now assume that the seasonal component for each period (such as summer) is stable and estimate that component by averaging Y_t^{DT} over all available observations for that period (e.g., all summers for which data are available). Often, the seasonal components are adjusted to have a zero mean, although this does not affect the forecasts. The seasonal factor for period t is denoted by $S_{(j,\,t)}$; the subscript j indexes the seasons and is included in the parentheses to remind us that there are only 4 (quarterly), 7 (days of the week), or 12 (monthly) such factors. Finally, we produce the deseasonalized series Y_t^{DS} and the error terms:

$$Y_t^{DS} = Y_t - S_{(j,\,t)}$$
$$E_t = Y_t - T_t - S_{(j,\,t)}.$$

Now that the seasonal effects have been removed, the deseasonalized series may be forecast with SES or LES, as appropriate, as described in Sections 3.3 and 3.4. The final forecast is then obtained by adding back the seasonal component.

EXAMPLE 4.2 ■ (*Examples_chapter_4.xlsx*)

The process of additive deseasonalization is illustrated for quarterly data in Table 4.3.

---

[1]We are working with estimates of the components, not their actual values. This point should be kept in mind, as the distinction is not made in the notation.

TABLE 4.3   ADDITIVE DESEASONALIZATION AND ITS USE IN FORECASTING

Part A: Deseasonalized Series

Obs	Series	MA(4)	Detrended Series	Seasonal Factor	Deseasonalized Series	Deseasonalized Forecasts	Series Forecasts	Error	Error Squared	Absolute Error	Absolute Percentage Error
1	115			20.63	94.38						
2	90			−15.21	105.21						
3	65			−38.54	103.54						
4	135			33.13	101.88						
5	130	101.25	28.75	20.63	109.38	109.60	130.22	−0.22	0.05	0.22	0.17
6	95	105.00	−10.00	−15.21	110.21	111.94	96.73	−1.73	2.99	1.73	1.82
7	75	106.25	−31.25	−38.54	113.54	113.28	74.74	0.26	0.07	0.26	0.35
8	150	108.75	41.25	33.13	116.88	115.43	148.56	1.44	2.09	1.44	0.96
9	135	112.50	22.50	20.63	114.38	118.38	139.01	−4.01	16.06	4.01	2.97
10	105	113.75	−8.75	−15.21	120.21	118.30	103.09	1.91	3.64	1.91	1.82
11	85	116.25	−31.25	−38.54	123.54	120.89	82.35	2.65	7.01	2.65	3.11
12	155	118.75	36.25	33.13	121.88	124.43	157.56	−2.56	6.53	2.56	1.65
13	145	120.00	25.00	20.63	124.38	125.39	146.02	−1.02	1.03	1.02	0.70
14	110	122.50	−12.50	−15.21	125.21	126.67	111.46	−1.46	2.13	1.46	1.33
15	85	123.75	−38.75	−38.54	123.54	127.41	88.87	−3.87	14.97	3.87	4.55
16	160	123.75	36.25	33.13	126.88	126.28	159.41	0.59	0.35	0.59	0.37

(continued)

TABLE 4.3   (CONTINUED)

Part B: Seasonal Calculations

Quarter	Year 1	Year 2	Year 3	Year 4	Seasonal Means	Adjusted Means
Q1		28.75	22.5	25	25.42	20.63
Q2		−10.00	−8.75	−12.5	−10.42	−15.21
Q3		−31.25	−31.25	−38.75	−33.75	−38.54
Q4		41.25	36.25	36.25	37.92	33.13
				Overall	4.79	0

Part C: Summary Measures

MSE	MAE	MAPE	RMSE
4.74	1.81	1.65	2.18

Data shown is from file Examples_chapter_4.xlsx. © Cengage Learning 2013.

In part A of the table, the third column gives the moving average of terms taken four at a time. To align the forecasts with the actual values, we place the average of the first four terms, $(115 + 90 + 65 + 135)/4 = 101.25$, in the row corresponding to observation 5, and so on. That is, we average the figures for the first year, thereby eliminating seasonal effects, and then use that average as a preliminary forecast of the level for the first period (quarter) of the second year. The fourth column contains the values of the *Detrended series*, computed with equation (4.7); that is, we subtract the initial trend values from the original observations. In part B of the table, we gather together the 12 detrended values (three observations for each quarter) and compute their average (*Seasonal Means*). Next, these quarterly averages are adjusted to have zero mean, yielding the seasonal index values (*Adjusted Means*) with values $(20.63, -15.21, -38.54, 33.13)$. The *Deseasonalized series* is then given in the sixth column by subtracting the adjusted seasonal component from each observation.

Finally, the deseasonalized series may be forecast by linear exponential smoothing (LES, described in Section 3.4, because a trend clearly exists). The resulting forecasts are shown in column seven (*Deseasonalized Forecasts*). The starting values were specified in Section 3.4.1, and the optimal values of the smoothing parameters turned out to be $\alpha = 0.37$ and $\beta = 0.68$. The seasonal components are then added back in to produce the final forecasts in the eighth column (*Series Forecasts*). The error analysis then proceeds in the usual way. Note that the values given are fitted values rather than pure forecasts, because all the observations were used to construct the seasonal index values and to estimate the smoothing parameters. However, given these estimates, proper forecasts can be constructed for future values. ∎

Analogously to the additive model just described, we may construct a mixed additive–multiplicative scheme based upon the model given by equation (4.6). The key difference is that we must divide the original series by the moving average to obtain the detrended series (fourth column in Table 4.3) and then adjust the seasonal indexes to average 1.0 rather than zero. The deseasonalized series (column 6) follows upon dividing the original series by the seasonal indexes. After forecasting this series, we obtain forecasts for the original series (column 8) upon multiplying the deseasonalized forecasts (column 7) by the seasonal indexes. This analysis is left to the reader as Exercise 4.12.

Once the notion of decomposition is recognized, a variety of forecasting methods becomes available. The process of decomposition and the methods for forecasting the deseasonalized and seasonal components must all be determined by the forecaster. We have described two variants of one simple form, but specialized software allows a range of more sophisticated approaches, as we shall see in Section 4.6. In particular, we do not need to assume that the seasonal factors are constant over time.

 ## 4.4   Pure Decomposition

As we noted at the beginning of the previous section, time series are sometimes analyzed in order to better understand underlying trends, rather than for forecasting. This orientation is particularly strong with macroeconomic data, for which seasonally adjusted data allow a clearer picture of current developments within the economy. Thus, although the discussion that follows strays somewhat from our primary focus, it is worth understanding how such deseasonalized series are developed.

The first key element to recognize is that such seasonal adjustment methods may rely upon both past and future observations, as the focus now is upon understanding rather than pure forecasting. To take an obvious example, if you know the weather on Monday and Wednesday, you have a better understanding of what happened on Tuesday than if you have just Monday's weather. However, Wednesday's weather could not be available for forecasting purposes.

To make this process operational, we use moving averages as before, but now we want to align the average with the current value of the series. Thus, if we are dealing with daily sales figures, we would align the average across Sunday, Monday, . . . , Saturday of a given week with Wednesday, the fourth of the seven days. However, a problem arises when the number of periods per season is even (four quarters or 12 months). If we take the average over January–December, the average is a half-period out of phase. That is, the average of the 12 months lands between June and July (the average of the numbers 1 through 12 is 6.5), so the moving-average term would not match up exactly in time with either month. To overcome this difficulty, we take a further average to produce a centered moving average.

Centered Moving Average

A *centered moving average (MA)* of order K, denoted by $CM(t|K)$, which is defined by taking the average of successive pairs of simple moving averages. Thus, denote the first average by $M(t - 1|K) = (Y_{t-1} + Y_{t-2} + \cdots + Y_{t-K})/K$ and the next one by $M(t|K) = (Y_t + Y_{t-1} + \cdots + Y_{t-K+1})/K$, then we define the centered MA as $CM(t|K) = [M(t - 1|K) + M(t|K)]/2$.

When K is odd, it is usually not necessary to calculate a CMA. However when K is even, $K = 2J$ say, the first average corresponds to an "average time" of $t - J - 0.5$ and the second to $t - J + 0.5$ so the centered MA corresponds to time $t - J$ as desired.

The effect of using the centered MA is to "lose" $K/2$ observations at the beginning of the series and another $K/2$ observations at the end of the series. Normally, this does not matter at the beginning of the series, but clearly it is critical at the end of the series, because the most recent observations are usually those of greatest interest. If the aim is only to produce a deseasonalized series, we can estimate the seasonal factors and proceed as in Table 4.3, as we show in Table 4.4. However, if we seek to identify underlying trends, we must find some way to extend the series. Earlier schemes used moving averages that assigned different weights to the last few observations in the series, but current "best practice" is to use a statistical model-based approach. The best-known such technique is

TABLE 4.4 MULTIPLICATIVE DECOMPOSITION FOR SEASONAL ADJUSTMENT

Part A: Deseasonalized Series

Obs	Series	MA(4)	CM(4)	Detrended Series	Seasonal Factors	Deseasonalized Series
1	115				1.18	97.65
2	90	101.25			0.88	102.83
3	65	105.00	103.13	0.630	0.67	97.64
4	135	106.25	105.63	1.278	1.28	105.35
5	130	108.75	107.50	1.209	1.18	110.39
6	95	112.50	110.63	0.859	0.88	108.54
7	75	113.75	113.13	0.663	0.67	112.66
8	150	116.25	115.00	1.304	1.28	117.06
9	135	118.75	117.50	1.149	1.18	114.64
10	105	120.00	119.38	0.880	0.88	119.97
11	85	122.50	121.25	0.701	0.67	127.68
12	155	123.75	123.13	1.259	1.28	120.96
13	145	123.75	123.75	1.172	1.18	123.13
14	110	125.00	124.38	0.884	0.88	125.68
15	85				0.67	127.68
16	160				1.28	124.86

Part B: Seasonal Calculations

Season	Year 1	Year 2	Year 3	Year 4	Averages	Adjusted
Q1		1.209	1.149	1.172	1.177	1.178
Q2		0.859	0.880	0.884	0.874	0.875
Q3	0.630	0.663	0.701		0.665	0.666
Q4	1.278	1.304	1.259		1.280	1.281
				Overall	0.999	1.000

© Cengage Learning 2013.

Census X-12-ARIMA and is discussed briefly in the next section. A simpler method involves fitting a trend line to estimate the last $K/2$ observations (used, e.g., in the Minitab decomposition routine).

The steps that follow describe the process based upon moving averages for quarterly data, assuming t observations; a similar procedure using 12-term moving averages is followed with monthly data. The description applies to the more commonly used multiplicative scheme; modifications for the additive scheme are shown in square brackets.

1. Calculate the four-term *MA(4)* and then the centered moving average, *CM(4)*. The first *CM* term corresponds to period 3 and the last one to period $(t - 2)$; $K = 4$, so we "lose" two values at each end of the series.
2. Divide [subtract] observations 3, . . . , $(t - 2)$ by [from] their corresponding *CM* to obtain a detrended series.
3. Calculate the average value (across years) of the detrended series for each quarter j ($j = 1, 2, 3, 4$) to produce the initial seasonal factors.
4. Standardize the seasonal factors by computing their average and then setting the final seasonal factor equal to the initial value divided by [minus] the overall average.
5. Estimate the error term by dividing the detrended series by the final seasonal factor [subtracting the final seasonal factor from the detrended series].

Note that this process is similar to the forecasting procedure described in the previous section. The key difference is that the moving-average values are now centered on the observations, whereas before they were used (asymmetrically) to predict future values in the forecasting framework.

EXAMPLE 4.3 ■ Seasonal decomposition—the calculations (*Examples_chapter_4.xlsx*)

For purposes of illustration, we revisit the data set considered in Example 4.2 but now apply a multiplicative *Decomposition*, rather than generating forecasts. Following steps 1–5, we arrive at the results shown in Table 4.4. Successive columns of interest in part A show the original series, the moving average, *MA(4)*, the centered moving average, *CM(4)*, centered *MA*, the *Detrended series*, the *Seasonal factors,* and, finally, the *Deseasonalized series*. The final seasonal factors are calculated in part B of the table and then inserted into part A. For example, the first *CM(4)* value is (101.25 + 105.00)/2 = 103.13, where the original *MA* values may be obtained from Table 4.3. However, it is important to observe that the *CM* values are now aligned with the corresponding time periods. In Table 4.3, the past moving averages were used to forecast. As in Table 4.3, the seasonal components are considered to be unchanging, and we can produce a deseasonalized series that covers all time periods.   ■

The principal purpose of decomposition is to generate the deseasonalized, or seasonally adjusted, series; such series are commonly used in macroeconomic policy discussions. For example, unemployment is heavily seasonal and the focus of much political debate. Because such issues are of critical importance, the decomposition methods used in practice are much more sophisticated than the simple procedure we have just described. Accordingly, we now provide a brief outline of the most commonly used decomposition method.

4.5* The Census X-12 Decomposition

The original seasonal adjustment program introduced in 1965 by the U.S. Bureau of the Census was known as X-11 (Shiskin, Young, and Musgrave, 1967). The name reflects the many years of improvement and modification (from Method 1 in 1954 and onwards) that elapsed before the method reached a standard form. The X-11 method was among the first such procedures to be computerized, and it became a standard for seasonal adjustment around the world. Its successor, X-12-ARIMA, was introduced in the 1990s and continues to use the smoothing operations developed in X-11 but extends the series, using the ARIMA models that will be described in Chapter 6. In effect, the ARIMA model enables us to "fill in the blanks" at the end of the series; the model also allows us to incorporate changing seasonal patterns, as in the forecasting procedures described in Sections 4.6 and 4.7. A full description of X-12-ARIMA[2] appears in Findley, Monsell, Bell, Otto, and Chen (1999) and on the Census Bureau website. Thus, we will summarize only a few key properties here. The detailed steps are given in appendices in Findley *et al.*

Step 1: The time series is first adjusted to take into account any anomalous observations. (An anomalous observation is an observation that stands out as incompatible with those around it.) This is begun by creating an initial time series model that provides one-step-ahead preliminary forecasts. Anomalous observations can then be identified and appropriate adjustments made to the data. For example, suppose production is interrupted by a strike or severe weather but returns to normal once the event is over. If no adjustment is made, the anomalous observation will distort future estimates of the trend and seasonal factors and so

---

[2] A more advanced seasonal adjustment procedure, X-13-ARIMA-SEATS, is in the later stages of development. This new software embraces the modeling approach more comprehensively. (For further details, see the U.S. Census Bureau website *www.census.gov/srd/www/x12a/index.html*.)

give misleading values for the seasonally adjusted series. The model is also used to extend the series for the trend and seasonal components so that standard moving averages can be applied throughout the series.

Step 2: The multiplicative (or, more rarely, the additive) version of seasonal adjustment is applied to the series, essentially as described in the previous section. However, rather than assume fixed seasonals, preliminary seasonal factors are estimated by taking a moving average of the initial seasonal estimates for each quarter or month.

Step 3: An initial set of seasonal adjustments is applied as in Table 4.4, but using more complex moving averages.

Step 4: He series is extended (using ARIMA; see Chapter 6) so that moving averages can be computed for each time period up to the end of the series, using the seasonally adjusted data. This leads to a revised estimate of the trend and seasonal factors.

Step 5: A final round of detrending is applied, and the error term is then estimated by dividing the observation by the trend and seasonal factors, to complete the decomposition.

Discussion Question   *In retail store sales of a product, what type of events might introduce anomalies into the observed sales figures?*

   For readers wishing to conduct "industrial strength" seasonal adjustments, the X-12-ARIMA program is available free of charge from the Census Bureau; the URL is *www.census.gov/srd/www/x12a*. In both the United States and Europe, a heavily used free program is TRAMO-SEATS; the URL is *www.bde.es/servicio/software/programase.htm*.

4.6   The Holt–Winters Seasonal Smoothing Methods

We now examine exponential smoothing methods for forecasting series that include both trends and seasonal patterns. We focus upon two particular schemes, known as the Holt–Winters' additive and multiplicative schemes, respectively, because they were first developed by Holt (2004, original published in 1957) and Winters (1960).

4.6.1   The Additive Holt–Winters Method

We consider a forecast function that combines, by addition, the level, trend (or slope), and seasonal components. That is, we add a seasonal component to the linear exponential smoothing (LES) scheme developed in Section 3.4. As before, we denote the level of the series by L_t, the trend by T_t, and the seasonal factor by S_t. When there are m seasons (e.g., $m = 12$ for monthly data), the forecast for one period ahead may be written as

$$F_{t+1}(1) = F_{t+1} = L_t + T_t + S_{t+1-m}.$$

For example, to forecast the sales in July 2011, we combine the level and trend elements derived up to and including June 2011 with the seasonal component from July 2010. If we wish to forecast h periods ahead, we use the more general expression

$$F_{t+h}(h) = L_t + hT_t + S_{t+h-m}. \tag{4.8}$$

Equation (4.8) takes the current local level of the series modified by h times the current trend and selects the appropriate monthly seasonal corresponding to period $(t + h)$ to estimate the h-step ahead forecast. The notation is designed to maintain the connection with exponential smoothing as developed in the previous chapter. If $h > m$, we select the appropriate seasonal index, cycling through every m periods; for example, the July index is used for future July forecasts, no matter how many years ahead.

The next step is to update these components. The new information we have is the latest observation or, equivalently, the latest error term, written as

$$e_t = Y_t - L_{t-1} - T_{t-1} - S_{t-m}$$
$$= Y_t - F_t(1).$$
(4.9)

The updating expressions for the level and trend are the same as those used for LES in Section 3.4.2:

$$L_t = L_{t-1} + T_{t-1} + \alpha e_t$$
$$T_t = T_{t-1} + \alpha\beta e_t.$$
(4.10)

To complete the process, we must also update the seasonal component, relative to the same period in the previous "year." That is, the seasonal update may be written as

$$S_t = S_{t-m} + \gamma e_t.$$
(4.11)

This expression is exactly that appearing in equation (4.4), save that we have changed the variable of interest from F to S to recognize that the seasonal component is now one part of the forecast. Each seasonal component will be updated just once per "year," when the corresponding "monthly" value has been recorded. So, if we were dealing with 12 months in a year, we would have 12 such components and each would be updated once every 12 time periods. From equations (4.10) and (4.11), we observe that each component is updated with the use of a partial adjustment for the error. As before, these equations are known as the *error correction* form. The more usual, but also more cumbersome, way of expressing these relationships is to substitute for e_t, using equation (4.9) to arrive at equation (4.12):

$$L_t = L_{t-1} + T_{t-1} + \alpha[Y_t - L_{t-1} - T_{t-1} - S_{t-m}]$$
$$T_t = T_{t-1} + \beta[L_t - L_{t-1} - T_{t-1}]$$
$$S_t = S_{t-m} + \gamma[Y_t - L_{t-1} - T_{t-1} - S_{t-m}].$$
(4.12)

Demonstrating the equivalence between the two versions is left as an end-of-chapter exercise. At this stage, we should note that the Holt–Winters equations are often written in a slightly different form, with L_t and T_t replacing L_{t-1} and T_{t-1}, appearing in the seasonal update. For the linear case, the two versions produce identical forecasts, although the parameter γ has a different value. We prefer the present formulation because it leads directly to an underlying model (see Section 5.3.2) whereas the more common version does not.

The Holt–Winters method allows for a number of special cases, such as the following:

- Fixed seasonal pattern: $\gamma = 0$ (no seasonal updating)
- No seasonal pattern: $\gamma = 0$ and all initial S values are set equal to zero
- Fixed trend: $\beta = 0$
- Zero trend: $\beta = 0$ and $T_0 = 0$
- All fixed components: $\alpha = \beta = \gamma = 0$ linear trend with fixed seasonal dummy variables as discussed.

4.6.2* Starting Values

When the time series is seasonal with m periods, we require a total of $(m + 2)$ starting values: one each for the level and trend, as before, and one for each period. We again refer to "months" within a "year" for convenience, while recognizing that broader definitions of seasonality are also included. The macros provided on the website and briefly described in

Appendix 4A use starting values specified in the way we shall show here, although we should stress that a wide variety of heuristic procedures exists. We use data for the first two years, written as $Y_1, Y_2, \ldots, Y_{2m}$, to initialize the level at period m (L_m), the trend (T_m), and the first m seasonals, $S_1, S_2, \ldots S_m$. The starting values may be written as

$$L_m = \frac{1}{m}(Y_1 + Y_2 + \cdots + Y_m) + \frac{(m-1)}{2}T_m$$

$$T_m = \frac{1}{m}\left[\frac{1}{m}(Y_{m+1} + Y_{m+2} + \cdots + Y_{2m}) - \frac{1}{m}(Y_1 + Y_2 + \cdots + Y_m)\right] \quad (4.13)$$

$$S_{(i)} = 1/2(Y_i + Y_{i+m}) - \frac{1}{2m}(Y_1 + Y_2 + \cdots + Y_{2m}), \quad i = 1, 2, \ldots, m.$$

The initial value for the level is defined as the average across the first year, plus an adjustment using the estimated initial trend to allow for the difference between the middle of the year and its end. Thus, for monthly data, $m = 12$, and we add 5.5 trend increments to move from midyear to December. The trend estimate is the average increase for the second year over the first year, and the seasonal estimates are the average value for the month in question taken over years 1 and 2 minus the average for all months taken over the first two years.

It is not too much of an exaggeration to suggest that no two statistical software packages define the start-up values in quite the same way. The net effects will be minor, provided that the series is of reasonable length and the smoothing coefficients are not too small. If greater precision is required, the starting values should be estimated from the full estimation sample; the more technically inclined reader should consult Hyndman, Koehler, Ord, and Snyder (2008, Chapter 5) for details and the software referenced in on-line Appendix C.

EXAMPLE 4.4 ■ Additive Holt-Winters forecasting—the calculations (*Examples_chapter_4.xlsx*)

An illustration of the basic calculations is shown in Table 4.5. We suppose that the time series is quarterly. The first part of the table provides a schematic layout setting up the calculations. Note that these values are aligned in the table in such a way that the forecast is obtained by adding elements in the same row. Thus, the forecast for period 5 is based upon L_4, T_4, and S_1, all located in the row corresponding to Y_5. Part B of the table provides a numerical example. We take the smoothing parameters to be $\alpha = 0.2$, $\beta = 0.1$, and $\gamma = 0.3$. The totals for the first two years are 405 and 450 respectively, so the two-year average is 106.875. Equations (4.13) provide the starting values:

$$T_4 = \frac{1}{4}\left[\frac{450}{4} - \frac{405}{4}\right] = 2.81$$

$$L_4 = \frac{405}{4} + 1.5 * 2.81 = 105.47$$

$$S_1 = 0.5 * (115 + 130) - 106.875 = 15.625$$
$$S_2 = 0.5 * (90 + 95) - 106.875 = -14.375$$
$$S_3 = 0.5 * (65 + 75) - 106.875 = -36.875$$
$$S_4 = 0.5 * (135 + 150) - 106.875 = 35.625.$$

These values are shown in boldface in the table. The updating begins after the first two years. The subsequent values in the table are then calculated with the use of equations (4.8–4.11). Note that although the initial seasonal values are constrained to sum to zero, this constraint is not retained. Fortunately, this does not affect forecasting performance. The seasonal values can be adjusted to sum to zero and an exactly compensating adjustment made to the level; see Archibald and Koehler (2003) for details.   ■

TABLE 4.5   ILLUSTRATIVE CALCULATIONS FOR THE ADDITIVE HOLT–WINTERS SCHEME (*The numbers in* **bold** *indicate the starting values.*)

(A) Illustration of Spreadsheet Layout for Forecasting

Series	Level	Trend	Seasonal	Forecast	Error
Y1					
Y2					
Y3					
Y4					
Y5	**L4**	**B4**	**S1**		
Y6	L5	**B5**	**S2**		
Y7	L6	**B6**	**S3**		
Y8	L7	**B7**	S4	F8=L7+B7+S4	Y8–F8
Y9	L8	B8	S5	F9=L8+B8+S5	Y9–F9
Y10	L9	B9	S6	F10=L9+B9+S6	Y10–F10
Y11	L10	B10	S7	F11=L10+B10+S7	Y11–F11

(B) Detailed Calculations (Alpha = 0.20, Beta = 0.10, Gamma = 0.30)

Obs	Series values	Level	Trend	Seasonal	Forecast	Error
1	115					
2	90					
3	65					
4	135					
5	130	**105.47**	**2.81**	**15.625**		
6	95	108.28	**2.81**	**−14.375**		
7	75	111.09	**2.81**	**−36.875**		
8	150	113.91	**2.81**	**35.625**	152.34	−2.3
9	135	116.25	2.77	15.625	134.64	0.4
10	105	119.09	2.77	−14.375	107.49	−2.5
11	85	121.36	2.72	−36.875	87.21	−2.2
12	155	123.64	2.68	35.625	161.95	−6.9
13	145	124.93	2.54	15.733	143.21	1.8
14	110	127.83	2.58	−15.121	115.29	−5.3
15	85	129.35	2.47	−37.538	94.28	−9.3
16	160	129.96	2.28	33.541	165.79	−5.8

Data: Examples_chapter_4.xlsx. © Cengage Learning 2013.

The same general format is used in the spreadsheet macros (*HW_quarterly.xlsm* and *HW_monthly.xlsm*) that are available on the book's website. The user may specify

- the method: additive, multiplicative, or logarithmic transform
- the observations to be used in the estimation sample
- the observations to be used in the holdout sample

Once we have decided upon these values, we can choose those values of the smoothing parameters that minimize the fitting criterion (*RMSE, MAE,* or *MAPE*), using Solver in Excel. In all cases, the first two "years" of data are used to establish starting values. Note that the HW models have three smoothing parameters and 6 (quarterly) or 14 (monthly) starting values: level, trend, and seasonals. Solver is not effective in optimizing over so many unknowns, so we always use heuristic starting values in these macros.

More sophisticated statistical software enables a search to determine optimal starting values for the states (level, trend and seasonals) as well as for the smoothing parameters. The macros provided here serve to illustrate the general principles and are not the final word in computational processes for forecasting! As noted previously, the current ad hoc starting values typically work well unless the series is short and some of the smoothing parameters are close to zero.

The next example relates to quarterly data and uses the macro *HW_quarterly.xlsm*. The procedures for monthly data follow essentially the same pattern.

EXAMPLE 4.5 ■ Additive Holt-Winters forecasting (*Autos_quarterly.xlsx*)

Figure 4.4 shows a plot of the total quarterly production of motor vehicles in the United States from the first quarter of 1966 (1966Q1) through the last quarter of 2006 (2006Q4), recorded at annual rates. The mean level shifts over time and a seasonal pattern is also evident.

An additive Holt–Winters forecasting scheme was fitted by using data over the period 1968Q1 to 1999Q4 after using the first two years of data to set the starting values. The performance of the system was then checked by means of the one-step-ahead forecasts over the 28 observations from 2000Q1 to 2006Q4. The results are summarized in panel A of Table 4.6 and the components are plotted in Figure 4.5.

In this example, the error criteria (*RMSE*, *MAE*, and *MAPE*) are higher for the estimation data than for the holdout sample. Such a situation is relatively rare, because the parameter estimates are based on the estimation sample. The reason for this reversal is that the series is more stable in later years, as seen in the plot of the errors after the mid-1970s. The series also reflects smaller seasonal components in later years, as the drop-off in production in the third quarter gradually disappears. In Minicase 4.2, you are encouraged to explore the effects of using smaller estimation samples; recall that a longer series is preferable only if the underlying properties of the series do not change. ■

FIGURE 4.4   MILLIONS OF MOTOR VEHICLES PRODUCED (AT ANNUAL RATES) FROM 1966Q1 TO 2006Q4

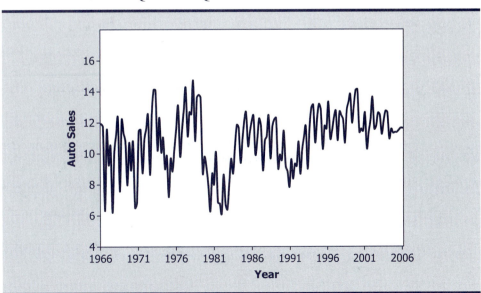

Source: U.S. Federal Reserve Board of Governors (*www.federalreserve.gov/releases*).
Data shown is from file Autos_quarterly.xlsx.

TABLE 4.6   OUT-OF-SAMPLE ACCURACY FOR HOLT-WINTERS FORECASTING METHODS: (*US Motor vehicle production, 2001Q1–2006Q4*)

	RMSE	MAE	MAPE	α	β	γ
PANEL A: Additive						
Fitting sample	1.16	0.87	8.92	0.68	0.03	0.20
Hold-out sample	0.72	0.57	4.83			
PANEL B: Multiplicative						
Fitting sample	1.46	1.09	11.14	0.55	0.03	0.18
Hold-out sample	0.86	0.70	5.94			
PANEL C: logarithmic						
Fitting sample	1.14	0.86	8.70	0.67	0.02	0.21
Hold-out sample	0.69	0.55	4.63			

Data: Autos_quarterly.xlsx. © Cengage Learning 2013.

FIGURE 4.5   COMPONENTS OF THE ADDITIVE HOLT–WINTERS SCHEME FOR THE MOTOR VEHICLES PRODUCTION SERIES

4.7   The Multiplicative Holt–Winters Method

An examination of the time series plot sometimes reveals seasonal fluctuations that increase with the level of the series; that is, the movements are proportional rather than absolute. In these circumstances, it makes sense to combine an additive trend with a multiplicative seasonal factor; in other words, we consider the forecast function

$$F_{t+1}(1) = F_{t+1} = (L_t + T_t)S_{t+1-m}. \tag{4.14}$$

Thus, the one-step-ahead error for period t becomes

$$e_t = Y_t - (L_{t-1} + T_{t-1})S_{t-m}. \tag{4.15}$$

In both equations, the seasonal component is now a multiplicative rather than an additive term. The *error correction* form of the updating equations is then

$$L_t = L_{t-1} + T_{t-1} + \alpha(e_t/S_{t-m})$$
$$T_t = T_{t-1} + \alpha\beta(e_t/S_{t-m}) \tag{4.16}$$
$$S_t = S_{t-m} + \gamma[e_t/(L_{t-1} + T_{t-1})].$$

The updating relationships involve removing the seasonal element in the error (now by division rather than by subtraction as in the additive scheme) before adjusting the level and trend. Similarly, the trend element is removed from the error before updating the seasonal component. As with the additive case, the seasonals are adjusted only once per "year," so we need $(m + 2)$ starting values in all. Exercise 4.14 provides the version of equation (4.16) that uses the observations and components in place of the error correction form. The macros *HW_quarterly.xlsm* and *HW_monthly.xlsm* are available on the book website; they include the multiplicative Holt-Winters case.

4.7.1*   Starting Values

As with the additive case, we use data for the first two years, written as $Y_1, Y_2, \dots, Y_{2m}$. The starting values for the level and trend are unchanged:

$$L_m = \frac{1}{m}(Y_1 + Y_2 + \cdots + Y_m) + \frac{(m-1)}{2}T_m$$

$$T_m = \frac{1}{m}\left[\frac{1}{m}(Y_{m+1} + Y_{m+2} + \cdots + Y_{2m}) - \frac{1}{m}(Y_1 + Y_2 + \cdots + Y_m)\right].$$

The seasonal values are created from the first "year's" values by division rather than subtraction:

$$S_{(i)} = 0.5*(Y_i + Y_{i+m})/\left[\frac{1}{2m}(Y_1 + Y_2 + \cdots + Y_{2m})\right], \quad i = 1, 2, \dots, m. \tag{4.17}$$

EXAMPLE 4.6   ■   Multiplicative Holt-Winters (*Autos_quarterly.xlsx*)

For purposes of comparison, we now examine the motor vehicles series, using the multiplicative Holt–Winters scheme. The results, based upon minimizing the *MSE*, are shown in panel B of Table 4.6. The estimated smoothing parameters are similar. Plots of the components are omitted, but they again show a reduction in the magnitude of the seasonal components from the mid-1970s on. Overall, the multiplicative scheme seems to perform much like the additive version in this example, probably because there is little trend in the data.   ■

Note again that the seasonal coefficients start out with an average of 1.0 but later values do not meet this constraint. Archibald and Koehler (2003) show how to adjust the seasonals to retain the average of 1.0; again, their adjustment does not affect the forecasts but makes interpretation easier.

4.7.2   Purely Multiplicative Schemes

A third variation is to allow both trend and seasonal components to be multiplicative. In these circumstances, we may make a (natural) logarithmic transformation, as described in Section 2.6.2, and apply the additive Holt–Winters scheme to the transformed data. The optimization step may then use either the *MSE* of the original data or the *MSE* of the transformed data. The macro on the website use the original data, because those data constitute the performance measure of interest. The forecasts for the original series are then found by application of the reverse transformation, or exponentiation. That is, if Z denotes the transformed variable, we make the transformation $Z = \ln(Y)$ and then, after generating the forecasts, transform the forecast F_Z back, using the inverse transform $F_Y = \exp(F_z)$ to regain forecasts of the original series. The subscripts have been added to the forecast variables to distinguish the transformed and original series.

EXAMPLE 4.7 ■ Purely multiplicative seasonality (*Autos_quarterly.xlsx*)
Application of this scheme to the motor vehicles series yields the results shown in panel C of Table 4.6. The forecasting performance is similar to that of the additive method. Plots of the components are omitted, but they again show a reduction in the magnitude of the seasonal components from the mid-1970s on.   ■

Weekly Data

Business time series based upon weekly observations have four distinctive features:

- They are often short, in the sense that each week of the year may be represented only a few times (e.g., two years of data provides 104 observations, but each week appears only twice).
- Key features of the series may fall into different weeks from year to year (e.g., Easter, Thanksgiving).
- There are often a large number of series to be forecast (e.g., stock-keeping units (SKUs) for a retail company or a manufacturer).
- Totals of forecasts for individual items should match up to aggregate forecasts for product groups.

We defer a detailed discussion of forecasting support systems to Chapter 12, but address some of the technical issues here. Figure 4.6 shows the sales figures for five bracelets of a particular line of bracelets sold by a leading costume jewelry company. These data are described and examined in detail in Minicase 12.2 in Chapter 12; the observations run from week 5 in year 1 through week 24 in year 3. The Christmas sales peaks are easy to recognize, and the seasonal patterns are similar for all five products even though the sales volumes differ.

FIGURE 4.6 WEEKLY SALES FIGURES FOR FIVE BRACELETS
(*Year 1, Week 5–Year 3, Week 24*)

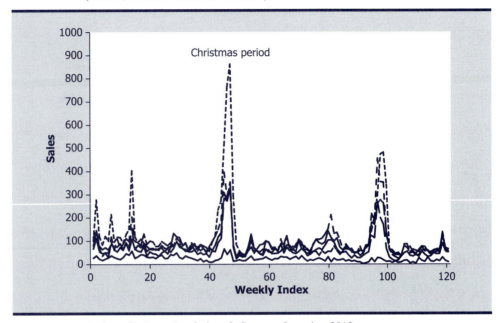

Data shown is from file Bracelet_5.xlsx. © Cengage Learning 2013.

Clearly, if we are to forecast such series, we must take the seasonal patterns into account. A single series will not provide very reliable information about seasonal patterns, but a well-defined cluster of these series (e.g., all bracelets with Christmas designs) will provide a strong indication of such shifts in sales. Further, we can see that although the sales volumes may change, the seasonal patterns are remarkably consistent. These two features are combined to provide users with a framework for dealing with weekly series; the ideas may apply equally well in other cases where there are a large number of "seasons" but relatively short series.

We adapt the multiplicative Holt–Winters scheme to allow for fixed seasonals, but we calculate the seasonals from the aggregate sales data. This approach has the effect of reducing the randomness in our estimates compared with what would happen if we had just used the individual SKU data. We can drop the trend term because it appears from the data that simple exponential smoothing will suffice once we have taken care of seasonality. Again, it is possible to retain the trend component, but for many series SES will suffice. Particularly in short-term forecasting at an SKU level, the trend has little relevance. Thus, we arrive at the scheme

$$F_{t+1}(1) = L_t S_{t+1-m}$$
$$L_t = L_{t-1} + \alpha(e_t/S_{t-m})$$
$$S_t = S_{t-m}.$$

Further, because the seasonal factors are fixed and prespecified, we may produce a deseasonalized series (Y_t/S_{t-m}), forecast this series by means of SES, and then multiply the results by the seasonal factors to obtain the final forecasts. The detailed calculations are illustrated on hypothetical data in Table 4.7.

TABLE 4.7   ANALYSIS OF HYPOTHETICAL WEEKLY SALES DATA

A	B	C	D	E	F	G	H	I	J	K	L
Week	SKU1 Sales	Group Sales (previous year)	Seasonal Factor	Adjusted SKU1 Sales	One-step-ahead forecasts	SKU1 Forecasts	Errors	Absolute Errors	Forecast (no adjustment)	Errors	Absolute Errors
1	54	557	0.87	62.1	62.1	54.0	0.0	0.0	54.0	0	0
2	29	533	0.83	35.0	62.1	51.6	−22.5	22.5	54.0	−25	24.9
3	51	539	0.84	60.8	55.4	46.6	4.6	4.6	46.5	5	4.6
4	52	700	1.09	48.0	56.7	61.9	−9.6	9.6	47.9	4	4.4
5	113	1100	1.72	65.6	53.9	92.4	20.2	20.2	49.2	63	63.3
6	58	672	1.05	55.8	59.9	62.8	−4.3	4.3	68.2	−10	9.8
7	79	602	0.94	84.0	58.6	55.0	23.9	23.9	65.3	14	13.6
8	48	603	0.94	51.0	65.8	61.9	−13.9	13.9	69.4	−21	21.4
9	76	598	0.93	81.1	61.6	57.5	18.2	18.2	63.0	13	12.7
10	32	508	0.79	40.8	67.1	53.1	−20.8	20.8	66.8	−34	34.4
Averages		609	1.00	58.4	60.31	60.30	−0.47	15.3	58.9	0.90	21.0

Data: Autos_quarterly.xlsx. © Cengage Learning 2013.

EXAMPLE 4.8 ■ Forecasting weekly sales

We consider a single-item *SKU1*, which is part of a larger product group. The sales for *SKU1* are given in column B, and last year's sales for the entire product group are given in column C. The seasonal factors in column D are created by dividing the total product sales in column C by the weekly average of 609. The adjusted *SKU1* sales are then given by the SKU1 Sales divided by the seasonal factor. Next, these adjusted sales are forecast one step ahead with SES. The one-step-ahead forecasts in column F are then multiplied by the seasonal factors to produce the *SKU1* forecasts in column G, with the corresponding errors shown in column H. The rest of the table provides forecasts based upon SES without any seasonal adjustment and compares the forecast errors.

The data were constructed to show peak sales in week 5; as it happens, both forecasts undershoot, but the error is much more serious when the seasonal pattern is not taken into account. The week-5 error would increase from 20 to 63 units; the overall *MAE* is 15.3 for the adjusted forecasts, as against 21.0 when the seasonal effects are ignored. Further, if seasonal effects appear in different weeks, as in Easter, it is a simple matter to shuffle the seasonal factors accordingly.   ■

One final point is worth noting. If we use this approach on a group of individual (sales) series with the same seasonal coefficients and a common value for α, the forecasts for the total group sales will be the same whether we sum the forecasts for the individual items (the so-called bottom-up approach) or whether we forecast the total sales directly. If only the total sales are forecast, it is then necessary to produce forecasts for individual items by partitioning the total (the so-called top-down approach). These ideas are explored further in Chapter 12.

4.8.1 Multiple Seasonalities

At various places in this chapter we have mentioned weekly, monthly and quarterly seasonal patterns. In forecasting electricity consumption and similar phenomena, time-of-day patterns are also extremely important. Such multiple seasonalities are becoming increasingly common as forecasting methods are extended to cover new situations with more frequently collected data.

We do not have space in this volume to discuss details, save to note that the general principles remain the same: we formulate an equation to describe each seasonal component such as hours within days, days within weeks and weeks within years. More detailed accounts are available in Taylor (2003) and Gould *et al.* (2008).

TABLE 4.8 ONE STEP-AHEAD PREDICTION INTERVALS FOR QUARTERLY U.S. AUTOMOBILE PRODUCTION (AT ANNUAL RATES) FOR 2006

Quarter	Actual	Forecast	Prediction Interval
2006Q1	11.63	11.91	(9.84, 14.38)
2006Q2	11.62	12.18	(9.65, 14.19)
2006Q3	11.65	10.75	(8.03, 12.57)
2006Q4	11.73	11.51	(9.53, 14.07)

© Cengage Learning 2013.

4.9 Prediction Intervals

The structure of prediction intervals for series with a seasonal component is essentially the same as that of the nonseasonal series discussed in Section 3.8. As in that discussion, we restrict attention, for the time being, to the construction of prediction intervals for one-step-ahead forecasts. (Intervals for forecasts made two or more periods ahead will be considered in Chapter 5.) As in Section 2.8, an approximate interval is given by

$$\text{Forecast} \pm z_{\alpha/2} * (RMSE).$$

EXAMPLE 4.9 ■ Prediction intervals for automobile production, one quarter ahead

As in Example 4.3, we use the Additive Holt–Winters scheme. The parameters are estimated with data over the years 1968Q1–1999Q4 after using the first two years to set starting values. Table 4.8 provides the one-step-ahead forecasts and 95 percent prediction intervals for the four quarters of 2006. As shown in Table 4.6 *RMSE* was estimated from the fitting sample to be 1.16 (million vehicles).

Two features stand out in the table. First, the intervals appear to be very wide compared with the differences between the actual and forecast values. This discrepancy reflects the greater stability (or lower variability) of the numbers in recent years and suggests that older observations are inflating the estimate of *RMSE*. At the same time, sales can be quite volatile and we should not be lulled into a false sense of security by a period of relative calm. Second, the forecast for the third quarter is well below that for the other quarters, although little variation is seen among the actual quarterly figures. As we observed earlier, the seasonal pattern has changed somewhat over time and the forecasting procedure may not fully reflect this shift. ■

Empirical prediction intervals may also be calculated by following the approach given in Section 2.8.2. The details are left as Exercise 4.15. Note that when we use the logarithmic transform, the prediction interval should be calculated for the transformed values and only then converted back to the original series.

4.10 Principles

The six principles described in Chapter 3 are equally valid for seasonal modeling. In addition, we should consider

[4.1] Carefully examine the structure of the seasonal pattern. The seasonal component may be additive or multiplicative, and it may also have certain biases that require systematic adjustment. Examples include Easter falling in March or April, some months having more weekend days than others, and certain days being national holidays. In each case, the resulting seasonal pattern could be distorted and preliminary adjustments to the data may be necessary prior to forecasting. Even in the absence of special holidays, some months have more weekend days than others. Programs such as Census X-12-ARIMA allow the user to make "trading day" adjustments so that the different levels of activity (e.g., higher retail sales on Saturday, stock markets closing on weekends) can be taken into account.

[4.2] When there are limited data from which to calculate seasonal components, consider using the seasonals from related data series, such as the aggregate. Alternatively, average the estimates across similar products.

Summary

In this chapter, we have considered time series that possess a seasonal component. There are two principal objectives in the analysis of such series. The first is to take account of the seasonal pattern when making forecasts. The second is seasonal adjustment, whereby we wish to estimate the seasonal effects and then remove them, to produce a seasonally adjusted series.

We began by considering a purely seasonal series—that is, one without a trend. Such series are rare in business applications but serve to illustrate how we can examine seasonal patterns, either by using a method that combines trends with seasonalality or by isolating the seasonal component. We then developed forecasting procedures based upon decomposition methods and explored decomposition as a tool for describing time series phenomena. The remainder of the chapter was taken up with using the Holt–Winters approach to extend exponential smoothing to series with additive or multiplicative seasonal components. As in Chapter 3, the seasonal and trend components are updated after each new observation is recorded. Finally, we briefly examined the construction of prediction intervals.

Discussion Question *In many forecasting applications, why is forecasting seasonality critically important?*

Exercises

4.1   Create seasonal plots for the Walmart quarterly sales data (*Walmart.xlsx*) by plotting
   a.   Sales against quarter, classified by year (as in Figure 4.2)
   b.   Sales against time, with years classified.

4.2   The data in the spreadsheet that follows refer to a quarterly series that is purely seasonal, as in Section 4.2. The values for year 1 are used as starting values (forecasts) for year 2. Use the purely seasonal version of exponential smoothing with $\gamma = 0.5$ to generate forecasts for year 3.

Quarter	Year	Data	Forecasts
1	1	50	
2	1	30	
3	1	20	
4	1	90	
1	2	55	50
2	2	35	30
3	2	15	20
4	2	80	90
1	3		
2	3		
3	3		
4	3		

Data shown is from file Exercise_4_2.xlsx.

4.3   The file *US_retail_sales.xlsx* includes the series *Seasonal Factors* for the monthly series
      on U.S. retail sales as developed by the Census Bureau. The data cover the period from
      January 1993 to December 2009.
      a.   Using the period from January 1993 to December 2007 as the estimation sample,
           develop a seasonal forecasting method for this series.
      b.   Generate one-year-ahead forecasts for the hold-out sample for the period from January
           2008 through to December 2009 using December 2007 as the forecast origin.
      c.   Recalibrate the forecasting equation by using all the data, and then forecast the next
           12 months. Compare the results.
4.4   Use the complete US_Retail_Sales series in *US_retail_sales.xlsx* to generate one-step-
      ahead forecasts for the period from January 2008 to December 2009, with the period from
      January 1993 to December 2007 as the estimation sample. Use the additive Holt–Winters
      method with the *macro HW_monthly.xlsm* or other software as appropriate.
4.5   Following on from Exercise 4.4, repeat the analysis for the multiplicative Holt–Winters
      scheme, using the macro *HW_monthly.xlsm* or other software as appropriate. Compare the
      performance of the two methods. Which one is preferable in this case?
4.6   Following on from Exercise 4.5, repeat the analysis for the purely multiplicative seasonal
      scheme by employing a logarithmic transform, using the macro *HW_monthly.xlsm* or other
      software as appropriate. Compare the performance of the three methods. Which one is
      preferable in this case?
4.7   The spreadsheet *GDP_quarterly.xlsx* gives the quarterly value of the U.S. gross domestic
      product from 1947Q1 through 2008Q4. Using the macro *HW_quarterly.xlsm* or other soft-
      ware as appropriate, develop an additive Holt–Winters scheme, with the period 1961Q1 to
      2005Q4 as the estimation sample. Then generate the one-step-ahead forecasts for the next
      12 quarters and compute the usual error measures. Repeat the exercise, using 1981Q1 to
      2005Q4 as the estimation sample, and compare your results.
4.8   Following on from Exercise 4.7, repeat the analysis for the multiplicative Holt–Winters
      scheme, using the macro *HW_quarterly.xlsm* or other software as appropriate. Compare
      the performance of the two methods. Which of the two Holt–Winters schemes is prefer-
      able in this case?
4.9   Following on from Exercise 4.8, repeat the analysis for the purely multiplicative seasonal
      scheme by employing a logarithmic transform, the macro *HW_quarterly.xlsm*, or other
      software as appropriate. Compare the performance with the results from exercises 4.7 and
      4.8. Which one is preferable in this case?
4.10 Use the data in the file *US_retail_sales.xlsx*.
      a.   With the period from January 1993 to December 2007 as the estimation sample, de-
           velop the LES forecasts for the deseasonalized series for the hold-out sample through
           to December 2009.
      b.   Combine your forecasts from part a, with the pure seasonal forecast generated in
           Exercise 4.2 to produce one-step-ahead forecasts for retail sales for January 2008 to
           December 2009.
      c.   Compute the usual error measures, and compare the results with those from Exercises
           4.8 and 4.9. [Note: Keep in mind that the seasonal series used a decomposition method,
           so the comparison is not a fair one. Why not?]
4.11 The spreadsheet Gas_*prices_1.xlsx* gives the average monthly prices of regular-grade
      gasoline for the period from January 1996 to December 2010. Use the period from Janu-
      ary 1996 to December 2008 as the estimation sample, and evaluate the usual error mea-
      sures for the one-step-ahead forecasts for 2009 and 2010 for each of the additive and
      multiplicative Holt–Winters schemes. Which method seems better in this case? Comment
      on the results.
4.12 Modify the spreadsheet corresponding to Example 4.2 in *Examples_chapter_4.xlsx* to fore-
      cast, by means of a multiplicative decomposition, on the data in Table 4.3.

4.13* Use equation (4.9) to substitute for the error term in the updating equations (4.10–11). Hence, derive the alternative form of the updating equations for the additive Holt-Winters scheme as given in equation (4.12):

$$L_t = L_{t-1} + T_{t-1} + \alpha[Y_t - S_{t-m} - L_{t-1} - T_{t-1}]$$
$$T_t = T_{t-1} + \beta(L_t - L_{t-1} - T_{t-1})$$
$$S_t = S_{t-m} + \gamma[Y_t - L_{t-1} - T_{t-1} - S_{t-m}].$$

4.14* As in Exercise 4.13, substitute for the error term in the updating equations (4.16). Hence, derive the alternative form of the updating equations for the multiplicative Holt–Winters scheme:

$$L_t = L_{t-1} + T_{t-1} + \alpha[(Y_t/S_{t-m}) - L_{t-1} - T_{t-1}]$$
$$T_t = T_{t-1} + \beta(L_t - L_{t-1} - T_{t-1})$$
$$S_t = S_{t-m} + \gamma[Y_t/(L_{t-1} + T_{t-1}) - S_{t-m}].$$

4.15 Following on from Example 4.9, develop empirical prediction intervals for the automobile data for the four quarters of 2006.

Minicases

Minicase 4.1 Walmart Sales

Consider the data on Walmart stores previously given in Table 2.11 and available in *Walmart.xlsx*. Plot the quarterly sales data and verify that the series exhibits a seasonal element. Contrast the additive, multiplicative, and logarithmic forms for forecasting sales, using the last eight quarters as a hold-out sample. Compare the results, using both approximate normal and empirical prediction intervals, with those obtained for Minicase 3.2.

Minicase 4.2 Automobile Production

Reexamine the automobile production series considered in Example 4.3 and later examples (*Autos_quarterly.xlsx*). Retain the same hold-out sample, but reduce the size of the estimation sample by starting in 1976, 1986, and again in 1996. Compare the results with those obtained for the complete series. Also, generate prediction intervals for the four quarters of 2006, using both approximate normal and empirical prediction intervals.

What are your conclusions regarding the relevance of the earlier data in the light of possible changes in production plans over time?

Minicase 4.3 U.S. Retail Sales

The spreadsheet *US_retail_sales.xlsx* contains the monthly values of U.S. retail sales over the period from January 1993 to December 2009. The series was plotted in Chapter 1 together with the deseasonalized series and the seasonal factors. Compare the options of

- forecasting the series by using the Holt–Winters approach
- forecasting the components separately and then combining them.

It is recommended that you use the period 1993–2005 for estimation and the remaining 48 months as the hold-out sample. Pay particular attention to the forecasts for December 2007 and beyond, when the economy was officially in a recession.

The onset of the "Great Recession" was determined to have occurred in December 2007 but was not confirmed until December 2008; would your one-step-ahead forecasts have provided earlier warning? Generate prediction intervals and see whether the actual values fall within the limits.

If you have access to suitable software, evaluate the ability of the multiple-step-ahead forecasts to predict the downturn. Conduct a rolling origin 1-12 evaluation, forecasting for the years 2008-2010. (If no suitable software is available, use just three forecast origins to compare results.)

Extend the data set to include the most recent months by going to the website *www.econ-stats.com/retsal/retsal_m1.htm* and then rework the analysis using the last four years as the holdout sample.

Minicase 4.4   UK Retail Sales

The spreadsheet *UK_retail_sales.xlsx* contains the monthly values of UK retail sales, both unadjusted and seasonally adjusted, over the period from January 1996 to December 2009. Create a purely seasonal series by dividing the unadjusted series by the seasonally adjusted one. Using one-step-ahead forecasts, compare the options of:

- Forecasting the series by using the Holt–Winters approach.
- Forecasting the components separately and then combining them.

It is recommended that you use the period 1996–2005 for estimation and the remaining 48 months as the hold-out sample.

Compare the performance of the two methods for forecasting retail sales in the United Kingdom with the results from Minicase 4.3 for the United States.

Minicase 4.5   Newspaper Sales

A small local bakery purchases a limited number of copies of the *Washington Post* on a "sale or return" basis. Sales and unsold copies were monitored over a six-week period, with the results shown in the table below. The data[3] are available in *Newspapers.xlsx*. The owner seeks advice regarding the number of copies to order in the coming week.

Week	Variable	Sun	Mon	Tue	Wed	Thu	Fri	Sat
1	Sales	15	12	10	12	13	14	16
	Returns	0	3	1	0	2	0	6
2	Sales	16	11	10	13	14	15	15
	Returns	5	0	0	0	6	6	5
3	Sales	15	11	13	16	14	15	14
	Returns	8	6	3	8	2	3	1
4	Sales	15	13	13	13	16	14	13
	Returns	3	7	3	8	7	4	5
5	Sales	14	11	12	14	13	16	12
	Returns	1	0	0	6	3	1	2
6	Sales	13	12	16	13	12	21	12
	Returns	6	7	0	*	4	8	0

*not reported

© Cengage Learning 2013.

---

[3]The data are genuine, but the name of the bakery is withheld for reasons of confidentiality.

What additional information would you like to see? How do you treat the days when there were no returns? Is there any seasonal structure? What do you recommend as an ordering policy?

References

Archibald, B.C., and Koehler, A.B. (2003). Normalization of seasonal factors in Winters' methods. *International Journal of Forecasting, 19*, 143–148.

Findley, D.F., Monsell, B.C., Bell, W.R., Otto, M.C., and Chen, B.C. (1998). New capabilities and methods of the X-12-ARIMA seasonal adjustment program (with discussion). *Journal of Business and Economic Statistics*, 16, 127–177. [For recent developments, consult the U.S. Census Bureau website for X1-12-ARIMA: *www.census.gov/srd/ www/x12a*]

Gould, P.G., Koehler, A.B., Ord, J.K., Snyder, R.D., Hyndman, R.J. and Vahid-Araghi, F. (2008). Forecasting time series with multiple seasonal patterns. *European Journal of Operational Research*, 191, 205–220.

Holt, C. (2004). Forecasting seasonals and trends by exponentially weighted moving averages. *International Journal of Forecasting*, 20, 5–10. Reprint of Office of Naval Research Memorandum 52/1957, Carnegie Institute of Technology.

Hyndman, R. J., Koehler, A. B., Ord, J. K., and Snyder, R. D. (2008). *Forecasting with Exponential Smoothing.* Berlin: Springer.

Shiskin, J., Young, A.H., and Musgrave, J.C. (1967). *The X-11 variant of the Census Method II seasonal adjustment program.* Technical Paper 15, Bureau of the Census, U.S. Department of Commerce, Washington, DC.

Taylor, J.W. (2003). Short-term electricity demand forecasting using double seasonal exponential smoothing. *Journal of the Operational Research Society*, 54, 799–805.

Winters, P.R. (1960). Forecasting sales by exponentially weighted moving averages. *Management Science,* 6, 324–342.

Appendix 4A   Excel Macro for Holt–Winters Methods

This appendix provides brief details of the Excel macros *HW_quarterly.xlsx* for quarterly data and *HW_monthly.xlsx* for monthly data. These macros are available on the book's website. Three methods are considered:

- Additive Holt–Winters (Section 4.6)
- Multiplicative Holt–Winters (Section 4.7)
- Holt–Winters with a logarithmic transform (Section 4.7.2)

1. The starting values for the level, trend, and seasonals are determined in accordance with Section 4.6.2.
2. The smoothing parameters are estimated by minimizing the *RMSE*. The solution is obtained numerically with Solver.
3. The user may specify the estimation and hold-out samples.
4. One-step-ahead forecasts are generated for the hold-out sample.

NOTE: The optimization procedure involves an iterative nonlinear search to determine the best fit. Different statistical software will give different results, depending upon the choices of starting values and the numerical recipes employed.

CHAPTER 5

State-Space Models for Time Series

CONTENTS

Our ideas must agree with realities, be such realities concrete or abstract, be they facts or be they principles, under penalty of endless inconsistency and frustration.

—William James [*Thinkexist.com*] (American philosopher and psychologist, leader of the philosophical movement of pragmatism, 1842–1910)

Introduction

In Chapters 3 and 4, we considered forecasting methods for a single time series. These methods provided forecasting flexibility by allowing the trend and seasonal components to evolve over time. Throughout that discussion, we stressed that these forecasting methods (or good intuitive approaches) lacked any theoretical foundations. Such methods can, as we have seen, provide good point forecasts and may be applied without regard to the form of the data, because all we are doing is applying a numerical recipe to the observations. However, when we wish to make statements concerning the level of uncertainty in a forecast, we must turn to a statistical model with a related set of assumptions. In turn, we must validate those assumptions if our assessment of the underlying uncertainty is to be accurate. In particular, a statistical *model* will enable us to construct prediction intervals. In retrospect, we cheated a bit and came up with such intervals in Sections 3.7 and 4.9 by assuming an additive error term that was normally distributed (but we did not mention that at the time!). Our objective in this chapter and the next is to develop underlying statistical models for exponential smoothing and then to explore possible extensions of those models. In doing so, we must keep in mind that, to be useful, a model must be validated; we seek the model that best conforms to the observations and the forecasting problem we face.

There are two principal approaches to modeling a single (univariate) time series. In this chapter, we focus upon state-space modeling, because a state-space framework is a natural extension of the exponential smoothing equations that we considered in earlier chapters. The second approach to model building is best known by the label ARIMA, which stands for *AutoRegressive Integrated Moving Average*. These models are considered in Chapter 6.

State-space models are extremely flexible, and, as a result, a number of different approaches exist. Following Hyndman *et al.* (2008), we adopt a state-space scheme because it provides the most transparent link between methods and models, as we shall see in Section 5.1. Other approaches exist that result in similar models,[1] but we do not examine them in detail.

In Section 5.1, we establish a state-space model for the simple exponential smoothing method introduced in Section 3.3 and describe the assumptions underlying this model. Once the model is established, we can develop prediction intervals, as in Section 5.2.

Hitherto, we have chosen from among this set of forecasting methods by comparing their performance over a hold-out sample. This procedure remains perfectly valid, but it may be inefficient when the time series is short, a circumstance that tends to be all too common in our fast-changing economy. Therefore, in Section 5.3 we introduce what is known as an *information criterion*—essentially, a penalty that is assigned to each of a number of candidate models. More complex models receive a larger penalty so that the models compete on an even playing field. The information criterion is then used to choose the best of the competing models. A brief discussion on extreme observations (known as outliers) follows in Section 5.4. The chapter ends with a discussion of some underlying principles in Section 5.5.

 ## 5.1   A State–Space Model for Simple Exponential Smoothing

All activities are based upon various assumptions, and forecasting is no exception. In order to forecast effectively, we must specify the underlying assumptions and verify that they hold, at least approximately. Thus, our purpose in this section is to build upon the forecasting framework developed in Chapters 3 and 4 to produce an appropriate underlying statistical model. We examine this process in the context of simple exponential smoothing (SES), since the same principles apply to all the forecasting methods we have so far considered.

---

[1]See, for example, the advanced discussions in Harvey (1989), West and Harrison (1997), and Durbin and Koopman (2001).

To achieve our goal, we use the basic forecasting equation to suggest an appropriate statistical model. When we introduced SES in Section 3.3.1, we specified the forecast function as

$$F_{t+1}(1) = F_t(1) + \alpha(Y_t - F_t(1)). \tag{5.1}$$

Recall that Y_t denotes the latest observation in the series and $F_t(1)$ is the forecast for period t, made one step earlier at time $t - 1$. The constant α is the smoothing parameter. Because this equation considers only the one-step-ahead forecasts, we rewrote it in terms of the simpler notation as

$$F_{t+1} = F_t + \alpha(Y_t - F_t). \tag{5.2}$$

That is, we set $F_t(1) = F_t$. Expressed verbally, the equation reads:

New forecast = Old forecast + Partial adjustment to account for the observed error.

At time t, after Y_t is observed, the term inside the parentheses represents the observed forecast error, which we may write as *Error = Observed Value − Forecast*, or

$$e_t = Y_t - F_t. \tag{5.3}$$

If we rearrange equations (5.2) and (5.3), we can write down the pair of equations

$$\begin{aligned} Y_t &= F_t + e_t \\ F_{t+1} &= F_t + \alpha e_t. \end{aligned} \tag{5.4}$$

Equations (5.4) involve the actual observation, the forecast made one step ahead and the observed error, which is the difference between the two. Future values of the series are *random variables* and will be described by a statistical distribution with a mean level (or expected value) and a random error term. The statistical model for the observations is then specified in terms of assumptions about the random error process. The mean level of the series, equal to the most recent forecast for SES, changes over time—precisely the local behavior we seek to describe.

Suppose now that the present time is $(t - 1)$, and let Y_t represent the random variable describing the possible observed values of the series in the next period, time t. Then the *true* mean level will be unknown, and we write it as L_{t-1}, where the subscript $(t - 1)$ is used to indicate that the model is being formulated at that time. In many traditional statistical models, the mean (level) does not change and it is represented by a single parameter (say, μ). By contrast, we will assume that the level changes over time. The level is not directly observable, but rather, is a time-dependent component that describes the nature of the process. To distinguish the unobservable level from the variable Y_t that we do observe in due course, we refer to L_{t-1} as a *state variable*. State variables are not directly observable but describe the underlying state of the process in question.

In more general forecasting models, the trend and seasonal terms, T_t and S_t, are also state variables. Thus, we have two kinds of random variables in the model: the observable variables and the unobservable state variables. These two elements constitute what we refer to as a state-space model.

State Space Models

A *state space model* consists of two parts:

- An *observation equation* that relates the random variables (Y_t) to the underlying state variable(s).
- One or more *state equations* that describe how the state(s) change(s) over time.

Starting from the first of the two expressions in (5.4), we write the *observation equation* as

New observation = mean level + random error.

That is, the observation equation is

$$Y_t = L_{t-1} + \varepsilon_t. \tag{5.5}$$

Equation (5.5) has a structure similar to that of the first equation in (5.4), but keep in mind that it refers to random variables (future observations), not (already) observed quantities.

The mean level changes over time by adjusting to the latest disturbance, and we may describe its development by the *state equation*

$$L_t = L_{t-1} + \alpha\varepsilon_t. \tag{5.6}$$

That is,

New mean level = Previous mean level + Partial adjustment for random error.

Equation (5.6) is known as the state equation because it describes how the underlying state (here, the mean level) changes over time. It is evident that equation (5.6) is similar in form to the second equation in equations (5.4), but again, we are dealing with unknown (random) quantities, whereas the forecasting equations dealt with observed values. Equations (5.5) and (5.6) represent the complete specification of the state-space model. If there were more states, we would have one state equation for each state.

To match up with our earlier development of SES, we impose the standard conditions upon the smoothing parameter as before—that is, $0 \leq \alpha \leq 1$. When α is small, the mean level changes only slowly; for larger values, it changes more rapidly. We note in passing that the state-space model may actually be applied for any α in the range $0 \leq \alpha < 2$, although when $\alpha > 1$, a given error induces an even larger adjustment to the mean level.

To summarize, the complete model may be stated as follows:

Observation equation: $Y_t = L_{t-1} + \varepsilon_t$
State equation: $L_t = L_{t-1} + \alpha\varepsilon_t.$

The one-step-ahead forecast for period $(t + 1)$ is then the updated mean level after Y_t is observed, or

Forecast function: $F_{t+1} = L_t = F_t + \alpha e_t.$

That is, the forecast function generates the SES forecasts, just as we discussed in Chapter 3.

All state-space models have these three elements: the forecast function, the observation equation, and one or more state equations. For example, LES has two state equations and the Holt–Winters seasonal models have three state equations. (See Appendix 5C for details.)

5.1.1 The Random Walk

When $\alpha = 1$, $L_t = L_{t-1} + \varepsilon_t$ and $Y_t = L_{t-1} + \varepsilon_t$; thus, the two right-hand sides are identical, and it follows that $L_t = Y_t$. The two equations may then be collapsed into the single equation

$$Y_t = Y_{t-1} + \varepsilon_t.$$

The preceding equation reflects a time series whose mean level is the previous observed value. This model is known as the *random walk* and is an appropriate description of short-term movements in stock prices: The best predictor for tomorrow's closing price is today's closing price. If the best forecast were not today's closing price, it would be possible to predict the movement of stock prices at least to some extent and thereby make money.

The random walk model for stock prices has an interesting history. It was first proposed by Louis Bachelier in 1900, but was virtually ignored for the next 50 years. Then, in 1953, Maurice Kendall conducted extensive empirical analyses which again suggested that stock prices followed a random walk. After more time elapsed, this empirical regularity was recognized as a theoretically justified conclusion that was based on an economic model of market transactions and the random walk hypothesis is now a cornerstone of financial theory (see, e.g., Reilly and Brown, 2009, Chapter 6). Nevertheless, investors continue to believe that they can somehow beat the market, and on any given day, about half of them do! Timmermann and Granger (2004) discuss the role of forecasting in financial markets, an important topic for everyone to consider.

5.1.2   The Random Error Term

Equations (5.5) and (5.6) together form the basis of the *state-space model* for a process with a local level that changes over time. Further, as we have seen, the forecast function derived from this model is exactly that given by equations (5.4). In order to complete the specification of the model, we must specify the properties of the random error term. In Table 5.1, we summarize the reason for each assumption, along with its statistical statement. Only when the assumptions are (at least approximately) justified can we use the model to make valid inferences (such as those involving tests of hypotheses and prediction intervals).

If we make these four assumptions, we are supposing that the random errors are independent and normally distributed with zero means and a common variance. The assumptions are exactly those we will make for the ARIMA models of Chapter 6 and for regression models (Section 7.5).

So, now we have a statistical model! Rather like a paddling duck, we do not see much happening on the surface, but a lot is going on underneath. In particular, our state-space model will enable us to formulate prediction intervals, and it is to this topic that we now turn.

TABLE 5.1   MODEL ASSUMPTIONS AND THE UNDERLYING RATIONALE

Statistical Assumption	Reason for Assumption
The expected value of each error term is zero.	We need to assume that there is no bias in the measurement process; otherwise the observed values would not reflect the true value of the process (e.g., some sales might go unreported or returned items might not be added to inventory figures).
The errors for different time periods are independent of (or at least uncorrelated with) one another and also independent of past states.	If errors are related, we can improve the forecast by using this information. If we have the correct model, such correlations will be zero.
The variance of the errors is constant. This common variance is denoted by σ^2.	If errors are increasing [decreasing] in absolute magnitude over time, the stated prediction intervals for future time periods would become too narrow [wide].
The errors are drawn from a normal distribution.	A distributional assumption is necessary in order to make inferences. The normal distribution is by far the most common choice, but the use of an empirical distribution of the errors that is based on observed errors in the past is becoming increasingly popular (see Section 2.8.2).

5.2 Prediction Intervals for the Local-Level Model

Given our assumptions about the random error term and the form of equation (5.5), it follows that the conditional mean of Y_t is the current mean level L_{t-1}, which we write as $E(Y_t|L_{t-1}) = L_{t-1}$. This equation follows from the fact that, for any random variables X and Y, $E(aX + bY) = aE(X) + bE(Y)$ and therefore $E(Y_t|L_{t-1}) = E(L_{t-1} + \varepsilon_t|L_{t-1}) = L_{t-1} + 0$.

Likewise, the conditional variance of Y_t, given the mean level, may be written as

$$V(Y_t|L_{t-1}) = \sigma^2 \quad \text{(see Appendix 5A).}$$

The preceding statements conform to the assumptions we have just specified; that is, we built these results into the state-space model. But what happens if we are interested in two, three, or more periods ahead? Now that we have an underlying model, we can substitute equation (5.6) into equation (5.5) to obtain

$$Y_{t+1} = L_t + \varepsilon_{t+1} = L_{t-1} + \alpha\varepsilon_t + \varepsilon_{t+1}. \tag{5.7}$$

Thus, going two steps ahead, we see that the conditional mean of Y_{t+1}, given the mean level at time $(t-1)$, is

$$E(Y_{t+1}|L_{t-1}) = L_{t-1},$$

which follows because the random errors have an expected value of zero.

The variance depends upon the variability of the errors at both time t and time $(t+1)$ and is given by

$$V(Y_{t+1}|L_{t-1}) = V(\varepsilon_{t+1}) + \alpha^2 V(\varepsilon_t) = \sigma^2(1 + \alpha^2),$$

which follows because the errors are independent and have equal variances. The details are provided in Appendix 5A. The important thing to notice is that the two-step-ahead variance is larger than that for one step ahead. The general equations for h steps ahead are

$$E(Y_{t+h-1}|L_{t-1}) = L_{t-1} \quad \text{and} \quad V(Y_{t+h-1}|L_{t-1}) = \sigma^2[1 + (h-1)\alpha^2]. \tag{5.8}$$

What these equations tell us is that, with SES, the point forecasts for periods $t, t+1, \ldots,$ $t+h$ made at time $(t-1)$ are all the same, just as we observed in Chapter 3. The second term shows how the variance increases with the forecasting horizon. The increase makes intuitive sense, because we would expect forecasts to become less accurate as the horizon increases. Of course, this statement does not mean that *every* forecast made *two* steps ahead will be less accurate than the corresponding forecast made *one* step ahead; rather, it is an average property, as we saw back in Table 2.10.

Equations (5.8), combined with the assumption of a normal distribution for the errors, provide us with the necessary information to construct a prediction interval, which may be written as

$$L_{t-1} \pm z_{\alpha/2}\sqrt{V(Y_{t+h-1}|L_{t-1})}. \tag{5.9}$$

In practice, the values of L and V will be unknown and must be estimated from the data; z represents the appropriate percentage point of the normal distribution, and the entire expression represents a $100(1 - \alpha)$ percent prediction interval. The estimated value of σ^2 in (5.8) is the *MSE* calculated over the estimation sample.

There is a notational difficulty here: The α for the normal tables is the usual probability, such as 0.10 and 0.05 (with corresponding cutoff values 1.645 and 1.960, respectively), and bears no relation whatever to the smoothing constant that we estimate from the data. Something to keep in mind!

Note that this interval is strictly valid only if we are willing to assume that the random errors have zero mean and are independent and normally distributed with equal variances. Contrary to popular belief, the Central Limit Theorem[2] is no help here, because we are making statements about a single future observation. The other option, as noted in Section 2.8.2, is to use empirical prediction intervals, but these constructs also rely upon the assumptions of independent errors with equal variances. These assumptions should be checked periodically in any forecasting application.

EXAMPLE 5.1 ■ Prediction intervals for the WFJ Sales data

As in Chapter 3, we used the first 26 observations in the series to estimate the SES parameters by ordinary least squares. We then forecast the next ten weeks with week 26 as the origin. The 90 percent prediction intervals ($z = 1.645$) were computed from expression (5.9). The results are given in Table 5.2. The values needed for calculating the prediction intervals are $\alpha = 0.729$, $RMSE = 3200$, and $L_{26} = 34,581$.

As expected, the prediction intervals gradually widen as h is increased. The final column, YES–NO, indicates whether the actual value fell within the prediction interval (PI); in this example, all the values fall well inside their respective intervals, suggesting that the sales in this part of the series may be more stable than in the estimation sample. This question is explored more fully in Minicase 5.2. ■

Violations of the assumption of constant variances may have relatively little impact upon the point forecast. However, they are critical for the construction of prediction intervals. In particular, extreme observations may greatly inflate the variance and, hence, the size of the prediction interval, as we will see in Section 5.4. The establishment of good prediction intervals is a difficult, but crucial, task, and the results should be carefully scrutinized before accepting them as the basis for planning.

TABLE 5.2   90 PERCENT PREDICTION INTERVALS FOR WFJ SALES
(One to ten steps ahead from forecast origin week 26, fitted using observations 1–26 and yielding $\alpha = 0.729$)

h	Forecast	Variance	Forecast RMSE	Lower Limit	Upper Limit	Actual	YES–NO
A	B	C	D	$E = B - Z*D$	$F = B + Z*D$	G	**
1	34581	10240000	3200	29317	39845	30986	1
2	34581	15681956	3960	28067	41095	33321	1
3	34581	21123912	4596	27020	42142	34003	1
4	34581	26565868	5154	26102	43060	35417	1
5	34581	32007823	5658	25274	43888	33822	1
6	34581	37449779	6120	24514	44648	32723	1
7	34581	42891735	6549	23808	45354	34925	1
8	34581	48333691	6952	23145	46017	33460	1
9	34581	53775647	7333	22518	46644	30999	1
10	34581	59217603	7695	21922	47240	31286	1

**YES–NO = 1 if Actual (=G) lies between Lower Limit (=E) and Upper Limit (=F)—that is, if the prediction interval includes the actual value. YES–NO = 0 otherwise.

The lettered entries at the head of the columns indicate the nature of the calculations with $Z = 1.645$ for a 90% interval.

Data shown is from file WFJ Sales sheet in PI_exponential_smoothing.xlsx.

---

[2]The Central Limit Theorem states that the sampling distribution of the sample mean approaches normality as the sample size increases. In the present case, no matter how long the observed series, only one future observation is under consideration.

FIGURE 5.1 ACTUAL VALUES AND PREDICTION INTERVALS FOR OBSERVATIONS 27–36 OF WFJ SALES

Data shown is from file WFJ_sales.xlsx.

WARNING: Some packages, even reputable ones, give incorrect prediction intervals for multiple steps ahead, often failing to allow for increasing h. Check before using!

Figure 5.1 shows the actual values of the series and the prediction limits. The plot is based upon Table 5.2.

The same approach can be adopted to produce prediction intervals for more complex state-space models; the details are summarized in Appendix 5C. (For further details, see Hyndman *et al.*, 2008, Chapter 6.)

5.3 Model Selection

In earlier chapters, we recommended the use of a hold-out sample as an effective way to choose among competing methods. At that time, we focused upon the simplest approach, which makes use only of the one-step-ahead forecasts. However, we may also consider forecasts over different lead times. This issue is explored in Section 5.3.1.

Although such approaches have gained widespread acceptance, two concerns emerge:

- Is it feasible to use a hold-out sample when the series is very short? Many series are very short—for example, after the launch of a new product.
- Can we find a criterion that uses all the data, rather than one that does not rely on excluding the most recent observations, when estimating the parameters in the alternative models?

The second question is also relevant when only a small number of observations are available. We know that it is not reasonable just to compare the *RMSE* (or a similar measure) for the estimation sample, because more complicated models involve more parameters. Given enough parameters, we can always achieve a perfect fit! So, how should we proceed? A different approach is explored in Section 5.3.2.

5.3.1 Use of a Hold-out Sample

Suppose we hold out N observations beyond the last observation (time T, say) in the estimation sample. As we work progressively through the data, we can generate one-step-ahead

TABLE 5.3 INDIVIDUAL AND CUMULATIVE MAE AND MAPE VALUES AT DIFFERENT FORECAST HORIZONS FOR THE AUTOMOBILES DATA
(*Using the fourth quarter of 1999 as the forecast origin*)

Forecast Horizon	Number of Replicates	MAE	Cumulative Average (MAE)	MAPE	Cumulative Average (MAPE)
1	15	0.601	0.601	4.95	4.95
2	14	0.709	0.653	5.97	5.44
3	13	0.838	0.710	7.06	5.94
4	12	1.024	0.780	8.68	6.55
5	11	1.024	0.821	8.71	6.91
6	10	1.054	0.852	9.08	7.20
7	9	0.956	0.863	8.38	7.33
8	8	0.773	0.855	6.47	7.25
9	7	0.727	0.846	6.02	7.17
10	6	0.803	0.844	6.79	7.15
11	5	1.008	0.851	8.39	7.20
12	4	1.168	0.862	9.57	7.29
13	3	1.201	0.871	9.89	7.35
14	2	1.291	0.878	10.86	7.41
15	1	0.611	0.876	5.44	7.39

Data shown is from file Autos_quarterly.xlsx.

forecasts for periods $T + 1, T + 2, \ldots, T + N$; that is, we generate N one-step-ahead forecasts in all. However, we can also generate two-step-ahead forecasts for periods $T + 2$, $T + 3, \ldots, T + N$; there are $(N - 1)$ of them. We proceed in this way until we finally generate just one forecast N periods ahead. Table 5.3 provides an example of such output for the automobiles data, using the period from the first quarter of 1966 through the fourth quarter of 1999 as the estimation sample and forecasting up to four years ahead.[3] The cumulative averages are weighted by the number of replicates; for example, the second term for the cumulative average *MAE*, for forecast horizon 2, is given by

$$\frac{(15 * 0.601 + 14 * 0.709)}{(15 + 14)} = 0.653.$$

Although we would expect the error measures to increase with the forecast horizon, the pattern is not entirely uniform because of the small sample sizes involved for the longer forecast horizons. Depending upon the forecasting horizon of interest, we could choose a method based on either that particular horizon or the average measure up to that horizon.

Again by way of example, Table 5.4 presents summary results for different models, taken as a summary from Forecast Pro output. The two non-seasonally-adjusted models are clearly inferior, but it is difficult to express a preference for any one of the other four. Intuitively, we might lean toward the trend-free models, because the addition of the trend term does not appear to provide any improvement, but none of these criteria allow explicitly for such a consideration to be taken into account. We now develop possible measures for model selection that are not based upon hold-out samples.

---

[3]*The results in this table are generated with Forecast Pro. The program has a default maximum of 15 periods and provides both MAE and MAPE as outputs; RMSE results are not available.*

TABLE 5.4   MAE AND MAPE VALUES FOR DIFFERENT MODELS FOR THE
AUTOMOBILES DATA

Trend	Seasonal	Method	MAE	Cumulative MAE	MAPE	Cumulative MAPE
No	No	SES	0.99	0.98	8.27	8.36
Yes	No	LES	0.99	0.98	8.27	8.36
No	Yes, A	Pure Add	0.60	0.88	4.96	7.39
No	Yes, M	Pure Mult	0.60	0.86	4.92	7.25
Yes	Yes, A	Add HW	0.60	0.88	4.96	7.42
Yes	Yes, M	Mult HW	0.60	0.86	4.92	7.25

Data: Autos_quarterly.xlsx. © Cengage Learning 2013.

"Cumulative" denotes the weighted average over 1–15 periods ahead with each lead time error measure weighted by the number of observations used in its calculation. A and M refer to the additive and multiplicative seasonality cases, respectively.

5.3.2   Information Criteria

The results obtained in the previous section suggest the need for a balance between forecasting performance and model complexity in selecting a model. Before we proceed, a brief recap is in order. Thus far, our approach to model selection has been to partition the observed series into an estimation sample and a hold-out sample. After the parameters are estimated from the estimation sample, performance is evaluated by means of the hold-out sample. The reason for the partition is to ensure that all the models under consideration can be evaluated by using the same hold-out data on an equal footing. This approach works well when sufficient data are available, but may be problematic for short series when we have to choose between poor parameter estimates and a small hold-out sample.

Discussion Question   *What problems arise when a small hold-out sample based on a single forecast origin is used? After all, statistical calculations are often based on small samples.*

The concern about a small hold-out sample leads to the idea of creating a performance measure that uses all the data, with some kind of *penalty function* to adjust for more complex models. The argument for such an approach is as follows: When the *RMSE* or any other error measure is minimized, we recognize that a more complex model has a built-in advantage because the inclusion of extra parameters reduces the value of the error measure for the estimation sample. Thus, we seek to level the playing field by adding a penalty and then choosing the best model on the basis of the combined criterion of minimizing:

$$[performance\ measure\ +\ penalty].$$

The penalty function approach was introduced by Akaike (1974) and has gained widespread use in statistics generally and time series forecasting in particular.[4] The theoretical work that has been done in this area uses the *MSE* as the performance measure, so we will also follow that path, even though it entails a slight disconnect from the previous section.

Given a time series with $n + n_0$ observations, we suppose that the first n_0 values are used to establish the starting values of the state variables. We then define an Information Criterion (*IC*) as

$$IC = \ln(MSE) + pQ(n), \tag{5.10}$$

---

[4]Akaike used a more general version, but we use a simplified form based upon the MSE.

where $Q(n)$ represents the penalty function and p denotes the number of parameters fitted (beyond the starting values). That is, for SES, $p = 2$ (α and σ^2); for LES, $p = 3$ (α, β, and σ^2), where the trend is included; and for the two Holt–Winters seasonal models, $p = 4$ (α, β, γ, and σ^2). If we are comparing models that are based upon series of different lengths, we must change the value of n appropriately.

How do we choose $Q(n)$? A number of alternatives have been proposed; the two best known are as follows:

    Akaike's information criterion (AIC; Akaike, 1974): $Q(n) = 2/n$
    Bayesian information criterion (BIC; Schwarz, 1978): $Q(n) = \ln(n)/n$.

The chosen criterion is then used in the following way:

Model Selection

Select the model with the minimum value of the Information Criterion.

The penalty in the *AIC* is selected so that the chosen model gives the forecasts with the minimum forecast *MSE*, at least for large samples. That is, we might think of a very large sample, and then the *AIC* would select the model that had the smallest *MSE* in the (large) hold-out sample. Even with the penalty, the AIC sometimes produces a model that seems overly complex, so the BIC is designed to avoid such extra terms. For example, when $n = 20$, the *AIC* has $Q(n) = 0.10$, whereas the *BIC* has $Q(n) = 0.15$. When $n = 100$, the *AIC* has $Q(n) = 0.02$, whereas the *BIC* has $Q(n) = 0.046$. Even though the formal justification relies on large samples being available, empirical studies have found that these criteria appear to do well (see, e.g., Billah, Hyndman, and Koehler, 2005).

The AIC and the BIC are formulated in various ways by different authors, which leads to different numerical values but similar or identical model choices. The important thing from our perspective is that a penalty is applied to neutralize the effects of fitting extra terms. Many forecasting programs provide either the *AIC* or the *BIC* or both, enabling a ready choice to be made among competing models.

EXAMPLE 5.2 ■ Model selection for the automobiles data

The automobiles data were fitted over the period from the first quarter of 1968 through the last quarter of 1999, with the first quarter of 1966 through the last quarter of 1967 used to establish the starting values. We fitted the local-level, the local-trend, and the three Holt–Winters models (respectively, additive, multiplicative, and additive with a logarithmic transform) using the macros described in Chapters 3 and 4. The results are shown in Table 5.5, with the models listed from best to worst. The Holt–Winters log additive model fares best. Recall that the *MSE* is calculated in the original units, after transforming back

TABLE 5.5   VALUES OF THE AIC AND BIC CRITERIA FOR DIFFERENT MODELS FOR THE AUTOMOBILES DATA

	HW: Log Additive	HW: Additive	HW: Multiplicative	SES	LES
MSE	1.3891	1.413	2.264	2.725	3.215
parameters	4	4	4	2	3
AIC	0.39	0.41	0.88	1.03	1.21
BIC	0.48	0.50	0.97	1.08	1.28

Data: Autos_quarterly.xlsx.

from the log transform. The local-trend (LES) model fares poorly because it tends to incorporate the seasonal component as a trend element. Note that the margin between the simpler SES and the seasonal models is less for *BIC* than for *AIC*, although both criteria produce the same final choice.   ∎

The discussion in the previous section used Forecast Pro to look at a somewhat different set of models. Up to this point, we have considered only the most commonly used versions of exponential smoothing models. However, we could mix and match components, for example, as follows:

- Trend: none (N), additive (A), multiplicative (M), or damped (D)
- Seasonal: none (N), additive (A), or multiplicative (M).

That is, we may choose from up to 12 different models. A summary description of these models is provided in Appendix 5B.

An automatic model selection method proceeds by fitting each of the 12 models and then selecting the one that achieves the minimum value of the information criterion. To illustrate the analysis, the results[5] in Table 5.6 provide the *BIC* for the automobiles data along with the *RMSE* values, fitted over the same period (quarter 1, 1966, to quarter 4, 1999).

As before, examination of the *RMSE* alone tells us only that a seasonal component exists. However, the *BIC* clearly indicates the preference for the simpler model: local level plus seasonal. Because the series does not contain a pronounced trend, the additive and multiplicative seasonal schemes produce similar results. This conclusion conflicts somewhat with the models considered in Chapter 4, probably because the analysis presented here results in a larger value for the seasonal smoothing parameter. The Forecast Pro© selection procedure leads to the (no trend, multiplicative seasonal) model with smoothing parameter estimates $\alpha = 0.64$, $\gamma = 0.40$. In conclusion, the *BIC* provides clear guidance, although it should be kept in mind that *BIC* (and *AIC*) relate only to one-step-ahead estimation errors.

TABLE 5.6   VALUES OF BIC AND RMSE FOR DIFFERENT MODELS FOR THE AUTOMOBILES DATA (*Based on the estimation sample from Quarter 1, 1966–Quarter 4, 1999*)

	BIC Seasonal			RMSE Seasonal		
Trend	None	Additive	Multiplicative	None	Additive	Multiplicative
None	1.85	**1.26**	**1.26**	1.81	1.20	1.20
Linear	1.89	1.29	1.28	1.81	1.21	1.20
Damped	1.93	1.31	1.31	1.80	1.20	1.20
Multiplicative	1.94	1.31	1.31	1.81	1.20	1.20

© Cengage Learning 2013.

The values are generated with Forecast Pro, whose definition of *BIC* is qualitatively similar to that given in this section. The best models are indicated in boldface type.

Discussion Question   *How might you modify AIC and BIC if you wished to select the best model for forecasting h steps ahead?*

---

[5]These calculations were performed with Forecast Pro, which provides an automatic selection procedure based upon *BIC* and also generates the rolling analysis of the hold-out sample described in Section 6.4.2. For further details of the Forecast Pro© software, see the online supplement.

5.3.3   **Automatic Selection**

It is evident from the table that the *RMSE* would not provide an adequate basis for choosing between the models, beyond favoring a model with seasonality. Once we incorporate the *BIC* penalty, it becomes clear that the best model would combine a seasonality component with local level only (no trend). That is, we would drop the trend equation completely from the model and just use the level and seasonal state variables. In applications, there is often no need to generate such a table, because most programs enable the user to opt for direct selection of the best model, but the user must still specify the list of alternative models from which the selection is to be made. Appendix 5B provides some additional guidance on this issue.

Although the *AIC* and *BIC* are now widely used, some forecasters (e.g., Armstrong, 2001) contend strongly that the use of a hold-out sample is much to be preferred. The study by Billah *et al.* (2005) suggests that the information criterion approach may often be preferable, but the matter is still open for debate. We believe that the answer is often to use both; the hold-out sample is particularly valuable for the detection of possible changes in the series' behavior, whereas the information criteria may be preferred when the series is stable and relatively short.

Discussion Question   *If you were responsible for developing forecasting methods for a large number of SKUs, what combination of hold-out samples and information criteria would you employ?*

5.4   Outliers

> ### Outliers
>
> An *outlier* is an extreme observation that, if not adjusted, may cause serious estimation and forecasting errors.

Most real series have occasional unusual observations. A sales series may have a sudden peak because of special promotions, or a macroeconomic variable such as overall employment may be affected by severe weather. In each case, the phenomenon observed is real enough, but the values are sufficiently atypical that they may distort the estimation process and, in turn, the derived forecasts. We cannot simply remove such observations, and we may wish to extend the model to account for such changes. However, at this stage we seek to do two things:

- Develop a way to identify such outliers
- Adjust the outliers once they have been identified

The approach we describe is purely graphical, and our intention is to illustrate some of the issues involved. Modern forecasting software systems usually provide a much more sophisticated procedure that involves fitting an initial model and then checking the residuals from the estimation process to determine whether any outliers exist. Outliers are then modified in a sequential fashion, because earlier outliers may generate further unusual observations later in the series.

Outliers may take one of several forms. For example, there could be a single extreme value, after which the series reverts to its previous pattern; such an outlier is known as an *additive outlier* (AO). Another possibility is a permanent change in the level, known as a *level shift* (LS). Various other possibilities exist, but we will consider only the AO and LS forms. From the forecasting perspective, it is often these single unusual observations that cause the most trouble. Figure 5.2A illustrates an AO and Figure 5.2B an LS.

FIGURE 5.2   TYPICAL PATTERNS FOR ADDITIVE OUTLIER AND LEVEL SHIFT

A: Additive outlier. B: Level shift. C: Additive outlier plus difference. D: Level shift plus difference.
© Cengage Learning 2013.

Taking first differences of the series, we see that the AO and LS provide the patterns shown in Figures 5.2C and 5.2D, respectively. Note that an LS after differencing is of the same form as an AO without differencing. Of course, the AO and LS may be either positive or negative.

The time plots are most useful if we first standardize the variables; that is, we compute and then plot the Z-scores as described in Section 2.4.4. We then compute first differences and compute and plot their Z-scores. The full procedure is as follows:

1. Plot the Z-scores for the original series and for the first differences; that is,
$$Z_t = \frac{Y_t - \bar{Y}}{\text{Stddev}(Y)} \text{ or the equivalent in first differences.}$$

2. Find the first absolute Z-value that exceeds 3.0. If there are no such values, end the search.

3. If the observation with the extreme Z-value suggests a pattern such as either of those shown in Figure 5.2A or 5.2C, an AO is suggested. If either of Figures 5.2B and 5.2D is more appropriate, consider an LS.

4. Replace the outlier by a suitable reduced value; we suggest replacing the current Z-score by 1.5, with the same sign as the original.

5. Return to step 1 and continue until no outliers remain.

The choice of a cutoff of 3.0 is a common one and generally viewed as reasonable, but some forecasters prefer a larger number. Likewise, the adjustment made in step 4 is one of many options that provide a compromise between the observed and fitted values. If it appears that a large number of outliers exists, a desirable extension of this approach is to refit the model after each adjustment—or even to consider a different model!

Again, we stress that the approach we have outlined is very basic and forecasting programs include much more sophisticated procedures. When the data are seasonal we need to develop a seasonal model (such as those discussed in Chapter 4) and then examine the residuals from the model to see if any are outliers; our basic method is not able to detect outliers in seasonal data. Rather, our primary aim is to draw attention to the problem and to provide a basic process for identifying and dealing with extreme values. By way of consolation, the very large outliers are the most important and they are usually quite easy to detect!

EXAMPLE 5.3 ■ Outlier detection and adjustment for Dulles domestic passengers

The number of passengers in millions per year is recorded in *Dulles.xlsx* and provides 48 annual observations (1962–2009). Because a log transform is clearly desirable, we analyze the transformed series. The Z-scores for the log series and its first differences are shown in Figure 5.3. The upward trend before differencing obscures the presence of outliers, but the plot of the differences clearly shows an LS in 1986, which was the first year of full operations with the expanded facilities.

The observed Z-score is 3.34 and we replace that by $Z = 1.5$ corresponding to the outlier observation 0.615. This means that the value in the differenced series changes from

$$Z = 3.34 = \frac{0.615 - 0.077}{0.161} \quad \text{to} \quad Z^* = 1.5 = \frac{y - 0.077}{0.161},$$

where y is the newly adjusted value: So 0.615 is so that 0.615 is replaced by $= 0.077 + 1.50*0.161 = 0.319$, or about half the original value. Rather than adjust all the later observations for the level shift, we scale all the earlier values by the multiplier $\exp(0.615 - 0.319) = \exp(0.296) = 1.344$. The original and changed values for 1983–88 are shown in Table 5.7; by design, the two series match from 1986 onward. Without a log transform, the adjustment would be adding an appropriate constant rather than multiplying.

After making the adjustments to the series, we can compute the forecasts as in Chapter 3. We use LES with the log transform and, as before, use the last four observations as a hold-out sample. The results are summarized in Table 5.8.

Several points emerge from Table 5.8. The *RMSE* for the estimation sample drops substantially, which produces narrower prediction intervals. However, the results for the hold-out sample are little changed. This pattern is quite common because the effects of the outliers diminish over time—and quite rapidly particularly if the smoothing parameters are large, as here; recall Figure 3.6, which showed how quickly the weights diminished with increases in the smoothing value. ■

FIGURE 5.3 Z-SCORE PLOTS FOR LOG DULLES SERIES AND ITS DERIVED FIRST-DIFFERENCE SERIES

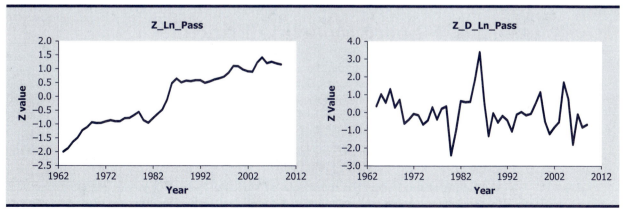

Data shown is from file Dulles.xlsx.

TABLE 5.7   ORIGINAL AND ADJUSTED DULLES SERIES FOR 1983–88

Year	Passengers	Passengers_modified
1983	2651	3564
1984	3136	4217
1985	4538	6102
1986 (level shift)	**8394**	**8394**
1987	9980	9980
1988	8650	8650

Data: Dulles.xlsx.

TABLE 5.8   SUMMARY RESULTS FOR DULLES PASSENGERS SERIES,
WITHOUT AND WITH AN ADJUSTMENT FOR THE 1986 OUTLIER

Data	Sample	RMSE	MAE	MAPE	α	β
Original	Estimation	1.41	0.82	12.1	1.00	0.51
	Hold-out	5.24	4.13	22.7		
Adjusted	Estimation	1.20	0.74	10.6	1.00	0.46
	Hold-out	5.12	4.08	22.4		

Data: Dulles.xlsx.

It would be possible to check for and perhaps remove further outliers. However, a word of caution is needed here: Removing all the outliers and then creating a modified prediction interval assumes that the future will be free from unusual events; the interval may be far too narrow as the result of this overoptimistic assumption!

Outlier adjustment for good reason, such as the Dulles expansion in 1986, leads to model-based intervention analysis, which is explored in Section 9.8. In general, outlier adjustment needs to be approached with care, and the overzealous removal of extreme values may hurt, rather than help, the forecasting process (see Koehler, Snyder, Ord, and Beaumont, 2012).

Discussion Question   *Suppose all the outliers in the estimation sample have been identified and adjusted. How should we construct prediction intervals to allow for the possibility of extreme observations in the future?*

5.5   State-Space Modeling Principles

The essence of model-building in a state-space context is to select states that describe the principal features of the series. The principles stated here are designed to facilitate that process. When the number of series under consideration is large, it is reasonable to select a sample stratified by key features such as length and reporting frequency and then to apply the analysis just to the sample. Automated checks for large errors may be applied to the remaining series once the general approach has been established. (For additional discussion, see Armstrong, 2001 and Section 13.1.5.)

[5.1] Plot the series (or a sample of series).   Plots of the series, augmented by seasonal plots, should be used to identify trends and seasonal patterns as well as to provide early warning of possible outliers.

[5.2] List all the relevant features of the series. On the basis of the initial plots, develop a list that indicates whether trend and seasonal effects are important and whether the seasonal effects, if present, are additive or multiplicative. Also, consider whether a transformation is likely to be beneficial to allow for trend-dependent variation.

[5.3] Select the best performing model, using an information criterion and/or a hold-out sample. If the series is short, an information criterion will perform better. For longer series, there is not usually a lot of difference, although some forecasters strongly prefer to use the hold-out sample. Either way, these criteria are readily automated.

[5.4] Check the model assumptions. This step involves plotting the observed error terms to determine whether the variance appears to be constant and whether any remaining dependence is apparent in the errors. Also, the empirical distribution of the residuals should be checked to see whether the normality assumption is appropriate.

[5.5] Check for outliers and make adjustments where appropriate. As noted in our discussion, such action should be taken sparingly and the outlier may reflect an omitted variable rather than an aberrant observation.

[5.6] Examine the prediction intervals. If the intervals appear much too wide or too narrow, this may suggest a change in the volatility of the series, a topic to which we return in Section 9.6.4. A transformation should be considered as a way to ameliorate the problem.

Summary

The state-space framework enables the development of underlying statistical models to support the forecasting methods discussed in Chapters 3 and 4. Such models are developed for the simple and linear exponential smoothing schemes for nonseasonal data and for the additive and multiplicative Holt–Winters schemes for seasonal data. We also considered the selection of a suitable model, using both a hold-out sample and an information criterion.

Overall, this chapter is rather theoretical, and it might seem that the forecaster interested only in applications could pass it by. We agree that it is not necessary for every automobile driver to be a mechanic, but some knowledge of what is going on under the hood contributes to carefree driving. For the modern driver, the many displays (dare we say metrics?) on the dashboard contribute to trouble-free driving, provided that warning signs are not ignored. The chapter provides the design for a forecasting dashboard: Valid forecasts depend upon a series of assumptions, and the forecasts work only when those assumptions are satisfied at least approximately. Good forecasting relies upon the skill and knowledge of the forecaster just as surely as good driving requires such attributes in the driver.

As elsewhere in the book, our focus is upon the development of the forecasting system. Once that step has been achieved, the system can operate in more automatically, a topic we return to in Chapter 12 when we discuss forecasting for operations.

Exercises

5.1 Forecasting by means of simple exponential smoothing (SES) with $\alpha = 0.3$ produces a one-step-ahead forecast of $F_t = 100$ and an estimation sample *RMSE* of 64. Determine the point forecasts and the prediction intervals for one through four steps ahead.

5.2 Consider the data on the change in real *GDP* (*GDP_change.xlsx*) previously examined in Exercises 4.1 and 4.3. Estimate the smoothing parameter and the *RMSE*, using the data through 2001 as the estimation sample. Then determine the point forecasts and the prediction intervals for one through six steps ahead. Repeat the exercise, using the data through 2004 as the estimation sample, and compare your results.

5.3   Consider the data on the change in the Consumer Price Index (*CPI_change.xlsx*) previously examined in Exercises 4.2 and 4.5. Estimate the smoothing parameter and the *RMSE*, using the data though 2001 as the estimation sample. Then determine the point forecasts and the prediction intervals for one through six steps ahead. Repeat the exercise, using the data through 2004 as the estimation sample, and compare your results.

5.4   Using the results from Exercises 5.2 and 5.3, develop one-step-ahead forecasts and prediction intervals for the *GDP* and the *CPI* for 2007 and compare your forecasts with the actual outcomes, commenting on any contrast.

5.5   An analysis of an annual sales series uses linear exponential smoothing (LES) to produce the following results:

$$L_t = 100, \quad T_t = 4.0, \quad \alpha = 0.3, \quad \beta = 0.2.$$

In addition, the estimation sample produces an estimated *RMSE* of 2.5. Determine the point forecasts and the prediction intervals for one through four steps ahead.

5.6   The spreadsheet *Google_volume.xlsx* contains data on the monthly volume of trading in Google stock (millions of shares) from May 2006 to January 2009. Generate one-step-ahead forecasts for May 2008 through January 2009, using May 2006 through April 2008 as the estimation sample. Compute the one-step-ahead prediction intervals, and check to see how many intervals include the actual values.

5.7* An analysis of an annual sales series uses linear exponential smoothing (LES) with a log transform to produce the following results:

$$L_t = 100, \quad T_t = 4.0, \quad \alpha = 0.3, \quad \beta = 0.2.$$

In addition, the estimation sample produces an estimated *RMSE* (for the logarithms) of 2.5. Determine the point forecasts and the prediction intervals for the original data for one through four steps ahead.

5.8* Reexamine the Google data described in Exercise 5.6, using a log transform. As before, generate one-step-ahead forecasts for May 2008 through January 2009, using May 2006 through April 2008 as the estimation sample. Compute the one-step-ahead prediction intervals for the original series, and check to see how many intervals include the actual values. Compare the intervals given by this approach with those obtained from the original LES.

5.9   Consider the data on Walmart stores given in Table 2.11, and examined in Minicase 5.1 (see the file *Walmart.xlsx*). Determine the most appropriate forecasting model for the quarterly sales data, using the last eight quarters as a hold-out sample. Compute the one-step-ahead prediction intervals for the original series, and check to see how many intervals include the actual values.

Minicases

Minicase 5.1 Analysis of UK Retail Sales

The file *UK_retail_sales.xlsx* contains indexes for the volumes of annual, monthly, and quarterly Retail Sales in Predominantly Non-Food Stores [code: EAGX] for the United Kingdom for the period 1988–2009. The indexes are not seasonally adjusted, and each index is based upon constant 2005 prices, with the average values for 2005 set at 100.

Determine the most appropriate model for forecasting each of the three series, and compare your forecasts for 2008 and 2009 (i.e., compare aggregate monthly with quarterly, and both monthly and quarterly with annual).

Do the forecasts fall within appropriate prediction intervals?

[Advanced] How would you generate prediction intervals for the forecasts you obtained by aggregation? Extend the data set to include the most recent data and rework the analysis for the last two years.

Minicase 5.2 Prediction Intervals for WFJ Sales

We make use of the data file *WFJ_sales.xlsx*. Around week 12, the WFJ Sales manager changed the advertising strategy for the product, which resulted in an increase in sales. To allow for this change, drop the first 12 observations and recompute the prediction intervals for weeks 27–36, using only observations 13–25 as the estimation sample. You will find that the *RMSE* is reduced and the width of the intervals increases more slowly, because α is smaller.

Repeat this analysis for other subsamples to see how the prediction intervals depend critically upon validating the assumptions listed in Table 5.1.

References

Starred items indicate more advanced reading.

*Akaike, H. (1974). A new look at the statistical model identification. *IEEE Transactions on Automatic Control,* 19, 716–723.

Armstrong, J. S. (2001). Extrapolation. In Armstrong, J.S. (ed.), *Principles of Forecasting: A Handbook for Researchers and Practitioners.* Boston and Dordrecht: Kluwer, pp. 215–243.

*Bachelier, L. (1900). Théorie de la speculation, *Annales Scientifiques de l'École Normale Supérieure,* 3, 21–86.

*Billah, B., Hyndman, R. J., and Koehler, A. B. (2005). Empirical information criteria for time series forecasting model selection. *Journal of Statistical Computation & Simulation,* 75, 831–840.

*Durbin, J., and Koopman, S. J. (2001). *Time Series Analysis by State Space methods.* Oxford, U.K: Oxford University Press.

*Harvey, A. C. (1989). *Forecasting, Structural Time Series Models, and the Kalman Filter.* Cambridge, U.K.: Cambridge University Press.

*Hyndman, R. J., Koehler, A. B., Ord, J. K., and Snyder, R. D. (2008). *Forecasting with Exponential Smoothing.* Berlin, Heidelberg, and New York: Springer.

Koehler, A. B., Snyder, R. D., Ord, J. K., and Beaumont, A. (2012). A study of outliers in the exponential smoothing approach to forecasting. *International Journal of Forecasting,* 28, 477–484.

Reilly, R. K., and Brown, K. C. (2009). *Investment Analysis and Portfolio Management,* 9th ed. Pacific Grove, CA: Thomson.

*Schwarz, G. (1978). Estimating the dimension of a model. *Annals of Statistics,* 6, 461–464.

Timmermann, A., and Granger, C. W. J. (2004). Efficient market hypothesis and forecasting. *International Journal of Forecasting,* 20, 15–27.

*West, M., and Harrison, P. J. (1997). *Bayesian Forecasting and Dynamic Models,* 2nd ed. Berlin, Heidelberg, and New York: Springer.

Appendix 5A* Derivation of Forecast Means and Variances

We consider the local-level model explored in Section 5.2 and rely upon the set of assumptions stated in Table 5.1. In technical terms, these assumptions about the random error terms (ε_t) may be stated as follows:

Zero bias: $E(\varepsilon_{t+i}|L_{t-1}) = 0, \quad i = 0, 1, \ldots$

Constant variance: $V(\varepsilon_{t+i}|L_{t-1}) = \sigma^2, \quad i = 0, 1, \ldots$

Independent (strictly uncorrelated) errors: $Corr(\varepsilon_{t+i}, \varepsilon_{t+j}|L_{t-1}) = 0, \quad i \neq j$

Using the idea of zero bias yields (and the formulae of Appendix A)

$$E(Y_t|L_{t-1}) = E(L_{t-1} + \varepsilon_t|L_{t-1})$$
$$= E(L_{t-1}|L_{t-1}) + E(\varepsilon_t|L_{t-1})$$
$$= L_{t-1} \text{ (since the first term is a constant).}$$

The variance for one step ahead may then be written as

$$V(Y_t|L_{t-1}) = V(L_{t-1} + \varepsilon_t|L_{t-1})$$
$$= V(L_{t-1}|L_{t-1}) + V(\varepsilon_t|L_{t-1})$$
$$= 0 + \sigma^2.$$

Following the same line of argument, we see that the variance for two steps ahead is given by

$$V(Y_{t+1}|L_{t-1}) = V(L_t + \varepsilon_{t-1}|L_{t-1})$$
$$= V(L_{t-1} + \alpha\varepsilon_t + \varepsilon_{t+1}|L_{t-1}) + V(\varepsilon_t|L_{t-1})$$
$$= V(L_{t-1}|L_{t-1}) + V(\alpha\varepsilon_t + \varepsilon_{t+1}|L_{t-1})$$
$$= 0 + V(\alpha\varepsilon_t + \varepsilon_{t+1}|L_{t-1}).$$

Because there is zero correlation between the two error terms, the equation becomes

$$V(Y_{t+1}|L_{t-1}) = V(\alpha\varepsilon_t + \varepsilon_{t+1}|L_{t-1})$$
$$= V(\alpha\varepsilon_t|L_{t-1}) + V(\varepsilon_{t+1}|L_{t-1})$$
$$= \alpha^2 V(\varepsilon_t|L_{t-1}) + V(\varepsilon_{t+1}|L_{t-1})$$
$$= \alpha^2\sigma^2 + \sigma^2 = \sigma^2(1 + \alpha^2).$$

Higher numbers of steps ahead are dealt with in the same way.

In the general case, the error terms in the model, for h steps ahead, may be written as

$$\varepsilon_{t+h-1} + A_1\varepsilon_{t+h-2} + \cdots + A_{h-1}\varepsilon_t.$$

By similar arguments, the variance becomes

$$V(Y_{t+h-1}|L_{t-1}) = V(\varepsilon_{t+h-1} + A_1\varepsilon_{t+h-2} + \cdots + A_{h-1}\varepsilon_t|L_{t-1})$$
$$= \sigma^2(1 + A_1^2 + \cdots + A_{h-1}^2).$$

Appendix 5B   Pegels' Classification

We have discussed seasonal forecasting methods in the context of three basic components: the trend, seasonal, and error components. It is evident that there are four possible settings for the trend, namely, none (N), additive (A), damped (D), and multiplicative (M). Likewise, three possibilities exist for the seasonal pattern: none (N), additive (A), and multiplicative (M). Together, these make 12 possibilities in all. To this arrangement may be added two options for the error term: additive (A) or multiplicative (M). An additive error implies

TABLE 5B.1   SOME STANDARD FORECASTING METHODS, LISTED IN ACCORDANCE WITH PEGELS' CLASSIFICATION

Method	ETS	Section(s)
SES	A,N,N	3.3
LES	A,A,N	3.4
LES (log transform)	M,M,N	3.5
Damped ES	A,D,N	3.6
Seasonal SES	A,N,A	4.2
Additive Holt–Winters	A,A,A	4.6
Multiplicative Holt–Winters	A,A,M	4.7
Holt–Winters (log transform)	M,M,M	4.7.2

© Cengage Learning 2013.

that the variance of the process is constant over time, thereby validating the use of the method of least squares to estimate the unknown parameters. By contrast, multiplicative errors imply an increase in the variance of the process when the expected value (or one-step-ahead forecast) increases.

The preceding classification has its origins in the scheme introduced by Pegels (1969) and extended by several others (see, for example, Hyndman *et al.*, 2008, pp. 11–12). Each forecasting model may be coded as an ETS scheme, where ETS stands for *Error, Trend, Seasonal*. For example, the SES scheme considered in Section 5.1 is ETS(A,N,N), corresponding to an additive error, no trend, and no seasonality. Likewise, ETS(A,A,A) means that the series has additive error, trend, and seasonal components, corresponding to the additive Holt–Winters model in Section 5.3.2. The various schemes we have discussed are summarized in Table 5B.1, along with the relevant section number; all may now be referred to as models, provided that we make explicit assumptions concerning the error terms.

A key element in the forecasting process is to decide upon the appropriate form of relationship. A convenient way to proceed, using either a hold-out sample or an information criterion, is to select a general form and then to evaluate the choice criterion with the use of some or all of the special cases, as illustrated in Example 5C.2 in Appendix 5C. When a large number of series must be considered, it is possible to guide the choice of model by evaluating the forecast performance of a sample, or subset, of the series. Such prescreening may reduce the computational effort considerably.

Appendix 5C*   State-Space Models for Other Exponential Smoothing Methods

The pathway we have established for exponential smoothing with simple models works for more complex models as well. We first establish the state-space model, then derive the variance, and finally create the prediction interval. We provide summary results for the principal cases we considered in Chapters 3 and 4. Interested readers can check Hyndman *et al.* (2008, Chapter 6) for details.

5C.1   The Local-Level-with-Trend Model for Linear Exponential Smoothing

The state-space model for SES involves underlying state variables and random errors in a way that parallels the estimated states and observed errors in the SES method. The same approach holds good for LES. We obtain the following equations:

Forecast function:

$$F_{t+h-1}(h) = L_{t-1} + hT_{t-1}, \quad h = 1, 2, \ldots$$

Observation equation:

$$Y_t = L_{t-1} + T_{t-1} + \varepsilon_t$$

State equations:

$$L_t = L_{t-1} + T_{t-1} + \alpha\varepsilon_t$$

$$T_t = T_{t-1} + \alpha\beta\varepsilon_t$$

The two state equations involve partial adjustments related to the random error. The trend term adjusts directly to the previous trend, but the level equation needs to account for the trend in the series (previous level plus trend) as well as making the partial adjustment. The reader is invited to compare these equations with equations (3.10) and (3.11) in Chapter 3, keeping in mind the switch from forecast updates to a statistical model, so that the actual forecasts are based upon the estimated values of the level and trend. If we put $\beta = 0$, we have a model with fixed trend. If, in addition, we set $\beta_0 = 0$, we are back at the model for SES.

The one-step-ahead variance for LES is just $V(Y_t|L_{t-1}, T_{t-1}) = \sigma^2$, as it is for all such models. The variance expression for h steps ahead is found by using the approach described in Appendix 5A:

$$V(Y_{t+h-1}|L_{t-1}, T_{t-1}) = \sigma^2[1 + (h-1)\{\alpha^2 + \alpha\beta h + \tfrac{1}{6}\beta^2 h(2h-1)\}].$$

When $\beta = 0$, these expressions revert to equation (5.8), because a fixed trend coefficient does not contribute to variability. The variance involves the third power of h, so it can increase quite rapidly.

EXAMPLE 5C.1 ■ Prediction intervals for the Netflix data

Table 5C.1 shows the results for the Netflix data first considered in Section 3.4. At that time, we observed that the forecasts seemed to lag the series, so it is not surprising that many of

TABLE 5C.1   90 PERCENT PREDICTION INTERVALS FOR NETFLIX SALES
(1–10 steps ahead, from forecast origin period 15)

h	Forecast	Variance	FMSE	Lower Limit	Upper Limit	Actual	YES–NO
1	80.4	8.5	2.9	75.6	85.2	81.2	1
2	88.6	26.9	5.2	80.1	97.1	99.8	0
3	96.8	59.0	7.7	84.2	109.5	119.7	0
4	105.0	108.7	10.4	87.9	122.2	140.4	0
5	113.3	179.7	13.4	91.2	135.3	140.7	0
6	121.5	275.9	16.6	94.1	148.8	152.5	0
7	129.7	401.0	20.0	96.7	162.6	164.0	0
8	137.9	558.9	23.6	99.0	176.8	172.7	1
9	146.1	753.3	27.4	100.9	191.2	193.0	0
10	154.3	988.2	31.4	102.6	206.0	224.1	0

YES–NO equals 1 if the prediction interval includes the actual value and equals 0 otherwise.
Data shown is from the Netflix sheet in *PI_exponential_smoothing.xlsx*.

the actual values lie outside the prediction intervals. The estimated parameter values are $\alpha = 1.00$, $\beta = 0.474$, and $RMSE = 2.91$. The state variables computed after period 15 are $L_{15} = 72.20$ and $B_{15} = 8.21$. The intervals widen considerably as the forecast horizon increases, because of the relatively large values of the estimated smoothing constants. ■

Even so, the relatively poor quality of the forecasts is illustrated by the fact that only two of the ten observations fall within their respective prediction intervals. The reason for this failure to cover the actual values is that the variability of the sales series is increasing with the mean, so the assumption of constant variance is not valid.

5C.2   The Holt–Winters Additive Scheme

In a similar fashion to the LES model, we obtain the state-space model for additive seasonals (m seasons) as follows:

Forecast function:

$$F_{t+h-1}(h) = L_{t-1} + hT_{t-1} + S_{t+h-1-m}, \quad h = 1, 2, \ldots$$

Observation equation:

$$Y_t = L_{t-1} + T_{t-1} + S_{t-m} + \varepsilon_t$$

State equations:

$$L_t = L_{t-1} + T_{t-1} + \alpha\varepsilon_t$$

$$T_t = T_{t-1} + \alpha\beta\varepsilon_t$$

$$S_t = S_{t-m} + \gamma\varepsilon_t$$

In addition to the level and trend equations, we now have a seasonal term, or rather a set of m seasonal terms, each of which is updated once per complete seasonal cycle. Again, a comparison with equations (4.8) through (4.11) reveals the same structural form, but with the crucial distinction between random variables and observed quantities. A comparison with the LES case indicates that we have added the seasonal state variables and corresponding state equations. Setting $\gamma = 0$ yields a model with fixed seasonals, and if we then set all the initial seasonal values to zero, we are back at LES. The h-step-ahead variance for the Holt–Winters additive scheme is

$$V(Y_{t+h-1}|L_{t-1}, T_{t-1}, S_{t-m+h-1}) = \sigma^2[1 + (h-1)\{\alpha^2 + \alpha\beta h + \tfrac{1}{6}\beta^2 h(2h-1)\}],$$

provided that $h < m$. That is, the variance matches that for LES for $h < m$ because the seasonal factors are not being updated during this period; we must wait for a full yearly cycle before adjustments are made. When $h \geq m$, the variance expression involves seasonal terms as well. (For full details, see Hyndman *et al.*, 2008, p. 82.)

EXAMPLE 5C.2 ■ Prediction intervals for the automobiles data

In Table 5C.2, we give the forecasts and PIs for the automobile series (*Autos_quarterly.xlsx*) considered Section 4.6, using the fourth quarter of 1999 as the forecast origin. The parameter estimates are $\alpha = 0.507$, $\beta = 0.033$, $\gamma = 0.001$, and $RMSE = 1.198$. The initial values of the state variables are $L_{136} = 12.616$ and $T_{136} = 0.042$. The seasonal values are given in the table, duly repeated once for each year. ■

TABLE 5C.2   90 PERCENT PREDICTION INTERVALS FOR THE AUTOMOBILES
SERIES (*1–12 quarters ahead, from forecast origin Q4 1999*)

h	S(t − m + h)	Forecast	Variance	RMSE	Lower Limit	Upper Limit	Actual	YES–NO
1	0.795	13.45	1.44	1.20	11.48	15.42	14.07	1
2	1.325	14.03	1.85	1.36	11.79	16.27	14.09	1
3	−2.065	10.68	2.32	1.52	8.17	13.19	11.36	1
4	0.120	12.90	2.85	1.69	10.13	15.68	11.58	1
5	0.795	13.62	3.44	1.85	10.57	16.67	11.44	1
6	1.325	14.19	4.09	2.02	10.87	17.52	12.61	1
7	−2.065	10.85	4.80	2.19	7.24	14.45	10.30	1
8	0.120	13.07	5.58	2.36	9.19	16.96	11.35	1
9	0.795	13.79	6.43	2.54	9.62	17.96	12.18	1
10	1.325	14.36	7.36	2.71	9.90	18.82	13.61	1
11	−2.065	11.01	8.37	2.89	6.26	15.77	11.57	1
12	0.120	13.24	9.45	3.07	8.18	18.30	11.75	1

Data shown is from the "Automobiles" sheet in *PI_exponential_Smoothing.xlsx*.

5C.3   The Holt–Winters Multiplicative Scheme

The multiplicative scheme follows in the way we would expect, with the seasonal term in the forecast function now involving a product in place of a sum:

Forecast function:

$$F_{t+h-1}(h) = (L_{t-1} + hT_{t-1})S_{t+h-1-m}, \quad h = 1, 2, \ldots$$

Observation equation:

$$Y_t = (L_{t-1} + T_{t-1})S_{t-m}(1 + \varepsilon_t)$$

State equations:

$$L_t = (L_{t-1} + T_{t-1})(1 + \alpha\varepsilon_t)$$

$$T_t = T_{t-1} + \alpha\beta(L_{t-1} + T_{t-1})\varepsilon_t$$

$$S_t = S_{t-m}(1 + \gamma\varepsilon_t)$$

If we compare this model with that for the additive Holt–Winters scheme, we see some major differences. The forecast is now given by the product of the trend and the seasonal factor, and the state variables are now updated by multiplicative factors involving the random error. In turn, when the random errors $\{\varepsilon_t\}$ have constant variance, the standard deviation of Y_t will be proportional to the current mean level rather than being constant. This idea makes sense; we have often noticed that the variability of the series increases with the mean. We note in passing that the one-step-ahead variance becomes

$$V(Y_t | L_{t-1}, T_{t-1}, S_{t+1-m}) = \sigma^2 F_t^2.$$

Unfortunately, the nonlinearity makes the analysis more complicated; equations for the variance for multiple steps ahead may be found in Hyndman *et al.* (2008, Chapter 4).

CHAPTER 6

Autoregressive Integrated Moving Average (ARIMA) Models

CONTENTS

All models are wrong, but some are useful.

—George Box

Introduction

In Chapter 5, we developed state-space models that grew naturally out of the exponential smoothing methods introduced in Chapters 3 and 4. However, there are other ways to model time series, of which the most prominent is the use of the *Autoregressive Integrated Moving Average (ARIMA)* class of models. These models are often referred to as *Box–Jenkins models*, because the first systematic treatment of modeling, estimation, and forecasting with such models appeared in the seminal work of those two researchers (Box and Jenkins, 1970; the most recent edition is Box, Jenkins, and Reinsel, 2008).

In Chapter 5, we developed a state-space model by specifying components such as level, trend, and seasonality; such models are sometimes known as *structural models*, given that they are developed in terms of these intuitive components. However, once we move over to ARIMA models, the approach to model building is data driven. Rather than identify particular components, the ARIMA modeler first develops the properties of basic ARIMA models as a class. He or she then examines various summary statistics that characterize the time series in order to find a model that matches the data summaries. The key measures used for this purpose are the sample *Autocorrelation Function* (ACF), described in Section 6.1, and the sample *Partial Autocorrelation Function* (PACF), described in Section 6.3. The basic properties of ARIMA models are explored in Sections 6.1, 6.2, and 6.3, and the issue of model selection is considered in Section 6.4. Then, in Section 6.5, we examine diagnostic methods for checking whether the model selected is adequate, although an alternative approach is simply to choose the best model from a prespecified short list, as we did with state-space models. In Section 6.6, we consider the problem of outliers; we then develop forecasting procedures in Section 6.7. We briefly consider seasonal ARIMA models in Section 6.8 and then, in Section 6.9, outline the linkages between state-space and ARIMA models. As we note, where relevant, many ARIMA models are equivalent to the state space models of Chapter 5 (and thus underlie the exponential smoothing formulations of Chapter 3).

Our analysis up to this point has always assumed that the error variance is constant. In Section 6.10, we relax that assumption and allow the variance to change over time. Finally, the section on principles provides a systematic approach to the development of ARIMA models.

The standard, albeit rather advanced, reference for ARIMA models is that of Box *et al.* (2008). A useful intermediate-level text is Chatfield (2004), but both require more mathematics than is used in this chapter.

6.1   The Sample Autocorrelation Function

From Chapter 2, we are familiar with the calculation of the mean and variance of an observed time series, but we have not so far developed any direct measures of the dependence that may exist among observations. If we are to develop a data-driven framework for time series modeling, the first requirement is to provide such a measure.

Just as we used the correlation coefficient in Section 2.5 to assess the association between two variables, we now introduce the concept of *autocorrelation*. As the name suggests, autocorrelations measure the correlation between the current and immediate past values of a time series. We refer to Y_{t-1} as the *(first-order) lagged value* of Y_t, or just the *lag*. We then define the *(first-order) sample autocorrelation* for Y as

$$r_1 = \frac{\sum_{t=2}^{n}(Y_t - \bar{Y})(Y_{t-1} - \bar{Y})}{\sum_{t=1}^{n}(Y_t - \bar{Y})^2}.$$

(6.1)

There are several things to note about this expression:

- The first value, Y_1, is being compared with the second value, Y_2, so the summation starts at $t = 2$, corresponding to the first pair available.
- The two series (Y and its first-order lag) have almost the same mean, differing by only one observation out of n. So, we use a common mean taken over all n values. By the same token, we use a common variance in the denominator, also taken over all n values.
- There are $(n - 1)$ pairs in the numerator, yet n terms in the denominator. One could argue for making an adjustment, but it has generally been found useful to retain this slight bias toward zero for reasons of numerical stability in higher order autocorrelations.

EXAMPLE 6.1 ■ Calculation of the first-order autocorrelation

The calculations are laid out in the following table:

Week, X	1	2	3	4	5	6	7	Sums
Sales (000s), Y_t	15	10	12	16	9	12	10	84
Lagged values, Y_{t-1}		15	10	12	16	9	12	
$Y_t - \bar{Y}$		-2	0	4	-3	0	-2	
$Y_{t-1} - \bar{Y}$		3	-2	0	4	-3	0	
$(Y_t - \bar{Y})(Y_{t-1} - \bar{Y})$		-6	0	0	-12	0	0	-18
$(Y_t - \bar{Y})^2$	9	4	0	16	9	0	4	42

Total sales over the seven weeks are 84, so the weekly average is 12.

From equation (6.1), we then have $r_1 = -18/42 = -0.429$, showing some negative autocorrelation. We interpret this as an indication that above-average sales one week tend to be followed by somewhat below-average sales the next week. We should keep in mind, however, that the autocorrelation is weak and the sample size is very small, so such a conclusion should be viewed as tentative. ■

We referred to equation (6.1) as the first-order autocorrelation because we lagged the series by one time period. In similar fashion, we could go 2, 3, ..., k steps back and define the second-, third-, ..., kth-order autocorrelations. We refer to Y_{t-k} as the lag of order k, so the *sample autocorrelation of order k* for Y is defined as

$$r_k = \frac{\sum_{t=k+1}^{n} (Y_t - \bar{Y})(Y_{t-k} - \bar{Y})}{\sum_{t=1}^{n}(Y_t - \bar{Y})^2}. \tag{6.2}$$

The sample autocorrelation of order k is an estimate of the population autocorrelation of order k, which we denote by ρ_k. Comments about equation (6.2) are essentially the same as those about r_1, except that we lose k terms in general. A good way to look for structure in a time series is to compute the first K autocorrelations, usually no further than $K = n/4$ or thereabouts. The autocorrelations are then plotted against k, and the plot is known as the *autocorrelation function*, abbreviated to ACF.

EXAMPLE 6.2 ■ The autocorrelation function for WFJ Sales

The ACF for WFJ Sales is shown in Figure 6.1. The broken boundary lines provide a quick visual test of the statistical significance of the autocorrelations. That is, if the

FIGURE 6.1   THE ACF FOR WFJ SALES (MINITAB)

Autocorrelation Function for WFJ Sales
(with 5% Significance Limits for the Autocorrelations)

Data shown is from file WFJ_sales.xlsx.

observed value lies outside the area enclosed by those lines, we may reject the null hypothesis that the population autocorrelation is zero (with significance level $\alpha = 0.05$ as the default value). From Figure 6.1, we can see that the first few autocorrelations are positive, indicating a carryover in sales level from one week to the next. As the lag increases, the correlation dies away.

6.1.1   Model Assumptions

The pattern of association illustrated in Figure 6.1 seems quite plausible: Successive weeks show similar levels of sales, but the similarity fades as the time between weeks is increased. But how do we translate such notions into a statistical model? Recall that, to make sense of the sample mean and the sample variance, we require that the observations come from a process with a constant mean and variance. To those requirements we now add the condition that any snapshot of the time series looks the same as any other of the same length (whatever the starting point). Formally stated, this condition means that the theoretical autocorrelation between observations k lags apart should be the same, no matter where those two observations occur in the series; it is only their *relative* position that matters. For example, the autocorrelation between observations for the months of January and May should be the same as that for the same months the previous year. For nonseasonal data, they should remain the same for March and July or for August and December; all pairs are four months apart. Fortunately for us, this assumption is often reasonable. Nevertheless, exceptions may arise, as with the sale of roses, for which February is atypical because of St. Valentine's Day. Some modifications to the analysis might then be necessary, but for now we ignore such complications.

Putting together these requirements for a constant mean and variance and a relative autocorrelation structure, we arrive at the concept of *stationarity*.

Stationarity

A time series is *stationary* if it has a constant mean and variance and its autocorrelations depend only on the relative time between the observations. Formally, we introduce the notation ω^2 for the variance of Y and ρ_k to denote the autocorrelation at lag k. Then, for stationarity, we require that

$$E(Y_t) = \mu$$
$$V(Y_t) = \omega^2$$
$$Corr(Y_t, Y_{t-k}) = \rho_k,$$

all independent of t.

Why does stationarity matter? We can always compute the mean, the variance, and autocorrelations from an observed time series, but the numbers make sense only if the assumption of stationarity holds. The following examples suggest, however, that this assumption may often be the exception, rather than the rule, for business forecasting:

- Sales of a product increase after it is introduced into the market and then flatten out as the market matures. As the product is superseded by an improved competitor, sales may begin to decline. The series is *nonstationary in the mean*.
- Gross domestic product (*GDP*) generally increases, but the fluctuations are measured in percentage terms rather than absolute terms. The series is *nonstationary in both the mean and the variance*.
- The price of a stock varies over time but does not show any tendency to fluctuate around a particular (mean) value. The series is *nonstationary in the mean, even though no systematic trend may exist*.

Fortunately, as we show later in the chapter, it is often feasible to restore stationarity by suitable transformations. For the time being, when we analyze a series, we will assume that the series is stationary and we will develop some statistical models under that assumption. We then relate these models to observed features of the data.

Autoregressive Moving Average (ARMA) Models

The models we now consider contain two components: *autoregression (AR)* and a *moving average (MA)*. Just as autocorrelation is an association between past and present values, autoregression is a regression-like relationship between the current value and past values of a series. We begin by considering only the autoregressive component and then examine the moving average element before combining the two in a single model.

6.2.1 The First-Order Autoregressive Model

The simplest autoregressive model is the first-order scheme, designated AR(1) and written as

$$Y_t = \delta + \phi Y_{t-1} + \varepsilon_t, \tag{6.3}$$

where ε_t denotes the random error term, subject to the same set of assumptions as those made in Section 5.1.2, namely,

- The errors are independent of each other
- The errors are normally distributed with zero means and constant variance σ^2

The parameter δ may be interpreted as an intercept term, whereas ϕ is a slope term. When ϕ is positive, high values in the series tend to be followed by high values (and low by low). When ϕ is negative, a pattern high–low–high–low is to be expected.

The AR(1) model is stationary if and only if $-1 < \phi < 1$. We then have

$$E(Y_t) = \mu = \delta/(1 - \phi)$$
$$V(Y_t) = \omega^2 = \sigma^2/(1 - \phi^2)$$
$$Corr(Y_t, Y_{t-k}) = \phi^k \quad k = 1, 2, \ldots$$

The proof is given in Appendix 6A. Note that the autocorrelations decline geometrically; for example, when $\phi = 0.8$, successive terms are 0.8, 0.64, 0.512, . . . , as illustrated in Figure 6.2. Note also that when ϕ is negative, the signs alternate. Further, when $\phi = 0.4$, the values die away much more quickly. These patterns can be used to assist in the choice of a suitable model, which we discuss in Section 6.4.

FIGURE 6.2   ACF FOR AR(1) SCHEME WITH $\phi = 0.8$, $\phi = -0.8$ AND $\phi = 0.4$

(Continued)

FIGURE 6.2 (CONTINUED)

© Cengage Learning 2013.

We can now gain more insight into the concept of stationarity. Suppose that $Y_1 = 120$, $\mu = 100$, and $\phi = 0.8$, and for the moment set the error terms equal to zero. Then successive terms in the series are, from equation (6.3),

$$Y_2 = 100 * (1 - 0.8) + 0.8Y_1 = 20 + 0.8 * 120 = 116$$
$$Y_3 = 20 + 0.8 * 116 = 112.8,$$

and so on, so that the next values in the series are 110.24, 108.19, and 106.55. By time 10, we have the value $Y_{10} = 102.68$, and by time 25, $Y_{25} = 100.09$. That is, the series converges toward the mean value; the series is said to be *mean reverting*. By contrast, if we take $\phi = 1.2$, successive values are 120, 124, 128.8, and 134.56. By time 10, we have the value $Y_{10} = 203.20$, and by time 25, $Y_{25} = 1689.94$. The series is *explosive*.

6.2.2 Higher Order Autoregressive Models

The second-order autoregressive scheme is specified by adding a *lag-2* term:

$$Y_t = \delta + \phi_1 Y_{t-1} + \phi_2 Y_{t-2} + \varepsilon_t$$
$$\delta = \mu(1 - \phi_1 - \phi_2).$$

The ACF now takes on a greater variety of forms, because there are two parameters to determine its shape rather than one. Some examples are shown in Figure 6.3. The abundance of possible shapes is evident, and we need to develop further tools to assist in model selection (see Section 6.3).

Higher order schemes follow by adding further lags. If we include p lags, we have the set of autoregressive parameters $\{\phi_1, \phi_2, \ldots, \phi_p\}$. The general form of the model is then

$$Y_t = \delta + \phi_1 Y_{t-1} + \phi_2 Y_{t-2} + \cdots + \phi_p Y_{t-p} + \varepsilon_t$$
$$\delta = \mu(1 - \phi_1 - \phi_2 - \cdots - \phi_p).$$

(6.4)

The above result for the mean μ comes from taking expectations of the equation for Y_t (see Appendix 6A). The conditions for stationarity become quite complex and we do not explore them here. Suffice it to say that these conditions are always checked in standard statistical software.

We can go as far back in time as we wish, but relatively small values of p usually suffice, unless the data are seasonal, in which case we might want to include lags of order 4 (quarterly

FIGURE 6.3   ACFs FOR AN AR(2) SCHEME WITH (A) $\phi_1 = 1.1$ AND $\phi_2 = -0.5$ AND (B) $\phi_1 = 0.3$ AND $\phi_2 = 0.5$

© Cengage Learning 2013.

series) or 12 (monthly series). Seasonal models raise additional issues, which we address briefly in Section 6.9.

6.2.3   Pure Moving Average (MA) Models

Pure MA models involve only lagged error terms. The simplest case is the first-order, or MA(1), scheme:

$$Y_t = \mu + \varepsilon_t - \theta\varepsilon_{t-1}. \tag{6.5}$$

No conditions are required to ensure that pure MA models are stationary. For MA(1), we have

$$E(Y_t) = \mu$$
$$V(Y_t) = \sigma^2(1 + \theta^2)$$
$$Corr(Y_t, Y_{t-1}) = -\theta/(1 + \theta^2)$$
$$Corr(Y_t, Y_{t-k}) = 0, \quad k \geq 2.$$

The MA(1) scheme is a short-memory process in that observations two or more periods apart are uncorrelated. Accordingly, it has only a single spike on the ACF, as illustrated in Figure 6.4.

FIGURE 6.4 ACF AND PACF FOR MA(1) SCHEME WITH (A) $\theta = -0.6$ AND
(B) $\theta = 0.6$

© Cengage Learning 2013.

EXAMPLE 6.3 ■ A first-order MA scheme

Suppose that $\varepsilon_1 = 10$, $\mu = 100$, and $\theta = -0.8$. Then, given the values for period 1, the equation for time 2 becomes $Y_2 = \mu - \theta\varepsilon_1 + \varepsilon_2 = 100 + 0.8 * 10 + \varepsilon_2 = 108 + \varepsilon_2$.

The overall summary statistics are

$$E(Y_t) = 100$$
$$V(Y_t) = 9(1 + 0.64) = 14.76$$
$$Corr(Y_t, Y_{t-1}) = 0.8/(1 + 0.64) = 0.488$$
$$Corr(Y_t, Y_{t-k}) = 0, \quad k \geq 2.$$

The MA(1) scheme has two other surprising properties. First of all, the maximum value of the first-order autocorrelation of MA(1) is only 0.5 when $\theta = -1$. (The minimum, -0.5, occurs at $\theta = 1$.) Intuitively, if observations *two* periods apart are uncorrelated, those values *one* period apart cannot be too closely related. The second property is that if $\theta > 1$, then the lagged error has greater weight than the current error. In turn, this state of affairs implies increasing importance for the distant past. To avoid this intuitively unattractive possibility, we make the restriction[1] that $-1 < \theta < 1$. ∎

---

[1] This condition is known as the property of *invertibility*. All the standard software packages impose conditions for invertibility in their estimation procedures, and we will not comment further on this matter.

The extension to higher order schemes, denoted by MA(q) follows directly:

$$Y_t = \mu + \varepsilon_t - \theta_1 \varepsilon_{t-1} - \cdots - \theta_q \varepsilon_{t-q}. \qquad (6.6)$$

As before, μ denotes the mean of the series and the coefficients $\{\theta_1, \theta_2, \ldots, \theta_q\}$ are the moving average parameters. Nonzero autocorrelations exist for only the first q lags for the MA(q) scheme. As q increases, so does the maximum value of the first-order autocorrelation.

6.2.4 Mixed Autoregressive Moving Average (ARMA) Models

The mixed ARMA models follow by combining the autoregressive and moving average elements of equations (6.4) and (6.6) to produce:

$$Y_t = \delta + \phi_1 Y_{t-1} + \cdots + \phi_p Y_{t-p} + \varepsilon_t - \theta_1 \varepsilon_{t-1} - \cdots - \theta_q \varepsilon_{t-q}. \qquad (6.7)$$

Equation (6.7) is referred to as the ARMA(p, q) model; the constant term is given by $\delta = \mu(1 - \phi_1 - \phi_2 - \cdots - \phi_p)$, as with the AR scheme.

EXAMPLE 6.4 ■ An ARMA(1,1) scheme
Suppose that $p = q = 1$, $Y_1 = 120$, $\varepsilon_1 = 10$, $\mu = 100$, $\phi = 0.5$, and $\theta = -0.8$. Then, given these values for period 1, equation (6.7) for period 2 becomes

$$Y_2 = 100(1 - 0.5) + 0.5 * 120 + \varepsilon_2 + 0.8 * 10$$
$$= 118 + \varepsilon_2. \qquad ■$$

6.3 Partial Autocorrelations and Model Selection

We have introduced a variety of possible ARMA models; how do we make an appropriate choice from among the whole set? We continue the approach begun in the last section; that is, we develop the theoretical properties of specific ARIMA models and then compare the sample results with these theoretical forms.

One approach is to prespecify a list of alternatives and try each of them. A number of software packages adopt this approach, and with the declining cost of computing, this option has much to commend it. When the time series seems rather complex and sufficiently long to merit the exploration, we seek to build a customized model. One approach would be to seek a model whose theoretical autocorrelation function matches the sample ACF. However, this matching process can be tricky, as suggested by the variety of shapes shown in Figures 6.2–6.4, so we now seek additional insights to assist in this task. One feature of these figures is that the ACF looks simpler for *MA* schemes than for AR schemes, so we now develop criteria that make it easier to identify AR structure.

6.3.1 The Partial Autocorrelation Function (PACF)

We saw in Figure 6.2 that the theoretical autocorrelations for the AR(1) scheme declined geometrically. It is not easy to look at a sample ACF and decide when it matches up with Figure 6.2. One direct way to explore AR structure would be to estimate successively higher order AR schemes AR(1), AR(2), AR(3), . . . , deciding to stop when the additional terms do not contribute to the explanatory power of the model. Box and Jenkins made use of this idea in creating the partial autocorrelation function (PACF), which we may define as follows:

1. For $k = 1, 2, \ldots$, fit an AR scheme of order k to the data and record the value of the autoregressive coefficient for lag k. Denote this quantity by C_k. That is, we generate a sequence of autoregressive models as given in equation (6.4) and check the last coefficient each time. Table 6.1 illustrates the process for the WFJ Sales data.
2. Plot C_k against k ($=1, 2, 3, \ldots$). For an AR(p) scheme, only the first p values will be nonzero.

TABLE 6.1   ESTIMATED COEFFICIENTS FOR AR(p) SCHEMES FOR WFJ SALES,
            $K = 1, 2, 3$, AND RESULTING VALUES OF THE PARTIAL
            AUTOCORRELATIONS

Lag (k)	ϕ_1	ϕ_2	ϕ_3	C_k
1	0.787			0.787
2	0.647	0.187		0.187
3	0.674	0.281	−0.157	−0.157

Data: WFJ_sales.xlsx.

The preceding statements about zero values apply to the theoretical values. In practice, sampling variation will mean that the coefficients are not exactly zero, but we can check the assumptions by setting 95 percent limits for each value. We should stress that more efficient computational methods exist than the one we have just outlined, but the foregoing definition helps to interpret the PACF. The sample PACF for WFJ Sales is shown up to lag 16 in Figure 6.5.

As with the sample ACF, we need some theoretical benchmarks for the PACF to guide model selection. The theoretical PACFs for some low-order schemes are plotted in Figures 6.6–6.8, which are located on the following two pages.

Now that we have both the ACF and the PACF, we may distinguish AR and *MA* components more readily. Table 6.2 (page 163) summarizes typical shapes that are expected for different schemes. In Section 6.3.2, we use these results to suggest possible models.

FIGURE 6.5   THE PACF FOR WFJ SALES DATA

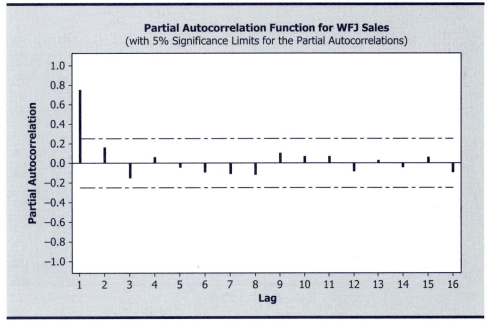

Data: WFJ_sales.xlsx.

FIGURE 6.6   PACF FOR AR(1) SCHEME WITH (A) $\phi = 0.8$, (B) $\phi = -0.8$ AND FOR MA(1) SCHEME WITH (A) $\theta = -0.6$, (B) $\theta = 0.6$

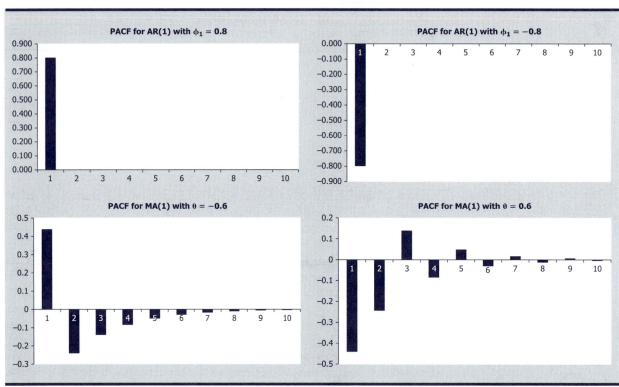

© Cengage Learning 2013.

FIGURE 6.7   PACF FOR AR(2) SCHEME WITH $\phi_1 = 1.1$ AND $\phi_2 = -0.5$

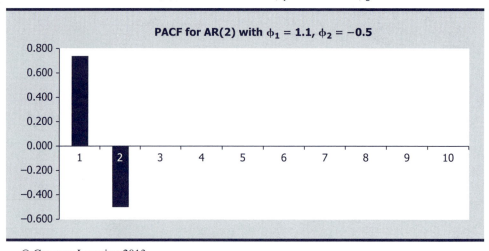

© Cengage Learning 2013.

FIGURE 6.8   ACF AND PACF FOR AN ARMA(1, 1) SCHEME WITH $\phi = 0.8, \theta = -0.7$

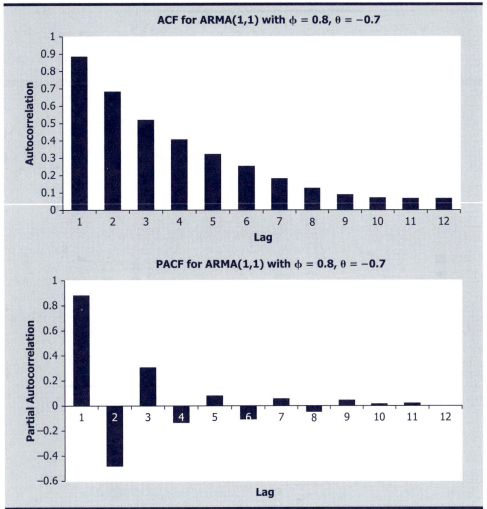

Source: Based upon a generated series of 1000 observations.

TABLE 6.2   ACF AND PACF PATTERNS FOR GENERAL AR, MA, AND ARMA SCHEMES

Function	AR(p) Scheme	MA(q) Scheme	Mixed ARMA Scheme
ACF	Tails off as a damped wave pattern or damped exponential	Finite, q spikes	Tails off as a damped wave pattern or damped exponential
PACF	Finite, p spikes	Tails off as a damped wave pattern or damped exponential	Tails off as a damped wave pattern or damped exponential

© Cengage Learning 2013.

6.3.2 **Model Choice**

We now examine some series to see how well they might conform to one of the ARMA schemes just described.

Figures 6.1 and 6.5 showed the sample ACF and PACF, respectively, for the WFJ Sales data; all 62 observations were used in the calculations. A comparison of these plots with Figures 6.2 and 6.6 suggests that an AR(1) model with a positive coefficient would be appropriate. Figure 6.7 shows the PACF for an AR(2) scheme. Figure 6.8 shows the ACF and PACF for an ARMA(1,1) scheme. Note that there will always be some sampling variation, but we can deal with that by testing whether individual coefficients differ from zero.

The test procedure contrasts a null hypothesis that the (partial) autocorrelation coefficient at a particular lag is zero against the alternative that it is nonzero. The ACF and PACF plots show the significance limits for tests at the 5 percent level. If the coefficient at a particular lag lies outside the limits, the null hypothesis is rejected for that lag.

Figure 6.5 shows that after lag 1 all the higher order partial autocorrelations lie well inside the significance limits. An examination of Figure 6.1 indicates that, although the autocorrelations lie inside the significance limits after lag 3, the systematic pattern of exponential decay in the ACF reinforces the AR(1) identification, as suggested by the description in Table 6.2.

Figure 6.9 shows the sample ACF and PACF for the quarterly Netflix percentage growth series from 2000 to 2007. The series is short and fairly volatile, and the plots suggest that either an AR(1) (check the PACF in Figure 6.6) or an MA(1) (check the ACF in Figure 6.4) scheme would be appropriate. An ARMA(1,1) scheme would be "overkill," because there is no evidence of either a wave pattern or exponential decay. The shorter series results in wider significance limits, as we would expect.

FIGURE 6.9   ACF AND PACF FOR NETFLIX PERCENTAGE GROWTH

(Continued)

FIGURE 6.9   (CONTINUED)

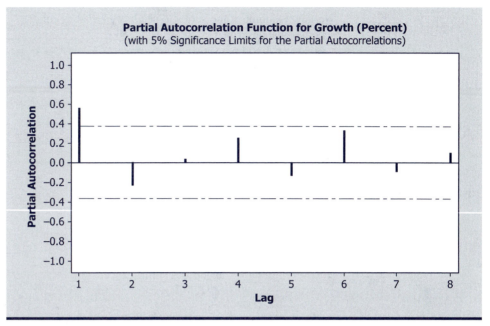

Data shown is from file Netflix.xlsx.

6.3.3 Nonstationary Series

We have stressed the need for a series to be stationary if the selection procedures just described are to be valid. What happens if the series is not stationary? Suppose we were to examine the original Netflix sales series rather than the growth figures? The resulting sample ACF and PACF are shown in Figure 6.10.

Two features stand out in Figure 6.10: The values of the autocorrelations decay very slowly, and the decay is linear rather than geometric. The first partial autocorrelation is close to 1.0, and the remaining ones are much closer to zero than we would expect. At first sight, we might be tempted to propose an AR(1) scheme, but the strong trend in the series, seen originally in Figure 3.9, is clearly a violation of the stationarity condition of a constant mean. The partial autocorrelations seem extraordinarily well behaved, what is sometimes called a Pollyanna effect. That is, they are just too good to be true.

Why does this happen? Suppose that, instead of using the Netflix series, we calculate the ACF and PACF for the sequence of numbers 1 to 32 (an artificial series of the same length). The results are shown in Figure 6.11 and look similar to the plots in Figure 6.10. In short, whenever a series has a strong trend, the resulting plots of the ACF and PACF will tend to display the characteristics found in Figure 6.10.

The appropriate action in these circumstances is to consider differencing the series, as discussed in Section 2.6:

Differencing a Time Series

The (first) difference of the series Y_t is defined as
$$DY_t = Y_t - Y_{t-1}.$$
The second difference of the series Y_t is defined as
$$D^2Y_t = D(DY_t) = DY_t - DY_{t-1}$$
$$= Y_t - 2Y_{t-1} + Y_{t-2}.$$

FIGURE 6.10   ACF AND PACF FOR NETFLIX QUARTERLY SALES

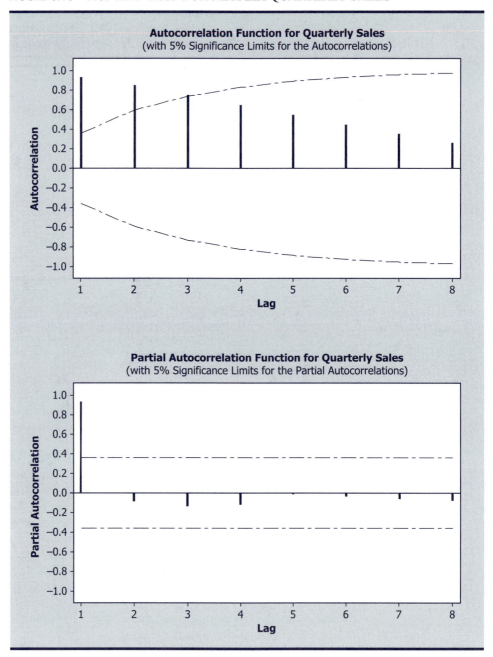

Data: Netflix.xlsx.

This step will often remove the trend and restore stationarity in the mean. If it does not suffice, a second differencing and/or a suitable transformation, such as a log transform (followed by differencing), or the use of growth rates may achieve that goal. Finally, we note that the original series should always be plotted, and that plot will often serve to determine whether the series needs to be differenced. The ACF and PACF for the first differences of the Netflix sales series are shown in Figure 6.12. They are similar to the plots in Figure 6.9 and suggest either AR(1) or MA(1).

FIGURE 6.11   ACF AND PACF FOR THE FIRST 32 NATURAL NUMBERS

© Cengage Learning 2013.

When a series has been differenced, the ARIMA model is written as ARIMA (p, d, q), with p giving the number of autoregressive parameters included in the model, d the degree of differencing, and q the number of moving average parameters. When a series needs to be differenced d times to induce stationarity, we say that the series is *integrated of order d*, written as $I(d)$. Thus, a stationary series is $I(0)$ and a series like the Netflix sales series is probably $I(1)$.

6.3.4   **The Random Walk**

It is important to note that a strong trend is not the only way in which stationarity may be violated. A series may meander, without showing any tendency to revert to a mean.

FIGURE 6.12   ACF AND PACF FOR NETFLIX SALES, DIFFERENCED ONCE

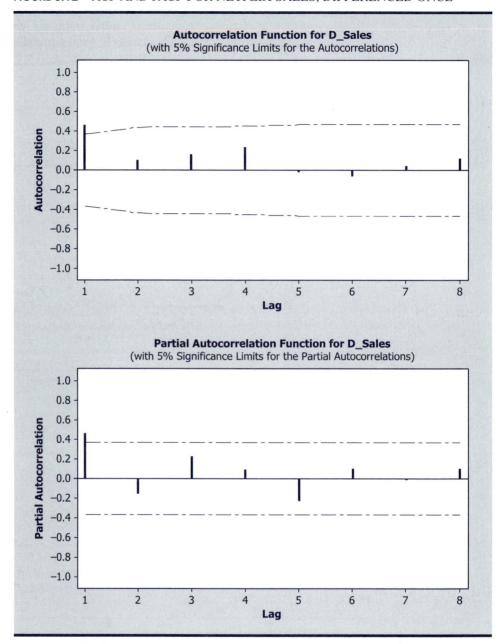

Data: Netflix.xlsx.

A particular example of this phenomenon is the random-walk model, introduced in Section 5.1.1, and so named because successive differences are independent:

$$Y_t = Y_{t-1} + \varepsilon_t \quad \text{or} \quad Y_t - Y_{t-1} = \varepsilon_t.$$

That is, ε_t is independent of ε_s for all $s \neq t$. Four examples of a random walk are shown in Figure 6.13, with $n = 50$. Each has initial value equal to 10, and the error terms are independent and identically distributed normal variables with mean 0 and variance 1. The

ACF and PACF for the first of these series are shown in Figure 6.14. Note the slow decay in the ACF and the Pollyanna effect in the PACF. When we take first differences we are left with only the error term, which is clearly stationary given our usual assumptions about the error process. The ACF and PACF for the first differences also are shown in Figure 6.14. The spike at lag 4 is statistically significant but has no real meaning; these things happen!

FIGURE 6.13   FOUR RANDOM WALKS (*with starting value equal to 10 and normal errors with mean 0 and variance 1*)

© Cengage Learning 2013.

FIGURE 6.14   ACF AND PACF FOR A RANDOM WALK WITH $n = 50$, BEFORE AND AFTER DIFFERENCING

(*Continued*)

FIGURE 6.14   (CONTINUED)

6.4 Model Estimation and Selection

Simpler methods of estimation for ARIMA models rely upon the method of ordinary least squares, in essentially the same way as the state-space models we considered earlier. Other, more sophisticated (and somewhat statistically more efficient) estimation procedures (e.g., maximum likelihood) are available as well. Those seeking a detailed description of these procedures should consult Box *et al.* (2008, Chapter 7) or any other theoretical text. Any standard time series software will provide estimation procedures based upon either least squares or maximum likelihood or both, and we will not dwell on the theoretical details except to note that different assumptions about starting conditions may lead to somewhat different estimates, particularly in shorter series. So don't be too surprised if different software gives different parameter estimates and even different forecasts!

We now examine the series discussed in the previous section.

EXAMPLE 6.5 ■ Fitted model for Netflix percentage growth

Our discussion of this series suggested an AR(1) model or possibly an MA(1) model. We fit both and compare the results in Table 6.3.

The output suggests a simple comparison: Which model has the smaller *RMSE*? Clearly, AR(1) does better, reinforcing our initial assessment that it was the preferred scheme. Further questions remain to be answered: Is it worth including additional terms? Does the current model show any unusual features that need further consideration? We return to these questions in the next section. ■

TABLE 6.3   FITTED MODELS FOR NETFLIX PERCENTAGE GROWTH SERIES
              USING MINITAB

AR(1) Model

Type	Coef	SE Coef	T	P
AR1	0.6654	0.1423	4.68	0.000
Constant	5.101	1.665	3.06	0.005
Mean	15.243	4.976		

Mean Square error = 85.94 with DF = 29

[RMSE = 9.27]

MA(1) Model

Type	Coef	SE Coef	T	P
MA1	−0.4985	0.1603	−3.11	0.004
Constant	14.660	2.667	5.50	0.000
Mean	14.660	2.667		

Mean Square error = 98.77 with DF = 29

[RMSE = 9.94]

Data: Netflix.xlsx.

FIGURE 6.15   ACF AND PACF FOR WFJ SALES DATA, DIFFERENCED ONCE

Data: WFJ_sales.xlsx.

EXAMPLE 6.6 ■ Fitted model for WFJ Sales

Our earlier analysis using Figures 6.1 and 6.5 suggested an AR(1) model. However, further examination of Figure 6.5 suggests that the series might be nonstationary, in which case differencing would be needed. After differencing, we have the ACF and PACF shown in Figure 6.15.

The original series seemed to be AR(1), and the differenced series might reasonably be represented by either an AR(1) or an MA(1), so we have three candidate models. The summary results for each model are given in Table 6.4.

Observe that all three models have 60 DF, based on $n = 62$. The AR(1) model has three parameters: constant, AR coefficient, and variance. However, only the first two parameters

TABLE 6.4   DIFFERENT MODELS FOR WFJ SALES DATA USING MINITAB

AR(1)

Type	Coef	SE Coef	T	P
AR1	0.7867	0.0807	9.75	0.000
Constant	6.8382	0.4460	15.33	0.000
Mean	32.063	2.091		

Mean Square error = 12.304 with DF = 60

[RMSE = 3.51]

ARIMA(1, 1, 0)

Type	Coef	SE Coef	T	P
AR1	−0.2766	0.1267	−2.18	0.033

Mean Square error = 12.933 with DF = 60

[RMSE = 3.60]

ARIMA(0, 1, 1)

Type	Coef	SE Coef	T	P
MA1	0.2686	0.1269	2.12	0.038

Mean Square error = 13.017 with DF = 60

[RMSE = 3.61]

Data: WFJ_sales.xlsx.

involve the loss of a degree of freedom. The models for the differenced series lose one observation through differencing but have only one parameter (other than the variance), so they also have DF = 60. Typically, as here, the models for the differenced series do not include a constant term, because that would imply a fixed trend, something that is not apparent in the WFJ Sales series. Nevertheless, a constant term is sometimes useful, as we shall see in Examples 6.7 and 6.8.

On the basis of the *RMSE*, the AR(1) scheme appears to be slightly better than the other two, but we should also take into account the underlying assumptions. The AR(1) scheme implies stationarity and a fixed mean, whereas the other two are based upon nonstationary schemes. ■

6.4.1   Should We Assume Stationarity?

Are we willing to assume stationarity? We suggest that, for most business series, the volatile nature of the modern economy is such that nonstationary models are usually to be preferred. The rationale for this claim is that if a series is subject to a shift of some kind, a nonstationary scheme adapts to the changing circumstances, whereas a stationary scheme wistfully seeks to return to its original level. This is not a sterile debate based upon statistical niceties, but one that has real policy implications. For example, there is considerable debate as to whether stock prices follow a random walk with drift or are mean reverting. (The series fluctuates about a long-term trend-adjusted mean.) Forecasts made one or two periods ahead may differ little between stationary and nonstationary models, but longer term trends and associated prediction intervals become very different.

TABLE 6.5   MSE FOR DIFFERENT ARIMA MODELS FOR NETFLIX SALES, LOG SERIES USING MINITAB

Model	MSE $\times 10^2$	RMSE $\times 10$	DF
AR(1), AR(2)	Cannot be fitted; violates stationarity assumption		
MA(1)	41.92	6.47	30
MA(2)	11.64	3.41	29
ARIMA(0,1,1)+C	0.693	0.83	29
ARIMA(1,1,0)+C	0.609	0.78	29
ARIMA(1,1,1)+C	0.619	0.79	28

Data: Netflix.xlsx.

EXAMPLE 6.7 ■ Fitted model for Netflix data

We have already seen that the percentage changes in Netflix sales follow an AR(1) scheme with a constant term to allow for the steady growth. Thus, we could either work with the percentage change series as in Section 3.5.2, or consider a logarithmic transform for the original series. The best-fitting model for the Netflix is ARIMA(1,1,0)+C, as shown in Table 6.5, where "+C" refers to the inclusion of a constant term. This model leads to a special case of the damped linear-trend forecast function described in Section 3.6. This is an example of the observation that many ARIMA models have state space (exponential smoothing) equivalents. Failure to recognize the need to difference would carry a huge penalty in this case.   ■

EXAMPLE 6.8 ■ Fitted model for U.S. Retail Sales (*US_retail_sales.xlsx*)

We now consider a longer series, that for monthly retail sales in the United States (de-seasonalized) for the period from January 1992 to November 2008. As seen in Figure 1.4 (reproduced here), the series has a very strong upward trend, so the ACF and PACF conform to the general shapes shown in Figure 6.14. After taking first differences, we arrive at the ACF and PACF shown in Figure 6.16.

FIGURE 1.4   SEASONALLY ADJUSTED SERIES FOR U.S. MONTHLY TOTAL SALES FOR RETAIL AND FOOD SERVICES

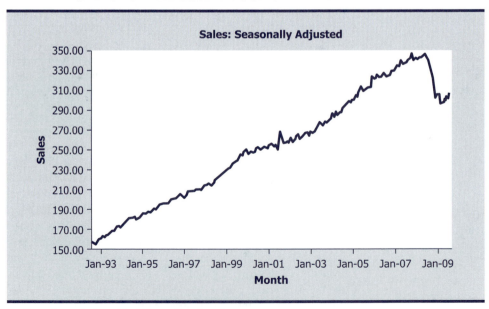

Data shown is from file US_retail_sales.xlsx.

FIGURE 6.16   ACF AND PACF FOR FIRST DIFFERENCES OF U.S. RETAIL SALES
                  (SEASONALLY ADJUSTED)

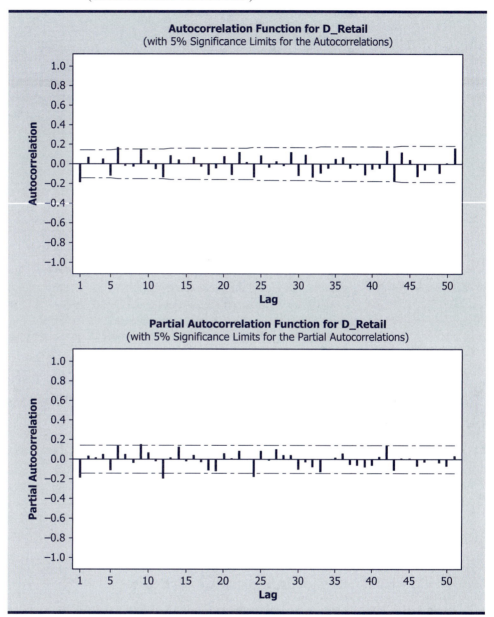

Data: US_retail_sales.xlsx.

The models suggested for the differenced series by the ACF and PACF are AR(1) and MA(1). We may or may not wish to include a constant term; these plots provide no guidance in that regard. Following these initial choices, both models were fitted, with and without a constant term. The summary results are given in Table 6.6. The need for a constant in the model may be determined with the use of the diagnostics to be developed in Section 6.5.

For the differenced data with $d = 1$, the results clearly indicate that the inclusion of a constant is desirable. There is little to choose between the AR(1) and MA(1) models for the differenced series and evidently no advantage to adding extra terms. The last entry is interesting. The ARIMA(0,2,2) scheme corresponds to Holt's linear exponential smoothing

TABLE 6.6   SUMMARY RESULTS FOR ARIMA MODELS FOR U.S. RETAIL SALES

ARIMA Model	Constant	MSE ($\times 10^{-4}$)	RMSE ($\times 10^{-2}$)
(1,1,0)	No	87.0	9.33
(1,1,0)	Yes	78.0	8.83
(0,1,1)	No	87.1	9.33
(0,1,1)	Yes	78.2	8.84
(2,1,0)	Yes	78.4	8.85
(0,1,2)	Yes	78.3	8.85
(1,1,1)	Yes	78.4	8.85
(0,2,2)	No	77.7	8.81

Data: US_retail_sales.xlsx.

(*LES*) method, introduced in Section 3.4. We demonstrate this equivalence in Section 6.8. The estimates for the ARIMA(0,2,2) scheme are as follows:

Final Estimates of Parameters

Type	Coef	SE Coef	T	P
MA1	1.1913	0.0694	17.16	0.000
MA2	−0.2854	0.0795	−3.59	0.000

Both parameters are statistically significant. These results lead to two questions:

- Is it reasonable to use *MSE* or, equivalently, *RMSE* as a basis for comparison when some models contain more parameters than others?
- Are we confident that the model chosen is the best available? We need to examine diagnostics, just as we did for the state-space models in Chapter 5.

As we observed in Section 5.3, for the state-space models, there are two ways to answer the first question. One is to use a hold-out sample in which, at each step, the next observation is included and the model is reestimated before generating a new set of forecasts. The second possibility is to use information criteria, as introduced in Section 5.3.2. Because the two approaches use different sets of information, the conclusions may vary and both can provide useful insights.

6.4.2   Use of Information Criteria

The Akaike information criterion was defined in Section 5.3.2, as

$$AIC = \ln(MSE) + 2p/n, \tag{6.8}$$

whereas the Bayesian information criterion was given by

$$BIC = \ln(MSE) + p\ln(n)/n. \tag{6.9}$$

The results for the eight models considered in Example 6.8 are summarized in Table 6.7. In general, the number of parameters (*NP*) involved is defined as follows for ARIMA models:

> *The number of parameters (NP) is*
> *NP* = number of AR parameters + number of MA parameters + 1 (for the variance)
>   + 1 (if a constant is included).

TABLE 6.7   VALUES OF INFORMATION CRITERIA FOR ARIMA MODELS FOR U.S. RETAIL SALES

		ARIMA				
Model	Constant	Sample size	NP	RMSE	AIC	BIC
1,1,0	no	202	2	2949	16.00	16.03
1,1,0	yes	202	3	2793	15.90	15.95
0,1,1	no	202	2	2952	16.00	16.03
0,1,1	yes	202	3	2797	15.90	15.95
2,1,0	yes	202	4	2799	15.91	15.98
0,1,2	yes	202	4	2798	15.91	15.98
1,1,1	yes	202	4	2799	15.91	15.98
0,2,2	no	201	3	2789	15.90	15.95

Data: US_retail_sales.xlsx.

The sample size should take account of differencing, so that although the original series contains 203 observations, we use $n = 202$ in the calculations of *AIC* and *BIC* after differencing once and $n = 201$ after differencing twice. Different programs vary in their exact definitions of the criteria, but the differences are typically minor in terms of how the programs rank competing models. The versions set forth here have the advantage that both criteria approach a stable value as the number of observations increases.

The results in Table 6.7 confirm the value of including the constant, as expected. *AIC* points to a virtual dead heat among the models with a constant term included, but *BIC* points to the value of the (1,1,0)+C model with fewer parameters. With shorter series, the differences would be more pronounced. A slight surprise comes with the additional entry in the last row of Table 6.7. The ARIMA(0,2,2) model underlies the linear exponential smoothing (Holt's) method and is tied with ARIMA(1,1,0)+C when *BIC* is used. The difference between the two models lies in whether to use a fixed or a changing slope. With the benefit of hindsight, we might prefer *LES*, which embodies a changing slope, given the recession that began in the United States in December 2007.

What should we conclude from this analysis? We would do well to recall the comment made by George Box at the beginning of this chapter. The ARIMA system produces a rich array of possible models, and it is quite common to find that two or more such models appear to perform equally well. Which version should we choose? From the perspective of point forecasts, it probably does not matter much, provided that we have incorporated an adequate amount of differencing and a constant where needed. The situation is more complex when we turn to interval forecasts, as we shall see in Section 6.7.1.

6.4.3   How Much Differencing?

We initially decided on the degree of differencing in a heuristic fashion, but, as illustrated by Table 6.7, the information criteria also provide useful guidance in this respect.[2] Overall, the following checks are worthwhile:

1. *Plot the series.* If a pronounced trend exists, differencing is probably required.
2. *Examine the ACF and PACF.* Slow decay in the ACF and a Pollyanna effect in the PACF are telltale signs that differencing is required.

---

[2]Some care is needed when we are using information criteria to decide on the order of differencing; see Hyndman, Koehler, Ord, and Snyder (2008, Chapter 12) for details. However, the forms stated in this chapter are usually adequate.

3. *Compare values of the information criteria.* As we saw in Example 6.7 with the Netflix data, an inadequate level of differencing will usually lead to a greatly inflated value of the MSE and the information criteria.

4. *Use a hold-out sample to compare forecasting performance.* As we have indicated throughout the book, this procedure is the ultimate test, provided that sufficient data exist.

6.4.4 Formal Tests for Differencing

A more formal approach to the decision on the degree of differencing is provided by hypothesis testing. The classical tests in this regard are known as the Dickey–Fuller tests, although several others have also been developed. A full description is provided by Box *et al.* (2008, pp. 281–287) and Diebold (2007, pp. 297–302), among others. These tests are complicated to apply, and we are not convinced that they provide sufficient additional value to justify the effort required. The problem arises because the tests are not powerful at discriminating between the alternatives (e.g., $d = 0$ and $d = 1$). But for econometricians, this is a hot topic, so we have included further details in Appendix 10C to illustrate the procedure.

 ## 6.5 Model Diagnostics

One approach to improving our initial model is to use diagnostic methods based upon the residuals. (The residual plots we use here are the same as those we shall use for regression analysis in Chapter 8.) We plot four figures that directly involve the residuals, along with the ACF and PACF of the residuals. The plots may be used to determine the key features of the residuals, as summarized in Table 6.8.

We first consider the diagnostics for the ARIMA(1,1,0) model for U.S. retail sales, fitted without a constant. The plots are given in Figures 6.17 and 6.18.

The plots in Figure 6.18 indicate that the addition of further AR or *MA* terms is not warranted since there is little pattern to be seen, although the slight spikes at lags 12 and 24 suggest that the seasonal adjustment process might not be perfect. The practical difference to the forecasts would be negligible. Figure 6.17 indicates a clear outlier in the differenced series (October sales minus September sales in 2001), an issue to which we return in Section 6.6. An outlier will often be signaled in the normal probability plot (NPP), as well as in the plots of the residuals. The series also shows increased volatility over recent years, casting doubt on the assumption of constant variance. The remaining feature is somewhat unusual: The model under consideration does not include a constant term, and a careful viewing of the two plots of residuals reveals that most of them lie above the horizontal axis, indicating the need for a constant in the model, as we saw from the results in Table 6.7.

When we include the constant and rerun the model, we obtain the residual plots shown in Figure 6.19. The residuals are now centered about a zero mean, but the other diagnostics are essentially the same as before. In particular, the NPP and the residuals plots still signal the large outlier. As we saw in Table 6.7, adding the constant produces a sizeable reduction in the *RMSE*.

6.5.1 The Ljung–Box Test

Our diagnostics so far have been based purely on graphical procedures. Such an approach is entirely reasonable, but can be somewhat subjective and may also be time consuming if a large number of series is to be investigated. The primary information that we glean from plots like those in Figure 6.18 is whether or not we have missed a significant element of the dependence structure of the series. This question may be formulated in a

TABLE 6.8   INTERPRETATION OF DIAGNOSTICS FOR RESIDUALS FROM ARIMA MODELS

Diagnostic Plots	Issues to Be Addressed	Indication of Problems	Remedial Action to Be Taken
Normal probability plot (NPP) and histogram (H)	1. The residuals may not be normally distributed. 2. Are there any outliers?	1. The residuals do not follow a straight line (NPP), or the histogram is not bell shaped (H). 2. Individual points are far removed from the overall plot (NPP) or other observations (H).	1. Consider a transformation. 2. Adjust outliers.
Residuals versus fitted values	1. Is there evidence of nonlinearity? 2. Are there any outliers? 3. Does the series show increasing or decreasing variance with the size of the observations (heteroscedasticity)? 4. (*Only when the model does not contain a constant term*) Is the model consistent with a zero mean for the errors?	1. The plot shows curvature. 2. Individual points are far removed from the overall plot. 3. The plot forms an increasing or decreasing funnel shape. 4. The residuals plot shows evidence of a nonzero mean.	1. Consider a transformation. 2. Adjust outliers. 3. Consider a transformation. 4. Add a constant term to the model.
Residuals versus observation order	1. Is there any evidence of residual autocorrelation? 2. Are there any outliers? 3. Does the series show increasing or decreasing variance over time (changes in volatility)?	1. The plot shows long runs of residuals with the same sign (positive autocorrelation) or a zigzag pattern (negative autocorrelation). 2. Individual points are far removed from the overall plot. 3. The plot forms an increasing or decreasing funnel shape.	1. Consider adding terms to the model. 2. Adjust outliers. 3. Use a transformation to stabilize the variance.
Autocorrelation function (ACF)	1. Are additional differences required? 2. Should more moving average terms be added? 3. Is there too much differencing?	1. The ACF shows a slow linear decay. 2. The ACF shows significant spikes. 3. The lag 1 autocorrelation is close to its minimum value of -0.5.	1. Try further differencing. 2. Include further MA terms. 3. Reduce the amount of differencing.
Partial autocorrelation function (PACF)	1. Are additional differences required? 2. Should additional AR terms be added?	1. A "Pollyanna" effect exists. 2. The PACF shows significant spikes.	1. Try further differencing. 2. Include further AR terms.

© Cengage Learning 2013.

hypothesis-testing framework as a comparison of the null hypothesis for the set of auto-correlations $\{\rho_k\}$,

$$H_0: \rho_1 = \rho_2 = \cdots = \rho_K = 0,$$

with the alternative,

$$H_1: \text{not all } \rho_k = 0, \quad k = 1, 2, \ldots, K$$

FIGURE 6.17   RESIDUALS PLOT FOR ARIMA(1,1,0) MODEL FOR U.S. RETAIL SALES

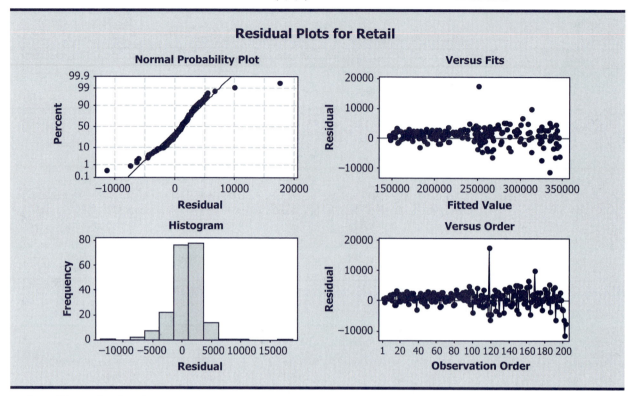

Data: US_retail_sales.xlsx.

FIGURE 6.18   ACF AND PACF FOR RESIDUALS FROM THE ARIMA(0,1,1) MODEL FOR U.S. RETAIL SALES

(Continued)

FIGURE 6.18 (CONTINUED)

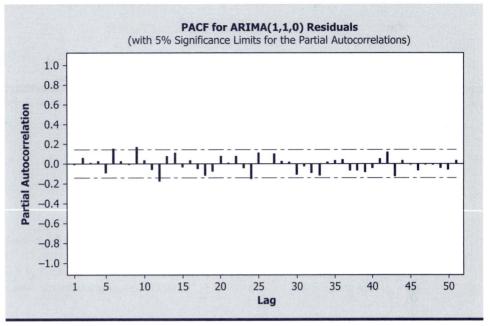

Data: US_retail_sales.xlsx.

FIGURE 6.19 RESIDUALS PLOTS FOR ARIMA(0,1,1)+C MODEL FOR U.S. RETAIL SALES

Data: US_retail_sales.xlsx.

A test for this purpose was developed by Box and Pierce and refined by Ljung and Box. (See Box *et al.*, 2008, pp. 338–343, for details.) The procedure is based upon sample auto-correlations $\{r_k\}$, using the criterion

$$Q = n(n + 2) \sum_{k=1}^{K} \frac{r_k^2}{n - k},$$ (6.10)

where

      n = number of observations in the series after any differencing
      k = lag
      K = number of time lags to be used in the test.

When the null hypothesis is true, the large-sample distribution of Q is chi-square with degrees of freedom $(K - p - q)$. The P-values are based upon this approximate distribution.

EXAMPLE 6.9 ■ An application of the Ljung–Box statistic to the U.S. retail sales model

It is common practice to use several values of K when testing these hypotheses. For example, for the ARIMA(1,1,0)+C model, Minitab provides the following output:

Modified Box-Pierce (Ljung–Box) Chi-Square statistic				
Lag	12	24	36	48
Chi-Square	18.9	35.2	53.2	78.9
DF	10	22	34	46
P-Value	0.042	0.037	0.019	0.002

Using the conventional testing procedure

      Reject H_0 if P-value < significance level (α),

we would reject the null hypothesis at the 5 percent level, but not the 1 percent level, for lags up to 12, 24, and 36 (i.e., up to three years ahead). The departures from the null hypothesis seem to become more severe as we move to four years ahead. These results suggest that the model is somewhat inadequate, but the ACF and PACF plots suggest that improvements in short-term forecasting are unlikely. ■

Similar analyses for the ARIMA(0,2,2) model are left as Exercise 6.10.

 ## 6.6   Outliers Again

The plots in Figure 6.17 reveal a large outlier. What should be done about this extreme value with respect to generating forecasts? The first point to observe is that our concern is to generate forecasts based upon what we believe to be an appropriate model or description of future events. If occasional extreme events are likely to be repeated (such as large sales of beer in the week before the Super Bowl) they can be modeled with techniques we describe in Section 9.7. However, when the events are unique, we may need to adjust the observations involved. A detailed discussion is beyond our scope, and the interested reader may consult Tsay (2005, pp. 558–565) and Koehler, Snyder, Ord, and Beaumont (2012). For the present, we resort to the simple fix of fitting the initial model and then replacing the outlier by its estimated value.

EXAMPLE 6.10 ■ ARIMA(1,1,0)+C model for U.S. retail sales after adjusting for an outlier

After adjusting for the outlier (October 2001), we may summarize the revised model as follows:

Type	Coef	SE Coef	T	P
AR 1	−0.1044	0.0718	−1.45	0.147
Constant	933.3	178.7	5.22	0.000

Differencing: 1 regular difference

Number of observations: Original series 203, after differencing 202

Residuals: RMSE = 2540,   DF = 200

Modified Box–Pierce (Ljung–Box) Chi-Square statistic

Lag	12	24	36	48
Chi-Square	20.9	37.0	47.7	67.0
DF	10	22	34	46
P-Value	0.022	0.024	0.060	0.023

Comparing these results with the earlier set, we see that the AR coefficient is no longer significant, being about half its previous size, and that the *RMSE* has been reduced from 2793 to 2540, a reduction of about 9 percent. The residuals plots, shown in Figure 6.20, are

FIGURE 6.20   RESIDUALS PLOTS FOR U.S. RETAIL SALES, AFTER ADJUSTING FOR THE OUTLIER

Data: US_retail_sales.xlsx.

similar to those obtained before, as seen in Figure 6.18, apart from the removal of the outlier. The ACF and PACF diagnostics are little changed, so we omit them. Additional outliers might be considered for adjustment, but we do not pursue the question further. ■

The ARIMA(0,2,2) yields a slightly lower *RMSE* but worse Ljung-Box diagnostics. Neither model does well at the very end of the series, when sales are declining. Because the residuals show clear evidence of increasing variation at the end of the series, a transformation should be considered, either along the lines of Section 6.7.2 or using a Box–Cox transform as in Section 3.9. This endeavor is left to the reader as Exercises 6.6 and 6.7.

 ## 6.7   Forecasting with ARIMA Models

Once an appropriate model has been identified, we can proceed to create forecasts. Referring back to the general form in equation (6.7) in Section 6.2.4, we observe that it is necessary to provide input values for both error terms and past values of the series. The general process is as follows:

Y_t values: Use observations already recorded where available; for values not yet recorded, insert the latest available forecast.

ε_t values: Use recorded one-step-ahead residuals where available; set future errors in the equation equal to zero (best available forecast).

EXAMPLE 6.11 ■ Forecasting for WFJ Sales using AR(1) and ARIMA(0,1,1)
From Table 6.4, the AR(1) model is

$$Y_{t+1} = 6.838 + 0.787Y_t + \varepsilon_{t+1}.$$

Applying the general process just given, we find that the one-step-ahead forecast for period 63, given period 62 as the forecast origin, is

$$F_{63} = F_{63}(1) = 6.8382 + 0.7867Y_{62}$$
$$= 6.8382 + 0.7867 * 34.1282$$
$$= 33.69.$$

Likewise, the two-step-ahead forecast is

$$F_{64}(2) = 6.8382 + 0.7867F_{63}$$
$$= 6.8382 + 0.7867 * 33.6878$$
$$= 33.34. \quad ■$$

The forecasts for the next four weeks, with period 62 as the forecast origin, are as follows:

Period	Forecast	Lower Limit 95% PI	Upper Limit 95% PI
63	33.69	26.81	40.56
64	33.34	24.59	42.09
65	33.07	23.34	42.80
66	32.85	22.56	43.14

The lower and upper limits in the table define the 95 percent prediction intervals for the forecasts. We discuss prediction intervals in Section 6.7.1.

A similar exercise may be carried out for the ARIMA(0,1,1) model:

$$Y_{t+1} = Y_t - 0.2686\varepsilon_t + \varepsilon_{t+1}$$
$$F_{63} = Y_{62} - 0.2686e_{62}$$
$$= 34.182 - 0.2686 * 5.7152$$
$$= 32.59.$$

The two-step-ahead forecast and all later forecasts are

$$F_{62+h}(h) = 32.59.$$

This result holds because the best forecasts for future error terms are zero. The complete summary is as follows:

Period	Forecast	Lower Limit 95% PI	Upper Limit 95% PI
63	32.59	25.52	39.67
64	32.59	23.83	41.36
65	32.59	22.42	42.77
66	32.59	21.18	44.01

In Section 6.8, we show that the ARIMA(0,1,1) model corresponds to the local-level state-space scheme, which underpins simple exponential smoothing—hence, the constant forecasts multiple steps ahead.

The two sets of forecasts are not materially different in this case. Indeed, in the short term AR(1) and ARIMA(0,1,1) models often produce similar short-term forecasts if the estimated AR parameter is close to 1.0. In the longer term, of course, AR(1) is mean reverting (to the mean of 32.06) whereas the other scheme is not.

6.7.1 Prediction Intervals

The prediction intervals are evaluated by means of the same general approach that we described in Section 5.2. The intervals require calculation of the variances for forecasts one or more steps ahead. We illustrate with the AR(1) and ARIMA(0,1,1) schemes. The principles are the same for other models, although the details become more involved.

We start with the AR(1) model

$$Y_{t+1} = \delta + \phi Y_t + \varepsilon_{t+1}.$$

For the time period $(t + 2)$, we can substitute the expression for Y_{t+1} to obtain

$$Y_{t+2} = \delta + \phi Y_{t+1} + \varepsilon_{t+2}$$
$$= \delta + \phi[\phi Y_t + \varepsilon_{t+1}] + \varepsilon_{t+2}$$
$$= \varepsilon_{t+2} + \phi\varepsilon_{t+1} + (\text{constant terms}).$$

The process can be repeated successively for longer lead times. This step is achieved by substituting the model back into itself so that we need only deal with independent error terms. Just the portion of the equation involving the error terms contributes to future uncertainty, so the error component for the one-step-ahead forecast is ε_{t+1}. Because the errors are independent with zero means and constant variance σ^2, it follows that the one-step-ahead forecast has variance σ^2. Likewise, the two-step-ahead forecast has variance $\sigma^2[1 + \phi^2]$ using the result from Appendix A that for independent random variables $\text{Variance}(AX + BY) = A^2\text{VAR}(X) + B^2\text{VAR}(Y)$. When we go out h steps ahead, the variance becomes $\sigma^2[1 + \phi^2 + \cdots + \phi^{2h-2}]$. The series is stationary, so as h increases, the variance levels out to $\sigma^2/[1 - \phi^2]$.

TABLE 6.9   FORECAST RMSE FOR WFJ SALES

Horizon, h	AR(1)	ARIMA(0,1,1)
1	3.51	3.61
2	4.47	3.74
5	5.42	4.10
10	5.66	4.64
20	5.69	5.56
50	5.69	7.69
σ	3.51	3.61
ϕ	0.7867	
θ		0.2686

Data: WFJ_sales.xlsx.

By similar arguments, it may be shown that the ARIMA(0,1,1) scheme has a one-step-ahead error variance equal to σ^2. Its two-step-ahead error variance is $\sigma^2/[1 + \theta^2]$, and when we go out h steps ahead, the error variance is $\sigma^2[1 + (h-1)\theta^2]$. As h increases, the variance increases without limit. This property reflects the nonstationarity and non-mean-reverting behavior of this scheme and contrasts sharply with that of the AR(1) scheme. Thus, although the one-step-ahead forecasts may be similar and have similar prediction intervals, the long-term implications of the two models are very different, which serves to make long-term forecasting a hazardous occupation!

EXAMPLE 6.12 ■ Forecast *RMSE* for WFJ Sales

We may compute the forecast *RMSE* for these two models by taking the square roots of the variances just obtained. The results for different forecasting horizons are shown in Table 6.9.   ■

Note: Although we have not discussed empirical prediction intervals for ARIMA models, the approach described in Section 2.8.3 may be used.

6.7.2   Forecasting Using Transformations

The same general approach follows for all transformations:

- Transform the series.
- Generate the point forecasts and prediction intervals for the transformed series.
- Convert the point forecasts and prediction intervals back to the original units.

We use the logarithmic transform to illustrate the process:

- Convert Y_t to the new series $y_t = \ln(Y_t)$.
- Develop the model for y_t.
- Generate forecasts for future values, say, f_{n+h}, with associated lower and upper prediction limits l_{n+h} and u_{n+h}.
- Convert back to the original units to obtain the forecast: $F_{n+h} = \exp(f_{n+h})$, the lower limit $L_{n+h} = \exp(l_{n+h})$, and the upper limit $U_{n+h} = \exp(u_{n+h})$.

The limits for the transformed series will be symmetric about the forecasts, so the limits for the original series, after transforming back, will not be.

EXAMPLE 6.13 ■ **Forecasting for Netflix Sales, using ARIMA(1,1,0)+C for the logarithms**

The fitted model may be summarized as follows:

Type	Coef	SE Coef	T	P
AR 1	0.6658	0.1426	4.67	0.000
Constant	0.04553	0.01402	3.25	0.003

Differencing: 1 regular difference
RMSE = 0.078, DF = 29

Modified Box-Pierce (Ljung-Box) Chi-Square Statistic

Lag	12	24
Chi-Square	12.6	23.8
DF	10	22
P-Value	0.245	0.360

The model may be written as

$$Dy_{t+1} = 0.04553 + 0.6658Dy_t + \varepsilon_{t+1}.$$

In turn, this expression becomes

$$y_{t+1} = y_t + 0.04553 + 0.6658(y_t - y_{t-1}) + \varepsilon_{t+1}$$
$$= 0.04553 + 1.6658y_t - 0.6658 \, y_{t-1} + \varepsilon_{t+1}.$$

Applying the process given earlier, we find that the one-step-ahead forecast for the transformed series is

$$f_{n+1} = 0.04553 + 1.6658y_n - 0.6658y_{n-1}$$
$$= 0.04553 + 1.6658 * 5.7116 - 0.6658 * 5.6835$$
$$= 5.7759.$$

Likewise, the two-step-ahead forecast is

$$f_{n+2}(2) = 0.04553 + 1.665f_{n+1} - 0.6658y_n$$
$$= 0.04553 + 1.6658 * 5.7759 - 0.6658 * 5.7116$$
$$= 5.8642. \qquad ■$$

The remaining forecasts for 2008 and the upper and lower 95 percent prediction interval limits for log Sales are as follows:

Year	Quarter	Forecast	Lower Limit 95% PI	Upper Limit 95% PI
2008	1	5.77589	5.62288	5.92889
2008	2	5.86421	5.56692	6.16149
2008	3	5.96854	5.52977	6.40732
2008	4	6.08354	5.51095	6.65614

The extra decimal places are retained for numerical accuracy because we must transform back to the original series of interest, Netflix Sales, only *after* completing the forecasting

TABLE 6.10   POINT FORECASTS AND PREDICTION INTERVALS FOR NETFLIX SALES FOR 2008

Year	Quarter	LOG Model ARIMA(1,1,0)			ARIMA(1,1,0)+C		
		Forecast	Lower Limit 95% PI	Upper Limit 95% PI	Forecast	Lower Limit 95% PI	Upper Limit 95% PI
2008	1	322.4	276.7	375.7	311.3	295.2	327.3
	2	352.2	261.6	474.1	320.4	291.8	348.9
	3	390.9	252.1	606.3	329.6	290.2	369.1
	4	438.6	247.4	777.5	338.9	290.0	387.9

Data: Netflix.xlsx.

operations. The first half of Table 6.10 shows the point forecasts and their prediction intervals, after transforming back to the original units. The final figures are rounded to a level of accuracy that is appropriate for presentation to management.

For comparison, the forecasts from the ARIMA(1,1,0)+C model without applying a transformation are shown in the second panel of Table 6.10. In both cases, the prediction intervals are very wide, although those for the model without the transformation are much narrower. Also, it is worth noting that the forecasts based upon the log transform are more optimistic than those based upon the untransformed data. Such forecast patterns tend to occur when strong growth has been observed in the past, given that the log model assumes a steady percentage growth. On further examination, the log model is seen to imply a steady-state growth (denoted by the subscript ss for steady state) of $Dy_{ss} = \dfrac{0.04553}{1 - 0.6658} = 0.136$, $\dfrac{0.04553}{1 - 0.6658} = 0.136$ or 13.6 percent per quarter! This figure is calculated from the expression

$$Dy_{ss} = 0.4553 + 0.6658 \, Dy_{ss}$$

by setting $Dy_t = Dy_{ss}$ for all t in the AR model and then solving for Dy_{ss}. Such a figure is seen to be unrealistic on the basis of recent results. Given the start-up nature of the company, the results in 2000 indicate a performance that could not be sustained in later years. In other words, the assumption of stationarity (for the differences of the logarithms) is not appropriate. Dropping the data for 2000 produces more plausible results; the details are left to the reader as Exercise 6.11.

 6.8 # Seasonal ARIMA Models

Seasonal ARIMA models can be developed along the same lines as those developed already, but the details become quite intricate. Rather than consider the complete framework, we will examine just one example, but one that has proved very useful in applications.

When we developed seasonal exponential smoothing methods in Chapter 4, we began with a purely seasonal scheme, and we may do the same for ARIMA modeling. Given m seasons, the purely seasonal ARIMA analogue to purely seasonal exponential smoothing is

$$D_m Y_t = Y_t - Y_{t-m} = \varepsilon_t - \theta_m \varepsilon_{t-m}. \tag{6.11}$$

We use D_m to denote the mth-order difference $Y_t - Y_{t-m}$, and the seasonal parameter is θ_m. Equation (6.11) would lead to the purely seasonal forecasting equation (4.4), with $\gamma = 1 - \theta_m$.

A full MA scheme is then achieved by superimposing regular and seasonal ARIMA components:

$$DD_m Y_t = \varepsilon_t - \theta_1 \varepsilon_{t-1} - \theta_m \varepsilon_{t-m} + \theta_1 \theta_m \varepsilon_{t-m-1}. \tag{6.12}$$

The left-hand side represents taking both a regular and a seasonal difference:

$$\begin{aligned} DD_m Y_t &= D(Y_t - Y_{t-m}) \\ &= (Y_t - Y_{t-m}) - (Y_{t-1} - Y_{t-m-1}) \\ &= Y_t - Y_{t-1} - Y_{t-m} + Y_{t-m-1} \end{aligned}$$

Differencing in the reverse order produces the same result, as the reader may verify. One final wrinkle to notice is that equation (6.12) has only two *MA* parameters rather than three. This results from the way the regular and seasonal elements have been overlaid.

Model (6.12) is represented as an ARIMA$(0,1,1)(0,1,1)_m$ scheme to denote that we have first-order differences and *MA* components for both the regular and seasonal components and the seasonal element is of m periods' duration. This scheme is known as the "airline model," because the initial application by Box and Jenkins related to a time series on numbers of airline passengers. We may include additional autoregressive and moving average terms, but we do not pursue that topic here. (See Box *et al.*, 2008, Chapter 9, or one of a number of other technical texts.) Fortunately for us, many specialized computer programs, such as Forecast Pro and Autobox, will perform model selection automatically, even with seasonal models. (See Appendix C for details.)

EXAMPLE 6.14 ■ Seasonal state-space and ARIMA schemes

As before, we start out from a state-space model. The particular form we consider is the additive Holt–Winters scheme set forth in Section 5.3.2, but with the trend term and equation omitted. That is, we consider the model

$$\begin{aligned} Y_t &= L_{t-1} + S_{t-m} + \varepsilon_t \\ L_t &= L_{t-1} + \alpha \varepsilon_t \\ S_t &= S_{t-m} + \gamma \varepsilon_t. \end{aligned}$$

We follow the same procedure as before and eliminate the state variables. We then arrive at the reduced form

$$\begin{aligned} D_m[DY_t] &= Y_t - Y_{t-1} - Y_{t-m} + Y_{t-m-1} \\ &= \varepsilon_t - (1 - \alpha)\varepsilon_{t-1} - (1 - \gamma)\varepsilon_{t-m} + (1 - \alpha - \gamma)\varepsilon_{t-m-1}. \end{aligned}$$

The reduced model differs slightly from that given in equation (6.12). We may set $\theta_1 = 1 - \alpha$, $\theta_m = 1 - \gamma$, but the final coefficient is then $1 - \alpha - \gamma = \theta_1 + \theta_m - 1$ rather than $\theta_1 \theta_m = 1 - \alpha - \gamma + \alpha\gamma$. Generally speaking, the state-space and ARIMA seasonal models in common use do have different parameter structures. ■

EXAMPLE 6.15 ■ Seasonal model for UK retail sales

Quarterly UK retail sales for the period 1988–2009 are plotted in Figure 6.21.

FIGURE 6.21   UK RETAIL SALES VOLUME, 1988Q1 TO 2009Q3

Data shown is from file UK_retail_sales.xlsx.

The series shows a strong seasonal pattern, with a peak in the fourth quarter as might be expected. Fitting the airline model produces the following results:

Type	Coef	SE Coef	T	P
MA 1	0.2186	0.1097	1.99	0.050
SMA 4	0.1183	0.1145	1.03	0.305

Differencing: 1 regular, 1 seasonal of order 4
Number of observations: Original series 87, after differencing 82
Residuals:

    RMSE = 1.53 DF = 80

Modified Box-Pierce (Ljung–Box) Chi-Square statistic

Lag	12	24	36	48
Chi-Square	15.6	24.2	30.6	37.4
DF	10	22	34	46
P-Value	0.113	0.338	0.635	0.813

The plots of residuals in Figures 6.22 and 6.23 suggest that all is well save that the variability increases over time, a feature that would indicate the consideration of a logarithmic transform. The seasonal *MA* term is not significant and should probably be dropped and the model then reestimated. We leave that as Exercise 6.14 for the reader.   ∎

FIGURE 6.22   RESIDUALS PLOTS FOR UK RETAIL SALES VOLUME, 1988Q1 TO 2009Q3

Data: UK_retail_sales.xlsx.

FIGURE 6.23   ACF AND PACF RESIDUALS PLOTS FOR UK RETAIL SALES
VOLUME, 1988Q1 TO 2009Q3

(Continued)

FIGURE 6.23   (CONTINUED)

Data: UK_retail_sales.xlsx.

6.8.1   Forecasts for Seasonal Models

The general approach is the same as that for the nonseasonal case. That is, we substitute values as follows:

Y_t values: Use observations already recorded where available; for values not yet recorded, insert the latest available forecast.

ε_t values: Use recorded one-step-ahead residuals where available; set future errors in the equation equal to zero (best available forecast).

EXAMPLE 6.16 ■ Forecasts for U.K. retail sales

When we substitute the parameter estimates into equation (6.12), we obtain

$$Y_t - Y_{t-1} - Y_{t-4} + Y_{t-5} = \varepsilon_t - 0.2186\varepsilon_{t-1} - 0.1183\varepsilon_{t-4} + 0.0259\varepsilon_{t-5}. \qquad ■$$

Substituting the values as before, we arrive at the one- through four-step-ahead forecasts shown in the following table (the appropriate prediction intervals are also provided; calculations are via Minitab):

Period	Actual	Residual	Forecast	Lower Limit 95% PI	Upper Limit 95% PI
2008Q4	137.7	−0.97			
2009Q1	102.9	−2.83			
2009Q2	109.5	−0.24			
2009Q3	111.6	0.74			
2009Q4			139.2	136.2	142.2
2010Q1			104.7	100.9	108.5
2010Q2			111.3	106.8	115.7
2010Q3			113.3	108.3	118.3
2010Q4			140.9	133.9	148.0

State-Space and ARIMA Models

This chapter has been devoted to ARIMA models in an apparent complete break from the exponential smoothing methods of Chapters 3 and 4 and the state-space models developed in Chapter 5. All too often, this is how the material is treated, perhaps along with an occasional (false) statement that exponential smoothing is "just a special case of ARIMA."

We first show how the state-space and ARIMA models are related and where differences arise. The discussion is presented in terms of simple models, but the ideas carry over to a much broader class.

In Section 5.1, we introduced the local-level model for random variable Y in terms of the local level (L) and random error (ε) as

$$
\begin{aligned}
Y_t &= L_{t-1} + \varepsilon_t \\
L_t &= L_{t-1} + \alpha\varepsilon_t
\end{aligned}
\tag{6.13}
$$

If we write down the observation equations for periods t and $t-1$ and then subtract one from the other, we arrive at

$$
Y_t - Y_{t-1} = L_{t-1} - L_{t-2} + \varepsilon_t - \varepsilon_{t-1}.
\tag{6.14}
$$

We can then use the state equation to eliminate the states from the observation equation:

$$
\begin{aligned}
Y_t - Y_{t-1} &= L_{t-1} - L_{t-2} + \varepsilon_t - \varepsilon_{t-1} \\
&= \alpha\varepsilon_{t-1} + \varepsilon_t - \varepsilon_{t-1} \\
&= \varepsilon_t - (1 - \alpha)\varepsilon_{t-1}
\end{aligned}
\tag{6.15}
$$

Equation (6.15) does not involve the state variables and so may be regarded as a *reduced form* of the state-space model (in the sense that the states have been eliminated). The left-hand side of the equation is just the difference, $DY_t = Y_t - Y_{t-1}$.

Finally, this model may be written in the standard ARIMA (0,1,1) notation as

$$
DY_t = \varepsilon_t - \theta\varepsilon_{t-1},
\tag{6.16}
$$

where $\theta = 1 - \alpha$. So, starting with a state space model, we have found the equivalent ARIMA model. Other state-space models may be reduced to ARIMA forms by the same process of eliminating the state variables. We present one more example and refer the reader to Hyndman *et al.* (2008, Chapter 11) for further details.

EXAMPLE 6.17 ■ The damped linear trend model as an ARIMA scheme
The damped linear trend model developed in Section 3.5 is underpinned by the model

$$
\begin{aligned}
Y_t &= L_{t-1} + \phi T_{t-1} + \varepsilon_t \\
L_t &= L_{t-1} + \theta T_{t-1} + \alpha\varepsilon_t \\
T_t &= \phi T_{t-1} + \beta\varepsilon_t.
\end{aligned}
$$

We may eliminate the local-level and trend terms to arrive at the ARIMA model:

$$
DY_t - \phi DY_{t-1} = \varepsilon_t - \theta_1\varepsilon_{t-1} - \theta_2\varepsilon_{t-2}.
\tag{6.17}
$$

Here, $\theta_1 = 1 + \phi - \alpha - \beta\phi$, $\theta_2 = -\phi(1 - \alpha)$, and model (6.17) is an ARIMA(1,1,2) scheme, because it contains one autoregression, one difference, and two moving average terms.

From Example 6.11, the ARIMA(0,2,2) model with $\theta_1 = 1.1913$, $\theta_2 = -0.2854$, and $\phi = 1$ corresponds to the LES scheme with coefficients $\alpha = 1 + \theta_2 = 1 - 0.285 = 0.715$ and $\beta = 1 - \theta_1 - \theta_2 = 1 - 1.191 + 0.285 = 0.094$. ■

TABLE 6.11   EQUIVALENCES BETWEEN STATE-SPACE AND ARIMA SCHEMES

State-space form	Parameter restrictions	ARIMA
Damped linear trend	None	(1,1,2)
Local linear trend (LES)	$\phi = 1$	(0,2,2)
Local level (SES)	$\phi = 0$	(0,1,1)

© Cengage Learning 2013.

The damped trend scheme includes a variety of special cases that arise for specific choices of the parameters, and we present a summary in Table 6.11. The reader is encouraged to check the details by making the appropriate substitutions.

> **Equivalence between State Space and ARIMA Models**
>
> We can express a *linear* state-space scheme in ARIMA form if and only if we assume that the random error terms satisfy the standard assumptions.

When both the error assumptions and linearity are satisfied, exponential smoothing methods do indeed correspond to an ARIMA scheme. However, methods such as the multiplicative Holt–Winters scheme have nonlinear forecast functions and cannot be derived from an ARIMA scheme. Further, even when the observation and state equations are linear, state-space schemes may have nonconstant variances and hence are not representable as ARIMA schemes.

There is a further subtle distinction that may be illustrated by considering *SES* with $\alpha = 0$. In state-space format, *SES* then reduces to the constant-mean version

$$Y_t = L_0 + \varepsilon_t.$$

This reduction is possible because the state-space scheme has a finite starting point (time zero). By contrast, the equivalent ARIMA(0,1,0) model breaks down because stationarity implies that the starting values become irrelevant, which is clearly not true here.

6.9.1 From ARIMA to a State-Space Form

Any ARIMA scheme may be expressed in state-space form, and a variety of state-space formulations have appeared over the years. (Again, see Hyndman *et al.*, 2008, Chapter 11, for details.)

EXAMPLE 6.18 ■ The first-order autoregressive scheme, AR(1)
The AR(1) scheme is written in the ARIMA format as

$$Y_t = \delta + \phi Y_{t-1} + \varepsilon_t.$$

To show that a corresponding state-space version exists, we start from the damped local-level model:

$$Y_t = \mu + \phi L_{t-1} + \varepsilon_t$$
$$L_t = \phi L_{t-1} + \alpha \varepsilon_t$$
$$\delta = \mu(1 - \phi).$$

Here, μ denotes the mean, or expected value, of the series; that is, $E(Y_t) = \mu$. After some manipulation, these equations reduce to the ARIMA form

$$Y_t = \delta + \phi Y_{t-1} + \varepsilon_t - \phi(1 - \alpha)\varepsilon_{t-1}.$$

The damped local-level model is represented by an ARIMA(1,0,1) scheme, and the AR(1) model results as a special case when $\alpha = 1$. The AR(1) model seems "natural," but so does the damped local-level state-space form. ∎

Two lessons emerge from this example:

1. There is a duality between the two approaches.
2. The models we select in practice may vary somewhat, depending upon whether we are working in the state-space or the ARIMA framework.

In general, the ARIMA version is obtained by eliminating the unobservable state variables.

The elimination of the state variables is both a blessing and a curse. The advantage of the state variables is that they provide insights into the structure of the model and help to guide model selection. Also, the state-space schemes can incorporate nonlinear structures such as the multiplicative Holt–Winters scheme, whereas ARIMA cannot. By contrast, the ARIMA forms are easier to link directly to functions of the data, so that model selection tends to be more data driven. Increasingly, forecasting software provides both options (see Appendix C).

Discussion Question *In what circumstances would you prefer the state-space approach or the ARIMA approach? Why?*

6.10* GARCH Models

One of the standard assumptions underlying most of the models we develop is that the error terms have constant variances. In many circumstances, this assumption is manifestly false for the original series. For example, when we consider sales or *GDP*, we automatically think of percentage changes over time, rather than changes in absolute amounts. That thought process in turn leads naturally to looking at percentage changes (or making a logarithmic transformation), and such steps will often resolve the difficulty, at least to a reasonable degree of approximation. However, this approach will not work in other circumstances, such as the variations (or volatility) in stock prices. An individual stock, or even a whole market index, tends to show quiet times intermingled with heavy (indeed, sometimes frantic) periods of trading. Such activity does not necessarily involve major movements up or down, so simple transformations (such as differencing or logs) will not work. Rather, we must recognize that the volatility is itself a stochastic process that needs to be modeled.

This insight was first developed by Rob Engle (1982), who introduced the notion of *Autoregressive Conditional Heteroscedasticity* (ARCH), whereby the variance at time *t* is an autoregressive (AR) function of past variances, updated by the latest squared error term. Thus, if periods of high volatility are likely to persist, the AR structure would have a positive coefficient, just as it does in the AR models considered in Section 6.2.1. The heteroscedasticity is local, because it is conditional upon immediate past values. Just as AR models have been extended to ARIMA models (see Section 6.2.3), ARCH models have been extended to include moving-average-like components (Bollerslev, 1986) and given the name *generalized ARCH*, or *GARCH*. Since these models were introduced, they have become extremely popular in econometrics, especially in the financial area, where predictions of volatility are the key to the efficient design of options contracts (see Hull, 2002). The article by Engle (2001) provides a nice overview of more recent developments.

We will focus upon only one special case, the so-called GARCH (1, 1) model, which has proved to be extremely popular in applications.

6.10.1 The GARCH (1, 1) Model

We begin with the random variable Y_t defined in the usual way but with time-dependent mean and variance:

$$E(Y_t) = \mu_t \quad \text{and} \quad V(Y_t) = \sigma_t^2.$$

Because our current interest is exclusively in the variance, we assume that the mean is known or has been estimated to a sufficiently high degree of accuracy so that we can focus upon the error process $\varepsilon_t = Y_t - \mu_t$. Such an assumption is usually appropriate for applications in finance when the random variable is defined as the return on an investment, typically over a short time period (e.g., days or even minutes). The expected value of that return would be close to zero. Accordingly, we may write

$$E(\varepsilon_t) = 0 \quad \text{and} \quad E(\varepsilon_t^2) = \sigma_t^2.$$

The GARCH (1, 1) model is now defined as

$$\sigma_t^2 = \omega + \alpha \varepsilon_{t-1}^2 + \beta \sigma_{t-1}^2. \tag{6.18}$$

The variable σ_t^2 represents the *conditional variance*, defined as a function of past elements of the series. To ensure that the model gives rise to strictly positive variances, we must impose the conditions

$$\omega > 0, \ \alpha > 0, \ \text{and} \ \beta > 0.$$

In addition, we impose the condition

$$\alpha + \beta < 1$$

to ensure that the long-term variance is finite. Equation (6.18) looks rather like an ARMA (1, 1) scheme but with the important difference that the term on the left-hand side does not represent an observable quantity. To make the model operational, we define the new variable

$$u_t = \varepsilon_t^2 - \sigma_t^2$$

and then rewrite equation (6.18) as

$$\varepsilon_t^2 = \omega + (\alpha + \beta)\varepsilon_{t-1}^2 + u_t - \beta u_{t-1}. \tag{6.19}$$

The new "error term" u_t has a zero mean, and its autocorrelations are zero when the model is valid. However, they are not independent and identically distributed, so the estimation process is more complex and we will not discuss the details. Fortunately computer software will deliver the estimates automatically (see Appendix C).

Once the model has been estimated, we may use the parameter estimates $(\hat{\omega}, \hat{\alpha}, \hat{\beta})$, the current estimate of the variance $(\hat{\sigma}_t^2)$, and the latest sample squared error (e_t^2) to forecast future values:

One step ahead: $\hat{\sigma}_{t+1}^2(1) = \hat{\omega} + \hat{\alpha} e_t^2 + \hat{\beta} \hat{\sigma}_t^2.$

Beyond the first period, we update this expression step by step:

h steps ahead: $\hat{\sigma}_{t+h}^2(h) = \hat{\omega} + (\hat{\alpha} + \hat{\beta})\hat{\sigma}_{t+h-1}^2(h-1), \ h = 2, 3, \ldots$

As the forecasting horizon increases, the variance approaches the limiting value

$$\frac{\omega}{1 - \alpha - \beta}.$$

From this expression, we can see that this limiting value is defined only if $\alpha + \beta < 1$.

EXAMPLE 6.19 ■ Variation in the Dow Jones Index

As an illustration of the GARCH methodology, we consider daily closing prices for the Dow Jones Index over the period from January 1, 2001, to September 30, 2005, a total of 1200 observations. The data are available in the file *DowJones.xlsx* and are plotted in Figure 6.24. The figure shows the plot of the returns data, with volatility clearly higher in the earlier part of the period. The summary statistics for the returns and the absolute values of the returns are shown in Table 6.12: The skewness and heavy tails in both distributions are quite evident. ■

Discussion Question *Some investment analysts continue to operate as through returns were normally distributed with a constant variance. How do you think this approach affects measures of risk?*

FIGURE 6.24   DAILY RETURNS ON THE DOW JONES INDEX, JANUARY 2001–SEPTEMBER 2005 (*Analysis completed with EViews*)

Data shown is from file DowJones.xlsx.

TABLE 6.12   SUMMARY STATISTICS FOR RETURNS AND ABSOLUTE RETURNS OF DOW JONES SERIES

	Return	Absolute Return
Mean	0.01	0.82
Median	0.02	0.61
Maximum	6.35	7.13
Minimum	−7.13	0.00
Std. Dev.	1.15	0.80
Skewness	0.15	2.31
Kurtosis	6.76	11.89
Observations	1199	1199

Data: DowJones.xlsx.

The Efficient Market Hypothesis, which states that stock prices incorporate all relevant (publicly available) information, implies a random walk model for prices:

$$Y_t = Y_{t-1} + \varepsilon_t.$$

That is, the current closing price at $(t - 1)$ contains all the information which is useful in predicting the next period's price. This equation had proved extremely useful in understanding many financial markets, including stock prices and exchange rates. Broadly, such a model holds for most markets in which the instrument is widely traded. However, there are interesting exceptions that have offered valuable trading opportunities. Still, it is a hard model to beat without inside information. (See Timmermann and Granger, 2004, for an interesting discussion of where there are forecasting opportunities.) Nonetheless, the efficient market model does not suggest any constraints on the error variance. An examination of Figure 6.24 reveals that there are periods of relatively high and low volatility, so it should be possible to predict future levels of volatility to a greater degree of accuracy than is implied by a constant-variance assumption. We therefore consider a GARCH (1,1) model for the error variance.

The output from EViews[3] for the GARCH (1, 1) model is shown in Table 6.13, which is based upon an estimation sample of the first 1160 observations. The constant term (mean return) is not significantly different from zero, so the results for the variance are almost identical if it is dropped. Thus, the fitted model is

$$\hat{\sigma}_{t+1}^2(1) = 0.0095 + 0.0775e_t^2 + 0.9160\hat{\sigma}_t^2.$$

Because EViews does not provide one-step-ahead forecasts, this equation was used to produce such forecasts via Excel. For comparison, we computed forecasts with the use of a ten-step moving average and the unconditional variance based on the same 1160 observations. The mean absolute errors (*MAE*, as defined in Section 2.7.2) are shown in Table 6.14, computed one step ahead for the hold-out sample of the last 40 observations. For comparison, the *MAE* values for the same three methods are shown for the last 200 and the last 600 observations. The results are remarkably consistent. We conclude that it is important to obtain local forecasts of the variance, but for that purpose a suitably chosen moving average scheme may perform just as well as a GARCH model.

Minicase 6.2 provides an opportunity for the reader to develop a GARCH model which uses a series that also includes a substantial ARIMA component.

TABLE 6.13   COEFFICIENT ESTIMATES FOR A GARCH(1,1) MODEL USING THE FIRST 1160 OBSERVATIONS OF THE DOW JONES SERIES (*Estimated with EViews 7*)

Variable	Coefficient	Std. Error	z-Statistic	Prob.
C	0.028642	0.025845	1.108225	0.2678
Variance Equation				
C	0.009478	0.004685	2.022987	0.0431
RESID(−1)^2	0.077483	0.011649	6.651471	0.0000
GARCH(−1)	0.915981	0.012865	71.19897	0.0000

Data: DowJones.xlsx.

[3]A brief introduction to the use of EViews is provided on the book's website. This software is especially useful for more advanced econometric modeling.

TABLE 6.14 COMPARISON OF MOVING AVERAGE, UNCONDITIONAL, AND
GARCH ESTIMATES OF THE VARIANCE FOR THE DOW JONES DATA

	MA(10)	**Unconditional**	**GARCH**
MAE last 40	0.325	1.037	0.342
MAE last 200	0.399	1.020	0.427
MAE last 600	0.511	1.018	0.532

Data: DowJones.xlsx.

Principles of ARIMA Modeling

One of the great strengths of the ARIMA framework is that Box and Jenkins developed a set of model-building principles. No simple summary exists beyond their injunction to "identify–estimate–test–forecast," so we have collated our own from a variety of sources.

6.11.1 ARIMA Models

[6.1] Identify the key features of the data. Is the series seasonal? Does it display (nonlinear) trends?

[6.2] Transform the data to stationarity. If the series appears to be nonstationary, consider differences and/or transformations to achieve stationarity.

[6.3] Consider a variety of models, compatible with the time series characteristics. Create a list of potential models, using the sample ACF and PACF and keeping in mind the characteristics of the series.

[6.4] Estimate the models, using your preferred software.

[6.5] Examine the diagnostic statistics—in particular, the residual autocorrelations. Look at the sample ACF or PACF for outliers and for lags that have been omitted. If the sample ACF shows a slow decay, consider additional differencing.

[6.6] Consider simplifying the model if the coefficients are insignificant.

[6.7] Use an information criterion supplemented, where possible, by an out-of-sample fit to choose among models.

[6.8] Compare your ARIMA forecasts with alternative methods of forecasting—in particular, with a naïve model.

6.11.2 GARCH Models

[6.9] Start with a constant-variance model, and then examine the auto-correlation structure of the squared residuals, using the methods of this chapter.

[6.10] The GARCH(1,1) model will suffice for most purposes. The KISS principle (keep it simple, statistician) should always be kept in mind.

Summary

We began this chapter by developing the autocorrelation function (ACF), which is a basic tool for describing the dependence structure of a time series, along with the partial autocorrelation function (PACF). We developed the class of ARIMA models and showed how the ACF and PACF may be used to select an appropriate model from within that class. Questions of parameter estimation and model diagnostics were then explored. When the data do not conform to the underlying assumptions of a model, we may use a combination of differencing, transformation, and outlier adjustment to achieve a better description of the observed series. Once these issues have been resolved, we may generate point and interval forecasts, as in earlier chapters. These ideas are then extended, albeit in brief fashion, to cover seasonal time series.

Although ARIMA and state-space models have a number of similarities and the two classes share a number of common models, there are some significant differences in applications and users may well select different models based on the two approaches. The discussion up to this point has assumed a constant variance over time. However, this assumption may not be true, and the final section of the chapter examined GARCH models, which enable us to consider processes whose error variances, as well as levels, change over time.

Exercises

6.1   Develop an ARIMA model for the growth rate of the U.S. gross domestic product (*GDP*) given in Table 3.17 (*GDP_change.xlsx*). Compare your model with the results obtained in Exercise 3.3. Use the diagnostics discussed in Section 6.5 to guide your choice of model.

6.2   Develop an ARIMA model for changes in the Consumer Price Index (*CPI*) given in Table 3.18 (*CPI_change.xlsx*). Compare your model with the results obtained in Exercise 3.5. Use the diagnostics discussed in Section 6.5 to guide your choice of model.

6.3   Develop an ARIMA model for the Saudi Arabian Light Oil spot price series given in Table 3.19 (*SA_oil_spot.xlsx*). Compare your model with the results obtained in Exercises 3.7 and 3.8. Use the diagnostics discussed in Section 6.5 to guide your choice of model.

6.4   Develop an ARIMA model for the Dulles Airport passengers' series given in Table 2.2 (*Dulles.xlsx*). Compare your model with the results obtained in Exercises 3.11 and 3.12. Use the diagnostics discussed in Section 6.5 to guide your choice of model.

6.5   Carry out diagnostic checks for the ARIMA(0,2,2) scheme for U.S. retail sales (*US_retail_sales.xlsx*), mentioned at the end of Section 6.5.

6.6   Using a log transform, develop an ARIMA model for U.S. retail sales and carry out appropriate diagnostic tests.

6.7*   Repeat the analysis of Exercise 6.6, using the Box–Cox transform with $c = 1/2$ and $c = 1/3$.

6.8   Adjust the U.S. retail sales series for the outlier in October 2001 and rerun the analyses from Exercises 6.6 and 6.7. Compare the parameter estimates with those obtained earlier.

6.9   The actual values of the U.S. retail sales series for December 2008–December 2009 are given in the file *US_retail_sales.xlsx*. Generate the point forecasts, with November 2008 as origin, and compare the forecasting performance of the log transform models with and without outlier adjustments, using *MAPE* and *MASE*. Comment on your results.

6.10*   Verify the two-step-ahead forecast variances for the AR(1) and MA(1) schemes given in Section 6.7.1.

6.11   Reanalyze the Netflix series (*Netflix.xlsx*) considered in Example 6.13 after dropping the data for 2000. How does this change in the in-sample data set affect your results? Which data set do you think is the more appropriate?

6.12   Use ARIMA models to generate point forecasts and prediction intervals for the following annual series, and compare your results with actual values obtained from the relevant data sources (United States, United Kingdom, or country of choice for the first two):
   a.   Gross domestic product (*GDP*)
   b.   Consumer Price Index (*CPI*)
   c.   Saudi Arabian Light Oil spot price
   d.   Dulles Airport passengers
   In each case, use the last four values of the series as the hold-out sample.

6.13   Compare the point forecasts and prediction intervals for U.S. retail sales (*US_retail_sales.xlsx*), using both ARIMA(1,1,0)+C and ARIMA(0,2,2) models.

6.14   Using a log transform, develop a seasonal ARIMA model for UK retail sales (*UK_retail_sales.xlsx*) and carry out appropriate diagnostic tests.

6.15*   Show that the $MA(1)$ scheme has $E(Y_1) = \mu$, $V(Y_1) = \sigma^2(1 + \theta^2)$ and $\rho_1 = \dfrac{-\theta}{1 + \theta^2}$. Further, show that all higher order autocorrelations are zero.

6.16*   Download the day-to-day percentage changes over the last three years for the Dow Jones Index and the FTSE 100 Index (or any other indexes in which you have an interest). These series may be found, for example, at *www.econstats.com*. Develop GARCH models for each series and compare the structures.

Minicases

Minicase 6.1

Use the data in *UK_retail_sales.xlsx* to develop ARIMA models for the quarterly series and for the monthly series. Generate forecasts for 2010 in each case, and compare the quarterly forecasts from each approach and the results for the year as a whole. Which forecasts would you use for the year 2010? Why?

   Given that the variability of the series increases over time, rework the analyses, using a logarithmic transformation. Compare your results and comment on which model you prefer to use.

Minicase 6.2

The data file *Run_miles.xlsx* records the miles run per month by a middle-aged forecaster (JKO) over the period January 1981–March 2007.[4] The period from January 1981 to September 1996 shows considerably greater variability than the subsequent period from June 1997 to March 2007. The five months in between these two periods record zeros, because the runner was injured during that time. These months may be excluded from the record.

   Use the observations through March 2005 as the estimation sample. After doing the usual preliminary data analyses,

   1.   Develop an ARIMA model, assuming a constant variance.
   2.   Use the model you developed to generate the one-step-ahead forecasts and corresponding prediction intervals for the next 24 months.
   3.   Repeat the analysis, incorporating a GARCH model for the variances.

Compare the results of the two analyses. In particular, examine the comparative widths of the prediction intervals and their coverage.

---

[4]These data were originally analyzed in Ord, Koehler, Snyder, and Hyndman (2009), who used the GARCH structure within a state-space framework.

References

*Bollerslev, T. (1986). Generalized autoregressive conditional heteroskedasticity. *Journal of Econometrics*, 31, 307–327.

*Box, G. E. P., and Jenkins, G. M. (1980). *Time Series Analysis: Forecasting and Control*. Upper Saddle River, NJ: Prentice-Hall.

*Box, G. E. P., Jenkins, G. M., and Reinsel, G. C. (2008). *Time Series Analysis: Forecasting and Control*, 4th ed. New York: Wiley.

Chatfield, C. (2004). *The Analysis of Time Series: An Introduction*, 6th ed. London and New York: Chapman and Hall.

Diebold, F. X. (2007). *Elements of Forecasting*, 4th ed. Mason, OH: Cengage (South-Western).

*Engle, R. F. (1982). Autoregressive conditional heteroscedasticity with estimates of variance of United Kingdom inflation. *Econometrica*, 50, 987–1008.

Engle, R.F. (2001). GARCH 101: The use of ARCH/GARCH models in applied econometrics. *Journal of Economic Perspectives*, 15, 157–168.

Hull, J. C. (2002). *Fundamentals of Futures and Options Markets*, 4th ed. Upper Saddle River, NJ: Prentice Hall.

Hyndman, R. J., Koehler, A. B., Ord, J. K., and Snyder, R. D. (2008). *Forecasting with Exponential Smoothing*. Berlin, Heidelberg, and New York: Springer.

Koehler, A. B., Snyder, R. D., Ord, J. K., and Beaumont, A. (2011). A study of outliers in the exponential smoothing approach to forecasting. *International Journal of Forecasting*, 28, 477–484.

Ord, J. K., Koehler, A. B., Snyder, R. D. and Hyndman, R. J. (2009). Monitoring processes with changing variances. *International Journal of Forecasting*, 25, 518–525.

Timmermann, A., and Granger, C. W. J. (2004). Efficient market hypothesis and forecasting. *International Journal of Forecasting*, 20, 15–27.

*Tsay, R. S. (2005). *Analysis of Financial Time Series*, 2nd ed. Hoboken, NJ: Wiley.

Appendix 6A*   Mean and Variance for AR(1) Scheme

We start with the AR(1) model as specified in equation (6.3):

$$Y_t = \delta + \phi Y_{t-1} + \varepsilon_t. \tag{6A.1}$$

Taking expected values in equation (6A.1), we have

$$E(Y_t) = E(\delta + \phi Y_{t-1} + \varepsilon_t)$$
$$= \delta + \phi E(Y_{t-1}) + E(\varepsilon_t). \tag{6A.2}$$

The last result follows by the property that the mean of a sum is equal to the sum of the means and by the fact that, because δ and ϕ are fixed values, we can "factor" them out of the expectation sign. From the stationarity conditions, we have

$$E(\varepsilon_t) = 0, \quad V(\varepsilon_t) = \sigma^2$$
$$E(Y_t) = \sigma, \quad V(Y_t) = \omega^2$$
$$Corr(Y_t, Y_{t-k}) = \rho_k \tag{6A.3}$$

for all values of t. Substituting the expected values into equation (6A.2), we arrive at

$$E(Y_t) = \mu = \delta + \phi E(Y_{t-1}) + E(\varepsilon_t)$$
$$= \delta + \phi\mu + 0.$$

It then follows that $\mu = \delta/(1 - \phi)$, provided that $-1 < \phi < 1$.

To obtain the variance, we employ the following rules:

1. The variance of a constant is zero.
2. If A is a constant, then $V(AY) = A^2 V(Y)$.
3. When two variables are independent, the variance of the sum is the sum of the variances.

Because the conditions for Rule 3 hold, we can write the variance of Y_t as

$$V(Y_t) = V(\delta + \phi Y_{t-1} + \varepsilon_t)$$
$$= V(\delta) + V(\phi Y_{t-1}) + V(\varepsilon_t).$$

By Rule 1, the first term is zero, and applying Rule 2 to the second term, we have

$$V(Y_t) = \phi^2 V(Y_{t-1}) + V(\varepsilon_t).$$

The values listed in equation (6A.3) reduce this equation to

$$\omega^2 = \phi^2\omega^2 + \sigma^2 \quad \text{or} \quad \omega^2 = \sigma^2/(1 - \phi^2).$$

The autocorrelation is a bit more difficult to determine. To simplify the notation, we first subtract the mean from the random variable and define

$$y_t = Y_t - \mu.$$

The first order autocorrelation may then be written as the autocovariance divided by the variance:

$$\rho_1 = \frac{E(y_t y_{t-1})}{\omega^2}.$$

Thus, we need to evaluate the autocovariance. We do this by the following steps. First note that $y_t = \phi y_t + \varepsilon_t$:

1. Multiply the entire equation by the y_{t-1}.
2. Take expected values:

$$E(y_t y_{t-1}) = E[y_{t-1}(\phi y_{t-1} + \varepsilon_t)]$$
$$= E(\phi y_{t-1}^2) + E(y_{t-1}\varepsilon_t).$$

The second term is zero because the two components are independent and have zero means. Thus, the equation reduces to

$$E(y_t y_{t-1}) = E(\phi y_{t-1}^2) = \phi E(y_{t-1}^2) = \phi\omega^2.$$

It then follows that $\rho_1 = \phi$. By a similar approach, we may show that $\rho_k = \phi\rho_{k-1}$, $k = 2, 3, \ldots$ from which it follows that $\rho_k = \phi^k$, $k = 1, 2, \ldots$

The mean, the variance, and autocorrelations for more complex schemes may be derived by similar, but more involved, methods. We encourage readers to test their understanding of the arguments by deriving the expressions for the MA(1) scheme in Exercise 6.15.

CHAPTER 7

Simple Linear Regression for Forecasting

CONTENTS

INTRODUCTION

Even trained statisticians often fail to appreciate the extent to which statistics are vitiated by the unrecorded assumptions of their interpreters. . . . It is easy to prove that the wearing of tall hats and the carrying of umbrellas enlarges the chest, prolongs life, and confers comparative immunity from disease. . . . A university degree, a daily bath, the owning of thirty pairs of trousers, a knowledge of Wagner's music, a pew in church, anything, in short that implies more means and better nurture . . . can be statistically palmed off as a magic spell conferring all sorts of privileges. . . . The mathematician whose correlations would fill a Newton with admiration, may, in collecting and accepting data and drawing conclusions from them, fall into quite crude errors by just such popular oversights as I have been describing.

—George Bernard Shaw, 1906, The Doctor's Dilemma[1]

---

[1]As abstracted in A. Stuart, J. K. Ord, and S. F. Arnold, *Kendall's Advanced Theory of Statistics*, Volume 2A (London: Arnold, 1999) p. 467.

Introduction

So far, we have looked at models that capture patterns within a single time series. A natural next step, in both forecasting and statistical modeling generally, is to look for relationships between the variable of interest and other factors, regardless of whether the data of interest are cross-sectional or defined over time. For example, when trying to predict a company's product sales, we expect such variables as the price of the product and the level of advertising expenditures to affect sales movements. These variables come to mind when we think of consumer choice, because consumers are usually price sensitive and advertising may be needed to bring the product to consumers' attention. Probing more deeply, we recognize that such variables are not absolutes, but must be judged relative to the pricing and advertising actions of the product's principal competitors. Ah, but here lies the rub! Information on our competitors' plans would be very valuable and often helps to explain fluctuations in sales with the benefit of hindsight. However, at the time we make our production and inventory decisions, the plans of our competitors are unknown; at best, we can hope to forecast those plans or to evaluate the impact of their different possible actions. This scenario is not unusual, and it contains the essential questions that plague any forecaster: *What do you know and when will you know it?* We will return to these key questions periodically.

Similar problems arise in cross-sectional studies. We may seek to evaluate an individual's potential for purchasing a particular product, such as a new automobile. We will have demographic information on that person, plus some financial data, but we cannot measure a host of other factors, such as the importance the person attaches to having a new vehicle, other interests that may compete for his or her funds, and information obtained from friends regarding that particular model.

We are now moving away from the purely extrapolative time series methods of the earlier chapters and into the realm of economic and market modeling. Our data may be cross-sectional or time indexed, or even both. The tools we develop in this and the next two chapters are commonly referred to as methods of *regression analysis*. Because our focus is on the development of quantitative models for economic activities, we also use the term *econometric modeling*.

We continue to denote the variable of interest by Y, but now refer to it as the *dependent variable* or the *output*. Our statistical model will then depend upon one or more *inputs*, or *predictors*, or *explanatory variables*[2] that are denoted by X, with subscripts if we have two or more such variables (e.g., X_1 and X_2). In this chapter, we follow the simpler path of assuming that only one such variable is important and we proceed to develop tools for that case before extending the ideas to multiple explanatory variables in Chapter 8. We urge the reader not to be overly impatient, but to think of the chapter as training for the more realistic problems to come.

In Section 7.1, we discuss the relationship between causality and correlation. Two variables may be correlated, and that information may be useful, but it does not imply causation. This discussion serves as a lead-in to Section 7.2, in which we specify a linear relationship between the variable of interest (Y) and the explanatory variable (X) and use the method of ordinary least squares to estimate this relationship; a case study on gasoline prices follows in Section 7.3. In order to determine whether an estimated relationship is useful, we first introduce the standard error and the coefficient of determination in Section 7.4. We then provide a systematic development of statistical inference for the regression model

---

[2]Many texts use the term *independent variable* to describe the X inputs. Because we employ the term "independent" in other, more critical contexts, we will not use it here.

in Sections 7.5 and 7.6, including the use of transformations. In Sections 7.7 and 7.8, we discuss forecasting by means of simple linear regression. Principles of regression modeling are left to Chapter 8.

7.1 Relationships Between Variables: Correlation and Causation

The ideal basis for forecasting is a *causal model*. In such a scheme, we are able to identify all the key factors that determine future values of Y and to measure them in sufficient time to generate the forecasts. In practice, at least three problems arise:

- We may not be able to identify all the causal variables (e.g., try listing all the factors that affect gasoline prices).
- We may not be able to obtain information to measure these variables (e.g., competitors' plans).
- The measurements may not be available in time to make the forecasts (e.g., measurements on macroeconomic variables such as gross domestic product (*GDP*) are not available until several weeks or even months after the forecasting horizon of interest).

The availability and timing of measurements affect the type of forecast that we can make, as we now describe.

Forecasting with a Regression Model

An *ex ante*, or *unconditional*, forecast uses only the information that would have been available at the time the forecast was made (i.e., at the forecast origin).

An *ex post*, or *conditional*, forecast uses the actual values of the explanatory variables, even if these would not have been known at the time the forecast was made.

A *what-if* forecast uses assumed values of the explanatory variables to determine the potential outcomes of different policy alternatives or different possible futures.

For example, consider the effect upon sales of the difference in price between a supplier and its competition. An *ex post* analysis would use actual price differentials to review forecasting performance over past data, an exercise that is useful for the determination of price sensitivity but does not provide genuine forecasts. An *ex ante* analysis would forecast the price differential and use that forecast in turn to forecast sales. Finally, a *what-if* analysis would use the model (previously validated by *ex post* and *ex ante* analyses of historical data) to determine the implications of different price-setting policies in the light of possible competitive prices.

Trying to track down all the causal variables in a real economic system is probably a fool's errand, but it is vital that we measure the key factors. If the measurements are not available in time for *ex ante* forecasts, we must seek appropriate substitutes. For example, the variable of interest may be the local unemployment rate, but for short-term forecasting we might use the relative numbers of "Help Wanted" advertisements in newspapers to gauge the health of a local labor market. Note that, in this last step, we are moving away from a causal model to a model in which an *available* input variable is substituted for the causal input variable. Of course, the available input variable may reasonably be assumed to be correlated with the input variable of interest. The apparent association may be due only to a common dependence upon other variables, but the relationship may still provide useful forecasts. Nevertheless, we will do well to heed George Bernard Shaw's warning whenever we seek to navigate such uncharted waters; that is, we must beware of interpreting correlation as causation and should recognize that apparent relationships are sometimes spurious.

7.1.1   What Is Regression Analysis?

With this background in mind, we now assume that we can identify a single output variable (Y) that is related to a single input variable (X). In the simplest possible case, the value of X may completely determine the value of Y. For example, consider Figure 7.1, which shows such a *mathematical relationship* between X and Y: A single value of X produces a single value of Y. The intercept, b_0, is the value of Y when $X = 0$, and the slope, b_1, denotes the increase in Y when X is increased by 1 unit. Thus, if $b_0 = 3$ and $b_1 = 1.5$, a value of $X = 4$ yields $Y = 3 + 1.5(4) = 9.0$. Such tidy relationships do not exist in the business world, so we must allow for uncertainty in the relationship between X and Y. The methodology for developing these relationships is known as *regression analysis*.

A regression line differs fundamentally from a mathematical relationship. We may observe one of many possible Y-values for a given value of X, and the regression line reflects the *expected value of Y given X*. For a particular observation, Y may be above or below our expectation. For example, in Figure 7.2 X denotes household size and Y represents monthly electricity usage (for this hypothetical data set).

The regression line indicates that the *average* household of size 4 consumes about 250 units of electricity; an individual household may consume more or less, depending on other factors such as house size, mode of heating, lifestyle, and so on. Also, it is worth noting that in this example the intercept value (the value of Y when $X = 0$) does not have any statistical meaning: It does not make sense to ask about consumption for a household containing zero people. Regression lines typically have restricted ranges of application (here, $1 \leq X \leq 8$). Also in this example, noninteger values of X are not sensible, but it is still convenient to draw a straight line to represent the relationship between the expected value of Y and a given X.

In our example, the equation of the straight line is $Y = 25.19 + 55.60X$; the approach described in the next section is used to determine the slope and intercept.

FIGURE 7.1   THE TERMS OF THE LINE $Y = b_0 + b_1X$

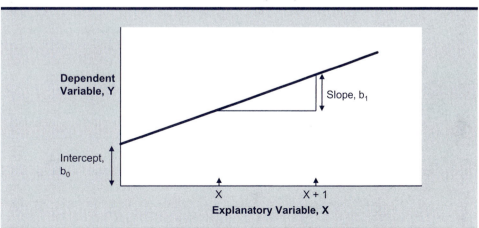

FIGURE 7.2   PLOT OF ELECTRICITY CONSUMPTION AGAINST HOUSEHOLD
SIZE, WITH A FITTED REGRESSION LINE

© Cengage Learning 2013.

7.2 Fitting a Regression Line by Ordinary Least Squares (OLS)

After we have identified the variables of interest, we create a scatterplot, as in Figure 7.2, to determine whether the relationship between X and Y could reasonably be described by a straight line, at least over the region of interest.

EXAMPLE 7.1 ■ Sales versus advertising

If a company increases its advertising budget, it expects to see a higher level of sales. In any particular week, that may or may not happen, because sales will be affected by the weather, the state of the economy, and the actions of competitors. Nevertheless, we would *expect* to see an increase in sales. At the same time, there comes a point where further increases in advertising expenditures cease to have much effect. The overall relationship between expected sales and advertising may be like that shown in Figure 7.3.

Now consider this figure from the perspective of a brand manager. On the one hand, if that person spends $8K or less on advertising, he or she is missing a range over which advertising becomes increasingly effective. On the other hand, if the manager spends more than $17K, the extra expenditures have limited impact. Accordingly, the manager will probably keep the budget in the range $8 \leq X \leq 17$, and the relationship is very close to a straight line over that range.   ■

Two conclusions emerge from this example. First, it may be feasible to use a linear relationship over the range of interest, even when the true relationship is nonlinear; second, the relationship may be valid only over the range of X for which observations are available. If the brand manager estimated the relationship over $8 \leq X \leq 17$ and then used the resulting line to estimate sales at $X = 25$, he or she would be in for a rude shock! We now assume (for the moment) that a straight-line relationship is appropriate over the range of interest, and we seek to determine a (regression) line that best describes the expected relationship between Y and X. We formulate the relationship as

$$Y = b_0 + b_1 X + e$$
$$= \textit{Explainable pattern} + \textit{Unexplained error}. \tag{7.1}$$

FIGURE 7.3   RELATIONSHIP BETWEEN SALES AND ADVERTISING

© Cengage Learning 2013.

The first two terms on the right-hand side of equation (7.1) show the extent to which Y can be linearly "explained" by X; the third term, e, known as the *error term*, represents the discrepancy between the observed value of Y and the value on the straight line. The errors are the *vertical* distances between the observed and fitted values. As is evident from the figure, we would like to choose values of the coefficients b_0 and b_1 so that the resulting line is a good representation of the relationship between Y and X. One approach would be to draw a freehand line, but this method is unreliable. An individual might draw different lines on different days, and two individuals might be quite unable to agree on whose line seemed better, as can be seen from the two lines in Figure 7.4. To resolve the argument, we must select an objective method of fitting so that, for a given set of data, everyone would arrive at the same result once the method had been agreed upon.

FIGURE 7.4   TWO POSSIBLE REGRESSION LINES RELATING Y TO X

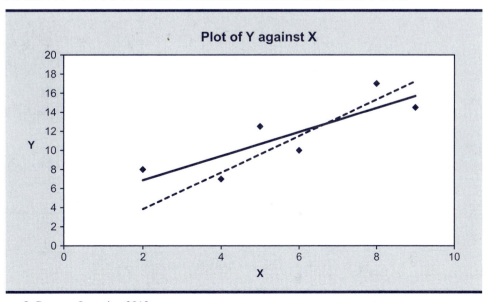

© Cengage Learning 2013.

7.2.1   **The Method of Ordinary Least Squares (OLS)**

The technique most commonly used to estimate the regression line is the *Method of Ordinary Least Squares*, often abbreviated to OLS.[3] Once we have formulated the nature of the relationship, as in equation (7.1), we define the OLS estimates as those values of $\{b_0, b_1\}$ which minimize the *Sum of Squared Errors (SSE):*

Given n pairs of observed values (X_i, Y_i), we have

$$SSE = \sum_{i=1}^{n} (Observed - Fitted)^2 = \sum_{i=1}^{n} (Y_i - b_0 - b_1 X_i)^2 = \sum_{i=1}^{n} e_i^2. \qquad (7.2)$$

> **Ordinary Least Squares**
>
> The method of ordinary least squares determines the intercept and slope of the regression line by minimizing the sum of squared errors (*SSE*).

We might compute the *SSE* for a range of values of the intercept and slope and search for the best values. Such an approach is illustrated in Figure 7.5, where we plot the *SSE* against b_0 and b_1. Given that we seek to minimize the *SSE*, inspection of that diagram suggests values in the range $2.5 < b_0 < 5.5$ and $1.0 < b_1 < 1.5$. A finer grid on the diagram would allow a more accurate determination of the best values. Such an approach is clearly tedious, but one of the nice features about the method of ordinary least squares is that we can determine exact computational formulas for the coefficients; the derivation is provided in Appendix 7A and the final formulas are presented next. Although the details of these calculations are relatively unimportant in the computer age unless you are a programmer, details for our simple example are laid out in spreadsheet form in Table 7.1.

FIGURE 7.5   MINITAB PLOT OF SSE AGAINST DIFFERENT INTERCEPT AND
SLOPE PARAMETERS FOR DATA IN TABLE 7.1

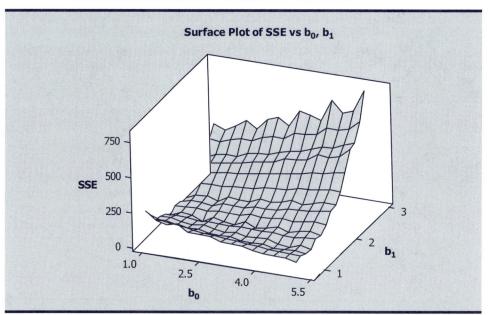

© Cengage Learning 2013; adapted from Minitab output.

---

[3]Other criteria could be—and are—applied, such as minimizing the sum of absolute errors, as defined in Section 2.7. However, the method of *ordinary least squares* is by far the most popular because of its numerical tractability. The method dates back to Carl Friedrich Gauss in the early nineteenth century. (For some historical insights, see the Wikipedia entry on Gauss at *http://en.wikipedia.org/wiki/Carl_Friedrich_Gauss*.) The method is labeled "ordinary" because there are a number of extensions, such as "*generalized least squares*," which we do not cover here.

TABLE 7.1   SPREADSHEET FOR REGRESSION CALCULATIONS USING EQUATION (7.5)

X	Y	$(X-\bar{X})$	$(X-\bar{X})^2$	$(Y-\bar{Y})$	$(X-\bar{X})(Y-\bar{Y})$	$(Y-\bar{Y})^2$
2	8	−3.67	13.44	−3.50	12.83	12.25
4	7	−1.67	2.78	−4.50	7.50	20.25
5	12.5	−0.67	0.44	1.00	−0.67	1.00
6	10	0.33	0.11	−1.50	−0.50	2.25
8	17	2.33	5.44	5.50	12.83	30.25
9	14.5	3.33	11.11	3.00	10.00	9.00
Sum 34	69	0.00	33.33	0.00	42.00	75.00
Mean 5.67	11.5	0.00	5.56	0.00		

$b_1 = 1.26$
$b_0 = 4.36$

Data shown is from file *Example 7_2.xlsx*. See Example 7.2 for details of calculations of intercept and slope.

The calculations may be summarized as follows: The sample means are

$$\bar{X} = \frac{\sum X_i}{n}, \quad \bar{Y} = \frac{\sum Y_i}{n}. \tag{7.3}$$

Now, denote the sum of squares for X by S_{XX} and the sum of cross products for X and Y by S_{XY}, defined respectively as

$$S_{XX} = \sum (X_i - \bar{X})^2 \quad \text{and} \quad S_{XY} = \sum (X_i - \bar{X})(Y_i - \bar{Y}). \tag{7.4}$$

OLS yields the intercept and slope as

$$b_0 = \bar{Y} - b_1 \bar{X} \quad \text{and} \quad b_1 = \frac{S_{XY}}{S_{XX}}, \tag{7.5}$$

Thus, we have exact solutions and do not need to follow the search process suggested by Figure 7.5. Nevertheless, it is useful to keep the idea of a direct search in mind when models are more complex; indeed, that was the process we followed when fitting the state-space models in Chapter 5 and the ARIMA models in Chapter 6.

EXAMPLE 7.2 ■ Calculation of slope and intercept
From the spreadsheet given in Table 7.1, we see that

$$\bar{X} = 5.67, \quad \bar{Y} = 11.50, \quad S_{XX} = 33.33, \quad \text{and} \quad S_{XY} = 42.00,$$

and it follows that $b_1 = 42.00/33.33 = 1.26$ and $b_0 = 11.50 - (1.26)(5.67) = 4.36$.

(Note that the figures have been rounded to two decimal places, so you may get slightly different answers.)   ■

We encourage the reader to work through the details of Table 7.1, if only this once, to aid understanding. Thereafter, we make use of one of the many statistical packages that are available for the calculation of regression lines.

We used Table 7.1 to determine the regression line for Y on X and came up with

$$\hat{Y} = 4.36 + 1.26X. \tag{7.6}$$

The "hat" notation is used to indicate that the line defined by expression (7.6) has been estimated by applying OLS. The equation refers to the fitted values of Y, not the observations. Note that the equation represents the fitted values of Y, *given different values* of X, and it is not appropriate to reverse the roles of X and Y. That is why we have included the "hat" only on the dependent variable.

Another way of thinking about this calculation is to return to Figure 7.3. The line is chosen to minimize the *SSE*, which is based upon the *vertical* distances between the observed and fitted Y values. Finally, leave the mathematics behind. What are you trying to forecast? Y! What are you using to make the forecast? X. Thus, equation (7.6) is the correct version to use.

EXAMPLE 7.3 ■ Baseball salaries

In 2003, a book appeared called *Moneyball: The Art of Winning an Unfair Game* (New York: W. W. Norton), written by Michael Lewis. In the book, Lewis describes how Billy Beane, general manager of the Oakland Athletics baseball team, used statistical methods to identify players who were undervalued. His teams had considerable success on the field despite having a very low budget for player salaries. The essence of Beane's approach was to identify those factors which were important to winning games but were often overlooked by other baseball managers. He then sought out players who could deliver those skills.

As a first step in such an analysis, we consider a simple regression for Y = player's salary (in thousands of dollars) on X = number of years in the major leagues.[4] The data are for the 1986 season, and in this example we use only the data relating to pitchers. The scatterplot for the data appears in Figure 7.6.

FIGURE 7.6   SCATTERPLOT OF BASEBALL PLAYERS' SALARIES AGAINST
THE NUMBER OF YEARS PLAYED IN THE MAJOR LEAGUES

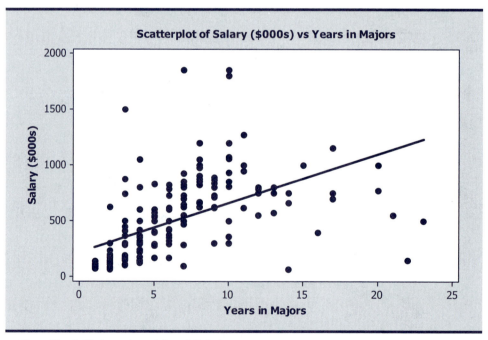

Data: Baseball.xlsx; adapted from Minitab output.

---

[4]The data are included in the file *Baseball.xlsx*, and we wish to acknowledge StatLib of the Department of Statistics at Carnegie Mellon University for allowing us access to these data. The data were originally compiled by Lorraine Denby as part of a project with the Graphics Section of the American Statistical Association.

The fitted regression line is of the form

$$Salary\ (\$000s) = 224 + 43.6 * Years\ in\ Majors.$$

One might interpret the line as an average baseline salary of $224K plus $43.6K per year of service, keeping in mind that this is the expected value and that individual salaries vary considerably. Common sense suggests that players tend to become less valuable toward the end of their careers, and we can see from Figure 7.6 that a number of veteran players (say, with 12 or more years in the major leagues) have salaries well below the fitted values. Nevertheless, this simple model suggests that career length is an important determinant of salary. (We examine the model further at the end of the chapter, in Minicase 7.3.). ■

Discussion Question *How might you modify the analysis to allow for the lower salaries of veteran players?*

7.3 A Case Study on the Price of Gasoline

Fluctuations in gasoline prices have an impact on most sectors of the economy. Although the transportation industry is the first affected, any price increases will eventually work their way through the system to have an impact on the prices of most goods and services. At the same time, price increases in other sectors will have an effect on gasoline prices primarily by changing demand. In addition, decisions by the Organization of the Petroleum Exporting Countries (OPEC) and other world events will have an impact on supply. Our purpose in this section is to illustrate the model-building process by starting to develop a statistical model that can account for the fluctuations in retail gasoline prices. We will revisit the model from time to time and improve it as we develop our model building principles.

Where should we start? Everything seems to be related to everything else! However, recalling Principle 2.1, we start by trying to identify the key variables of interest and come up with the following (albeit incomplete) list of factors and corresponding time series:

- Price of gasoline to U.S. consumers (variable to be forecast): price of unleaded gasoline
- Producer price: price of crude oil
- Consumer income: personal disposable income
- Level of economic activity: unemployment; retail sales
- Weather conditions: average monthly temperature
- Leading indicator of economic activity: U.S. housing starts, S&P 500 Index

We also need to decide on the precise way to measure each variable—for example, weather conditions: Should we measure average temperatures or extreme temperatures? Equally, there are many alternative measures of consumer income and economic activity. Measures of these variables are all readily available from standard sources,[5] and monthly data for January 1996 through December 2010 are included in the file *Gas_prices_1.xlsx*.

Discussion Questions *What other variables might have an impact? How could they be measured effectively, and what possible sources of data might be available?*

---

[5]These series are part of the library of Official Energy Statistics from the U.S. Government. They are located on the website of the Energy Information Administration: *www.eia.doe.gov*. Background information on petroleum markets is also available on this site.

7.3.1   **Preliminary Data Analysis**

Before we leap into any attempts at model building, we start out by developing a feel for the data. The first step is to take a look at a time plot of the data, as shown in Figure 7.7; prices are quoted in dollars per U.S. gallon. Observations are plotted through December 2008; we have retained January 2009 to December 2010 as a hold-out sample. The plot is very revealing: Prices were reasonably steady over the first eight years of the period examined and then climbed before dropping sharply in the last six months of the period. Automobile drivers will not need to be reminded of the recent wild fluctuations in gasoline prices!

The next step is to think about the variables of interest and how they relate to gasoline prices. A full analysis should include an examination of each variable, using the methods of Chapter 2, plus checks for unusual observations and so on. In the interest of space, we do not report those details here, but encourage the reader to probe in greater depth. Instead, we move to the next phase and look at a matrix plot to relate gasoline prices to some of the explanatory variables. We have restricted the list to the more interesting items to make the plot more readable.

The variables plotted in Figure 7.8 are monthly average gasoline prices for the current month and the one-month lagged values for the explanatory variables to ensure that the data would be available for forecasting:

- The price of unleaded gasoline in the United States ("*Unleaded*"; in dollars per U.S. gallon)
- The price of crude oil ("*L1_crude*"; in dollars per barrel)
- Unemployment ("*L1_Unemp*"; Overall percentage rate for the United States)
- The S&P 500 Stock Index ("*L1_S&P*").
- Total personal disposable income ("*L1_PDI*"; in billions of current dollars)

The prefix *L1* is used to indicate that the variable is lagged by one month.

FIGURE 7.7   TIME PLOT OF U.S. GASOLINE PRICES, IN DOLLARS PER GALLON (*January 1996–December 2008*)

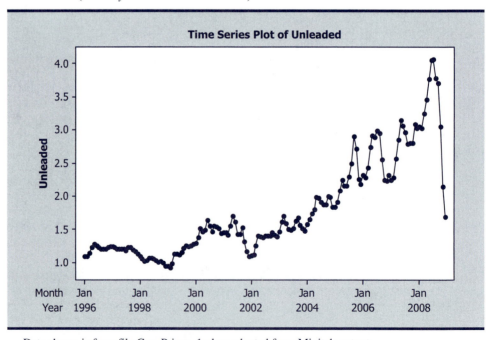

Data shown is from file Gas_Prices_1.xlsx; adapted from Minitab output.

FIGURE 7.8   MATRIX PLOT FOR GASOLINE PRICES AGAINST DISPOSABLE INCOME, LAGGED PRICE OF CRUDE OIL, UNEMPLOYMENT, AND THE S&P INDEX

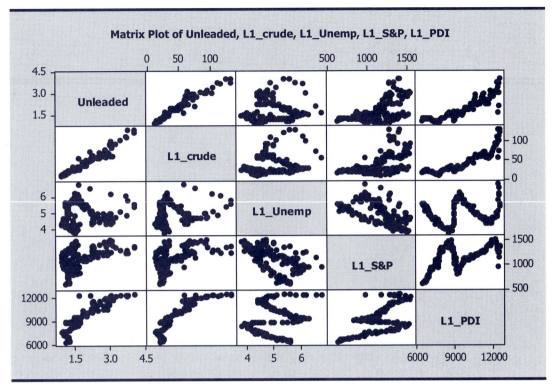

Data: Gas_prices_1.xlsx; adapted from Minitab output.

We use the lagged values for two reasons. First, from an economic perspective, increases in production costs and other changes will take some time to pass on to consumers. Second, as forecasters, we need to make sure that the input data are available. The previous month's figures may become available relatively early in the current month, but the current month's value clearly could not be available in time for *forecasting* purposes.[6]

The plots provide a couple of insights:

- Gasoline prices appear to be most closely related to *L1_crude*.
- There is a strong upward sloping relationship between gasoline prices and PDI, and a somewhat weaker one between gasoline prices and the S&P 500 Index.

Finally, we may confirm our visual impressions by computing the correlations between these pairs of variables. The full set of correlations is given in Table 7.2. Because correlations measure linear relationships, the values should accord with the intuition gained from the matrix plot, and they do.

---

[6]There are a number of different ways in which forecasts might be generated. We defer discussion of this topic until Sections 7.7 and 7.8.

TABLE 7.2   CORRELATIONS WITH GASOLINE PRICES

	Unleaded	L1_crude	L1_Unemp	L1_S&P
L1_crude	0.971 0.000			
L1_Unemp	0.070 0.385	0.128 0.114		
L1_S&P	0.533 0.000	0.496 0.000	−0.556 0.000	
L1_PDI	0.893 0.000	0.882 0.000	0.150 0.063	0.628 0.000

Data: Gas_prices_1.xlsx. The upper figure denotes the correlation and the lower figure is the *P*-value for testing whether the correlation differs from zero.

On the basis of this preliminary analysis, we will focus our attention upon the relationship between gasoline prices and the lagged crude oil price. However, our preliminary investigations suffice to indicate that *L1_crude* alone is unlikely to provide the whole story. In this chapter, we develop simple regression models, using this relationship as a running example. In Chapter 8, we return to the more general issue of developing a full model for gasoline prices that includes other variables.

Although the price of crude passes the test as the best single predictor in this case, we must recognize that forecasts based upon that model will be useful mainly in the short term. Longer term forecasts would need to capture more details about the infrastructure of the industry and proven reserves, as well as worldwide demand, which in turn affect the price of crude oil.

7.3.2   The Regression Model

Figure 7.9 shows an enlarged view of the plot for gasoline prices on *L1_crude*, with the fitted regression line superimposed. The relationship appears to be linear, although there does seem to be more scatter at the upper end of the range. The fitted line has the equation

$$Unleaded = 0.688 + 0.0271L1\_crude. \tag{7.7}$$

We may interpret equation (7.7) as stating that an increase of $1 in the price of a barrel of crude may be expected to increase the price at the pump next month by $0.027, or just under 3 cents per gallon. It is tempting to conclude that the intercept term represents overhead cost plus markup, but this conclusion is highly speculative, because we have no observations that correspond to *X* near zero. As previously noted in Section 7.1.1 such relationships should be viewed as valid only within the existing range of the explanatory variable, which is about $18 to $130 per barrel. Such a position is theoretically sound, but at times it is too restrictive. Commodity prices such as oil fluctuate dramatically. In addition, many economic aggregates grow over time. Thus, future values of variables such as *L1_crude* are likely to lie outside the "valid range" when it comes to making forecasts. The problem of *extrapolation* is not easily avoided, but we should always ask whether it makes sense to extend the relationship beyond the current range of *X*. Further, we must recognize that all forecasts are extrapolations, since they use the past to forecast the future. Consequently, we must assume that expressions like equation (7.7) hold both for future time periods *and*

FIGURE 7.9   PLOT OF UNLEADED PRICES AGAINST LAGGED CRUDE OIL
PRICES (L1_CRUDE)

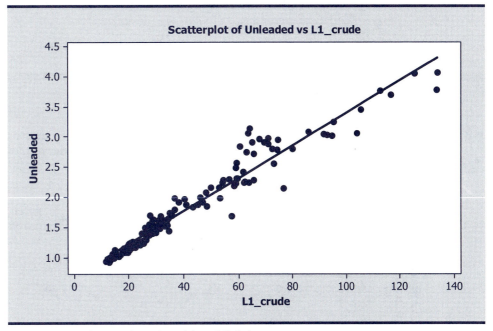

Data: Gas_prices_1.xlsx; adapted from Minitab output.

for *X*-values that may lie outside the current range of observations.[7] Because of the need
to extrapolate, business forecasters should rightly maintain a certain degree of humility[8]
about their craft: There are plenty of assumptions in their models that may well go wrong!

How Good Is the Fitted Line?

Once the line has been fitted, the next question is how effective is it as a basis for forecasting? In Section 7.2, we decided to fit the line by minimizing the sum of squares. That is, we
started from the total sum of squares for *Y*, measured about its overall mean. We denote this
sum by *SST* or S_{YY}:

$$SST = S_{YY} = \sum_{i=1}^{n} (Y_i - \bar{Y})^2. \tag{7.8}$$

This quantity is sometimes called the *variation in Y*. We then used OLS to choose the line
in order to make the sum of the squares of the errors about the fitted line as small as possible. That sum, denoted *SSE*, is the variation in *Y* left unexplained by the model, written as

$$SSE = \sum_{i=1}^{n} (Y_i - \hat{Y}_i)^2. \tag{7.9}$$

In this equation, $\hat{Y}_i = b_0 + b_1 X_i$ denotes the fitted value for the *i*th observation and therefore, $Y - \hat{Y}$ estimates the error made in predicting the *i*th observation.

---

[7]At times, we can improve matters somewhat by looking at changes rather than absolute levels (see Section 9.5.1). We should
also consider whether to examine prices in real dollars (i.e., dollars adjusted for inflation) rather than current dollars; this
question is explored in Minicase 7.1.

[8]It is sometimes suggested that shrewd forecasters always ensure that the forecast horizon is longer than they expect to stay
in their current job. That way, someone else takes the heat when the forecasts fail. Such people often run for political office.

SSE represents the error sum of squares, where $Y_i - \hat{Y}_i$ is the error incurred in using the regression model to calculate the ith fitted value. Therefore, the smaller the value of SSE, the smaller is the average squared difference between the fitted and observed values. Further, we define the *sum of squares explained by the regression equation*, or the reduction in SST, as

$$SSR = SST - SSE.$$

It can be shown that

$$SSR = \sum_{i=1}^{n} (\hat{Y}_i - \bar{Y})^2.$$

These sums of squares provide a basis for examining the performance of the model, as we now explain.

7.4.1   The Standard Error of Estimate

In Section 2.4, we introduced the standard deviation as a measure of variability. The average of the squared deviations about the sample mean defined the variance, and the standard deviation is then the square root of the variance. Recall that we then defined the standardized score for an observation X, or Z-score, as

$$Z = \frac{(X - \bar{X})}{S},$$

where S is the standard deviation. Provided the distribution of X is approximately normal, we may then make probability statements such as

The probability that $|Z| > 2$ is approximately 0.046.

We now seek to make similar statements about the errors (deviations from the OLS line), and to do so we define the standard error of estimate, often just called the standard error.

The Standard Error of Estimate

The *standard error of estimate*, denoted by S, is defined as

$$S = \frac{SSE}{\sqrt{n - 2}}.$$

The standard error is a key measure of the accuracy of the model and is used in testing hypotheses and creating confidence intervals and prediction intervals.

We may define the Z-score for the ith observation as (approximately)

$$Z_i = \frac{Y_i - \hat{Y}_i}{S}$$

and make similar probability statements for these error terms. The assumptions necessary to justify this procedure are listed in Section 7.5.1.

The denominator in the definition of the standard error is $(n - 2)$ rather than the $(n - 1)$ that we used to define the sample variance in Section 2.4. The reason for this choice is that, from a sample of n observations or degrees of freedom (DF), we use 2 DF to specify the intercept and slope. ("A straight line is defined by two points.") Intuitively speaking, this leaves $(n - 2)$ observations from which to estimate the error variance. We say that S is based upon $(n - 2)$ degrees of freedom, or $(n - 2)$ DF. We have given up or "lost" 2 DF in order to estimate the slope and intercept. Another way to think about this situation is that when $n = 2$, we have a "perfect fit," so it is only with more than two observations that we can hope to estimate the residual uncertainty in the model. In the next chapter, we will use models with more parameters and lose more DF.

From the computer output, we find that

$$S = 0.176121$$

Thus, unusual values would be about 35 cents (or two standard errors) away from the expected values. Analysis of the differences between observed and fitted values shows a period from April through July 2007 when prices were higher than expected. From August through December 2008, prices were lower than expected.

7.4.2   The Coefficient of Determination

A second measure of performance is defined as the proportion of variation accounted for by the regression line. This measure is known as the *coefficient of determination* and is denoted by R^2:

$$R^2 = \frac{SSR}{SST} = 1 - \frac{SSE}{SST}. \tag{7.10}$$

Because SSR and SSE are sums of squares, they cannot be negative. It then follows that $0 \le R^2 \le 1$.

Some properties

1. A value of $R^2 = 1$ means that the regression line fits perfectly ($SSE = 0$).
2. $R^2 = 0$ when $SSE = SST$, an equality that occurs only when every prediction $\hat{Y}_i = \bar{Y}$. This condition in turn means that X is of no value in predicting Y.
3. For *simple linear regression only*, the square of the correlation (denoted by r in Section 2.5) between X and Y is equal to R^2.
4. R is known as the *coefficient of multiple correlation* and represents the correlation between Y and $\hat{Y}$. For simple regression with one explanatory variable, $R = |r|$.

In our gasoline price example, we find that $R^2 = 0.943$, or 94.3 percent. (Both formats are used and referred to as R^2, a notational quirk that needs to be remembered.) Accounting for over 90 percent of the variation seems pretty good, but how good is it? There are several parts to this question:

-   Is the relationship meaningful, or could such results arise purely by chance?
-   Are the assumptions underlying the model valid?
-   Are the predictions from the model accurate enough to be useful?
-   Are there other variables that could improve our ability to forecast Y?

> ### R^2, the Coefficient of Determination
>
> R^2, the *coefficient of determination*, measures the proportion of the variation in the dependent variable, Y, explained by the regression model.

We will defer discussion of the last three points, but even to examine the first one, we need a more formal framework than we have considered hitherto.

7.5   The Statistical Framework for Regression

In Section 7.2, we specified the fitted line in terms of an explainable (linear) pattern and an unexplained error, as given in equation (7.1). The coefficients for the fitted line were then determined with the use of OLS. No underlying theory was involved; we just applied a numerical recipe. However, in order to make statistical inferences, we must formulate an underlying statistical model, just as we did in Chapter 5 for the exponential smoothing methods developed in Chapters 3 and 4. Once the model is specified, we can use it to make probability statements about the estimated coefficients, the forecasts, and associated assessments of the accuracy of those forecasts by constructing prediction intervals. These statements are predicated on the supposition that the model is correctly and fully specified. Such an ideal state of affairs is unlikely, but we must take steps to ensure that the model we use conforms at least approximately with the assumptions we have made. Thus, statistical model building is a critical element of the forecasting process.

7.5.1   The Linear Model

The method of ordinary least squares is a pragmatic procedure for describing the relationship between variables, based upon the notion that putting a straight line through the cloud of observations provides a convenient numerical summary. We now go further and assume that there truly is an underlying linear relationship between X and Y. We recognize that different samples, or different pieces of a time series record, will lead to different OLS estimates for the slope and intercept. However, we postulate that there is a linear relationship relating the expected value of Y to X, even though individual observations will deviate from that straight line because of random errors. The structure of the assumed relationship between Y and X is illustrated in Figure 7.10.

In order to develop a statistical model and use it for data analysis, we must make a set of assumptions. We express these assumptions formally as follows:

Assumption R1: For given values of the explanatory variable X, the expected value of Y given X is written as $E(Y|X)$ and has the form

$$E(Y|X) = \beta_0 + \beta_1 X.$$

FIGURE 7.10   LINE SHOWS THE EXPECTED VALUE OF Y FOR EACH X
(The vertical distance from the line to the observed value denotes the error.)

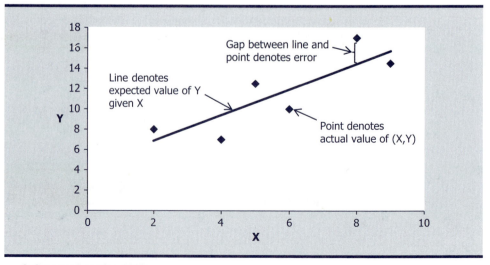

That is, $E(Y|X)$ shows how X affects Y and forms the explainable, or predictable, component of the model. Here, β_0 denotes the intercept and β_1 is the slope; the values of these parameters are unknown and must be estimated from the data. The remaining assumptions provide a framework for this estimation process.

Assumption R2: The difference between an observed Y and its expected value is known as a *random error*, denoted by ε (epsilon). The random error represents the unexplained component of the model. Thus, the full model may be written as

$$Y = E(Y|X) + \varepsilon = \beta_0 + \beta_1 X + \varepsilon$$
$$= (Expected\ value) + (Random\ error). \qquad (7.11)$$

This specification applies *before* the observations are recorded; hence, the error term is random and we can discuss its statistical properties. After the value of Y has been recorded for a particular value of X, the error may be estimated from the fitted model; this estimate is referred to as the *residual*, denoted by e.

Assumptions R1 and R2 constitute a *linear model*. The meaning of this term is not as obvious as would first appear. Intuitively, we would expect the adjective "linear" to indicate that the expected value of Y is a linear function of X. However, in the statistical literature, a linear model is a model that is linear *in its parameters*. We will refer to a model as being "linear in X" or "linear in the parameters" whenever there is any possibility of confusion. For the present, the models we examine are linear in both senses; when we consider transformations of X and Y in Section 7.6.3, the model remains linear in the parameters, but not in X.

The reason for specifying a formal model is to enable us to use the observed data to make *statistical inferences*. Given n observations $(X_1, Y_1), (X_2, Y_2), \ldots, (X_n, Y_n)$, we wish to make probability statements concerning the values of the unknown parameters. To do so, we must make some assumptions about the nature of the random errors. These assumptions could be aggregated into a single statement, but we separate them out because we wish to check them separately later.

Assumption R3: The expected value of each error term is zero.

That is, there is no bias in the measurement process. For example, biases would arise if sales were systematically overreported by counting advance orders that later were cancelled.

Assumption R4: The errors for different observations are uncorrelated with other variables and with one another.

Thus, the errors should be uncorrelated with the explanatory variable or with other variables not included in the model. When we examine observations over time, this assumption implies no correlation between the error at time t and past errors. When correlation exists over time, the errors are said to be *autocorrelated*.

Assumption R5: The variance of the errors is constant.

That is, the error terms come from distributions with equal variances. This common variance is denoted by σ^2, and when the assumption is satisfied, we say that the error process is *homoscedastic*.[9] Otherwise, we say that it is *heteroscedastic*.

---

[9]From the classical Greek: *homo* = same and *scedastos* = scattered; similarly *hetero* = different. The original use of the term "scedastos" was not related to variation. We are grateful to Professor Alex Sens, Department of Classics at Georgetown University, for this clarification.

Assumption R6: The random errors are drawn from a normal distribution.

If we take assumptions R3–R6 together, we are making the claim that the random errors are independent and normally distributed with zero means and common variance. These four assumptions are exactly the same as those made for the state space models in Chapter 5 and the ARIMA models in Chapter 6. In the next few sections, we suppose these assumptions to be valid so that we can develop our statistical tools. However, in applications of regression analysis, each assumption must be carefully checked, and if any of them are not satisfied, corrective action must be taken. Some, of course, are more critical than others for effective forecasting. We return to the question of checking the assumptions in Chapter 8.

Random Errors and Residuals

The *random error* represents the difference between the expected and observed values.

In a valid model, the random error for a particular observation is *completely unpredictable*, in that it is unrelated to either the explanatory variable(s) or the random errors of other observations. Assumption R4 is designed to ensure that this requirement holds.

Because the intercept and slope are unknown, we must estimate the error from the fitted model; we refer to this estimate as a *residual*.

7.5.2 Parameter Estimates

In the course of our assumptions, we specified three unknown parameters: the intercept, the slope, and the error variance. The method of ordinary least squares may now be invoked in the context of our linear model. The estimates of the intercept and slope are precisely those given in equation (7.5); that is,

$$b_0 = \bar{Y} - b_1\bar{X} \quad \text{and} \quad b_1 = \frac{S_{XY}}{S_{XX}}. \tag{7.12}$$

Further, the estimate for the error variance is the square of the standard error of the estimate:

$$S^2 = SSE/(n-2). \tag{7.13}$$

As noted earlier, the denominator in equation (7.13) reflects the loss of two *degrees of freedom*, corresponding to the two parameters that must be estimated to define the regression line.

To make the distinction clear between the unknown parameters and the sample quantities that are used to estimate them, we summarize the notation in the following table:

Term	Unknown parameter	Sample estimate
Intercept	β_0	b_0
Slope	β_1	b_1
Error variance	σ^2	S^2

So far in this section, we have introduced three new quantities and specified how to estimate them from sample data. We do not appear to have made much real progress! However, we have established a framework that will enable us to answer questions about the value of the proposed model, and it is to these questions that we now turn.

7.6 Testing the Slope

So far, using least squares, we have estimated the regression line's parameters. But these estimates are themselves random (because they are based on random data). This situation leads us back to the question raised in Section 7.4: Is the relationship that we have produced meaningful, or could such results arise purely by chance? We are now in a position to address that question. First of all, we formulate the question in terms of two hypotheses:[10]

The *null hypothesis* is denoted by H_0 and states that the slope (β_1) in expression (7.11) is zero; that is, there is no linear relationship between X and Y.

The *alternative hypothesis* is denoted by H_A and states that the slope is not zero; that is, there is a linear relationship between X and Y.

These two hypotheses are mutually exclusive and exhaustive; that is, only one of them can be true, and exactly one of them must be true. Algebraically, we write these competing hypotheses as

$$H_0 : \beta_1 = 0 \text{ versus } H_A : \beta_1 \neq 0.$$

One-sided alternatives may also be used if there is prior information that the slope should have a particular sign. Thus, if we wish to test for a positive slope, we consider

$$H_0 : \beta_1 \leq 0 \text{ versus } H_A : \beta_1 > 0.$$

Likewise, for a negative slope we compare the hypotheses

$$H_0 : \beta_1 \geq 0 \text{ versus } H_A : \beta_1 < 0.$$

The null hypothesis always includes an equals sign, which specifies the benchmark value of the parameter to be used in the test.

We assume the null hypothesis to be true and then formulate a test based upon this assumption. We use the test statistic

$$t = b_1 / SE(b_1), \tag{7.14}$$

where $SE(b_1)$ denotes the standard error of the sample slope. (Remember that our estimated regression line moves around, depending on the random data.) For simple regression, the algebraic form of the standard error is given in Appendix 7A, in equation (7A.7), but there is rarely any need to make direct use of this expression with statistical software.

We refer to the observed value of t obtained from (7.14) as t_{obs}; this value is to be compared with the appropriate value[11] from Student's t-distribution with $(n - 2)$ DF. If we set the significance level equal to α, we denote the critical value for the two-sided test as $t_{\alpha/2}(n - 2)$ [and for a one-sided test by $t_\alpha(n - 2)$ with the appropriate sign attached]. The classical decision rules for these tests are as follows:

Two sided: If $|t_{obs}| > t_{\alpha/2}(n - 2)$, reject H_0; otherwise, do not reject H_0.

Positive slope: If $t_{obs} > t_\alpha(n - 2)$, reject H_0; otherwise, do not reject H_0.

Negative slope: If $t_{obs} < -t_\alpha(n - 2)$, reject H_0; otherwise, do not reject H_0.

---

[10]For a more detailed introduction to hypothesis testing, see Anderson, Sweeney, and Williams (2011, Chapter 9) or any other introductory statistics text.

[11]Most tests are now conducted with the use of P-values, which are described in Section 7.6.1. When needed, values of the percentage points of the t-distribution may be obtained with Excel or any statistical software (see Appendix 7B).

FIGURE 7.11   THE *t*-DISTRIBUTION WITH DF = 15: SHADED AREAS
CORRESPOND TO $\alpha = 0.05$ FOR (A) A TWO-TAILED TEST AND
(B) A ONE-TAILED (UPPER TAIL) TEST

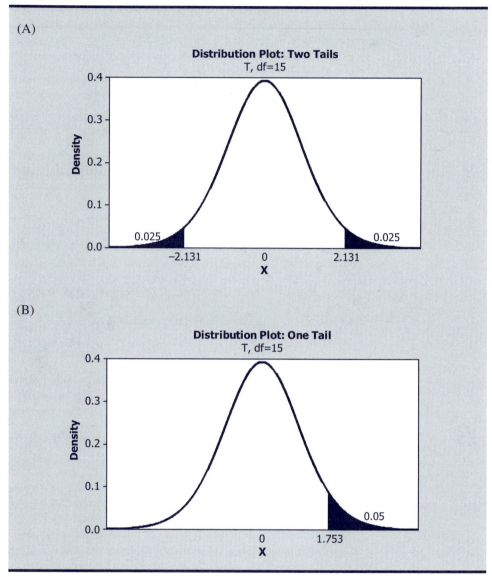

© Cengage Learning 2013.

Figure 7.11 shows the rejection region (shaded) for the *t*-distribution with DF = 15 and
significance level $\alpha = 0.05$ for the two-tailed and positive-slope cases; the negative-slope
case is just the mirror image of the positive-slope case.

7.6.1 *P*-Values

An equivalent procedure and one that is more convenient for computer usage is to determine the *observed significance level*, denoted by *P*. The *P-value* denotes the probability,
under H_0, of observing a value of the test statistic at least as extreme as that actually
observed. Most statistical software now provides *P*-values as part of the standard output for

regression analysis; see Anderson, Sweeney, and Williams (2011, Section 9.3) for further details. The decision rule for the two-tailed test is then written as

$$\text{If } P = Prob[|t| > |t_{obs}|] < \alpha, \text{ reject } H_0; \text{ otherwise, do not reject } H_0.$$

For a one-tailed test, the rules are also straightforward:

Upper tail: If $P = Prob[t > t_{obs}] < \alpha$ *and* the sign of the coefficient is compatible with H_A, reject H_0; otherwise, do not reject H_0.

Lower tail: If $P = Prob[t < t_{obs}] < \alpha$ *and* the sign of the coefficient is compatible with H_A, reject H_0; otherwise, do not reject H_0.

(Note that most computer programs provide only the *P*-value for the two-sided test. In such cases, when a one-sided test is used, the *P*-value in the output should be divided by 2 before making the comparison with α.)

Use of the *P*-value has two advantages; first, we can perform the test by inspecting this value without the need to enter a significance level into the program. Second, the rule just stated is "one size fits all," in that virtually all the tests we consider may be expressed in this format. In view of the importance of this result, we provide the output from both Excel and Minitab in the next example, by way of illustration. Other programs produce similar outputs.

Hypothesis Testing with *P*-Values

Tests based upon *P*-values are completely equivalent to those which use the same statistics with reference to tables of the *t*-distribution.

EXAMPLE 7.4 ■ A test of the slope

The Excel and Minitab outputs for the simple example given earlier as Example 7.2 are shown in Figure 7.12. From the output, we see that $t_{obs} = 3.10$ and the *P*-value for the slope is 0.036. [The numbers in the Excel output have been rounded for ease of comparison; in addition, we never need so many decimal places in the final answer!] We set $\alpha = 0.05$ and conduct a two-tailed test. Because $P = 0.036 < \alpha = 0.05$, we reject H_0 and conclude that there is evidence in favor of a relationship between *X* and *Y*. In general, it is much easier to use *P*-values, and we shall usually do so without further comment.

Note 1: As may be seen from the computer output, it is also possible to set up a test for the intercept. Such tests, however, rarely provide any useful information, because the value $X = 0$ is usually well outside the range of applications. Further, the value of the intercept can be changed by shifting the origins of the *X* and *Y* measurements. Thus, an intercept test is useful *only* when we wish to test that the regression line goes through a prespecified origin.

Note 2: A $100(1 - \alpha)$ percent confidence interval for the slope may be established as $b_1 \pm t_{\alpha/2}(n - 2) * SE(b_1)$. The *t* value in this expression must be obtained from the *t*-distribution. Thus for the data in this example, the 95 percent CI for the slope is $1.26 \pm (2.78) * (0.4069) = [0.13, 2.39]$. Because the sample size is so small, we do not have an accurate assessment of how *X* affects *Y*, even though the test tells us that there appears to be a relationship.

Note 3: For the time being, we ignore the *Analysis of Variance (ANOVA)* table. For simple regression, it provides no new information relative to the two-tailed *t*-test, as can be seen from the fact that the *t*-test and ANOVA test have the same *P*-values. We will discuss this further in Section 8.3.

FIGURE 7.12 EXCEL AND MINITAB OUTPUTS FOR SIMPLE EXAMPLE

(A) Excel output

	A	B	C	D	E	F	G	H
1	*X*	*Y*						
2	2	8						
3	4	7						
4	5	12.5						
5	6	10						
6	8	17						
7	9	14.5						
8								
9	SUMMARY OUTPUT							
10								
11	*Regression Statistics*							
12	Multiple R	0.84						
13	R Square	0.7056						
14	Adjusted R Square	0.632						
15	Standard Error	2.349						
16	Observations	6						
17								
18	ANOVA							
19		*df*	*SS*	*MS*	*F*	*Significance F*		
20	Regression	1	52.92	52.92	9.59	0.0364		
21	Residual	4	22.08	5.52				
22	Total	5	75					
23								
24		*Coefficients*	*Standard Error*	*t Stat*	*P-value*	*Lower 95%*	*Upper 95%*	
25	Intercept	4.36	2.50	1.75	0.16	-2.57	11.29	
26	X	1.26	0.41	3.10	0.04	0.13	2.39	
27								
28								
29								

Sheet1 / Sheet2 / Sheet3

(B) Minitab output

Regression Analysis: Y versus X

The regression equation is
Y = 4.36 + 1.26X

Predictor	Coef	SE Coef	T	P
Constant	4.360	2.498	1.75	0.156
X	1.2600	0.4069	3.10	0.036

S = 2.34947   R-Sq = 70.6%   R-Sq(adj) = 63.2%

Analysis of Variance

Source	DF	SS	MS	F	P
Regression	1	52.920	52.920	9.59	0.036
Residual Error	4	22.080	5.520		
Total	5	75.000			

Data: Example 7_2.xlsx. ∎

Numerical Accuracy and Presentation of Results

Using a large number of decimal places to ensure numerical precision in the calculations is desirable. However, once the calculations are complete, we must decide how many decimal places to retain for presentation purposes.

EXAMPLE 7.5 ■ Test and confidence interval for gasoline prices

The relevant output for the data on gasoline prices is as follows:

Predictor	Coef	SE Coef	T	P
Constant	0.68760	0.02591	26.54	0.000
L1_crude	0.0270690	0.0005367	50.44	0.000
S = 0.176121	R-Sq = 94.3%	R-Sq(adj) = 94.3%		

Note that the P-value is quoted to only three decimal places, so the output does not imply that P is exactly zero; rather, it means that $P < 0.0005$, which rounds down to 0.000 to three decimal places. Here we reproduce the computer output exactly as it appears. Elsewhere in the book for presentation purposes, we simplify the output to an appropriate number of significant figures. In this example, we expect a positive slope, so a one-sided upper-tail test is appropriate. Using $\alpha = 0.05$ (or any other plausible value!), we clearly reject H_0 and conclude that there is a strong positive relationship between the two variables, as expected. The intercept might conceivably be interpreted as the transport and marketing costs of gasoline, but this interpretation is a stretch when the smallest observed value of $L1\_crude$ is so far from the origin.

To determine the 95 percent confidence interval for the slope, we first obtain the critical value from the t-distribution to get $t_{.025}(153) = 1.975$, very close to the limiting value of 1.960 obtained from the normal distribution. The confidence interval for the slope is given by $0.027069 \pm (1.975) * (0.0005367) = [0.0260, 0.0281]$. That is, an increase of \$1 in the price of a barrel of crude oil produces an *expected* increase of 2.6 to 2.8 cents per gallon of gasoline at the pump. In this case, the large sample provides a clear idea of the relationship between X and Y. ■

7.6.2 Interpreting the Slope Coefficient

We have shown that when the slope coefficient is significant we can sensibly regard X as a suitable explanatory variable in our model. As before, suppose our linear model for the dependent variable is

$$Y = \beta_0 + \beta_1 X + \varepsilon.$$

That is, X has a linear impact on Y. Specifically, a unit change in X produces an impact of β_1 in Y. So, does the size of β_1 measure the importance of X in forecasting Y? No, because a change of units in either Y or X will affect the estimate. In our gasoline example, the price of unleaded was measured in dollars. If we changed the units of measurement to cents, this would affect β_1 and give a revised estimate of $100\beta_1$ (and similarly with β_0). However, the tests in the previous section would again show the same P-value and R^2, and, of course, the same predictions, but this time in cents.

Discussion Question *What is the impact on the standard error of a change in the units in which X is measured? In which Y is measured? Does R^2 change?*

An easily interpretable measure that eliminates the effects of the units used in measuring both X and Y is the *elasticity*, which measures the responsiveness of changes in Y to changes in X. For example, if the elasticity of the price of unleaded to the price of crude was 1, then a doubling of the price of crude would lead to a doubling of the expected price of unleaded at the pump.

Elasticity

The *elasticity* is defined as the proportionate change in Y relative to the proportionate change in X and is measured by

$$\frac{\Delta E(Y|X)}{E(Y|X)} \bigg/ \frac{\Delta X}{X} = b_1 \frac{X}{E(Y|X)} = \frac{b_1 X}{b_0 + b_1 X},$$

where ΔY is the change in Y and ΔX is the change in X.

In November 2008, the price of crude was \$57.31 per barrel of oil. From that dollar amount, together with the expected December price of unleaded, \$2.239, the elasticity of the price of unleaded to the price of crude is estimated to be

$$b_1 \frac{X}{E(Y|X)} = (0.02707) \frac{57.31}{2.239} = 0.69.$$

As X increases, the elasticity also increases, since $b_0 > 0$. This result seems counterintuitive and suggests that we should modify our analysis; accordingly, we now explore a logarithmic transformation, which leads us to a simpler, more intuitive definition of elasticity.

7.6.3 Transformations

The increased fluctuations in the later part of the series, when the price of crude oil is higher, suggest that some kind of transformation is desirable. Two possibilities come to mind:

1. A logarithmic transformation, as in Chapters 3 and 4;
2. Conversion from current dollars to real dollars through division by a price index.

These two options are not mutually exclusive. We pursue the second option and their combination in Minicase 7.1 but now examine the first possibility, letting ln Y and ln X denote the logarithms of the two variables of interest. The output is as follows:

Predictor	Coef	SE Coef	T	P
Constant	−1.70805	0.03771	−45.30	0.000
ln_L1_crude	0.62815	0.01056	59.46	0.000
S = 0.0763061	R-Sq = 95.9%	R-Sq(adj) = 95.8%		

Transforming back to the original units, we have

$$Unleaded = exp(-1.70805) * (L1\_crude)^{0.62815}.$$

The log–log model has a constant elasticity, given by the coefficient of the slope. That is, the elasticity is $b_1 = 0.628$ for all values of X, implying that an increase of 1 percent in the price of crude leads to an increase of about 0.063 percent in the price at the pump. This value is somewhat lower than that obtained in the previous analysis. The key difference is that for the log transformed model, the elasticity is constant. But before we can make a reasoned choice between the two models, we need to develop diagnostic procedures, a task we defer to Section 8.5.

Forecasting by Using Simple Linear Regression

Once we have established our statistical model, we are ready to use it for forecasting. With X as the explanatory variable in the model, we must first establish values of X for which the model is to be used to forecast future time periods. Similarly, when we forecast from a cross section to new members of the population, again we need to establish the relevant X values. For simplicity, we present the discussion in terms of a single future value, although multiple forecasts will often be needed.

The value of X may arise in any of three ways:

a. X is known ahead of time (e.g., the size of a sales force, or demographic details concerning a consumer)
b. X is unknown but can still be forecast (e.g., gross domestic product)
c. X is unknown, but we wish to make what-if forecasts (e.g., the effects of different advertising or pricing policies)

Consider the gasoline prices example that we have used throughout this chapter. We deliberately used X with a one-month lag so that the value of X would be available when we wish to make forecasts *one month ahead*. However, if we forecast gasoline prices two or more months ahead, we must either invoke case (b) and provide forecasts of the price of crude oil or construct new regression models that progressively use X lagged by two, three, . . . , months. For the present, we stay with forecasts one period ahead. The use of models with longer lags is explored in Section 7.7.4.

Finally, case (c) represents an important use of regression models whereby several alternative values of the input may be considered and the effects on Y examined. For example, we might specify different possible prices for a barrel of crude oil and examine the subsequent changes in price at the pump as a guide to decision making.

7.7.1   The Point Forecast

If we are given the value of the input for the next time period as X_{n+1} and we have estimated the regression line, the point forecast (F_{n+1}) is

$$F_{n+1} = b_0 + b_1 X_{n+1}. \qquad (7.15)$$

Many people and texts refer to equation (7.15) simply as *the* forecast. However, it is important to recognize that is the *point forecast* and that statistical models provide much more information and greater insights than just one number. In particular, the regression model may be used to generate prediction intervals, as we show in the next section.

Note: We have used $\hat{Y}$ to denote the fitted values in the regression line, as in equation (7.6), and now we use F_{n+1} to denote the forecast in equation (7.15); the two formulas are the same, so why the different notation? The reason is that the *fitted* values correspond to those observations which were used in the estimation process. By contrast, forecasts pertain to new observations that were not used to estimate the model parameters.

EXAMPLE 7.6 ■ Forecasting gasoline prices

The model for gasoline prices was fitted with the use of data from January 1996 through December 2008. We now generate one-step-ahead forecasts, using equation (7.15) for the 24 months from January 2009 to December 2010 so that, for example, the forecast for May 2009 uses the crude price for April 2009 and the calculation is as follows:

$$X_{n+1} = 49.65 \quad \text{and} \quad F_{n+1} = 0.6876 + 0.027069 * 49.65 = 2.032.$$

The first few point forecasts and the overall summary measures are given in Table 7.3. The various error measures are computed in accordance with the formulas in Section 2.7.

TABLE 7.3   SELECTED ONE-STEP-AHEAD FORECASTS FOR GASOLINE PRICES, WITH PREDICTION INTERVALS AND OVERALL (24-MONTH) SUMMARY MEASURES (*January 2009–December 2010*)

Forecast Month	Actual Price	L1_Crude	Forecast	95% PI, Lower Limit	95% PI, Upper Limit
Jan-2009	1.788	41.71	1.801	1.452	2.150
Feb-2009	1.923	39.09	1.817	1.468	2.166
Mar-2009	1.959	47.94	1.746	1.397	2.095
Apr-2009	2.049	49.65	1.985	1.636	2.334
. . .	. . .	. . .	. . .	. . .	. . .
	ME	0.019			
	MAE	0.092			
	RMSE	0.126			
	MAPE	3.73			

Data: Gas_prices_1.xlsx.

The full set of forecast and actual values appears in Figure 7.13. The forecasts lagged the upturn in prices from March to June 2009 but otherwise did quite well. The root-mean-square error over the hold-out period was 0.126, consistent with the standard error for the model ($S = 0.176$). ∎

7.7.2   Prediction Intervals

Given that our forecasts are not going to be exact, what can we say about their likely accuracy? This is the critical question that arises in building a forecasting model. The random variation in the forecasts comes from three sources: the inherent variation of the process (i.e., the error term), the uncertainty caused by needing to estimate the unknown parameters, and misspecification of the model. For the time being, we assume that assumptions R3 through R6 are valid, so we focus only on the first two of these sources.

If we denote the future (unknown) value of the dependent variable by Y_{n+1} and the forecast of that value based upon the estimated regression line by F_{n+1}, then the overall mean square error for the forecast in relation to the future value is

$$var(Y_{n+1} - F_{n+1}) = \sigma^2 \left[1 + \frac{1}{n} + \frac{(X_{n+1} - \overline{X})^2}{\sum (X_i - \overline{X})^2} \right]. \qquad (7.16)$$

The details are given in Appendix 7A. Note that the term on the left-hand side of equation (7.16) is written as the variance rather than the mean square error because the forecast is unbiased when the linear model is correct. Given that we must estimate σ by S, the estimated variance is

$$\widehat{var}(Y_{n+1} - F_{n+1}) = S^2 \left[1 + \frac{1}{n} + \frac{(X_{n+1} - \overline{X})^2}{\sum (X_i - \overline{X})^2} \right].$$

Finally, we define the standard error of the forecast as

$$SE(Y_{n+1} - F_{n+1}) = \sqrt{\widehat{var}(Y_{n+1} - F_{n+1})}.$$

Now, recall from Section 7.5 that assumptions R3–R6 combine to assert that the error terms follow a normal distribution with zero mean and variance σ^2. It can be shown that the forecast error then follows a normal distribution with variance given by equation (7.16).

Because we must estimate σ by S, we replace the normal distribution by Student's t with the appropriate DF. Putting all this together, we arrive at the prediction interval:

$$F_{n+1} \pm t_{\alpha/2}(n-2) * SE(Y_{n+1} - F_{n+1}). \qquad (7.17)$$

The $100(1-\alpha)$ percent prediction interval is a probability statement. It says that the probability that a future observation will lie in the interval defined by equation (7.17) is $(1-\alpha)$. For example, if we set $(1-\alpha) = 0.95$, then, given that the price of crude (X) for April 2009 is 49.65, then the prediction interval for May 2009 is $2.032 \pm 1.975 * 0.1767$, and it follows that

> With probability 0.95, the actual gasoline price will lie in the range from \$1.68 to \$2.38 per gallon when the previous month's crude price was \$49.65.

Prediction Interval for the Future Observation, Y_{n+1}

The *prediction interval* for a forecast measures the range of likely outcomes for the unknown actual observation, for a specified probability and for a given X value.

The detailed calculation is shown in the next example.

EXAMPLE 7.7 ■ Calculation of a prediction interval

We continue our consideration of the forecasts for May 2009, begun in Example 7.6. The various numbers we need are

$$n = 155, X_{n+1} = 49.65, F_{n+1} = 2.032, S = 0.1761,$$

$$\overline{X} = 40.44, \text{ and } \sum(X_i - \overline{X})^2 = 361163.6.$$

We now substitute into equation (7.16) to obtain

$$SE(Y_{n+1} - F_{n+1}) = S\left[1 + \frac{1}{n} + \frac{(X_{n+1} - \overline{X})^2}{\sum(X_i - \overline{X})^2}\right]^{1/2}$$

$$= 0.1761\left[1 + \frac{1}{155} + \frac{(49.65 - 40.44)^2}{361163.6}\right]^{1/2}$$

$$= 0.1761[1 + 0.00645 + 0.000235]^{1/2}$$

$$= 0.1767.$$

Because the sample is large, the extra terms have a very slight effect on the SE. Returning to equation (7.17), we obtain the 95 percent prediction interval by using $t_{0.025}(153) = 1.975$:

$$2.032 \pm (1.975) * (0.1767) = 2.032 \pm 0.349 = [1.682, 2.381].$$

In practice, the prediction intervals are evaluated with the use of standard software, which implements the analysis just described. The steps in Minitab and SPSS are summarized in Appendix 7C. Excel does not provide the intervals as a standard function.

The actual and one-step-ahead forecast values and the 95 percent lower and upper prediction interval limits for January 2009 through December 2010 are shown in Figure 7.13. All 24 actual values fall within the PI, which might be expected when one is using 95 percent prediction intervals. However, the intervals are of the order of ± 35 cents, which is too wide to be very useful. In Chapter 8, we will develop improved models that narrow the PIs. ■

FIGURE 7.13   PLOT OF ACTUAL VALUES WITH ONE-STEP-AHEAD FORECASTS
AND 95% PREDICTION INTERVALS FOR UNLEADED PRICES
(January 2009–December 2010)

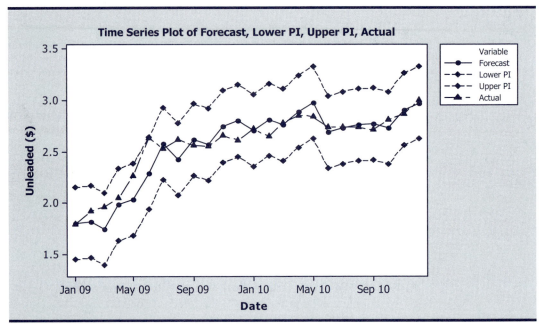

Data: Gas_prices_1.xlsx; adapted from Minitab output.

7.7.3   An Approximate Prediction Interval

The previous example suggests that when n is reasonably large, the term in square brackets in equation (7.16) is close to 1.0. This result is generally true, and as a quick calculation, the 95 percent prediction interval may be reasonably approximated by $F_{n+1} \pm 2S$. This approximation gives us an easy way of interpreting whether our predictions are useful. Effectively, the standard error S measures the predictive accuracy of our model. When $Y > 0$, as is true for most business variables, the comparison of S with $\bar{Y}$ is a rough measure of a model's accuracy. With the gasoline example, $\dfrac{S}{\bar{Y}} = \dfrac{0.1767}{1.778} = 0.099$, which suggests a prediction interval of around 20 percent of the average price level. However, the increases in price in recent years mean that using the overall average is not as useful as relating S to the most recent data.

> **Discussion Question**   *Ideally, prediction intervals should be narrow. How would you decide whether a prediction interval was sufficiently narrow to be useful? How might you recognize that an interval was too narrow?*

7.7.4   Forecasting More than One Period Ahead

Suppose we were living at the end of December 2008 and wished to make forecasts further ahead than January 2009. There are two[12] possible approaches:

1. Generate forecasts for X and apply these to the original model.
2. Reformulate the model so that X is lagged by two (or more) periods, as appropriate.

---

[12]We may also use vector autoregressive (VAR) models, which we discuss in Section 10.5.

The first approach is more commonly applied, but suffers from the drawback that the uncertainty in X is not reflected in the prediction intervals for the forecasts. It has the advantage that different what-if paths for X can be formulated and compared with the use of a single model. The second approach is somewhat more tedious, but it will be more valuable when good forecasts for X are unavailable. It has the advantage of providing accurate prediction intervals, especially when forecasts for X are inaccurate.

EXAMPLE 7.8 ■ Forecasting gasoline prices two periods ahead

To illustrate the preceding two points, we generated two-step-ahead forecasts for gasoline prices by each method:

- We generate one-step-ahead forecasts for the crude oil price series and then insert these forecasts into equation (7.7). The forecasts are produced by means of the additive Holt–Winters model (see Section 4.4).
- We fitted a regression model for the crude price, lagged two periods.

The results are summarized in Table 7.4. The following points may be noted:

i. The standard error increases and R^2 falls when we move to two steps ahead, as expected.
ii. Forecast performance also falls off when we move to two steps ahead.
iii. The two sets of forecasts are broadly comparable in performance. (The second method does somewhat better here, but we should not read much into such a finding for just one example.).
iv. The prediction intervals for one step ahead and for two steps ahead with method 2 seem to provide the right level of *coverage*; that is, we would expect 95 percent of future observations to fall within the 95 percent prediction intervals. The prediction intervals for method 1 appear to be too narrow, with 4 out of 24 values lying outside the 95 percent limits for the two-step-ahead predictions.

The first two results are as expected and the third is reasonable. However, point (iv) is often overlooked in applications and can lead to overoptimistic conclusions about forecast accuracy, as assessed by the width of the prediction intervals.

TABLE 7.4 SUMMARY RESULTS FOR ONE-STEP-AHEAD AND TWO-STEPS-AHEAD FORECASTS FOR GASOLINE PRICES

Statistic	One Step Ahead	Two Steps Ahead	
		Lag-1 Model + Forecast	Lag-2 Model
Intercept		0.688	0.73
Slope		0.0271	0.0262
R^2		94.3	88.6
S		0.176	0.250
ME	0.019	0.064	0.066
MAE	0.092	0.179	0.145
RMSE	0.126	0.235	0.202
MAPE	3.73	8.64	6.49
MWPI	0.70	0.70	1.00
# outside PI	0/24	4/24	1/24

Data: Gas_prices_1.xlsx.

[*Note:* MWPI = mean width of the prediction interval, the difference between the upper and lower limits in equation (7.17).]

7.8

Forecasting by Using Leading Indicators

When we are developing a forecasting system, we must always ask, "What do we know and when do we know it?" An economic model would naturally relate current sales to the current value of the gross domestic product (*GDP*). However, the figure for current *GDP* will be available only well after the current quarter is over, so it is of limited value for *forecasting* sales over the next few weeks.

An alternative approach is to seek a suitable *leading indicator*—that is, a series produced early enough to be usable and reflective of likely future movements in sales. One such series is the Index of Consumer Sentiment, produced by the University of Michigan. A second major source of this kind of information is the Conference Board, which produces several such indexes: Consumer Confidence, CEO Confidence, U.S. Leading Indicators, and Help Wanted Advertising. (For further details, see *www.conference-board.org*.) Another natural leading indicator is the stock market, whether a general index like Dow Jones for the economy as a whole, an industry-level index, or the stock of a single company.

In each case, we are seeking, not a causal relationship, but rather an indicator that is published in timely fashion. Indeed, the causal pattern will often be of the form that some factor (say, Z) causes movements both in the leading indicator (*LI*) and in the variable of interest (Y). If Z is observed in time to make the forecast, clearly we will use it. If Z is unavailable, but *LI* is, we use *LI*. The forecasts may not be as effective as they would have been if Z were available, but *LI* will generally provide some improvements over forecasting with no knowledge of the inputs. We follow up on these ideas in Minicase 7.2 at the end of the chapter.

Summary

This chapter introduced the notion of modeling the relationship between two variables. After a discussion of the distinction between correlation and causation, we developed an estimation procedure by using the method of ordinary least squares and we went on to develop a statistical framework for the evaluation of regression models. We ended the chapter with a discussion of forecasting methods that provide both point and interval forecasts.

We do not discuss the relevant forecasting principles at this stage, but prefer to wait until the end of Chapter 8, when the full multiple regression model, which can include more input variables, has been developed.

Exercises

7.1   A soft-drink company monitored its television advertising over an eight-week period to evaluate the effect on sales (in millions of dollars) with respect to the number of 30-second spots aired in that week. Estimate the regression equation. The data are as follows:

Week	1	2	3	4	5	6	7	8
No. of spots	8	12	16	10	8	12	16	10
Sales	25	34	39	32	22	30	43	31

Data shown is from file Exercise_7_1.xlsx.

a.   Estimate the regression line for sales on spots.
b.   Test whether the slope is significantly different from zero, using $\alpha = 0.10$.
c.   Compute S and R^2 and interpret the results.
d.   The company has reserved 20 spots for week 9. Forecast the sales and construct a 90 percent prediction interval.
e.   Comment on the level of accuracy this analysis provides.

7.2 A company experiments with different price settings over a 12-week period. The weekly sales and revenue figures are shown in the following table:

Week	1	2	3	4	5	6	7	8	9	10	11	12
Price	6	8	10	6	8	10	6	8	10	6	8	10
Sales	28	30	28	30	24	22	34	26	20	36	32	26
Revenue	168	240	280	180	320	220	204	208	200	216	256	260

Data shown is from file Exercise_7_2.xlsx.

a. Estimate the regression lines for sales on price and for revenues on price.
b. Test whether the slopes are significantly different from zero, using $\alpha = 0.05$.
c. Compute R^2 and interpret the results.
d. Why does the line for sales fit the data better than the line for revenues?

7.3 A linear time trend may be estimated by means of simple linear regression for Y on time.
a. Estimate the time trend for the sales data given in Exercise 7.1.
b. Compute S and R^2 and interpret the results.
c. Test whether the slope is significantly different from zero, using $\alpha = 0.05$.
d. Which model is more useful, the regression of sales on spots or that of sales on time? Give reasons for your answer.

7.4 Estimate a linear time trend for the Netflix data (*Netflix.xlsx*), using data for the period 2000Q1 to 2008Q4.
a. Carry out a preliminary analysis of the data and interpret your results.
b. Estimate the time trend.
c. Test whether the slope is significantly different from zero, using $\alpha = 0.05$.
d. Compute S and R^2 and interpret the results.
e. Compute point forecasts for sales in each quarter of 2009, and construct 95 percent prediction intervals.
f. Comment upon your results.

7.5 Consider the data on rail safety previously examined in Exercise 2.2 (*Rail_safety.xlsx*).
a. Carry out a preliminary analysis of the data and interpret your results.
b. Estimate the regression line for injuries on train miles.
c. Test whether the slope is significantly different from zero, using $\alpha = 0.05$.
d. Compute S and R^2 and interpret the results.
e. Compute a point forecast for the number of injuries, given an estimated level of train miles equal to 100. Construct a 95 percent prediction interval.
f. Comment upon your results.

7.6 Develop a simple linear regression model for the median price of a new home as a linear function of time, using the data in *New_home_prices.xlsx*, which shows monthly prices from January 1981 through December 2007. (Prices are quoted in thousands of dollars and include the price of the land.) Use the data through December 2005 to estimate the parameters and then predict monthly sales for 2006 and 2007. Generate 90 percent prediction intervals for your forecasts and compare your forecasts with the actual values. Repeat the analysis for the mean prices and compare the results. What other variables might be useful for forecasting purposes?

7.7 Develop a simple linear regression model for the number of new housing starts as a linear function of the mortgage rate, using the data in *Housing_starts.xlsx*, downloaded from *www.EconStats.com*. The data relate to monthly housing starts (in thousands, seasonally adjusted) and mortgage rates (end-of-month 30-year percentage rate) from January 1981 through December 2010. With the data through December 2006, estimate the parameters and then predict monthly sales for 2007 and 2008, using the actual mortgage rates as inputs. Generate 90 percent prediction intervals for your forecasts and compare your forecasts with the actual values. Comment upon your results and then refit the model using the data through December 2010. Compare the two sets of parameters. Interpret the results.

7.8   Reanalyze the gasoline prices data, using the data in *Gas_prices_1.xlsx* after transforming both variables to logarithms, as in Section 7.6.3. Generate forecasts for the hold-out sample, and convert the point forecasts and prediction interval limits back to the original units. Compare your results with the model developed earlier that does not use any transformations. Which model would you recommend?

Minicase 7.1 Gasoline Prices Revisited

Use the data in *Gas_prices_1.xlsx*, or go to the U.S. Department of Energy website, *www.eia.doe.gov*, and download the most recent data on the monthly series for retail gasoline prices and crude oil prices. Use the last ten years of data as the estimation sample and keep the last two years as the hold-out sample to test the forecasting performance of your model.

1. Rerun the model described there and compare the results with those obtained earlier.
2. Repeat the analysis, using the log transformed series, and compare your results.
3. Use the Consumer Price Index (*CPI*) to create real (constant-dollar) prices rather than observed prices for both variables. Repeat the analysis described in steps 1 and 2. Does this approach lead to improved forecasts? (This question is harder than it looks!) What if any economic arguments suggest using a constant-price model.
4. Repeat the analysis for weekly data from the same source, using a lag of one week or two weeks and the last five years of data. Keep the last year as the hold-out sample.

Summarize your findings.

Minicase 7.2 Consumer Confidence and Unemployment

Measures of consumer confidence are readily available from sample surveys and often serve as useful leading indicators when data on causal macroeconomic variables are not yet available. Use the data in the spreadsheet *Unemp_conconf.xlsx* to examine the regression for U.S. unemployment on the Conference Board Index of Consumer Confidence. Try the current month as the predictor variable and also try the Index of Consumer Confidence at lags one, two and three. Which model provides the best fit?

Hold out the last 12 months of data and generate forecasts, using each model. Compare the forecasting performance of each model, using the measures developed in Chapter 2. Summarize your findings.

Minicase 7.3 Baseball Salaries Revisited

Use the data in *Baseball.xlsx*. It is evident from Figure 7.6 that salaries start to level off or even decline once players' careers extend beyond 12 years or so. Also, the spread of salaries increases considerably as the number of years played increases. To allow for these features of the data,

1. Eliminate players with 12 or more years of experience from the data set and rerun the analysis. Compare your results with those reported in Example 7.3.

2. Transform the salaries by taking logarithms and determine whether the regression assumptions outlined in Section 7.5 seem to be better approximations to the transformed data.
3. Generate 95 percent prediction intervals for all players, and check to see how many actual salaries fall within those intervals.

What conclusion do you draw from eliminating the unusual observations?

References

Anderson, D. R., Sweeney, D. J., and Williams, T. A. (2011). *Statistics for Business and Economics*, 11th ed. Mason, OH: South-Western.

Kutner, M., Nachtsheim, C., Neter, J. and Li, W. (2005). *Applied Linear Statistical Models*, 5th ed. New York: McGraw-Hill.

Appendix 7A   Derivation of Ordinary Least Squares Estimators[13]

In Section 7.2, we stated that the regression line relating the dependent variable Y to the explanatory variable X should be determined by the method of ordinary least squares. That is, we choose the intercept b_0 and the slope b_1 so as to minimize the quantity given in equation (7.2):

$$SSE = \sum_{i=1}^{n}(Observed - Fitted)^2 = \sum_{i=1}^{n}(Y_i - b_0 - b_1X_i)^2.$$

Here, SSE denotes the sum of squared errors, with the sum taken over all n observations. A feature of SSE is that it is quadratic in the coefficients $\{b_0, b_1\}$, so that obtaining the partial first derivatives with respect to these coefficients and setting the partial derivatives to zero yields a pair of linear equations. That is, if we set

$$\frac{\partial(SSE)}{\partial b_0} = 0 \quad \text{and} \quad \frac{\partial(SSE)}{\partial b_1} = 0, \qquad (7A.1)$$

we arrive at the equations

$$\sum_{i=1}^{n}(Y_i - b_0 - b_1X_i) = 0$$

$$\sum_{i=1}^{n}X_i(Y_i - b_0 - b_1X_i) = 0. \qquad (7A.2)$$

We now define the sample means of the two variables as

$$\overline{X} = \frac{\sum X_i}{n} \quad \text{and} \quad \overline{Y} = \frac{\sum Y_i}{n} \qquad (7A.3)$$

---

[13]This appendix provides only a brief outline of the derivation. For a complete treatment, see a standard text on regression analysis, such as Kutner, Nachtsheim, Neter, and Li (2005).

and the sums of squares and cross products as

$$S_{XX} = \sum (X_i - \bar{X})^2, \; S_{XY} = \sum (X_i - \bar{X})(Y_i - \bar{Y}), \text{ and } S_{YY} = \sum (Y_i - \bar{Y})^2. \quad (7A.4)$$

We then simplify equation (7A.4), using equations (7A.2) and (7A.3), to arrive at

$$b_0 = \bar{Y} - b_1 \bar{X} \quad \text{and} \quad b_1 = \frac{S_{XY}}{S_{XX}}. \quad (7A.5)$$

The standard error is estimated as

$$S = \frac{SSE}{\sqrt{(n-2)}}. \quad (7A.6)$$

The estimated standard error of the slope is given by

$$SE(b_1) = S/\sqrt{S_{XX}}. \quad (7A.7)$$

Further, it may be shown that the solution given in equation (7A.2) produces a minimum for *SSE* and that this minimum value is

$$SSE = S_{YY} - b_1^2 S_{XX}. \quad (7A.8)$$

Equation (7A.8) is just a restatement of the partition of the sum of squares given in Section 7.4 and may be rewritten as $SSE = (1 - R^2)S_{YY}$.

Extension to K explanatory variables

The discussion thus far relates to simple regression, with estimates given by two linear equations in two unknowns, as we can see in equation (7A.2). When we turn to multiple regression in the next chapter, we include *K* predictor variables in the model and *SSE* becomes

$$SSE = \sum_{i=1}^{n} (Observed - Fitted)^2 = \sum_{i=1}^{n} (Y_i - b_0 - b_1 X_{1i} - \cdots b_K X_{Ki})^2.$$

The partial first derivatives lead to the $(K + 1)$ linear equations

$$\sum_{i=1}^{n} (Y_i - b_0 - b_1 X_{1i} \cdots - b_K X_{Ki}) = 0.$$
$$\sum_{i=1}^{n} X_{ji}(Y_i - b_0 - b_1 X_{1i} \cdots - b_K X_{Ki}) = 0, \quad j = 1, 2, \ldots, K \quad (7A.9)$$

Equations (7A.9) reduce to equations (7A.2) when $K = 1$. However, for any value of K, we may still write

$$SSE = (1 - R^2)S_{YY}. \quad (7A.10)$$

That is, R^2 denotes the proportion of variance explained by the model. To emphasize, equations (7A.5) through (7A.8) apply only when $K = 1$, but equations (7A.9) and (7A.10) apply for any value of K.

Prediction intervals

The uncertainty in the forecasts depends on the difference between the forecasted value (F_{n+1}) and the actual value of Y. If we knew the underlying model, a (future) new observation Y_{n+1}, with the explanatory variable taking on the value X_{n+1}, would be given by

$$Y_{n+1} = \beta_0 + \beta_1 X_{n+1} + \varepsilon_{n+1}.$$

However, we had to estimate the intercept and slope, so the forecast is

$$F_{n+1} = b_0 + b_1 X_{n+1}. \tag{7A.11}$$

The difference between these two expressions is

$$\begin{aligned}Y_{n+1} - F_{n+1} &= (\beta_0 + \beta_1 X_{n+1} + \varepsilon_{n+1}) - (b_0 + b_1 X_{n+1})\\ &= \varepsilon_{n+1} + (b_0 - \beta_0) + (b_1 - \beta_1)X_{n+1}.\end{aligned}$$

The first term in the rightmost expression represents the inherent variation in the process. Even if we knew the parameters of the model, so that the second and third terms were zero, this element would still be present. The second and third terms represent the estimation error; as the sample size increases, they will diminish in importance. Because the error term pertains to the new observation, whereas the estimates are based upon the original sample, it follows that the two terms are statistically independent when the errors are independent. Thus, the variance of the forecast error is

$$var(Y_{n+1} - F_{n+1}) = var(\varepsilon_{n+1}) + var\{(b_0 - \beta_0) + (b_1 - \beta_1)X_{n+1}\}. \tag{7A.12}$$

For simple linear regression, we may derive the variance of the fitted value from the variances for the intercept and slope. It can be shown that

$$var\{(b_0 - \beta_0) + (b_1 - \beta_1)X_{n+1}\} = \sigma^2\left[\frac{1}{n} + \frac{(X_{n+1} - \overline{X})^2}{\sum(X_i - \overline{X})^2}\right]. \tag{7A.13}$$

We substitute equation (7A.13) into equation (7A.12) to arrive at the final expression for the *forecast variance in simple linear regression*:

$$var(Y_{n+1} - F_{n+1}) = \sigma^2\left[1 + \frac{1}{n} + \frac{(X_{n+1} - \overline{X})^2}{\sum(X_i - \overline{X})^2}\right]. \tag{7A.14}$$

Note that the further X_{n+1} is from the sample mean, $\overline{X}$, the larger the variance. Because the variance is unknown, we use the estimate given in equation (7A.6) to obtain

$$\widehat{var}(Y_{n+1} - F_{n+1}) = S^2\left[1 + \frac{1}{n} + \frac{(X_{n+1} - \overline{X})^2}{\sum(X_i - \overline{X})^2}\right].$$

The second and third terms in equation (7A.14) decline as the sample size increases, but the first remains constant. Thus, in sufficiently large samples, we can approximate the forecast variance by S^2.

Appendix 7B   Computing *P*-Values in Excel

In this appendix, we explain how to calculate *P*-values in Excel. Most statistical packages include similar procedures, and further details for select packages may be found on the book's website.

In all cases, begin by clicking on f_x and select the *Statistical* functions. Continue using the appropriate choices for the *t* or *F* distributions as needed. The table specifies both the function to be used for each tail area and the required inputs. The final column provides numerical examples.

Distribution and Tail Area	Function	Items to enter	Example
t: Lower tail	T.DIST	*X = Observed t-value* *Deg_freedom = Degrees of freedom* *Cumulative = TRUE*	$X = -1.58$ *Deg_freedom = 20* *P-value = 0.0649*
t: Upper tail	T.DIST.RT	*X = Observed t-value* *Deg_freedom = Degrees of freedom*	$X = 1.58$ *Deg_freedom = 20* *P-value = 0.0649*
t: Two tails	T.DIST.2T	*X = Observed t-value* *Deg_freedom = Degrees of freedom*	$X = 1.58$ *Deg_freedom = 20* *P-value = 0.1298*
F: Upper tail	F.DIST.RT	*X = Observed F-value* *Deg_freedom1 = Numerator degrees of freedom* *Deg_freedom2 = Denominator degrees of freedom*	$X = 2.50$ *Deg_freedom1 = 3* *Deg_freedom2 = 25* *P-value = 0.0826*

Appendix 7C Computing Prediction Intervals

In practice, prediction intervals are evaluated with the use of standard software, which implements the analysis just described. The steps in Minitab and in SPSS are summarized in the box that follows. Excel does not provide the intervals as a standard function.

Calculation of Prediction Intervals in Minitab

1. Stat > Regression > Regression
2. Enter the *Y* (Response) and *X* (Predictor) variables.
3. Click on *Options*.
4. Enter the column containing the *X* values to be used for forecasting.
5. Specify the confidence level.
6. Click on OK to return to main dialog box, and click on OK again.

Calculation of Prediction Intervals in SPSS

1. Analyze > Regression > Linear
2. Enter the *Y* (Dependent) and *X* (Independent) variables.
3. Click on *Save*.
4. Check *Predicted Values–Unstandardized* and *Prediction Intervals–Individual*.
5. Specify the confidence level.
6. Click on *Continue* to return to main dialog box, and click on OK.

Note that SPSS computes prediction intervals for the *X* values already entered. Enter any additional *X* values in the *X* column(s), with blanks (for missing values) in the *Y* column.

Examples of both these commands can be found on the book's website.

CHAPTER 8

Multiple Regression for Time Series

CONTENTS

INTRODUCTION

Why have you included so many variables in your regression model?

—Anonymous Statistician

Why have you included so few variables in your regression model?

—Anonymous Economist

Introduction

One of the key restrictions we faced in Chapter 7 was the inability to consider more than one explanatory variable at a time. Yet both the discussion there and basic common sense indicate that events in the business world are typically affected by multiple inputs. We may not be able to measure all of them, but we do need to identify the main factors and incorporate them into our forecasting framework. A first step toward identifying an appropriate set of variables is to examine plots of the data, which we do in Section 8.1, although we need to proceed with caution because multiple dependencies in the data may make interpretations complex. Then, in Section 8.2, we proceed to formulate a statistical model that incorporates multiple inputs and to interpret the coefficients in that model. Estimation of the parameters follows the method of ordinary least squares developed in Section 7.2 and is extended to cover multiple regression in Section 8.2.1.

Once we have developed a model, we need to know whether it is useful. For simple linear regression, the answer to this question was straightforward. We checked to see whether or not there was a statistically meaningful relationship between X and Y, and that completed the analysis, as in Section 7.6. The question now is more complex. For example, sales of a product may depend upon both advertising expenditures and price. Either variable alone may provide only a modest description of what is going on, whereas the two taken together may give a much better level of explanation. Conversely, a model for national retail sales that includes both consumer expenditures and consumer incomes may be only marginally better than a model that includes only one of them. The reason for this apparent anomaly is that if X_1 and X_2 are highly correlated and X_1 is already in the model, X_2 will not bring much new information to the table. To resolve such questions, we need to proceed in two steps:

1. We ask, "Is the overall model useful?" If the answer is NO, we go back to the drawing board.
2. If the answer is YES, we check whether individual variables in the model are useful for forecasting purposes.

These two steps are explored in Sections 8.3 and 8.4. As we explained in Section 7.5, our analysis is based upon a set of standard assumptions. In Section 8.5, we briefly revisit those assumptions and present graphical procedures to determine whether the assumptions are reasonable. Taking action to deal with failures of the assumptions is a more difficult step, which we defer to Chapter 9.

Once the model has been shown to be effective and the assumptions appear to be reasonable, we are in a position to generate forecasts. Point forecasts and prediction intervals are considered in Section 8.6. Finally, in Section 8.7, we consider some of the key principles that underlie the development of multiple regression models.

At the end of the chapter, we offer six minicases. Rather than work through "prepackaged" problem sets, these examples provide a more realistic approach to model building using multiple regression methods. The same minicases will be revisited at the end of Chapter 9, to make use of the more advanced skills developed in that chapter.

8.1 Graphical Analysis and Preliminary Model Development

We return to the study of gasoline prices, initially examined in Section 7.3 (see *Gas_prices_1.xlsx*). The matrix plot we considered there is reproduced as Figure 8.1 here for convenience. The variables in the plot are as follows:

- The price of regular unleaded gasoline ("*Unleaded*"; in dollars per U.S. gallon)
- Total disposable income ("*PDI*"; in billions of current dollars)

FIGURE 8.1 MINITAB MATRIX PLOT FOR GAS PRICES AGAINST DISPOSABLE INCOME, LAGGED PRICE OF CRUDE OIL, UNEMPLOYMENT, AND THE S&P INDEX

Data shown is from file Gas_prices_1.xlsx; adapted from Minitab output.

- The Price of Crude Oil ("*L1_crude*"; in cents per barrel, lagged one month)
- Unemployment ("*Unemp*"; overall percentage rate for United States)
- The S&P 500 Stock Index ("*S&P*").

Examination of the plot had already revealed that the strongest linear relationship for unleaded gas price appeared to be the lagged value of the price of crude oil. However, we also see a somewhat upward-sloping relationship between price and disposable income, possibly due to the effect of inflation on both series. The general level of economic activity is reflected in a downward-sloping relationship with unemployment and an upward-sloping relationship with the S&P Index. None of these last three relationships appears to be nearly as strong as that with *L1_crude* (the lagged crude price), but they all make economic sense and might improve our overall ability to forecast gas prices. Also, as we saw in Table 7.1, all their correlations with gas prices are significantly different from zero, so they may add value to the model.

With this example as background, we now examine the specification of the multiple regression model.

8.2 The Multiple Regression Model

The multiple regression model is a direct extension of the simple linear regression model specified in Section 7.5. Note that we now move directly to the specification of the under-lying model, having already motivated the basic ideas in Chapter 7. We consider K explanatory variables $X_1, X_2, \ldots, X_K$ and assume that the dependent variable Y is linearly related to them through the following model:

$$Y = \beta_0 + \beta_1 X_1 + \beta_2 X_2 + \cdots + \beta_K X_K + \varepsilon. \tag{8.1}$$

The coefficients in equation (8.1) may be interpreted as follows:

β_0 denotes the intercept, which is the *expected* value of Y when all the $\{X_j\}$ are zero, in which case the equation reduces to $Y = \beta_0$.

β_j denotes the slope for X_j: When X_j increases by one unit *and all the other Xs are kept fixed*, the *expected* value of Y increases by β_j units.

Beyond the extended form of the expected value that now includes all K variables (the explained component of the model), the underlying assumptions are the same as for simple regression presented in Section 7.5.1. That is, we need only extend assumption R1 appropriately.

Assumption R1: For given values of the explanatory variables, $X = (X_1, \ldots, X_K)$, the expected value of Y is written as $E(Y | X)$ and has the form

$$E(Y | X) = \beta_0 + \beta_1 X_1 + \beta_2 X_2 + \cdots + \beta_K X_K.$$

Assumption R2: The difference between an observed Y and its expectation is a random error, denoted by ε. The complete model is

$$Y = E(Y | X) + \varepsilon = [Expected\ value] + [Random\ error]. \tag{8.2}$$

Assumption R3: The errors have zero means.

Assumption R4: The errors for different observations are uncorrelated with one another and with other explanatory variables.

Assumption R5: The error terms come from distributions with equal variances.

Assumption R6: The errors are drawn from a normal distribution.

As in Section 7.5, if we take assumptions R3–R6 together, we are making the claim that the random errors are independent and normally distributed with zero means and equal variances.

8.2.1 The Method of Ordinary Least Squares (OLS)

The method of ordinary least squares (OLS) may be used to estimate the unknown parameters. As with simple linear regression, we choose the sample coefficients, now $\{b_0, b_1, \ldots, b_K\}$, to minimize the sum of squared errors, *SSE*. That is, we choose $\{b_j\}$ to minimize

$$SSE = \sum_{i=1}^{n} e_i^2 = \sum_{i=1}^{n} [Observed - Fitted]^2$$

$$= \sum_{i=1}^{n} (Y_i - b_0 - b_1 X_{1i} - b_2 X_{2i} - \cdots - b_K X_{Ki})^2. \tag{8.3}$$

The technical details were summarized in Appendix 7A, and we will not consider the computational issues further.[1] After we have determined the best fitting model, we estimate the error terms, using the (*least squares*) *residuals*, defined as

$$e_i = Y_i - b_0 - b_1 X_{1i} - b_2 X_{2i} - \cdots - b_K X_{Ki}. \tag{8.4}$$

The residuals form the basis of many of the tests and diagnostic checks that we employ to validate the model, as we shall see in later sections.

---

[1]Standard texts on regression analysis provide the necessary details; see, for example, Kutner *et al.* (2005, pp. 15–20 and 222–227).

EXAMPLE 8.1 ■ Multiple regression model for unleaded gasoline prices

(*Gas_prices_1.xlsx*)

We employ the observations for January 1996–December 2008 as the estimation sample, as before. The OLS solution is

$$Unleaded = 1.01 + 0.0220 \; L1\_crude - 0.164 \; L1\_Unemp - 0.000406 \; L1\_S\&P \\ + 0.000125 \; L1\_PDI$$

Examination of the coefficients indicates that an increase of $1 in the price of a barrel of crude may be expected to increase the price at the pump by about 2.2 cents per gallon, somewhat lower than the figure we got with simple regression. Likewise, an increase in disposable income (*PDI*) produces an increase in the expected price, whereas an increase in unemployment (*Unemp*) reduces the expected gas price. These coefficients have the signs we would expect. The coefficient for the S&P Index is also negative; initially, we might have expected an increase in the *S&P* to signal increased economic activity and thus exert upward pressure on gas prices. However, the issue of timing is important, and the negative sign could reflect the impact of good news in the crude oil markets, lowering pump prices and boosting the overall economy. Alternatively, the observed nonzero coefficient might have arisen due to chance alone, a topic we pick up in Section 8.4. ■

No matter how good the statistical fit, the forecaster should always check the face validity of the proposed forecasting model.[2] If the model passes the face-validity test, we go ahead and check to see whether it makes sense statistically.

8.3 Testing the Overall Model

We specify the null hypothesis as the claim that the overall model is of no value or, more explicitly, that none of the explanatory variables affects the expected value. Formally, this statement is written as

$$H_0 : \beta_1 = \beta_2 = \cdots = \beta_K = 0.$$

When the null hypothesis is true, none of the variables in the model contribute to explaining the variation in *Y*. The alternative hypothesis, H_A, states that the overall model *is* of value, in that at least one of the explanatory variables has an effect:

$$H_A : \text{Not all } \beta_1 = \beta_2 = \cdots = \beta_K = 0.$$

That is, there is some statistical relationship between *Y* and at least one of the *Xs*. If we fail to reject H_0, we conclude that the overall model is without value and we need to start over. If we reject H_0, we may still wish to eliminate those variables which do not appear to contribute, so as to arrive at a more parsimonious model.[3]

---

[2]Toward that end, imagine standing in front of your boss in his or her office. Can you give a plausible justification of the model and all the coefficients? If not, develop a different model!

[3]When the model is based upon sound theoretical considerations, it makes sense to retain all the variables in it, even if some are not statistically significant, so long as the parameter estimates make sense. This is typically true in econometric modeling. By contrast, if we optimistically include variables on a "see if it flies" basis, we will usually prefer to prune the model to the smaller number of statistically significant and interpretable variables.

8.3.1 The *F*-test for Multiple Variables

The *F*-test is based upon partitioning the total sum of squares and is known as the *Analysis of Variance*, often referred to as *ANOVA*. The total sum of squares and the sums of squares resulting from the partition are as follows:

$$\text{Total sum of squares: } SST = S_{YY} = \sum_{i=1}^{n}(Y_i - \bar{Y})^2$$

$$\text{Sum of squared errors: } SSE = \sum_{i=1}^{n}(Y_i - \hat{Y}_i)^2$$

$$\text{Sum of squares explained by the regression model: } SSR = \sum_{i=1}^{n}(\hat{Y}_i - \bar{Y})^2$$

As was true in the case of simple regression, it can be shown that

$$SST = SSR + SSE. \tag{8.5}$$

The ANOVA test is usually summarized in tabular form, and the general framework is presented in Table 8.1. Note that

- The first column describes the partition into the two sources of variation: the sums of squares explained by the regression model and the sum of squared errors.
- The second column gives the number of degrees of freedom (DF) associated with each of the sums of squares; the total DF is $(n - 1)$, because we always start out with a constant term in the model.
- The third column provides the numerical values of the sums of squares.
- Column four gives the mean squares, defined as [sum of squares/DF] for each source: *MSR* and *MSE*, respectively.
- Column five yields the test statistic $F = MSR/MSE$.

The reason for introducing the new term *Mean Square Error* is that, when the null hypothesis is true, both *MSR* and *MSE* have expected values equal to the error variance, σ^2. Thus, the test statistic[4] $F = MSR/MSE$ should have a value in the neighborhood of 1.0 if the null hypothesis is appropriate. When the regression model is useful, the amount of variation explained by the model will increase, so *MSR* will increase relative to *MSE* and *F* will increase. Thus, we reject H_0 for sufficiently large values of *F*.

We refer to the observed value of *F* generated from this table as F_{obs}. The decision rule becomes

$$\text{Reject } H_0 \text{ if } F_{obs} > F_\alpha(K, n - K - 1); \text{ otherwise do not reject } H_0.$$

TABLE 8.1   GENERAL FORM OF THE ANOVA TABLE

Source	DF	Sums of Squares	Mean Squares	F
Regression	K	SSR	$MSR = SSR/K$	MSR/MSE
Residual error	$n - K - 1$	SSE	$MSE = SSE/(n - K - 1)$	
Total	$n - 1$	SST		

© Cengage Learning 2013.

---

[4]The method of analysis of variance was first derived by Sir Ronald Fisher, the father of modern inferential statistics. The ratio was labeled *F* in his honor.

The critical value for F depends upon the number of degrees of freedom for both SSR (in the numerator, DF = ν_1) and the SSE (in the denominator, DF = ν_2).[5]

In keeping with our previous discussions, we use the P-value with the following decision rule:

Reject H_0 if $P < \alpha$; otherwise do not reject H_0.

Should it prove necessary to compute the P-value for some observed value of the F statistic, we follow the procedure outlined in Appendix 7A.2.

EXAMPLE 8.2 ■ ANOVA for unleaded gas prices (*Gas_prices_1.xlsx*)

The ANOVA table for the gas prices model given in Example 8.1 with $K = 4$ is as follows (consistent with our usual convention, we specify $\alpha = 0.05$):

Analysis of Variance					
Source	**DF**	**SS**	**MS**	**F**	**P**
Regression	4	79.949	19.987	807.50	0.000
Residual Error	150	3.713	0.025		
Total	154	83.662			

Because $P < 0.05$, we reject H_0. Recall that a P-value of 0.000 does not mean zero; rather, it signifies that $P < 0.0005$ and the result is rounded down. We conclude that there is strong evidence that the overall model is useful as an explanation of the price of unleaded gasoline. The next step is to determine the contribution made by each of the variables. ■

The relationship between F and R² There is a simple relationship between F and R^2. It can be shown that

$$F = \frac{(n - K - 1)R^2}{K(1 - R^2)}. \tag{8.6}$$

The details are left to Exercise 8.11. From inspection of equation (8.6), it is evident that an increase in R^2 leads to an increase in F, so the *ANOVA* test is completely equivalent to a test based upon the coefficient of determination. Either from the *ANOVA* table or directly from the computer output, we find that, for Example 8.2,

$$R^2 = \frac{SSR}{SST} = \frac{79.949}{83.662} = 0.956.$$

Thus, the coefficient of determination shows an increase over that for the single-variable model, which had $R^2 = 94.3$ percent. Indeed, whenever we add a variable to the model, we find that R^2 increases (or, strictly speaking, cannot decrease). However, the value of the F statistic often falls because of the K in the denominator of equation (8.6). There is no inconsistency here, but we need to recognize that the decline in F does not signal a weakness in the model.

The increase in R^2 seems modest, but more important is the change in S. The single-variable model has $S = 0.176$, whereas the current model has $S = 0.157$, so the prediction interval is about four cents narrower.

---

[5]Detailed tables for the upper 5 percent and 1 percent points of the F distribution are available from the National Institute of Standards and Technology [NIST] website, *www.itl.nist.gov/div898/handbook/eda/section3/eda3673.htm#ONE-05-11-20.*

8.3.2 ANOVA in Simple Regression

We did not consider analysis of variance in Chapter 7 because it did not provide any additional information. When there is only one variable in the model, the test of the overall model is formally equivalent to the two-sided test of the single slope. Referring back to the computer output in Figure 7.12, we see that the *P*-value for ANOVA is identical with that for the *t*-test of the slope parameter. That is, in *simple linear regression*, the *F*-test and (two-sided) *t*-tests provide identical information. Another way of saying this is that, in *simple linear regression*, $F = t^2$, as can readily be verified numerically in Figure 7.12.

8.3.3 *S* and Adjusted *R²*

The steady increase in R^2 as new variables are added is a matter for some concern. A better guide to the performance of the model is to look at *S*, the standard error, now defined as

$$S^2 = \frac{\sum_{i=1}^{n} e_i^2}{(n - K - 1)} = \frac{SSE}{(n - K - 1)} = MSE. \qquad (8.7)$$

If *S* is smaller, the model has improved as the result of including the extra variable, although the improvement may be marginal. As we argued in Section 7.7.3, *S* has a straightforward interpretation as the accuracy of the predictions, because it is an estimate of the standard deviation of the error.

An alternative route to interpreting the overall accuracy of a multiple regression model is through the adjusted form of R^2, which we abbreviate to $R^2(adj)$. The general algebraic expression is

$$R^2(adj) = \frac{(n - 1)}{(n - K - 1)}\left[R^2 - \frac{K}{(n - 1)}\right]. \qquad (8.8)$$

The term inside the brackets removes that part of R^2 which could arise just by chance, and the ratio in front of the brackets then rescales the expression so that $R^2(adj) = 1$ when $R^2 = 1$.

The plot of $R^2(adj)$ is shown in Figure 8.2 for $n = 21$ and $K = 5$. For example, when the observed value of $R^2 = 0.20$, it follows that $R^2(adj) = -0.067$, a model distinguished only in the sense that you would have been better off using random numbers!

FIGURE 8.2 $R^2(adj)$ PLOTTED AGAINST R^2 FOR $n = 21$, $K = 5$

An alternative form for $R^2(adj)$ is

$$R^2(adj) = 1 - \frac{(n-1)S^2}{SST}.$$

Thus, when we add a variable to the model, $R^2(adj)$ will increase if and only if S decreases. Hence, any decisions about the choice of model that use $R^2(adj)$ or S will reach identical conclusions.

EXAMPLE 8.3 ■ $R^2(adj)$ and S for the gas prices model (*Gas_prices_1.xlsx*)
We have $K = 4$ and $n = 155$, so

$$S^2 = \frac{3.713}{150} = 0.025 \text{ and it follows that } S = 0.157.$$

We then obtain

$$R^2(adj) = 1 - \frac{155 * 0.025}{83.662} = 0.954.$$

As we see in this example, when K is small relative to n, the adjusted value is only marginally less than the original R^2.

Computer programs generally provide all the information discussed in this section in summary form, such as

$$S = 0.157, \quad R^2 = 95.6\%, \quad R^2(adj) = 95.4\%. \qquad ■$$

8.4 Testing Individual Coefficients

Once we have established that the overall model is of value, we need to determine which variables are useful and which, if any, do not contribute. The process is similar to that described in Section 7.6, but there are some crucial differences. First, because there are K variables in the model, we will perform K separate tests. We describe the procedure for variable X_j, $j = 1, 2, \ldots, K$.

The null hypothesis, now denoted by $H_0(j)$, states that the theoretical slope for X_j in the regression is zero, *given that the other variables are already in the model*. We are not testing for a direct relationship between X_j and Y; rather, we seek a conditional relationship, that asks the question: Given that the other variables are already in the model, does X_j add anything? This is captured by the null hypothesis

$$H_0(j) : \beta_j = 0, \text{ given that } X_i, i \neq j, \text{ are in the model.}$$

The alternative hypothesis is now denoted by $H_A(j)$ and states that the slope is not zero, again assuming that the other variables are in the model. That is, there is a relationship between X_j and Y even after accounting for the contributions of the other variables. We write the alternative hypothesis as

$$H_A(j) : \beta_j \neq 0, \text{ given that } X_i, i \neq j, \text{ are in the model.}$$

As before, we assume the null hypothesis to be true and then test this assumption. We use the test statistic

$$t = \frac{b_j}{SE(b_j)}. \qquad (8.9)$$

Let t_{obs} denote the observed value of this statistic. The observed value is to be compared with the appropriate value from a table of Student's t distribution with $(n - K - 1)$ DF; the number of degrees of freedom is determined by the number of observations available to estimate S. That number is now $(n - K - 1)$, as seen from Table 8.1. If we use a significance level of 100α percent, we denote the value from the t tables as $t_{\alpha/2}(n - K - 1)$. The decision rule for the test is

$$\text{If } |t_{\text{obs}}| > t_{\alpha/2}(n - K - 1), \text{ reject } H_0(j); \text{ otherwise, do not reject } H_0(j).$$

As in Chapter 7, it is more convenient to use the P-value to perform the test. The decision rule is then written as

$$\text{If } P < \alpha, \text{ reject } H_0(j); \text{ otherwise do not reject } H_0(j).$$

A benefit of using the P-value approach is that, once the value of P is available, the decision rule always has this standard form: Reject $H_0(j)$ if $P < \alpha$.[6]

Because we are performing a test on each slope in turn, standard computer packages typically summarize the set of K tests in a single table. Figure 8.3 provides the output for the gas prices example.

As in Chapter 7, we ignore the test for the intercept or constant because such a test is not meaningful in this case. All four input variables have $P < 0.05$, and there is strong evidence that they should be retained in the model. Even though there are also some strong correlations among the explanatory variables (see Figure 8.4), the contribution of each variable is well defined and the signs are consistent with our previous expectations.

FIGURE 8.3   SINGLE-VARIABLE TESTS FOR THE GAS PRICES MODEL

Predictor	Coef	SE Coef	T	P
Constant	1.0137	0.2163	4.69	0.000
L1_crude	0.022001	0.001068	20.60	0.000
L1_Unemp	−0.16398	0.03752	−4.37	0.000
L1_S&P	−0.0004063	0.0001360	−2.99	0.003
L1_PDI	0.00012541	0.00002324	5.40	0.000

Data shown is from file Gas_prices_1.xlsx.

FIGURE 8.4   CORRELATIONS BETWEEN VARIABLES IN GAS PRICES MODEL

	Crude	Unemp	S&P
Unemp	0.123		
	0.125		
S&P	0.494	−0.557	
	0.000	0.000	
PDI	0.874	0.179	0.609
	0.000	0.025	0.000

Data: Gas_prices_1.xlsx. *Note:* P-values appear below the correlation coefficients.

---

[6]The authors' tombstones will probably bear the inscription "RIP $< \alpha$", or "Reject if the P-value is less than the significance level."

8.4.1 Case Study: Baseball Salaries

We now revisit the baseball salaries data and examine some other factors that might affect a player's salary. Some will have to do with his overall career performance and others with his recent results. Although baseball is arguably the most statistically oriented of all sports, a few brief explanations are in order for those who are not baseball fans:

1. A pitcher may be recorded as the winner or the loser of a game. He may also record "No decision". Thus, the numbers of wins ("*Career Wins*") and losses ("*Career Losses*") in the course of a career are important factors in a player's remuneration.
2. The quality of a pitcher's performance over the years may be assessed by the average number of runs given up in the equivalent of a full game, known as the earned run average ("*Career ERA*"); the lower the ERA, the better the pitcher is seen to be.
3. The player's recent activity level can be judged by the number of innings pitched in the previous season ("*Innings Pitched*"); the more activity, the more the team is seen to rely on the pitcher.

Baseball fans will be able to suggest a number of other criteria, and some are listed in the file *Baseball.xlsx*, but these four additional factors (wins, losses, earned run average, and innings pitched) will suffice for our purposes. The extended model is summarized in Figure 8.5(B). It is apparent that the "*Career Wins*" and "*Career Losses*" variables do not appear to add much to the overall explanation; further, "*Career Wins*" has the wrong sign. The other variables are highly significant and have the appropriate signs.

Should we drop both variables with high *P*-values? Not necessarily: Pitchers with long careers have time to accumulate a lot of wins, but also a lot of losses, so the variables may be highly correlated, as indeed can be seen from Figure 8.5(A).

One solution to the question is to drop the variables one at a time and see what happens. We leave that as an exercise for the reader. The other approach is to test the variables as a group, comparing models with and without the "*Wins*" and "*Losses*" variables. We now explore this alternative.

8.4.2 Testing a Group of Coefficients

We have seen how the *t*-test may be used to evaluate individual variables. Now, we go a step further and consider whether it is necessary to include a group of variables. The question is, "Does the group of extra variables add anything to the predictive power of the model?"

We may solve this problem by comparing two models: M_1, which contains all the variables, and M_0, which contains only a subset:

Model M_1 (with error sum of squares SSE_1),

$$Y = f(X; \beta_0, \beta_1, \beta_2, \ldots, \beta_q, \beta_{q+1}, \ldots, \beta_K), \tag{8.10}$$

and Model M_0 (with error sum of squares SSE_0),

$$Y = f(X; \beta_0, \beta_1, \beta_2, \ldots, \beta_q, 0, 0, \ldots, 0) \tag{8.11}$$

In equation (8.10), M_1 contains the $(K + 1)$ parameters $\{\beta_0, \beta_1, \ldots, \beta_q, \beta_{q+1}, \ldots, \beta_K\}$ while the simpler model M_0 in equation (8.11) contains the $(q + 1)$ parameters $\{\beta_0, \beta_1, \ldots, \beta_q\}$. In each case, the sum of squared errors is

$$SSE_j = \sum_{i=1}^{n} e_{ji}^2, \text{ for Model } j, j = 0, 1.$$

FIGURE 8.5 CORRELATIONS AND REGRESSION MODELS FOR BASEBALL SALARIES

(A) Correlation Analysis

	Salary ($000s)	Years in Majors	Career ERA	Innings Pitched	Career Wins	Career Losses
Salary ($000s)	1.00					
Years in Majors	0.53	1.00				
Career ERA	−0.34	−0.22	1.00			
Innings Pitched	0.27	0.11	0.09	1.00		
Career Wins	0.51	0.89	−0.21	0.33	1.00	
Career Losses	0.49	0.91	−0.14	0.30	0.97	1.00

(B) Regression Analysis: Five Explanatory Variables

The regression equation is

Salary ($000s) = 547 + 53.6 Years in Majors − 152 Career ERA
+ 1.71 Innings Pitched − 0.59 Career Wins − 1.12 Career Losses

Predictor	Coef	SE Coef	T	P
Constant	547.4	167.2	3.27	0.001
Years in Majors	53.65	13.62	3.94	0.000
Career ERA	−152.37	39.81	−3.83	0.000
Innings Pitched	1.7112	0.4207	4.07	0.000
Career Wins	−0.590	1.846	−0.32	0.749
Career Losses	−1.123	2.400	−0.47	0.640

S = 292.804   R-Sq = 39.8%   R-Sq(adj) = 38.0%

Analysis of Variance

Source	DF	SS	MS	F	P
Regression	5	9639078	1927816	22.49	0.000
Residual Error	170	14574798	85734		
Total	175	24213875			

(C) Regression Analysis: Three Explanatory Variables

The regression equation is

Salary ($000s) = 620 + 36.8 Years in Majors − 154 Career ERA + 1.42 Innings Pitched

Predictor	Coef	SE Coef	T	P
Constant	620.2	150.2	4.13	0.000
Years in Majors	36.850	5.023	7.34	0.000
Career ERA	−154.21	36.88	−4.18	0.000
Innings Pitched	1.4156	0.3556	3.98	0.000

S = 292.643   R-Sq = 39.2%   R-Sq(adj) = 38.1%

Analysis of Variance

Source	DF	SS	MS	F	P
Regression	3	9483783	3161261	36.91	0.000
Residual Error	172	14730092	85640		
Total	175	24213875			

Data shown is from file Baseball.xlsx; adapted from Minitab output.

More formally, $(K - q)$ restrictions are placed on model M_1 to obtain the simpler model M_0, so we consider the null hypothesis

$$H_0: \beta_{q+1} = \beta_{q+2} = \cdots = \beta_K = 0, \text{ given that } X_1, \ldots, X_q \text{ are in the model}$$

and the alternative hypothesis

H_A: *At least one of the coefficients $\beta_{q+1}, \ldots, \beta_K$ is nonzero* when $X_1, \ldots, X_q$ are in the model.

To compare the two models, we just examine their explanatory power through their residuals. We therefore estimate the sum of squared errors from both the extended model M_1 and the simpler model M_0. We define the statistic

$$F = \frac{(SSE_0 - SSE_1)/(K - q)}{SSE_1/(n - K - 1)}.$$

This statistic has an F distribution with $(K - q, n - K - 1)$ degrees of freedom, and the P-value can be found by using the Excel function FDIST-RT as before.

Discussion Question *Why is SSE_0 always greater than SSE_1?*

EXAMPLE 8.4 ■ Testing a group of coefficients (*Baseball.xlsx*)
From Figure 8.5, $SSE_1 = 14574798$. The analysis without the two variables "*Career Wins*" and "*Career Losses*" yields $SSE_0 = 14730092$. With $n = 176$, $q = 3$, and $K = 5$, the F statistic has the value

$$F = \frac{(14{,}730{,}092 - 14{,}574{,}798)/2}{14{,}574{,}798/170}$$

$$= \frac{77{,}647}{85{,}734} = 0.906.$$

The P-value is 0.406, so, clearly, we do not reject the null hypothesis; indeed, whenever $F < 1$, the null hypothesis will not be rejected. The two variables in question do not add to the explanatory power of the model, so we will use the three-variable model summarized in Figure 8.5(C). Tests of the residuals are deferred to Exercise 8.5.

The test can also be used to test for nonlinearities (of polynomial form) or any other set of parameter restrictions, so long as the simple model M_0 is a restricted version of the full model. ■

8.5 Checking the Assumptions

In both this chapter and the previous one we laid out a set of assumptions. However, up to now, we have not attempted to validate those assumptions; rather, we have proceeded as though our model was fully and completely specified and all the assumptions were valid. In short, we have been living in a forecasting fool's paradise. In this section, we take the model for gas prices selected in Section 8.4 and try to determine how well it matches up to the assumptions stated in Section 8.2.

We examine these assumptions and devise ways to check the validity of each. Because we have available only a sample, we can never guarantee a particular assumption, but we can check whether it seems plausible. We tend to be very pragmatic: If the data suggest that a particular assumption holds, we stay with that assumption. Given a reasonably sized sample, such evidence suggests that any violation of the assumption is likely to be modest, as will be the likely impact of that violation. However, we should always keep in mind that this argument applies only if we are confident that the system will continue to operate under the same regime as in the past; if major structural changes take place, all bets are off, unless we can incorporate such changes into the model.

If a particular assumption breaks down, the nature of the breakdown will often indicate how the model might be improved. We use the residuals, as defined in equation (8.4), to develop our diagnostics. A comparison with the material in Section 6.5 serves to indicate that many of the analyses suggested here are the same as those for state-space and ARIMA models.

Assumption R1: The expected value of Y is linear in the values of the selected explanatory variables.

Potential violations: We may have missed an important variable, or the relationship may not be linear in the Xs.

Diagnostics:

1. Plot the residuals against the fitted values. Nonlinear relationships will show up as curvature in the plot.
2. Plot the residuals against potentially important Xs not currently in the model. If a particular new X has an impact on Y, it should show up as a nonzero slope on the scatterplot.

Possible actions

1. Include omitted variables in the model.
2. Consider nonlinear models (see Section 9.6).

Assumption R2: The difference between an observed Y and its expected value is due to random error.

Discussion: The assumption states that the error is an "add-on" and serves to justify the least squares formulation for estimating the parameters. The error can always be expressed in this way, but its properties will depend critically upon the next four assumptions. Therefore, we do not check this assumption directly, but examine aspects of it as described next.

Assumption R3: The errors have zero means.

Discussion: Typically, this assumption is not testable, at least when we are looking at a single series. The inclusion of a constant term in the model ensures that the mean of the in-sample errors is zero. However, when the model is used for forecasting, the forecast errors may show bias. For example, many macroeconomic series are released in preliminary form and then updated. Thus, the model may have been constructed on a particular set of final figures but then used in forecasting with the preliminary data. Cross-checks between the preliminary and final versions of such variables may reveal biases.

Assumption R4: The errors associated with different observations are uncorrelated with other variables and with one another. Thus, the errors should be uncorrelated with the explanatory variable or with other variables not included in the model. In examining observations over time, this assumption implies that there is no correlation between the error at time t and past errors; otherwise, the errors are autocorrelated.

Possible violations: Assumption R4 lies at the heart of model building and boils down to the claim that the model contains all the predictable components, leaving only noise in the error term. The residuals therefore should not be related to factors omitted from the model, such as the input variables themselves. Where the data form a time series, there should be no relationship with past values of the inputs, the dependent variable, or past errors. Such a relationship can obtain if there is a carry-over effect from one period to the next, which could be due to such factors as the weather, brand loyalty, or economic trends. Thus, a positive residual in one time period is likely to be followed by a positive residual in the next period. High–low sequences are also possible, such as a drop in sales after high volumes because of a special promotion. In cross-sectional studies, we should check whether subgroups in the population exhibit correlations, be it from locational, demographic, or other shared properties.

Diagnostics:

1. Plot the residuals against both the predicted value of Y and the input variables included in the model (as well as any other potential explanatory variables that have been excluded).
2. For time series, plot the residuals against time. If positive autocorrelation exists, lengthy sequences of values above zero and then below zero, rather than a random scatter, will appear. If a negative autocorrelation exists, a sawtooth pattern will prevail.
3. For time series, plot the sample autocorrelation function (ACF) and partial autocorrelation function (PACF) for the residuals (see Section 6.3) and look for departures from a random series by performing tests for the presence of autocorrelation. A test that is sometimes recommended for this purpose is based on the Durbin–Watson statistic, described in Appendix 8A. However, this test applies only to first-order autocorrelation so we prefer to use the ACF and PACF along with the Ljung–Box statistic of Section 6.5.1 as useful overall diagnostics. In Chapter 10, we consider more efficient tests.

Possible actions

1. For cross-sectional data, examine the data collection process carefully. For example, check whether the sample includes multiple respondents from the same company; if it does, the result could be correlation among the responses from these individuals.
2. For time series, consider the use of lagged values (see Section 9.3).

Assumption R5: The error terms come from distributions with equal variances.

Possible violations: The most common pattern is that the variability increases as the mean level of Y increases. We naturally talk about percentage movements up or down in GDP, in sales, and in many other series. The implication behind such terminology is that the variations are proportional to the level of the mean, rather than displaying constant variance.

Diagnostics:

1. Plot the residuals against the fitted values. If the errors are heteroscedastic, the scatter will often be greater for the larger fitted values.
2. Various test statistics are available (see Anderson *et al.*, 2011, Chapter 11), but we do not pursue that topic further here; such tests are illustrated in Chapter 10. Procedures for dealing with changing variances by transforming the raw data are discussed in Section 9.6.

Assumption R6: The errors are drawn from a normal distribution.

Possible violations: One or more outliers may render the distribution nonnormal, or the whole pattern of the residuals may suggest a nonnormal distribution.

Diagnostics:

1. Plot the histogram of the residuals, and look for an approximate bell shape.
2. Use the normal probability plot. A plot that deviates significantly from a straight line indicates nonnormality.
3. Examine the plots of residuals against both time and fitted values for extreme observations.

Possible actions

1. There is an interaction between normality assumption R6 and the heteroscedasticity assumption, R5. Often, correcting for extreme observations will lead to the data having an approximately constant variance.
2. Consider transformations of the dependent variable and possibly of the predictors as well (see Section 9.6).

It is evident from the preceding summary that some plots—notably, that of the residuals against fitted values—serve multiple purposes. It is important to keep these several objectives in mind in examining the plots.

8.5.1   Analysis of Residuals for Gas Price Data

Most forecasting packages will generate the plots we have just discussed, some more easily than others. In particular, Minitab produces a "Four in One" plot as part of its regression component, a feature that is particularly useful for the analyses we have been discussing.

The four-variable model of unleaded gas prices was identified in Figure 8.3, and the residuals are shown in Figure 8.6. We examine these plots in the order they appear in the output:

a. The probability plot (top left) shows several outliers at either end, partially a reflection of the increased volatility in the later part of the series. The histogram (bottom left) tells much the same story: The long tails shown afford some evidence of a departure from the normal curve.

FIGURE 8.6(A)   RESIDUALS PLOTS FOR THE FOUR-VARIABLE MODEL OF UNLEADED GAS PRICES

Data: Gas_prices_1.xlsx; adapted from Minitab output.

FIGURE 8.6(B) RESIDUAL PLOTS VERSUS POSSIBLE ADDITIONAL INPUT
VARIABLES FOR UNLEADED GAS PRICES

Data: Gas_prices_1.xlsx; adapted from Minitab output.

b. As we noted earlier, the plot of residuals against fitted values (top right) may tell
several stories. The residuals for fitted values in the range from $1 to $2 are tightly
bunched, showing low variability. However, the higher fitted values show considerable variation, a clear demonstration of nonconstant variances. The plot of residuals against order (bottom right) shows runs of positive values followed by runs of
negative values, indicative of autocorrelation. Also, we observe that larger values
are clustered together at the end of the series, suggesting a possible change in conditions that should be examined more closely.

c. Figure 8.6(B) explores possible relationships between the residuals and the price
level, measured by the *CPI*. Although there is no evidence of a linear relationship,
the increased fluctuations in the later part of the series suggest that constant-dollar
prices might produce a better model. This figure also checks for a possible relationship with the price of crude lagged two periods, *L2_crude*, but there is no evidence of such dependence.

The issue of residual autocorrelation is particularly important because it indicates persistence in the time series that has not been fully captured by the current model. To investigate
this phenomenon, we look at the ACF of the residuals, shown in Figure 8.7.

The ACF and PACF indicate a degree of persistence, with a significant positive autocorrelation at lag 1. The spikes at lag 6 and lag 12 suggest possible seasonality, which also merits further examination.

Collectively, these plots provide plenty of food for thought and indicate that we have
some work ahead of us before we can be satisfied with the model. We will return to the
model-building endeavor in Chapter 9; for now, we explore the use of such models in
forecasting.

FIGURE 8.7 ACF AND PACF FOR THE RESIDUALS OF THE FOUR-VARIABLE UNLEADED GAS PRICES MODEL

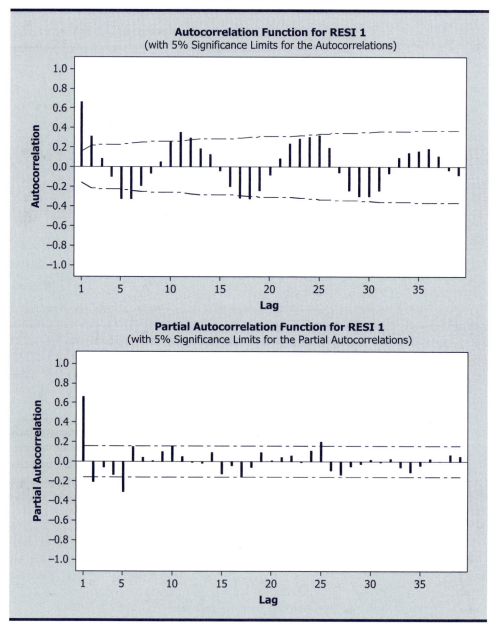

Data: Gas_prices_1.xlsx; adapted from Minitab output.

8.6 Forecasting with Multiple Regression

The general procedure for forecasting with several explanatory variables is essentially the same as that for the single-variable case described in Section 7.7. The interested reader is referred to Kutner *et al.* (2005, pp. 229–232) for further details. The first question we must answer relates to the nature of the explanatory variables. Recall that any particular *X* may arise in one of three ways:

    a. X is known ahead of time
    b. X is unknown but can itself be forecast
    c. X is unknown but we wish to make "what-if" forecasts

For example, consider a model for sales. Clearly, variables that designate particular seasons are known in advance, as may be substantive variables that have been sufficiently lagged in time. Policy variables—for example, price and advertising expenditures—may be explored with the model to make "what-if" forecasts so that the sensitivity of expected sales to policy changes can be explored. Finally, some variables, such as the price charged by competitors or the level of GDP, will require forecasts themselves. These forecasts are often generated by industry analysts, government sources, or macroeconomic panels (see, e.g., *www.consensuseconomics.com*). Alternatively, time series methods, such as the exponential smoothing methods discussed in Chapters 3 and 4, could be used.

8.6.1   **The Point Forecast**

We suppose that values for the next time period are available for each of the K variables and denote these values by $X_{n+1,\,1}, X_{n+1,\,2}, \ldots, X_{n+1,\,K}$. Given the estimated regression line, the point forecast is

$$F_{n+1} = b_0 + b_1 X_{n+1,\,1} + b_2 X_{n+1,\,2} + \cdots + b_K X_{n+1,\,K}. \qquad (8.12)$$

As before, we need to distinguish between the fitted values $\hat{Y}$ and the forecast F_{n+1}. The two formulas are the same, but the fitted values correspond to those observations which were used in the estimation process, whereas the forecasts are based on new observations. These new values may be part of a hold-out sample or values as yet unobserved, but they are not used to estimate the model parameters.

EXAMPLE 8.5 ■ **One-step-ahead forecasts for gas prices** (*Gas_prices_1.xlsx*)
We use the four-variable model for gas prices as an illustration. One-step-ahead forecasts were generated from equation (8.12), so for example, the forecast for January 2009 uses the December 2008 values of the explanatory variables. The regression model (from Figure 8.3) is

$$Unleaded = 1.01 + 0.0220 \ L1\_crude - 0.164 \ L1\_Unemp - 0.000406 \ L1\_S\&P \\ + 0.000125 \ L1\_PDI$$

The values for December 2008 are as follows:

    L1_crude: 41.12
    L1_Unemp: 7.3
    L1_S&P: 888.6
    L1_PDI: 12257.7

The forecast for January 2009 is then

$$F = 1.01 + 0.0220 * 41.12 - 0.164 * 7.3 - 0.000406 * 888.6 + 0.000125 * 12257.7 \\ = 1.889.$$

More accurate calculations by computer to avoid rounding errors give 1.897. The forecasts for the 24 months (January 2009 to December 2010) are plotted in Figure 8.8; all the forecasts are one-step-ahead, using the previous month's values as inputs. ■

FIGURE 8.8   ACTUAL PRICES FOR UNLEADED GASOLINE, ALONG WITH ONE-STEP-AHEAD FORECASTS AND 95 PERCENT PREDICTION INTERVALS (*January 2009–December 2010*)

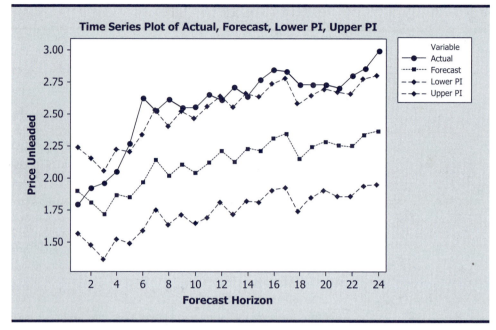

Data: Gas_prices_1.xlsx; adapted from Minitab output.

8.6.2 Prediction Intervals

We now require prediction intervals to provide an indication of the accuracy of the forecasts. We omit the technical details and simply note that, relative to the unknown future value Y_{n+1}, the point forecast has an estimated standard error that we write as

$$SE(Y_{n+1} - F_{n+1}) = \sqrt{var(Y_{n+1} - F_{n+1})}. \tag{8.13}$$

Given assumptions R3–R6, the forecast error follows a normal distribution, and after allowing for the estimation of σ by S, we may use the Student's t distribution with the appropriate DF to specify the prediction interval.

Prediction interval for the future observation Y_{n+1}:

$$F_{n+1} \pm t_{\alpha/2}(n - K - 1) * SE(Y_{n+1} - F_{n+1}). \tag{8.14}$$

The $100(1 - \alpha)$ percent prediction interval is a probability statement: The probability that the future observation will lie in the interval defined by equation (8.14) is $(1 - \alpha)$.

EXAMPLE 8.6 ■ **Construction of a prediction interval** (*Gas_prices_1.xlsx*)
We continue our consideration of the forecasts for January 2009, begun in Example 8.5. With $K = 4$ and $n = 155$, we have DF = 150. The SE for the point forecast is found to be 0.1695. Using $t_{0.025}(150) = 1.976$, we find that the 95 percent prediction interval is

$$1.8975 \pm (1.976) * (0.1695) = 1.8975 \pm 0.335 = [1.563, 2.233].$$

The one-step-ahead point forecasts for January 2009 to December 2010 are plotted in Figure 8.8, along with the actual values and the 95 percent prediction intervals. From the plot, we can see that the forecasts systematically underestimated the actual values and that this error was not corrected over time.

As with simple regression, when n is large, an approximate 95 percent prediction interval is given by $F \pm 2S$. From Example 8.3, $S = 0.157$, giving an approximate prediction interval of $+/- 0.314$, only a slight underestimate. ∎

8.6.3 Forecasting More than One Period Ahead

When we wish to forecast more than one period ahead, we must provide values for all the predictor variables over the forecasting horizon. As we discussed in Section 7.7.4, there are two possible approaches:

1. Generate forecasts for all the Xs and apply the forecasts to the original model.
2. Reformulate the model so that all unknown Xs are lagged by two (or more) periods, as appropriate.

The first approach is more commonly applied, but suffers from the drawback that the uncertainty in X is not reflected in the prediction intervals for the forecasts. This approach has the advantage that only a single model need be used to compare different "what-if" paths formulated for X. The second approach is somewhat more tedious, but it will be more valuable when good forecasts for X are unavailable and it will provide more accurate prediction intervals.

As before, neither approach is necessarily better than the other. Where forecasts of the Xs are unreliable, it will usually prove better (and easier) to adopt the second approach. Exploration of the gas prices model for multiple steps ahead is left as Exercises 8.8 and 8.9.

8.7 Principles

[8.1] Aim for a relatively simple model specification. The researcher must strike a balance between failing to include key variables and cluttering the model with variables that have very little effect upon the outcome. For example, the number of consumers in a market area clearly has an impact on the level of sales. However, for a particular market area, that figure is not going to change much over the course of a few months. Accordingly, we would not bother to include a variable for population in a short-term model for sales forecasting (Allen and Fildes, 2001).

[8.2] Tailor the forecasting model to the horizon. As noted in Principle 8.1, we need to identify those variables which are important for the forecasting horizon under consideration (Armstrong, 2001).

[8.3] Identify important causal variables on the basis of the underlying theory and earlier empirical studies. Identify suitable proxy variables when the variables of interest are not available in a timely fashion. Expertise and earlier research should be used to formulate a model whenever possible. Statements such as "The stock market goes up when the AFC team wins the Super Bowl" may be factually correct over a period of years, but they are not a reliable guide to investment! (Adapted from Allen and Fildes, 2001)

[8.4] If the aim of the analysis is to provide pure forecasts, you must either know the explanatory variables in advance or be able to forecast them sufficiently well to justify their inclusion in the model.

This principle is a more formal statement of the necessary response to the questions "What do you know?" and "When will you know it?" (Adapted from Allen and Fildes, 2001)

[8.5] Use the method of ordinary least squares to estimate the parameters. The method of ordinary least squares is strictly valid only when Assumptions R3–R5 apply, but it is often a good place to start, and the basic multiple regression model presented in this chapter can be extended to deal with more complex models (Allen and Fildes, 2001).

[8.6] Update the estimates frequently.   Frequent updating involves little effort beyond recording the latest data. The new parameter estimates will better reflect the relationships among the variables and also help to alert the modeler to any lack of stability in those values (Armstrong, 2001).

Summary

In this chapter, we have extended regression models to multiple explanatory variables, thereby greatly increasing the range and value of models that we may use for forecasting purposes. We have also provided the basic inferential framework in terms of parameter estimation and model testing, as well as identifying the key assumptions underlying the models. This structure will enable us to check assumptions and refine the models in the next chapter.

Exercises

8.1   Exercise 7.1 provided the following data on television advertising and sales for a soft-drink company over an eight-week period:

Week	Spots	Price	Sales
1	8	11	25
2	12	11	34
3	16	12	39
4	10	10	32
5	8	12	22
6	12	12	30
7	16	10	43
8	10	10	31

The purpose was to evaluate the effect on sales (in millions of dollars) with respect to the number of 30-second spots aired during that week. In further analysis, additional price data were collected (in *Exercise_7_1.xlsx*). Conduct a multiple regression analysis for sales on spot and price.

a.   Carry out tests on the overall model and on the individual coefficients. Summarize your conclusions.

b.   Compare the performance of the two models. Which model would you recommend?

8.2   The following table, from *Exercise_7_2.xlsx*, contains additional data on a company's sales on advertising expenditures, beyond the data quoted in Exercise 7.2:

Week	Price	Advertising	Sales
1	6	10	28
2	8	20	30
3	10	30	28
4	6	10	30
5	8	10	24
6	10	10	22
7	6	20	34
8	8	10	26
9	10	10	20
10	6	30	36
11	8	30	32
12	10	20	26

a.   Conduct a regression analysis of sales on advertising and price.

b.   Carry out tests on the overall model and on the individual coefficients. Summarize your conclusions.

c.   Compare the performance of the overall model and the price-only model. Which model would you recommend?

8.3   Create constant-dollar series for the unleaded gas prices data [*Gas_prices_1.xlsx*] by dividing *Unleaded, Crude, S&P 500*, and *PDI* by the Consumer Price Index (*CPI*). Repeat the analysis, using these new series and *Unemp*, and check the assumptions underlying this model. Finally, comment on the model's adequacy for explaining the price of unleaded gasoline.

8.4   Use the model developed in Exercise 8.3 to generate forecasts for the period from January 2009 through December 2010. Compare the performance of this model with that developed in Section 8.2. (This is not as easy as it looks!)

8.5   Use the file *Baseball.xlsx* to carry out the analysis of residuals for the three-variable baseball model developed in Section 8.4.1. Summarize your conclusions.

8.6   Use the file *Baseball.xlsx* and logarithms to transform the salaries data, and repeat the model development process. Compare your results with those given in Figure 8.5, and comment upon your results.

8.7   Use the file *Baseball.xlsx*. Modify the database by removing all the veterans, defined as players with ten or more years in the major leagues. Repeat the analyses of Exercises 8.5 and 8.6 and compare results.

8.8   Use the four-variable gas prices model to generate forecasts three periods ahead for the period from March 2009 to December 2010 by first generating forecasts for both the lagged crude oil price and disposable income. Compare the estimates with those for the model developed in the chapter. Compute the forecast accuracy measures and generate the 90 percent prediction intervals, using equation (8.14). How many of the actual values fall inside these intervals?

8.9   Develop the four-variable gas prices model, using explanatory variables with lag = 3 to allow for direct prediction of the prices three periods ahead over the period from March 2009 to December 2010. Compute the forecast accuracy measures and generate the 90 percent prediction intervals, using equation (8.14). How many of the actual values fall inside these intervals? Compare the results with those obtained for Exercise 8.8.

8.10* Repeat Exercises 8.8 and 8.9, using the empirical prediction intervals (recall Section 2.8.3).

8.11* Verify the relationship between F and R^2 given in equation (8.6).

Minicases

The purpose of these minicases is to provide opportunities for you to use data analysis to tackle important real-world problems. The format is essentially the same in each: A dependent variable of interest is identified, along with a plausible set of explanatory variables. The aim is to develop a valid forecasting model for at least one period ahead, and multiple periods ahead should also be considered.

The full set of modeling steps should be examined:

- Create plots of the data to look for relationships and possible unusual observations.
- Perform basic data analysis.
- Develop a multiple regression model and check the model's adequacy with regard to the regression assumptions.
- Evaluate your chosen model's forecasting performance, preferably using a hold-out sample.

Keep in mind that there are no "right" answers, but some solutions will be more effective than others. After you complete your statistical analysis, do not fail to ask the following questions:

- Would the data be available to enable me to make timely forecasts?
- Are there other variables that should be included in the model?
- Would you feel able to justify your model to a senior manager?

If the answer to any of these questions is NO, you have more work to do!

Minicase 8.1 The Volatility of Google Stock

[Contributors: Christine Choi, Alex Dixon, Melissa Gong, Michael Neches, and Greg Thompson. Data for Minicase 8.1 can be found in file *Google_Data.xlsx*.]

Volatility is a measure of the uncertainty of the return realized on an asset (Hull, 2009). Applied to financial markets, the volatility of a stock price is a measure of how uncertain we are of future stock price movements. As volatility increases, the possibility that the stock price will appreciate or depreciate significantly also increases. The volatility measure has widespread implications, particularly for stock option valuation and also for volatility indices (VIX), portfolio management, and hedging strategies. Since its initial public offering, Google, Inc. (GOOG: NASDAQ), stock has become one of the most sought-after and popular investment opportunities. The search engine giant's stock price has fluctuated from an IPO price of $85/share, to a high of $741/share (adjusted close, Nov. 27, 2007), down to a low 2009 closing price of $345/share (adjusted close, Feb. 25, 2009). This fluctuation reveals the uncertainty associated with any stock, especially that of high-tech companies with Web-based models for which the monetization of services can confuse even the most sophisticated investor.

The aim of the project is to develop a multiple regression model to forecast the volatility of Google's stock price over the next three months. After an initial review of Google-specific and macroeconomic data, we identified the following potential explanatory variables:

STDEV: the volatility measure for Google stock

VOLUME: amount of trading in Google shares

P/E: the price-to-earnings ratio of Google stock

GDP: quarterly growth in GDP at an annualized rate (quarterly, repeated for each month)

VIX: the market volatility index

CONF: the Conference Board Consumer Confidence Index®

JOBLESS: the number of claims posted for benefits

HOUSING: the number of new housing starts.

Monthly data are available for the period from May 2006 through January 2009 on the preceding variables. The data were downloaded from Bloomberg.

Minicase 8.2 Economic Factors in Homicide Rates

[Contributors: Daniel Adcock, Sybil Desangles, Gerald McSwiggan, John Siminerio, Marc Steining, and Katherine Wood. Data for Minicase 8.2 can be found in file *Homicides.xlsx.*]

This project is an analysis of annual homicides in the United States in which historical data are used to predict future homicide rates. The purpose is to develop a predictive model that estimates future homicide rates on the basis of a number of potential explanatory and predictor variables. The project has significant ramifications: If an effective model is devised to forecast future homicides, the variables underlying the model could be used as a focal point for police and government officials. The model would help law enforcement by heightening awareness, leading to more effective homicide prevention.

Annual data are available for the period 1972–2001. The variables measured are as follows:

HOMICIDE: the rate of homicides per 100,000 of the population

GDP: Real GDP per capita

UNEMPLOY: the national unemployment rate (percent)

DROPOUT: the high school dropout rate (percent)

RECESSION: the presence (=1) or absence (=0) of a recession

CABLE: cable subscription rates

Minicase 8.3 Forecasting Natural Gas Consumption for the DC Metropolitan Area

[Contributors: Sameer Aggarwal, Parshant Dhand, Yulia Egorov, and Natasha Heidenrich. Data for Minicase 8.3 can be found in file *Natural_Gas.xlsx.*]

The intent of this project was to develop a model to forecast natural gas consumption for the residential sector in the Washington, DC, metropolitan area. The level of natural gas consumption is influenced by a variety of factors, including local weather, the state of the national and the local economies, the purchasing power of the dollar (because at least some of the natural gas is imported), and the prices for other commodities. The following variables have been identified and recorded on a quarterly basis (the data cover the period 1997Q1 through 2008Q3, with all data measured quarterly):

GASCONS: consumption of natural gas in DC metro area (million cubic feet)

AVETEMP: average temperature for the period in the DC metro area

GDP: annualized percentage change in GDP

UNEMP: percentage unemployment in the DC metro area

GAS_PRICE: price of natural gas ($/100 cubic feet)

DOLLAR: value index for the U.S. dollar relative to a basket of international currencies

OIL_PRICE: price of crude oil ($/barrel)

RESERVES: reserves of natural gas (million cubic feet)

FUTURES: price of futures contract on natural gas ($/100 cubic feet).

Minicase 8.4 Economic Factors in Property Crime

[Contributors: Jay Cafarella, Jordan Krawll, Caroline Levington, Allen Lin, and Steven Schuler. Data for Minicase 8.4 can be found in file *Property_crime.xlsx*.]

The purpose of this project is to determine the relationship between crime and the country's economic health. The drop in wealth that accompanies a recession may result in an increase in the crime rate. It is reasonable to believe that if people don't have jobs, have less money, and are no longer able to pay for their daily expenses, some will resort to crime. Various economic indicators were identified to address this issue. The following variables are measured annually for the period 1960–2007:

CRIME_pc: number of property crimes reported per capita

POP_GROWTH: the percentage change in population over the previous year

GDP_GROWTH: change in real GDP over the previous year

UNEMP: percentage unemployment in the United States

CREDIT: percentage growth in credit card indebtedness

S&P RETURN: the annual return on the S&P 500 Index

CPI_GROWTH: percentage change in the Consumer Price Index

INCOME_GROWTH: percentage growth in average household income

RECESSION: the presence (=1) or absence (=0) of a recession.

Other variables in the spreadsheet were used in the calculation of these rates.

Minicase 8.5 U.S. Retail & Food Service Sales

[Contributors: Doug Goff, Rich Marsden, Jeff Rodgers, and Masaki Takeda. Data for Minicase 8.5 can be found in file *Retail_food_sales.xlsx*.]

The purpose of this project is to forecast how U.S. retail and food sales will fare over the coming months. The variables considered include personal income and savings, consumer sentiment, and various macroeconomzic variables. Because manufacturing costs and levels of activity are clearly important, these factors are also included. Considered in the analysis as well were three seasonal factors associated, respectively, with the Easter, Thanksgiving, and Christmas holidays.

The data set includes monthly figures for the period January 2000–December 2008.

RSALES: U.S. retail and food service sales [$ millions]

CONSENT: University of Michigan Index of U.S. Consumer Sentiment

PRICE_OIL: spot price of oil ($/barrel)

IND_PROD: Index of U.S. Industrial Production

PERSINC: U.S. personal income ($ per capita)

PERSSAV: net U.S. personal savings ($ per capita)

POPULATION: total U.S. population (thousands)

UNEMP: U.S. unemployment rate

CPI: U.S. Consumer Price Index

TGIVING: indicator for Thanksgiving (November)

EASTER: indicator for Easter (March or April)

XMAS: indicator for Christmas (December).

Minicase 8.6 U.S. Unemployment Rates

[Contributors : Matt Egyhazy, Jay Kreider, Jim Platt, Ashley Wall, and Rob Whiteside. Data for Minicase 8.6 can be found in file *Unemployment_2.xlsx.*]

Unemployment has multiple causes, among which five potentially important factors are minimum-wage laws, labor unions, efficiency wages, job searches, and general economic conditions. Minimum wages help maintain a certain standard of living for individuals, but also create an artificial bottom that prevents wages from dropping to a level where a greater percentage of workers would be employed. Like minimum wage laws, labor unions create higher wage levels by increasing the wages and benefits of union workers, potentially at the expense of others. Efficiency wages, or paying employees above the market equilibrium in order to produce more productive employees, creates an excess in the labor supply that also may increase unemployment. The amount of time taken in job searches as employees move from one job to another has a direct effect on unemployment because those employees are considered unemployed between jobs. Finally, U.S. economic conditions have a direct effect on the unemployment rate: As the economy slips, unemployment rises.

In order to build an appropriate forecasting model, monthly data were collected for the following economic indicators:

UNEMPLOYMENT: U.S. unemployment (percent)

MINIMUM WAGE: nominal minimum wage, as enacted by Congress ($/hour)

NONFARM EARNINGS: average income in the nonfarming sector ($/year, monthly series, annualized data)

CPI: Consumer Price Index

UNION MEMBERSHIP: percentage of labor force that is unionized

NOM GDP: U.S. gross domestic product (nominal $ millions; quarterly).

Data Sources for Minicases

1. National Climatic Data Center (National Oceanic and Atmospheric Administration, Department of Commerce), *http://lwf.ncdc.noaa.gov/oa/climate/research/cag3/md.html*
2. Bureau of Labor Statistics (U.S. Department of Labor), *www.bls.gov*
3. Energy Information Administration (U.S. Department of Energy), *www.eia.doe.gov/overview_hd.html* and *http://tonto.eia.doe.gov/dnav/ng/ng_stor_sum_ dcu_nus_m.htm*
4. Bureau of Economic Analysis (U.S. Department of Commerce), *www.bea.gov*
5. Bureau of Justice Statistics (U.S. Department of Justice), *www.ojp.usdoj.gov/bjs*
6. FBI Uniform Crime Reports (National Archive of Criminal Justice Data), *www.fbi.gov/ucr*
7. University of Michigan Index of Consumer Sentiment, *www.sca.isr.umich.edu*

References

Allen, P. G., and Fildes, R. (2001). Econometric forecasting. In J. S. Armstrong (ed.) *Principles of Forecasting: A Handbook for Researchers and Practitioners*, Boston and Dordrecht: Kluwer, pp. 300–362.

Anderson, D. R., Sweeney, D. J., and Williams, T. A. (2011). *Statistics for Business and Economics*, 11th ed. Mason, OH: South-Western.

Armstrong, J. S., ed. (2001). *Principles of Forecasting: A Handbook for Researchers and Practitioners*. Boston and Dordrecht: Kluwer.

Hull, J. C. (2009). *Options, Futures, and Other Derivatives*, 7th ed. Upper Saddle River, NJ: Pearson Prentice Hall.

Kutner, M. H., Nachtsheim, C. J., Neter, J., and Li, W. (2005). *Applied Linear Statistical Models*, 5th ed. New York City: McGraw-Hill.

Appendix 8A # The Durbin–Watson Statistic

The Durbin–Watson test is often used to check for first-order autocorrelation in the random error terms in time series regression. The test compares the null hypothesis:

H_0: error terms are not autocorrelated

to the alternative

H_A: error terms display first order autocorrelation.

Given a sample of size n and residuals $\{e_t, t = 1, 2, \ldots, n\}$ the Durbin–Watson statistic has the form:

$$DW = \frac{\sum_{t=2}^{n}(e_t - e_{t-1})^2}{\sum_{t=1}^{n}e_t^2}.$$

When H_0 is true, DW is close to 2.0. The minimum value is 0.0 and the maximum value is 4.0; small values indicate positive autocorrelation and large values indicate negative autocorrelation. The exact test requires detailed tables, which may be found in texts such as Kutner *et al.* (2005, pp. 1330–31). The test is invalid when lagged values of the dependent variable are included in the regression model.

Because we use the sample autocorrelations as diagnostics and are often interested in autocorrelations at other lags as well, we prefer to use the sample ACF and PACF, as in Section 8.5. However, many software packages provide the value of the DW statistic but not the sample ACF. To make use of this information, we match up the values of DW with the test for first-order autocorrelation shown in Figure 8.7; this leads to the decision rule:

$$\text{Reject } H_0 \text{ with } \alpha = 0.05 \text{ if } |DW - 2.0| > \frac{3.92}{\sqrt{n}}; \text{ do not reject otherwise.}$$

The right-hand side is $1.96 * 2/\sqrt{n}$. The expression is based upon the assumption that DW is approximately normally distributed in large samples; the number 1.96 is the percentage point from normal tables and the other part represents the approximate standard error of DW.

Example

The gas prices model in Section 8.5.1 is found to have $DW = 0.576$. The sample size is $n = 155$ so the lower critical value is $2.0 - 3.92/\sqrt{155} = 2.0 - 0.315 = 1.685$. The observed value is well below this, so we reject the null hypothesis of no first order autocorrelation, reaching the same conclusion as we did from Figure 8.7.

CHAPTER 9

Model Building

CONTENTS

Two hikers were walking through a forest when they were confronted by a large grizzly bear. One of the hikers promptly opened his backpack and started to lace up his running shoes. Dumbfounded, the other looked at him and said, "You can't outrun a grizzly!" "No need to," replied the first hiker, "I only need to outrun you!"

Introduction

Even the simplest business process is likely to be driven by a large number of different factors. Many of these will have only a minor impact. Our objective in statistical modeling is to identify the key elements and then to be prepared to ascribe the remaining variation to the random or unexplained error term that appears in all our models. In Chapters 7 and 8 we listed our key assumptions, and the model will be effective only if those assumptions are satisfied, at least approximately. In Section 8.5, we saw how to examine some of these assumptions by graphical means. In this chapter, guided by these diagnostic procedures, we develop more accurate forecasting models. However, we should always remember two things:

- Our forecasts rely on the future being governed by the same rules and relationships as in the past;
- Our conclusions about the behavior of processes are based upon sample data and can never be definitive.

The model specified in Assumptions R1 and R2 in Section 8.5 assumes that we have identified all of the relevant variables; however, key variables may have been omitted, including possible changes in conditions (e.g., seasonal effects or changes in legal requirements). Some of the possible departures from the basic assumptions about the error process are the presence of (auto)correlation, the lack of constancy in the variance, and a nonnormal distribution, possibly caused by outliers. We explore each of these issues in turn. In Section 9.1, we introduce indicator (or dummy) variables and show how these tools can be used to address various problems, including seasonal patterns. In Section 9.2, we consider the introduction of lagged values of the dependent variable into the model in order to account for autocorrelation. A natural extension is to combine lagged values of the dependent variable with other variables, and this option is explored in Section 9.3.

In principle, we might consider a large number of predictor variables and incorporate lags of various orders for each of these input variables. If we are guided by strong theoretical considerations, such steps can be very valuable. More commonly, we are guided only by the vague intuition or fond hope that some of these variables might be useful. Without clear guidelines, we may arrive at a plethora of variables and no strong reason to prefer one set of inputs over another. We therefore need to develop methods that identify plausible models from among the many alternatives; we refer to these methods as variable selection methods and introduce them in Section 9.4. An additional problem arising from an increased number of inputs is that we may find that some or all of the variables are very highly correlated. This finding would have two undesirable effects: (1) Our estimates of the individual slope coefficients may become highly unstable, to the point that identifying the "best" forecasting model becomes difficult, and (2) the magnitudes of the estimated effects may be unrealistic. We refer to the condition in which two or more of the variables are highly correlated as *multicollinearity* among the inputs. In Section 9.5, we consider how to check for the presence of multicollinearity and use variable selection methods as one way to handle the difficulty.

When the level of the dependent variable increases over time (as does, e.g., *GDP* or the sales of a new product), the inherent variability in the series often increases as well. Sometimes, our intuition comes to the rescue. We talk naturally about percentage changes and would expect to see greater constancy in percentage swings over time than in absolute levels. Thus, a switch (or transformation) of the dependent variable to deal with percentage changes will often take care of increasing variances. Indeed, if the "forecasting gods" are smiling on us, such a transformation may well take care of nonlinearity in the relationship as well. These issues are explored in Section 9.6.

In Section 9.7, we consider how to deal with influential observations and with outliers. Extreme observations may arise from data-recording errors or from unusual events such as a strike or a hurricane. Left alone, such items may distort model estimates and subsequent forecasts. On other occasions, process-changing events may be recognized or anticipated, such as a change in legal requirements. We usually refer to the methods for handling such events as intervention analysis, which is the subject of Section 9.8. Interventions and outliers have a close affinity in terms of the methods used to deal with them; the difference is that interventions are deliberate policy changes whereas outliers are unexpected events.

Although the chapter focuses on model building, the ultimate objective is still forecasting. In Section 9.9, we close the loop by using the models to derive forecast functions. The chapter concludes with a discussion of new principles and a summary.

 # Indicator (Dummy) Variables

Many variables of interest are defined as (unordered) categories; gender and profession are two obvious examples. Nevertheless, such data may be valuable in building a regression model. Suppose we wish to examine a company's compensation policy in order to establish whether there is any gender bias in setting salary levels. It is certainly possible that males and females are equally recognized for such factors as years of experience, and yet a pay gap may exist. In order to allow for such a possibility in a regression model, we define an indicator variable:

Indicator (Dummy) Variables

When observations fall into one of two categories, we distinguish them by means of an *indicator* (*or dummy*) *variable*, defined as

   $X = 1$ if the observation falls into category A;

   $X = 0$ if the observation falls into category B.

In general, when there are K categories, we need only $(K - 1)$ indicator variables, which can be defined as follows for $i = 1, \ldots, (K - 1)$:

   $X_i = 1$ if the observation falls into the ith category;

   $X_i = 0$ otherwise. Thus, all indicator variables have the value zero for category K.

EXAMPLE 9.1 ■ Use of an indicator variable

Let Y = salary (in thousands of dollars), X_1 = years of experience, and X_2 = gender (1 if female, 0 if male).

Suppose that the expected salary progressions are as follows:

$$\text{Males: } E(Y) = 47 + 3X_1 \quad \text{Females: } E(Y) = 42 + 3X_1$$

That is, each group is expected to receive an annual increase of $3000, and males start out with a salary that is $5000 higher, as illustrated in Figure 9.1.

We could estimate the two relationships separately for each gender, but such a strategy may be problematic if we have to deal with small sample sizes. More generally, in time series, we may switch from one category to another and back again (e.g., weekday and weekend sales patterns). The simplest way to incorporate such differences into the statistical model is to combine the two relationships into one by using an indicator variable X_2.

In this example, we may use the indicator to combine the expectation statements into a single expression, coding $X_2 = 0$ for males and $X_2 = 1$ for females. Thus, the combined expression is

$$E(Y) = 47 + 3X_1 - 5X_2.$$

FIGURE 9.1   EXPECTED SALARIES FOR EACH GENDER, BY YEARS OF
EXPERIENCE

© Cengage Learning 2013.

When $X_2 = 0$, we recover the expression for males, and when $X_2 = 1$, we obtain that for females. If we define $X_3 = (0$ if female, 1 if male), we arrive at the formula

$$E(Y) = 42 + 3X_1 + 5X_3. \tag{9.1}$$

This relationship recovers the same initial formulae, so it does not matter which of the two gender variables is used. That is, it does not matter whether we use X_2 or X_3; the two models will yield the same sets of fitted values, forecasts, and summary statistics. This equivalence continues to hold when there are more than two categories.   ■

The Use of Indicator Variables

All (valid) choices of indicator (dummy) variables will yield the same regression relationship, provided that a full set of $(K - 1)$ variables is included in the model. Thus, in Example 9.2, we may use any four of the five indicator variables.

EXAMPLE 9.2 ■ *WFJ Sales* and TV advertising [*WFJ_sales_2.xlsx*]
WFJ can choose between 15-second and 30-second spots in its television advertising. In the absence of other information, we suppose that the total budget for TV advertising is fixed, so only the mix of commercials matters. WFJ employs five options: 100 percent 15-second slots, 75:25 in favor of 15- vs. 30-second slots, and then 50:50, 25:75, and 0:100 splits. These five categories may be represented by the following indicator variables that respectively identify them:

	X1	X2	X3	X4	X5
If advertising split is 100:0 for 15-second to 30-second commercial slots	1	0	0	0	0
If advertising split is 75:25 for 15-second to 30-second commercial slots	0	1	0	0	0
If advertising split is 50:50 for 15-second to 30-second commercial slots	0	0	1	0	0
If advertising split is 25:75 for second to 30 second commercial slots	0	0	0	1	0
If advertising split is 0:100 for 15-second to 30-second commercial slots	0	0	0	0	1

We may use any four of the five indicator variables in a regression model. Using the first four (with no other variables), we have, for the fitted model,

$$WFJ\ Sales = 34488 - 8019\ X1 + 119\ X2 - 305\ X3 - 1356\ X4$$

Predictor	Coef	SE Coef	T	P
Constant	34488	3315	10.40	0.000
X1	−8019	3564	−2.25	0.028
X2	119	3636	0.03	0.974
X3	−305	3436	−0.09	0.930
X4	−1356	3584	−0.38	0.707

The summary measures are

$$S = 4688.03 \quad R\text{-}Sq = 31.9\% \quad R\text{-}Sq(adj) = 27.1\%$$

If we use the last four indicators, the fitted model and summary measures are as follows:

$$WFJ\ Sales = 26470 + 8138\ X2 + 7714\ X3 + 6663\ X4 + 8019\ X5$$

Predictor	Coef	SE Coef	T	P
Constant	26470	1309	20.23	0.000
X2	8138	2064	3.94	0.000
X3	7714	1590	4.85	0.000
X4	6663	1819	3.66	0.001
X5	8019	3564	2.25	0.028

$$S = 4688.03 \quad R\text{-}Sq = 31.9\% \quad R\text{-}Sq(adj) = 27.1\%$$

The two models look very different at first sight. However, note that the summary measures [S, R-Sq, and R-$Sq(adj)$] are identical. Further, when we substitute a valid set of (0,1) values into these expressions, we necessarily obtain the same fitted values (see Exercise 9.3). It is important to recognize that the coefficients have different interpretations in the two models. In the first model, the coefficient for X_2 measures the difference between policy 2 (75:25 in favor of 15-second slots) and policy 5 (all 30-second slots); in the second model, the coefficient for X_2 measures the difference between policy 2 and policy 1 (all 15-second slots). Other coefficients are interpreted similarly.

At this point, another question arises: Only one coefficient in the first model has a significant t-value, whereas the t-values of all four coefficients are significant in the second model, so should we drop the nonsignificant values? The short answer is *no*! The more complete answer is that the two versions indicate that the 100 percent 15-second choice is a poor one, resulting in lower sales than the other four choices, all of which yield similar results. Thus, a more parsimonious representation might be achieved by using a modified X_1 alone (100 percent 15-second slots, versus all other options), but the policy implications of that choice should be recognized first; only then should the simpler model be considered. Consequently, choosing different subsets of the indicators may provide useful insights. Although the resulting models may look different, this does not affect the fitted values or the forecasts.

Interpreting Dummy Variables

The coefficient of the dummy variable for a particular state measures the differential effect of being in that state compared with some baseline state (in which all the dummies equal 0).

9.1.1 Seasonal Indicators

We now introduce a data set that will be used as the running example for the next few sections of this chapter. Recall that in Minicase 4.2 we used single-series methods to explore the Walmart sales data. The series represents quarterly sales figures for Walmart from 1995Q1 through 2010Q4, with $n = 64$. We now extend that analysis to include gross domestic product (GDP), lagged one period, $L1\_GDP$, as an explanatory variable. The measure we use is obtained from the U.S. Department of Commerce and represents GDP by quarter in current dollars (i.e., there is no adjustment for inflation); this series has also been seasonally adjusted. A scatterplot of the relationship is shown in Figure 9.2.

The regression results are as follows:

Model 1: **Walmart** [*Walmart_2.xlsx*]

Predictor	Coef	SE Coef	T	P
Constant	−63.236	3.057	−20.69	0.000
L1_GDP	0.0114637	0.0002688	42.64	0.000

S = 5.06494   R-Sq = 96.8%   R-Sq(adj) = 96.7%

At first sight, the fit appears to be fairly good; but examination of the diagnostics in Figure 9.3 reveals several problems, most notably a pattern in the ordered residuals and evidence of nonnormality. To confirm the suspected seasonal pattern, we also generate the ACF and PACF of the residuals, shown in Figure 9.4. These autocorrelation functions show a very clear seasonal pattern (a spike at lag 4), confirming the suspicions just raised.

FIGURE 9.2   SCATTERPLOT FOR QUARTERLY WALMART SALES ON GDP, LAGGED ONE MONTH (*Current dollars, seasonally adjusted, 1995Q1–2010Q4*)

Data shown is from file Walmart_2.xlsx; adapted from Minitab output.

FIGURE 9.3 RESIDUALS PLOTS FOR WALMART SALES ON LAGGED GDP

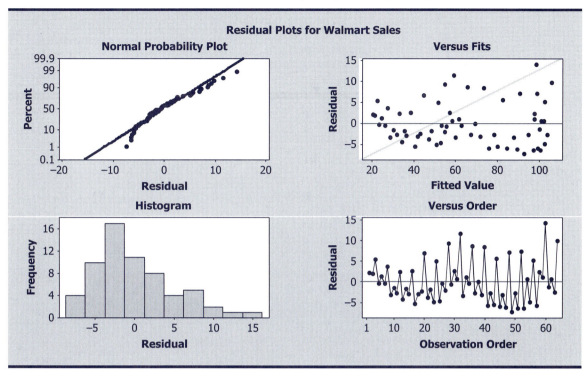

Data: Walmart_2.xlsx; adapted from Minitab output.

FIGURE 9.4 ACF AND PACF OF RESIDUALS (*From the Regression of Walmart Sales on Lagged GDP*)

(Continued)

FIGURE 9.4   (CONTINUED)

Data: Walmart_2.xlsx; adapted from Minitab output.

In order to incorporate any seasonal pattern into the model, we specify three indicator variables:

	X_1	X_2	X_3
If the observation pertains to the first quarter	1	0	0
If the observation pertains to the second quarter	0	1	0
If the observation pertains to the third quarter	0	0	1

The fourth quarter is then identified by default as that quarter in which $X_1 = X_2 = X_3 = 0$. The first few rows of the data file are shown in Table 9.1.

TABLE 9.1   DATA FILE SHOWING INDICATOR VARIABLES FOR WALMART SALES

Date	Walmart Sales	L1_GDP	Quarter_1	Quarter_2	Quarter_3
1995Q1	20.4		1	0	0
1995Q2	22.7	7307.7	0	1	0
1995Q3	22.9	7355.8	0	0	1
1995Q4	27.6	7452.5	0	0	0
1996Q1	22.8	7542.5	1	0	0
1996Q2	25.6	7638.2	0	1	0
1996Q3	25.6	7800.0	0	0	1
1996Q4	30.9	7892.7	0	0	0

Data: Walmart_2.xlsx.

We then rerun the regression for *Walmart Sales* on lagged *GDP* and the three indicator variables. The results are as follows:

Model 2: **Walmart** [*Walmart_2.xlsx*]

Predictor	Coef	SE Coef	T	P
Constant	−55.703	1.674	−33.28	0.000
L1_GDP	0.0114216	0.0001373	83.18	0.000
Quarter 1	−11.2437	0.9293	−12.10	0.000
Quarter 2	−7.5465	0.9147	−8.25	0.000
Quarter 3	−9.7294	0.9142	−10.64	0.000

S = 2.58527   R-Sq = 99.2%   R-Sq(adj) = 99.1%

At first sight, an increase in the adjusted R^2 from 96.7 percent to 99.1 percent may not seem such a big deal, but the more important measure is S, which relates to the width of the prediction interval; S has dropped from 5.06 to 2.59, a considerable improvement in the width of the interval. When we wish to compare the fits of competing models, the standard error is a better guide than R^2. The residuals plots in Figure 9.5 show that we are not yet out of the woods, because the residuals still show a systematic pattern and their ACF and PACF (not shown) still indicate some dependence over the first four lags. In order to make further progress, we need to develop additional tools, and to do so, we now turn to the use of lagged values of the dependent variable.

FIGURE 9.5   RESIDUALS PLOTS (*From the Regression of Walmart Sales on Lagged GDP and Seasonal Indicators*)

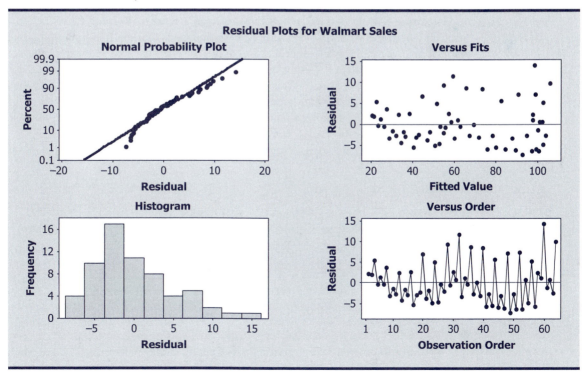

Data: Walmart_2.xlsx; adapted from Minitab output.

9.2   Autoregressive Models

Whenever the ACF of the residuals shows significant autocorrelation, it is worth thinking about autoregressive models—that is, models that use past values of the dependent variable to describe future developments. The general form of such models is

$$Y_t = \beta_0 + \beta_1 Y_{t-1} + \cdots + \beta_p Y_{t-p} + \varepsilon_t. \tag{9.2}$$

Equation (9.2) represents the autoregressive model of order p, written as AR(p), previously discussed in Section 6.2.2. Several points are worth noting before we proceed:

- Not all lags 1, 2, . . . , p need to be included. This point is particularly important in dealing with seasonal series, as we shall see shortly.
- The assumptions regarding the error term are the same as those for standard regression models and need not be repeated here (see Section 8.5). The same diagnostics may be used for model checking.
- The parameters may be estimated by ordinary least squares (OLS), as before. By virtue of the central limit theorem, the estimators are approximately normally distributed, provided that the sample size is not too small. (For a detailed discussion of this issue, see Box *et al.*, 2008, pp. 323–326.)
- OLS can be used even when the process is *nonstationary*, as defined in Section 6.1.1. For example, in the AR(1) scheme, we may allow $|\beta_1| > 1$. Nevertheless, when this occurs, the absolute values of the forecasts will increase without limit, so such models should not be used for other than short-term forecasting.
- The pure autoregressive model can be extended to also include a regression component, as we discuss in Section 9.3.

Example 9.3 ■ An AR model using lags 1 and 4 [*Walmart_2.xlsx*]
The plot of the Walmart sales series clearly indicates that the final quarter of each financial year (actually, November and December of one year and January of the next year) has higher sales than the other quarters. This observation was confirmed in the previous section by our analysis using seasonal indicators. Also, the series shows a strong upward trend over time. Accordingly, lags 1 and 4 seem reasonable initial choices for modeling purposes. The resulting analysis, using a standard regression program, yields the following results:

Model 3: **Walmart** [*Walmart_2.xlsx*]				
Predictor	**Coef**	**SE Coef**	**T**	**P**
Constant	4.9224	0.8780	5.61	0.000
L1_Sales	0.05939	0.04081	1.46	0.151
L4_Sales	0.94496	0.04053	23.32	0.000
	S = 2.57060 R-Sq = 99.1% R-Sq(adj) = 99.1%			

The results provide two surprises. First of all, the model performs as well as Model 2, the regression with dummy (indicator) variables. Second, lag 1 is seen to be relatively unimportant. Dropping this lag, we finish up with the following simpler model:

Model 4: **Walmart** [*Walmart_2.xlsx*]

Predictor	Coef	SE Coef	T	P
Constant	5.3554	0.8340	6.42	0.000
L4_Sales	1.00109	0.01256	79.72	0.000

S = 2.59526   R-Sq = 99.1%   R-Sq(adj) = 99.1%

The overall properties are similar, but it is worth noting that Model 4 implies an annual increase of about $5.36 million for a given quarter over the same quarter in the previous year. Such a result implies that the growth rate for Walmart is slowing; that may be so, but it is not a conclusion to be reached lightly and we should at least consider a log transform; we leave this to the reader as Exercise 9.4. For the model to be stationary, we would need to restrict the lag 4 coefficient to be less than 1.0 in absolute value; such a restriction would clearly be inappropriate in this case, because the series has a strong upward trend. Here, the coefficient is approximately 1.0 and differencing should be considered (see Section 9.5.1 and Exercise 9.5). ■

A purely autoregressive scheme will not usually be totally effective when important explanatory variables are available. Our purpose in this section has been to show how to incorporate autoregressive terms into a regression framework. We now consider a more complete model.

9.3 Models with Both Autoregressive and Regression Components

Now that we have developed a way to incorporate autoregressive terms into the model, we may combine our findings and consider a model that includes *GDP*, lagged sales, and the three seasonal factors. It remains to be seen whether all these elements are needed, but we can start out with the five explanatory variables and then eliminate redundancies as necessary.

The results for this model are as follows:

$$Walmart\ Sales = -26.8 + 0.00597\ L1\_GDP + 0.486\ L4\_Sales - 6.11\ Quarter\_1$$
$$- 4.25\ Quarter\_2 - 5.52\ Quarter\_3$$

Model 5: **Walmart** [*Walmart_2.xlsx*]

Predictor	Coef	SE Coef	T	P
Constant	−26.790	3.525	−7.60	0.000
L1_GDP	0.0059660	0.0006297	9.47	0.000
L4_Sales	0.48566	0.05480	8.86	0.000
Quarter 1	−6.1120	0.8413	−7.27	0.000
Quarter 2	−4.2543	0.7215	−5.90	0.000
Quarter 3	−5.5173	0.7934	−6.95	0.000

S = 1.63975   R-Sq = 99.7%   R-Sq(adj) = 99.6%

At first sight, the adjusted R^2 seems only marginally higher, but the key result to note is that S has fallen to 1.64, a worthwhile reduction over the earlier models we considered. Although all three dummy variables show small P values, it is evident that this reflects higher sales in the fourth quarter and fairly similar levels during the rest of the year.

FIGURE 9.6   DIAGNOSTICS FOR THE AUTOREGRESSIVE REGRESSION MODEL FOR WALMART SALES (MODEL 5)

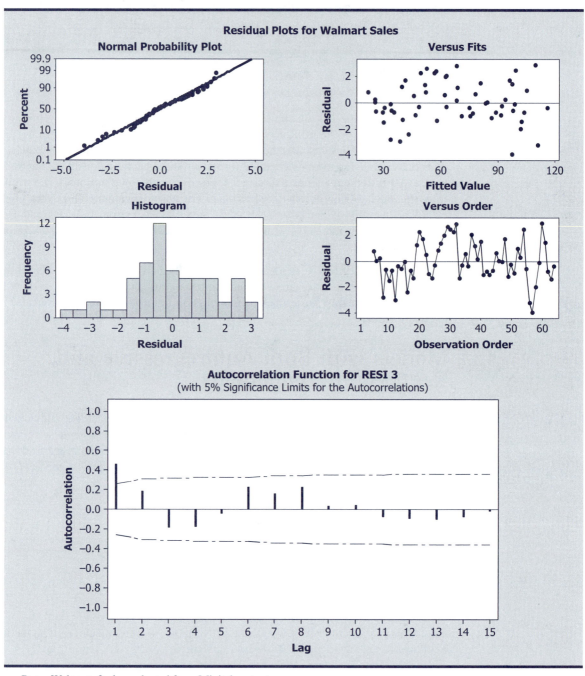

Data: Walmart_2.xlsx; adapted from Minitab output.

The residuals diagnostics are shown in Figure 9.6. There is some suggestion of residual first-order autocorrelation, but the inclusion of such a term does little to improve the model, as we see in the output for Model 6.

Discussion Question   *In Model 5, what are the relative advantages and disadvantages of using both the 4-period lag for unleaded and the seasonal dummy variables?*

Model 6: **Walmart** [*Walmart_2.xlsx*]

Predictor	Coef	SE Coef	T	P
Constant	−19.949	5.570	−3.58	0.001
L1_GDP	0.0048760	0.0009310	5.24	0.000
L1_Sales	0.15368	0.09776	1.57	0.122
L4_Sales	0.42595	0.06607	6.45	0.000
Quarter_1	−8.296	1.618	−5.13	0.000
Quarter_2	−4.5216	0.7319	−6.18	0.000
Quarter_3	−6.4163	0.9694	−6.62	0.000

S = 1.61786   R-Sq = 99.7%   R-Sq(adj) = 99.6%

TABLE 9.2   SUMMARY STATISTICS FOR DIFFERENT MODELS FOR WALMART SALES

Model	X Variables	R^2(adj)	S
Model 1	L1_GDP	96.7	5.06
Model 2	L1_GDP + Seasonals	99.1	2.58
Model 3	L1_Sales, L4_Sales	99.1	2.57
Model 4	L4_Sales	99.1	2.60
Model 5	L1_GDP, Seasonals, L4_Sales	99.6	1.64
Model 6	L1_GDP, Seasonals, L1_Sales, L4_Sales	99.6	1.62

Data: Walmart_2.xlsx.

It is always difficult to know when to stop in a model-building exercise, but we will call a halt here. The summary statistics shown in Table 9.2 indicate the progress we have made through the various stages of the model's development. Using Model 5, we find that the one-step-ahead forecast for 2011Q1 is 103.95, with 95 percent prediction interval (100.48, 107.42).

Selection of Variables

When the number of variables is relatively small, inspection of the individual slope coefficients is feasible and enables us to prune marginal variables from the model. These are the variables for which there are no strong reasons for their inclusion *and* their slope estimates yield insignificant *t*-values. At each step, we can check how the removal of a variable affects our model in terms of diagnostic statistics, predictive power, and interpretation. By the same token, we may plot the residuals against other variables that are not currently in the model to determine whether we have missed any important effects and then expand the model accordingly. The final stage is reached when the model is as simple as possible but incorporates all relevant variables and satisfies the underlying assumptions—a tall order!

When we have a large number of possible explanatory variables, with little to guide us in choosing one set over another, a more automated procedure is desirable. Conceptually, we might think in terms of running all the possible models and choosing the one that is best in some sense. However, such a process can be a daunting task. If we have K possible variables, there are $2^K - 1$ possible models, based upon all possible patterns of including or excluding a particular variable. (Test this out with two variables, with three variables, and so on.) When $K = 10$, we have 1023 candidate models, but by the time we reach $K = 20$, there are over a million possibilities! Such numbers are easy to reach when lagged variables are included in the general model. Thus, when the number of variables is large, we employ various partial searches. Standard approaches are *forward selection*, *backward selection*, and *stepwise regression*. Most statistical software, including Minitab, SAS, and SPSS, has these options.

If K is small enough (some programs have efficient search algorithms that enable them to search up to $K = 16$ or thereabouts), then we can consider all the possibilities and choose the *best subsets*. (For further details of the algorithms used, see Kutner *et al.*, 2005, pp. 361–369.)

Model Selection Algorithms

Forward selection starts by including the variable that has greatest explanatory power (and most significant *t*-value). Next, those variables not yet included in the model are evaluated, and the variable that adds most to the model's explanatory power is added to the model. This step is then repeated.

Backward selection starts by including all the variables in the model and then deleting the variable with least explanatory power (and least significant *t*-value). This step is then repeated for the variables remaining in the model.

Stepwise regression alternately adds a new variable to the model and then evaluates existing variables for possible deletion. When the same variable is successively deleted and immediately added back, the search considers additional variables. The aim is to achieve the highest value of R^2 (or some other preselected criterion) at each stage, but not all possibilities are considered.

Best subsets regression considers all possible subsets of the variables and so guarantees finding an optimum on whatever the preselected criterion. This approach is computationally more expensive than the other ones.

9.4.1 Forward, Backward, and Stepwise Selection

In this section, we use data on the price of unleaded gasoline to examine various model selection approaches. By way of illustration, we show only the SPSS summary printout for the different models.

A substantial number of macroeconomic variables could be considered as possible explanatory variables for movements in U.S. unleaded gasoline prices. Because we are concerned primarily with forecasting, we use only lagged variables. However, many econometricians would make use of contemporaneous observations, as well as lagged values, in model building. Minicase 9.1 encourages the exploration of model development using such an approach.

Our analyses take into account the following eight variables, all lagged by one month:

- Price of unleaded gas (*L1_Unleaded*)
- Price of crude oil (*L1_Crude*)
- Unemployment (*L1_Unemp*)
- S&P 500 Index (*L1_SP500*)
- New housing starts (*L1_Housing*)
- Personal disposable income (*L1_PDI*)
- Consumer price index (*L1_CPI*)
- Time (*Time*)

These data series are contained in *Gas_prices_2.xlsx*. The estimation sample used throughout the following discussions covers the period from January 1996 to December 2008; the hold-out sample covers the period from January 2009 to December 2010.

Forward Selection

	Model Summary: Forward Selection			
Model	R	R Square	Adjusted R Square	Std. Error of the Estimate
1	.978[a]	.956	.956	15.517
2	.980[b]	.961	.960	14.702
3	.983[c]	.966	.965	13.711
4	.984[d]	.969	.968	13.194

a. Predictors: (Constant), L1_Unleaded
b. Predictors: (Constant), L1_Unleaded, L1_Crude
c. Predictors: (Constant), L1_Unleaded, L1_Crude, L1_Housing
d. Predictors: (Constant), L1_Unleaded, L1_Crude, L1_Housing, L1_Unemp

Data shown is from file Gas_prices_2.xlsx; adapted from SPSS output.

The selection terminates when none of the excluded variables (if added) would prove significant (on the basis of the F-test with $\alpha = 0.05$). Does the final model (Model 4) make sense? The details are provided in Table 9.3 and the answer to the question is "Yes". There is a positive autoregressive effect such that a higher past price of unleaded gasoline leads to higher current prices and previous crude prices are working through into current retail prices

TABLE 9.3 UNLEADED PRICE MODELS: FORWARD AND BACKWARD SELECTION PROCEDURES COMPARED

	Coefficients				
	Unstandardized Coefficients		Standardized Coefficients		
Model	B	Std. Error	Beta	T	P(Sig.)
4 (Forward)					
(Constant)	23.559	11.004		2.141	.034
L1_Unleaded	.541	.073	.543	7.454	.000
L1_Crude	1.326	.207	.476	6.397	.000
L1_Housing	.021	.004	.084	5.297	.000
L1_Unemp	−5.860	1.622	−.053	−3.614	.000
2 (Backward)					
(Constant)	1603.484	205.980		7.785	.000
Time	2.278	.325	1.387	7.000	.000
L1_Unleaded	.864	.088	.867	9.807	.000
L1_Crude	1.607	.196	.577	8.206	.000
L1_Unemp	−8.055	3.484	−.073	−2.312	.022
L1_SP500	−.055	.012	−.175	−4.725	.000
L1_PDI	.055	.014	1.322	3.820	.000
L1_CPI	−12.269	1.846	−2.989	−6.646	.000

Note: Dependent Variable: *Unleaded*

N.B. SPSS also includes "Standardized Coefficients," which attempt to measure the importance of one explanatory variable relative to another. The interpretation is not straightforward, and we will omit this column in later SPSS-based tables. One simpler route to measuring the relative impact of a variable is to estimate the effect of a 10 percent change in each of them upon the expected value of the dependent variable.

Data: Gas_prices_2.xlsx; adapted from SPSS output.

of unleaded gasoline with the expected positive coefficient. In addition, Housing has a positive sign, reflecting overall economic conditions, and the negative sign for Unemployment reflects the impact of reduced demand.

Backward Selection

Model Summary: Backward Selection

Model	R	R Square	Adjusted R Square	Std. Error of the Estimate
1	.988[a]	.975	.974	11.902
2	.987[b]	.975	.974	11.916

a. Predictors: (Constant), L1_Housing, L1_Unemp, L1_PDI, L1_SP500, L1_Crude, L1_Unleaded, Time, L1_CPI
b. Predictors: (Constant), L1_Unemp, L1_PDI, L1_SP500, L1_Crude, L1_Unleaded, Time, L1_CPI

Data: Gas_prices.2.xlsx; adapted from SPSS output.

The backward selection method leads to a more complicated model that includes the lagged *SP500, Unemployment, PDI, CPI,* and *Time,* but *Housing* does not appear. The coefficients for the lagged values of *Unleaded, Crude,* and *Unemployment* are broadly comparable for the two models, but certainly not the same. Such a discrepancy between the two methods is common and relates to the different criteria for adding new variables to a model or for removing existing ones. Note that, in this example, the "best" model obtained through backward selection yields a smaller standard error than forward selection does.

In this particular case, using stepwise selection is found to give the same results as forward selection. Such differences among the selection procedures may occur because of multicollinearity (see Section 9.5) but also because of outliers (a topic we discuss in Section 9.7). Accordingly, we will defer making a choice between the models until we have examined matters further; see Section 9.5.

9.4.2 Searching All Possible Models: Best Subset Regression

Alternatively, we may examine all possible regressions, using, for example, Minitab or SAS. Results are shown in Table 9.4.

TABLE 9.4   RESULTS OF BEST SUBSETS ANALYSIS FOR UNLEADED PRICES

Number of Variables Selected	Model	Adjusted R²	S
1	L1_Unleaded	95.6	15.5
2	L1_Unleaded, L1_Crude	96.0	14.7
3	L1_Unleaded, L1_Crude, L1_Housing	96.5	13.7
4	L1_Unleaded, L1_Crude, L1_CPI, Time	96.8	13.2
5	L1_Unleaded, L1_Crude, L1_CPI, Time, L1_PDI	97.0	12.7
6	L1_Unleaded, L1_Crude, L1_CPI, Time, L1_PDI, L1_SP500	97.3	12.1
7	L1_Unleaded, L1_Crude, L1_CPI, Time, L1_PDI, L1_SP500, L1_Unemp	97.4	11.9

Data: Gas_prices_2.xlsx.

The best subsets results are encouraging, in that there is a steady reduction in the value of S. But now we are faced with a second problem: How should we choose among these best subset models?

The seven-variable model has the smallest value of S and matches the choice obtained from backward selection. (This is bound to occur when only one variable is omitted.) We must also keep in mind that we have examined (at least implicitly) $2^8 - 1 = 255$ different models. Clearly, if we choose from among so many possibilities, we run the risk of being overoptimistic about the performance of the model selected. One remedy is to split the sample: Use an estimation sample to select the preferred model, and then use the hold-out sample for final estimation and forecasting. When sufficient data exist, this is the best method, and it should be routinely applied in, for example, data-mining applications, as we discuss in Chapter 10. The approach is straightforward with the large cross-sectional data sets that are typically available, such as those concerned with customers' purchasing habits. With the smaller data sets that are usual in time series, we recommend the careful use of a hold-out sample, as on other occasions.

Model Selection

In comparing models with reference to a hold-out sample, consider only models that are interpretable and that pass the standard diagnostic tests.

Discussion Question *Why might using best subsets or stepwise regression not deliver the most accurate forecasting model?*

9.4.3 Using a Hold-out Sample to Compare Models

Which model wins? To answer this question, we may compare the models chosen by forward and backward selection with an ARIMA(0,1,1) model by computing the mean error (ME), the mean absolute error (MAE), and the mean absolute percentage error (MAPE) [all introduced in Section 2.8]. Our hold-out sample covers the period January 2009–December 2010. The ME, MAE, and MAPE for the three sets of forecasts are shown in Table 9.5.

Something has gone badly wrong! Our hold-out period coincided with the start of the "Great Recession" in the United States and elsewhere. In brief, oil prices shot up, the economy slumped, and our models failed to take those possibilities into account. (Neither did most economists!) Although the two models included lagged price variables, both versions recorded large positive residuals in January 2009 (the forecasts were too low and never recovered, as can be seen from the fact that ME = MAE; all 24 one-step-ahead errors were positive! The ARIMA scheme was more successful because it allowed more rapid adjustments based upon recent errors.

TABLE 9.5 SUMMARY MEASURES OF ONE-STEP-AHEAD FORECAST PERFORMANCE FOR THE ARIMA SCHEME AND THE SELECTED MODELS, 2009–2010

Method of Forecasting	ME	MAE	MAPE
ARIMA(0,1,1) with $\theta = -0.56$	3.9	11.1	4.4
Model 2: Forward	49.0	49.0	19.5
Model 7: Backward	44.1	44.1	17.7

© Cengage Learning 2013.

9.4.4   A Regression Model with Autoregressive Errors

The superior performance of the ARIMA model suggests that we might combine the regression terms with a component that adjusts for the errors. We set up the model as follows:

$$Y_t = \beta_0 + \beta_1 X_{1,t} + \cdots + \beta_K X_{K,t} + u_t$$
$$u_t = \phi u_{t-1} + \varepsilon_t. \tag{9.3}$$

Dropping the regression terms reduces the model to a first-order autoregressive scheme, whereas setting $\phi = 0$ reduces the model to the usual multiple regression formulation. This model is known as the *Cochrane–Orcutt scheme* (Kutner *et al.*, 2005, pp. 492–495). Estimation proceeds by OLS but involves an iterative solution. Conceptually, it is easiest to think of trying a range of values for ϕ and fitting a multiple regression model for each choice. A practical approach is to use Solver in Excel, and the spreadsheet *Gas_prices_Cochrane.xlsx* is available on the website for the model we describe next.

EXAMPLE 9.4 ■ Cochrane–Orcutt model for unleaded gas prices [*Gas_prices_Cochrane.xlsx*]

We consider model (9.3) with the two explanatory variables *L1_Unleaded* and *L1_Crude* and use *Solver* to estimate the model. The resulting forecast function is

$$F_t = 43.066 + 0.369 * L1\_Unleaded + 1.704 * L1\_Crude + 0.41 u_{t-1}.$$

That is, $\phi = 0.41$, so that a positive residual in one time period leads to an upward adjustment for the next forecast. The standard error of estimate is $S = 14.01$. The resulting error measures for the forecasts are

$$ME = 4.27, \quad MAE = 9.74, \quad \text{and} \quad MAPE = 4.30.$$

These results are only marginally better than those obtained with the simple ARIMA scheme, but the causal form of the model, which now includes the lagged crude oil price, makes the model more desirable than the simple extrapolative scheme. ■

The latest econometric packages feature new approaches that aim to do a better job of automatic model selection as well as describing more general error structures (see, e.g., EViews (available through *www.eviews.com*) or PCGIVE (*www.oxmetrics.net*). In this example, we have included only one-period lags, but some effects, such as those for crude oil prices, may take longer to feed through into the unleaded price. Exercise 9.9 explores more general structures, and other, more advanced alternatives are considered in Chapter 10.

 9.5   Multicollinearity and Structural Change

Model building for business processes is frequently fraught with uncertainty. We are often able to identify a considerable number of variables that *may* have an effect, but we lack a strong theoretical foundation for making a selection from among those variables. Further, the variables we choose may be highly correlated among themselves (different lags of the same variable, different measures of household income or various stock price indexes), or the relationships may change over time.

The questions we raise are similar to those posed earlier: How do we identify such problems and what do we do about them? If the explanatory variables are highly correlated with one another, there is potentially an element of redundancy. Whenever such a condition arises, we say that the data display *multicollinearity* and that some of the variables *may* be superfluous. Once some of them are included in the model, it may be possible to exclude others. Conversely, a variable may be important at some times and less so at others. We first examine multicollinearity and then return to consider structural change in Section 9.5.2.

When we developed the multiple regression model, we used the *t*-test to examine the contribution of a particular variable, given that all the others were included in the model. The same idea may be exploited here: For each explanatory variable, we may perform a regression analysis on all the other explanatory variables. If a particular variable has a very high value of R^2 in such a setting, it means that most of the explanation which that variable can provide is already available from those other variables. As a consequence, it may be feasible to remove that variable from the model without any serious loss of performance.

Let R_j^2 denote the coefficient of determination for variable X_j on all the other explanatory variables. We define the *Variance Inflation Factor* (or VIF) as

$$VIF(j) = \frac{1}{1 - R_j^2}. \tag{9.4}$$

If X_j is completely uncorrelated with the other variables, then $R_j^2 = 0$ and $VIF = 1$, its minimum value. As the overall correlation gets higher, the coefficient of determination increases and so does VIF. If X_j is perfectly correlated with a linear function of the other variables, VIF becomes infinite, which is what happens when we try to include all four quarterly seasonal indicators in the model. That is a clear signal that we can drop one of the indicator variables without any loss of explanatory power.

In other cases, VIF remains finite but may be large. There are no formal rules about how large a value of VIF is too large, but the following guidelines are reasonable:

- If $n < 30$, consider dropping a variable if its VIF is greater than 5.
- If $n \geq 30$, consider dropping a variable if its VIF is greater than 10.
- As before, for any n, we consider dropping a variable if $P > \alpha$ (our chosen significance level).

Remember, these are guidelines, not sacred laws! A high VIF may be acceptable if $P < \alpha$, although such mixed signals usually mean that a more careful investigation is in order. As a practical matter, we proceed cautiously and remove variables only one at a time, to avoid casting out the baby with the bathwater. There is hardly any problem with dropping a variable when other variables included in the model measure much the same phenomenon (e.g., GDP and personal disposable income). However, sometimes two quite distinct variables, such as company expenditures on television advertising and in-store promotions, may be very highly (negatively) correlated because the overall marketing budget is fixed. A change in policy could lead to a very different relationship. In such a situation, the multicollinearity is *data-based*. In that case, if we think that the apparent relationship between the variables may break down during the forecast period, we really need to obtain better estimates of the slope coefficients. While this is easier said than done, the only straightforward route is to collect more relevant data to use in the model; companies sometimes do this by test marketing in restricted areas (e.g., a small number of metropolitan regions).

In contrast, when the variables are *definitionally related*, as with different measures of income, we can usually be confident that the collinearity will continue into the forecast period. In this situation, it is perfectly reasonable to drop one or more of the variables and simplify the model.

When the data are cross-sectional, the same arguments apply. Dropping variables that theory suggests are important is dangerous.

Multicollinearity

Multicollinearity occurs when the explanatory variables are themselves strongly related.

Definitional Multicollinearity occurs when two variables are strongly related because they share a similar definition and are similarly measured; in this case, the multicollinearity will persist.

Causal Multicollinearity arises when the explanatory variables are strongly related because of the nature of the underlying phenomena: the multicollinearity can therefore be expected to persist.

Data-based Multicollinearity occurs when the relationship exists in the data being analyzed and there is no strong reason to believe that it will persist during the forecast period.

EXAMPLE 9.5 ■ Multicollinearity in the unleaded prices data [*Gas_prices_ 2.xlsx*]
We may examine the two previously selected models, given in Table 9.3, and compute their VIF values. The output is given in Table 9.6. The model obtained by forward selection shows the very high correlation between the lagged values of *Unleaded* and *Crude*. This relationship is not surprising, being an example of causal multicollinearity, as there is no reason to suspect that the price of gasoline at the pump will become disconnected from crude oil prices. Also, both variables are significant with interpretable coefficients. Accordingly, we will keep both variables in the model.

The situation with the model obtained by backward selection is rather different. The VIFs are horrendously high, and there is no particular reason to expect *PDI* and *CPI* to move linearly with time, although they will tend to be highly correlated because of inflation. The model is unacceptable and we must consider a reformulation. In particular, we need to consider whether some of the variables, including the unleaded price itself (as well as *PDI*), should be measured in real terms (with inflation removed) or in current dollars, as it is now measured. This question is explored in Exercise 9.10.

TABLE 9.6 *VIF* VALUES FOR THE GAS PRICE MODELS OBTAINED BY FORWARD AND BACKWARD SELECTION

Model	Slope	Std. Error	T	P	VIF
(Constant)	23.559	11.004	2.141	.034	
L1_Unleaded	.541	.073	7.454	.000	25.491
L1_Crude	1.326	.207	6.397	.000	26.585
L1_Housing	.021	.004	5.297	.000	1.210
L1_Unemp	−5.860	1.622	−3.614	.000	1.024
(Constant)	1603.484	205.980	7.785	.000	
Time	2.278	.325	7.000	.000	231.398
L1_Unleaded	.864	.088	9.807	.000	45.995
L1_Crude	1.607	.196	8.206	.000	29.089
L1_Unemp	−8.055	3.484	−2.312	.022	5.795
L1_SP500	−.055	.012	−4.725	.000	8.038
L1_PDI	.055	.014	3.820	.000	705.901
L1_CPI	−12.269	1.846	−6.646	.000	1191.818

Data: Gas_prices_2.xlsx; adapted from SPSS output.

In retrospect, the poor quality of the forecasts, as summarized in Table 9.5, provides additional evidence that such models are not to be trusted. VIF values should always be checked in multiple regression models. ∎

9.5.1   Use of Differences

Time series often change relatively slowly over time, so we must deal with large auto-correlations as well as the high correlations that exist among some of the predictors. To keep multicollinearity in check, we need to find a way to retain the richness of the model with multiple variables and yet remove the instability caused by the high correlations. As we have seen, one solution is to use model selection procedures, but this may eliminate key variables. Another solution is to examine *changes* in the variables, rather than looking at their *absolute levels*. That is, we consider differences, as originally introduced in Section 2.6.2. As before, we define the first-order difference in the dependent variable as

$$DY_t = Y_t - Y_{t-1},$$

with similar expressions for the differences of the explanatory variables. We continue to lag all the predictor variables by one month and explore forward and backward selection.

The models selected are summarized in Table 9.7. The model obtained by forward selection is very simple; only the lagged change in the price of crude has any effect. The model obtained by backward selection also includes the lagged change in Unleaded and the changes in PDI and CPI, but we observe that the *VIF* values are now at acceptable levels. Further, all the slopes have the appropriate signs.

The summary statistics for these models are as follows:

Forward selection: $R^2(adj) = 0.432, S = 11.82$
Backward selection: $R^2(adj) = 0.521, S = 10.96$

The much lower value for $R^2(adj)$ may come as a shock, but keep in mind that it relates to the variance explained for the *change* in the unleaded price; much of the variability has already been eliminated by using the difference rather than the original price variable. More relevant is the value of S, which is smaller for the case of backward selection than for any of the models discussed earlier.

Discussion Question   *Why can S be used to compare a model in levels with a model in differences?*

TABLE 9.7   SUMMARY RESULTS FOR FORWARD AND BACKWARD SELECTION MODELS FOR UNLEADED GASOLINE PRICES, BASED UPON DIFFERENCED SERIES

Model	Slope	Std. Error	T	P	VIF
Forward (Step 1)					
(Constant)	−.172	.954	−.180	.857	
DIFF(L1_Crude,1)	2.243	.209	10.742	.000	
Backward (Step 4)					
(Constant)	3.469	1.499	2.315	.022	
DIFF(L1_Unleaded,1)	.597	.132	4.528	.000	5.090
DIFF(L1_Crude,1)	2.016	.287	7.031	.000	2.194
DIFF(L1_PDI,1)	.035	.019	1.785	.076	1.037
DIFF(L1_CPI,1)	−14.153	2.883	−4.909	.000	4.173

Note: Dependent Variable: $DY_t = $ DIFF(Unleaded,1). The notation DIFF(X,1) represents the first difference of X.

Data: Gas_prices_2.xlsx; adapted from SAS output (with default names).

TABLE 9.8   ONE-STEP AHEAD FORECAST ERROR STATISTICS COMPARING
FORWARD AND BACKWARD SELECTION STRATEGIES
(Based Upon a Hold-out Sample from January 2009–December 2010)

Model	ME	MAE	MAPE
Forward	3.1	13.4	5.6
Backward	1.1	14.0	5.9

© Cengage Learning 2013.

We may briefly summarize the diagnostic plots (not shown). The *ACF* and *PACF* suggest slight seasonal patterns, and the probability plot indicates heavier tails than for the normal distribution. Most critically, the plot of residuals against time shows increasing variability; we take up this issue again in Section 9.6.2.

The summary measures for forecasts based on the two models are given in Table 9.8.

The models incorporating differences do not appear to be as effective in adjusting for past errors as is the final model in Section 9.4.4. However, differencing often serves to eliminate multicollinearity, and it is an important tool when we believe that changes, rather than levels, should be modeled.

Model Evaluation

When comparing a model with a differenced dependent variable with a model in the raw data,

- R^2 cannot be used to make a sensible comparison.
- The predictive accuracy of the models in forecasting the original data should be used to make the comparison.
- S is the key measure to consider.

9.5.2   Structural Change

In using a multiple regression model for forecasting, one very strong assumption is made implicitly: That the regression model and its coefficients remain constant into the forecast period.

Discussion Question   *If the impact of the price of Crude changes (say, doubles) during the forecast period, what would you expect to happen to the accuracy of your forecasts? If the constant term doubles (because of some variable, such as tax, omitted from the equation), what would you expect to happen?*

How might such changes affect the forecasts if they happened in the estimation sample?

A number of tests have been proposed that allow us to examine whether there have been any structural changes in the model (i.e., changes in the model's coefficients). These tests can, of course, be applied only to the available data, so there remains the judgmental question that any forecaster must ask: Do we expect stability in the forecast period? But if there has been little stability during the estimation period, we would surely be more nervous about assuming stability into the future.

We start out with a general regression model in K variables and assume that there are n_1 observations in the estimation sample:

$$Y_t = \beta_0 + \sum \beta_i X_{it} + \varepsilon_t, \quad t = 1, 2, \ldots, n_1.$$

Further, we assume that n_2 observations are retained in the hold-out sample, so that there are $n = n_1 + n_2$ observations in all. If the model has undergone a structural change, the parameters for the hold-out sample will differ from those in the estimation sample. We may write the two versions as

$$Y_t = \beta_0 + \sum \beta_i X_{it} + \varepsilon_t, \quad \text{for } t \le n_1$$

$$Y_t = \gamma_0 + \sum \gamma_i X_{it} + \varepsilon_t, \quad \text{for } t > n_1. \tag{9.5}$$

A convenient way of combining these equations so that we can use standard regression software is to set

$$\gamma_i = \beta_i + \delta_i, \quad i = 0, 1, \ldots, K.$$

Then the assumption of no structural change corresponds to the null hypothesis,

$$H_0 \colon \delta_0 = \delta_1 = \cdots = \delta_K = 0.$$

We test this null against the alternative hypothesis,

$$H_A \colon \text{not all } \delta_i = 0.$$

By equations (9.5), the combined equation becomes

$$Y_t = \beta_0 + \delta_0 U_t + \sum \beta_i X_{it} + \sum \delta_i U_t X_{it} + \varepsilon_t.$$

The indicator variable U serves to identify the two subsamples and is defined as

$$U_t = 0, \quad t = 1, 2, \ldots, n_1$$
$$= 1, \quad t = n_1 + 1, \ldots, n.$$

Under the usual assumption that the error terms are independent and identically distributed normal random variables, an F-test may be used. Let SSE_0 and SSE_1 denote the sums of squared errors under the null and alternative hypotheses, respectively. Then the test statistic is

$$F = \frac{(SSE_0 - SSE_1)/(K + 1)}{SSE_1/(n - 2K - 2)}.$$

Under the null hypothesis, this statistic has an F distribution with $(K + 1, n - 2K - 2)$ DF. This test is known as the *Chow* test and is equivalent to testing whether the slopes for each variable are the same in each period.

EXAMPLE 9.6 ■ Chow test for an unleaded gas prices model

We will use the backward selection model for the differenced series, as given in Table 9.6. The estimation sample covers the period up to December 2008, and the hold-out sample covers the period from January 2009 to December 2010. The analysis-of-variance tables for the null and alternative models are as follows:

Null Model (adapted from SPSS output)

ANOVA					
Model	Sum of Squares	DF	Mean Square	F	P
Regression	16281.303	4	4070.326	29.052	.000
Residual	24238.213	173	140.105		
Total	40519.516	177			

Alternative Model (adapted from SPSS output)

		ANOVA			
Model	Sum of Squares	DF	Mean Square	F	P
Regression	20416.625	9	2268.514	18.958	.000
Residual	20102.892	168	119.660		
Total	40519.516	177			

The test statistic is evaluated as

$$F = \frac{(24338.2 - 20102.9)/5}{20102.9/168} = 6.91,$$

with (5, 168) DF. The P-value is 0.000 to three decimal places, so, clearly, changes have taken place over the last two years. The individual coefficients are shown in the following table, where $U*L1\_Crude\_1$ denotes the product of U with the lagged first-order difference of the crude oil price (and so on):

	Null Model Coefficients	P-Value	Alternative Model Coefficients	P-Value
1 (Constant)	3.450		3.469	
L1_Unleaded_1	.525	.015	.597	.000
L1_Crude_1	1.506	.000	2.016	.000
L1_PDI_1	.022	.221	.035	.076
L1_CPI_1	-11.688	.000	-14.153	.000
U*L1_Unleaded_1			-.636	.079
U*L1_Crude_1			-1.633	.016
U*L1_PDI_1			.002	.957
U*L1_CPI_1			8.462	.270
U			2.633	.390

From the table, we see that the biggest (and statistically significant) change has been in the Crude coefficient, perhaps lending support to the popular argument that prices at the pump were set with little regard to the price at the wellhead. Further analysis of the price of unleaded gasoline should take this shift into account.

We have illustrated how the Chow test can be implemented using standard statistical software. This test and several others are included as standard outputs in various econometric packages. Key extensions include the case in which there are a number of possible structural breaks. For example, such tests are available automatically in PCGive.

9.6 Nonlinear Models

Sometimes the response of the dependent variable (Y) to a particular input variable is unlikely to be linear *over the range of the application*. (See Figure 7.3, describing the sales–advertising relationship.) One example is the effect of temperature on the consumption of energy or foodstuffs such as beer and ice cream. Small changes from the average temperature typically have little effect on consumption, but above a certain threshold, a particularly hot day drives up airconditioner use and people enjoy a cold drink and ice cream even more than usual.

FIGURE 9.7   A NONLINEAR RELATIONSHIP BETWEEN SALES AND PRICE

Data shown is from file Advert.xlsx.

Sometimes too the data are highly suggestive of a nonlinear relationship. Figure 9.7 shows that when the price of a product is too high, the product ceases to be competitive in the marketplace and sales dwindle toward zero. If regression modeling is to capture all the possible relationships between the explanatory variables and the dependent variable, then we need to model such nonlinear relationships.

9.6.1   Polynomial Schemes

The simplest approach is to include nonlinear variables such as X^2, leaving the model still linear in the parameters. The quadratic model is

$$Y_t = \beta_0 + \beta_1 X_t + \beta_2 X_t^2 + \varepsilon_t.$$

This model can be estimated by means of the standard methods for multiple regression because it is *linear in the parameters:* You just add an additional variable, defined as the square of X, into the spreadsheet or worksheet. To see how this is done, consider Example 9.7, which shows sales as they are affected by advertising. The data set also includes a classification of the different types of advertising.

EXAMPLE 9.7 ■ Modeling the advertising–sales relationship

Sales	Advert	Promotion Type	AdvertSq
874.53	100.57	1	10114.32
928.1	106.8	2	11406.24
937	109.26	2	11937.75
928.9	121.78	1	14830.37
.	.	.	.

Data: Advert.xlsx.

A graph of the data is plotted in Figure 9.8, which shows clear nonlinear effects, with sales tailing off at the higher levels of advertising but a rapid response from levels from 100 to 170. The first observation may be unusual (see Section 9.7).

With the two input variables (*Advert* and *AdvertSq*), we can now estimate the parameters β_0, β_1, and β_2 as a standard linear model and compare it with the model that is linear in *Advert*. Results are shown in Table 9.9.

How might we have known that there was a problem with the linear model (which included just *Advert*)? In general, we would expect a nonlinear relationship between sales

FIGURE 9.8   THE NONLINEAR RELATIONSHIP BETWEEN SALES AND ADVERTISING

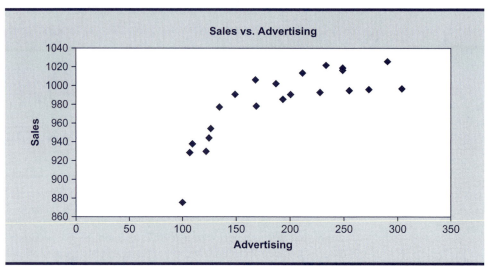

Data: Advert.xlsx.

TABLE 9.9   SALES VERSUS ADVERTISING: USING SPSS TO ESTIMATE NONLINEAR EFFECTS (*Model 1 is linear in advertising, model 2 quadratic in advertising*)

Model Summary

Model	R	R Square	Adjusted R Square	Std. Error of the Estimate
1	.791[a]	.626	.607	23.67525
2	.909[b]	.826	.807	16.56919

a. Predictors: (Constant), Advert
b. Predictors: (Constant), Advert, AdvertSq

Model	Unstandardized Coefficients		T	P
	B	Std. Error		
1 (Constant)	890.717	16.248	54.822	.000
Advert	.470	.081	5.780	.000
2 (Constant)	722.143	37.826	19.091	.000
Advert	2.390	.415	5.760	.000
AdvertSq	−.005	.001	−4.673	.000

Data: Advert.xlsx; adapted from SPSS output.

and advertising; any marketing text would point this out. In addition, we should, of course, always look at the residuals, and those for Model 1 do not look at all random, showing a distinct nonlinear pattern (an exercise we leave to the reader). Because *AdvertSq* has a negative sign, the fitted value for *Sales* is now lower; that is, the quadratic term has a damping effect on the sales response at higher advertising levels.   ■

Higher order (e.g., cubic) terms could be included in the model, but this is rarely a good idea for business data because the higher order terms can create unstable models. However, when there are two or more explanatory variables, it is often a good idea to include cross-product terms to capture interactions. For example, the two-variable model with quadratic and interaction terms may be written as

$$Y = \beta_0 + \beta_1 X_1 + \beta_2 X_1^2 + \beta_3 X_2 + \beta_4 X_2^2 + \beta_5 X_1 X_2 + \varepsilon.$$

As before, these kinds of models can be estimated by ordinary least squares. It should be kept in mind that quadratic models display a single turning point (maximum or minimum). If the turning point is natural in the context of the problem (e.g., profit as a function of price), all is well. If not, as in the advertising example just discussed, the model is valid only in the range of X values for which the expected values are increasing—generally, $X < -b_1/2b_2$ or $X < 2.39/0.01 = 239$ in the example. The model fits may be unreliable for $X > 239$.

9.6.2   Nonlinear Transformations

Some models are nonlinear in the *parameters*, not just the input variables. An example is

$$Y = \alpha X_1^{\beta_1} X_2^{\beta_2} * (\text{error}).$$

As we discuss in Chapter 12, models such as these are needed to model a product's market share where price and promotional effects have been shown to have a multiplicative relationship. (The effect of a price change is amplified proportionately by how much the change is promoted.)

However, these models can be handled quite easily by taking natural logarithms (the function in Excel and several other packages is LN) to get

$$\ln(Y) = \ln(\alpha) + \beta_1 \ln(X_1) + \beta_2 \ln(X_2) + \ln(\text{error}).$$

For obvious reasons, such models are often called log–log models. Of course, the preceding model does not look like a conventional regression equation, but if we set

$$Y^* = \ln(Y), \quad \alpha^* = \ln(\alpha), \quad X_1^* = \ln(X_1), \quad X_2^* = \ln(X_2), \quad \varepsilon = \ln(\text{error}),$$

we get the standard regression model

$$Y^* = \alpha^* + \beta_1 X_1^* + \beta_2 X_2^* + \varepsilon.$$

By adding the log transforms, Y^*, X_1^*, and X_2^* into the data matrix, we can use OLS to obtain the parameters, α^*, β_1, and β_2, and, therefore, an estimate of $\alpha = \exp(\alpha^*)$. The results are as shown in Table 9.10 for the advertising data (with no other input variables). The parameter $\alpha = \exp(\alpha^*)$ has the estimated value $\exp(6.392) = 597.05$.

Although R^2 here is less than that of the AdvertSq model, the standard error is much smaller. Have we found a particularly good model? No, we've transformed the variables into logarithms and cannot compare apples (Y) with oranges ($\ln Y$). To make an appropriate

TABLE 9.10   SUMMARY STATISTICS AND PARAMETER ESTIMATES IN THE LOG–LOG MODEL

	Coefficients	Standard Error	T	P	Regression Statistics	
Intercept	6.392	0.070	91.537	0.000	Multiple R	0.846
Advert	0.095	0.013	7.099	0.000	R Square	0.716
					Adjusted R Square	0.702
					Standard Error	0.022

Data: Advert.xlsx.

TABLE 9.11   COMPARING THE FORECAST ERRORS FROM LOG MODEL WITH THE ADVERTSQ MODEL

Observation	LnSales	Predicted Lnsales	Ln Residuals	Sales	Predicted Sales Log Model	Residuals from Log Model	Predicted Sales AdvertSq	Residuals from AdvertSq Model
1	6.77	6.83	−0.058	874.5	926.6	−52.1	912.8	−38.3
2	6.83	6.83	−0.004	928.1	931.9	−3.8	921.4	6.7
3	6.84	6.83	0.003	937.0	933.9	13.1	924.6	12.4
4	6.83	6.85	−0.016	928.9	943.6	−14.7	940.3	−11.4
.	.	.	.	.				
					RMSE	19.7		15.4
					MAPE	1.52		1.3

Data: Advert.xlsx.

comparison, we need to take two steps. The first is to examine the residuals to see if they conform to the regression assumptions. (Here, both models have their weaknesses.) The second step is to make a quantitative comparison of the two models' predictions. This can be done by transforming the fitted values of the log model back to the original units by taking exponentials of the column labeled "Predicted Lnsales" in Table 9.11. That is, we use the equation $\hat{Y}_{\text{logmodel}} = \exp(\hat{Y}^*)$, so, for example, the first observation has fitted value $\exp(6.832) = 926.59$. We can then compare the accuracy of the two models, as shown in the table.

In addition to producing a model that is linear in the parameters, the logarithmic transform often helps to stabilize the variance, as we illustrate in the next section.

An easily interpretable measure of the impact of changes in the levels of the explanatory variables that eliminates the effects of the units used in measuring both X and Y is the *elasticity*, introduced in Section 7.6.2. The advantage of the log–log model just discussed is that the parameter estimates of the slope are estimates of the elasticities. In such a model, these elasticities are constant, so the crude price elasticity is given by the coefficient β_1. In our example, the estimated elasticity for sales on advertising is low, only 0.095; a doubling of advertising expenditures increases expected sales by 9.5%.

9.6.3   Intrinsically Nonlinear Models

Finally, some models are intrinsically nonlinear, and no transformation will make them linear in the parameters. They can be estimated with nonlinear least squares methods (using Solver or other programs designed for nonlinear estimation). The spreadsheet program, available on the book's website, *Trend.xlsm* demonstrates how this can be done.

One example is the model involving unknown powers of the variables with additive errors:

$$Y_t = \alpha X_t^\delta + \beta Z_t^\gamma + \varepsilon_t.$$

Discussion Question   *How does this equation differ from the multiplicative model with the same variables?*

Another example is the Gompertz (S-shaped) trend curve, illustrated in Figure 9.9:

$$Y_t = ae^{-be^{-ct}} + \varepsilon_t.$$

This curve takes the limiting a when t tends to infinity and has the value ae^{-b} when $t = 0$. Larger values of c lead to the curve flattening out more quickly. We discuss the uses of such curves and how they can be modeled in Chapter 12.

FIGURE 9.9 INTRINSICALLY NONLINEAR MODELS

© Cengage Learning 2013.

9.6.4 Changing Variances and the Use of Logarithmic Models

Many business and economic variables display growth over time, and the magnitude of the variations in the series likewise increases. There are also other reasons the variance may change over time, such as increased trading volatility in the stock market or reductions in product variability caused by improved quality assurance procedures. In this section, we address only growth-related variations, keeping in mind that this approach also encompasses negative growth (or decline). The other form of volatility was discussed in Section 6.10, where we considered GARCH models as extensions of ARIMA schemes. Similar extensions could be considered for regression models, using PCGive or EViews, but a detailed discussion lies beyond the scope of this book.

A change in the variance typically has only a modest effect upon the estimation of the intercept and slope parameters and, in turn, upon the point forecasts. However, the prediction intervals depend critically upon the estimate of the variance, which is why we seek to satisfy the assumption of a constant variance, at least approximately. Because the price series for *Unleaded* displayed increasing volatility that was somewhat related to higher prices, we continue to examine those data.

Recalling the discussion in Section 3.8, we may hope to stabilize the variance by using a transformation; a logarithmic transform is the logical choice here, because it corresponds to steady proportional growth. By way of illustration, we examine only the simple model for *Ln_Unleaded* (the natural logarithm of unleaded gas prices) on the lagged variables *Ln_L1_Unleaded* and *Ln_L1_crude*. Forecasts derived from this model and from more extensive models based upon log transforms are left to the reader (Exercises 9.7 and 9.8). The fitted model is summarized in the following table:

Model	Unstandardized Coefficients		T	P
	B	**Std. Error**		
1 (Constant)	1.114	.220	5.053	.000
Ln_L1_Unleaded	.620	.076	8.176	.000
Ln_L1_Crude	.235	.049	4.811	.000

Note: Dependent Variable: *Ln_Unleaded*

In addition, $R^2(adj) = 0.971$ and $S = 0.0638$.

298 Chapter 9 Model Building

FIGURE 9.10 RESIDUALS PLOTS FOR Ln(UNLEADED) MODEL

Data: Gas_prices_2.xlsx.

The plot of the residuals is shown in Figure 9.10. The log transform goes some way towards stabilizing the variance, but the later part of the series (higher prices) still shows somewhat greater volatility. The implication behind our discussion in this section is that nonconstant variances may not be recognized until the diagnostic stage, but the remedy is to go back to the original series and seek a suitable transformation. Then model building can proceed in the manner of earlier sections, with the assumption of constant variances known to be at least approximately satisfied.

We can also use the elasticity definition given in the previous section to interpret the model: A doubling of the price of crude would lead to an expected increase of 23.5 percent in the price at the pumps in the next time period. The 23.5 percent figure represents the *short-term elasticity*, which describes the change in the price during the next time period. However, greater changes would be expected over the long term as higher prices work their way through the supply chain and refineries adapt to the new realities. We examine these longer term effects by assuming that *Ln_L1_Crude* is increased to a new level and then is kept at this new level while the dependent variable (and hence its lagged values) updates in response to these conditions. The complete effect is known as the *long-term elasticity*. When the model is defined in terms of logarithms, as it is here, the long-term elasticity is

$$\beta_2/(1 - \beta_1)$$

where β_1 is the coefficient of the lagged dependent variable and β_2 is the coefficient of *Ln_L1_Crude*. In this case, the long-term elasticity becomes $0.235/(1 - 0.620) = 0.618$, so that the long-term effect of a doubling of the price of crude would be to increase the price at the pump by 62 percent. As expected, prices respond more over the longer term.

9.7 Outliers and Leverage

Two further types of data characteristic may affect model building: outliers and leverage points. They affect both time series and cross-sectional data, and are illustrated in Figure 9.11.

A leverage point is an observation that exerts an undue influence on the regression line (or model). Leverage points are situated far away from the average X-values. In Figure 9.11, we see that the point labeled as a leverage point affects the regression line quite dramatically. The line labeled "All" was estimated on the basis of all the data points, whereas the line labeled "Omit" dropped both the leverage point and the outlier. The inclusion of the leverage point has dragged the "Omit" line down toward it, as shown by the position of the "All" line. An outlier in the dependent variable is an observation that is far away from its expected or forecast value. An outlier typically has less effect on the regression line, as Figure 9.11 shows: The "Omit" line has not shifted much relative to the outlier.

9.7.1 Leverage Points and What to Do About Them

Obviously, it is undesirable if the inclusion of a single data point dramatically affects the estimated regression line and therefore the corresponding forecasts. Often, this will occur because of a data error. Sometimes, however, the observation will be measured correctly, but no model that adequately captures the remaining observations could also describe the leverage point(s). The first step is to identify whether the data set contains such potentially influential data points. Several diagnostics can help here to come to a commonsense decision whether or not to omit the point on the basis of knowledge of the problem.

Various statistics are included in Minitab, SAS or SPSS that check whether an observation affects the regression results in a particular manner. Standardized DFITS[1] gives

FIGURE 9.11   OUTLIERS AND LEVERAGE POINTS

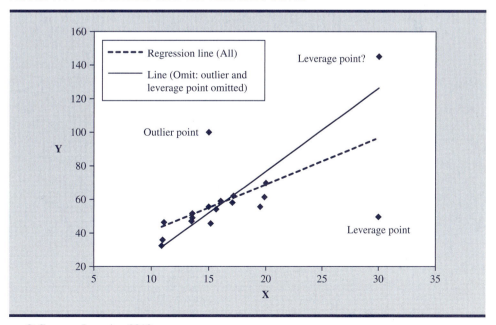

© Cengage Learning 2013.

---

[1] See the HELP commands in the statistical software for further details, or see Kutner *et al.* (2005, pp. 401–402).

an overall measure of how unusual an observation is. The rule is that one should check an observation if $abs(Standardized\ DFITS) > 2\sqrt{p/n}$. Alternatively, we can examine *Cook's distance D*, which is another measure of the influence of an observation. Cases with larger D values than the rest of the data are those which have unusual leverage. A cutoff for detecting influential observations is to examine values of D greater than $4/(n - p - 1)$, where n is the number of observations and p is the number of independent variables.

Some programs allow the user to examine the effects on the individual regression coefficients. As an example, suppose the model building was focused on forecasting the effects of a promotion. Here, the sensitivity of the promotional coefficient to a particular data point could be examined through the *DFBetas* function (available in SPSS and SAS but not Minitab); this function measures the change in the individual regression coefficients when a particular observation is excluded.

These measures of leverage are not based on hard-and-fast rules. Although one measure may point to a potentially damaging observation, another may suggest that the model is just fine. What the modeler must do is check the effects both with and without the potential leverage observation and, where the software makes it available, test those results by using out-of-sample data. Often, in time series forecasting, where the latest data are most relevant to producing the forecasts, these data represent exactly the points that are furthest from the center of the X observations and therefore are more likely to be leverage points.

We can examine the results obtained from the advertising data set *Advert.xlsx*. We use the full set of explanatory variables now, where, in addition to advertising and sales, we have included a quadratic term to capture possible saturation effects. We also use data on the promotional type. There are three types of promotion: high, low, and special. We will therefore need two dummy variables:

> *Newdum1* = 1 if the promotion type is high.
> *Newdum2* = 1 if the promotion type is special.

With all observations included, we reach the regression model shown in Table 9.12.

Cook's distance measure (with a cutoff of $4/(n - p - 1) = 0.24$) identifies observations 1 and 22 as suspect. Standardized *DFITS* (cutoff = 0.85) comes to the same conclusion, but

TABLE 9.12   THE SALES–ADVERTISING PROMOTION MODEL (*all data*)

Model Summary				
Model	**R**	**R Square**	**Adjusted R Square**	**Std. Error of the Estimate**
1	.969	.939	.925	10.37369

	Unstandardized Coefficients			
Model	**B**	**Std. Error**	**T**	**P**
1 (Constant)	755.833	30.545	24.745	.000
Advert	1.912	.325	5.886	.000
Newdum1	19.864	5.138	3.866	.001
Newdum2	−13.106	8.176	−1.603	.127
AdvertSq	−.004	.001	−4.416	.000

Note: Dependent variable: *Sales*

Data: Advert.xlsx; adapted from SPSS output.

TABLE 9.13 THE SALES–ADVERTISING PROMOTION MODEL WITH LEVERAGE POINTS 1 AND 22 REMOVED

Model Summary				
Model	**R**	**R Square**	**Adjusted R Square**	**Std. Error of the Estimate**
1	.975	.951	.937	7.73157

	Unstandardized Coefficients			
Model	**B**	**Std. Error**	**T**	**P**
1 (Constant)	760.599	24.593	30.927	.000
Advert	1.916	.265	7.227	.000
newdum1	20.309	3.855	5.268	.000
newdum2	−5.791	6.700	−.864	.401
AdvertSq	−.004	.001	−5.556	.000

Note: Dependent Variable: Sales

Data: Advert.xlsx; adapted from SPSS output.

also alerts the user to observation 6. We just omit the two common points, 1 and 22, which gives the results shown in Table 9.13.

A comparison of Tables 9.12 and 9.13 indicates that only the coefficient estimating the special promotion effect changes. Despite the fact that now other points are identified as potentially influential, we can regard the model that uses all the variables and estimates all the data as robust (apart from forecasting special promotions, where a few data points include the extreme observation 1).

Note that the summary statistics cannot readily be used to compare the two models because the data set has been changed. However, the elimination of extreme points typically leads to a reduction in S, as here.

9.7.2 The Effects of Outliers

An outlier is an extreme residual (or observation) in the data set.

> ### Outliers
> An *outlier* is an observation (or residual from a model) that lies far away from its expected or forecast value.

To fix ideas, we examine aggregate monthly U.S. retail sales (deseasonalized), shown in Figure 9.12, panel A. The data are available in the file *US_retail_sales_2.xlsx.*

The series exhibits a strong trend, so, keeping in mind the discussion in the previous section, we take differences; because the series has been seasonally adjusted, first-order differences are appropriate. The resulting series is shown in Figure 9.12(B), and it is evident that the variance of the differences is increasing over time. As in the previous section, we aim to stabilize the variance by using a logarithmic transformation. The plot of Ln(*Sales*) is shown in Figure 9.12(C) and the difference of that series in Figure 9.12(D). Comparing the plots of differences, we see that the log transform goes some way toward stabilizing the variance, but the later part of the series still shows somewhat greater volatility.

FIGURE 9.12   PLOTS OF U.S. RETAIL SALES, LOG(SALES), CHANGE IN SALES
(D_SALES), AND CHANGE IN THE LOGARITHM OF SALES
(D_LOGSALES)
*(The actual series represents total sales, in millions of dollars, in the retail
and food services industries. The series has been seasonally adjusted but
is not adjusted for inflation.)*

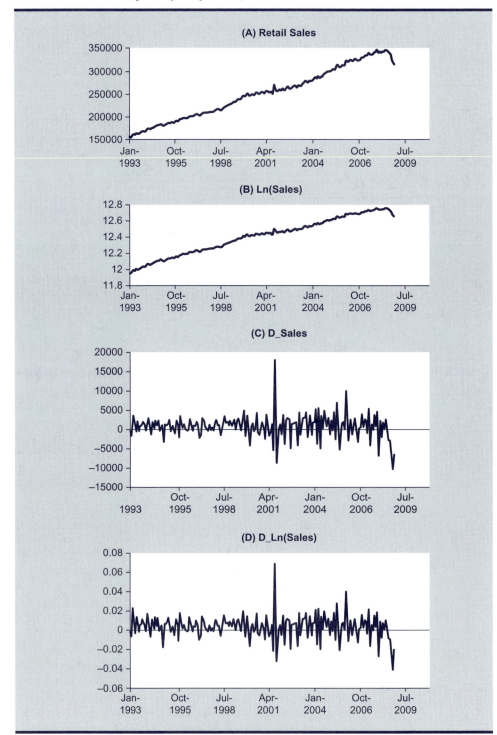

Source: U.S. Census Bureau. *Data:* US_retail_sales_2.xlsx.

TABLE 9.14   VALUES OF COEFFICIENTS FOR AR(1) MODEL FOR THE
DIFFERENCES OF THE LOGARITHM OF U.S. RETAIL SALES
(*January 1993–January 2008*)

Model	AR(1)	AR(1)+IV_Oct01
β_0 = intercept	0.006	0.005
β_1 = slope of AR term	−0.334	−0.267
β_2 = coefficient for IV_Oct01	–	0.059
R^2(adjusted)	0.107	0.275

Data: US_retail_sales_2.xlsx.

The plots in Figure 9.12, panels (B) and (D), show an extreme outlier associated with October 2001; recall that the first differences are plotted, so this observation represents (October sales minus September sales). The outlier is positive, showing the bounce back of sales following the September 2001 terrorist attack on the United States. Such outliers can distort the estimates produced by a time series model with an autoregressive component, in contrast to a standard regression model where the impact is less pronounced. One solution to the problem is to use a robust estimation procedure, which gives less weight in the fitting criterion to such observations. This approach is theoretically demanding and beyond our scope; the interested reader should consult Kutner *et al.* (2005, pp. 437–449).

We follow the second approach, which is to make use of indicator variables. We may define an indicator with value $I = 1$ for October 2001 and value $I = 0$ at all other times. We then include that indicator in the regression model. The net effect is to set the residual for that observation to zero, which seems rather extreme but typically works much better than doing nothing. The analyst should not get carried away with this procedure, however: In principle, we could define an indicator for every observation and be back where we started! Rather, we follow a three-step procedure:

- Identify the outlier(s); a rough guideline is to fit an initial model and then find those residuals which lie outside the interval $\pm 3S$.
- Check the history of the process to see whether an omitted variable might have been important at the time in question; if so, include it in the regression.
- If not, check for unusual events around the time in question and use the indicator variable with a tentative attribution to the event(s) identified.

In the current example, we can attribute the event to exceptional circumstances, so we go ahead and use an indicator variable (*IV_Oct01*). For purposes of illustration, we consider a first-order autoregressive model for the differences of Ln(*Sales*). The effect upon the model is shown in Table 9.14, and the modified residuals are plotted in Figure 9.13. The adjustment for the outlier improves the overall fit of the model but reduces the magnitude of the AR(1) coefficient.

The advertising–sales example also contains outliers—in particular, the first observation. We leave the outlier analysis by indicator variables as Exercise 9.11.

9.7.3   The Role of Outliers and Leverage Points: A Summary

Outliers and leverage points are often neglected in building a model. But both of these data characteristics can do considerable damage if they are ignored. Whether the data are cross-sectional or time series, such points should not be automatically omitted. Instead, they raise questions, both about the data (Is the suspect observation correct?) and about the model (Have we omitted a key variable from the model? Has a structural change been introduced into the problem, such as a new policy or a new competitor?). Outliers and leverage points must always be investigated.

FIGURE 9.13   RESIDUALS FOR THE AR(1) MODEL FOR U.S. RETAIL SALES
AFTER INCLUDING THE OCTOBER 2001 INDICATOR VARIABLE

Data: US_retail_sales_2.xlsx.

9.8 Intervention Analysis

The outlier adjustment process just described is a quick fix that is useful in circumstances in which a single aberrant observation can be identified. However, shocks to the system may produce more complex changes than a one-period outlier, so we now examine a more systematic approach to dealing with such events. Known as *intervention analysis*, this approach is often associated with ARIMA model building, but the methods are equally valuable in building standard regression models.

The goal of intervention analysis is to make adjustments to the model when the underlying structure changes, either permanently or temporarily. Consider the following interventions or changes (shocks) to the system:

a. Monthly production figures are down because of a disruption in the supply of raw materials (e.g., an industrial action, bad weather).
b. An automobile manufacturer plans to offer zero percent financing to new buyers for a four-week period.
c. A competing product is introduced into the market, affecting your own product's sales.

The first case represents what we have already termed an outlier, in that a single month is likely to be affected. Such events may be represented by an indicator variable of the form

$$X_t = 1, \quad \text{if } t = t_0$$
$$= 0, \quad \text{otherwise.} \tag{9.6}$$

In equation (9.6), t_0 denotes the time period in which the event occurs. The special promotion in the second example extends over a finite period, and then financing plans revert to their usual form. We may represent this phenomenon by the indicator

$$X_t = 1, \quad \text{if } t_0 \le t \le t_0 + h$$
$$= 0, \quad \text{otherwise.} \tag{9.7}$$

In equation (9.7), $(h + 1)$ represents the duration of the change. Finally, if the change is permanent, as in the third example, we represent the intervention by a *step function*:

$$X_t = 1, \quad \text{if } t \geq t_0$$
$$ = 0, \quad \text{otherwise.}$$

$$(9.8)$$

In all three cases, the estimated coefficient in the regression equation measures the impact of the intervention. These three examples may be viewed as basic building blocks from which more complex interventions may be constructed. For example, if lost production extends over, say, one-and-a-half months, we might use a two-period indicator weighted by the number of weeks affected in each month. Likewise, special promotions might lead to increased sales during the lifetime of the promotion, but some of those sales would be the result of consumers moving up their buying plans. Thus, post-promotion sales might be lower than normal. We could check for this possibility by using one indicator for the period of the promotion and a second for two or three weeks after the promotion. The first one would be expected to have a positive sign, demonstrating the increase in sales, whereas the second could be negative and would indicate that some sales had been shifted in time rather than being sales made to newly recruited customers.

Minicase 9.2 provides a classic example of intervention analysis related to the introduction of seat-belt requirements in the United Kingdom.

An Update on Forecasting

This chapter has focused upon model building, and little mention has been made of forecasting, which is our ultimate objective. The emphasis is deliberate, because forecasts can be only as good as the model upon which they are based. Once we are satisfied with the model we have constructed, we must reexamine the forecasting issues.

The process of forecasting follows exactly the same steps as were laid out in Section 8.6, so we do not repeat them here. Nevertheless, prior to making forecasts, we should recall the three principal bases upon which explanatory variable values are specified. The explanatory variables may be

- perfectly known,
- estimated from past values, or
- specified hypothetically for "what-if" or policy analysis purposes.

Features of all three varieties may appear in a single model. For example, we may wish to predict seasonal sales for a company that depend upon overall economic activity levels and upon specific company policies, with the values of the seasonal variables known, as in Minicase 9.2. The macroeconomic variables must be forecast; sometimes a company will purchase such forecasts from a specialist econometric forecaster or rely on internal expert judgment. At other times an internal model based upon either regression or exponential smoothing methods may be used. Finally, there will be some policy variables that are under the control of the company, such as prices and special promotions. These are the variables that can be set at different levels to simulate likely outcomes. Indeed, a more involved simulation may also involve varying the input values of the macroeconomic variables.

The impact of these different approaches upon the estimated prediction intervals must be recognized, always under the assumption that the model is correctly specified. When the inputs are known, the nominal coverage (90 percent or whatever) will be correct. When the values of the variables are specified on a "what-if" basis, the coverage is correct, *conditionally upon those specified values*. Finally, when we insert forecasts for the inputs, the true prediction interval should be wider; that is, the actual probability of coverage will be less than that stated.

   A more detailed discussion of how to handle this problem is included in Section 13.3.1. But one simple approach that is sometimes useful is to build into the model a time delay equal to the forecasting horizon. That way, the values of the inputs will be available for forecasting purposes. This approach was considered in Section 7.7.4 and is explored in greater detail in Exercise 9.8.

Principles

The principles discussed in Chapter 8 clearly continue to apply, but the additional skills in model building that have been described in this chapter lead to some further issues that need to be addressed. These principles are based upon the work of Armstrong (2001) and Allen and Fildes (2001).

[9.1] Rely upon theory and domain expertise to select explanatory variables. Use all important variables. The need for such care in model building has been stressed at various points in this chapter. Excessive data mining can lead to models that have no solid foundation in theory or in practice. However, it is best to start with a general model that includes all variables which have the potential to be important.

[9.2] Plot, inspect, and test the residuals for departures from the assumptions, including departures such as outliers and leverage points. As we have seen throughout the chapter, the residuals plots (including the residual ACF) form the most effective means to signal possible breakdowns in the assumptions. Once such problems are identified, we can draw upon the developments in this chapter to improve the model.

[9.3] Aim for a relatively simple model specification.

[9.4] When theory provides a guide to functional form (e.g., when you know that there is an upper limit to the market penetration level of a new technology) or when data strongly suggest a functional form that is compatible with theory, follow the theory.

[9.5] If the date of a possible structural break is known, test whether the parameters remain constant.

[9.6] Test all models for performance with data not used in the estimation process, comparing the results with baseline extrapolative or judgmental alternatives. Criteria such as MAPE and MASE, described in Chapter 2, are particularly useful in this context. This topic was examined in Section 9.5.1 and is also pursued in several of the end-of-chapter exercises.

[9.7] Apply the same principles to forecasts of the explanatory variables.

[9.8] Aim for an interpretable model with adequate forecasting capabilities that captures the key data characteristics. Don't rely on automatic selection procedures to deliver such a model.

Summary

In this chapter, we have developed enhanced model-building procedures to deal with possible violations of assumptions such as autocorrelation, nonlinearity, heteroscedasticity, and the presence of outliers. Model building can be an exhausting activity—although we find it fun! The principles enunciated here and in the previous chapter, along with the examples provided, will help the modeler to arrive at a forecasting model that is grounded in both theory and empirical observation.

As regards automatic model selection, whatever approach you adopt and software you use, the final model should

- Be interpretable, making good sense in the context of the problem
- Be compatible with the data used, in that the regression assumptions should be met, at least approximately
- Have adequate forecasting accuracy for the problem under consideration, compared with benchmark alternatives.

Exercises

9.1   Verify that equation (9.1) produces exactly the same regression lines as those shown in Figure 9.1.

9.2   Use your favorite software to try to fit a model containing all four seasonal indicator variables for a quarterly series, and see what happens. (Versions of Excel are particularly interesting in this regard!)

9.3   Verify that the forecasts for WFJ Sales (*WFJ_sales_2.xlsx*) will be the same, no matter which subset of four indicator variables is used.

9.4   Reanalyze the Walmart data (*Walmart_2.xlsx*), using Model 5 in Section 9.3, but keep the observations for 2009 and 2010 as a hold-out sample. Use this hold-out sample to compute MAE and MAPE for the model. Comment on your results.

9.5   Rework the analysis for Walmart outlined in Exercise 9.4, but transform the *Sales* and *GDP* variables to logarithms before conducting the analysis.

9.6   Rework the analysis for Walmart outlined in Exercises 9.4 and 9.5, but use the differences of the logarithms.

9.7   Reanalyze the unleaded gas prices data (*Gas_prices_2.xlsx*), using logarithmic transforms for all the variables. Use January 2009–December 2010 as a hold-out sample. Compute MAE and MAPE for *the forecasts of the original series*. Compare your results with those given in the text.

9.8   Re-analyze the unleaded prices data (*Gas_prices_2.xlsx*), using the model selected in Exercise 9.7 but with a sufficient number of lags to enable forecasting three months ahead. Use the same hold-out sample to check the model's forecasting performance. Compute MAE and MAPE for the forecasts, and compare your results with the one-step-ahead forecasts. Comment on your results.

9.9   Use EViews or PCGive (or some other appropriate software) to examine a more general lag structure for the error process in the model for unleaded prices (*Gas_prices_2.xlsx*) discussed in Example 9.4. Interpret your results.

9.10 Reanalyze the unleaded prices data (*Gas_prices_2.xlsx*) after transforming all the financial variables to real terms, using *CPI* as the deflator. Consider the six models developed in the text and determine a preferred model. Use this model to generate one-step-ahead point forecasts for the months of 2009 and 2010, and compare your results with those given in the text.

9.11 For the sales–advertising data set (*Advert.xlsx*), use the full model, as set forth in Section 9.7.1, to identify the effects of any outliers. Use indicator variables to deal with any outliers you identify. Compare your results with those given in the text. Does a model based on logarithms of advertising and sales lead to an improved description of the data?

9.12 The WFJ Sales (*WFJ_sales_2.xlsx*) series shows an extreme peak in week 52 (post-Christmas sales). Incorporate a suitable indicator variable into the model and reanalyze the data. Compare your results with the original models for WFJ Sales.

Minicases

The six minicases introduced in Chapter 8 are all open to further analysis. Return to the case you examined originally and proceed as follows:

- Use a hold-out sample of the last 10–15 percent of the observations and run the original model.
- Check the residuals plots, including the residuals ACF, for any departures from the assumptions: autocorrelation, heteroscedasticity, nonlinearity, and possible outliers.
- Depending upon the severity of the violations of particular assumptions, proceed in a step-by-step fashion to revise the model so as to bring it closer to the assumptions.
- When you have reached a final model, generate the one-step-ahead forecasts and associated prediction intervals. Compute the MASE and MAPE, and check how many of the observations lie inside the prediction intervals.
- Revise your model to make forecasts three steps ahead, and evaluate the performance. [OPTIONAL]
- Summarize your results.

Minicase 9.1 An Econometric Analysis of Unleaded Gasoline Prices

(Data for Minicase 9.1 can be found in file *Gas_prices_2.xlsx*.)

In Section 9.4 and in later sections, we developed models for the price of unleaded gasoline at the pump, but always using lagged values of the variables to enable real-time forecasting. Revisit some of these models, but now allow for contemporaneous values of the explanatory variables as well as lags. The possible variables are as follows:

- Price of unleaded gas (*L1_Unleaded*)
- Price of crude oil (*Crude*)
- Unemployment (*Unemp*)
- S&P 500 Index (*SP500*)
- New housing starts (*Housing*)
- Personal disposable income (*PDI*)
- Consumer price index (*CPI*)
- Time (*Time*)

What would you expect to find in the new model that was not present before? Do your results support your previous views?

Discussion Question *Are the aims of the econometrician and the forecaster fundamentally different?*

Minicase 9.2 The Effectiveness of Seat–Belt Legislation

(Data for Minicase 9.2 can be found in file *Road_accidents.xlsx*.)

Harvey and Durbin (1986) provided a classic illustration of the value of intervention analysis to determine the effectiveness of new legislation that required drivers to wear seat belts. The data they used are plotted in Figure 9.14 and represent monthly totals of deaths and serious injuries (labeled DSI) on roads in the United Kingdom over the period from January 1975 to December 1984. The legislation became effective on February 1, 1983, although drivers began to comply in increasing numbers during January of that year.

FIGURE 9.14 MONTHLY TOTAL DEATHS AND SERIOUS INJURIES (DSI) ON
UK ROADS (*January 1975–December 1984*)

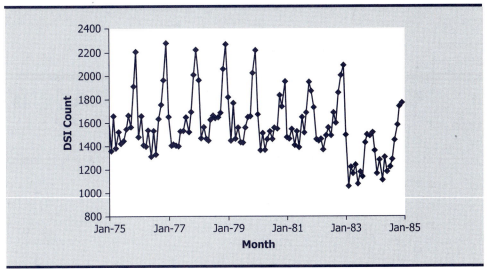

Source: Harvey and Durbin, 1986. Data shown is from file Road_accidents.xlsx.

The data clearly exhibit a strong seasonal pattern but little trend. Develop a model for this series, using only 11 seasonal indicators, plus a step function defined as

$$X_t = 1, \quad \text{if February 1983 or later}$$
$$= 0.5, \quad \text{for January 1983}$$
$$= 0, \quad \text{prior to January 1983}.$$

The value 0.5 for January 1983 is somewhat arbitrary but seems intuitively reasonable given that drivers were using seat belts in increasing numbers during that month; this was the form of step function used by Harvey and Durbin.

Because the model uses only indicator variables, forecasting is straightforward, but longer term projections would clearly need to take into account other safety measures, total traffic volumes, and similar variables. Such forecasts are clearly important in guiding policy makers.

Did the legislation achieve the desired effect of reducing deaths and serious accidents? By how much? If you were a policy maker in 1985 (when the study was conducted), would you support similar requirements for passengers? Why?

References

Allen, P. G., and Fildes, R. (2001). Econometric forecasting. In J. S. Armstrong (ed.), *Principles of Forecasting*. Boston and Dordrecht: Kluwer, pp. 300–362.

Armstrong, J. S., ed. (2001). *Principles of Forecasting: A Handbook for Researchers and Practitioners*. Boston and Dordrecht: Kluwer.

Box, G. E. P, Jenkins, G. M., and Reinsel, G. C. (2008). *Time Series Analysis: Forecasting and Control*, 4th ed. Hoboken, NJ: Wiley.

Harvey, A. C., and Durbin, J. (1986). The effects of seat belt legislation on British road casualties: A case study in structural time series modelling. *Journal of the Royal Statistical Society*, series A, 149, 187–227.

Kutner, M. H., Nachtsheim, C. J., Neter, J., and Li, W. (2005). *Applied Linear Statistical Models*, 5th ed. New York City: McGraw-Hill.

CHAPTER 10

Advanced Methods of Forecasting*

CONTENTS

No matter how advanced your camera you still need to be responsible for getting it to the right place at the right time and pointing it in the right direction to get the photo you want.

—Ken Rockwell, *Your Camera Does Not Matter*, 2005

Introduction

In this chapter, we consider a number of advanced methods of forecasting. They are all widely used in applications. However, these methods do require the reader to work harder, because they are all more complex than those discussed so far and demand more out of the user, either to get the method to work at all or to build an appropriate model and interpret the results. As a consequence, the chapter can be omitted without affecting the book's flow. (The methods are discussed further only in Chapter 12.) Still, for an "advanced forecaster," knowledge of these topics is valuable if not essential.

We first introduce a new type of forecasting problem: predictive classification, in which the aim is to predict the probability of an event happening (or not). This question arises in many contexts: sports forecasting where the aim is to predict the winner, forecasting customer purchasing behavior, and forecasting whether a company will go bankrupt, among others. After introducing the data-mining problem of predictive classification in Section 10.1, we describe three new forecasting methods, all with the capability of predicting the outcome of a binary event: classification trees (Section 10.2), logistic regression (Section 10.3), and neural networks (Section 10.4). Neural network methods can also be used in time series forecasting when the variable of interest is continuous (see Section 10.4.2).

Econometric modeling has undergone many developments in recent years. In Section 10.5, we aim to overcome the problem of deciding which variables are determined within the system being modeled and which are determined exogenously (i.e., outside the system). Vector autoregressive models (VARs) can overcome this confusion and have delivered strong out-of-sample forecasting performance compared with standard regression methods. What is more, they have the added advantage of not relying on separate (exogenously determined) forecasts of the explanatory input variables. As usual, we conclude with some principles that aim to help the forecaster who is implementing these more complex methods.

10.1 Predictive Classification

Although many forecasting problems are concerned with predicting a continuous interval-scaled variable, such as sales, whether by value or by volume, some important forecasting problems require us to predict a binary outcome, such as whether a potential customer will purchase a product or whether a recession will happen next year. A particularly important example that has generated a major industry is betting on the outcome of a sporting event. Such classification problems don't easily fit into the models we have developed so far because we've assumed (both in regression and in time series analysis) that the errors are unbounded and at least approximately normal.

A typical data set is illustrated in Table 10.1, in which the dependent (target) variable is whether a household owns a computer. (*Nocomp* = 1 if no computer is available in the household, and *Nocomp* = 0 if a computer is available.) The input, or predictor, variables are *Income*, *Education*, whether there are children in the household (*Kids* = 1 for households with children, and *Kids* = 0 otherwise), and, finally, a measure of the respondent's attitudes toward technology (*TAM*). The data set, created through a survey of owners and nonowners of computers in the United Kingdom, is cross-sectional (i.e., the survey was conducted over a single short time period). For ease of interpretation of British English, we have rephrased the definitions used in the survey and converted income levels to U.S. dollars. All the variables are categorical, so, for example, the income level has been broken up

TABLE 10.1   CROSS-SECTIONAL DATA FOR PREDICTING HOUSEHOLD OWNERSHIP OF COMPUTERS

Panel (A)

Variables	Definition	Type
Computer user (*Nocomp*)	Do you own a computer? (*Nocomp* = 1 if no computer, *NoComp* = 0 if own computer)	Target
Income	Ordinal: 1 (<$20K) to 5 (>$100K)	Input
Education	Ordinal: 1 (No qualifications) to 5 (Further degree)	Input
Kids	Binary (Yes = 1, No = 0)	Input
TAM: Attitude toward Technology	Different levels of response to technology (with dummy variables, *TAM1* = 1, negative attitude, to *TAM3* = 1, positive attitude)	Input

Panel (B)

Household Computer Ownership [Nocomp]	Income	Attitude to Technology	Education	Kids
1	$31K ($20K–$49K): Inc2	Negative	High School: level2	0
0	$57K ($50–$69K): Inc3	Neutral	Degree: level3	1
0	$95K ($70–$99K): Inc4	Positive	Further degree: level4	1
1	$22K ($20K–$49K): Inc2	Neutral	No qualifications/ Other: level1	0
0	$135K (>$100K): Inc5	Positive	Prof level5	1

Data shown is from file Compdata.xlsx.

into five groups, with *Inc1* representing the lowest level of household income and *Inc5* the highest. Similarly, there are four education levels and a professional category (level 5). Panel (A) defines the variables and Panel (B) illustrates typical entries.

For example, the first observation shows a household that does not own a computer and has an income of $31K (which is assigned into an income class between $20K and $49K). The household has a negative attitude toward technology. Each household in the sample falls into one of five distinct income classes,[1] thereby requiring the inclusion of four dummy variables in the regression model (see Section 9.8). The simplest model of these classifications is a regression of the form

$$Y_i = \beta_0 + \beta_1 X_{1i} + \cdots + \beta_K X_{Ki} + \varepsilon_i,$$

where Y_i = *Nocomp* = 1 if the *i*th household has no computer and Y_i = 0 if the *i*th household has at least one computer, and we include four (K = 4) income dummy variables as the explanatory variables. The model can be estimated by the usual ordinary least squares method (see Chapter 8), with the data set split into an estimation data set and a test (out-of-sample) data set. The regression model gives a table of regression coefficients, as shown in Figure 10.1, with the coefficients of the dummy variables for the different income classes all significant and increasing in absolute magnitude. Whichever computer program is used, the model will generate a set of predictions such as those labeled *PRE_1* in Table 10.2.

---

[1]Our thanks for this data set are due to Alastair Robertson, who collected the data as part of his Ph.D. thesis research.

FIGURE 10.1 REGRESSION COEFFICIENTS IN A CLASSIFICATION PROBLEM: HOUSEHOLD COMPUTER OWNERSHIP AS A FUNCTION OF INCOME

		Coefficients			
		Unstandardized Coefficients			
Model		B	Std. Error	T	P
1	(Constant)	.436	.032	13.603	.000
	Inc2	−.137	.043	−3.183	.001
	Inc3	−.283	.042	−6.701	.000
	Inc4	−.299	.041	−7.309	.000
	Inc5	−.373	.035	−10.680	.000

Note: Dependent variable is Nocomp

Data: Compdata.xlsx; adapted from SPSS output.

TABLE 10.2 DATA INPUT AND PREDICTIONS OF THE PROBABILITY OF HOUSEHOLD COMPUTER NONOWNERSHIP ON THE ESTIMATION AND VALIDATION (OUT-OF-SAMPLE) DATA

Nocomp	Inc2	Inc3	Inc4	Inc5	filter_$	PRE_1	RES_1	Prednocomp
0	0	0	0	1	1	0.063	−0.063	0.063
1	0	0	0	1	1	0.063	−.937	0.063
0	0	0	0	1	1	0.063	−0.063	0.063
0	0	0	0	1	0			0.063
0	0	1	0	0	0			0.153
0	0	0	0	0	0			0.436
0	0	0	0	1	0			0.063
1	0	0	0	1	0			0.063
0	0	0	1	0	0			0.137

Data: Compdata.xlsx; the filter variable, *filter_$*, defines the estimation sample (for *filter_$* = 1) and the validation (out-of-sample) data (*filter_$* = 0).

The regression model was fitted on the estimation data set, taken as a random sample of approximately 80 percent of the full data set. This data set is identified (in SPSS) through the *filter_$* variable, so all observations used in the regression were labeled with a 1. The test data were not used in estimation (*filter_$* = 0), but predictions for this data set are easily calculated with the foregoing regression equation, so

$$Prednocomp = 0.436 − 0.137 Inc2 − 0.283 Inc3 − 0.299 Inc4 − 0.373 Inc5$$

gives a prediction of whether or not a household owns a computer. A high value corresponds to a high probability of nonownership, a low value to a low probability of nonownership. Not surprisingly, as income increases, so does the predicted probability of owning a computer. Note that the value calculated from the preceding formula is the same as the predictions produced automatically by SPSS on the estimation data set. Using the preceding equation allows us to calculate both the predictions and the residuals for the 20 percent sample of the data omitted in the model building.

To use the model in classification, a threshold value has to be chosen so that every observation above the threshold is taken as predicting nonownership = 1 and every observation below the threshold predicting that the household does in fact own a computer. There are two approaches to defining the threshold as stated in the following box:

Threshold Values

After ranking the observations according to their fitted (or projected) values, we may define the threshold as either

1. The top so many percent of the ranked values (the cutoff percentage), or
2. All observations whose fitted or predicted values exceed a certain value (the cutoff value)

In general, the two definitions will result in different numbers of cases being assigned to a particular category.

For example, if the cutoff percentage is taken as 20 percent, the top 20 percent would be predicted to be nonowners. The purpose of such an exercise might be to segment the market. For example, if we were selling computer games, we would seek to identify the characteristics of households that already own computers. Conversely, the manufacturer of an entry-level laptop would be interested in technology-oriented nonowners.

Various error statistics may be calculated to describe the accuracy of the classifications, as we next explain.

10.1.1 Evaluating the Accuracy of the Predictions

In evaluating the accuracy of the the predictive classifications, the first step is to rank the observations by the value of the predictions (scores) they receive from the model. Therefore, households that the model predicts as more likely to own a computer will fall at one end of the score distribution while those the model predicts as less likely will lie at the other end. Here, the higher values represent customers who are more likely to fall into the target event class (e.g., those who do not own a computer in the preceding example). Typically, members of the target class are often called the "bads," as they often have undesirable characteristics (as far as the analysis is concerned). Examples are mobile phone customers who are likely to churn (i.e., switch providers) and loan customers who are likely to default.

For a chosen percentage of customers predicted to fall into the target class (say, the top 50 percent of the ranked predictions), when the model is appraised on either the estimation or out-of-sample (test) data sets, its performance can be characterized by the errors made in predicting the target. This characterization, sometimes called the *Classification, or Confusion, Matrix*, may be presented in tabular form, as shown in Table 10.3.

TABLE 10.3   THE CLASSIFICATION (OR CONFUSION) MATRIX

		Predicted	
		Nontarget Event [Owner]	**Target Event [Nonowner]**
Actual	**Nontarget** = 0 [Owner]	h_{00}	h_{01}
	Target = 1 [Nonowner]	h_{10}	h_{11}

TABLE 10.4   THE CLASSIFICATION MATRIX FOR THE LINEAR REGRESSION
MODEL FOR IDENTIFYING HOUSEHOLDS NOT OWNING
COMPUTERS (THE TARGET EVENT)

		Cutoff 49% Predicted				Cutoff 21% Predicted		
		0	**1**	**Row Total**		**0**	**1**	**Row Total**
Actual	0	682	537	1219	0	1018	201	1219
	1	44	158	202	1	101	101	202
	col. Total	726	695	1421	col. Total	1119	302	1421

Data: Compdata.xlsx. Cutoff percentages 48.9% and 21.3% have been used with the full data set.

Using the prediction equation (based on all the data and including just the income dummy variables) gives the following results for the five distinct income classes:

Predicted probabilities	.436	.299	.153	.137	.063
Percentage in given class	9.6	11.7	12.7	14.9	51.1
Cumulative percentages	9.6	21.3	34.0	48.9	100

Table 10.4 shows the classification matrices for cut-off percentages of 48.9% and 21.3%. Usually exact cut-off percentages can be calculated from the predicted probabilities which fall on a continuous scale (rather than into discrete classes as here).

The overall proportion classified as correct is $\dfrac{(h_{00} + h_{11})}{N} = \dfrac{682 + 158}{1421} = 0.59$. The

$sensitivity = \dfrac{h_{11}}{(h_{10} + h_{11})} = \dfrac{158}{(44 + 158)} = 0.78$ measures the proportion of target events that are correctly predicted (i.e., nonowners).

The $specificity = \dfrac{h_{00}}{(h_{00} + h_{01})} = \dfrac{682}{(682 + 537)} = 0.56$ measures the proportion of correctly predicted nontarget events.

With the totals for target events and nontarget events (e.g., bad risks and good risks, respectively) known in the sample, once the cutoff is decided, the various percentages can be calculated.

Two examples of different cutoff percentages are shown for an extended model of computer nonownership. A cutoff of 49 percent (21 percent) assigns 49 percent (21 percent) of the scored observations to the target class, and we use these cutoff percentages in Table 10.4. The higher cutoff percentage yields more nonowners predicted (with a corresponding decrease in errors) while we predict fewer owners successfully. The 21 percent cutoff has sensitivity 0.50 and specificity 0.84.

Ideally, we would like the misclassifications, h_{01} and h_{10}, to both be zero, and our model would then correctly identify all the targets (nonowners in this case) and also all the owners. But no model has such capabilities. Moreover, as the output in Table 10.4 shows, as one type of error falls (type h_{10}, a predicted owner who turns out to be a nonowner), the other (type h_{01}, a predicted nonowner who owns a computer) increases.

The effects of the different cutoff values can be shown graphically for different cutoff percentages. By way of example, we consider a regression-type model (technically, a logistic regression, which we discuss in the Section 10.3). The result is a curve like Figure 10.2(a), which shows the cumulative percentage of the target event (the nonowners) that has been

correctly predicted $= \dfrac{100 h_{11}}{(h_{10} + h_{11})}$, for different cut-offs.

FIGURE 10.2   CAPTURED (CORRECTLY IDENTIFIED) RESPONSE CURVES FOR
DIFFERENT CUTOFF PERCENTAGES: PERCENTAGE OF THE
TARGET RESPONSE, (A) CUMULATIVE, and (B) NONCUMULATIVE

(A) Cumulative % Captured Target Response   **(B)** Noncumulative % Captured Target Response

Data: Compdata.xlsx; adapted from SAS output.

Figure 10.2(A) shows the percentage of the target response (the nonowners here, often the "bads" in credit applications) that has been predicted (or captured) when the different cutoff rates are used. Thus, a random benchmark model with a 10 percent cutoff will, on average, predict 10 percent of the target population, a 20 percent cutoff will capture 20 percent, etc., as shown. With a 20 percent cutoff, the regression model gets (approximately) 40 percent correct. Of course, with a 100 percent cutoff, because every observation is classified as a "bad," any method captures all those falling into the target class (the nonowners here) but, unfortunately, this will misclassify all the owners.

Shown in Figure 10.2(B) is the noncumulative % captured response curve, which is useful for identifying where the model is proving effective and where it is not. For each 10th percentile, a random selection would expect to capture 10 percent of the owners (or "bads"). Here, the regression model captures between 10 and 30 percent in the lower percentiles and, by way of compensation, drops below 10 percent past the 50th percentile cutoff mark.

A second tool for understanding performance is a graph of the *sensitivity* (proportion of captured target events) $= \dfrac{h_{11}}{(h_{10} + h_{11})}$ versus the proportion of falsely predicted non-target events $= \dfrac{h_{01}}{(h_{00} + h_{01})}$ ($=1 - \textit{specificity}$). This graph is called the *Receiver Operating Characteristic* curve, shown in Figure 10.3. The shape of the curve gives a visual impression of how good the classification model is: The closer the curve gets to the upper left corner (position (0, 1)), the better is the model.

When there is no specific use in mind for the proposed models, but it is still regarded as desirable to compare them, a summary measure, known as the *Gini coefficient*, is sometimes used. Based on the area under the model performance curves in Figure 10.3, the measure is defined as

$$Gini = 2 * (\text{Area under the } ROC \text{ curve}) - 1.$$

FIGURE 10.3 THE RECEIVER OPERATING CHARACTERISTIC (ROC) CURVE FOR THE LOGISTIC REGRESSION MODEL

Data: Compdata.xlsx; adapted from SAS output.

A perfect model would have a sensitivity = 1.0 for all values of the specificity <1.0, which yields a Gini coefficient of 1.0, as can be seen from the figure. The measure should not be given much credence, because it does not focus on the cutoff values of interest.

In considering the benefits of a model in helping identify the target class, it would be desirable to consider the profitability of adopting alternative cutoffs. Rather than just relying on statistical properties of the models, we can instead consider the expected profit from using a 10 percent cutoff versus, say, a 20 percent cutoff. Let us suppose that the expected profit from a "good" customer is P_G and the expected profit (typically negative) from a "bad" customer is P_B, so that the expected net profit is

$$Profit(Cutoff) = P_G h_{11} + h_{01} P_B, \tag{10.1}$$

and this quantity can be calculated for different cutoffs to give a profit curve and identify an appropriate cutoff. This approach is readily expanded to include the lost profits from failing to identify the good targets and the benefits from excluding the bad prospects.

Discussion Question *For a Web-based insurance provider, what costs and profits should be considered in deciding whether to offer a policy to a new customer?*

10.1.2 A Comment

With only two possible Y values in the data, the error term cannot be normal, as we explained in Section 10.1, so other models are needed (if we are to be strict about the regression assumptions holding). In the sections that follow, we discuss three different methods for tackling the problem that do not conflict with the regression assumptions: classification trees, logistic regression, and neural networks. All are useful for predictive classification.

Classification and Regression Trees

An intuitively appealing procedure for making predictions, especially in dealing with cross-sectional data, is to divide the cases into homogeneous subgroups such that the members of a given subgroup might be expected to behave in a similar way. For example, local areas might be identified whose residents strongly favor one political party or where demographic factors might point to prospective customers for a product or service. However, such subdivisions of available data come at a cost; for example, classifying cases according to ten two-category factors produces over a thousand subclasses, too many for all but the largest databases. This realization leads to the idea that we should subdivide the data according to the most relevant factors and stop when we have reached a sufficiently fine-grained classification system. Such an approach is best represented by a *tree diagram*, which shows the successive partitions that are made in the data set to try to improve the predictions for future cases.

EXAMPLE 10.1 ■ Hypothetical data on bank loans

A bank that is interested in improving its ability to identify good loan customers (i.e., those who repay their loans on schedule) might select a sample of past loan histories and classify each account as "good" or "bad" according to the account history. Hopefully, the bank has made a relatively small number of bad loans, so the sample might include most, if not all, such problem cases to ensure that the model has the potential for capturing the key features of bad customers. Only a relatively small percentage of good loans would be included, so as not to overweight the good loans at the expense of the bad (see Section 12.5.2). In this example, the target class is "bad loans."

By way of illustration, we assume that the bank has selected 200 records, consisting of 150 good loans and 50 bad loans. Included in each record is information such as the customer's employment history, credit rating, home ownership, and other, similar background information. A classification tree analysis might proceed as shown in Figure 10.4. The best single variable relates to credit history (*Credit score* > 600 or *Credit score* ≤ 600), which

FIGURE 10.4   CLASSIFICATION TREE BASED UPON HYPOTHETICAL DATA ON BANK LOANS

© Cengage Learning 2013.

serves to separate out most of the good cases. The employment record is found to provide useful information on those with a good credit score, but for those with a score below 600, home ownership proves the key factor. At that point, we terminate the process on the grounds that further partitions are dealing with small numbers that would produce questionable improvements.

Initial screening of new applicants could then proceed, using this tree for decision-making purposes. For example if, on average, a bad loan costs five times as much as the profit from a good loan, we might approve a loan when the applicant fell into a box for which the proportion of "goods" exceeded 83 percent (when the expected profit would be positive). Thus, (*Credit score* > 600 *and Employed for last 3 years*) or (*Credit score* < 600 *and Own home*) would qualify. The lowest level boxes are often called *leaves* on the tree's branches.   ∎

Discussion Question   *Why might a customer with (Credit score > 600 and Own home) not qualify?*

The example serves to illustrate the key issues that must be addressed in the construction of such trees:

- The process of recursive partitioning of cases
- A stopping rule that determines when the tree is sufficiently developed.

Some researchers prefer to develop a complete tree (i.e., until every last possible partition has been identified) and then to operate a *pruning rule*. This approach compares with the one we have described, which involves a *stopping rule* that comes into play when the improvements in predictive accuracy are negligible. Conceptually, the two approaches should arrive at the same final tree, although differences in detailed application may lead to minor differences in the final result.

10.2.1   Performance Measures: An Example

If we possess cost or profit information concerning the relative impact of wrong decisions, we can use this information to optimize the decision-making process. By way of example, suppose that granting a bad loan costs an average of $10,000 whereas granting a good one nets an average profit of $2000. On the basis of only the first box, and making the assumption that the proportion of good and bad loans is as shown, the bank would not make any loans, because the total profit under each policy, from equation (10.1), is as follows:

No loans: *Total profit* = 0;

All loans approved : *Total profit* = (150 * $2000 − 50 * $10,000) = −$200,000.

Using the credit rating criterion to make loans only to those with scores greater than 600 produces a *Total profit* of (130 * $2000 − 20 * $10000) = $60,000. Using all the criteria listed and then lending to those with a "yes" response at the second level produces a *Total profit* of (110 * $2000 − 10 * $10,000 + 15 * $2000) = $150,000.

In many circumstances, data on potential profit and costs may be either not available or not relevant and we must then employ other criteria. We will continue to employ the classification matrix introduced in Table 10.3. Using a 50 percent cutoff, Figure 10.4 produces the results shown in Table 10.5. From the latter table, with 135 loans approved, the sensitivity is 40/50 = 0.80 and the specificity is 125/150 = 0.83.

If we were to stop at the first level, we would have a sensitivity equal to 0.60 (30/50) and a specificity of 0.87 (130/150). Thus, the extension of the tree from one level to two leads

TABLE 10.5   THE CLASSIFICATION MATRIX FOR THE HYPOTHETICAL DATA
ON BANK LOANS

		Predicted		
		Good	**Bad**	**Row Total**
Actual	**Nontarget = Good**	125	25	150
	Target = Bad	10	40	50
	Column Total	135	65	200

© Cengage Learning 2013.

to an improved sensitivity of 0.80 (40/50), although the specificity declines slightly, to 0.83 (125/150). As we have seen, the use of the second level also improves profitability.

10.2.2   Computer Ownership Example Revisited

We now consider a realistic example using the computer ownership data we introduced in Section 10.1. For this example, we used the same partition of the data as in Section 10.1, with approximately 80 percent of the observations in the estimation sample and the remaining 20 percent in the hold-out sample. The software employed was the SPSS add-in for classification and regression trees, evolving from the original work of Breiman, Friedman, Olshen, and Stone (1984). For ease of reproduction, the output we present is restricted to two levels of partitioning. There are several tree-building algorithms that may be employed, and we opted for the CHAID method, defined as follows in the SPSS Help notes:

> CHAID. Chi-squared Automatic Interaction Detection. At each step, CHAID chooses the independent (predictor) variable that has the strongest interaction [as measured by a chi-squared criterion] with the dependent variable. Categories of each predictor are merged if they are not significantly different with respect to the dependent variable.

This method works by splitting the data into subclasses. When the data are nominal, as in the present example, no additional splits are required, but for ordinal or interval-scaled data, the procedure involves trying multiple splits at each node and then selecting the split that provides the best partition (the highest value of the chi-squared statistic for that binary split, a value that measures the improvement in predictive power arising from the split).

EXAMPLE 10.2 ■ Chi-square calculations

This example illustrates the use of the chi-square statistic and the basis of the calculations. If a split on the tree produces the same proportions of goods and bads at the next level, it has zero value as a predictor. This notion is akin to the usual use of the statistic in testing for independence. Consider the second split on the left-hand branch of the tree in Figure 10.4. The data may be summarized in the following table:

	Decision (Predicted)		
Actual	**Good**	**Bad**	**Total**
Good	110	20	130
Bad	10	10	20
Total	120	30	150

If there was no association between the actual classifications and the decisions made, the expected number of {Good/Good} cases would be given by

$$\frac{Predicted\ Number\ of\ Good\ Cases\ *\ Actual\ Number\ of\ Good\ Cases}{Total\ number} = \frac{120 * 130}{150} = 104.$$

This result compares with the 110 of those accepted for a loan (on the basis of the prediction "Good") that actually turned out good. The other expected numbers may be calculated in the same way. The chi-square statistic is then

$$\sum_{all\ cells} \frac{(observed - expected)^2}{expected}.$$

That is,

$$\frac{(110 - 104)^2}{104} + \frac{(20 - 26)^2}{26} + \frac{(10 - 16)^2}{16} + \frac{(10 - 4)^2}{4} = 12.98.$$

If there was no association between the two variables, this statistic would have a small value. (In a formal test, the upper 5 percent point is 3.84 and the upper 1 percent point is 6.63.) Tree development can stop when "nonsignificant" values are encountered, although some users prefer to develop the tree the whole way and then "prune" noninformative branches. Because multiple classifications are attempted at each branching, the actual significance levels are larger than the nominal values cited, and the user should not rely upon them, but rather test the performance of the classification by using a hold-out sample. ■

An initial analysis of the computer ownership data produced a classification in which owners outnumbered nonowners in all parts of the tree. Seeking to improve the analysis, we combined the two lowest income groups (*Inc1* and *Inc2*) to form *Inc12* and repeated the analysis. The second split variable was the respondents' negative attitude to technology ($TAM1 = 1$). The results proved more satisfactory, and the tree for the estimation sample is shown in Figure 10.5, in which those respondents with a negative attitude ($TAM1 = 1$) who fall into the low-income group ($Inc12 = 1$) were much less likely to own a computer (51/111, or 46 percent) than the respondents as a whole (90.4 percent). The output in Figure 10.5 includes the chi-square statistic measuring the benefits of the split and its significance through a *P*-value. The tree for the test sample has, of course, the same structure, and the proportions assigned to each branch are similar. The relative classifications of cases are summarized in Table 10.6. As expected, the performance on the test sample is slightly inferior to that of the training (estimation) sample, but the difference is not pronounced.

TABLE 10.6   CLASSIFICATION OF CASES IN THE ESTIMATION (TRAINING) AND TEST SAMPLES FOR THE COMPUTER OWNERSHIP DATA

		Predicted		
Sample	**Observed**	**0**	**1**	**Percent Correct**
Training	0	935	51	94.8%
	1	113	60	34.7%
	Overall Percentage	90.4%	9.6%	85.8%
Test	0	221	12	94.8%
	1	22	7	24.1%
	Overall Percentage	92.7%	7.3%	87.0%

Growing Method: CHAID   Dependent Variable: *Nocomp*
Data: Compdata.xlsx; adapted from SPSS output.

FIGURE 10.5   PREDICTING COMPUTER OWNERSHIP: THE CHAID TREE FOR 1159 CASES
IN THE ESTIMATION SAMPLE (*Nocomp* = 1 *for a nonowner and Nocomp* = 0
for an owner).

Data: Compdata.xlsx; adapted from SPSS output.

10.3 Logistic Regression

Logistic regression employs a model that is superficially similar to the linear regression
model with which we introduced the topic of classification in Section 10.1, but the
model is now specified in terms of probabilities rather than a linear scale. The model
we consider is sometimes known as *binary* logistic regression, because other versions
may involve more than two categories, which, in turn may be either ordered or
unordered. (For a detailed discussion of these more advanced schemes, see Kutner *et al.*,
2005, Chapter 14.)

To continue our example on computer ownership, let P_i denote the probability that the *i*th
household does not own a computer [*Nocomp* = 1]. Then the logistic model is written as

$$P_i = \frac{\exp(Q_i)}{1 + \exp(Q_i)} \tag{10.2}$$

or, equivalently, as

$$\ln\left(\frac{P_i}{1 - P_i}\right) = Q_i.$$

The quantity Q_i is known as the *log odds ratio*. Q_i contains the explanatory variables in a regression-like form, written as

$$Q_i = \beta_0 + \beta_1 X_{1i} + \cdots + \beta_K X_{Ki}. \tag{10.3}$$

Logistic regression has two advantages over linear regression: The fitted values of P_i ($\hat{P}_i$, say) are constrained to lie in the range (0, 1), and the observations are generated by a simple binomial distribution with parameters ($n = 1, p = P_i$). P_i represents the probability of an observation with characteristics $\{X_{1i}, X_{2i} \ldots X_{Ki}\}$ being bad: a nonowner in our example.

We consider the variables listed in Table 10.1, but exclude *Education*. As in linear regression, for each multiple-category variable, we use one fewer indicator variable than there are categories. The estimated logistic regression model for computer ownership is summarized in Table 10.7, based upon the 1159 cases (approximately 80 percent of the total) previously selected as the estimation sample. The selected cases are identified in the data file by "*filter_$ = 1*".

Column B lists the regression coefficient for each explanatory variable, and S.E. is the standard error of estimate of the coefficient. The Wald statistics, equal to $(B/S.E.)^2$ perform a role analogous to the t statistics in linear regression, and we may simply evaluate the contributions of the individual variables via the set of P-values, listed in the column marked Sig.

The results presented in Table 10.7 show that the highest income level (*Inc5*) has a strong negative effect, as would be expected. The other income levels all have negative, but progressively smaller, effects relative to the lowest income level (*Inc1*, which was the omitted category). Likewise, having children (*kids* = 1) and being pro technology (*TAM2* and *TAM3*) both increase the probability of ownership and hence have negative signs in a prediction equation for nonownership. The final column denotes the *Odds Ratio* for each variable [exp(Q)] so that, for example, being technologically savvy (*TAM3*) decreases the odds in favor of nonownership by a factor of 4.28 (1/0.234) relative to someone with the same income and family structure—a considerable effect.

TABLE 10.7 LOGISTIC REGRESSION MODEL FOR COMPUTER OWNERSHIP DATA

		Variables in the Equation					
		B	**S.E.**	**Wald**	**DF**	**P(Sig.)**	**Exp(B)**
Step 1	Kids	−.662	.231	8.231	1	.004	.516
	Inc2	−.532	.276	3.709	1	.054	.587
	Inc3	−1.223	.307	15.847	1	.000	.294
	Inc4	−1.333	.303	19.350	1	.000	.264
	Inc5	−2.202	.265	69.163	1	.000	.111
	TAM2	−.718	.201	12.838	1	.000	.488
	TAM3	−1.453	.304	22.811	1	.000	.234
	Constant	.188	.214	.771	1	.380	1.206

Note: Variable(s) entered on step 1: Kids, Inc2, Inc3, Inc4, Inc5, TAM2, TAM3.

Data: Compdata.xlsx; adapted from SPSS output.

If we set the cutoff percentage at 50, we arrive at the classification shown in Table 10.8(A). In that table, this leads to a sensitivity of 20.2 percent but a specificity of 44.6 percent. Table 10.8(B) uses the alternative classification approach of classifying an observation as "bad" if it has a fitted or projected probability higher than the cutoff value, here taken to be 0.5. This leads to many fewer observations falling into the target class. The overall percentage of correctly classified cases is 85.9 percent, but only 18.5 percent of nonowners are correctly identified (sensitivity). In the hold-out sample, only 10.3 percent of nonowners are correctly identified. By contrast, the specificity in the estimation sample is 97.8 percent, which indicates that almost all computer owners were correctly identified.

The problem of misclassification errors is particularly acute when we seek to identify small subgroups (such as those suffering from a rare disease). Unless the model can be improved, the only choice is to modify the cutoff level. The appropriate choice of cutoff depends upon the objectives of the study and the relative costs of misclassification for the two categories.

TABLE 10.8 CLASSIFICATION TABLES FOR LOGISTIC REGRESSION: ESTIMATION AND TEST SAMPLES ((A) *With 50% sample cutoff percentage defining the top 50% of cases to be nonowners*; (B) *with those cases with a predicted probability above the cutoff value of 0.5 predicted to be nonowners (as calculated by SPSS or SAS)*)

(A) 50% cutoff, with approximately the top 50% predicted to be nonowners

		Estimation Sample Nocomp 0	1	Percentage Correct	Test Sample Nocomp 0	1	Percentage Correct
Nocomp	0	549	437	55.7%	125	108	53.6%
	1	31	142	82.1%	6	23	79.3%
Overall Percentage		580	579	59.6%	131	131	56.5%

(B) Cutoff value of 0.5, classifying those cases with a predicted probability of nonownership of 0.5 or greater as nonowners

		Estimation Sample Nocomp 0	1	Percentage Correct	Test Sample Nocomp 0	1	Percentage Correct
Nocomp	0	964	22	97.8	229	4	98.3
	1	141	32	18.5	26	3	10.3
Overall Percentage				85.9			88.5

Data: Compdata.xlsx; adapted from SPSS output.

The 50% cutoff has been calculated by ranking the predictions and classifying the top 50% as non-owners. This assumes the observations are listed in random order with regard to ownership.

The figures in Table 10.8(B) are all based on the predicted probabilities. Contrasting Tables 10.8(A) and 10.8(B) demonstrates the importance of defining the cutoff procedure clearly. (See Exercise 10.5, which examines the value of additional explanatory variables in improving classification accuracy.)

10.3.1 Issues in Logistic Regression Modeling

A number of issues arise in logistic modeling:

1. How do we define residuals and identify outliers?
2. How do we measure overall fit?
3. Does the model work equally well across different cases, i.e. for all values of the log-odds ratio?
4. Does the hold-out sample indicate real separation between the two groups?

We provide a brief discussion here; for a more detailed account see Kutner *et al.* (2005, pp. 591–601).

Residuals A number of definitions exist, but we focus on the standardized residuals

$$e_{st} = \frac{Y - \hat{P}}{\sqrt{\hat{P}(1 - \hat{P})}}.$$

The observed values (Y) are either 0 or 1, so although the standardized residuals have a mean close to 0 and variance close to 1, they clearly are not normally distributed. Nevertheless, large values indicate exceptional cases. For example, case #435 has kids, is in income class *Inc5*, and has a technology rating *TAM3*, yet is a nonowner. These values yield $Y = 1$, $\hat{P} = 0.016$, $e_{st} = 7.88$, indicating an unusual case.

Overall Fit The simplest measure, known as *Efron's R*, is

$$R^2 = 1 - \frac{\sum (Y - \hat{P})^2}{\sum (Y - \overline{Y})^2}.$$

The estimation sample yields $R^2 = 0.155$. This value cannot be interpreted in the same way as the coefficient of determination in Chapter 8, but values from different models are useful for comparative purposes, with a set of perfect predictions having $R^2 = 1$.

Performance Across Different Cases We may divide the estimation sample into G groups and then perform a chi-square-like test to determine whether the observed group sizes match expected sizes. The groups are defined by ordering the observations according to their fitted P_i values and then splitting them into groups by size. Ten ($G = 10$) such groups is a common choice. The average P_i is then computed for each group. If the group has N_i members, the expected number of cases with $Y = 1$ in the subgroup is $E_{i1} = N_i P_i$. Likewise, the expected number of cases with $Y = 0$ is $E_{i0} = N_i (1 - P_i)$. This measure is known as the *Hosmer–Lemeshow statistic*:

$$H = \sum_{i=1}^{G} \frac{(O_{i0} - E_{i0})^2}{N_i P_i (1 - P_i)} + \sum_{i=1}^{G} \frac{(O_{i1} - E_{i1})^2}{N_i P_i (1 - P_i)}$$

The test statistic asymptotically follows a chi-square distribution with $G - 2$ degrees of freedom. For $G = 10$, the results for the present example are as follows:

| | | **Contingency Table for Hosmer–Lemeshow Test** | | | | |
| | | **Nocomp = 0** | | **Nocomp = 1** | | |
Group		**Observed**	**Expected**	**Observed**	**Expected**	**Total**
Step 1	1	160	158.775	3	4.225	163
	2	97	99.453	6	3.547	103
	3	116	114.548	6	7.452	122
	4	117	117.534	9	8.466	126
	5	38	39.608	5	3.392	43
	6	132	134.104	20	17.896	152
	7	99	97.921	15	16.079	114
	8	100	98.540	27	28.460	127
	9	72	67.090	25	29.910	97
	10	55	58.426	57	53.574	112

The number of cases per group varies because of ties among the expected values. The value of the test statistic is 5.225 and with 8 DF this is insignificant at the 5% level, so the results are clearly consistent with an even performance across groups.

Performance in the Hold-out Sample The simplest way to examine the performance of the logistic regression in the hold-out sample is to calculate the chi-square statistic, using the results in Table 10.8. The observed values for the test sample in part (A) of that table are shown as follows, followed by the expected values in parentheses, for each cell under the null hypothesis of no association between the observed and predicted classifications.

| | | **Predicted** | | | |
		Nocomp = 0	**Nocomp = 1**	**Total**	**Percentage Correct**
Actual	Nocomp = 0	125 (116.5)	108 (116.5)	233	53.6
	Nocomp = 1	6 (14.5)	23 (14.5)	29	79.3
	Total	131	131	262	

The resulting value of the chi-square statistic is 11.2, with associated P-value equal to 0.001. The proposed model clearly provides some separation between owners and nonowners. The same test procedure for Table 10.8(B) results in the lower value of 3.9, with P-value equal to 0.048. The same test procedure for the holdout sample in Table 10.8(B) results in the slightly lower value of 7.4, with a P-value equal to 0.007, although the counts in the second column are very small.

10.4 Neural Network Methods

Neural network (*NN*) forecasting methods provide a flexible set of nonlinear forecasting tools. The methods can be used for extrapolative time series forecasting, causal modeling, or classification (where the dependent variable is categorical, usually binary, as we discussed earlier in the chapter). The initial formulation of neural networks was based on an analogy with how the brain processes information. As the literature developed separately from statistics, neural networks began to adopt their own terminology; here, we will use both sets of terms for clarity. Although neural network methods have a history that encompasses more than 50 years, it is only as increasing computer power has become available that the methods

FIGURE 10.6   SCHEMATIC VIEW OF A NEURAL NETWORK, KNOWN AS THE
MULTILAYER PERCEPTRON

© Cengage Learning 2013.

have gained wide acceptance in practical applications. Even now, however, their applications in forecasting are limited, with electricity demand being the most established. Still, research has shown neural networks to be potentially useful in a wide range of circumstances, from demand forecasting to predictions of individual consumer or business behavior.

Figure 10.6 illustrates a neural network with inputs (explanatory variables) $X_1 \ldots X_4$, that may be transformed to $(I_1 \ldots I_4)$. These transformed variables [to $(I_1 \ldots I_4)$], together with a bias (constant) term, are connected through a "hidden layer" of K (here, $K = 3$) nodes $(H_1, H_2, \ldots, H_K)$ to the dependent (output) variable. The four input variables shown are connected together with the bias term to the three nodes shown in the hidden layer. (There could be more or fewer than three nodes.) Each of these nodes is connected to all the inputs by producing a linear combination of inputs.

For node H_1, the input is given by

$$Z_1 = w_1 Bias + \sum_i w_{i1} I_i.$$

This input is then transformed by means of a nonlinear function (the *activation* function; the most common choice is the logistic function) so that the output from node H_1 is

$$f(Z_1) = \exp(Z_1)/[1 + \exp(Z_1)].$$

The final stage in the process is to take a weighted average of the outputs from the hidden layer to predict Y_1. (Alternatively, another nonlinear transform can be used.)

EXAMPLE 10.3 ■ Special cases of neural networks

a. If the network has no hidden layer and the activation function is linear, the network corresponds to multiple linear regression.

b. If we use a single hidden layer with only one node and no transformations, so that $Z_1 = w_1 Bias + \sum_i w_{i1} X_i$, and then use the logistic function, we are back to logistic regression, as discussed in Section 10.3. ■

As the reader will have realized, there is a lot of flexibility in neural network modeling. In fact, it can be shown mathematically that a neural network can approximate pretty much any type of relationship between inputs and outputs. But as with the nonlinear models we introduced in earlier chapters, such as the multiplicative seasonal models of Section 4.7, this very flexibility generates its own problems. In particular, overfitting the estimation sample ("training" is the term used by neural network specialists) results in poor performance out of sample, as with any other overfitted model. One effective route used to overcome this problem is to split the data into three segments: the training sample, the validation sample, and the test (hold-out) sample.

The key decisions a neural network modeler must make are the following:

i. Which input (explanatory) variables to use

ii. The number of hidden nodes.

In addition, the interval-scaled input variables may need to be preprocessed through a transformation, typically by scaling them between 0 and 1—for example,

$$X_i^* = \frac{X_i - Min(X_i)}{Max(X_i) - Min(X_i)}.$$

Dummy variables are, of course, coded as 0 or 1.

The output variable is also scaled to be inside the range of the nonlinear activation function (e.g., between 0 and 1 if a logistic function is used) and is then transformed back to produce the final forecast of Y. In commercial neural network software, this step is performed automatically.

Of less importance for forecasting applications are the choices of the nonlinear activation function (the logistic function as defined in equation 10.2 will usually suffice) and of the number of hidden layers (one is enough in most applications).

The parameters are then selected, often by minimizing the mean squared error function. However, because there are usually many parameters to estimate, it is necessary to carry out the estimation a number of times, with different starting values, to improve the likelihood of finding the global minimum (rather than a local minimum). These initializations can be done automatically by choosing random starting values. The error statistics are then calculated by taking an average of the error statistics for each of the training, validation, and test data sets.

Choosing the Input Variables   For a causal (explanatory) model, the modeler should just follow the guidelines given in Chapter 9 and identify possible drivers, including them all initially. For extrapolative models or causal models with lags, there is a potentially vast number of inputs to consider. One simple, but effective, approach is to use stepwise regression to reduce the number of variables for inclusion (Crone and Kourentzes, 2010).

Selecting the Number of Hidden Nodes   The number of hidden nodes can be ascertained automatically by the program searching through a range of alternatives and selecting the architecture (the number of hidden layers and the number of nodes within each layer) that delivers the minimum of the (squared) error function. Alternatively, as we show next, neural networks with different numbers of hidden nodes can be compared by calculating the RMSE on the validation sample for each individual architecture.

The Process of Building a Neural Network

1. Choose the input variables.
2. Divide the sample into training (estimation), validation, and test (hold-out) data sets.
3. Ensure that the input variables are standardized and coded appropriately (e.g., with dummy variables for categorical inputs).
4. Ensure that a number of different sets of starting values are used in estimation.
5. Ensure that your neural network program removes unimportant variables.
6. Compare the results from using different numbers of hidden nodes.
7. Choose the neural network architecture that leads to the best performance on the validation data.
8. Use the performance on the test data to measure the likely future performance of the network.

10.4.1 A Cross-Sectional Neural Network Analysis

We return again to the data on computer usage (*Compdata.xlsx*), as described in Table 10.1. We use just *Income* and *Education* as possible explanatory variables.

Three alternative neural networks are considered, with one, three, and five hidden nodes, respectively. The results from this analysis are given in Table 10.9. The table shows the *RMSE* (or Root Average Squared Error in SAS) for the training set, the validation data set, and the test set. We have used a split of 50 percent, 30 percent, and 20 percent in the database to define these three sets. The misclassification rate is calculated on the validation data set as follows: A predicted output above 0.5 is taken to be a prediction for the output (target) variable of 1 (i.e., a computer non-owner), whereas a predicted value below 0.5 is taken to be a predicted output of 0 (i.e., an owner). The cutoff value can be taken to be any value between 0 and 1, as noted in Section 10.2.

Although both NN3 and NN5 seem poorer than the simpler configurations, this arises in part because of the cutoff rule of assigning a case with a predicted probability of 0.5 or more to the nonowner class. Here, the models perform similarly. However, the ROC curve shown in Figure 10.7 is more helpful and suggests that the simplest neural network, with just one node, is outperformed at lower cutoffs by networks with three or five nodes.

TABLE 10.9 SUMMARY MEASURES FOR NEURAL NETWORK ANALYSIS OF COMPUTER USAGE DATA

	Root ASE			Misclassification Rate		
	Training Set	Validation Set	Test Set	Training Set	Validation set	Test Set
NN5	0.323	0.300	0.357	0.149	0.115	0.165
NN3	0.325	0.302	0.360	0.136	0.115	0.165
NN1	0.329	0.300	0.358	0.149	0.115	0.165

Data: Compdata.xlsx; adapted from SAS output.

FIGURE 10.7   ROC CURVE FOR COMPUTER USAGE EXAMPLE (VALIDATION DATA)

Data: Compdata.xlsx; adapted from SAS output.

For a particular neural network, we can examine the classification matrix, which depends on the cutoff we choose (e.g., with cutoff values of 50 percent and 20 percent, shown in Table 10.10, for NN1, with a single hidden node). With a cut-off of 20 percent rather than 50 percent, fewer households (86, as opposed to 214) are predicted as not owning a computer.

Overall, the misclassification rate for the 50 percent value is $(173 + 8)/426$, or 42.5 percent, found by using the left half of Table 10.10. The same tables can be produced for the training and test sample data sets, because all the models produce estimated probabilities that can be ranked. The summary results giving the misclassification rates for the 0.5 cutoff value are shown in Table 10.9.

TABLE 10.10   CLASSIFICATION MATRICES FOR 50% AND 20% CUTOFFS
(*Using the 30% validation data set*)

		50% Cutoff Predicted				20% Cutoff Predicted		
		0	**1**	**Total**		**0**	**1**	**Total**
0	Frequency	204	173	377	**0** Frequency	316	61	377
	percent	48%	41%	88%	percent	74%	14%	88%
	Row Pct	54%	46%		Row Pct	84%	16%	
	Col Pct	96%	81%		Col Pct	93%	71%	
1	Frequency	8	41	49	**1** Frequency	24	25	49
	percent	2%	10%	12%	percent	6%	6%	12%
	Row Pct	16%	84%		Row Pct	49%	51%	
	Col Pct	4%	19%		Col Pct	7%	29%	
Total		212	214	426	**Total**	340	86	426
		50%	50%	100%		80%	20%	100%

Data: Compdata.xlsx; adapted from SAS output.

10.4.2 A Time Series Neural Network Analysis

Neural nets can equally well be used to forecast time series data. Figure 10.8 shows the time series for UK retail sales that we analyzed earlier in Chapter 5 (Minicase 5.1). With 22 years of data, there are more than enough observations to identify any nonlinearities. For this example, we will use feed-forward multilayer perceptrons, the most common type of neural network employed in forecasting.

It is apparent that the time series has an upward changing trend, easily demonstrated through the use of a 12-period centered moving average (also shown in Figure 10.8). As in the Box–Jenkins ARIMA approach of Chapter 6, we model the trend by considering the differenced time series, which can be seen in Figure 10.9. Notice that there is no trend now and only a seasonal pattern is apparent. In both Figure 10.8 and Figure 10.9, it is apparent that the seasonality is changing over time, implying some nonadditive form of seasonality. Employing the ability of neural networks to model nonlinearities, we will not preprocess the time series any further; instead, we model the differenced time series directly, letting the network identify the ideal mapping of the seasonality.

In this application, we will use a relatively simple neural network that is easy to build and replicate. We will use a single hidden layer that, together with the input and output layers, results in a standard three-layer perceptron as illustrated in Figure 10.6. In the hidden nodes, we will use the S-shaped logistic function that allows us to model flexibly any type of linear and nonlinear mapping between the inputs and the outputs of the network, given an adequate number of hidden nodes. The selection of the logistic function requires a further transformation of the time series before we can model it with the neural network. We will linearly scale

FIGURE 10.8   UK RETAIL SALES, NOT SEASONALLY ADJUSTED, IN CONSTANT 2006
PRICES (*January 1988–December 2009*)

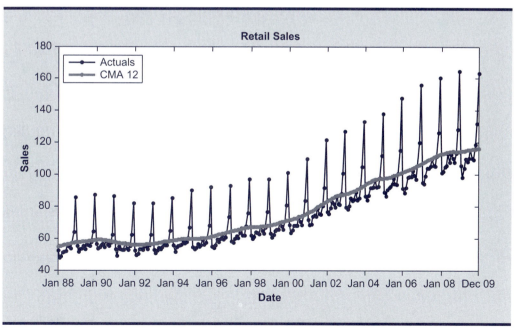

Source: www.ons.gov.uk/ons/rel/rsi/retail-sales/august-2011/tsd-retail-sales.html.
Data shown is from file UK_retail_sales.xlsx.

FIGURE 10.9   DIFFERENCED UK RETAIL SALES TIME SERIES

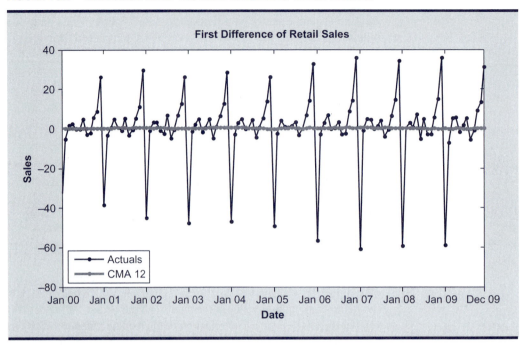

Data: UK_retail_sales.xlsx.

the time series between –0.75 and 0.75 to ensure efficient estimates of the weights. The transformation is produced with the use of the standard scaling function

$$y = \frac{(y_{max} - y_{min})(x - x_{min})}{(x_{max} - x_{min})} + y_{min}$$

where x is an observation of the unscaled time series; x_{min} and x_{max} are, respectively, the minimum and maximum of the time series; y is the scaled output; and y_{min} and y_{max} are, respectively, the desired minimum and the desired maximum of the scaled time series (here ±0.75).

The design parameters that we have to consider are the number of inputs, the size of the hidden layer, the activation functions, and the training parameters of the network. We will use 12 lags as inputs for the network, allowing it to model the seasonal pattern. The output node will use a standard linear function, essentially summing and scaling the results from the hidden nodes. To decide the number of hidden nodes, we perform a grid search from 1 to 10 hidden nodes. In typical neural network computer packages, the user can select the particular estimation method. We will minimize the sum of squared errors, using the standard gradient descent with momentum and adaptive learning rate backpropagation. This training algorithm requires a number of settings, such as the learning rate and the momentum. (See Exercise 10.7, which explores the effects of these choices.) The example we are presenting has been implemented in MatLab, and we use the default settings.

As before, to avoid overfitting, we adopt the standard approach of splitting the time series into three subsets: training, validation, and test sets. We train the network on the training set and simultaneously track the prediction error in the validation set. Thus, 18 years are used to train the data, 2 years for the validation sample, and 2 years for testing the results through out-of-sample forecasts.

FIGURE 10.10   ERROR PROGRESSION DURING TRAINING

Data: UK_retail_sales.xlsx.

As the network trains during the first passes through the data, using an iterative procedure (the "initial epochs" in neural network terminology), both training and validation error measures decline, indicating that the network is learning the time series structure (i.e., on each pass through the data, the revised parameter values are getting closer to the optimum values). As usual, the parameters are estimated by minimizing the one-step-ahead mean squared error—the error that will be tracked during training. (Other error measures could be used, of course.) After some epochs, the validation error levels out and may start to increase, signaling that the network has started to overfit to the training set and cannot accurately generalize to unseen data, such as the validation set data. This signal allows us to track when to stop training the network, so that it can generalize to the out-of-sample test data and provide accurate predictions. The process of error progression during training is shown in Figure 10.10. The best network is identified at the minimum validation error.

The test, or out-of-sample, data set is not involved in the training process and is used to assess the network on completely unseen data, because stopping the training on the basis of minimum validation error can lead to a bias towards the validation set, thereby giving a false sense of the model's accuracy. Note how the training mean squared error is lower than the validation error, which in turn is lower than the out-of-sample test error.

Training a neural network is a complex multidimensional nonlinear optimization problem. The training algorithms can easily get trapped in a local minimum with poorly chosen parameters and corresponding poor forecasts on the test data. A way around this problem is to train the network several times with different initial weights. For this example, we will use five initializations, resulting in five different neural networks.

Training neural networks is computationally expensive. Therefore, ideally, we would prefer to stop the training as soon as possible. This is done by using some early-stopping criteria. In this case, we will use two. First, we stop if the minimum performance gradient is less than or equal to 10^{-10} or the validation error increases for 100 epochs. This allows us to stop the training well before the set maximum of 6000 epochs is reached. It is important to ensure that the networks are allowed to train for enough epochs. The training continues

FIGURE 10.11   ONE-STEP-AHEAD PREDICTIONS AND ACTUALS FOR THE TRAINING, VALIDATION, AND TEST SUBSETS (*January 2000–December 2010*)

Data: UK_retail_sales.xlsx.

for another 100 epochs in case a better network is identified and then stops as indicated by the early-stopping criterion.

Now the modeler is facing what is essentially a model selection problem: Which of the initializations to use in forecasting? A common approach used to solve this problem is to select the best initialization, based on the minimum validation set error. A preferred alternative is to use a combination of all initializations as our final model. We employ a simple unweighted average to calculate the predictions of the final model. The one-step-ahead predictions for the three subsets can be seen in Figure 10.11.

Note that, in order to get the final forecasts, the linear scaling and the differencing employed previously need to be reversed.

The results depend on the number of hidden nodes; here, we have set a maximum of 10. Table 10.11 gives the results for 1 to 10 hidden nodes for the training, validation, and test data sets, with the minimum value shown in bold. We chose to use 2 hidden nodes as the minimum value on the validation data set, using *MAPE* and *MdAPE* (and with second-best performance using *RMSE*).

Table 10.12 compares the results produced by the two-hidden-node neural network on the test data set with output from benchmark Holt–Winters methods (with the minimum values again shown in bold). We utilized the macros described in Chapter 4 to fit the Holt–Winters methods; data from January 1994 on. As expected, the multiplicative and logarithmic transform methods are better able to handle the growth in seasonal fluctuations over time. The results illustrate a number of points: (i) The additive Holt–Winters model is unsuccessful at capturing the growing seasonality, (ii) the logarithmic model, which permits exponential growth, is poorer at longer lead times, (iii) different lead times suggest different models, and (iv) despite their flexibility, neural networks do not invariably improve on simpler methods.

This example has been implemented in MatLab, and the program used is downloadable from the book's website.

TABLE 10.11 ERROR MEASURES ONE STEP AHEAD FOR DIFFERENT
NUMBERS OF HIDDEN NODES IN THE NETWORK
(*Training, validation, and test data sets*)

Hidden Nodes	RMSE			MAPE			MdAPE		
	Training	Valid.	Test	Training	Valid.	Test	Training	Valid.	Test
1	1.828	3.397	3.949	0.020	0.021	0.029	0.016	0.012	0.017
2	2.257	1.729	3.127	0.024	**0.012**	0.022	0.019	**0.007**	**0.013**
3	1.732	2.027	3.161	0.019	0.014	**0.020**	**0.013**	0.009	0.022
4	1.859	2.220	3.042	**0.017**	0.016	0.024	0.017	0.008	0.020
5	1.560	2.076	3.074	0.018	0.015	0.023	0.017	0.011	0.019
6	**1.516**	2.115	3.268	**0.017**	0.015	0.023	0.017	0.009	0.019
7	1.584	1.935	3.070	0.019	0.014	0.023	**0.013**	0.012	0.022
8	1.546	**1.641**	3.522	**0.017**	0.013	0.026	0.014	0.010	0.020
9	2.836	2.539	3.856	0.029	0.018	0.024	0.015	0.012	0.024
10	1.987	2.276	**2.728**	0.024	0.016	0.028	0.020	0.010	0.017

Data: UK_retail_sales.xlsx.

TABLE 10.12 FORECAST COMPARISONS ON THE TEST DATA: NEURAL
NETWORKS VS. SMOOTHING MODELS (*Years 17 and 18: 2008
and 2009*)

Method	Lead 1			Lead 1-12		
	RMSE	MAPE	MdAPE	RMSE	MAPE	MdAPE
Neural network	3.56	2.63%	1.71%	3.95	2.87%	**1.70%**
Holt–Winters, additive	2.68	2.01%	1.72%	3.51	2.61%	1.93%
Holt–Winters, multiplicative	**2.35**	**1.69%**	1.56%	**3.31**	**2.51%**	1.77%
Holt–Winters, logarithmic	2.45	1.75%	**1.51%**	3.82	2.99%	2.50%

Data: UK_retail_sales.xlsx.

10.4.3 Neural Networks: A Summary

Neural network models make up a flexible class of nonlinear models that can be used for ordinary time series modeling, causal modeling, or predictive classification. An extensive literature exists, and a comprehensive discussion in a business context may be found in Shmueli, Bruce, and Patel (2010). However, the very flexibility offered by neural network models means that there are many choices a modeler must make. Poor choices will often lead to poor results. The guidelines we have provided should be followed.

Unfortunately, although many software programs are available, they are not standardized, and some may well produce poor forecasts or misleading results due to inadequate programming. We have used MATLAB and SAS for our calculations. But because there are no accepted benchmarks for checking the calculations, all that can be done is to check whether the output (particularly the performance of the neural network on test data) improves on some standard classification or forecasting benchmark.

Vector Autoregressive (VAR) Models

In regression analysis, the modeler must distinguish between the explanatory input variables and the dependent variable. A major innovation in forecasting (made famous by Sims in 1980; in 2011, a Nobel prize winner) was to argue that, in many circumstances, it is impossible to clearly distinguish between these two classes of variables, particularly in macroeconomic forecasting. Instead, he suggested that we model a set of output variables in terms of their own lagged values. An example is the retail price of *Unleaded* gasoline used in Chapter 9. Other key variables that might be best thought of as "jointly determined" are the Consumer Price Index (*CPI*) and the price of crude oil (*Crude*). A first-order vector autoregression model using these three variables is

$$Unleaded_t = \beta_{10} + \beta_{11}Unleaded_{t-1} + \beta_{12}\,Crude_{t-1} + \beta_{13}\,CPI_{t-1} + e_{1t}$$
$$Crude_t = \beta_{20} + \beta_{21}Crude_{t-1} + \beta_{22}\,Unleaded_{t-1} + \beta_{23}\,CPI_{t-1} + e_{2t} \quad (10.4)$$
$$CPI_t = \beta_{30} + \beta_{31}Crude_{t-1} + \beta_{32}Unleaded_{t-1} + \beta_{33}\,CPI_{t-1} + e_{3t}.$$

These equations are similar to the single-equation regression models considered in Chapter 9, but they contrast in that all the variables on the right-hand side are lagged. (Such a set of equations is called a VAR in standard form.) Any standard statistical software, such as Minitab or SPSS, can be used to estimate the parameters, but when there are a large number of lags to include (with monthly data here, we could contemplate including 12 lags), it is easier to use an econometric package. We again use EViews (version 7)[2] to estimate the model specified in equation (10.4); the results are shown in Table 10.13.

The retail unleaded price (*Unleaded*) is strongly affected by past crude prices (*Crude*); the *CPI* is positively affected by past crude prices, partially balanced (with a perhaps counterintuitive negative sign) with the past unleaded price. Note that the models for *Crude* and *CPI* are close to an autoregressive model in first differences, given that the coefficients of their first-order lag terms are close to 1.0 (see Section 6.2). We might well choose to model *Crude* as a first difference. There is apparently no feedback to *Crude* from *CPI*, because the coefficient is insignificant, whereas unleaded price increases apparently damp the next period's crude price. Also, our earlier considerations of these series in Section 9.6.4 suggested using logarithmic transformations rather than the original series. Further, in developing this simple model, we arbitrarily chose a lag length of 1 as shown in equation (10.4). However, there are often longer lags in an economic system. We might therefore wish to select an "optimal" lag length. There are many criteria that help a user choose the maximum length. An analysis using EViews includes the results shown in Table 10.14, where we have shown just two of the available criteria for selecting the lag length.

Of the various selection criteria, those which aim to produce a simple model (i.e., The Schwartz information criterion (*SC*), previously denoted by *BIC*) have been shown to produce better forecasting performance: here the Schwarz criterion points to a maximum lag length of 3. Akaike's Information Criterion (the *AIC*) usually recommends a longer lag, as it does here: The recommendation of 13 suggests some possible residual seasonality, which should be examined with residual tests. Where a lag is recommended that makes no sense in the context of the problem, it is better to use a shorter interpretable maximum lag. However, there is no strong economic reason that the maximum lag lengths of the endogenous variables should all be the same, so the criteria outlined in Table 10.14 may miss higher order terms for some of the variables. Some programs, such as PCGive (through its automatic model selection option), will simplify each individual equation automatically. The user can then choose to test or impose further constraints. As an investigative check, we provide

---

[2]See on-line Appendix C for a discussion of alternatives and the rationale behind the use of specialist software.

TABLE 10.13   A SIMPLE VECTOR AUTOREGRESSION OF UNLEADED, CRUDE, AND THE CONSUMER PRICE INDEX

Vector Autoregression Estimates
Date: 04/03/11 Time: 19:58
Sample (adjusted): 1996M02 2008M12
Included observations: 155 after adjustments
Standard errors in ( ) & t-statistics in [ ]

	CRUDE	**UNLEADED**	**CPI**
CRUDE(-1)	1.103865	0.009444	0.037175
	(0.07025)	(0.00220)	(0.00922)
	[15.7143]	[4.29954]	[4.03118]
UNLEADED(-1)	-5.705355	0.613553	-1.165751
	(2.81102)	(0.08790)	(0.36903)
	[-2.02964]	[6.98039]	[-3.15896]
CPI(-1)	0.055435	0.001370	0.995205
	(0.05458)	(0.00171)	(0.00717)
	[1.01567]	[0.80254]	[138.894]
C	-3.999061	0.059934	1.807983
	(7.94843)	(0.24854)	(1.04347)
	[-0.50313]	[0.24115]	[1.73267]
R-squared	0.968797	0.960896	0.998841
Adj. R-squared	0.968177	0.960119	0.998818
Sum sq. resids	3346.034	3.271517	57.66687
S.E. equation	4.707352	0.147193	0.617980
F-statistic	1562.740	1236.834	43372.29
Log likelihood	-458.0237	79.07281	-143.3080
Akaike AIC	5.961596	-0.968681	1.900748
Schwarz SC	6.040136	-0.890141	1.979288
Mean dependent	40.58174	1.782219	182.3606
S.D. dependent	26.38785	0.737062	17.97351

Determinant resid covariance (dof adj.)	0.017068
Determinant resid covariance	0.015780
Log likelihood	-338.2593
Akaike information criterion	4.519475
Schwarz criterion	4.755095

Source: Output adapted from EViews 7. *Data*: Gas_prices.xlsx. Note that for presentation purposes, the number of significant figures in the table should be much smaller.

details of the model for lags of order 2, the recommended order using Schwartz's criterion on the log transformed series, with the results shown in Table 10.15.

The extended model suggests that retail prices are also affected by a two-period lag in crude prices, with a positive impact of 0.400, moderated the next period by a damping of −0.220. Again, the coefficients indicate that differencing may be appropriate (see Appendix 10A; further exploration is left to the reader).

Another advantage of using a fully functional automatic econometric package is that a wide range of tests of the model's assumptions is usually included as standard output. As we argued in the last chapter, the in-sample residuals contain a lot of information as to whether our proposed model captures the characteristics of the data. Typical tests of

TABLE 10.14   VAR LAG ORDER SELECTION CRITERIA

VAR Lag Order Selection Criteria
Endogenous variables: CRUDE UNLEADED CPI
Exogenous variables: C
Date: 04/03/11 Time: 19:58
Sample: 1996M01 2008M12
Included observations: 143

Lag	AIC	SC
0	15.14710	15.20926
1	4.733544	4.982174
2	3.689127	4.124230
3	3.445643	4.067218*
4	3.426309	4.234358
5	3.324741	4.319262
6	3.214579	4.395573
7	3.321803	4.689270
8	3.197473	4.751413
9	3.048888	4.789300
10	2.850198	4.777083
11	2.553266	4.666624
12	2.608478	4.908309
13	2.418193*	4.904496

* indicates lag order selected by the criterion
AIC: Akaike information criterion
SC: Schwarz information criterion

Data: Gas_prices.xlsx; output adapted from EViews7.

the residuals include various tests for autocorrelation in the residuals, tests for heteroscedasticity and normality, and tests for outliers. An (edited) example taken from PCGive for the foregoing models with two lags included in the VAR is given in Appendix 10A.

The final stage in the process is producing the forecasts. The sample period for estimating the model has to be set. Here, it is 2008M12, leading to the 24 periods in 2009–2010 for which we can compare data with actual observations. The forecasts can either be rolling-origin, one-period-ahead conditional forecasts where the actual lagged values are used to produce the forecasts or fixed-origin forecasts where, for each lead time greater than 1, the lagged values are estimated (i.e., for two periods ahead), the forecast is based on the previous lagged values, which themselves have been estimated. (This type of forecasting is sometimes described as dynamic forecasting.)

Forecasting with a VAR Model

In a VAR model, the forecasts may be produced automatically, without any need to forecast the dependent variables *separately*. However, most programs also allow the user to include *exogenous variables*, to avoid creating an excessive number of variables and parameters in the model.

TABLE 10.15   SECOND-ORDER VAR MODEL FOR THE LOG TRANSFORMED
UNLEADED, CRUDE, AND CPI SERIES

Vector Autoregression Estimates
Date: 04/03/11 Time: 20:00
Sample (adjusted): 1996M03 2008M12
Included observations: 154 after adjustments
Standard errors in ( ) & t-statistics in [ ]

	LN(CRUDE)	**LN(UNLEADED)**	**LN(CPI)**
LN(CRUDE(−1))	1.305219	0.399645	0.019384
	(0.10868)	(0.06524)	(0.00320)
	[12.0093]	[6.12545]	[6.05575]
LN(CRUDE(−2))	−0.329113	−0.219738	−0.013275
	(0.11860)	(0.07120)	(0.00349)
	[−2.77495]	[−3.08635]	[−3.80049]
LN(UNLEADED(−1))	−0.179097	1.189029	−0.003947
	(0.22459)	(0.13482)	(0.00661)
	[−0.79745]	[8.81930]	[−0.59677]
LN(UNLEADED(−2))	0.105673	−0.543476	−0.005972
	(0.21460)	(0.12882)	(0.00632)
	[0.49243]	[−4.21881]	[−0.94490]
LN(CPI(−1))	3.418897	−3.822748	1.178728
	(4.32873)	(2.59855)	(0.12749)
	[0.78981]	[−1.47111]	[9.24596]
LN(CPI(−2))	−3.091305	4.055036	−0.177869
	(4.27602)	(2.56691)	(0.12593)
	[−0.72294]	[1.57974]	[−1.41241]
C	−1.585642	−1.656303	−0.019480
	(1.09680)	(0.65841)	(0.03230)
	[−1.44569]	[−2.51559]	[−0.60306]
R-squared	0.979308	0.981961	0.999360
Adj. R-squared	0.978463	0.981225	0.999334
Sum sq. resids	1.066112	0.384188	0.000925
S.E. equation	0.085161	0.051123	0.002508
F-statistic	1159.520	1333.672	38246.57
Log likelihood	164.3994	242.9889	707.2533
Akaike AIC	−2.044148	−3.064790	−9.094199
Schwarz SC	−1.906104	−2.926747	−8.956156
Mean dependent	3.530607	0.506896	5.202244
S.D. dependent	0.580300	0.373096	0.097165
Determinant resid covariance (dof adj.)	2.20E-11		
Determinant resid covariance	1.91E-11		
Log likelihood	1244.940		
Akaike information criterion	−15.89532		
Schwarz criterion	−15.48119		

Data: Gas_prices.xlsx; output adapted from EViews.

TABLE 10.16   ONE-STEP-AHEAD FORECAST ERROR STATISTICS FOR
UNLEADED FOR OUT-OF-SAMPLE, 2009–2010: VAR MODELS VS.
BENCHMARK AUTOREGRESSION

	In-Sample Standard Error	RMSE (Lead1)	MAPE (Lead1)	MdAPE (Lead1)
AR(1)	0.155	0.350	3.7%	3.4%
AR(2)	0.129	0.382	4.8%	3.7%
First-order VAR	0.146	0.318	3.0%	2.4%
Second-order VAR(*)	0.107	0.371	4.2%	3.2%

(*) For the VAR models in logs, fitted values and forecasts were transformed back before calculation of the error measures.

Data: Gas_prices.xlsx.

Looking at Table 10.16, we see a very substantial deterioration in the out-of-sample *RMSE* (compared to the in-sample standard error). The explanation for that lies in the dramatic structural changes seen as the economic crisis starting in 2007 developed (see Example 9.6 and Figure 10.12). Note also that, although the additional complexity of the two-period lag VAR system seems to offer a reasonably substantial in-sample improvement over the first-order model, this thesis does not hold out of sample. Thus, we have yet another example in which a simple model turns out to deliver the best forecast. But the VAR model does outperform the univariate AR models.

FIGURE 10.12   UNLEADED GAS PRICES, 2000–2010

Data: Gas_prices.xlsx.

Principles

Many of the principles we have listed in earlier chapters apply to these more advanced methods, but we repeat them here to underline their importance.

Classification Methods

[10.1] Consider a variety of different classification methods, using as much data as is computationally feasible.

[10.2] Use a variety of error measures (such as the classification matrices and the ROC curves) to evaluate the methods.

[10.3] In developing classification models, always retain a subset of the data with which to test the effectiveness of the proposed methods.

[10.4] Always compare the new method with a benchmark classification approach.

Neural Networks *(see Remus and O'Connor, 2001)*

[10.5] Scale the data before estimating the neural network model.

[10.6] Use a variety of starting values (typically selected at random) to avoid local minima.

[10.7] Use techniques such as validation samples to avoid overfitting.

VAR Models *(see Allen and Fildes, 2001; 2005)*

[10.8] Use a VAR model (based on lags), as opposed to a set of single equations based upon concurrent values of the explanatory variables.

[10.9] Reduce the lag length on each variable separately.

[10.10] Model the data in levels, rather than differences, initially.

[10.11] Examine all the model's variables for potential nonstationarity. Use theoretical analysis, graphs, autocorrelations, and such tests as the augmented Dickey–Fuller test (discussed in Appendix 10C) to decide whether the variables are nonstationary. Beware: Relying on tests alone is dangerous because these tests have weak power.

[10.12] For nonstationary data, develop an Error Correction Model (ECM) and compare it with an unrestricted model and a model in differences. As we argue in Appendixes 10D and 10E, the general VAR model can be successively constrained, first to the ECM and then to a model in differences. These constraints will generally lead to improved forecast accuracy when they are justified by the data. But it is worthwhile carrying out the straightforward comparison of the ECM model with a model in levels and a model in differences.

Summary

In this chapter, we have presented a number of new methods suitable for a wide class of forecasting problems that collectively go under the name *predictive classification*. We have also extended the range of time series methods we considered to include the relatively new approaches of neural networks and VAR models. All these methods and models are part of the required armory for a forecaster who aspires to be on top of the latest techniques. They are harder to use than the regular methods and models described in earlier chapters. But that problem arises in part because the software needed is more specialized (see on-line Appendix C) and in part because it is not easy for a forecaster to switch between packages. So, if there are these barriers to implementing the models in practice, why are the models used at all?

For classification problems, the industry-standard approach is logistic regression. Although the other methods we have described—classification trees and neural nets—have often been shown to outperform logistic regression in particular situations, the differences have not proved consistent enough to supplant the standard. One particular advantage of logistic regression compared with neural nets is that the output of the former is readily interpretable whereas neural networks act as a black box. It turns out that predictive accuracy is not the only criterion for users.

VAR models are used regularly in macroeconomic modeling but much less frequently, as far as we can tell, in industry models. Again, the software and the output are not as user friendly as they are for standard regression models. Nevertheless, the use of such software as EViews and PCGive (Oxmetrics) puts a lot of econometric power at the user's fingertips. Do these methods work better than simpler approaches? Allen and Fildes (2001) suggest that they do, but the differences are not as substantial or consistent as theory suggests.

In short, for important problems, the methods described in this chapter have the potential to improve accuracy. But success cannot be taken for granted. This tension emphasizes an important message in this book and a core forecasting principle: "Always compare your proposed model with some simple alternative."

Discussion Question *Why do these advanced methods often fail to outperform simple benchmarks?*

Exercises

10.1   Using the computer owner data set (*Compdata.xlsx*) and regular regression, take a random sample of approximately 80 percent of the data. Then use the variables *Income* and *Education* to develop a linear regression model. (You should consider pooling the classes.)
  a.   Calculate the classification matrix on the estimation sample and compare the results, for 50 percent and 20 percent cutoffs. Does knowledge of the household's education level add anything to your ability to identify non-owners?
  b.   Use your preferred model to score the out-of-sample test data. Compare your results with a model that uses income only.
  c.   Use logistic regression to carry out the same task. Are there any substantial differences between the results of the two approaches?

10.2   Using the computer owner data set (*Compdata.xlsx*), and 80 percent of the sample, develop a classification tree. Compare the classification performance you achieve with the model given in Section 10.3. Does combining the two lowest income classes as was done in Section 10.3 still improve the model's performance?

10.3   Using a three-node neural network and the computer owner data set (*Compdata.xlsx*), compare the results obtained from using five different random starting seeds.
  Using the rule "classify an observation as a '1' if the average score over the five runs is above 0.8," compare the misclassification performance of this new rule with (a) the best of the five runs and (b) the average performance.

10.4   Using regression (or logistic regression) and the data set *Compdata.xlsx*, include the variable *Income* as well as the additional variables *Kids* and attitude to technology (*TAM1–TAM3*) to develop a classification model, and then compare the performance of the model at the 0.50 cutoff. What advantages do you see to adopting one cutoff approach rather than the other. Do the additional variables improve the classification performance of the models compared with the performance of the simple model that uses just *Income*?

10.5 Using the time series NN3-001 from the data set *N3.xlsx*, develop a neural network time series forecasting model. Produce forecasts for up to 18 periods ahead. Compare the out-of-sample results with benchmark models of your choosing (e.g., random walk, simple exponential smoothing). Does the choice of the best performing method depend on the error measure you have chosen or the forecast origin you have chosen?

10.6* In the Exercise 10.5, what are the effects on the performance of the neural network, including computational times, of (a) changing the learning rate and (b) changing the momentum?

10.7 Carry out Exercises 10.5 and 10.6 on a time series data set of your choice.

10.8 Using the data set *Gasprices_full.xlsx*,
   a. Test whether *Crude*, *CPI*, and *Unemployment* are stationary variables.
   b. Develop a regression model for *Unleaded*, using the methods of Chapter 9.
   c. Develop a three-variable VAR model that includes the price of *Unleaded*. In so doing, include only those variables you expect to have an economic impact on the unleaded price. Use a maximum of two lags.
   d. Examine whether there is evidence for including lags longer than two in your model.
   e. Evaluate the forecasting performance of your chosen model.
   f. Develop a model in differences (for any of the nonstationary variables). Is this model a "better" model than the model developed in levels in parts (b) and (c)? Explain. Does the forecasting performance of the model improve on that of any of the earlier models?

10.9 Durkin, Ord, and Walker (2010) examined the growth of credit markets in the United States since 1946. The data file *Credit.xlsx* contains annual values for real mortgage credit (*RMC*), real consumer credit (*RCC*), and real disposable personal income (*RDPI*) for the period 1946–2006. All the observations are measured in billions of dollars, after adjustment by the Consumer Price Index (*CPI*). Develop a VAR model for these data for the period 1946–2003, and then forecast the last three years, 2004–2006. Examine the relative advantages of a logarithmic transform and the use of differences.

10.10 Using the data set *Gasprices_1.xlsx*, but setting aside the data for 2006 through 2010, develop an unrestricted VAR model, an ECM, and a model in stationary variables. Use appropriate error statistics to examine the residuals and test their respective forecasting performances.
   a. Do the residuals of the various models suggest any inadequacies in the model?
   b. If you now consider the more recent data, from 2006 to 2010, does your chosen model show any instability in its performance?
   c. If you also bring into consideration the performance of the models over the years 2009–2010, which model would you use for forecasting for the period 2011–2012? Explain your reasons.

10.11* Using the data set *Exchange_rates.xlsx*, covering data on the $US–Euro and $US–£Sterling exchange rates from June 13, 1991, to June 13, 2011,
   a. Test the stationarity of each series
      i. with the subset with data from October 13, 1997, to June 13, 2002.
      ii. with the full data set.
   b. For each time series, develop an ARIMA model that produces one-step-ahead daily forecasts. Then do the same for monthly average exchange rates.
   c. Are the two series cointegrated? Consider both the full and the shorter data sets.
   d. Is there any evidence of structural breaks in the full data series?
   e. Carry out a literature review of the comparative accuracy of alternative methods of exchange rate forecasting. Do you find any evidence that any of the methods you have discovered have proved successful beyond the random-walk naïve alternative?

Minicase 10.1 KMI BioPharma, Inc.: Biocide[3]

Ed Wheeler, marketing manager for KMI BioPharma, Inc.'s (KMI's) industrial products division, was developing a marketing strategy for its first new product, a biocide for metalworking fluids. KMI was a small, but rapidly growing, biopharmaceutical firm heavily funded by venture capitalists because of its promising technologies that extracted chemical elements from exotic plants. These elements were then used to develop innovative consumer and industrial products.

Although KMI had several products in various stages of development, only one consumer product—CelluLife Body Cream—had been launched. The relatively new product had been on the market for 48 months and was considered a commercial success, becoming profitable in just the past year. CelluLife was a general-purpose skin cream which contained proprietary ingredients that promoted the healing of damaged skin cells. KMI positioned CelluLife as an all-natural product with secret healing ingredients from exotic plants. While major competitors emphasized the "skin-caring" qualities of their products, KMI focused on its powerful effectiveness.

The new biocide product was KMI's first industrial market application. Using special chemical ingredients obtained from hundreds of analyses of various kinds of plant vegetation, KMI's chemists were able to develop a product that helped solve two key problems: killing bacteria and providing a pleasant odor to a normally pungent operating environment. The new biocide product was effective in killing bacteria, fungi, and other microorganisms in metalworking fluids and promised to be useful for other applications as well.

Ed was meeting with his launch marketing team to discuss the results of a market research survey. Ed commented on the survey results: "It seems that the results and analyses may have created more problems and decisions for us than we expected." Nan Kelly, a product manager on the team, said, "These aren't really problems, but rather opportunities for us. The fact that we have four viable target market segments lets us focus our limited resources. I think we should pick one segment and go with it."

Jim Burton, the R&D manager, was quick to respond, "What's the point of picking one segment? Why don't we take the simplest approach and develop our marketing strategy to reach the entire market? We have a great product, and all of these metalworking firms are going to jump on the bandwagon once they see how effective our new product is." Art Kanjian, the controller, said, "I think you are each at the extremes. The best strategy may be to take two or three of the segments and target them accordingly."

Ed responded to the group, "Look we need to make some decisions rather quickly. We have to make commitments soon if we want to make an April launch date. Depending on our marketing strategy, we may have to buy space in trade magazines, put together an Internet site, hire and train a sales force, or develop relationships with distributors. Furthermore, if we are really going to be successful, we have to determine how to best position this new product in the market. After all, the competition is well entrenched."

The Market

The process of working with metal generates heat and metal scraps. While the metal is ground, drilled, turned, milled, or otherwise machined, a fluid from a nozzle is directed toward the

---

[3] We wish to acknowledge Professor Robert Thomas of Georgetown University, who developed this case and kindly consented to our reproducing it herein. Minor changes have been made to the text and to the assignment that follows to meet present needs, but the principal details and the data set *Biocide.xlsx* are entirely as originally written.

work area to cool, lubricate, and keep the metalworking surfaces clean of scraps. The metal scraps are caught in a special tray, and the fluid is filtered and returned to the work area. The fluid passes through a reservoir, or sump, the size of which depends on the application.

Several problems with such a metalworking operation are due to the bacteria and other microorganisms that grow in the warm watery mixture. First, the bacteria can breakdown the effectiveness of the basic metalworking fluid by clogging filters, flow lines, and drains. Second, the bacteria give off a foul odor that contaminates the area for workers. Third, workers often complain that, when the fluid gets on their skin, it causes dermatitis and other problems. Because of this problem, workers are reluctant to go near the reservoir to recondition the fluid as necessary. They often resort to such tactics as dumping in liquid bleach, deodorants, and other household products to reduce the smells. In many cases, this only exacerbates the problem.

To deal with these metalworking problems, the 10 major metalworking fluid formulators in the United States add a biocide to the concentrate. The concentrate is composed of emulsified oils, additives, and biocides that are mixed with 95 percent water. However, once the fluid is in place, firms rarely change it. In most cases, they add so-called maintenance biocides. Concentrate biocides accounted for about 40 percent of the market for all metalworking biocides, with maintenance biocides at 60 percent. Importantly, concentrate biocides were decreasing in sales while maintenance biocides were increasing. This trend, expected to increase over the next ten years, made the market attractive.

The market was structured such that some 300 firms with an estimated 1,500 metalworking machines used large central system reservoirs with capacities of 10,000 gallons or more. This market was well served by such firms as Rohm and Haas, with its Kathon MW product, that had a 30 percent market share. There were, however, another 140,000 firms with some 1.4 million metalworking machines. These firms were served by some 14,000 supply houses in the United States, generating, in total, about $50 billion in sales of metalworking supplies, including various fluids and biocides.

The smaller metalworking firms were not as well served in the market as the larger ones, although there were at least two major competitors that recently had developed products for stand-alone machines rather than those with large central reservoir systems.

Angus Chemical offered the so-called Tris-Nitro "Sump Saver" 2-ounce tablets. Two such tablets were required to treat a 50-gallon tank, the average size for firms with stand-alone systems. Each tablet sold for about $1.00 to distributors and $2.00 to customers. The tablets were not completely effective in eliminating bacteria, did not kill fungus, and lasted for only about a week. Nevertheless, Tris-Nitro was liked because it was easy to use. Workers had to drop the tablets into the sump only when they suspected problems. Ed Wheeler estimated that Tris-Nitro was used in about 20 percent of the market for stand-alone metalworking systems.

Dowicil 75, made by Dow Chemical, was a water-soluble package that could simply be dropped into the reservoir. Each package was about 2 pounds and sold for $10 to distributors and about $30 to customers. Dowicil 75 was quite effective for about a month against bacteria and fungi. However, it had a strong ammonia odor that occasionally released formaldehyde, which could be a safety factor with employees. Ed Wheeler estimated that, like Tris-Nitro, Dowicil 75 had about a 20 percent share of the market for stand-alone systems.

Ed saw the other 60 percent of the market as a large opportunity. Although all of the aforementioned firms adopted local solutions (such as bleach, deodorants, and disinfectants), these products were more harmful than helpful to the metalworking process—although an employee who had a hard time working with the foul odors would not agree. Ed saw the market situation as strongly motivating KMI's product development program.

The New Product

After talking with a few potential users, Ed and his team of chemists initially formulated the product into a cakelike tablet that could be dropped into the sump of metalworking machines. However, this approach proved to be problematic because tests showed that there was considerable variation in how the tablet dissolved. There were also problems in how well the tablet was dispersing the chemical in the reservoir.

The team of chemists then improved the tablet's composition and developed a system for holding the tablet just below the surface of the liquid in the sump. This adjustable and corrosion-resistant triangular frame could be hung over the edge of the sump and retrieved weekly for replacement of the dissolved cake tablets. A handgrip helped to hold the frame in place. It also facilitated the placement of a new tablet in a mesh basket at the end of the triangular arm. The tablet was sized to last about one week in a typical 50-gallon reservoir application. The cost to make each tablet averaged $1.00. The cost to make a corrosion-resistant frame was about $25.00. The frames were expected to last the lifetime of a typical reservoir.

Beta tests conducted at five sites over a three-month period revealed that the new product worked well under average operating conditions. KMI chemists visited the plant at the beginning of each week, initially to train metalworkers in the use of the new system, but later to follow up to make sure that the workers had learned how to use it most effectively.

Ed was satisfied with the product, but when he started to develop his marketing program launch decisions, he discovered that he had several unanswered questions: How should he position the new product? How should he communicate its virtues? How should he price it? Should he use distributors or go directly to customers? Most importantly, to which firms should he target his new program? To begin to answer these questions, he turned to market research.

The Market Segmentation Study

Ed retained a local market research firm to conduct a survey of the market for metalworking biocides. After hearing Ed's major questions, the research firm designed a study that included the major features or benefits of a biocide used in metalworking applications. The study also included questions about the reaction to the new KMI biocide concept, brand usage, satisfaction with the current system, media usage, the use of distributors, usage of biocides, and so on.

Data were collected via telephone contact with a random sample of customers in order to identify the survey respondent, followed by a faxed, mailed, or e-mailed questionnaire (according to the respondent's preference). A total of 130 completed surveys were obtained. Summary results for the sample (and the basic questions in the questionnaire) are presented in Exhibit 1.

Ed also asked the firm if it could segment the market. In particular, he wanted to do so on the basis of the importance of the various biocide features to respondents.

Assignment

1. Management feels that the following features are most important to potential customers: cost, ease of replacing biocides, ease of use, and reduction in the number of bacteria. Management also feels that any potential customer recording 1 or 2 on the satisfaction scale is a likely purchaser. Define a binary variable to describe potential purchasers (*Potpurch*), and run a binary logistic regression to determine which factors should be emphasized in marketing the product.

2. To develop a market segmentation, select the appropriate variables for analysis. Generate a classification tree (as in Figure 10.5), using *Potpurch* as the dependent variable to determine an appropriate set of segments (clusters of terminal nodes). How many clusters are appropriate?

3. Use the selected clusters as the basis for analyzing the survey results to determine whether there are any advantages to taking a segmentation approach to the market. To do this, first create dummy variables to indicate cluster membership. (Remember,

you need one fewer dummies than clusters.) Then, continuing to use *Potpurch* as the dependent variable, carry out logistic regression analysis on the dummy variables to determine whether the segmentation is effective for marketing purposes.

EXHIBIT 1   OVERALL SURVEY FINDINGS

	N	*Mean*	*Std. Deviation*
How important are each of the following to you on a 5-point scale, with 5 = very important?			
Ease of using the biocide	130	4.48	.80
Ease of replacing the biocides	130	4.55	.68
Safety of handling the biocides	130	4.09	.92
Installation costs of the biocide system	130	3.95	1.01
Cost of replacement biocides	130	4.36	.77
Cost to maintain the system	130	4.12	.85
Biocide extends metalworking fluid life	130	3.67	1.19
Consistency of biocide dispersion in fluid reservoir	130	3.35	1.15
Stability of biocide chemicals (e.g., no formaldehyde leakage)	130	3.70	1.02
Biocide is effective over a wide pH range	130	3.72	1.19
Reducing bacteria that causes dermatitis	130	4.23	.98
Elimination of odors in machine fluid reservoir	130	4.43	.82
How effective are the following communication options to you on a 5-point scale, with 5 = very effective?			
Trade shows	130	3.02	1.36
Advertising in trade media	130	3.50	1.15
Telemarketing	130	1.98	1.04
Direct mail brochures	130	3.38	1.04
Internet	130	2.94	1.41
Visit by Distributor's sales force	130	3.89	1.09
Manufacturer's sales force	130	3.75	1.14
What is your degree of satisfaction, interest, intention to buy (higher number = greater degree)?			
Satisfaction with current biocide system (scale from 1 to 5)	130	3.06	.99
Interest in changing biocide systems (scale from 1 to 5)	130	3.06	1.19
Intention to buy the new concept as pictured and described (scale from 1 to 4)	130	2.62	.90
Overall, what is your rating of the following brands of biocide?			
Dow Chemical	130	3.22	1.25
Angus Chemical	130	3.04	1.07
Biocide usage			
Average packet equivalents used	130	183.5	149.9
Use Dowicil 75 (number used and % of 130)	28	22%	
Use Tris-Nitro "Sump Saver" (number used and % of 130)	26	20%	
Use other (number used and % of 130)	76	58%	

4. Complete a report to the management that summarizes your findings. In particular, you should address the following questions:
   - Should the market be segmented or treated as a whole?
   - If segmented, which segments should be targeted?
   - What additional analyses are needed with these data, and should another market research study be conducted before launching the product? If so, what information requirements are necessary in the next study?

References

*These papers are theoretical in nature and are listed for completeness and for those readers seeking an understanding of advanced topics.

Allen, P. G., and Fildes, R. (2001). Econometric forecasting, in J. S. Armstrong (ed.), *Principles of Forecasting: A Handbook for Researchers and Practitioners.* Boston and Dordrecht: Kluwer, pp. 303–362.

Allen, P. G., and Fildes, R. (2005). Levels, differences and ECMs: Principles for improved econometric forecasting. *Oxford Bulletin of Economics and Statistics*, 67, 881–904.

*Breiman, L., Friedman, J., Olshen, R., and Stone, C. (1984). *Classification and Regression Trees.* Boca Raton, FL: Chapman and Hall (CRC).

Crone, S. F., and Kourentzes, N. (2010). Feature selection for time series prediction: A combined filter and wrapper approach for neural networks. *Neurocomputing,* 73 (10–12), 1923–1936.

Doornik, J. A., and Hendry, D. F. (2009) *Modelling Dynamic Systems: PCGive™ 13, Vol. II,* London, Timberlake Consultants.

Durkin, T. A., Ord, J. K., and Walker, D. A. (2010). Long-run credit growth in the U.S. *Journal of Economics and Business*, 62, 383–400.

Elder, J., and Kennedy, P. E. (2001). Testing for unit roots: What should students be taught. *Journal of Economic Education*, 32, 137–146.

*Enders, W. (2010). *Applied Econometric Time Series*, 3rd ed. Hoboken, NJ: Wiley, 2010.

*Engle, R. F. & Granger, C. W. J. (1987). Cointegration and error correction: Representation, estimation, and testing. *Econometrica*, 55 (2), 251–276.

Fuller, W. A. (1996). *Introduction to Statistical Time Series*, 2nd ed. New York: Wiley.

Granger, C. W. J., and Newbold, P. (1974). Spurious regressions in econometrics. *J. Econometrics*, 2, 111–120.

*Harvey, D. I., Leybourne, S. J., and Taylor, A. M. R. (2009). Unit root testing in practice: Dealing with uncertainty over the trend and initial condition. *Econometric Theory*, 25, 587–63.

Hendry, D. F., and Mizon, G. E. (1978). Serial correlation as a convenient simplification, not a nuisance: A comment on a study of the demand for money by the Bank of England. *Econ. J.*, 88, 549–563.

*Johansen, S. (1988). Statistical analysis of cointegration vectors. *Journal of Economic Dynamics & Control*, 12 (2–3), 231–254.

Kutner, M., Nachtsheim, C., Neter, J. and Li, W. (2005). *Applied Linear Statistical Models*, 5th ed. New York: McGraw-Hill.

Murray, M. P. (1994). A drunk and her dog: An illustration of cointegration and error-correction. *American Statistician*, 48 (1), 37–39.

Remus, W., and O'Connor, M. (2001). Neural networks for time-series forecasting, In J. S. Armstrong (ed.), *Principles of Forecasting: A Handbook for Researchers and Practitioners*. Boston and Dordrecht: Kluwer, pp. 245–258.

Shmueli, G., Bruce, P. C., and Patel, N. R. (2010). *Data Mining for Business Intelligence*, 2nd ed. New York: Wiley.

*Sims, C.A. (1980). Macroeconomics and reality. *Econometrica*, 48, 1–48.

Timmermann, A., and Granger, C. W. J. (2004). Efficient market hypothesis and forecasting. *International Journal of Forecasting*, 20, 15–27.

Appendix 10A   PcGive Analysis of Oil Prices Data

A key issue in deciding whether a model is adequate is that it should capture the principal features of the data (be data congruent, as it is called) with no patterns remaining in the residuals.

In examining the residuals from the 2-lag model for the oil prices data, it is seen that no residuals exceed 3.5 standard errors; therefore, outliers are unlikely to be a major problem in this model. Recall that outliers have their greatest effect on prediction intervals.

The tests that follow are automatically carried out in most econometric packages. In this appendix, we use OxMetrics™ 6.2, a recently developed econometrics package, to evaluate alternative model specifications. A discussion of these tests, together with details of how the significance levels are calculated, is given in Doornik and Hendry (2009). Interpretation of the various tests is subjective: With so many tests being carried out on a system of equations such as that for the oil price model for unleaded gasoline, almost certainly some of the tests will suggest a potential problem with one or more of the model's assumptions. The aim for the forecaster is to establish whether the collective evidence points to a major misspecification and a possible improved model.

Analysis Based Upon the Estimation Sample

Individual model analysis:

Here, we include just the statistics relating to ln(*Unleaded*). Similar summary statistics are provided for all equations. In all cases, the number in square brackets represents the *P*-value for the test. We have

> ln(*Unleaded*): Portmanteau(12): $\chi^2 (10) = 39.495$ [0.0000]**[4]
>
> (This is usually called the Ljung–Box statistic; it tests for autocorrelation over the first 12 lags against χ^2 critical values. See Section 6.5. Results suggest autocorrelation.)
>
> ln(*Unleaded*): AR 1–12 test: $F(12,135) = 2.9973$ [0.0010]** (suggesting autocorrelation)
>
> ln(*Unleaded*): Normality test: $\chi^2(2) = 7.8096$ [0.0201]* (suggesting some remaining nonnormality despite the transform)
>
> ln(*Unleaded*): White's heteroscedasticity test: $F(12,141) = 6.6269$ [0.0000]** (suggesting some remaining heteroscedasticity despite the transform)
>
> ln(*Unleaded*): Hetero-X test: $F(27,126) = 5.0998$ [0.0000]** (suggesting some remaining heteroscedasticity despite the transform)

Overall, the model seems to suffer from some residual autocorrelation.

Autocorrelation test for all equations (the residuals should not be autocorrelated):

Vector portmanteau statistic (testing all equations simultaneously with null hypothesis that there is no autocorrelation) for 12 lags and 154 observations: 169.25 [0.0000]**. This is the vector equivalent of the Ljung–Box statistic.

---

[4]We use the usual convention here: ** denotes significance at the 0.01 level and * denotes significance at the 0.05 level.

Testing for vector error autocorrelation from lags 1 to 12:

$\chi^2(108) = 186.18\ [0.0000]$** and F-form $F(108,327) = 2.0973\ [0.0000]$**

These two tests together show evidence of residual autocorrelation.

Vector normality test for residuals:

Vector normality test: $\chi^2(6) = 63.206\ [0.0000]$** (suggesting nonnormality)

Testing for vector heteroscedasticity by using squares of the residuals:

$\chi^2(72) = 151.88\ [0.0000]$** and F-form $F(72,745) = 2.4934\ [0.0000]$**

Testing for vector heteroscedasticity by using squares and cross products:

$\chi^2(162) = 293.11\ [0.0000]$** and F-form $F(162,719) = 2.4323\ [0.0000]$** (suggesting strong evidence of heteroscedasticity

Finally, test statistics are given on the model's forecasting ability and the proposed model's stability, using the out-of-sample data we set aside—here, 12 periods. A key requirement in building a successful econometric forecasting model is that the parameters remain constant. These tests use a hold-out sample to check whether this is true at least over the hold-out.

One-Step (ex post) Forecast Analysis
(Periods 157–168; i.e., 2009m1–2009m12)

Three tests can be carried out, all of which examine the one-step-ahead forecast errors from the three equations. The forecaster needs to specify the data to be used—here, observations from 2009. These errors should, of course, be compatible with the assumptions of constant parameters both within and across the hold-out sample.

Parameter constancy forecast tests:

using Omega, $\chi^2(36) = 58.407\ [0.0105]$* and $F(36,147) = 1.6224\ [0.0242]$*
using V[e], $\chi^2(36) = 51.124\ [0.0488]$* and $F(36,147) = 1.4201\ [0.0765]$
using V[E], $\chi^2(36) = 52.847\ [0.0347]$* and $F(36,147) = 1.4680\ [0.0590]$

These results all suggest some structural change affecting the model. We would therefore search hard to find other variables that could offer a more robust explanation of movements in the price of unleaded gasoline. Possible variables to include would be some measure of the exchange rate and world trade, both of which could offer a fuller explanation of movements in the price of crude oil.

Parameter constancy forecast tests (including the Chow test) are conducted by PCGive when you reserve some of the observations (specifying an input in *less forecast* when you specify the range of the model, so, in the preceding example, *less forecast* = 12).

In addition, PCGive conducts another parameter instability test, testing whether the model parameters change jointly or individually on the basis of the full sample (so you don't have to reserve any observations for postsample analysis). This test should always be carried out.

Forecasting

We now use the model to produce forecasts. In estimating the model, we have set aside the last two years' data. The forecasts from the VAR model can be compared with the forecasts produced by the single-equation model we estimated in Table 9.6 and corresponding

TABLE 10A.1   FORECAST COMPARISONS: VAR VS. SINGLE-EQUATION
APPROACHES USED IN FORECASTING THE PRICE OF
UNLEADED GASOLINE (*Forecasts for 2009 and 2010*)

Model/measure	Average Across 24 One-Step-Ahead Forecasts (2009–2010)		Average 1- to- 12-Step-Ahead Forecasts (2009–2010)	
	MAPE	**MdAPE**	**MAPE**	**MdAPE**
ARIMA	4.6%	4.1%	28.5%	31.5%
Single-equation ADL model (including concurrent variables forecast using an ARIMA model)	8.8%	6.3%	70.6%	80.1%
VAR	5.1%	3.1%	5.6%	4.5%

Data: Gas_prices.xlsx.

forecasts in Table 10.8. If the ADL model had excluded concurrent variables then its 1-step-ahead forecasts would have been identical to those from the VAR for lead $h = 1$. For longer lead times there are two choices, ex ante and ex post. Ex post uses actual values of explanatory variables even if these would be unknown at the time the forecast is being made. Ex ante, more realistically, uses actual values of lagged explanatory variables when these would be known and forecasted values otherwise (see Section 8.6.3). Usually ex post forecasts are more accurate than ex ante. For the ADL model in the above, extrapolative models can be used to forecast the two explanatory variables and in Table 10A.1 we've used ARIMA models to forecast *Crude* and *CPI*.

The VAR model automatically produces longer lead time forecasts for the hold-out period successively substituting the latest forecast values for each variable. PCGive delivers both the h-step-ahead forecast based on a rolling origin and "dynamic" fixed-origin forecasts in which the unknown lagged values of the endogenous variables are replaced iteratively by the previously calculated forecasts up to the chosen lead time. The model is not reestimated. For example, for $h = 3$-step-ahead forecasts, a model using two lags would first calculate $\hat{Y}_{t+1}$, then $\hat{Y}_{t+2}$ using the forecast of $\hat{Y}_{t+1}$, and finally the forecast of $\hat{Y}_{t+3}$ using the previous two forecasts. If the model was based on three lags, the actual value of Y_t would be used together with the two forecast values $\hat{Y}_{t+1}$ and $\hat{Y}_{t+2}$. (In a so-called rolling regression, the parameters are reestimated each period, a useful technique to adopt when the system is changing.) In Table 10A.1 the dynamic forecasts are sequentially calculated by moving the origin of the 1–12 step-ahead forecasts one period at a time until the 12 step-ahead forecast coincides with the last observation in the holdout sample. The average forecast error is calculated for each of these sets of dynamic forecasts and the overall average across the 12 forecast origins reported in the table.

Appendix 10B   The Effects of Nonstationary Data

In Section 9.5.1, we noted that modeling the data in differences sometimes has the effect of removing autocorrelation and limiting multicollinearity. However, we need to be certain that the proposed model, whether in level form or in differences, makes sense. Let us suppose we include *CPI* as part of our model of unleaded prices. A graph of the two variables is shown in Figure 10B.1, with the variables standardized (i.e., the mean of the series is removed and

FIGURE 10B.1   TIME SERIES PLOT OF UNLEADED PRICE, PRICE CHANGE, AND *CPI*
(*Log Transformed and Standardised*)

Data: Gas_prices.xlsx; Standardisation over the period 1996–2010.

then divided by the standard deviation of the series: $Z = (Obs - Mean)/Stddev$, as introduced in Section 2.4.4).

After taking logarithms, we see that, for the period from 2005, *CPI* shows steady growth (apart from the wild flucation of end-2008 due to the emerging recession), whereas the unleaded price fluctuates around a constant mean. With such different characteristics, there can be no sensible relationship between the *Unleaded* price and *CPI*. The unleaded price is a stationary variable fluctuating around a constant mean (see Chapter 5), whereas *CPI* is nonstationary. Although a regression of one on the other might lead to an apparent relationship, it could never be used successfully in forecasting. Essentially, a model of a stationary variable has to be explained by stationary variables, while a model of a nonstationary variable requires some nonstationary explanatory variables. (In fact, a longer database suggests that *Unleaded* may not be stationary after all.)

Historically, one suggestion for overcoming the problem of nonstationary variables has been automatic differencing. Granger and Newbold (1974) showed how easy it was to decide that two randomly chosen variables were related. This spurious relationship is revealed by examining the residuals, which will be found to be autocorrelated. Modeling in differences was (and remains) one possible response. Here, the model explains changes in, rather than the actual levels of, the Y_t.

Note that if the theoretical model is

$$Y_t = \alpha_0 + \alpha_1 t + \alpha_2 X_t + v_t \qquad (10A.1)$$

then

$$DY_t = \alpha_1 + \alpha_2 DX_t + e_t. \qquad (10A.2)$$

Thus, a model in differences has implications for a model in levels and vice versa.

Figure 10B.1 also shows the inflation rate (measured here by the first differences in ln(CPI)). In principle, the inflation rate, a stationary variable, could explain unleaded prices. It also makes economic sense in that the price of *Unleaded* will be determined by the price of the raw material (*Crude* oil) together with more general costs in the economy as well as various demand indicators, of which housing starts is a possible measure. However, a non-stationary trending variable cannot be explained only by stationary variables and vice versa. We therefore need to establish when a variable is stationary.

Appendix 10C   Differencing and Units Roots

In ARIMA model building (see Chapter 6), it proved necessary to render the time series data stationary, usually by differencing, before the model building proper starts. Because economic data such as prices or income typically trend together, this leads to the taking of first differences, usually rendering the data stationary. As a response to the relative forecasting success of ARIMA modeling, and as a response to the pervasive autocorrelation experienced in many economic models proposed in the 1970s, economic models were developed, almost automatically, in differenced data.

But automatically differencing the data was an ad hoc procedure, and if the error term v_t in equation (10A.1) was independent, then e_t in equation (10A.2) could not be, and vice versa, so the procedure itself might induce autocorrelation. What was needed were more rigorous procedures.

We now proceed to explain a method by which a variable can be tested for stationarity. We first consider the simple autoregressive model with a one-period lag:

$$Y_t = \gamma Y_{t-1} + e_t. \tag{10A.3}$$

Suppose for the moment that $\gamma > 0$. Then, as we discussed in Chapter 6, if the model is to make any sense, then $\gamma \leq 1$. Otherwise the model is explosive (i.e., $EY_{t+n} = \gamma^n EY_t$, which will increase exponentially). Two distinct alternatives now occur: $\gamma < 1$, in which case the observations tend toward zero, rapidly if γ is small and Y_t is stationary; and $\gamma = 1$ when there is no tendency to zero and the series appears to move up and down aimlessly (see Figure 6.12). This gives the equation $DY_t \equiv Y_t - Y_{t-1} = e_t$. The series Y_t is then said to possess a unit root and is not stationary, whereas DY_t is. We can write equation 10A.3 as

$$DY_t = (\gamma - 1)Y_{t-1} + e_t, \tag{10A.4}$$

and a test of $\gamma - 1 = 0$, or whether Y_t possesses a unit root, was proposed by Dickey and Fuller; see Fuller (1996) for details. The test statistic is $(\hat{\gamma} - 1)/(Std.\ error\ \hat{\gamma})$, but because it does not have the usual t-distribution, special tables were produced to perform the test. A key characteristic is that rejection of the null hypothesis implies that Y_t is stationary. As a consequence, failure to reject the null hypothesis tells us that the series *might* have a unit root. This in turn leads to other possibilities, involving the following equations:

Added constant: $$Y_t = \alpha + \gamma Y_{t-1} + e_t \tag{10A.5}$$

Added constant and linear trend: $$Y_t = \alpha + \beta t + \gamma Y_{t-1} + e_t \tag{10A.6}$$

In each equation, the test statistic looks like a t statistic based upon $(\gamma - 1)$, but each test statistic requires special tables; see Fuller (1996).

TABLE 10C.1   THE RESULTS FROM AN AUGMENTED DICKEY–FULLER (ADF) TEST FOR THE STATIONARITY OF LN(CRUDE)

Null Hypothesis: LNCRUDE has a unit root
Exogenous: Constant, Linear Trend
Lag Length: 1 (Automatic - based on SIC, maxlag = 12)

		t-Statistic	Prob.*
Augmented Dickey-Fuller test statistic		−1.962199	0.6098
Test critical values:	1% level	−4.115684	
	5% level	−3.485218	
	10% level	−3.170793	

*One-sided *P*-values.
Data: Gas_prices.xlsx.

Why should we have to consider all three versions? The reason is that the tests are not particularly powerful (i.e., we all too often accept the null hypothesis when the alternative is true). We will therefore all too rarely reject the null hypothesis of a unit root to detect a stationary series.

These tests are all typically included in more advanced econometric software. For example, to test whether ln(*Crude*) is nonstationary (see Table 10C.1), we can use PCGive or EViews7. The actual equations that are estimated are augmented by the addition of a user-specified number of lags. (The test is called the augmented Dickey–Fuller test.) We first need to specify which of the three tests we wish to examine.

As we see, with both a constant and a trend term included, the unit root test accepts the null hypothesis of a unit root. Testing the other two options—no constant and just a constant without any trend—also suggests that the series is nonstationary. A problem arises, however, if the tests are contradictory. One strategy is to follow Elder and Kennedy (2001), who recommend (as we do) thinking about your data—first plotting it, but also using your knowledge of what makes the time series behave as it does. From theory and a plot of the data, three cases are possible:

a. Y_t is growing (or shrinking) in the long run. Then
  – Estimate equation (10A.6) with the trend term, and test for unit roots. Either there is a unit root $\gamma = 1$, but no time trend, but with α nonzero to create the observed growth; or there is no unit root, but there is a time trend $\beta \neq 0$. We can use a *t*-test of $\gamma = 1$ to distinguish between these two alternatives.

b. Y_t is not growing (or shrinking) in the long run. Then
  – Estimate equation (10A.5), omitting the trend term. Either there is a unit root, but $\alpha = 0$; or there is no unit root and α is nonzero. Again, conduct a *t*-test for $\gamma = 1$ to distinguish between these two alternatives.

c. We are unclear as to Y_t's growth pattern.
  – This is a more complicated story, and if the forecaster faces such a problem, we recommend checking Elder and Kennedy (2001).

One effective and quite simple alternative implementation is due to Harvey, Leybourne, and Taylor (2009), who propose using equation (10A.4) and conducting the test (i) on the series for which the mean has been removed (i.e., where the average $\overline{Y}$ is subtracted from each observation) and (ii) on the series for which the mean and the trend have been removed (i.e., where the OLS estimates of $Y_t - (\alpha + \beta t)$ are used in the ADF test). The original series is accepted as stationary if either of these tests rejects the null hypothesis.

Now, how does unit root testing affect how we build econometric models? Consider the model in which both Y and X are nonstationary:

$$Y_t = \beta_0 + \beta_1 X_t + \beta_2 X_{t-1} + \gamma Y_{t-1} + e_t. \tag{10A.7}$$

Modeled in differences, the equation is

$$DY_t = \alpha_0 + \alpha_1 DX_t + v_t. \tag{10A.8}$$

Note also that equation (10A.8) is a constrained dynamic regression with $\gamma = 1$ and $\alpha_2 = -\beta_2 = \beta_1$. These constraints can and should be tested for, rather than just assumed (see Hendry and Mizon, 1978).

> Do not automatically model in first differences.

Allen and Fildes (2001) give some insight into how best to carry out the tests of the constraints. The key issue is whether all this matters very much for forecasting. Here, unfortunately, the jury is still out, but we summarize the recommendations from the literature as follows:

> ### Testing for Stationarity and Forecasting
>
> Test dependent and explanatory variables for stationarity:
>
> - If variables are stationary, model in levels.
> - Include sufficient lags to remove autocorrelation.
> - If the dependent variable is nonstationary, model in differences, removing residual autocorrelation by including lags.
> - Compare the forecasting accuracy of the model in differences with the model in levels whilst requiring interpretability of the model finally selected.

We take these recomendations further in Appendixes 10D and 10E.

Appendix 10D   Introduction to Cointegration

Consider a possible (linear) relationship between two variables X and Y: $Y = \alpha + \beta X + \varepsilon$. If X is stationary and Y is nonstationary, then ε cannot be stationary. Similarly, if X is nonstationary and Y is stationary, then ε cannot be stationary. Essentially, the equation does not "balance". Of course, if X and Y are both stationary, then ε will be stationary and the normal regression methodology can be implemented. However, there is an important fourth case: where both X and Y are nonstationary. There are then two possibilities: (i) the error is nonstationary; this is the case of spurious regressions discussed in Appendix 10B. (ii) the error is stationary (a situation that arises fairly frequently in economics). In this case, we describe the variables as *cointegrated*.

> ### Cointegration
>
> Two nonstationary I(1) variables X and Y are said to be *cointegrated* if $\{Y - (\alpha + \beta X)\}$ is stationary.
>
> N.B. An I(1) variable is stationary in its first difference (see Section 6.3.3).

Using a comparison of a drunk walking with her dog, Murray (1994) offered an intuitive explanation: Like the drunk and the dog, the variables meander about (the short-term effect), but the dog never strays too far from its mistress (the long-term effect).

Using the gas prices example, let us examine the relationship between crude oil price (*Crude*) and *Unleaded*. Figure 10D.1 shows a graph of the two variables, with each observation standardized (around a mean of 2).

An important point to note is that we would expect there to be a relationship between the two: Unleaded prices depend on the price the distributor must pay for the crude oil. Sure enough, a regression of the standardized variables, *Unleaded* against *Crude*, delivers a slope estimate of 0.98, which, based on a conventional *t*-test, is highly significant. (Note that such a test would most often be invalidated because the error term does not conform to the regression assumptions.) Taking logs and applying the ADF tests of Appendix 10C shows the residuals to be stationary. The two variables can therefore be considered to be cointegrated.

In the previous discussions of how we might develop a model for *Unleaded*, we didn't concern ourselves directly with the stationarity or otherwise of the variables we included. However, in the discussions, we noted that a number of the first-order lagged coefficients were close to 1 (see Table 10.13) and that we should therefore consider a constrained model with some variables included in first differences. This can be best be seen by starting with the equation

$$Y_t = \alpha^* + \lambda^* Y_{t-1} + \beta_1^* X_t + \beta_2^* X_{t-1} + \varepsilon_t,$$

FIGURE 10D.1   AN EXAMPLE OF COINTEGRATED SERIES: UNLEADED PRICES AND CRUDE OIL PRICES

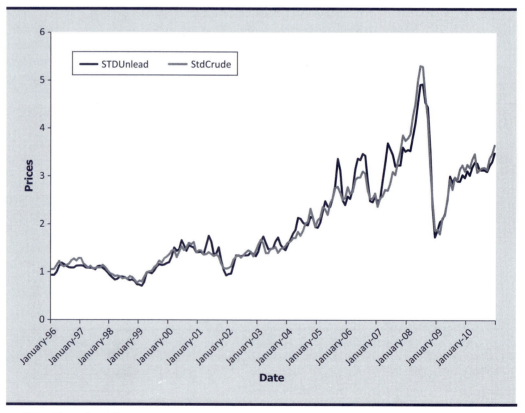

Data: Gas_prices.xlsx.

or, in first differences,

$$DY_t = \alpha^* - (1 - \lambda^*)Y_{t-1} + \beta_1^* DX_t - (\beta_1^* - \beta_2^*)X_{t-1} + \varepsilon_t, \qquad (10A.9)$$

We can see that the first-difference model is just a constrained form of the general model with $\lambda^* = 1$ and $\beta_1^* = \beta_2^*$.

Engle and Granger (1987) showed that when there is a cointegrating relationship between Y and X, their relationship can be expressed as

$$DY_t = \alpha + \lambda e_{t-1} + \varphi DX_t + v_t, \qquad (10A.10)$$

where

$$e_{t-1} = Y_{t-1} - (\beta_0 + \beta_1 X_{t-1}).$$

The equilibrium value of Y (for an unchanged X with $DX_t = 0$) is $\beta_0 + \beta_1 X$. Essentially, e_{t-1} represents the disequilibrium in the previous period between Y and its expected value. The parameter λ must be negative and $\lambda^* \leq 1$, because otherwise Y_t would automatically increase above Y_{t-1} when Y_{t-1} was above its expected value (i.e., Y_t could not be stationary). It is worth noting that equation (10A.9) has four parameters whereas equation (10A.10) has only three. That is, *cointegration implies cross-equation parameter constraints.* In the simplest approach, due to Engle and Granger (1987), the constraint is imposed by regressing Y on X (in a separate equation) and obtaining estimates of e_{t-1} that are used to replace Y_{t-1} and X_{t-1} in equation 10A.10.

In a vector system, X can be defined similarly to the way it is defined in equation (10A.9), which leads to equations similar to equation (10A.10) for DX and with the same long-term relationship. The implication is that in the vector system the cointegrated model leads to constrained estimators of the more general autoregressive distributed lagged model.

Equation (10A.9) usually is extended to include more than a single-period lag. Specialized computer programs are available to estimate such *Error (or Equilibrium) Correction Models (ECMs)*. The two programs we have considered here, PCGive and EViews7, offer the user the ability to estimate such models as equation (10A.10) and use the resulting parameter estimates to produce forecasts. Because the equations include just lagged values, they require exactly the same inputs as do the unconstrained VAR models we considered in Section 10.5.

The same ideas apply when there are more than two nonstationary variables. In this case, Johansen (1988) developed a test that can be applied to cover the case of more than one cointegrating relationship. First, the number of cointegrating vectors that are significant is tested. The crucial thing to remember is that including cointegrating relationships in the model has the effect of constraining its parameters. (A detailed examination is beyond the scope of this text, but see Enders, 2010, for a fuller discussion.)

Why might cointegration matter in forecasting? First, the interpretation of an equation is always important, and equations (10A.9) and (10A.10) offer the neat interpretation of the existence of a long-term equilibrium relationship between Y and X, as well as short-term movements in the series. A model that is expressed just in differences cannot capture the long-term development of a series.

Discussion Question   *Why does a model that is expressed solely in differences, such as equation (10A.8), fail to capture the long-term development of Y?*

Equation (10A.8), a model expressed in differences, is, as we noted, a strongly constrained version of the general autoregressive distributed lag (ADL) model. In fact, it turns out that it is also a constrained version of the ECM, which in turn is a constrained version of the general ADL model.

Discussion Question *Wouldn't it be much easier and just as effective if we simply estimated the ADL model?*

In developing an econometric forecasting model, imposing constraints justified by the data leads to a model with fewer parameters that are therefore estimated more efficiently (with tighter bounds on their standard deviations). In turn, this model leads to tighter prediction intervals. So, yes, imposing justifiable constraints will theoretically lead to better forecasts. But there is always the doubt that, despite the statistical testing, the constraints aren't justified. The empirical evidence (summarized by Allen and Fildes, 2005) is not strong. But overall, it seems that imposing valid constraints generally leads to improved forecasts.

Appendix 10E Modeling with Nonstationary Data: A Summary

When the variable to be forecast is nonstationary, the forecaster would benefit from having a clear path to determining the appropriate specification for the model. Current econometric text-books are of relatively little help and often contradictory in their recommendations, as Allen and Fildes (2005) have explained. With a view to deciding among the alternative approaches, Figure 10E.1 illustrates a number of different strategies that have been recommended in various texts.

FIGURE 10E.1 MODEL SELECTION STRATEGIES FOR NONSTATIONARY VARIABLES

Source: From Allen and Fildes, 2005.

TABLE 10E.1   FORECASTING COMPARISONS OF UNLEADED PRICES FOR THE ECM MODEL

	(Forecast Period, 2007–2008; 1–12 Step-Ahead Forecasts)					
	2007m1–2007m12		2008m1–2008m12		2007–2008 Average Performance	
Period Model	**MAPE**	**MdAPE**	**MAPE**	**MdAPE**	**MAPE**	**MdAPE**
Unrestricted ADL model including contemporaneous variables	15.3%	16.5%	21.6%	15.1%	18.45%	15.80%
Unrestricted VAR model	11.3%	10.8%	22.2%	12.2%	16.75%	11.50%
VAR model in stationary variables	16.6%	18.0%	22.9%	19.5%	19.75%	18.75%
VECM model	13.6%	13.8%	22.0%	15.0%	17.80%	14.40%

© Cengage Learning 2013.

After summarizing the evidence, Allen and Fildes argue for a strategy that first tests for stationarity and then attempts to identify cointegrating restrictions.

Here, we compare the results from the following models:

(i) An unrestricted model of *Unleaded* (with *CPI* and *Crude* the explanatory variables), taking logarithms of all variables. Forecasts of the *CPI* and *Crude* were obtained through an ARIMA model.

(ii) An unrestricted VAR model.

(iii) A VAR model with variables transformed to stationarity.

(iv) A vector ECM model.

Table 10E.1 presents only very limited results: the 1–12-step-ahead forecasts for the years 2007 and 2008. We leave it as an exercise for the reader to carry out the calculations for 2009 and 2010.

Although in this particular case the unrestricted VAR performs the best of the four variants, the forecaster needs to bear in mind that, overall, the ECM model outperforms the VAR model with stationary variables—but the margin is small, and certainly the latter model is the easier to operationalize. It is also easy to compare the constrained model with the unconstrained model, so this is a sensible practice to adopt.

CHAPTER 11

Judgment-Based Forecasts

CONTENTS

They couldn't hit an elephant at this dist. . . .

—Last words of General John B. Sedgwick at the Battle of Spotsylvania, 1864.

Introduction

In our introduction to forecasting in Chapter 1, we drew a distinction between forecasts based upon the judgments of individuals and those based upon quantitative analysis. Most of this book has been taken up with a discussion of quantitative approaches to forecasting, yet companies continue to report that the bulk of their forecasting operations are based upon judgments made by their managers.[1] Is the current emphasis by companies appropriate? Should forecasting books devote most of their pages to quantitative methods, as we and many others have done? Before rushing to answer this question, we need to look more closely at the role of judgment in forecasting. Thus, in this chapter we describe various judgmental methods and then attempt an assessment of the relative strengths of the different approaches. We should note that *all* forecasting methods contain judgmental elements, so, in some respects, the choice is one of degree rather than an absolute difference. The choice between adopting a quantitative approach or relying on judgment will also reflect the availability of data, but the choice should not be the result of managerial ignorance of the relative strengths and weaknesses of these two approaches!

The forecasting literature uses various terms to describe the two basic approaches to forecasting. Forecasting based on individual judgments is also known as *managerial*, *subjective*, or *qualitative* forecasting (although researchers sometimes use these terms slightly differently). Likewise, quantitative forecasts are also labeled as *statistical*. We employ the following formal definitions:

Judgmental or Quantitative Forecasting

Judgmental forecasting: The process of producing forecasts based on combining information and the subjective beliefs of individuals. The integration may be made informally or through a structured process. The forecast may also be obtained by aggregating the subjective forecasts of a number of individuals.

Quantitative forecasting: Forecasting based on the application of a prescribed explicit analysis of numerically coded data. This kind of forecasting may be *causal*, *extrapolative*, or a blend of both.

It is also useful to distinguish the *forecaster* from the *user* of the forecasts. The forecaster generates the forecasts, whereas the user employs the results in planning and decision making. The two functions may be performed by the same individual, but the distinction serves to emphasize that they are separate functions. When the same individual or group does both activities, considerable care must be taken to ensure that that the resulting forecasts indicate what is *likely* to happen, not what the forecaster/user would *like* to happen. Sales *targets* describe what management would like to achieve, whereas sales *forecasts* should describe likely outcomes.[2] By contrast, when the two functions are performed by separate individuals or groups, it is important to maintain proper communication between them, a point to which we return in Chapter 13.

Forecasting, Plans and Targets

Forecasts should represent the most likely (or expected) value.

Plans are a response by the organization to its forecasts in order to move toward its objectives.

Targets represent estimates of what might be achieved. A realistic target should therefore be based on the corresponding forecast.

---

[1] See, for example, the reports of surveys by Dalrymple (1987), Sanders and Manrodt (1994), and Table 13.1 taken from McCarthy, Davis, Golicic, and Mentzer (2006).

[2] Every sports team or individual has the target of winning a championship. Clearly, forecasts recognize that only one winner will emerge, a reality reflected in bookmakers' odds.

In Section 11.1, we consider the two approaches of judgmental and quantitative forecasting and suggest circumstances in which one may have advantages over the other. Then, in Section 11.2, we examine several judgmental methods and outline their relative strengths and weaknesses. In Section 11.3, we move on to look at the Delphi method, which has become increasingly popular with the widespread use of personal computers and which overcomes some of the criticisms leveled at other judgmental methods. Some methods require the assessment of probabilities, a topic that we consider in Section 11.4. On occasion, completely distinct situations may arise (e.g., war and peace) that call for quite different contingent forecasts; we may then use scenario analysis and role-playing, the subjects of Section 11.5. Prediction markets are the topic of Section 11.6; such markets represent a different way of obtaining subjective forecasts from a group of individuals. We conclude the chapter with a general summary and an analysis of some useful principles that underlie effective judgmental forecasting.

 ## 11.1 Judgmental or Quantitative Forecasting?

The distinction between judgmental and quantitative forecasts is perhaps most easily seen in the following example.

EXAMPLE 11.1 ■ Two approaches to sales forecasting

Suppose that we wish to forecast the demand for a particular type of refrigerator in a department store. A quantitative forecast might be based upon simple exponential smoothing, as introduced in Section 3.3. A judgmental forecast might be provided by the store manager, upon the basis of her past experience. Which forecast is better? The store manager may well be setting a target rather than stating a forecast, or she may be thinking about inventory levels and wishing to make sure that demand can be met. In contrast, she may have reasons to expect higher demand because of external factors that are not reflected in the simple exponential smoothing estimate. Given sufficient time and effort, she might well arrive at accurate forecasts for every unit the store has in stock, but such an activity would probably not be a valuable use of her time.   ■

From this example, it is evident that a number of factors must be taken into account in deciding upon the type of forecast to use. Table 11.1 provides a summary of the pros and cons.

The weaknesses listed in the table are often captured in the phrase "heuristics and biases," due to Tversky and Kahneman (1974). The words describe the deficiencies and, to a certain extent, the strengths of judgmental forecasting. In essence, the judgmental forecaster uses various simple mental strategies or heuristics to produce the forecast, and these are often deficient in predictable ways.

Heuristics and Biases in Judgmental Forecasting

Forecasters succumb to:

1. An *availability bias*, wherein the forecaster relies on easily available and memorable information.
2. The *representativeness heuristic*, in which the forecaster matches a situation to a similar earlier event without taking into account its frequency of occurrence.
3. The *anchoring and adjustment heuristic*, whereby the forecaster uses (anchors onto) an initial value such as the last observation and then adjusts the value to give a revised forecast.
4. *Overconfidence* in their beliefs as to the accuracy of their forecasts.

TABLE 11.1 COMPARISON OF JUDGMENTAL AND QUANTITATIVE FORECASTS

Forecasts	Strengths	Weaknesses
Judgmental	• Responsive to latest changes in environment • Can include inside information • Can compensate for one-time or unusual events • Forecaster "owns" the resulting forecast	• Human cognitive limitations (e.g., limited attention span, limited memory) • Biases (e.g., the desire for a particular outcome) • Possible lack of consistency • Subject to optimism or wishful thinking • May be very costly or time consuming • Overresponsive to salient, easily accessed information • Leads to overconfidence in forecasts
Quantitative	• Objective and consistent • Can process large amounts of data • Can consider many variables and complex relationships	• May be slow to react to changing environments • Only as good as the model used and the available data • Can be costly to model soft information • Requires a technical understanding (by both forecaster and user)

Source: Adapted from Sanders, 2005.

Goodwin and Wright (2009) discuss these and other heuristics in more detail. Crucially, none of these approaches will consistently deliver unbiased and efficient forecasts. Still, despite these damaging disadvantages, judgmental forecasting can prove remarkably effective (see Goldstein and Gigerenzer, 2009).

If we now compare quantitative with qualitative forecasting methods, we see that the table indicates that the two approaches may be complementary: A property that is a strength in some circumstances may be a weakness in others.

As with any forecasting exercise, the PHIVE items listed back in Section 1.2 need to be considered: *Purpose, Horizon, Information, Value,* and *Evaluation.* For the present, we assume that the questions relating to purpose, horizon and value have been resolved. Typically, judgmental forecasts are most useful when they involve unique forecasting assignments where past information is not directly relevant therefore, we cannot use summary numerical evaluation measures, such as *MAPE,* discussed in Section 2.7. However, the same individuals may be called upon to make a variety of judgments, in which case the performance of those individuals can be tracked over time through a forecasting support system (to be discussed in Chapter 12). The information we learn by such tracking may be used both to evaluate the relative performance of individuals and to provide feedback to them so that they can improve their forecasting abilities.

The preceding analysis leaves us with the following information and value questions that are pertinent to deciding whether to use judgmental or quantitative forecasting:

1. *Are quantitative data available?* If quantitative data are limited or nonexistent, a judgmental forecast will be needed, as in forecasting the sales of a new product. However, even here, it may be possible to use information on past launches of similar products.

2. *How valuable is the forecast?* If the forecast has limited value, the time spent on it should be limited also. If data are readily available, we may use a simple extrapolative method, as discussed in Chapters 3 and 4. If not, a speedy subjective assessment will generally suffice. By contrast, when a forecast relates to a major issue, we will want

to devote considerable resources to the exercise, quite probably involving both judgmental and quantitative components. The final forecast will need to be "owned" by the forecaster; that is, he or she must be willing to stand by the forecast and justify it to senior staff.

3. *How many items need to be forecast?* In some applications, such as inventory management, the numbers of units kept in stock can run to the tens of thousands or more. The cost of subjectively assessing each product would be enormous. In that case, the effective manager can operate by using exponential smoothing methods and then looking only at those products whose recent forecasts do not match up with actual demand.

4. *Would the numerical data be available in a timely fashion?* Data may become available only at certain points in time (e.g., quarterly or monthly macroeconomic data) and may not be available in time to make quantitative forecasts for the next time period.

5. *Are there any data that cannot be incorporated into a quantitative forecast?* For example, we may have a perfectly reasonable quantitative method that forecasts the quarterly earnings of a company on the basis of previous figures. However, by the time we get close to the next earnings announcement, there will be information available (at the company, industry, or even national level) that is relevant, but that cannot be incorporated directly into the model. Thus, we would start with the quantitative forecast and then adjust it upon the basis of more recent information.[3]

The issues we have just raised are illustrated in the following example.

EXAMPLE 11.2 ■ The U.S. Prime Rate

Table 11.2 and Figure 11.1 show the U.S. Prime Rate as reported by the *Wall Street Journal*. The data cover all changes from the beginning of January 2000 to May 2010. The rate, based upon a poll of major banks, changes when a sufficient majority of banks (currently 7 of 10 major banks) have changed their rates.

The banks will usually adjust their rates in response to a change made to the Federal Funds Rate (*FFR*), set by the Federal Reserve Board at its monthly meeting. The banks' rate is typically 3 percent above the *FFR*. We know the current rate and the date of the next Board meeting. The slightly bizarre scatterplot shown in Figure 11.1 enables us to see both the timing of changes and their direction. Since December 2008, the *FFR* has been close to zero, so any future change would be upward. Further, the Board recently made changes on the order of 0.25 percent, so we might expect the next change to be of that order of magnitude.

Are quantitative data available? Clearly the answer is yes, but the numbers need to be qualified by the background information just provided.

How valuable is the forecast? For any organization considering major investment decisions (as lender or borrower), the decision made at the next Board meeting has major implications. Getting it right is crucial.

How many items need to be forecast? Only one number is of direct interest, but the decision of the Board is based upon a balanced assessment of employment figures, economic growth, and the competing risks of deflation and inflation. Thus, we would seek to track these factors as well as the prime rate itself.

Would the numerical data be available in a timely fashion? Macroeconomic data are available only with a certain time lag and may not be published every month (e.g., the gross domestic product series is published quarterly in the U.S. and the UK). Forecasters will look for leading indicators such as stock indexes that incorporate expectations about changes in the prime rate. Typically, such activities will involve quantitative causal modeling, as we discussed in Chapter 8.

---

[3]See Bandyopadhyay, Brown, and Richardson (1995) for further discussion of this topic.

TABLE 11.2   CHANGES IN THE U.S. PRIME RATE AS REPORTED BY THE *WALL STREET JOURNAL*

Date of Rate Change	Rate (%)	Date of Rate Change	Rate (%)
3-Feb-00	8.75	22-Mar-05	5.75
22-Mar-00	9.00	3-May-05	6.00
17-May-00	9.50	30-Jun-05	6.25
4-Jan-01	9.00	9-Aug-05	6.50
1-Feb-01	8.50	21-Sep-05	6.75
21-Mar-01	8.00	1-Nov-05	7.00
19-Apr-01	7.50	13-Dec-05	7.25
16-May-01	7.00	31-Jan-06	7.50
28-Jun-01	6.75	28-Mar-06	7.75
22-Aug-01	6.50	10-May-06	8.00
18-Sep-01	6.00	29-Jun-06	8.25
3-Oct-01	5.50	18-Sep-07	7.75
7-Nov-01	5.00	31-Oct-07	7.50
12-Dec-01	4.75	11-Dec-07	7.25
7-Nov-02	4.25	22-Jan-08	6.50
27-Jun-03	4.00	30-Jan-08	6.00
1-Jul-04	4.25	18-Mar-08	5.25
11-Aug-04	4.50	30-Apr-08	5.00
22-Sep-04	4.75	8-Oct-08	4.50
10-Nov-04	5.00	29-Oct-08	4.00
14-Dec-04	5.25	16-Dec-08	3.25
2-Feb-05	5.50		

Source: www.wsjprimerate.us/wall_street_journal_prime_ rate_history.htm

FIGURE 11.1   PLOT OF CHANGES IN THE U.S. PRIME RATE AS REPORTED BY THE *WALL STREET JOURNAL*

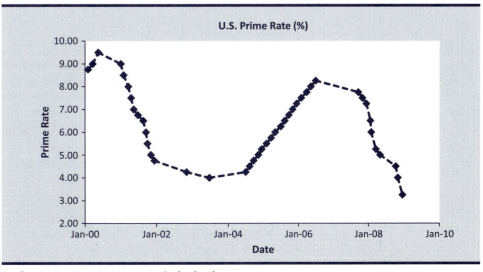

Source: www.wsjprimerate.us/index.html

Do we have data that cannot be incorporated into a quantitative forecast? Quantitative methods rely upon an assumption that the future will, in some sense, evolve in a manner that reflects the past. Although the Board considers rate changes only at its monthly meeting, there is a continuous stream of information on changing consumer confidence and financial and economic activity. A naïve extrapolation based solely upon the data in Table 11.2 and that ignored the background information would be hazardous to the forecaster's health! ■

This example illustrates some of the complexities of judgmental forecasting. By going through the PHIVE steps, we can identify relevant background information and assess the importance of the task. In turn, that knowledge will guide us to a suitable choice of forecasting procedures.

11.1.1   An Appraisal

On the one hand, judgmental forecasting is often labor intensive; that is, it is likely to be an expensive proposition. On the other hand, the judgmental approach will be particularly effective when quantitative data are lacking and the decisions to be made are few, but important. Also, judgmental adjustments to forecasts are valuable when data on recent events cannot be directly incorporated into quantitative forecasts.

When historical data are not directly relevant and potential effects are large, judgmental adjustments are likely to be both necessary and effective. By contrast, as Fildes and Goodwin (2007) point out, "making judgmental adjustments to statistical forecasts is not only a popular activity (75 percent of the forecasts [in their study] were adjusted) but one that is far *too* popular for the good of the companies." A key issue is whether the judgmental adjustment is made on the basis of strong, relevant information. For example, in Section 12.2.1 we discuss making such adjustments when forecasting the impact of sales promotions. In the remainder of this chapter, we will focus upon how to generate purely judgmental forecasts and leave issues of adjustment until the later chapters.

From the preceding discussion, it is evident that both judgmental and quantitative forecasts are potentially useful and that they should not be viewed as mutually exclusive. In the remainder of this chapter, we focus upon a description of judgmental methods. Then, in Chapter 13, we consider good forecasting practice as an amalgam of the two approaches. That is, whenever possible, we should use the best available combination of judgment and quantitative modeling. Good judgment should inform the structure of numerical forecasts, and good numerical forecasts should provide the basis for informed judgmental adjustments.

Judgmental Methods

We now examine various judgmental forecasting methods; there are many variants on these basic themes, and some of the approaches may be used in combination. However, the basic ideas outlined here provide building blocks for more general approaches. In this section, we consider four variants: the single expert, a jury of expert opinion, sales force projections, and customer surveys. We then look at Delphi methods in Section 11.3.

11.2.1   The Single Expert (or Unaided Judgment)

In its simplest form, this method relies on the judgment of a single expert. If that expert is truly well qualified, the forecasts may be excellent. But such experts, if they exist, will be hard to identify. Often the single individual will have certain prejudices that lead to systematic biases in the forecasts. The problem traces back to Plato's discussion of the "philosopher–king." Who chooses the single wise leader (or forecaster) who can enlighten the rest of us? All too often,

the most senior manager may be that person, and, as noted in Table 11.1, the resulting forecasts will reflect his or her personal biases or wishful thinking. Of course, the right person
may in fact have the knowledge and insight to provide superior forecasts; the next example
provides food for thought in that respect.

EXAMPLE 11.3 ■ The successful consultant?

Some years ago, one of us (KO) attended a seminar by a consultant whose basic forecasting methodology was to claim that everything grew at the rate of 8 percent per year. He was
apparently quite successful. My students gazed at him and then at me in disbelief. How
could this be?

One explanation is survivor bias. Were we listening to a wild-eyed prophet who had survived by pure chance, rather like the one person who wins the lottery? Possibly not, and
eventually a more cogent reason dawned. Apparently, he was advising companies whose
forecasting functions resided in the sales and production departments. If forecasts and
targets get confused, the sales force may understate likely sales so that it is rewarded with
lower targets. The marketing team will tend to overestimate demand so that it can be sure
of supplies. A third viewpoint comes from the production folks, who may instinctively tend
to underestimate so that they will not be left responsible for any unsold inventory. With all
this politicking going on, senior management might find the lone expert's views reasonably
palatable. Indeed, an 8 percent growth forecast was probably a nice political compromise!
And, of course, there was rarely a retrospective analysis of forecast errors.   ■

Discussion Question *Identify a current "hot" topic that relies on expert forecasts.
What do you think makes the forecast acceptable and convincing? What makes the forecast
questionable?*

11.2.2 Jury of Expert Opinion

Because of the weaknesses just noted with the single-expert approach, many organizations tend to prefer a *jury of executive opinion* that brings together leading executives with
different responsibilities, such as sales, production, and finance. The advantage is that a
range of managerial viewpoints can be incorporated into the discussion. The drawback is
that forecasts (what is likely to happen) and targets (what we would like to happen)
get confused and political considerations enter into the debate, a topic we return to in
Chapter 13.

If a group of experts with distinct competencies is brought together to agree to a forecast, such an approach can be highly effective, although it can also be costly and slow. If
the group is internal to the organization, political considerations will often prevail. Even
more damaging, the group may operate to suppress dissenting viewpoints, thereby ne-
glecting any uncertainty in the forecasts (or expected outcomes of policy decisions).
Here, contradictory information is rejected in favor of information, invented or more substantial, that apparently gives some support for the chosen course. A recent example is in
the 2003 invasion of Iraq, in which, in both the United States and the United Kingdom,
information on the low likelihood of weapons of mass destruction was discounted. Such
a response, wherein the members of a group of decision makers or forecasters feel that
their predictions cannot be wrong and should not be challenged, is often called *groupthink*. At a less dramatic level, these kinds of political motivations may lead the forecaster
astray, as we discuss in Section 13.2.3.

Such limitations led Armstrong (2006) to argue that, for forecasting purposes, face-to-
face meetings of an expert group should be avoided altogether. O'Connor (2006) suggests
that the purpose of a face-to-face meeting should be to achieve management buy-in but not
to generate forecasts. Overall, the research points overwhelmingly to the conclusion that

the senior management group should set the forecasting agenda and elaborate the key assumptions but leave the actual forecasting operations to a forecasting team.

11.2.3 Sales Force Projections (or Sales Force Composite)

Because a company's sales force is in regular contact with customers, its members constitute a natural source of information about prospective sales. Not only can members of the sales force provide details of likely orders in their territories, but they may also provide information on the timing of such orders. These reports may then be aggregated to produce overall forecasts for the company's operations. The method is similar to the jury of expert opinion, in that it draws upon company expertise and may be applied in situations where quantitative data are not sufficiently available (e.g., for new products). However, it usually has the advantage that the individual forecasts are independent of each other to a certain extent, because, although common information (such as the state of the economy or the company's marketing strategy) should be shared, area- or product-level forecasts are produced independently and thus with lower likelihood of common mistakes. Although members of the sales force may have similar backgrounds, their specific expertise relates to their particular sales areas.

The advantages of this approach include increased availability of timely information and tapping into an information source that would not otherwise be available. The principal weakness is that management may be tempted to use the forecasts to set sales targets; such an action would encourage biased forecasts from the sales force (by reporting a low figure in order to beat the target). This kind of procedure is poor management practice and should be avoided. In cases where the sales force survey is used on a regular basis, regression analysis (as described in Chapters 8 and 9) may be employed and the aggregate sales composite figure calibrated against actual sales so that an improved sales forecast is produced by removing any reporting bias (see Goodwin, 1996).

Discussion Question *Your role as the forecast manager of a company that manufactures and sells machine tools worldwide is to organize the company's forecasting process of gathering the area and regional sales forecast to produce the company's total sales by product. What considerations should you bear in mind, what information would you collect, and what information would you share? What role might quantitative methods have in this process?*

11.2.4 Customer Surveys

From the forecasting perspective, surveys of consumer (or business) intentions to buy (or use) a product or service may be treated much like the sales force figures. Data are collected directly from customers regarding their purchasing intentions, either by a direct survey or with some other method, such as a reply card used to register the guarantee for a newly purchased product. The question whether a potential customer intends to buy a product (such as a new car) within a given period of time can be phrased in a number of different ways. Asking respondents to estimate the probability that they will purchase the product in the future improves the accuracy of the survey (Morwitz, 2001). An example of a suitable question, taken from Morwitz, is as follows:

During the next 12 months, what do you think the chances are that you will buy a new car?

1. Certain, practically certain (99 in 100)
2. Almost sure (9 in 10)
3. Possible (5 in 10)
4. Unlikely (1 in 10)
5. Definitely will not (1 in 100)

The usual questions of validity related to survey work arise: Does the sample represent the population of interest (i.e., potential buyers)? Are the responses a true reflection of purchasing intentions? When such surveys are conducted on a consistent basis over time, biases can be corrected by calibration; that is, we could use the regression methods described in Chapter 8 to relate data on intentions to subsequent observed sales levels. These methods have the advantage of gaining direct access to the views of the customer and can provide information on such intangibles as customer satisfaction as well as sales forecasts. A good overview of methods that use such data for forecasting is given in Morwitz (2001).

Customer surveys can also be extended to understand why people (or organizations) make the choices they do. The surveys are based on data on respondents' preferences and attitudes to the choices they face (such as whether or not to buy a new product), and these preferences and attitudes are linked to demographic characteristics as well as to factors directly characterizing the choices (such as a product's price or its brand). We expand on the advantages of *choice modeling* in Section 12.4.5.

11.2.5 Use of Analogies

One way we all make judgments is to look at the problem we face and then try to identify analogous situations in the past to help inform the current choice. A simple example of this approach is in forecasting the impact of a promotion on product sales. (We develop various statistical methods for this kind of forecasting in Section 12.2.1.) Standard industry practice is to estimate the effect by using the most recent similar promotional effect. Such reliance upon a single analogy may lead to many of the biases discussed in Section 11.1. Further, a forecaster may be tempted to rely upon on a single characteristic to identify the analogy or analogies. Green and Armstrong (2007) employ detailed case descriptions (or scenarios, see Section 11.5) to ensure that all the main characteristics of the problem are taken into account. Effective use of this methodology requires that we identify a number of analogies and then to attempt to capture explicitly all their similarities and differences (often called *attributes*) that characterize the analogous situation.

Discussion Question *How would you characterize the similarities and differences between various retail promotions you have experienced?*

The first issue is what attributes (of the forecasting problem) should be included in comparing two situations. If we wished to compare alternative investments, we might examine their recent returns history and their volatility as well as recent comments by financial advisers. With similar new products, experts might identify the type of product, the availability of the product, and the speed of initial uptake as appropriate similarity measures. It might also be worthwhile including dissimilarity measures: The *absence* of some key characteristic might be important in identifying similar situations.

For most forecasting problems, there will be a range of measures with which to compare the current situation with situations in the past. Some of these measures may be subjective and rely on experts to estimate the similarity—for example, the similarity between boards of directors in two takeover situations where the aim is to decide whether a bid will be accepted. The next stage is to develop a scoring mechanism that weights the attributes to give an overall score. This technique is illustrated in Example 11.4.

EXAMPLE 11.4 ■ Forecasting the upcoming U.S. presidential election

The situation faced is to forecast the outcome of the next presidential election. The attributes shown in Table 11.3 were identified as potentially important. An expert panel identified the factors describing the state of the nation in an election year and assigned a weight to reflect their relative importance in presidential elections.

TABLE 11.3 SIMILARITY MATRIX FOR ESTIMATING THE SIMILARITY BETWEEN ELECTIONS

Attributes	McCain vs Obama: 2008	Bush vs Kerry: 2004	Gore vs Bush & Nader: 2000	Clinton vs Dole & Perot: 1996	Bush Snr vs Clinton & Perot: 1992	Weights
Economy	U	N	N	F	U	40%
Social Issues	F	F	U	U	N	20%
Third Party	N	N	U	N	N	10%
Outlook	U	F	F	F	F	10%
War	N	F	N	N	F	10%
Incumbency	N	F	U	F	F	10%
Unweighted	*	0.58	0.42	0.42	0.58	
Weighted	*	0.60	0.40	0.25	0.70	

F = favorable to incumbent or incumbent party (scored as +1)
N = neutral for the incumbent or incumbent party (scored as 0.5)
U = unfavorable to incumbent or incumbent party (scored as 0)

N.B. The first named candidate represents the incumbent party. © Cengage Learning 2013.

Each factor is scored as *F*, *N*, or *U* depending on whether or not it was viewed favorable, neutral, or unfavorable to the incumbent or the incumbent party. The website History Central (*www.historycentral.com/elections*) presents brief summaries of each election, thereby providing a basis for an individual wishing to generate scores independently. The last two rows of the table show the similarity between the 2008 race and the earlier campaigns.

The unweighted similarity score is defined as:

$$1 - \text{average absolute difference in ratings for the two elections.}$$

For example, comparing the 2008 and 1996 elections, the absolute differences in scores are 1, 1, 0, 1, 0, and 0.5. These values correspond to complete agreement on *Third Party* and *War*, and neutrality on *Incumbency*. Note that these ratings do not reflect similar circumstances, but rather the impact of those circumstances upon the election. It follows that the unweighted average is $3.5/6 = 0.58$, yielding a similarity score of 0.42. Likewise, the final row shows the similarity score based upon the averages using the weights in the last column, so that the entry for 1996 relative to 2008 is:

$$1 * 0.4 + 1 * 0.2 + 0 * 0.1 + 1 * 0.1 + 0 * 0.1 + 0.5 * 0.1 = 0.25.$$

Both these scores measure the similarity between the elections. Other measures are possible such as the correlation—this would be particularly appropriate if quantitative scores are assigned to the attributes.

The final step in the process is to select the closest analogy to that being forecast; here both similarity scores point to the 1992 election being the one most similar to McCain vs Obama, leading to the prediction that McCain would lose. Exercise 11.5 uses this same approach to make predictions for later elections. ∎

Just as with the presidential forecasting example, many attributes are relevant in identifying similar time series, from the correlation to key summary statistics such as the number of outliers and the most recent trend. Meade (2000) offers suggestions, but in addition to using statistical measures, series can often be naturally grouped by their substantive features—for example, the nature of the crime committed (crimes of violence) or the regions of the country where the product is sold (the Southwest). Then, the behavior of analogous series can be considered together, as we discuss further in Section 12.3.2.

11.3 The Delphi Method

The various judgmental methods described so far can all be successful under the right conditions:

- They may be used in the absence of detailed quantitative data.
- Management is more likely to buy into the forecasting process because managers can be directly involved in it.
- Forecasts can be more timely when numerical data are available only on an occasional basis.
- The forecaster has control over the resulting forecast and is therefore committed to it.

Unfortunately, this flexibility comes with some definite weaknesses:

- The process may be very costly.
- Some opinion leaders may exert undue influence over others in arriving at the forecasts.
- Underlying assumptions may be left unstated.
- Information may not be shared, so that forecasts are developed on the basis of incomplete knowledge (even when the relevant information is available).
- Targets and forecasts may become entwined.
- It is difficult to assess uncertainty.

Some of these problems can be addressed by good organizational practice, as noted earlier. That is, we should use judgmental forecasting only for tasks of sufficient importance and use management input primarily to formulate problems rather than to forecast activities. But even with these policies in place, the methods we have described may lead to biased forecasts that lack a proper evaluation of the issues. In the sections that follow, we describe two different approaches that can help to overcome such problems.

The first method we examine is known as the Delphi[4] technique. This method was developed by the Rand Corporation in the 1950s and, for a long time, was used most heavily in defense-related industries. Improvements in web technology and available software have now made the method feasible for asynchronous use involving participants scattered around the world, thereby greatly increasing its appeal. We provide only a brief outline here and recommend that the reader consult Rowe and Wright (2001) and Rowe (2007) for fuller details.

A Delphi project consists of a panel of experts, along with a facilitator whose responsibilities are to manage the operation and protect the integrity of the project. The aim is to elicit the unbiased views and forecasts of the participants without any distortions resulting from personal interactions. The key difference between this approach and a group meeting of experts is that the participants' viewpoints are provided anonymously. Thus, members of the panel usually do not know who else is involved in the forecasting exercise. Inputs may be provided simultaneously by the participants, but this is not necessary. Indeed, computer-based Delphi systems are becoming increasingly common (see Appendix 11A). The essential ingredients of the Delphi approach are as follows:

- *Anonymity and confidentiality:* Ideally, the panelists should not be aware of one another's involvement and their answers should be confidential. Thus, each panelist should be able to provide his or her views and forecasts without feeling any pressure to adopt a particular viewpoint.
- *Controlled feedback:* Panelists will have different types and degrees of background knowledge. At each stage, the project facilitator processes the inputs and sends out

---

[4]In ancient times, the Oracle at Delphi was famed for her cryptic predictions. For example, she advised Athenians to "defend the wooden walls" so that they might win a famous victory. The literalists built wooden fortifications and were routed by the Persian army; the more perceptive put to sea in their (wooden) ships and defeated the Persian navy. Notwithstanding this example, we urge forecasters to report their findings in a clear manner (see Chapter 13).

comments to all the other panelists. (This step may be automated.) Panelists may then revise their assessments in light of the new information and may provide new comments.

- *Repetition:* The process is repeated until the results appear to stabilize. Typically, three rounds are found to be sufficient and often only two rounds are employed.
- *Statistical summary:* The responses from the panelists are summarized in some convenient way. Numerical summaries often use the median (to avoid the effect of extreme values) and a measure of variability (e.g., a group of nine panelists might report the second smallest value and the second-largest value). Particularly with larger groups, graphical summaries are useful. Qualitative summaries of panelists' viewpoints may also be provided.
- *Consensual forecasts:* The final report is often termed a consensual forecast; this does not mean that total agreement has been reached, but rather that the variation among the respondents' answers has been reduced as far as possible.

Once the panel is established, the facilitator presents the members with the set of questions that they are to consider. These questions should be carefully framed so that their answers will provide the decision maker with the information and forecasts necessary to make an informed decision. An important aspect of the process is that a major question should be broken into parts so that assumptions are clearly stated. The next example shows how a Delphi study might work.

EXAMPLE 11.5 ■ Framing questions for Delphi: A new product

An automobile company is planning to launch a new vehicle. It is well known that such projects take five to seven years from drawing board to full production, but the decision on the type of automobile must be made now. We will suppose that the company definitely plans to go ahead with a new vehicle and that it has the resources to invest in only one such model at this time. The strategic question before the board of directors is whether to go for a medium-size hybrid or for an SUV. Direct questions such as "Should we go for the hybrid or the SUV?" or "Will the product be successful?" are too broad and are likely to elicit prejudices rather than any useful information.

The board of directors ultimately seeks to see how each choice might affect the company's bottom line. Forecasts in response to the following questions (among others) may be considered:

- What will be total sales of personal cars in the country over the next seven years?
- What will be the market share of hybrids and SUVs over the next seven years?
- What would be the company's share of those markets if the new product was launched?
- What are the development costs for each project?
- What profit margin is likely on individual sales of such vehicles?
- What would be the effect of a 10 percent government subsidy in the purchase price of hybrids? (Such a subsidy exists in some countries. See Section 12.4.4)

The marketing group could provide initial inputs, such as the total current market for hybrids and SUVs, along with a summary of recent trends and the company's current share of that market. Similarly, the engineering group could provide a range of cost estimates for each project. That is, we use quantitative information wherever and whenever we can find it. The forecasting team would then need to identify the principal factors that have an impact on future demand, such as income trends, future costs of gasoline, and the development of biofuels over the next five to seven years. In each case, some quantitative data sources are available and a preliminary analysis of the data from those sources could be provided to members of a Delphi panel. From the results of this exercise, it would be possible to create different scenarios (see Section 11.5). The final steps involve an assessment of the profitability of each policy under a given scenario and the probability that scenario would come to pass. ■

The launch of a new product is often a suitable subject for an in-house Delphi analysis. However, even the brief discussion just set forth indicates that a considerable amount of information may be available from previous launches and overall operations. The study will have a greater chance of success if the panel is provided with as much of this background information as possible. A useful start-up procedure before the Delphi analysis gets under-way is to ask panelists for recommendations about the information relevant to the question so that an information pack can be produced for the panel. It is also important to note that the last element of the proposed study examines the effects of a possible policy (of subsidizing the purchase price), a slightly different style of forecasting question than the others listed, because it permits the comparison of different policies.

Classroom illustrations of the Delphi process often involve assessments of *almanac events* rather than true predictions. An almanac event is a known, but relatively obscure fact, such as a historical date. With almanac events, the "answer" is always available and the responses of the panel might be examined in light of this "truth." Another approach, illustrated in the next example, is to ask about an event that will occur in the near future. Note that each approach is only illustrative: The real purpose of the Delphi technique is to elicit views on major issues. Nevertheless, the simple example that follows provides an illustration of the Delphi process as summarized in the following box:

Key Steps in Delphi

Key steps in a Delphi analysis (see Rowe, 2007):

1. Determine the question(s) and objectives.
2. Choose the panelists.
3. Circulate an information pack of agreed trends, reports, etc.
4. Request responses to a structured questionnaire by the end of round 1.
5. Summarize responses statistically, and summarize the rationale behind the responses.
6. Update information and complete round 2 of the survey. Repeat if necessary.

EXAMPLE 11.6 ■ A Delphi exercise

Students in an MBA class were given the current price of a gallon of regular gasoline at a local gas station and asked to predict the price a month later. Two rounds of the Delphi exercise were completed, and only limited comments were allowed. Twenty-eight students completed the first round, of whom twenty-four responded in the second round.

The results are summarized in Table 11.4, where the various inputs are as follows:

Mean = mean of point estimates

SD = standard deviation of point estimates

LPL, UPL = average lower and upper 95 percent prediction interval limits (to be discussed in Section 11.4)

Coverage = percentage of people whose prediction interval included the actual value (again, see Section 11.4)

The price at the beginning of the study was $1.96 per U.S. gallon, and a month later it had risen to $2.08. (Those were the days!) One principal feature of the results is the tendency to anchor onto (or stay overly close to) the current price; this is not an unreasonable reaction but may reflect a reluctance to take into account recent events that could change the price level. A second feature is that there is a reduction in the variability of the point forecasts. (The standard deviation drops from 0.07 to 0.05.) Such a closing-in of estimates is common in Delphi studies and reflects some sharing of information. We will discuss the rest of the table in the next section.

TABLE 11.4   RESULTS OF A DELPHI STUDY ON GASOLINE PRICES

Round	Mean	Median	SD	LPL	UPL	Coverage
One	1.96	1.96	0.07	1.86	2.08	13/28; 46%
Two	1.99	1.98	0.05	1.92	2.06	8/24; 33%

© Cengage Learning 2013.   ■

Discussion Question *Demographic changes—in particular, the effects of immigration as well as an aging established population—are affecting the demand for health services, both public and private, in Miami, Florida (or, for that matter, North West England). How would you develop a Delphi study to consider the broad question of the effects of these changes? (RF was involved in just such a study.)*

 ## Assessing Uncertainty Judgmentally

All too often, judgmental forecasting methods generate a single number that is viewed as the forecast. Managers frequently take comfort from a single point forecast, yet the failure to consider variation may lead to erroneous decisions. We need to identify different possible outcomes and associate each outcome with a probability of occurrence. Quantitative methods provide such information in a standard probabilistic form, given an underlying model, as we saw in Chapters 5 and 6. The judgmental forecaster needs to build such a framework from scratch.

11.4.1 Assessing Percentage Points and Probabilities

There is a rich literature on the detailed assessment of probabilities and statistical distributions by subjective methods. We consider only a few simple methods and refer the reader to Önkal-Atay, Thomson, and Pollock (2002) for a more detailed discussion.

The simplest approach to understanding the distribution of forecast errors is to calculate a measure of uncertainty, such as the standard deviation reported in Table 11.4, from the panel responses. The theory of sampling distributions (see Anderson et al., 2011, Chapter 7) tells us that this approach is valid for quantitative (interval scaled) data, but no such theory underpins the use of such measures for subjective assessments. The best that can be said about such measures is that they at least reflect uncertainty among the assessors.

A second approach is to ask panelists for estimates of, say, the 5 percent and 95 percent points of the distribution. These upper and lower limits are sometimes referred to more informally as pessimistic and optimistic values, respectively. Limited empirical evidence suggests that when people are asked for pessimistic and optimistic values, the results often correspond approximately to the 5th and 95th percentage points. That is, in the terminology of Section 2.8, these assessments aim to provide, at least approximately, a 90 percent prediction interval. However, the intervals may afford less coverage than desired, as shown in the next example.

EXAMPLE 11.7 ■ Delphi exercise on gasoline prices (continued)

The panelists in the study described in Example 11.5 were also asked to provide 5 percent (*LPL*) and 95 percent (*UPL*) probability limits; the results are summarized in Table 11.4. The average levels for these probability limits are seen to be too narrow: Coverage across the different groups was less than 50 percent. This shortfall could simply be a feature of the particular (small) study, but the same problem has been observed in other studies. A more general feature, seen in Round 2, is that, as information is shared, the group becomes more confident of its predictions and the width of an average interval is further reduced. In turn, the proportion of intervals that covers the actual outcomes falls even further. Such overconfidence is not an uncommon judgmental bias but makes subjective interval estimates of questionable value.   ■

A more effective way of assessing the uncertainty in the judgmental forecasts is to choose a simple statistical experiment with well-defined outcomes to estimate the prediction intervals for different percentage points. We now illustrate one such method.

EXAMPLE 11.8 ■ Assessing percentage points

We continue with the gasoline example and suppose that we wish to identify the 95th percent point of the price distribution. As a comparison, we visualize drawing a ticket from a hat with 100 tickets numbered from 1 to 100. For simplicity, we phrase the questions only with respect to the upper prediction level.

> Activity A: Draw a ticket from the hat; you win if it is numbered 1 through 95, and you lose if it is 96 through 100.

> Activity B: Set the upper price limit, say, at $2.00 for next month; you win if the actual price is below that level, and you lose if it is at or above that level.

Next, we ask the respondent which activity she would prefer. If she selects A, her choice implies that she believes that the probability that the price will be below $2.00 is less than 0.95. Accordingly, we then select a higher value for the price limit (e.g., $2.10) and repeat the question. Had she selected B, we would have lowered the price. The process continues until our respondent is indifferent between the two bets, and that price is her estimate for the upper limit. The same process may be repeated for the lower limit. The final step is to average the results across respondents.   ■

This process seems, and indeed is, rather convoluted, and getting participation from managers is difficult unless the problem is both important and relevant to them. However, such methods are more effective than straightforward questions of the "What is the 95 percent upper confidence limit" kind. Thus, on important issues, the extra effort is worthwhile. Probabilities may be assessed in a similar way. Activity B (the price of gasoline) would now be fixed, and the number of winning tickets varied. It is seldom worthwhile to try to assess probabilities on a finer scale than increments of 0.10, unless we are dealing with very rare events.

11.4.2   Decomposition

Forecasting complex and very rare events requires special treatment. Typically, the question is multifaceted and the problem should be decomposed into its components, as illustrated in the next example. The benefits of decomposition are that objective information about some elements may be available and, even when such data are not available, assessments of simpler events are typically more reliable. (For details, see MacGregor, 2001.)

EXAMPLE 11.9 ■ Tornado insurance

Insurance companies often offer protection against catastrophic risks for seemingly modest premiums. Is such insurance worthwhile? A tornado strike is one example of a catastrophic event over which we have no control and might consider purchasing insurance.

A decomposition of this event might involve the following steps:

1. How many tornados per year are sighted in my area (county, state)?
2. What proportion of these tornados touch down and cause damage?
3. Over what proportion of the total area is the damage severe?
4. What would the total (reimbursable) cost be to me of my business being wiped out?

Thus, the probability of your business being severely damaged by a tornado in the course of a year can be estimated approximately[5] by the formula

$$Number * Touchdown * Damage,$$

---

[5]For commonly occurring events, more precise calculations are appropriate. For very rare events, the probability of two or more happening is exceedingly small, so it suffices to use *expected number * probability*.

where

> *Number* = Expected number of tornados in my area,
>
> *Touchdown* = Proportion that touch down and cause damage, and
>
> *Damage* = Proportion of my area with severe damage, given touchdown.

Some of these estimates are available from the National Weather Service or similar sources, although the definition of "area" will be governed by the data-reporting procedures of the source. Areas with severe damage may have to be estimated from newspaper reports.

Next, this composite probability may be used together with the cost estimate of damage to those businesses which were hit to produce your expected loss for the year. The purchase of tornado insurance can then be evaluated by comparing the premium with the expected loss. Of course, any final comparison of the damage and premium costs must also take into account your level of risk aversion. Even a high premium might be worthwhile if it allows you to sleep well at night. ■

The final answer from the decomposition approach, though imprecise, will usually be more accurate than any direct attempt to answer the question "Will my business be damaged by a tornado in the coming year?" In sales forecasting, similar issues arise in estimating the impact of various marketing activities. Although such events as a promotional price change are not rare, their effects often reflect the nature of the promotional package, including the advertising, retail display, and retailer commitment. These factors can all be estimated separately to give the forecaster the information needed to produce a final sales promotion profile of incremental sales over the period of the promotion.

Discussion Question *How would you decompose the possible effects of global warming (a predicted increase of 0.3 degrees Fahrenheit, or 0.2 degrees Celsius, per decade) on the eastern seaboard of the United States? On the Mediterranean?*

11.4.3 Combining Judgmental Forecasts

When separate forecasts are produced by a number of experts or organizations, how should we combine the results? Table 11.5 shows results of several opinion polls taken in October 2007 regarding the level of popular support for the U.S. presidential candidates of the two

TABLE 11.5 RESULTS OF EARLY OPINION POLLS REGARDING THE 2008 U.S. PRESIDENTIAL ELECTION

Date	Source of Poll or Forecast	Republican Two-Party	Republican	Democrat	Other
Oct. 8, 2007	NPR Poll	42.5	36	49	3
Oct.15, 2007	CNN/Opinion Research Corporation Poll	45.5	39	52	0
Oct. 17, 2007	CBS News Poll	40.5	33	48	1
Oct. 24, 2007	Democracy Corps Poll	46.5	40	53	1
Oct. 30, 2007	Quinnipiac University Poll	40.5	37	44	

Note: Republican Two-Party = Republican share of two-party vote, excluding "Don't Know" and "Refused".

Source: http://forecastingprinciples.com/Political/pollyvote2008.html

major parties. What should be the final forecast as of the end of October 2007? Some claims could be made for each of the following:

- The latest survey, because it captures the most recent information. This survey gives a Republican share $R = 40.5$ percent. But we should note that such surveys are often performed over several days and may not be published immediately.
- The median for the Republican share, 42.5 percent.
- The arithmetic mean for the Republican share, 43.1 percent.
- An average that is weighted by the number of voters polled, requiring information that is not in the table.
- Some other weighted average that reflects the forecasting accuracy of the different organizations.

This issue is not a multiple-choice test; rather, the aim is to illustrate that even when we can obtain independent forecasts, we may not know how to put them together. Graefe, Armstrong, Cuzán, and Jones (2009) show how effective combinations can be in forecasting the outcome of elections. As ever, a simple average does well, although the forecaster should check for outliers. We return to the issue of combining forecasts in Chapter 12.

11.5   The Use of Scenarios

We might define a *scenario* as a story that depicts possible future events. In this sense, a scenario may be used for persuasion rather than forecasting. Like any story, it needs to include the causes of, and interactions among, its different elements. The box that follows gives a more formal definition. Our interest in scenarios lies in the elicitation of different possible outcomes as a basis for forecasting. Other uses include the development of an organizational strategy and the gaining of acceptance for a forecast or the strategy that it necessitates. (See, for example, Gregory and Duran, 2001, or van Der Heijden, 2005, who discuss these other interpretations.)

> ### Scenarios
>
> A *scenario* is a *consistent* set of statements about possible future events and trends and their *dependencies*. A scenario traces the *progression* of the present to the future through a *descriptive narrative*.

A critical feature of scenario construction is to include the interactions among the different events and trends. With many components to the scenario and even more interactions, scenario construction, as Schoemaker (1995) remarks, aims to "simplify an avalanche of data into a limited number of possible states."

In developing scenarios, various steps need to be undertaken (adapted from Schoemaker, 1995):

1. Define the scope of the study—its horizon, decision points, geographical range, etc.
2. Identify the major stakeholders and actors. Major stakeholders are those people, groups, or organizations that are affected by the events in the scenario; major actors are those who directly affect the outcomes of the scenario.
3. Identify the basic trends (e.g., demographic changes, medical advances, pipeline technologies).
4. Identify key uncertainties, four or five in the first instance.
5. Construct initial scenario themes.
6. Check for consistency and plausibility.
7. Develop initial scenarios aimed at identifying key themes. Name the scenarios (e.g., environmental degradation, peak oil) to capture the essence of the story.
8. Fill research gaps and model (or role-play) aspects of the subproblems to check for consistency.
9. Revise the initial scenarios to focus on key decisions being contemplated.

To be of any value, a scenario must be directly relevant to the decisions being contemplated. A scenario-building exercise should include the major internal stakeholders and actors. It should be internally consistent and plausible. The range of scenarios also needs to capture the key uncertainties being faced in the future ("archetypal" uncertainties, in Schoemaker's words). Finally, a scenario should represent a relatively stable (rather than transient) state of the envisaged future; the aim in its construction is not to capture short-term fluctuations.

It's possible to think of scenarios as the extremes and midpoint of a multivariate distribution that describes the future. Scenario analysts, however, reject such an interpretation: There are just too many possible stories, so any individual story has close to zero probability. Nevertheless, the aim in their construction is to provide a central (archetypal) view around which a series of less compelling stories cluster. Bunn and Salo (1993) have enlarged on some of these ideas and some of the difficulties of achieving a comprehensive range with sufficient detail. The use of scenarios for dealing with uncertainty is discussed in Section 13.3.3.

The step-by-step process of constructing such scenarios is challenging, so we will pass over the topic, apart from offering Goodwin and Wright (2009) as a reference. Nevertheless, there are some pitfalls that need attention. In particular, because scenarios are constructed primarily by individuals and groups using judgment (all too often unaided judgment), the pitfalls highlighted earlier in this chapter remain dangerous. Key issues include the need to overcome cognitive biases. This need suggests that explicit justification (perhaps through Delphi-like interactions) should be required. Also, outsiders should be involved because they are less prone to *groupthink*. Further, judgments tend toward the optimistic, so more time should be spent on threatening rather than nonthreatening scenarios. Finally, we know that people give more attention to stories that are vividly told. But that doesn't make those stories more likely or more important to an organization, so Bunn and Salo suggest that the various scenarios should be "balanced" and similar in format.

EXAMPLE 11.10 ■ Scenarios to gain acceptance of forecasts vs. scenarios as forecasts—Drilling for oil

The Mammoth Oil Company [MOC] is considering whether to set up an oil rig in a deep-water location. The rig is expected to operate with a 20-year life-span. Several issues have already been resolved: The presence of a large oil field in the area has been established, and the depth of the water (and hence the approximate costs of the platform and pipelines) is known. We will also assume that acceptable forecasts of increasing crude oil prices are available. If a scenario is used for purposes of persuasion, the CEO of MOC might paint an optimistic picture for shareholders as he describes profits gushing up from the seafloor to enhance the value of their holdings. The CEO could use the information just listed in support of the claim of increased long-term profitability. In this version of the story, the scenario is clearly being used for persuasion.

Now consider a second version, wherein the CEO is more cautious about the prospects. He might lay the available information before the MOC board and initiate a brainstorming session concerning additional factors to be considered. Factors that might emerge include the following:

- The possibility of bad weather in the area and its potential for disrupting supplies or damaging the rig
- Risks of sabotage or terrorist attacks
- The possibility of an explosion, as happened to the BP rig in the Gulf of Mexico in 2010
- Uncertain growth in the world economy following the U.S. recession of 2007–2009
- Enhanced government safety regulation.

The risks attributable to these factors could be reduced by building a stronger rig, including security personnel on the rig, and using more advanced technology to control the flows of oil and natural gas. Each solution clearly carries a substantial cost, as do decisions not to take action. At this stage, the board would probably pass the assignment over to an internal planning group or a group of consultants to provide a more detailed analysis.

Each potential cost needs to be identified, including the loss of operating revenues, the cost of legal actions, and compensation payouts. Risks to the company's reputation are also important, but there are advantages to be gained from the experience with new technology. The next step is to consider how likely each of the possible events is to occur. Some of these assessments will be based upon hard data, but others will depend upon subjective assessments using the methods discussed earlier in this chapter. The expected costs and benefits of different policies can then be assessed across all consequences following on the decision. Finally, the planning group can report back to the board, which will make its decisions on the strategies to adopt and, ultimately, whether to go ahead with the drilling project. In this second approach, scenarios are used to expand understanding of the forecasting issues and to identify potential sources of uncertainty. ∎

As illustrated by the example, the focused use of scenarios can enable decision makers to identify issues and key uncertainties that might otherwise be overlooked. Used in a structured fashion, scenarios can reduce heuristics and biases. Even in more structured modeling frameworks, the consideration of different scenarios will often be a constructive way to examine alternatives on a "what if" basis, a topic we discuss further in Chapter 13.

11.5.1 Role-Playing

The essence of role-playing is a scenario that describes a conflict among two or more interested parties. The idea is perhaps best illustrated by an example, taken from Green (2002), who describes a situation that he labels "Nurses' Dispute." Although the material was designed for a laboratory exercise, it is based upon a real conflict and the description illustrates the nature of role-playing. Green writes (p. 327):

> The situation was a dispute over pay between nursing staff and management. The nurses went on strike angry that they were being offered a much lower pay increase than management had already given to intensive care nurses and junior doctors. A mediator was appointed by a government agency.

For his experiment, Green used five participants, who were assigned the roles of government mediator, management representative (two), and union representative (two). The participants were provided with a detailed description of the dispute and were told to adopt the role that they had been assigned for the duration of the exercise. The group then negotiated until it either reached a decision or ran out of time (the time allotted to a lab exercise).

Clearly, in a genuine role-playing activity, participants would be aware of their roles, but the experimental approach allows multiple replicates with different subjects so that the value of the role-playing can be assessed. Green reports encouraging results on the effectiveness of role-playing in this and five other situations, when compared to unaided judgment and to judgment based on a structured economic modeling approach (game theory).

From this brief summary, it is evident that a scenario can be developed which outlines various options (e.g., go on strike, tender a better offer), but the role-playing adds the dynamic of interaction among the players. Either side in such negotiations (or even the mediator) could use a role-playing exercise to evaluate the effectiveness of different approaches prior to actually making the decision. The benefit of role-playing is that participants place themselves in the situation facing the various actors in the conflict and this avoids some of the biases that arise with a more hands-off, unstructured approach.

Forecasting Using Prediction Markets

Just as technological developments have simplified the implementation of Delphi methods, improved communications have led to other methods of data collection for judgmental forecasting. These methods are most often used to capture respondents' future intentions (as we discussed in Section 11.2.4). The most obvious source of data is the ubiquitous online survey, although this kind of instrument may be highly unreliable, unless the investigator is able to select the set of potential respondents. When such control is feasible, available software systems can collect and analyze responses with a minimum of user effort.

As with conventional surveys, the quality of information obtained is determined by the survey design, the size and selection of the sample, and the response rate. This last item is probably the weakest link in electronic surveys, because many users tend to opt for a large initial sample without follow-up, instead of a careful follow-up procedure to avoid nonresponse bias. An emerging example of nonresponse bias comes with the electronic reporting of students' evaluations of instructors. For many years, students filled out scan sheets in class, so that most students completed an evaluation. Increasingly, assessments are now done online outside class. Anecdotal evidence indicates much lower response rates and lower scores. (Only the angry respond?)

For the most part, the techniques just mentioned represent better "mousetraps" rather than true innovations. A fascinating exception to this characterization is the use of prediction markets. The notion of prediction markets is not new, but their implementation via electronic access provides a new tool for forecasting, as we now describe.

11.6.1   The Structure of a Prediction Market

Many structures are possible for electronic prediction markets. Our description is based upon the form used by the Iowa Electronic Market (IEM), operated by the University of Iowa and accessible on the Web at *www.biz.uiowa.edu/iem*.

For expository purposes, we use a hypothetical two-party presidential election as a running example. An electronic market is set up by considering the following two contracts:

> *Contract A delivers $1 if the Republicans win and $0 if the Democrats win.*
>
> *Contract B delivers $1 if the Democrats win and $0 if the Republicans win.*

Depending on the purposes of the market, traders may be recruited freely or by invitation only. A would-be trader enters the market by purchasing (or being provided with) shares in multiples of, say, $1 up to a specified maximum. Each initial share consists of one unit of contract A and one unit of contract B. Once the market opens, a trader may act in one of several ways.[6] We consider only the simplest situation, in which a trader seeks to buy or sell shares in one of the contracts, subject to finding someone to trade with and subject to having the funds or shares available. Trading costs are zero and an individual's trades are kept confidential. Thus, in all basic respects, the market operates like a simple stock exchange, but without any brokers. Because the market defines competing choices, such as choices for presidential candidates, the value of the share may be interpreted as an estimate of the probability of that candidate winning.

Do Prices Stay Aligned?   Suppose the price for each of the two contracts dropped to 40 cents. Clearly, opportunities for gain now exist. A trader could purchase both

---

[6]For example, the guidelines for the Iowa Electronic Market state that a trader may perform one of the following actions: "place a bid (an order to buy), place an ask (an order to sell), withdraw an outstanding bid or ask, make a purchase at the current market price, and execute a sale at the market price."

contracts for a total of 80 cents and be guaranteed $1 in return. Similarly, if both contracts then went up to 60 cents, traders would rush to cash in the guaranteed profits by selling both contracts until the total price was back in the region of $1. Thus, market forces ensure orderly operations, provided sufficient liquidity exists, and that participants can buy and sell. The issue of liquidity is not usually a problem in fast-moving markets such as those relating to elections, but can make trading difficult in other cases (e.g. in-house markets with a limited number of active participants).

Extensions to Multiple Options   The framework readily extends to multiple options. If, say, K alternatives $A_1, A_2, \ldots, A_K$ exist, we simply define contract j as

> *Contract j delivers $1 if the alternative A_j occurs and $0 otherwise.*

New traders are then issued one each of the K contracts for each $1 invested.

The issue of *combination* is resolved by using the market mechanism. When the market is open to all comers, the question of *recruitment* is also solved, provided that participants are concerned with maximizing expected returns and are not in collusion to manipulate the results.

Readers are encouraged to visit the IEM website, both to browse historical records and, if so desired, to participate in current markets.

11.6.2   How Might Prediction Markets Be Used in Business?

An electronic market is a suitable vehicle for forecasting when the time horizon is not too distant and the flow of information is sufficient to generate a reasonable volume of trading. The issue must also be of sufficient importance to justify the setup costs. Thus, at one extreme we can eliminate short-term inventory decisions, at the other major issues that may be years away. Although it is not essential, a specific target event, such as the release of an earnings statement, a Treasury bond auction, or a meeting of the Federal Reserve Board (with a decision about the prime rate), will make operation of the market more straightforward.

As with the Delphi method, if participants are to be invited rather than freely recruited, it is important to ensure that a range of interests be represented. As far as possible, no restrictions should be placed upon the traders' activities, although it would be desirable to capture some feedback, such as the final dollar balance for each participant.

One last consideration is the question of who stands to benefit from the results obtained from a prediction market. For example, if political markets were found to sway voters' opinions, those markets could become corrupted; fortunately, there is scant evidence of such problems. Alternatively, if the results are made public, others may be able to make use of the conclusions. For example, at one stage, the U.S. Department of Defense proposed to use an electronic market to assess the risk of a terrorist attack. If those results were made public, they would provide useful insights to potential terrorists on timing their assaults to coincide with a low risk assessment. Fortunately, that proposal was abandoned.

11.6.3   Usefulness of Prediction Markets

Miles (2008) suggests that prediction markets offer the following advantages:

- Incentives to be accurate
- The elimination of bias
- Elicits (latent) views that may not otherwise be heard
- A reduction in the time spent in meetings
- Dynamic updating of the prices and forecasts each time a trade is made (although this property is somewhat questionable because not all participants may be active traders at a particular time).

Miles (2008) summarizes several successful applications, and Gebert (2008) describes the challenges to successful implementation in a pharmaceutical application. Berg, Nelson, and Rietz (2008) examine the forecasting accuracy of prediction markets for presidential elections and find that the market approach systematically outperforms survey methods when the forecasting horizon is relatively long (100 days or more in their study).

Green, Armstrong, and Graefe (2007) and Graefe and Armstrong (2011) contrast Delphi methods with prediction markets and generally come down in favor of Delphi. For the application areas they consider, this conclusion is reasonable, but our discussion suggests that the two approaches are complementary and both can produce forecasts that are relatively free from bias.

 # Judgmental Forecasting Principles

The application of sound judgment can be a problem in any discipline and especially in forecasting. The principles we summarize next are by no means a complete guide, but adherence to these ideas will help to avoid some of the most egregious errors that can arise. (For more detailed discussions of underlying principles of judgmental forecasting, see Harvey, 2001; Stewart, 2001; MacGregor, 2001; and Rowe and Wright, 2001, all in Armstrong, 2001.)

[11.1] Identify the decision to be made and the inputs required to make that decision. We start out with the decision to be made and then work backward to determine what information is needed in order to make that decision. As we follow this reverse process, we should identify the key variables and how to measure them. Oftentimes, we may have to modify our objectives somewhat, because either the desired variable is not measurable or the information will not be available in time. At the end of this step, we should have a clear idea of the variables whose values we need to forecast.

[11.2] Different individuals should perform the planning and forecasting tasks. As we observed in Example 11.3, the area of responsibility of an individual manager may bias his or her assessments. Forecasts are not targets!

[11.3] Develop clear wording for the questions, consider alternative versions, and always pretest. Consider the following two questions:

- In extreme circumstances in a labor dispute, should employees have the right to withdraw their labor?
- Should employers have legal means to terminate lengthy strikes that are damaging to the economy?

The two questions could both be interpreted as asking "Do you support employees' right to strike?" yet the responses may be very different. Even the two terms "withdraw their labor" and "strike" may evoke different responses. Thus, it is important to phrase questions clearly, to avoid emotive or ambiguous terms, and to pretest with individuals who are representative of those likely to respond, in order to ensure that the results will be meaningful.

[11.4] Ask experts to justify their forecasts in writing. If some forecasts differ markedly from others, statements that justify each forecast may help to reveal hitherto unknown facts or different perceptions. Such statements may or may not reduce differences, but the increased pool of common knowledge should improve the quality of the forecasts.

[11.5] Keep records of past forecasts and use them to provide feedback. Past records can yield insights about both the events forecast and the performance of individual experts. This second feature is particularly useful when similar situations are examined on a continuing basis (e.g., new product evaluations or investment opportunities). Confidential feedback to individuals can also help them to calibrate their own forecasting performance.

[11.6] De-bias judgmental forecasts when there is a continuous record. When past records have been kept, they can be used to compare the actual outcomes with the forecasts. A regression of the actual outcomes on the forecasts can be run to produce an adjusted judgmental forecast with all biases removed. See Goodwin (1996) for details.

[11.7] When using analogous situations to produce a forecast, determine the attributes with respect to which the situations can be compared so that a more objective identification of relevant analogies can be made. Analogies for most situations are easily identified, but the various biases in such judgments make them prone to error. The likelihood of error can be lessened by formalizing the comparisons made to identify close analogous situations.

[11.8] Use decomposition when uncertainty is high or when the task is complex; otherwise use global or holistic estimation. Complexity and high uncertainty often go hand in hand, although not necessarily so. As we illustrated in Example 11.8, more reliable estimates may be obtainable when the project is decomposed. Indeed, it may happen that reliable estimates are already available for some parts of the problem, thereby simplifying the overall task. By contrast, simpler issues are often dealt with more expeditiously by a single estimate rather than by formulating elaborate decompositions.

[11.9] When carrying out a Delphi study, use between 5 and 20 experts who possess domain knowledge yet have heterogeneous backgrounds. The number of panelists may be determined by organizational factors such as the need to represent all departments, but such influences should be minimized. If internal politics make the subject a "hot" issue, the facilitator should seek outside expertise. There are extra costs to a large panel as it leads to slower responses and a potentially higher drop-out rate.

[11.10] Continue Delphi polling until the responses show stability; generally, three structured rounds are enough. After a while, panelists will tend to lock into a final answer, and they are unlikely to make appreciable changes to their forecasts. At that point, the exercise should end. Most new information tends to emerge between the first and second rounds, so the changes from the second to third rounds are modest, indicating that further shifts are likely to be slight. Possible criteria are discussed in Exercise 11.6.

[11.11] Focus scenario construction on key strategic questions and uncertainties facing the organization between now and the horizon year (rather than on general questions that fail to delineate key uncertainties). Many scenarios are used to assess the timing of future events, such as when electric-powered automobiles will capture 25 percent of the U.S. market. Careful wording is needed to ensure that everyone is considering the same issues.

[11.12] Use multiple scenarios to focus on uncertainties. The progress of electric vehicles will depend upon relative fuel prices, technological issues relating to the development of batteries, the provision of recharging facilities, and government subsidies. Different scenarios should emphasize particular developments.

[11.13] Develop scenarios that characterize "extreme" archetypes aimed at capturing possible diverse futures. Using archetypal cases allows the range of possibilities to be circumscribed so that it will be relevant to the context of the decision.

[11.14] In constructing scenarios, follow judgmental forecasting principles to overcome the biases that occur when experts forecast. These principles assume that the scenarios are being used for forecasting purposes. If the intent is only to persuade, these ideas remain useful but may not be essential.

[11.15] In prediction markets, the electronic predictions must be understandable, be perceived as important by the participants, and involve a choice of

specific actions. These requirements are necessary both to justify the expense and to ensure that participants are committed to achieving a valid outcome (Gebert, 2008).

[11.16] The number of participants in prediction markets need not be large, but the participants must be active. In-company markets may benefit from their competitive aspect and from personal interaction among traders. Real incentives must be provided. Overall, participants must be convinced of the value of the exercise and must receive some kind of payoff, financial or otherwise. Also, trading volume must be sufficient to ensure timely changes as new information becomes available (Gebert, 2008).

Summary

Judgmental forecasting is valuable when the nature of the question under discussion does not lend itself readily to quantitative assessments, when key data are not available, or when data are available only after unacceptable delays. A variety of judgmental methods exists, including the use of customer surveys, assessments by the sales force, and expert opinions. General aspects of judgmental forecasting were presented in Section 11.1 and several methods explored in Section 11.2. It should be remembered that these methods may benefit from linkage with more quantitative analyses, a topic to which we return in the forthcoming chapters.

In Section 11.3, we explored the Delphi method in detail and found that it avoids many of the problems inherent in other techniques and is increasingly accessible now that appropriate software is available. Judgmental methods were then used in Section 11.4 to provide assessments of uncertainty. One of the difficulties facing the forecaster is the identification of all the relevant issues, and we briefly examined the use of scenarios for this purpose in Section 11.5. An approach that has generated increasing interest recently is the use of (electronic) prediction markets, a topic that was described in Section 11.6. A number of underlying principles for judgmental forecasting were laid out in Section 11.7. Our key lesson to be learned from this discussion of judgmental forecasting is that, in common with quantitative methods, a structured approach to its use delivers substantial benefits.

Exercises

11.1 What is your forecast for the high temperature tomorrow in the area where you currently reside, given your current state of knowledge? What limits would you place on that value, with a view to being correct 80 percent of the time; that is, you would tend to undershoot one day in ten and overshoot one day in ten. Add to your database progressively: today's high, the seasonal high temperature, and tomorrow's forecast. Then see how your forecast changes.

11.2 Examine Table 2.6 to see how close forecasts tend to be to actual high temperatures (at least in Washington, DC, in winter). Modify your probability limits in light of this information.

11.3 Repeat Exercises 11.1 and 11.2 for ten days, and see whether you can do better than the meteorologist. How do you measure relative performance?

11.4 Repeat Exercises 11.1 and 11.2 for a major stock (or index) for ten days, and see whether you can outperform the simple random walk (the forecast for tomorrow's closing price is today's closing price).

11.5 Consider predicting the results of the most recent presidential election, examine the list of attributes in Example 11.4, and add any attributes you think are important that have been missed. Estimate the weight associated with the new list of attributes (weights to add to 100 percent), and complete the missing entries for the earlier elections (justifying your estimates). Which of the past elections looks most similar to the latest election, and does this similarity successfully predict the outcome of the latest election? If not, what factors made the difference? Looking to the next election, make a prediction of the outcome. (*Hint*: Consider *www.historycentral.com/elections.*) Non-U.S. readers may choose to refer to their own national elections.

11.6 [Group project] Consider a set of high-technology consumer products (e.g., 4G mobile phones, notepads, laptops, Twitter). What attributes would you consider important in rating their similarity in the context of forecasting their uptake by the U.S. or UK population? Which attribute do you regard as the most important? Assign weights (adding to 100 percent) to each of the attributes you have identified.

11.7 The numbers of medals won by the United States and by China in the summer Olympics from 1984 through 2008 are shown in the following table:

	United States			China		
Year	Gold	Silver	Bronze	Gold	Silver	Bronze
1984	83	61	30	15	8	9
1988	36	31	27	5	11	12
1992	37	34	37	16	22	16
1996	44	32	25	16	22	12
2000	36	24	32	28	16	15
2004	35	39	27	32	17	14
2008	36	38	36	51	21	28

Note: The 1984 Games were held in Los Angeles, the 1996 Games in Atlanta, and the 2008 Games in Beijing. Russia (then USSR) boycotted the 1984 Games.

Complete the table for the 2012 London Olympics. What are your estimates of the medal counts for the next Olympic Games?

11.8 The Delphi method is often illustrated by *almanac event*—that is, items which are known facts, but likely to be unknown to the panel. Cover the information in the footnote[7] at the bottom of the page so that you can add items one at a time. Update your answer to the following question, taking into account one additional piece of information each time:

Question A: On what day & month and in what year did Pickett's Charge take place?

Question B: In what day & month and in what year did the Charge of the Light Brigade take place?

Provide both point estimates and upper and lower 10 percent points for each of "day & month" and "year." For reference, the answer appears at the end of these exercises.

Do you think that "almanac events" provide a useful test ground for evaluating the effectiveness of judgmental forecasting procedures?

---

[7]In successive rounds, use the following information for question A:

Round 2: It took place in a battle on a hot day.
Round 3: It took place during the American Civil War.
Round 4: It took place at the Battle of Gettysburg.

For question B, use the following items:

Round 2: Queen Victoria was the reigning British monarch.
Round 3: It took place during the Crimean War which ended in 1856.
Round 4: The Crimean autumn was just ending.
         The Crimean harvest season was just ending.

11.9 A group of 26 economists was asked to predict the number of new jobs in the U.S. economy in April 2010; a survey took place during that month. How would you summarize the results and what additional information would you seek?

Number of Jobs Gained (in thousands)	Number of Economists
Less than 100	1
101 to 125	1
126 to 150	3
151 to 175	8
176 to 200	6
201 to 225	3
226 or more	4

Source: Dow Jones Newswires.

11.10 A group of seven experts was asked to forecast the percentage growth in *GDP* over the next 12 months, using the Delphi approach. At the end of each round, they were asked to justify their forecasts and to provide any additional comments they could think of. Four rounds of forecasts were generated, and the results are shown in the following table:

Expert	Round 1	Round 2	Round 3	Round 4
Alfred	1.8	2.2	2.1	2.1
Betty	2.5	2.5	2.5	2.5
Charles	2.7	3.0	2.9	3.0
Doug	2.9	2.9	2.9	2.9
Elaine	3.2	3.3	3.2	3.2
Freda	3.7	3.5	3.6	3.5
George	4.2	3.4	3.4	3.5

a. Summarize the results for each round by calculating the median, mean, range, and standard deviation.
b. Calculate the round-by-round changes made by each panelist (round 2 value minus round 1 value, etc.), and summarize the changes, using the same measures as in part (a).
c. After how many rounds would you have stopped, or would you continue? Why?

11.11 [Group project] Using the software described in Appendix 11A or similar software, conduct a Delphi analysis to generate forecasts for an agreed-upon event. One person should act as group administrator and the others as panelists. Go through three rounds and examine the extent to which your forecasts converge.

Answers for Exercise 11.8: Pickett's Charge took place on July 5, 1863, the last day of the Battle of Gettysburg. The Charge of the Light Brigade took place on October 25, 1854.

References

Anderson, D. R., Sweeney, D. J., and Williams, T. A. (2011). *Statistics for Business and Economics*, 11th ed. Mason, OH: South-Western.

Armstrong, J. S. (ed.) (2001). *Principles of Forecasting: A Handbook for Researchers and Practitioners*. Boston and Dordrecht: Kluwer.

Armstrong, J. S. (2006). How to make better forecasts and decisions: Avoid face-to-face meetings. *Foresight*, 5, 3–8.

Bandyopadhyay, S. P., Brown, L. D., and Richardson, G. D. (1995). Analysts' use of earnings forecasts in predicting stock returns: Forecast horizon effects. *International Journal of Forecasting*, 11, 429–445.

Berg, J. E., Nelson, F. D., and Rietz, T. A. (2008). Prediction market accuracy in the long run. *International Journal of Forecasting*, 24, 285–300.

Bunn, D. W., and Salo, A. A. (1993). Forecasting with scenarios. *European Journal of Operational Research*, 68 (3), 291–303.

Dalrymple, D. J. (1987). Sales forecasting practices: Results from a United States survey. *International Journal of Forecasting*, 3, 379–391.

Deschamps, E. A. (2005). Six steps to overcome bias in the forecast process. *Foresight*, 2, 6–11.

Fildes, R., and Goodwin, P. (2007). Good and bad judgment in forecasting: Lessons from four companies. *Foresight*, 8, 5–10.

Galbraith, C. S., and Merrill, G. B. (1996). The politics of forecasting: Managing the truth. *California Management Review*, 38, 29–43.

Gebert, C. (2008). Prediction markets: A guide to practical adoption in the pharmaceutical industry. *Foresight*, 9, 25–29.

Goldstein, D. G., and Gigerenzer, G. (2009). Fast and frugal forecasting. *International Journal of Forecasting*, 25 (4), 760–772.

Goodwin, P. (1996). Statistical correction of judgmental point forecasts and decisions. *Omega: International Journal of Management Science*, 24, 551–559.

Goodwin, P., and Wright, G. (2009). *Decision Analysis for Management Judgment,* 4th ed. Chichester, U.K.: Wiley.

Graefe, A., and Armstrong, J. S. (2011). Comparing face-to-face meetings, nominal groups, Delphi and prediction markets on an estimation task. *International Journal of Forecasting*, 27 (1), 183–195.

Graefe, A., Armstrong, J. S., Cuzán, A.G., & Jones, R. J., Jr. (2009). Combined Forecasts of the 2008 Election: The Pollyvote. *Foresight* (12), 41–42.

Green, K. C. (2002). Forecasting decisions in conflict situations: A comparison of game theory, role-playing and unaided judgment. *International Journal of Forecasting*, 18, 321–344.

Green, K. C., and Armstrong, J. S. (2007). Structured analogies for forecasting. *International Journal of Forecasting*, 23, 365–376.

Green, K., Armstrong, J. S., and Graefe, A. (2007). Methods to elicit forecasts from groups: Delphi and prediction markets compared. *Foresight*, 8, 17–20.

Gregory, W. L., and Duran, A. (2001). Scenarios and acceptance of forecasts. In J. S. Armstrong (ed.), *Principles of Forecasting: A Handbook for Researchers and Practitioners*. Boston and Dordrecht: Kluwer, pp. 519–540.

Harvey, N. (2001). Improving judgment in forecasting. In J. S. Armstrong (ed.), *Principles of Forecasting: A Handbook for Researchers and Practitioners*. Boston and Dordrecht: Kluwer, pp. 59–80.

MacGregor, D. G. (2001). Decomposition for judgmental forecasting and estimation. In J. S. Armstrong (ed.), *Principles of Forecasting: A Handbook for Researchers and Practitioners*. Boston and Dordrecht: Kluwer, pp. 107–123.

McCarthy, T. M., Davis, D. F., Golicic, S. L., and Mentzer, J. T. (2006). The evolution of sales forecasting management: A 20-year longitudinal study of forecasting practices. *Journal of Forecasting,* 25, 303–324.

Meade, N. (2000). Evidence for the selection of forecasting methods. *Journal of Forecasting*, 19 (6), 515–535.

Miles, J. (2008). A primer on prediction markets. *Foresight*, 9, 33–35.

Morwitz, V. G. (2001). Methods for forecasting from intentions data. In J. S. Armstrong (ed.), *Principles of Forecasting: A Handbook for Researchers and Practitioners*. Boston and Dordrecht: Kluwer, pp. 33–56.

O'Connor, M. (2006). Commentary: Forecasting meetings are really not about forecasting. *Foresight*, 5, 9–10.

Önkal-Atay, D., Thomson, M. E., and Pollock, A. C. (2002). Judgmental forecasting. In M. P. Clements and D. F. Hendry (eds.), *A Companion to Economic Forecasting*. Oxford, UK and Malden, MA and Oxford: Blackwell, pp. 133–151.

Rowe, G. (2007). A guide to Delphi. *Foresight*, 8, 11–16.

Rowe, G., and Wright, G. (2001). Expert opinions in forecasting: The role of the Delphi technique. In J. S. Armstrong (ed.), *Principles of Forecasting: A Handbook for Researchers and Practitioners*. Boston and Dordrecht: Kluwer, pp. 125–144.

Sanders, N. R. (2005). When and How to Judgmentally Adjust Statistical Forecasts. *Foresight*, 1, 5–7.

Sanders, N. R., and Manrodt, K. B. (1994). Forecasting practices in U.S. corporations: Survey results. *Interfaces*, 24, 92–100.

Schoemaker, P. J. H. (1995). Scenario planning: A tool for strategic thinking. *Sloan Management Review*, 36 (2), 25–40.

Stewart, T. R. (2001). Improving reliability of judgmental forecasts. In J. S. Armstrong (ed.), *Principles of Forecasting: A Handbook for Researchers and Practitioners*. Boston and Dordrecht: Kluwer, pp. 81–106.

Tversky, A., and Kahneman, D. (1974). Judgment under uncertainty: Heuristics and biases. *Science*, 185, 1124–1131.

van der Heijden, K. (2004). *Scenarios: The Art of Strategic Conversation*, 2nd ed. Chichester, UK: Wiley.

Appendix 11A   Delphi Software

An interactive freeware program for a Delphi analysis, named Delphi Decision Aid, is available at *www.forecastingprinciples.com*. Select *Software* and then *Delphi*. We may use this software to specify the question of interest and to identify the expert panel. E-mails are then sent automatically to each panel member, indicating the name of the study, the question, the name of the study administrator (facilitator), and how to post an electronic response. The software also provides for subjective assessments of prediction intervals. Once the replies have been received by the due date, the data are analyzed. After an evaluation of the results, the facilitator may request an update from panel members, with the option to provide feedback from the previous round. Panelists might also be asked to justify earlier responses.

This implementation of the Delphi technique has a number of advantages: Anonymity is protected, a diverse panel can be assembled and may respond asynchronously, and overall costs are low because the panel does not have to be physically assembled. At the forecasting stage, the aim is to maximize agreement and understanding of the key assumptions. Based on the Delphi forecasts there can then be a debate on possible policy options.

CHAPTER 12

Putting Forecasting Methods to Work

CONTENTS

INTRODUCTION

Production is not the application of tools to materials, but logic to work.

—Peter F. Drucker

Introduction

Forecasting applications are many and are implemented in a wide variety of organizational settings. In this chapter, we focus on how the methods we have introduced can be put to work in an organizational setting. First, in Section 12.1, we discuss a problem that is common to any organization wishing to appraise its current forecasting methods with a view to improving those methods. We seek also to establish how such an appraisal is best carried out. Most organizations employ a forecasting support system to produce their forecasts. (Such a system is computer based and consists of data, user interventions, and forecasting models.) Next, in Section 12.2, we examine the characteristics of the system and how users interact with it. Then, in Section 12.3, we examine perhaps the most common applications area for quantitative forecasting methods: forecasting to support operations in manufacturing, services, government, and retail. The key features here are that the forecasts are regularly updated and that the data are readily available. Of course, judgment is also used in arriving at the final forecasts. Next, in Section12.4 we are concerned with marketing, where there is a requirement for longer term forecasts that include various features of the market, such as whether the product is new, the competition the product faces, and the effects of various marketing drivers, such as price. Then, Section 12.5 considers how the methods we have introduced can be applied to the choices made by individuals to predict their behavior—in particular, their behavior as consumers. We round out the chapter with a discussion of other key areas in which quantitative methods are applied, such as macroeconomic forecasting. As with Chapters 10 and 11, we include many references in order to justify or amplify our argument so that the methods we describe can be more easily operationalized by the reader.

 ## 12.1   Evaluating a Forecasting Process

In earlier chapters, we introduced a variety of different forecasting methods, both simple and complex (e.g. simple exponential smoothing models, in contrast to regression models and neural networks). How should a forecasting manager with the responsibility of maintaining and developing a forecasting process appraise its current success and its potential for improvement? To answer this question, we need to define the criteria to be used in judging success: It can't be just a question of forecasting accuracy, which we've focused on so far. Typically, the criteria will be organization specific and will certainly include accuracy, but also to be taken into account are the costs and resources needed, the availability of the data, and the speed with which the forecasts are produced. A critical issue is the impact on the organization's bottom line, be it profit, service level, etc. In addition, users often require their forecasts to be produced by a process that they understand and that captures the key features of the activity system being modeled, such as its ability to include the effects of promotional activities and special events. In sum, we need to consider all the components of PHIVE, as defined in Chapter 1.

Forecasts often have a motivational element to them. For example, when a sales force is asked to produce forecasts of its expected sales, before a figure is offered back to the head office, it will certainly be examined for its effect on the target sales that might be set by senior management and on any resulting bonuses. Similarly, the sales forecasts need to be developed prior to the annual budget and must remain distinct from budgeted figures through the year. Whereas the budgeted financial figures depend critically on sales (and associated costs), the regularly updated forecasts through the year should reflect *current* market conditions and may well be incompatible with a budget set months earlier. Budgets also tend to have a motivational aspect to them that conflicts with our concept of a forecast as our best estimate of the most likely (or expected) outcome. In appraising the forecasting process, the interaction between setting targets and budgeting within an organizational setting may lead to distorted "best estimates" that are biased, less accurate forecasts, and poor decisions (Galbraith and Merrill, 1996). This topic is discussed in detail in Section 13.2.3. However, it is important to put in a proviso here: In this book, we assume that the aim of forecasting is accuracy (and authors of similar books assume the same thing). However, in some forecasting situations, the aim may well be to affect policy or to motivate, when scenarios might be more effective (Section 11.5). In that case, accuracy would be subservient to these other organizational demands.

One popular route to appraising forecasting performance is through benchmarking studies, whereby an organization compares its practices with those of its peers. The Institute of Business Forecasting and Planning (*www.ibf.org*) regularly conducts surveys of attendees at the organization's training workshops. However, such benchmarks have to be accepted with a large grain of salt because they have many problems. For instance, their samples often are small and not random within any given sector, and the answers obtained from them are not based directly on empirical data and are probably biased. But if such surveys are to be distrusted, and yet benchmarking is desirable, what is the alternative? In the next section, we discuss how to carry out a benchmarking study through a so-called forecasting competition. The aim of such a competition is to use an organization's own data to compare various methods with the organization's current approach. This strategy focuses effectively on the key benchmarking question "How are we doing?" Answering this question also points a way forward toward an improved forecasting system.

Forecasting competitions are most often used in organizations that are considering replacing their current forecasting software or forecasting process. An organization seeking to embark on changes will wish to ensure that the replacement software system is at least as good as the current system in terms of forecasting accuracy.

In the next section, we will focus on just one aspect of the appraisal: the comparison of forecasting accuracy. However, there are many other aspects that need to be taken into account, and these are discussed later, in Section 12.2.

12.1.1   Evaluating Forecasting Methods: Forecasting Competitions

Most manufacturing and retailing companies need to forecast the sales they expect of the many hundreds, if not thousands, of products they sell. Some companies, such as electricity suppliers or call center operators, focus on just the small number of variables that interest them. For government departments, there is a similar limited forecasting need, although local, regional, and national forecasts of a variable such as unemployment benefit claimants often are required. Periodically, the forecaster needs to evaluate the forecasting accuracy of the chosen method over a number of series and to compare the method with plausible alternatives. As noted earlier, the need is most acute when a new forecasting system or process is being considered.

Carrying out the Evaluation

Step 1: Specify the population of time series to be considered. For a supermarket, for example, this population could include the products sold (in stockkeeping units, or SKUs—the most detailed information about a product, including brand, pack size, packaging, and more) in a number of product categories, such as fresh vegetables, beer, cleaning products, and health care. We may then need to choose a sample from various important subpopulations or segments (the whole population being too large to analyze fully in a cost-effective manner).

Step 2: Define the forecasting task precisely. We can refer back to the PHIVE framework introduced in Chapter 1. The specification includes the information that is available in producing the forecasts, whether human intervention is permitted (or whether the method should be automatic), the forecast horizon(s), whether the method's parameters (such as the smoothing parameter) are reestimated, and the frequency with which the forecasts are updated.

Step 3: Specify the forecasting methods to be considered. The range of methods should include a standard benchmark such as damped trend smoothing (discussed in Section 3.6), as well as a naive method (e.g., random walk). If the data may be seasonal, a simple seasonal benchmark based on decomposition (Chapter 4) should be included. Although some of the methods used in a competition might not be practical for the organization (i.e., they may be too complex), including them in the competition may give some insight into the level of improvement possible.

Step 4: Define the measures of performance to be used in the evaluation. These measures should correspond as closely as possible to those used by the organization (including measures of profitability or service level) and should incorporate both standard measures and measures that are organization specific.

Step 5: Specify the data to be used in parameterizing the methods under consideration (the fit, or in-sample, data), as well as the data to be used in the out-of-sample (or hold-out) evaluation.

We have already introduced various measures of accuracy in Section 2.7—in particular, mean error (ME) and mean percentage error (MPE) as measures of bias, and mean absolute error (MAE) and mean absolute percentage error (MAPE) as measures of accuracy. When we wish to measure performance across a population (or sample), we need to decide what weight to give to each of the series in the sample. Table 12.1 illustrates the problem; in the table, we examine monthly electricity consumption by two households (extending the data in *Electricity.xlsx*, analyzed in Table 2.8).

Two forecasting methods—Smooth and Random Walk—have been used to produce forecasts of the two time series on household electricity consumption. In practice, there are often many more. In household 1, Smooth outperforms Random Walk, whether measured by MAE or MAPE. For household 2, Random Walk is the consistent winner. When the two measures are averaged across households, they give conflicting results. The conflict arises because of the difference in the mean consumption level of the two households and, consequently, the difference in scale of the MAE: 163 compared with 6.6. Thus, household 1 counts much more in the overall comparison when the MAE is used. However, when MAPE is the chosen error measure, the two households are of almost equal importance and Random Walk is identified as the better forecasting method (although the differences are

TABLE 12.1 COMPARING TWO FORECASTING METHODS FOR TWO TIME SERIES

	Household 1		Household 2		Overall	
	Household Mean	939.2	Household Mean	46.3	Overall Mean	492.7
	Smooth	Random Walk	Smooth	Random Walk	Smooth	Random Walk
Mean Error (ME)	−160.0	−149.2	2.59	0.17	−78.71	−74.50
MPE	−18.67	−17.30	3.86	−0.41	−7.40	−8.85
MAE	163.3	169.2	6.64	5.20	84.99	87.18
MAPE	19.08	19.82	13.76	11.10	16.42	15.46

Data: Competition.xlsx.

small). The electric utility company would want to use *MAE* when planning production, but might prefer *MAPE* when estimating consumption by individual customers. (Many companies charge customers monthly on the basis of estimated consumption, but check meters only every two or three months.)

This simple example, of course, generalizes: When error measures are aggregated across time series, the scale of the series might matter, implicitly affecting the weighting given to each series. So, how should a forecaster choose between conflicting measures? The differences can be substantial. In Step 4, in which we define a forecasting competition, we underlined the need to choose a measure that fits an organization's requirements such as profit or service level. In the preceding example, with the aim of forecasting overall electricity consumption, the *MAE* (or the *RMSE*) would be the more appropriate measure because the costs of generation or the marginal profit derived from selling electricity are proportional to the level of consumption.

Other approaches can be used to weight the individual error measures, such as weighting by product profit margin. The danger is that a forecasting method will be chosen that suits only a few products (or time series). The remedy is to segment the time series into more homogeneous subgroups and choose a (potentially different) method for each separate group. As large a sample of series as is practical should be used in evaluating performance, particularly when the population being examined has to be segmented into many important subgroups.

In general, in carrying out a forecasting competition, a variety of error measures should be used. They should all conform to the requirements of a reliable and valid error measure. Key criteria to consider are the following:

i. Sensitivity to outliers in the errors (or relative errors)
  ✓ *RMSE* is based on squared errors and therefore accentuates extreme outlying errors.

ii. Sensitivity to performance on individual series
  ✓ *MAE* can be dominated by large errors because the data values are large, as are those in Table 12.1.
  ✓ *MAPE* can be affected by series in which the actual value is close to zero.

iii. Effect of scale
  ✓ *MAPE* and percentage errors are scale-independent.
  ✓ Relative error measures, which measure the performance of one method relative to another, are scale-independent (for example, *MASE*; see Section 2.7).

iv. The measure's interpretability
  ✓ *RMSE* is not easily interpretable unless it is translated into inventory holding. Most forecasters find that *MAPE* conveys their understanding of accuracy, although relative error measures are also easily interpretable with regard to the extent to which one measure is better than another.

A number of major forecasting competitions have been described in the research literature. Notable among them are those discussed by Newbold and Granger (1974), Makridakis and Hibon (1979), and the M1 and M3 Competitions (Makridakis *et al.*, 1982; Makridakis and Hibon, 2000). All these publications have stimulated sometimes critical commentary. In the last of the studies, the M3 Competition used 3000 time series and 24 methods.[1] According to Fildes *et al.* (1998), key conclusions coming out of this research are as follows:

a. Statistically sophisticated or complex methods do not typically produce more accurate forecasts than simpler ones.

b. The rankings of the performance of the various methods vary with the error measures used.

---

[1]The discussion of the M3 Competition appears in the *International Journal of Forecasting*, 2001, 17(4).

    c. The relative performance of the various methods depends upon the length of the forecasting horizon.

    d. The characteristics of the data series are important factors in determining relative performance between methods; therefore, a method designed to capture the particular characteristics of a forecasting situation may well outperform standard benchmarks.

    e. The sampling variability of performance measures renders comparisons based on a single time series and a single forecast origin unreliable; thus, comparisons based on multiple time series and on multiple forecast origins are recommended.

In addition, the damped trend method of exponential smoothing (see Section 3.5) has proved to be a benchmark that is very hard to beat, so a forecaster using only time series data should always compare performances with a damped trend (as well as a naïve) benchmark. These principles for carrying out a forecasting competition and the general findings just presented suggest that a new method should be adopted (or an established method continued in use) only if, in a forecasting competition that includes standard benchmarks, its performance is no worse than the benchmarks' performance when evaluated across a wide range of series and appropriate error measures. The same principles apply in appraising a new causal method. Here, the forecaster should take care to ensure that the same data set is used in building and evaluating each model.

    However, there is an alternative approach to selecting a forecasting method; we consider this approach in the next section.

12.1.2 Combining Forecasting Methods

Suppose we have developed two separate forecasting methods, each of which delivers one-step-ahead forecasts of Y_t, which we denote F_{1t} and F_{2t}. Instead of trying to decide which of the two methods is better, we can produce a combined forecast for Y_t by averaging the two individual forecasts:

$$F_t = 0.5F_{1t} + 0.5F_{2t}. \tag{12.1}$$

More generally, we can try to weight the forecasts optimally so that the combined forecast produces the best forecast of Y_t by using least squares regression to estimate the weight w in the formula

$$F_t = wF_{1t} + (1 - w)F_{2t}. \tag{12.2}$$

When there are more than two forecasts available, the formulas generalize to

$$F_t = average(F_{1t}, F_{2t}, \ldots, F_{Kt})$$

and

$$F_t = w_1F_{1t} + w_2F_{2t} + \cdots + w_KF_{Kt},$$

where it is sometimes assumed that

$$\sum_{i=1}^{K} w_i = 1.$$

In addition, some forecasters prefer to restrict attention to nonnegative weights, an approach that has some intuitive appeal.

    Table 12.2(a and b) shows four sets of out-of-sample forecasts of call center data: a random-walk benchmark (*RW*), an exponentially smoothed forecast (*Smooth*), a causal model (*Causal*), and the company's judgmental forecast (*Company*). The table shows (some of) the raw data included in spreadsheet *Combination.xlsx* and some of the corresponding error statistics.

TABLE 12.2(A)   THE COMBINATION OF FORECASTS COMPARED (*Absolute percentage error statistics for four forecasting methods*)

		Forecast Method				Average Percentage Error			
Period	Actual	RW	Smooth	Causal	Company	RW	Smooth	Causal	Company
1	32.25	25.00	35.00	44.77	30.00	22.48	8.53	38.83	6.97
2	36.62	32.25	34.45	46.70	33.35	11.93	5.92	27.55	8.92
3	50.52	36.62	34.88	48.98	60.81	27.52	30.95	3.04	20.37
4	43.43	50.52	38.01	46.98	44.26	16.32	12.48	8.19	1.92
.									
.									
18	40.38	42.90	50.45	48.39	51.00	6.24	24.94	19.83	26.30
19	50.48	40.38	48.44	54.35	44.41	20.01	4.05	7.66	12.03
20	47.70	50.48	48.85	53.00	50.92	5.84	2.41	11.10	6.75
					MAPE	11.29	12.27	9.97	11.51
					MdAPE	9.34	12.98	7.13	8.80

Data: Combination.xlsx.

TABLE 12.2(B)   THE COMBINATION OF FORECASTS COMPARED (*Absolute error statistics for the forecast combinations*)

	Absolute Percentage Errors Combination			
Period	RW+Smooth	RW+Causal	RW+Company	All
1	6.97	8.18	14.72	4.48
2	8.92	7.81	10.42	0.20
3	29.23	15.28	3.58	10.29
4	1.92	12.26	9.12	3.49
.				
.				
18	15.59	13.04	16.27	19.33
19	12.03	6.18	16.02	7.11
20	4.12	8.47	6.30	6.53
MAPE	10.37	7.30	9.61	7.02
MdAPE	8.80	6.99	9.13	6.57

Data: Combination.xlsx.

Of the four individual methods, *Causal* performed best (10.0 percent *MAPE*). Combining by simple averaging improves the performance when the random walk (*RW*) is combined with the causal forecasting model (*RW + Causal*) but also when it is combined with the quite inaccurate company forecasts. However, combining all four methods outperforms not only all of the individual methods, but also the paired combinations. The improvement from 7.3 percent down to 7.0 percent in *MAPE* (and also in *MdAPE*) and this improvement is probably worth the extra effort.

Equation (12.2) for combining unequally weighted forecasts can be transformed to

$$Y_t - F_{2t} = w(F_{1t} - F_{2t}). \tag{12.3}$$

So, to estimate the unknown weight parameter w, the preceding regression is run with dependent variable $Y_t - F_{2t}$; note the constant term is suppressed. Using the regression estimate for w, however, does not improve the results much at all in the foregoing example—a finding of other researchers as well (see Exercise 12.1).

In general, the combination of a set of forecasts, based on a simple weighting scheme such as equal weights, produces more accurate forecasts than trying to select the best individual method. This conclusion has been reached in many studies, including the competitions discussed in the previous section as well as the many studies summarized by Clemen (1989) and Armstrong (2001a). But why should combining methods work so well when, surely, identifying the correct method would prove more accurate? The fundamental reason that combining is so effective is that all methods (and forecasts) suffer from deficiencies: Statistical approaches and judgmental approaches all offer simplifications of the system being forecast, with nonlinearities and variables omitted. Even if a method is satisfactory for a period of time, the market or the economy will change, and then the method and its parameters become suboptimal. Each of the alternative methods is likely to contain some information that is helpful in improving the overall combined forecast. In addition, there is an element of insurance to using a number of methods, so that when market circumstances change, one method takes over from another as offering the best forecasts. Ord (1988) provides a simple model that explains this effect.

Intuitively, the combination will work best when the error from one method is counterbalanced by the error from another; in statistical terms, they are negatively correlated. If the errors are positively correlated, they accumulate, which is less helpful. Typically, errors from similar methods are positively correlated while errors from very different approaches have a low or even a negative correlation. Thus, an extrapolative method that exploits the autocorrelation structure in the time series can best be combined with a causal model (that includes some of the key explanatory variables) or managerial judgment. By including managerial judgment, the combination may have access to new information that could not have formed a part of the historical data. In general, however, forecast errors from different sources tend to be positively correlated, even when different methods are used (they tend to make the same mistakes), so the benefits that may be achieved from combining are sometimes limited.

In most practical situations, only a limited number of forecasting methods can contribute to the combination. When there are many alternative forecasts (see Exercise 12.2), it is often better (as in the preceding example) to use them all, although the gains from using many more than five are usually limited. Note that benefits may be derived from excluding the extreme forecasts through trimming (removing, say, 20 percent of the extreme forecast errors in the calculation of the average; see Jose and Winkler, 2008).

When forecasts are consistently biased with a nonzero mean error, combining is unlikely to prove beneficial if the foregoing formulas are used. Instead, the forecasts require modification to remove the bias (see Exercise 12.1(b)).

Discussion Question   *How is the process of combining forecasts similar to portfolio diversification in finance? Why might such procedures reduce the forecast error (or investment risk)?*

12.2   The Role of Forecasting Support Systems

So far, we have discussed how forecasting methods can be evaluated, including the simple method of combining different forecasts, which generally delivers a more accurate result. But how are these forecasts produced in an organizational setting, whether for a manufacturer, in the service sector, in government, or by an economic analyst? The forecaster will often be faced with a multitude of variables that could conceivably affect the future outcome. At the same time, the forecaster may face the situation with very limited retrievable historical information with which to build a formal forecasting model. As a consequence, he or she often does not use a causal forecasting method, but instead adopts an approach through a forecasting support system, as shown in Figure 12.1.

   Here, the limited data in the system (within which demand is generated or other key variables are determined) is used to produce a method-based forecast. The method used is usually based on some variant of exponential smoothing: a simple causal model or a naïve method. The organizational forecasters know more (or at least think that they do) about what's going on with the variable being forecast, such as product demand. In forecasting demand and corresponding sales, this knowledge of factors influencing demand may often spring from a lengthy consultation process with colleagues such as account managers (who manage important customers) and brand managers (who manage the particular brand). In forecasting corporate earnings, the knowledge may originate in the Web or in meetings with industry specialists or company managers. Macroeconomists also gather information about the state of the economy from surveys, press reports, and other sources. In all these examples, forecasters should know how accurate their previous forecasts have been. Drawing on different sources of knowledge, they may judgmentally adjust the method-based forecasts by changing the parameters or even using a different method (the loop between the method-based forecast, the

FIGURE 12.1   THE FORECASTING SYSTEM

judgmental adjustment and the model form). They may even select a different method or change the method's parameters, as Figure 12.1 shows with the dashed line. Or they may combine the statistical forecast with judgment. More commonly, the forecaster will decide whether to adjust the statistical forecast and the size and direction of the adjustment, influenced in this decision by developments in the economic and market environment as well as past forecast errors. The result of these interactions is a *final forecast*, which, in demand forecasting, forms the input into other parts of the organization's (enterprise-wide resource planning, or ERP) information system.

Whatever the forecasting need, the data history, the algorithms, and the forecasts usually form a part of a forecasting support system.

Forecasting Support System (FSS)

A set of (typically computer-based) procedures that facilitate interactive forecasting of key variables in a given organizational context. An FSS enables users to combine relevant information, analytical models, and judgements, as well as visualizations, to produce (or create) the forecasts and monitor their accuracy.

Indeed, many organizations use an FSS, particularly when the forecasting problem is complex and the effects of forecast error are important. Some of these systems may cost well over a million dollars, whereas homegrown systems based upon good forecasting software may be much less expensive. Evidence from surveys (Sanders and Manrodt, 2003) suggests that the most used software in forecasting is Excel, despite its limited forecasting capability and well-documented numerical problems (McCullough, 2000). We hope that readers of this book will by now recognize that Excel is a valuable tool for data entry and storage, but much less so for forecasting. It is therefore important to organizations that they assess the candidate systems carefully when implementing an FSS. Fildes *et al.* (2006) discuss various aspects of the design of such systems. The key dimensions that need to be considered are the following:

1. The forecasting methods
   a. Range of methods
   b. Ability to include additional variables (such as weather effects)
   c. Suitability of the methods for the organization's data
   d. Accuracy of methods compared with current performance
2. Data aspects
   a. Categorization of data (into new products, established products, etc.; we discuss this further in Section 12.3)
   b. Frequency of data and their match to the decision problem (e.g., if there is a requirement for weekly forecasts, the database and the models should operate at a weekly level)
   c. Ability to include a range of variables both hard and soft.
   d. Links to other information systems (such as the ERP or inventory system)
3. Computer interface
   a. Ease of learning and ease of use
   b. Report-writing capabilities
4. Company characteristics
   a. Viability, history, list of clients
   b. Project team
5. Cost (purchase price, maintenance, and consulting/training).

One method for deciding among alternative forecasting systems would be to develop a scorecard with weights assigned to each dimension and each question within each dimension. The systems with the highest scores would be short-listed. However, some attributes of the proposed system would be absolute requirements, and those systems which failed to meet the standard would be excluded from the short list.

12.2.1 **Forecast Adjustment**

The forecaster is usually faced with many factors that influence the variable to be forecast. As Figure 12.1 illustrates, the initial system forecast is produced with an oversimplified model, which ignores some of this complexity. But forecasters and their colleagues know of at least some of these omitted influences, and for those series which are important to forecast accurately, they aim to improve accuracy by adjusting the statistical forecast to take the various factors into account.

Evidence pertaining to such judgmental adjustment is sparse, beyond the fact that manufacturing organizations will adjust around 70–80 percent of statistical forecasts (Fildes and Goodwin, 2007). Retailers adjust proportionately fewer forecasts but have many thousands of products on their shelves, so, in total, the adjustment process is even more significant. The main reason organizational forecasters give for making adjustments is to account for promotions, but other factors they find relevant include weather effects, holidays, and price changes. Other groups of forecasters also make adjustments to their formal models: Weather forecasters and macroeconomists adjust their forecasts, often to take into account recent information not included in their formal model-based forecasts.

But do such adjustments work to the organization's benefit? The first point to make is that they allow forecasters and their colleagues to own and take responsibility for the forecasts, because the adjustments give the final revised forecast an appearance of credibility that the initial statistical forecast lacked. The second related aspect is that there is now a story to be told around the forecast beyond the bald statistics, and the forecaster's expert role gains credibility. However, forecasters are paid a salary, and the whole adjustment process is expensive and time consuming. There is mixed evidence on whether the adjustments do in fact achieve improved accuracy. Such adjustments of course suffer from the usual problems of judgmental forecasts, as discussed in Chapter 11. On balance, for demand forecasting, judgmental adjustments do improve accuracy, particularly in those cases where the adjustment is downward (that is to say, where it is believed that the statistical forecast is too optimistic and there are factors driving sales off course). Also, in those cases where the forecaster believes that he or she has strong evidence of a major impact on sales, judgmental adjustments lead to improved accuracy. But many small adjustments, particularly upward, are damaging. The key questions are, first, when to adjust the statistical forecast (the answer is, only when substantial new information becomes available) and, second, by how much. As usual, both the initial statistical and the judgment-adjusted forecasts should be monitored continuously.

The problem of judgmentally estimating the size of the adjustment can be alleviated in a number of ways. One approach is to develop an extended database that describes the reasons an adjustment was made (e.g., a two-for-the-price-of-one promotion) and the effect on sales (e.g., sales increased 45 percent, sales of a competing product dropped 37 percent). To estimate the effects of a promotion, a benchmark forecast needs to be developed. Figure 12.2 shows weekly sales of an SKU and typical profiles for a number of four-week promotions. Forecasting can be done in a variety of ways, and we discuss two of them here.

Adjusting a Statistical Forecast

Model-based forecasts should be adjusted:

- Only if the forecaster has substantial information about factors that are excluded from the statistical forecast.

Adjustments can be made more effective:

- by developing a database of their past effectiveness and the reasons the adjustments were made, or
- by developing statistical summaries of past adjustments to provide advice on the size of the adjustment.

FIGURE 12.2   PROMOTIONAL SALES WITH A BASELINE FORECAST

Data shown is from file Promotions.xlsx.

The first and simplest is to develop a baseline model using just the nonpromoted periods. A simple exponential smoothing model with the smoothed value updated only in the non-promoted periods is one possibility. The results of this approach are also shown in Figure 12.2, with the baseline estimated from the exponentially smoothed nonpromoted periods. This is done by developing a simple exponential smoothing model on early data with no promotions. When the forecaster is faced with a promotion, the smoothed value is just not updated until the promotion is finished. Once into the next nonpromoted period, the smoothed baseline value can be updated again. (Check the calculation on the spreadsheet *Promotions.xlsx.*) The promotional effects are estimated as the difference between the baseline estimates and the observed sales.

A second method, theoretically better, but more complex, is to use the methods described in Section 9.8 to estimate a regression-based intervention model, incorporating variables to capture the marketing drivers, including promotions (see Section 12.4.5 for a fuller discussion of marketing effects). This approach may involve strong assumptions about the similarity from promotion to promotion, ignoring the possibility that each promotion has its own unique features. A simplified version of the approach is described next.

Using an autoregressive baseline, and dummy variables to estimate the effects of the promotion, we can derive average promotion effects for the period of the promotion (here taken as four periods and any aftermath). An alternative to using the autoregressive baseline is to use the statistical baseline as just described. We have added in a dummy variable for the week beyond the promotion's end to check whether there is any carry-over (positive or negative). The forecast equation is

$$\hat{Y}_t = \alpha + \lambda Y_{t-1} + \gamma_0 D_{0t} + \gamma_1 D_{1t} + \gamma_2 D_{2t} + \gamma_3 D_{3t} + \gamma_4 D_{4t},$$

where $D_{it} = 1$ in the ith period of the promotion after the start of the promotion, $i = 0 \ldots 4$. The dummy variables indicate the difference between the promotional periods and the non-promoted baseline.

TABLE 12.3   ESTIMATING PROMOTIONAL EFFECTS:
BASELINE VS. REGRESSION METHOD

		Promotion Effect	
Period	**Actual**	**Baseline Estimates**	**Regression Estimates**
0	53.50	55.54	53.71
1	53.50	53.29	51.54
2	35.67	38.80	37.04
3	26.75	27.37	25.54
4	8.92	6.36	6.21

Data: Promotions.xlsx.

Table 12.3 shows the results from these two approaches. (The spreadsheet is *Promotions.xlsx.*) The results are similar. (For simplicity, the regression model used in this example excluded lagged sales, Y_{t-1}.) The second column shows the actual promotional effect, the second the effect calculated from the baseline approach, and the third the effect obtained with regression.

Discussion Question   *In forecasting sales during promotions periods, what factors might limit the effectiveness of the two approaches we have described?*

Both approaches suffer from a potential problem of seasonality. For example, many products are promoted around Christmas; therefore, it is difficult, if not impossible, to sort out the seasonal uplift from the promotional uplift. An additional complication arises when lagged sales are significant: There is a carry-over effect from one period to the next (see Exercise 12.5).

The optimal approach is also limited, because of data constraints, with different promotional types having potentially very different effects. As a consequence, there may be insufficient data to estimate the effects SKU by SKU. In part, this difficulty can be overcome by developing a database of past promotions to help the forecasters adjust their forecasts in the face of a similar forthcoming promotion. Once the promotional effects are estimated (however roughly), the information can be collated in a database that contains detailed information about the type of promotion. Then, when making a judgmental adjustment, the forecaster consults the database to identify a number of similar promotions that help guide him or her in deciding the size of the adjustment. This approach has been shown to be effective in an experimental appraisal (Lee *et al.*, 2007).

In sum, judgmental adjustments can lead to improved accuracy. To obtain the best results a well-developed FSS is needed. But the potential for bias remains high, for many of the reasons we discussed in Chapter 11. Providing the organizational forecaster with information such as base estimates of past promotional effects to guide the adjustment has been shown to improve accuracy.

Discussion Question   *Why might a demand forecaster or planner be biased when forecasting sales as growing compared with the baseline?*

12.3 Operations

Short-term forecasts are needed to support the operational activities of most organizations, public and private. Such forecasts are necessarily detailed so that the operational decisions that have to be made can be based on the best possible information about future requirements. For a manufacturing company, this means that demand for a particular product at the

SKU level must include such details as pack size, packaging, and, sometimes, the name of the customer (or the distribution center that will store the product). The forecast horizon may be as short as a few days. For a service activity such as a call center or a government job center, forecasts of incoming calls by type of call (complaints, new business, etc.) are needed, perhaps at half-hourly intervals, to help in staff scheduling. The reason is that the number of incoming calls (or visitors) will typically depend on the time of day, as well as on the regular seasonality arising from the day of the week and the month.

Discussion Question   *What forecasts are needed by a chain of supermarkets to support their operations? By a criminal justice court?*

While the detailed forecasts are needed by product (or activity) and by short forecast horizon, more aggregate forecasts are also required, to support the purchase of new materials or decisions on staff numbers. At an even higher level of aggregation, overall forecasts of sales (or activities) are used for short-term financial management. In short, there is a hierarchy of forecasts needed to support operational decision making and planning in marketing. Figure 12.3 illustrates this hierarchy.

At each level of the hierarchy, various economic and market factors come into play, so, for example, the state of the economy will affect the aggregate demand for a company's products, as will the competitive products the company faces. At a product or brand level, various marketing factors come into play (such as brand advertising), whereas at the detailed SKU level, promotional activity by a retailer and calendar effects such as national holidays are the driving forces. The figure also shows how various SKUs are transported through distribution centers to the final clients: the retailers. The demand for space and transport also needs to be forecast.

Operational forecasting with a forecast horizon beginning from a day (or less) and looking ahead three months (sometime surprisingly longer) is at the heart of an organization's

FIGURE 12.3   THE HIERARCHY OF MARKET DRIVERS

© Cengage Learning 2013.

short-term management. Most companies face a complex problem of forecasting demand (or activities) at this detailed level. Demand is affected by factors such as the economy, marketing and promotional activities, and, often, local considerations such as the weather or the local competition. In Section 12.4.5, we describe various causal models for including some of these factors. But producing the forecasts on a day-to-day basis requires considerable organization. A survey estimated the median number of data series an organization has to produce at 400; however, the range is wide. An energy supplier will have only a small number of series to focus on; a national retailer would need to make many more—in the tens or even hundreds of thousands. This effort requires databases and staff with expertise relevant to the market and an information system to integrate the sources of information and produce the forecasts—the FSSs discussed in Section 12.2. These forecasts are then used by various customers elsewhere in the organization, in their operational planning, distribution, staffing, and cash management, and often form part of an integrated ERP information system. The next three sections discuss in more detail the methods and processes used to support this expensive and important organizational activity.

12.3.1 Supply Chain Forecasting and the Bullwhip Effect

Supply chain forecasting is the term we use to describe the forecasting activities of retailers, manufacturers, and their upstream suppliers. Figure 12.4 characterizes the information flows that affect demand at each level. The retailers' sales are affected by many factors, ranging from the state of the economy, to promotional activities, holidays, sporting events, and the

FIGURE 12.4   FORECASTING ACROSS THE SUPPLY CHAIN

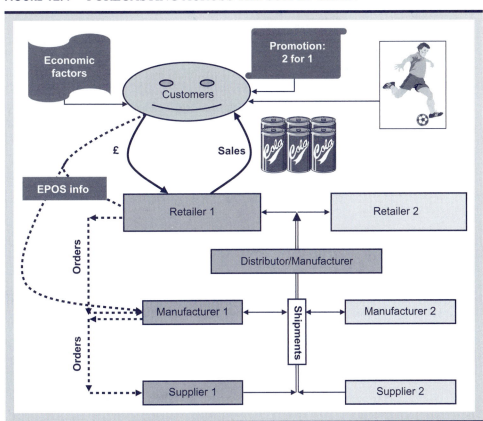

weather, to more localized factors (a festival or even a street closure). In response to these factors and the corresponding demand forecasts, the stock controllers (perhaps through an automated system) will take into account the stock on hand for each SKU and the orders already placed, if any. Then the controller will place a further order with the manufacturer. Fortunately, retailers will usually have up-to-date information on store SKU-level sales through their electronic point of sales (EPOS) information system.

The manufacturer suffers from a lack of knowledge, often knowing little about what's happening to the retailer's customers. The manufacturer knows only the orders placed for its own products by the retailer, the distributor, or the manufacturer. It may not even know what price is being charged or the promotional support in place, both of which affect consumer purchases. Increasingly, information may be shared on retailer sales through the retailer's EPOS data, as the figure shows.

The supplier is in an even worse situation than the manufacturer, being a further step removed from the final customer. As a consequence, the suppliers may use simple forecasting models of sales (at the retailer level), and the practice can lead to the *bullwhip effect*, whereby the variability of sales at the retailer level is amplified by the manufacturer's response to retail orders. This variability, in turn, is amplified by the supplier in response to the manufacturer's orders. Figure 12.5 illustrates the effect.

As the figure shows, the manufacturer's orders often lag the retailer's sales and the parts/raw material supplier's orders lag the manufacturer's—a delayed response to market changes and unexpected orders. The problem posed by the bullwhip effect is that variability and the corresponding forecast errors lead to heavy additional costs at all levels of the supply chain.

Various solutions have been proposed to mitigate the damaging effects, all of which involve sharing information so that the supply chain participants know, at the very least, their retail (or downstream) customers' sales. Most large companies collect EPOS data, which can readily be made available. In addition, some companies share inventory data and their own forecasts as part of what has become known as *Collaborative Planning, Forecasting, and Replenishment* (CPFR). The aim is to ensure the smooth, timely flow of goods throughout the supply chain by the effective use of the shared information. Lee *et al.*

FIGURE 12.5   THE BULLWHIP EFFECT ACROSS THE SUPPLY CHAIN: RETAILER, MANUFACTURER, AND PARTS/RAW MATERIALS SUPPLIER

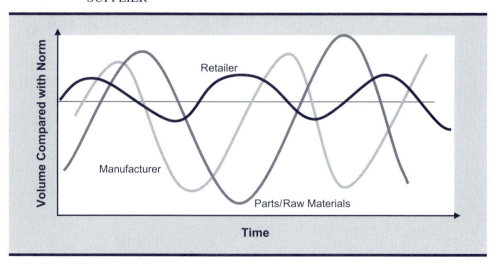

(1997) offer an accessible introduction to this potentially important subject. But research on how companies have operationalized these collaborative concepts suggests that their implementation is difficult: Using the downstream information requires both an effective information-sharing system through an FSS and forecasting methods that utilize the information. Software suppliers (who design the collaborative interfaces) and consultants have tended to overstate the benefits. In a real example in which the customer forecasts produced by a car manufacturer were shared, they added little to the parts manufacturer's own forecasts. So what can go wrong? Of course, the customer's own shared forecasts can be inaccurate, perhaps because they are not deemed valuable, or game playing may bias the forecasts to ensure that the manufacturer always has a readily available supply.

Discussion Question *How would a manufacturer best use a retailer's forecasts to improve the accuracy of its own forecasts?*

The database available to the forecaster upstream in the supply chain is often limited and confused, in that downstream demand is unknown, with only orders available. Many of the forecasts needed in the manufacturing resource planning system (MRP) are composed of two parts: an *independent demand*, determined by the organization's customers, and a *dependent demand*, often calculated from the production schedule itself. For example, if the manufacturer produces computers, the company will also require its own computers to be used in the production process itself. A second example of dependent demand is the number of hard disks needed in computer manufacture, a number that is calculated from the number of computers produced (taking into account rejections based on poor quality). The two types of demand need to be distinguished and forecast separately if both are potentially large and volatile.

In addition, the data may well not record demand at all, but instead record only sales (for a retailer) or shipments (for a manufacturer). An important aspect is to distinguish between the sales variable (which is observed) and demand (which is unobserved), where the latter includes such factors as lost or backlogged sales due to lack of supply (such as empty shelves in a retailer). In a call center, the record may exclude abandoned calls or lack a clear classification of the type of call received. All such limitations make the forecaster's life more difficult. Essentially, the first step when one is forecasting must be to "clean" the data. In operations, the process must usually be automatic so that corrections are put in place for a retailer to take into account lost sales due to the item's being out of stock or the effect of returns. A typical correction rule is to estimate demand as

$$Demand = Sales \ if \ Demand < Stock.$$

But when an out-of-stock situation is observed,

$$Demand = Initial \ Stock + Expected(Excess \ Demand) * P(Demand > Stock).$$

We use this revised estimate of demand to replace the raw sales figures in the forecast calculations (Lau and Hing-Ling Lau, 1996). To make this estimate, we will need to generate an estimate of the probability that demand exceeds the stock, and this requires us to assume an appropriate distribution for the demand, such as the normal distribution, and then estimate its parameters. For a manufacturer, the sales history again does not always reflect underlying activity and the sales data may require correction once more, with distorted values corrected or replaced. For example, for shipment patterns that are unusual, the shipments may be smoothed over a number of adjacent periods. Unlike the corrections made in the case of the retailer, the ones made here are likely to be made on a case-by-case basis, using judgment.

12.3.2 Hierarchical Forecasting: A Top-down or Bottom-up Approach?

Different parts of the organization require different levels of detail in order to support planning decisions. With the focus on distribution, the manager will require sales by region (perhaps transformed into container loads). In marketing, the emphasis will be on brand sales whereas the sales department is interested in customers. In Figure 12.6, we show two perspectives on this problem. In the first, annual sales are broken down into product categories, then brands, and finally SKUs. In the second, the overall world market is decomposed into countrywide sales and then to the different within-country areas and regions so that sales can be allocated to the various distribution centers and production facilities. These two hierarchies can be thought of equivalently from the bottom up, whereby daily SKU sales contribute to the weekly, monthly, and annual totals. A third perspective is aggregation across products. From an information systems viewpoint, to carry out this aggregation, the raw data must be very detailed, by SKU, time, and region at the very least.

In producing a forecast at the highest level of the hierarchy, two distinct approaches are possible. A model can be developed on the basis of past high-level aggregate data. Alternatively, forecasts can be produced (by whatever method) at a lower level and can then be aggregated up to produce the high-level forecast. This second approach is a bottom-up approach to forecasting.

The two alternatives are shown in Table 12.4 for a two-level hierarchy. Although the notation gets more complicated for a larger number of levels, the principles remain the same. There are L_1 product groups in the first level. In the second level, each of those L_1 groups is broken down into $L_{j2}, j = 1, \ldots, L_1$ SKUs. There are therefore L_{12} SKUs in the first product group, L_{22} in the second, etc.

A top-down approach forecasts the level 1 and level 2 sales by first forecasting the top-level total and then forecasting the proportion of level 1 sales that contribute (in groups) to

FIGURE 12.6 HIERARCHICAL ATTRIBUTES OF DEMAND DATA

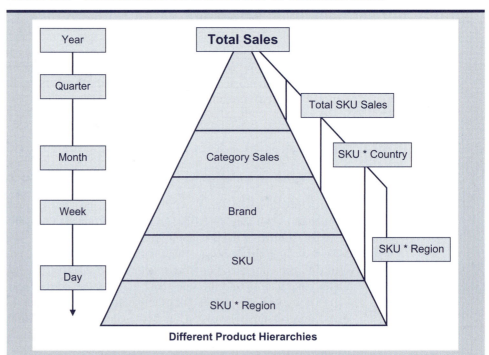

TABLE 12.4   TOP-DOWN AND BOTTOM-UP FORECASTS FOR A TWO-LEVEL
SYSTEM

	TOP DOWN↓	
Top	Total (T_t)	$T_t = \displaystyle\sum_{j=1}^{L_1} S_{jt}$
Level 1	$P_{jt} * T_t, j = 1, \ldots, L_1$, where P_{jt} is the proportion of total sales in the jth group	Sales of the jth group $S_{jt} = \displaystyle\sum_{k=1}^{L_{j2}} S_{kjt}$
Level 2	$P_{kjt} * (P_{jt} * T_t) \, k = 1, \ldots, L_{j2}$, where P_{kjt} is the proportion that the kth SKU contributes to the jth group's sales	S_{kjt} = sales of the kth SKU in the jth group
		BOTTOM UP↑

© Cengage Learning 2013.

the total. The historical proportions are known for each level 1 group, and often the historical average is used to estimate them. Alternatively, exponential smoothing can be used to forecast the proportions. The danger with using a fixed average is that this does not permit the different components of total sales to change.

The bottom-up approach first forecasts the level 2 sales for each SKU in each of the $j = 1, \ldots, L_1$ groups, and these are then summed to give the level 1 sales for each of the groups S_{jt}. These level 1 sales for each group can then be summed to estimate the (top-level) total sales.

Which method is better? They both have one advantage over the alternative approach of forecasting each level independently: The resulting forecasts are consistent. In effect, the organization is working with one set of numbers while other approaches can deliver conflicting forecasts. At the extreme, marketing could be working with one set of expected sales while production and distribution could be planning to produce and deliver a quite different mix of product volumes. However, there is no statistical reason that one method should be better than the other, and in fact, the empirical evidence is contradictory. A recent article (Athanasopoulos *et al.*, 2009) compares the two approaches and recommends a variant that combines them. Minicase 12.2 provides an opportunity to compare the approaches.

Discussion Question   *What advantages and disadvantages do you see in adopting either a top-down approach or a bottom-up approach?*

Within a particular disaggregated level of the hierarchy, there are typically many similar (analogous) series—for example, within a retailer, fresh food products. Methods have been developed that use information across the series to get better estimates of the individual series sales. The most obvious feature that similar series often share is a common seasonality. This feature is particularly helpful when the data history is relatively short and seasonal estimates based on the individual series will be error prone and noisy. Seasonality for such series may be estimated by averaging the seasonal estimates of the individual series and applying the group seasonal estimates to all the series (Duncan, Gorr, and Szczypula, 2001; Leonard, 2007; Williams, 2007).

Applying the same logic, but this time to the trend, yields an estimate of the smoothing constant for a group of series as the average (or median) of the individually estimated constants. Such methods have generally proved more accurate than relying on the parameter estimates for individual series.

12.3.3   **Demand Data and Intermittent Demand**

Demand data, even after it has been cleansed, does not always fall neatly into a time series such as those described in Chapter 2. Each year, retailers stock many new products for which there is little or no history. Manufacturers face the same problem. In Section 12.4, we discuss the new-product forecasting problem from a longer term marketing perspective that delivers (usually judgmentally) a forecast of total sales for the year. Simple methods such as adopting a seasonal profile based on similar products may then be applied to estimate the period-by-period sales. A variant of this approach involves the class of fashion goods, which is a particular type of new product (e.g., the issue might be sales of summer outfits). Here, there is a considerable history on the profile of sales of women's clothing, although not on the sales of this year's latest fashions.

Other types of demand pattern that require special attention include (i) seasonal products that are unavailable through much of the year and (ii) end-of-line items that are being run down. In addition, products are usually thought about and categorized into three classes (although it might be more) in terms of their importance, from those products which are most profitable (or have the highest value, class A) to those which matter least (class C). Further, the impact of forecasting error on stock suggests an additional classification running from those with low forecast error (class X) to those exhibiting high errors (class Z). Thus, class AZ products are important products which exhibit large forecasts errors. The database will then record the fact that a particular SKU can be regarded as having regular sales, being an important class A product, being a new product, etc. Standard forecasting procedures will apply only to the "regular" SKUs, while the remainder will usually be dealt with individually. This topic is dealt with more fully in Section 13.1.5.

Intermittent Demand   One particular class of product requires more detailed discussion, because it poses a common problem and corresponding formal models are included in many software products. *Intermittent-demand* SKUs frequently have zero sales, and any nonzero demand is often highly variable (so-called lumpy demand). Retailers and spare parts suppliers regularly experience this type of demand for many hundreds of SKUs, and it requires special statistical models.

Accordingly, let us define two time series. The first is the history of nonzero demands, Y_t, and the second is the number of periods between successive nonzero demands, p_t. Then the h-step-ahead forecast of the demand rate made at time t is given by

$$F_{t+h}(h) = \frac{Y_t'}{p_t'}, \tag{12.4}$$

where p_t' denotes the exponentially smoothed interdemand interval, updated only if demand occurs in period $t - 1$, and Y_t' is the exponentially smoothed (or moving-average) forecast of the size of demand, updated only if demand occurs in period $t - 1$.

This method, first proposed by Croston (and named after him), has been compared to standard exponential smoothing. Table 12.5 compares the two calculations, using a smoothing constant of 0.2, while Figure 12.7 shows the results graphically.

The first stage is to develop a time series of the number of periods observed between intervals of nonzero demand: 0 is observed between periods 3 and 2 because period 3 demand is 0, while period 4 has a nonzero demand of 5. Therefore, the observed interval between intervals of nonzero demand is 2. The standard exponential smoothing formula is then used to forecast the interval between nonzero demands. With smoothing parameter 0.2, the interval forecast for period 12 is .2 * 5 + .8 * 2 = 2.6. The demand size forecast is similarly calculated for period 12 as .2 * 6 + .8 * 2.690 = 3.352.

The final Croston forecast is

Demand size forecast/Interval forecast = 3.352/2.6 = 1.289.

Croston's method does not always perform better than SES, whether appraised by standard error measures such as the mean absolute error or by inventory cost measures. Performance

TABLE 12.5   CALCULATING FORECASTS FOR INTERMITTENT DEMAND BASED ON
CROSTON'S METHOD (*The value of the smoothing parameter is 0.2 in all cases.*)

Period	Actual Demand	Demand Forecast	Actual Intervals	Interval Forecast	Croston Forecast	Exponential Smoothing Forecast
1	0	No forecast	Can't be			
2	2	No forecast	calculated		No forecast	0.00
3	0	2.000	0	2.000	1.000	0.40
4	5	2.000	2	2.000	1.000	0.32
5	0	2.600	0	2.000	1.300	1.26
6	8	2.600	2	2.000	1.300	1.00
7	0	2.690	0	2.000	1.345	2.40
8	0	2.690	0	2.000	1.345	1.92
9	0	2.690	0	2.000	1.345	1.54
10	0	2.690	0	2.000	1.345	1.23
11	6	2.690	5	2.000	1.345	0.98
12	0	3.352	0	2.600	1.289	1.99

FIGURE 12.7   CROSTON'S METHOD FOR INTERMITTENT DEMAND
COMPARED WITH SIMPLE EXPONENTIAL SMOOTHING

depends on the coefficient of variation for demand size, as well as the expected number of periods between intervals of nonzero demand. Broadly, the less "intermittent" the time series, with
smaller coefficient of variation and less time between orders, the better simple exponential
smoothing performs compared with the Croston competitor (Syntetos, Boylan, and Teunter,
2011). Snyder, Ord, and Beaumont (2012) found that better results are obtained by using
different smoothing constants for the order size and the period between intervals of nonzero demand. Further, they found that the benefits derived from this approach were usually in the provision of more accurate prediction distributions (required for inventory planning, etc.) than
for point forecasts. Snyder *et al.* used a forecasting competition based upon the demand for

automobile parts to validate this conclusion. In general, no single method can always be relied on to produce the more accurate forecasts. In a particular application, a forecasting competition of the form described in Section 12.1.1 should be undertaken.

One potentially important issue in any FSS is how the error measures are calculated. Including intermittent demand in the calculation of the *MAPE* can lead to major distortions because of the zero values in the actual observations. Such SKUs must therefore be excluded and be evaluated separately, or else a different error measure, such as the *MASE*, should be used. In appraising different methods of forecasting for intermittent demand, the recommended error measure is the percentage of time one method outperforms an alternative benchmark (such as exponential smoothing). Using measures of the service level delivered for fixed inventory investment is also useful (though harder to calculate because it requires a simulation model to derive the estimates: See Syntetos and Boylan, 2006).

12.3.4 Operations Forecasting: Summary

Forecasting in order to support operations remains the most common applications area for forecasting methods. The data usually fall naturally into a hierarchy, raising important questions about the level in the hierarchy at which the forecasts are needed. The database itself is not usually particularly rich, in that few, if any, explanatory variables are included in the FSS that lies at the heart of most operational forecasting. Instead, as we argued in Section 12.2, the FSS relies heavily on managerial judgment to take into account all the special circumstances that affect future demand.

Most of the methods used in operations forecasting are based on exponential smoothing. However, for those special products which exhibit lumpy and intermittent demand, special methods that modify exponential smoothing may well be needed. Typically, there are many such products in a retail company or spare parts supplier. In choosing between the different methods, a forecasting competition may be needed (see Section 12.1.1). But beware: In any appraisal of forecasting performance where there is intermittent demand, the most popular error measure, *MAPE*, may be unusable (due to zero sales in the denominator). As regards point forecasts, the performance of Croston's method is mixed. However, the method appears to provide better prediction intervals for intermittent demands (see Snyder *et al.*, 2012).

12.4 Marketing

The major reason most organizations are concerned with forecasting is that they need to forecast the demand for their products and services. Without predictions of future demand, they are unable to put capacity in place to supply potential consumers. Without understanding the factors that stimulate a consumer to buy or use the product (or service), the organization cannot influence its demand and, in particular, cannot decide on those crucial aspects of marketing, such as pricing, promotions, and product design, that lead to success.

The methods suitable for forecasting demand for a product or service (from now on, we will use just "product" to include both concepts) depend quite critically on the data available, which in turn depend on the product's history and how much information has been collected from consumers. Figure 12.8 illustrates the various stages in the life cycle of an individual customer, from the earliest stage when she is only a prospective customer, yet to decide whether to purchase. Of these prospective customers, some proportion will adopt the new product and become an established user of it (and perhaps related services). Consider, for example, a fourth-generation mobile phone (such as the iPhone), offering music, Internet access, and many add-on applications. The profitability of such a phone to the telecoms supplier will depend on both the features of the new phone and the consumer's susceptibility to them (based on economic and demographic drivers such as income, age, and gender). The final stage in the consumer life cycle is retention, whereby the company competes to retain the profitable customers, rejecting those who may prove to be costly.

FIGURE 12.8 PREDICTION OF INDIVIDUAL AND AGGREGATE DEMAND IN A
CUSTOMER LIFE CYCLE

Source: Adapted by Fildes *et al.* (2008) from Berry and Linoff (2004) and Olafsson *et al.* (2008).

At each stage in the individual customer life cycle, more information is gathered on the customer and her behavior, adding value incrementally in the modeling of the customer's decisions. In the first stage, the market analyst aims to forecast the numbers of new customers that can be acquired, after first deciding on the target population. One of the most common applications of forecasting techniques is to decide to whom to mail promotional material, with a view toward acquiring new customers. (See Bose and Chen, 2009, for a technical survey of this area.) At this earliest stage, the analyst will know little of the target customers beyond their addresses and the demographics of the areas in which they live. At the end of the life cycle, the analyst will wish to identify those customers at risk from "churning"—that is to say, leaving their current supplier. Here the analyst should be able to access the customer's history of using the product (and the company), including such features as whether complaints have been made.

Forecasting individual customer behavior is only part of the story; we will discuss suitable models in Section 12.5. For market planning and related decisions, *aggregate* forecasts need to be made. For example, the capacity of the production line for a new product requires long-term forecasts of the product's potential market. Depending on the manufacturing complexity of the product, these forecasts may need to look many years ahead. As with the individual consumer, there is little, if any, history available at the earliest stages from the launch of new product. Sometimes market experiments are used, prior to the full-scale launch of the product, in order to gather data on such factors as the percentage of the target market who are willing to try the new product (if it's a fast-moving consumer product such as a new barbecue sauce). In contrast, after the product is established, the company has a time series history of sales, as well as prices and how much it spends on promoting the product. In addition, the company can buy similar information on its competition. A key issue the forecaster faces in deciding the methods to use is the availability of time series data. For example, the new-product forecasting problem must be treated differently from the situation where there is a substantial sales history.

Thus far, we have written as if the market demand we are concerned with is generated by an individual's demand for an organization's product or service (i.e., business to consumer, or B2C). However, many market forecasting problems focus on demand between businesses (B2B). Where there are many customers, the two problems are similar. Where there are few, judgment and customer information are applied to the individual purchase decisions, to estimate each customer's probability of purchase and the expected value of the purchase. The estimates obtained can then be aggregated to estimate overall demand. When the number of customers is small, information-sharing approaches to forecasting become important, as noted in Section 12.3.

Discussion Question   *How would you go about forecasting the demand for large airliners (e.g., Airbus 380) over the next five years?*

How do the techniques we have discussed so far in this book apply to these various market demand forecasting problems? In the remainder of this section, we discuss both new-product forecasting and forecasting when there is a substantial history. As we will see, the methods and the ideas all remain useful, but the special circumstances of market demand forecasting often require modifications to ensure that they match up to the specific features of the problem.

12.4.1   New Products and Services

New-product forecasting is important to organizations. The history of forecasting is full of major mistakes, usually in circumstances of overoptimism, in which the company's product champion has convinced colleagues that consumers were just waiting to whip the product off the shelf (or the dealer's lot). It is estimated that between 50 and 80 percent of new products fail to establish themselves. Although the failure to forecast demand is not the only reason, it is by far the most important.

Sometimes the forecasting problem is one of predicting how quickly the new product replaces an existing product. This is the situation where the product is not completely new but has some of the same attributes as products already on the market (termed a *product improvement*). However, sometimes there is a key attribute in the new product—a feature which is sufficiently distinct from established alternatives that it has the potential to be viewed quite differently by consumers. An example is the electric car. More rarely, the product (often based on a new technology) delivers a service to the consumer that was previously unavailable (*new to the world*). An example is the personal computer, which delivered personally controlled desktop access to computing. (It could be argued that computer time-sharing arrangements, popular in the 1970s, also had attributes similar to the PC, although we suggest that the issue of personal control is a critical difference.)

Numerous researchers have surveyed organizations in order to learn the techniques that are used to forecast these various types of new product or service. (See, for example, Lynn *et al.*, 1999, and Kahn, 2002.) Overwhelmingly, various types of judgmental forecasting are used—in particular, opinions of customers, company executives, and the sales force, which lead to an aggregate forecast. Both Lynn et al.'s and Kahn's surveys found that statistical models were used more rarely. However, reliance on judgment has often proved to generate overly error-prone forecasts, and as the failure history of new products makes clear, over-optimism is the typical result. We look next at models of how people (and companies) adopt a new product, for such models can be used to develop suitable benchmarks for appraising the more common judgmental approaches.

12.4.2   Long-Term Trends

For a new product that is not competing directly with others already established in the market, the question for the consumer is whether to try the product. For a frequently purchased product, the question is whether that product is sufficiently enjoyable to claim a regular spot in the consumer's shopping basket. If it is a product with a potentially long lifetime (such as a mobile phone), the decision to adopt or not to adopt is more important. We now consider models to describe the adoption decision. (For frequently purchased products, the frequency of purchase also needs to be considered; see Fader and Hardie, 2001, and the references therein.)

FIGURE 12.9   VARIOUS TREND CURVES

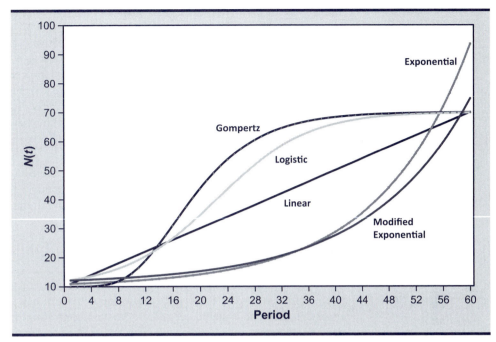

© Cengage Learning 2013.

Let $N(t)$ represent the number of people (or businesses) who have adopted (or tried) the product for the first time by time period t; this is the cumulative total of adopters. What might the time path of $N(t)$ look like? Figure 12.9 shows some alternative curves.

The curves included in the figure are the linear, $N(t) = a + bt$; the exponential,

$$N(t) = a\exp(bt);$$
(12.5)

and three new nonlinear curves:

i. the *modified exponential*,

$$N(t) = c + a\exp(bt),$$
(12.6)

This damps the growth of the exponential curve when a and b are negative.

A useful special case arises when $c = -a = M$ and $b < 0$. The curve is then bounded with upper limit M. We will refer to this scheme as the *bounded exponential*.

ii. the *Gompertz curve*, defined as

$$N(t) = M\exp(-a\exp(-bt)).$$
(12.7)

iii. the *extended logistic curve*, which has a shape similar to that of the Gompertz curve:

$$N(t) = M\left(\frac{1 - c\exp(-bt)}{1 + d\exp(-bt)}\right).$$
(12.8)

The simple logistic arises when $c = 0$. With each of the last two curves, as t gets large, $N(t)$ tends to a finite limit M (60 in the diagram). M is called the *asymptote*, the limiting value (of $N(t)$) as t increases without limit. These curves are often described as S-shaped; by contrast, the linear and exponential curves increase without limit as t increases: They are unbounded. In fact, the exponential curve was the basis of one of the first forecasting models that predicted cataclysmic disaster: Malthus's prediction of the effects of an exponentially increasing population. According to Malthus, if each family has, on average, more than two children, and they in turn have more than two children, the effect is an exponentially increasing population that quickly explodes through the finite capacity of the Earth to feed itself.

Discussion Question *What went wrong with Malthus's forecast of starvation for the planet? Or is the predicted catastrophe just taking longer than expected?*

When there are substantial past data, we can fit alternative curves by using an extension of the principles we introduced in Chapters 7 and 8, known as nonlinear least squares estimation. Most statistical software programs have such procedures, involving iterative solutions to obtain the parameter estimates. Also, a spreadsheet, *Trend.xlsm*, which illustrates how this analysis can be done with Excel's Solver, is available on the book's website.

Alternatively, we could linearize the exponential by taking natural logarithms to obtain

$$\ln(N(t)) = \ln(a) + bt + (error),$$

with the parameter estimated by the usual least squares procedure. However, this approach does not extend to the other models. Further, to compare the fit from a linear model with a nonlinear model, we have to make sure that the errors are in the same units; therefore, we cannot use R^2 or the standard error from the regression. As we discussed in Section 9.6 on nonlinearity, the forecasts have to be transformed back to the original units and then their *RMSEs* or other measures compared.

Are such trend curve methods useful for forecasting? As they stand, they cannot be used for new-product forecasting because they require sufficient data to estimate the parameters. Perhaps more important, forecasters would need to convince themselves and their colleagues that the trend is stable over the forecast horizon. Now, there are many reasons that a trend might persist for some considerable length of time. For example, a population may well start as Malthus feared, exponentially growing; but as the population gets richer and better educated, with a higher probability of children surviving, the growth will typically damp, leading to a modified exponential as a possibility, bounded or not. Where slow, continuous change is expected, growth curves such as these offer a benchmark with which to judge other methods. Working with Yongil Jeon, Nobel Prize winner Clive Granger (Granger and Jeon, 2007) has argued that such curves provide useful long-term forecasts. Using the growth of U.S. consumption, the two researchers compared the linear, exponential, and modified exponential curves. Their results establishing which curve provides the better forecast are left for the reader to consider in Exercise 12.10.

EXAMPLE 12.1 ■ The growth of Netflix

The various curves described in this section were used to fit quarterly sales figures for Netflix (see Minicase 3.1) for the period 2000Q1 through 2007Q4, as in Table 3.20. The results obtained from fitting each of the five models are given in Table 12.6. The *RMSE* and the first and last fitted values are included, along with the limiting values for the Gompertz and logistic curves. The two curves with finite upper limits fit much better and look similar, but show quite different asymptotic limits.   ■

TABLE 12.6   MINITAB MODEL FITS FOR NETFLIX GROWTH DATA

Model	Upper Limit	S	Fit(1)	Fit(32)
Linear	No limit	26.40	−45.2	290.3
Exponential	No limit	21.85	24.4	359.1
Mod. Exponential	No limit	14.07	−9.8	338.5
Gompertz	598	9.44	2.5	323.1
Logistic	400	8.54	1.6	317.4
Actual			5.2	302.4

Data: Netflix.xlsx.

Discussion Question *What other information might you require before you relied on the forecasts shown in Table 12.6? Which model would you use?*

In short, growth curves offer a description of trends that are most useful with highly aggregated data. We often cite such curves colloquially, particularly the exponential curve, as we express our fear of population growth or welcome growth in world trade. But they are rarely the best forecasting tools, because long term trends tend to damp down. Thus, the S-shaped curves have more potential, and as we argue next, can form the basis of new-product forecasting methods.

12.4.3 Diffusion Curves: Modeling the Adoption of New Technologies and Products

The curves we have just described offer descriptions of past data and are not based on any model of the underlying process. (It could be argued, as Malthus did, that the exponential growth model is based on a simple birth-and-death process.) Models of the adoption of new technology have at their heart some simple schemes that attempt to describe how a person (or organization) comes to adopt the technology. The distinction drawn is that between consumption (of a product or service), which is potentially continuous, and adoption, which is usually thought of as a one-time irreversible choice. The most famous of the various models of adoption is due to Bass, (1969).

Suppose the market potential of a new product is M. The potential may be the number of individuals within some age group or income bracket, the number of households in a country, etc. Potential differs from sales in a number of important respects including the fact that it excludes replacement products and multiple purchases (e.g., a consumer owning more than a single mobile phone). Nor may the potential ever be achieved due to, for example, supply constraints.

Discussion Question *What determines the market potential for a new high-speed rail link between San Francisco and Los Angeles (or London and Scotland)? What comparisons would you make with existing transportation systems? As a second example, consider the market potential of a new technological product such as a notepad.*

First let us define $N(t)$ as the cumulative number of individuals (or more generally, potential adopters) who have adopted or tried the product or service by the end of time period t. Then if $n(t)$ is the number of people who adopted in period t, it follows that $n(t) = N(t) - N(t-1)$. Now, let $g(t)$ be the probability that an individual adopts a new product in period t. Then the expected number $n(t)$ of people who adopt in period t is given by the probability $g(t)$ of adopting in period t, multiplied by the number $M - N(t-1)$ of people who have not yet adopted, or

$$n(t) \equiv DN(t) \equiv N(t) - N(t-1) = g(t)(M - N(t-1)). \qquad (12.9)$$

Various models for $g(t)$ have been proposed. The simplest would assume that $g(t)$ is a constant; that is, there is a constant probability of someone who has not yet tried the product trying in the next period. If we allow the model to be extended to continuous time, we can solve equation (12.9) algebraically. This assumption leads to the bounded exponential model discussed as a special case of equation (12.6). Bass (1969) proposed a more complex and more plausible model which assumes that the probability of adoption has two components: a constant probability that applies to each member of the population (sometimes called the coefficient of innovation, p) and a probability that increases with the number of people who have already adopted (a "word-of-mouth" effect proportional to those who have adopted, $qN(t-1)$, where q is the coefficient of imitation).

It follows that $g(t) = p + q(N(t)/M)$. Equation (12.9) can then be solved *for* $N(t)$. In continuous time the solution is a logistic curve given by equation (12.8) with $b = p + q$, $c = 1$ and $d = q/p$:

$$N(t) = M\left(\frac{1 - \exp(-(p + q)t)}{1 + \dfrac{q}{p}\exp(-(p + q)t)} \right). \tag{12.10}$$

Figure 12.10 shows how the logistic curve shifts with the values of these two coefficients. Observe that when $q = 0$ we are back at the bounded exponential curve.

FIGURE 12.10   THE EFFECTS OF INCREASING THE DIFFUSION
PARAMETERS p AND q

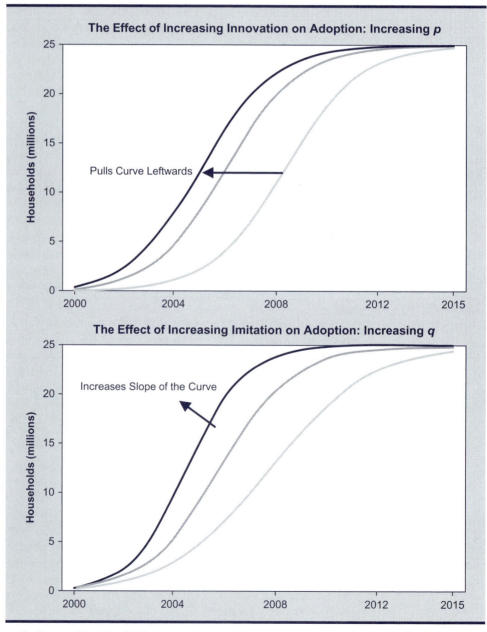

As the two coefficients increase, they affect how quickly the adoption reaches its potential. A larger imitation coefficient q raises the rate of adoption through an increasing probability of someone adopting as more and more of the potential market has succumbed. A larger coefficient of innovation p increases the early take-up.

There are various ways of estimating the coefficients. A number of algorithms can be used to estimate the diffusion parameters, but nonlinear least squares estimation using Solver is adequate for our purposes, as demonstrated in the macro *Trend.xlsm*. (An alternative, not recommended, however, is to estimate a linearized version of the Bass model.) The nonlinear model that is usually estimated is

$$N(t) = M\left(\frac{1 - \exp(-(p + q)t)}{1 + \frac{q}{p}\exp(-(p + q)t)}\right) + \varepsilon_t. \tag{12.11}$$

But it is important to note that the error term is assumed to be additive (i.e., it is equally important to minimize an error made for a large value of $N(t)$ as it is the small values in the early stages of the adoption cycle). Alternative assumptions could be made to minimize the percentage error, but for most purposes, it is the absolute value of the error that affects management decisions such as how much to invest in production capacity.

Much of the earlier research and estimation methods used assumed that substantial data were available, but that approach is of no help in new-product forecasting, where, by definition, there are few observations. Instead, the parameters can be estimated by analogy. In many new-product forecasting situations—even those in which the product can be thought of as being *new to the world*, there will have been examples of earlier products entering similar markets. Take the Internet as an example: In Figure 12.11, we see the various diffusion curves for radio and for both black-and-white and color television, as well as the as yet incomplete forecasts for the Internet.

FIGURE 12.11   PENETRATION LEVELS, DIFFUSION CURVES, AND PARAMETER ESTIMATES FOR VARIOUS MEDIA IN THE UNITED STATES

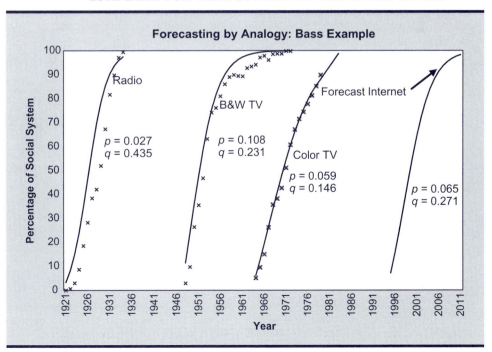

Source: Lilien, Rangaswamy, and Van den Bulte, 2000.

The parameters from the past products have been estimated from the full data set (from Lilien, Rangaswamy, and Van den Bulte, 2000). Note that, for radio in the 1920s, diffusion was initially slow, but word of mouth (represented by the parameter q) proved effective. Color television, replacing an established product (black-and-white television) had a slower diffusion path, perhaps because the early availability and range of programs were both limited. So how would we estimate the Internet diffusion parameters? We suggest that it is more like radio or black-and-white television, with a low coefficient of innovation and a high coefficient of imitation as people discover its benefits. There are also *network effects* whereby the attractiveness of the medium becomes higher the more people have adopted. In Figure 12.11, the forecast function shown is based on the averages of the parameter values for the three products judged to be similar.

Sometimes the problem of estimating the parameters for adoption in one country is helped by knowledge of the adoption path in another country, but the danger with this approach is that different countries and their populations differ in their willingness to try new products and services.

To help estimate the parameters by analogy, Lilien and Rangaswamy (2004) have provided a set of historical parameter estimates with an overall median value of $p = .025$ and $q = .280$. These historical values establish a starting point that immediately provides forecasts once a group of analogous products is chosen. Because the choice of analogous products cannot be based on a similar adoption history (our focus product is new, after all), the decision must be made on the grounds of their having similar attributes and with the methods we described in Section 11.2.5. (For further discussion of some of the issues surrounding defining analogies, see Goodwin, Dyussekeneva, and Meeran, 2011.)

12.4.4 Market Potential of a New Product or Technology

The Bass model and the Gompertz trend curves introduced in Section 12.4.2 both include the market potential M as a third parameter. In principle, if substantial data are available, this parameter can be estimated as any other would be. One example is the level of Internet adoption likely to be achieved, information that is important to Internet service providers, retailers, and governments. Using data in *Telecoms.xlsx*, Table 12.7 shows the results obtained from estimating the Bass model and the Gompertz curve to derive the market potential M as well as the diffusion parameters p and q. Two different time spans and

TABLE 12.7 DIFFUSION ESTIMATES: SAMPLE SIZE, MODEL, AND COUNTRY EFFECTS

	UK		Germany	
	4 years ($n = 16$)	all ($n = 27$)	4 years ($n = 16$)	all ($n = 27$)
Logistic/Bass				
p	0.0626	0.064	0.034	0.036
q	0*	0.0027	0*	0.019
M	23.57	23.18	42.47	38.11
S	0.593	0.572	1.248	1.063
Gompertz				
a	2.21	2.21	3.30	2.43
b	0.12	0.12	0.04	0.09
M	20.90	20.52	102.23	32.79
S	0.127	0.121	0.164	0.571

Source: Data shown is from file Telecoms.xlsx, derived from Analysys Mason Limited: database—Telecoms Market Matrix, Western Europe, version November 8, 2010.

*The optimization procedure identified the boundary value $q = 0$ as optimal, leading to the bounded exponential model.

two different countries—the United Kingdom and Germany—were analyzed. For the United Kingdom, we are able to establish stable parameters and similar estimates of market potential for the two time periods. The same, however, is not true of Germany, for which the Gompertz curve turns out to be unstable and the choice of diffusion curve has a considerable effect on the estimates. However, the Gompertz models fit much better than their logistic counterparts, as the smaller values of S indicates.

Market potential is a particularly important managerial variable. Whether the product is new to the world or, essentially, an improvement competing with established alternatives, its potential affects planning decisions at the earliest stage in the product's life cycle, before it is even fully designed for its market: It also influences more tactical decisions later in the product life cycle, from early adoption through growth, to saturation. After all, with a substantial market available to exploit, the managerial argument shifts from whether there are opportunities for profit to how such opportunities can be capitalized upon. In addition, the forecasts derived from the trend curve modeling exercise are often sensitive to the estimates of market potential and are themselves highly uncertain, as Table 12.7 shows for Germany. To make matters worse, the expected final penetration level itself can be increased (or decreased) by changes in the marketing of the product through pricing, distribution, and advertising, as well as by a factor such as *GDP*, which changes the affordability of the product.

One route to establishing the product's potential is through the use of an intentions survey, a survey that asks potential customers what their likelihood of purchase is (see Section 11.2.4; see also Morwitz, 2001). Various alternative approaches can be used to ask equivalent questions—for example, the constant-sum method, whereby potential customers are asked to allocate (or spend) part of a fixed amount among competing products, preferably in a simulated purchasing environment that is close to reality. Once the overall likelihood of purchase is calculated for different market segments, the total forecast of market potential is the product of the expected numbers of consumers falling into the segments and the likelihood.

But where a product or service has features that a purchaser must trade off against an alternative set, or where the potential customer is unfamiliar with some aspects of the product, a more complex approach is needed. The goal is to explain the choices consumers may make through various explanatory models that link the range of product attributes to the likelihood of purchasing a particular product. The core assumption is that customers value a product overall by valuing its individual attributes (or benefits), with one attribute compensating for another. (See, for instance, Figure 12.12, where running costs counterbalance purchase price.) *Conjoint Choice Models* based on a survey of potential consumers can be used to assess the relative value of the various attributes of the product or service that are expected to influence future intentions to purchase.

FIGURE 12.12   A SAMPLE OF CHOICE SCENARIOS IN THE CHINESE CAR MARKET

	Vehicle 1	**Vehicle 2**	**Vehicle 3**
Fuel type	Gasoline	Hybrid	Electric
Purchase price (RMB)	75,000	97,500	135,000
Annual running cost (RMB)	15,000	9,000	12,000
Government incentives to purchase	Not applicable	Priority lane	30,000 RMB subsidy
Availability of charging facility	Not applicable	Not applicable	40% of parking slots
Vehicle range with full charging	Not applicable	Not applicable	80 km
Your choice:	☐	☐	☐

Source: Qian and Soopramanien (2011). NB: RMB is the Chinese currency.

After the identification of the target population for the product, the first stage in the process is to identify the key attributes that characterize the product or service. This can be done through interviews and focus groups, as well as by reviewing the literature on analogous products. Then, a survey of potential customers is carried out that asks them how they value the new product or service (compared with a range of alternatives) on the basis of its attributes and also their likelihood of purchase (see Section 11.2.4). In so doing, the survey collects information on the characteristics of the respondent. Respondents either rank a range of alternatives or choose among them. The product attributes are often measured as dummy variables showing the presence or absence of an attribute or its level. Thus, different levels of the price of a product would each be assigned a dummy variable. For example, Qian and Soopramanien (2011) used a choice model to estimate the market potential for alternative-fuel cars (gasoline, hybrid, or electric) based on the attributes shown in Figure 12.12.

Discussion Question *Consider the choice you make when deciding how to communicate with someone at a distance (e.g., mobile, landline, IMS, VoIP). What are the key attributes that affect your choice, and what circumstances affect their relative value to you?*

Where potential purchasers (respondents) choose between different products, a choice model can infer how much weight they are giving to the different attributes that distinguish between the different choices which are on offer. This same set of approaches can be used to *indirectly* estimate a consumer's preference; the approach is referred to as *self-explicated conjoint*. The first stage is to ask participants to rate the importance or value of the different attributes (using one of the different rating or ranking methods). Then they score each product or choice on these attributes. For example, a participant might rate *brand* as having a weight of 0.33 (the weights should sum to 1) and then, with a new branded product in mind, could score this rating as being valued at 0.5 (compared with other products' ratings scoring higher or lower). This attribute would then contribute 0.5 * 0.33 = 0.167 to the overall value of the product. In selecting the attributes, it is important that they remain distinct, lest double counting give undue weight given to both attributes together (Goodwin and Wright, 2009, p. 36).

What all these methods have in common is that the preference for a product is some function of a weighted sum of the value imputed to the attributes (sometimes called *part worths*), which together sum to provide an estimate of the overall relative value for the particular alternative under consideration. Essentially, the valuable attributes of a product compensate for weaker performance of other attributes. (These values are more generally called *utilities*; see, e.g., Goodwin and Wright, 2009, which discusses the differences between the two. For our purposes here, we do not need to make the distinction.) The overall value, V_j is given by the weighted sum of the individual attributes values, $V_j = \sum_k w_{kj} A_{kj}$. Finally, the ith individual's preference or choice for the jth product is taken as a (sometimes linear) function of the overall value (or utility). We thus have

$$Preference_{ij} = f\left(\sum_{k=1}^{p} w_{ijk} A_{jk}\right) = f(V_{ij}),$$

where $Preference_{ij}$ is the preference of the ith respondent for the jth alternative (product) and w_{ijk} is the weight the ith respondent assigns to the kth attribute of the jth product, A_{jk}. The weights can be estimated over a group of participants in the survey and by the inclusion of sociodemographic dummy variables. This process leads to aggregate estimates of the potential for different market segments. In a choice model, the relationship between purchase intentions and preference scores is usually assumed to be logistic (see Equation 10.2 and the accompanying discussion), with the parameters representing the odds of preferring one product to another. (Classification trees, discussed in Section 10.2, can also be used, although they are not based on a compensatory model. However, the results do lead to a ranking of the importance of the various explanatory attributes.) There are various preference or choice functions, such as assuming that each consumer chooses the alternative which maximizes his value function. For the logit model, this becomes the probability of choosing alternative j from J alternatives, which is

$$P_{ij} = \frac{\exp(V_{ij})}{\sum_j \exp(V_{ij})}.$$

Various demographic variables can be included in the value function to explain different levels of interest from the different market segments.

Qian and Soopramanien (2011) used this approach to derive probabilities of selecting each of the three alternative types of car, depending on the market segment into which the respondent falls. (Demographics include family size, income, and age.) Illustrative results from estimating the logit model give weights of -1.3 for the electric car, $+0.87$ for the hybrid (compared with the gasoline-driven car), a price effect of -0.01, and a running cost of -0.06. As with any logit model, these weights translate into percentage increases (or decreases) in the probability of selecting the choice (e.g., $\exp(-1.3) = 0.27$, or a 27 percent chance of choosing the electric car compared with the base choice of the gasoline-fueled car). When type of car is supplemented with the government incentives and various demographic weights, the probability of purchase for the three types can be calculated.

The final stage in estimating the market potential (or market share) uses simulation of the individuals or market segments, based on the probabilities (or preferences) of the individuals or segments. In sum, conjoint choice modeling (or, more generally, conjoint analysis) offers a partial solution to the difficult problem of modeling market potential and market shares for a new product or service. However, putting the approach into practice is far from straightforward, starting with the problem of identifying the target market and the attributes to consider. Wittink and Bergestuen (2001) offer a useful summary of the "major elements of a conjoint study" as well as the "conditions under which conjoint should work well" (pp. 151–152). For example, customer preferences and estimates of market potential should be mediated by variables such as the availability of the product. (If, say, only 50 percent of the potential market has access to fast broadband, then the current operational market potential for this product is halved.)

Accessible references that expand on the alternative approaches to estimating market potential are available through Sawtooth, one of the major suppliers of software, training, and analysis (*www.sawtoothsoftware.com/solutions/conjoint_analysis.shtml*). Marder (1999) expands on the relationship between self-explicated approaches and indirect choice models (*http://emaprinciples.com/articles/cjmr1.pdf*). Lilien and Rangaswamy (2004) offer a more detailed summary of some of these issues at a mathematical level similar to that presented in this text. More advanced references are Wind and Green (2005, Section 5) and Gustafsson, Herrmann, and Huber (2001).

The final approach in our discussion of estimating market potential is to use analogous products (with Lilien *et al.*, 2000, providing a useful database) as a basis for making a judgmental estimate of the final penetration level, as we explained in Section 11.2.5. But as we previously noted, finding useful analogies is not an automatic recipe for success, although there may be no other route forward without collecting survey data (Goodwin, Dyussekeneva, and Meeran, 2011).

Whichever approach is taken, it is important that the choices be contextualized as effectively as possible so that the respondent feels that the purchase situation is realistic. This requirement means that the attribute set has to include all the most important factors and that the context of the purchase (including, e.g., competitive products) should be realistic. Computer-based simulations of the shopping experience have been used to meet the requirement. As ever, a combination of the applicable methods for forecasting market potential is likely to work best.

Discussion Questions *(1) What factors may affect the final uptake of 3-D high-definition TV in the United States? In France?*
(2) Thinking of the latest new major product or service just coming available, write down an estimate of the percentage of the population (or households) that you expect will adopt the product or service in its final penetration level. What factors may affect its final uptake? After the class discussion of the final uptake, do you want to revise your estimate?

12.4.5 Market Response Models

Market response models are used both to forecast aggregate medium-term movements in product sales or market shares and in market planning—for example, in deciding pricing strategies. Such models extend the promotional modeling framework discussed in Section 12.2.1 that focused exclusively on promotional effects at the SKU level. They aim to include the key explanatory "sales driver" variables in a causal model of demand. The dependent variable modeled is sales volume, at the product, brand, or category level.

Although there seems to be no ambiguity about how sales should be measured at the disaggregate SKU level, in practice there are many different measures, from factory shipments to store scanner data. As ever, we need to distinguish between sales, which are observed, and demand, which is unobserved (see Section 12.3.1). Hanssens, Parsons, and Schultz (2001) provide a thorough discussion of these various sources of data and their advantages and disadvantages. A further difficulty of definition arises as we move from an individual SKU to a brand and attempt to aggregate the result (e.g., from beer in four-packs of 250 ml to cases of 330 ml bottles). More difficult still would be to measure the sales of a particular brand of detergent for use in washing machines that comes not only in powder and liquid forms, but also in different levels of concentrate. Because of these difficulties, the variables to be forecast are often best kept as disaggregated as the data permit.

> **When Modeling Demand**
>
> - Use a measure of sales volume that removes the effects of price changes and package size.
> - Take into account lost sales due to supply shortages.

Price and income should be among the explanatory variables typically included in market response models of sales. Both need careful thought as to how they should be measured. Price data are collected in current money: dollars, pounds, etc. In a cross-sectional study designed to explain consumer behavior, this is unproblematic, but if price data are collected over time, general inflation (the overall price movements in an economy) may affect consumer response so that a dollar in one year buys less than a dollar did the year before. The problem is overcome by measuring price (or any variable expressed in money terms, including income) in real terms by dividing money prices by a price index such as the Consumer Price Index (published monthly by the Bureau of Labor Statistics in the United States and by government statistics offices in most countries). The issue of real vs. nominal measures of money was explored briefly in Exercise 9.10, which contrasted a model of unleaded prices in money terms with one in real, or inflation-adjusted, form.

Once the effect of general inflation is taken out of the price measure, it still leaves the question of how consumers perceive price when contemplating a purchase. Often, consumers, perceptions are based on alternative purchases in the category; therefore, the appropriate measure is the brand's own price, relative to the average market price, which is an average of prices, weighted by their respective sales volumes. That is, when there are J products in a category, the relative price of the ith product is given by

$$Relative\ Price_{it} = \frac{p_{it}}{\sum_{j=1}^{J}(Vol_{jt}p_{jt}/Total\ Vol_t)},$$

where Vol_{jt} represents the sales volume for the jth brand at time t. Sometimes the relative price is lagged or an average taken over time, because it denotes the consumers' subjective understanding, which would affect demand.

Income, in the aggregate or for an individual consumer, can also be measured in many ways. First, like price, it must be measured in real terms, with inflation effects removed (if a time series is being analyzed). Second, there is the question of whether any taxes paid should also be subtracted (the result of which is called *Disposable Income*). In addition, we might wish to focus on *Discretionary Income* after basic living costs, such as housing and energy, are removed as well. Finally, in considering purchases of consumer durables, it may be worth identifying *Permanent Income*, which is essentially a smoothed average of current and past income. The argument here is that major financial commitments are likely to be based on expectations that one's income will continue. A pragmatic route forward is to include current and lagged values of income in the response model.

Response models also include the price of competing products or services. For example, in models of tourism demand, the price of staying in alternative tourist destinations should be included in the initial, most general models considered (Song and Li, 2008).

Often, marketing activities—for example, advertising or a promotional mail, have effects on sales that last over a period of time. The basic model

$$Y_t = \beta_0 + \beta_j X_{jt}^* + (other\ factors) + (error)$$

includes a particular marketing activity, X_j^*, that is related not only to current spending (on, say, a mail promotion) but also to past spending. For example, if effects persist for $p_j + 1$ periods, then

$$X_{jt}^* = \sum_{k=0}^{p_j} \lambda_k X_{j,t-k},$$

where $\lambda_0 = 1$. If $\lambda_k = 0$ for all $k > 0$, then there is only an immediate effect of β_j, due to X_{jt}s affecting Y. Nonzero λ_k for $k > 0$ implies that past levels of X_j also affect current levels of Y. Advertising is such an example, because it is often thought of as having just such a cumulative effect over time. X_j^* is sometimes called *Adstock*. (See the discussion in Hanssens *et al.*, 2001, for further details.) Similarly, in the important example of forecasting calls to a call center, the number of incoming calls is stimulated by mail promotions; however, the mailings neither go out on the same day they are scheduled nor get delivered on the same day, so the telephone response on a particular day depends on past mailings over quite a number of periods. (See Minicase 12.1.)

An important influence on current demand is the consumer's habits; that is, past behavior carries over into the present. In an extreme case, the product is addictive, as in cigarette or alcohol consumption. In essence, past demand affects current demand, so it is often natural to include lagged values of Y as one of the drivers of current consumption. The basic model then becomes

$$Y_t = \beta_0 + \gamma_1 Y_{t-1} + \beta_j X_{jt}^* + (other\ factors) + (error).$$

Additional lags beyond 1 may also be justified empirically, so the simple model of demand now includes lags in both the dependent variable and some of the explanatory market drivers. Seasonal lags may capture behavioral seasonal effects, so a four-period lag would be considered for quarterly data.

The opposite idea is that of the stock of a product that consumers already own. As in the example of cars, the stock of cars already on the road and the average age of that stock are likely to influence the next period's purchases. Suppose the stock at time $(t-1)$ is S_{t-1}, with Y_t the current purchases. Then the stock at time t is given by

$$S_t = S_{t-1} - \delta S_{t-1} + Y_{t-1},$$

where δS_{t-1} is the number of cars scrapped at time $t-1$. Thus, a demand model that explains car sales Y_t in period t, in terms of stocks, is

$$Y_t = \beta_0 + \beta_{stock}S_t + (other\ factors) + (error).$$

By substituting for S_t, the model becomes a model in lagged values of Y_t, the other factors, and the error. In the example of modeling and forecasting car demand, running costs could be included, in addition to the stock of used cars on the road (de Jong, Fox, Pieters, Daly, and Smith, 2004).

EXAMPLE 12.2 ■ Model for air travel

Various air travel models have included lag effects to include habit formation as well as trade growth to capture economic activities (Fildes *et al.*, 2011). For the route between the United Kingdom and Canada, an autoregressive distributed lag model of the annual growth rate in passengers (measured in logarithms of differences) and of the form

$$Dy_t = \alpha_0 + \sum_{j=1}^{2}\alpha_j Dy_{t-j} + \sum_{k=1}^{2}\sum_{j=0}^{2}\beta_{kj}Dx_{k(t-j)} + \varepsilon_t$$

was proposed, where $t = 1, 2, \ldots, T$ (time periods); Dy_t is the growth rate of the number of passenger in year t; and Dx_{kt} is the growth rate of the kth explanatory variable, here international trade and ticket price, in year t. A maximum lag length of 2 was needed, and the model was simplified as illustrated below. The data for a number of countries, including Canada, are given in *Air_passenger.xlsx*. The model was estimated from 1961–2002 to give

$$Dy_t = 0.0260 + 0.509^* Dy_{t-1} + 0.199^* DTrade_{t-2} - 0.196^* DTicketPrice_t \quad R^2\ adj = .426$$
$$\quad (0.013)\quad (0.125)\qquad\quad (0.085)\qquad\qquad\quad (0.058),$$

where the asterisks (*) denote coefficients that are significant at the 1 percent level. (Standard errors are shown in parentheses.) The model was estimated in differences in order to capture the fact that all the variables were nonstationary (see Appendix 10A.3). In the model, the persistence of a habit is shown by the lagged impact of the previous year's growth. In addition, both *Trade* between the two counties and the *TicketPrice* have the expected sign, although the two period lag on *Trade* is perhaps counter-intuitive. The model also passes various diagnostic tests, including autocorrelation and, in particular, parameter constancy. Extending the analysis to look across five routes from the United Kingdom, including a route to the United States, showed (unsurprisingly) that the terrorist attacks of September 11, 2001, had a significantly negative impact on travel (see Exercise 12.9). Some other modes of transportation such as rail were much less affected by the event.   ■

Market response models have also been developed to forecast the demand for particular brands of goods at the individual store level. A typical causal model is of the form

Market response$_{ijt}$
 $= f$(*marketing instruments*: *price, display, feature, store, competition, events, promotion, . . . ; seasonality; exogenous factors*),

where i is the ith brand (or SKU) in a category of closely related products, j is the jth store, and t is time.

Building Market Response Models

In building a market response model, the key decisions to make are:

(i) which explanatory variables to include in the proposed model; and
(ii) the appropriate level of aggregation at which to build the model.

EXAMPLE 12.3 ■ Market response model for soft drinks

Divakar, Ratchford, and Shankar (2005) used the preceding model to examine the soft-drink market in the United States. They considered two leading brands (Pepsi and Coke) and data on different distribution channels to market, such as grocery stores, convenience stores, gas stations, and restaurants. They considered a log–log model where sales volume and the explanatory variables that measure price have been logged. Two additional promotional variables were included: *Display* (indicating whether the product is displayed to best advantage at the point of sale), measured as percent of total volume only on display, and *Feature*, measured as percent of total volume only featured (i.e., in a local store, leaflet advertising promoted products). Also measured was percent of total volume both featured and displayed.

Part of Divakar and colleagues' model for the grocery channel is

$$\ln(Pepsi\ volume) = 17.645 - 2.342\ln(Pepsi's\ price) + 0.583\ln(Coke's\ price)$$
$$(-23.9) \qquad\qquad\qquad (5.88)$$

$$+ 0.0028Pepsi's\ Display + \cdots + 0.0018Temp + (Dummies)$$
$$(3.15) \qquad\qquad\qquad (6.64)$$

t-statistics are shown in parentheses. $R^2 = 90$ percent. There is no indication of any autocorrelation in the residuals.

Estimated price and cross-price elasticities, at −2.34 and +0.58, respectively, accorded with other studies, so a 10 percent increase in Pepsi's price is forecast to lead to a drop of 23.4 percent in sales volume while the impact of a 10 percent increase in Coke's price is estimated to lead to a 5.83 percent increase in Pepsi's volume.

Additional variables included in the model were dummy variables for U.S. regions, for different periods of the year, and for sporting events (e.g., the Super Bowl). Temperature (*Temp*) also had an effect, as shown in the model, with higher temperatures leading to higher sales. Because *Display* and *Feature* are measured in percentages, their impact is calculated by multiplying by 100 and taking the exponential of the result. For example, the display effect when 100 percent of volume is on display is $\exp(0.0028 * 100) = 1.32$; that is, display increases volume by 32 percent (ranging from no store level display to 100 percent of volume being displayed).

When the model was used to forecast sales in individual regions (in the grocery channel) out of sample, *MAPE* one week ahead was around 5.5 percent, dropping to 3.1 percent when aggregated across regions.

Of course, some of the explanatory variables would be unknown when the model is put to use, so variables such as competitor price, as well as feature and display, are market drivers outside the manufacturer's control. Accordingly, models were then developed to forecast these explanatory variables, using the same variables as included in the original model. ■

Models have been proposed to capture the relative attraction of one brand compared with that of its competitors or, more generally, one SKU within a brand. A particular SKU may compete with other *product forms* within the same brand (e.g., different pack sizes), as well as competing with other brands (and their various product forms). For a full discussion of the various forms, the reader should consult Hanssens *et al.* (2001, pp. 121–129); however, be warned that this is a demanding read. Koehler, Snyder, Ord, and Beaumont (2012) use logistic transforms to examine exponential smoothing models for market share.

A model that captures the various market complexities must include competing brands and the different product forms. Let $p = 1, \ldots, P$ represent the different product forms and $b = 1, \ldots, B$ the different competing brands. Then if Q_{bp} represents the demand for brand b's product form p, where Q_{bp} could, in principle, depend on K variables and where each variable (e.g., price) could affect Q via all its competing products, it follows that if the price of a competing 20-oz pack goes down, then the drop in price could affect the quantity demanded of product bp (brand b in product form p). Perhaps the simplest model that captures competitive effects would be of the form

$$\ln Q_{bp,t} = \beta_{bp0} + \beta_{bp,bp} \ln X_{bp,t} + \beta_{bp,b1} \ln X_{b1,t} + \beta_{bp,1p} \ln X_{1p,t} + \beta_{bp,11} \ln X_{11,t} + \varepsilon_{bp,t}.$$

Here, product form p in brand b is thought only to compete through price directly with form 1 of the same brand and competing brand 1: The parameters represent the own-price elasticity ($\beta_{bp,bp}$) and cross-price elasticities (for form 1 of the same brand, $\beta_{bp,b1}$; for the competitor's form b, $\beta_{bp,1p}$, and for the competitor's form 1, $\beta_{bp,11}$). Although $\beta_{bp,bp}$ is expected to be negative, the cross-elasticities on product bp are expected to be positive. The higher the price of a competing product or a competing product form, the higher are the sales of the product we focus on.

These same ideas can be used to develop market response models to capture the share of a product's sales through a market share model in which

$$Market\ Share = \frac{Our\ Sales}{Total\ Market\ Sales}, \quad \text{or} \quad MS_{bp} = \frac{Q_{bp}}{\sum\limits_{i=1}^{B} \sum\limits_{j=1}^{P} Q_{ij}}.$$

An alternative multiplicative model of market share is

$$\ln(MS_{bpt}) = \beta_0 + \sum_{k,i} \beta_{bp,ki} \ln(X^*_{bpk,t}) + \varepsilon_t,$$

where $X^*_{bpk,i}$ represents the kth competitive marketing variable, such as relative price, promotional deals, and various retail characteristics (e.g., distribution and advertising), each of which may be lagged one or more periods. (Of course, a linear version of the same model could also be used.) Market share models should be logically consistent in that, summed over the whole market, $\sum_{b,p} MS_{bp} = 1$. However, the multiplicative form does not have that characteristic (but this does not prevent it from being a reasonable approximation).

Models such as these are complex, with too many parameters to estimate. Alternatively, these cross-effects could all be set to zero, but doing so would often render the model unrealistic. Instead, perhaps the best approach would be to set most cross-effects to zero and consider only products that are believed by market experts to compete.

A more heuristic, but still often effective, approach is to run a stepwise regression analysis (Section 9.4) with the cutoff value $\alpha = 1/N$, where N denotes the total number of predictor variables. The use of an extreme cutoff value ensures that the risk of including spurious variables in the model is low so that most terms are excluded, but the decision is made with the use of data-driven rules rather than prior judgments.

Other variables entered into such models include display (which describes how the product is displayed in the store) and feature (which describes whether the product is in retail advertisements) as well as lags in some the variables. As if this wasn't complicated enough, if we are a retailer, we may wish to understand and forecast at a store level. So the model can be extended to include store-level effects. It is unfortunate for the forecaster that stores differ in terms of their local markets and therefore experience different elasticities, depending on the preferences of their local consumers. With such complexities, how do practicing forecasters deal with the problem? The next section suggests some solutions.

12.4.6 Expert Adjustments and Promotional Effects

For most organizations, developing models of the complexity described in the previous section has historically proved just too difficult. There were probably no staff with the necessary expertise, nor were the data and the software available. Instead, forecasters resorted to taking a simple statistical approach and then would modify the baseline statistical forecast (see Section 12.2.1) to take into account the expected promotional effects. With recent improvements in data collection (e.g., point-of-sale data capture, the use of social networks) and more sophisticated models and software available, this state of affairs is beginning to change.

Returning to the question of promotional adjustments, we saw in Section 12.2.1 how this might be done statistically. But typically, there are many different types of promotion (e.g., buy one, get one free; half price; 30 percent extra), and forecasters see their role as taking all the particular characteristics of these promotions into account by adjusting the statistical forecast. So, do they do this well?

Empirical evidence presented in Fildes *et al.* (2009) suggests that forecasters often fail quite spectacularly. An analysis of four companies revealed that all the companies typically overestimated the expected positive effects of factors such as promotions. (There was a positive bias to the adjusted forecasts.) What was worse is that often the adjustments made by the company forecasters were in the wrong direction, due perhaps to competitive factors being neglected. There is therefore an obvious need to develop forecasting support systems (FSSs) so as to help practicing forecasters take account of promotions and other market drivers more successfully.

Discussion Question *How might an FSS be extended beyond the purely statistical to help forecasters take into account promotions and other market drivers?*

12.4.7 Implementation Issues

Market response modeling has been established in the research literature for many years. However, implementing the models we have examined has proved difficult for many companies, for reasons we will discuss in the last chapter of this book. In fact, Montgomery (2005) summarized the retail evidence on the practice of market modeling as follows: "the market is ready . . . although widespread adoption has not happened yet." Occasionally, we find evidence of an advanced application; see, for example, Natter, Reutterer, Mild, and Taudes (2007), which uses the price elasticities at store level in an Austrian–German do-it-yourself chain to both forecast and price the stores' products. But such examples are unusual. Even when a farsighted manager is successful in taking a marketing analytic view forward, it seems rare for these ideas to become embedded in the firm. All too often, the manager moves on and the system fails. It even seems rare to find companies with databases sufficiently rich to include a substantial and accessible history of their own price and promotion data, never mind that of their competition. Instead, simple models are often used, but as we have noted, new data sources are likely to drive change in this area, giving organizations all the detail they might require.

Forecasting Individual Behavior

In Chapter 10, we introduced various methods of mining rich databases of customer (or potential customer) characteristics in order to predict behavior. Companies want to forecast individual customer behavior (and sometimes firm behavior) in order to gain and keep additional profitable customers. A second important application is the granting of customer credit. Besides private companies, other organizations—for example, governments—want to forecast individual behavior for some of the same reasons, in order to predict the uptake of services. More ominously, they might wish to identify criminals who might reoffend (recidivists, who then would not be released from jail) or potential terrorists, who would undergo more intensive screening (prior to an aircraft flight, for example).

The information the organization has to help it in this regard depends on the nature of the customer relationship—in particular, whether a past history is available from a previous relationship with the organization or whether the customer is new. Figure 12.13 breaks down the process of forecasting individual behavior into four stages: (i) target marketing, in which the aim is to identify potentially profitable customers, (ii) new-customer acquisition, wherein the potential customer, having received an offer, must provide further information, (iii) maintaining a relationship, in which, after the new customer has established early patterns of behavior (e.g., through mobile calling or credit card spending), the company aims to increase the customer's profitability through cross-selling of complementary products or through promotional offers that make further spending more attractive (these are high-value customers), and (iv) churning, wherein the company loses a customer, usually because the customer has identified a better offer or because the customer is dissatisfied.

Target Marketing: If there has been no contact between the organization and the potential customer, then some limited sociodemographic information may be readily available—in particular, the zip code and gender of the person in the United States or the post-code, sex, and eligibility to vote in the United Kingdom. The zip code[2] (or postcode in the United Kingdom) can be used to classify the address so that it provides proxy (indirect) information on such characteristics as income, marital status, lifestyle, and housing. Systems such as Mosaic, Tapestry, and Prism are now available in much of the developed world, although such classifications are limited in that they associate with each person an average value for the area he or she lives in, rather than affording individual information.

FIGURE 12.13   FORECASTING INDIVIDUAL BEHAVIOR
(Adapted from Figure 12.8)

---

[2]In the United States, there are legal restrictions on the use of information such as zip codes and ethnicity in making decisions on credit applications, etc.

> ## Geodemographic Segmentation Systems (GSS)
>
> A GSS classifies neighborhoods (e.g., census tracts) into segments (e.g., 60 or so in the United States) by grouping tracts with similar demographic characteristics. The basic premise of geodemographic segmentation is that people tend to gravitate toward communities with people of similar backgrounds, interests, and financial means.

Sociodemographic data can be enhanced by using credit agencies to add such important details as whether the person has incurred debts that have led to legal proceedings. In addition, many of the companies that provide credit pool some of their information, including such key variables as the outstanding balance on a debt and the current and historical arrears record. The dependent variable here is whether to make an offer or to target a particular customer.

New Customers: In some applications, the stage after contacting the individual through target marketing is when the potential customer responds to the offer. The additional information the company learns from a customer's response offers the opportunity for understanding the customer's characteristics. Using the credit card application as an example, we see that the additional information would include personal sociodemographic information such as marital status, length of time at the current address, and income. This additional information can then be used to accept or reject an application or, more ambitiously, to price the offer through the terms of credit offered. The dependent variable here is whether to accept the customer's application.

Discussion Question *Is the use of such targeting methods ethical in considering (i) credit approvals, (ii) the identification of potential tax evaders, or (iii) the identification of potential terrorists?*

Established Customers and Churning: Valuable information is collected once the customer relationship is established with the company. Be it a phone company, a bookseller, or a credit card company, it can observe how the customer uses the product or service. Taking Amazon as an example, we see that once the purchasing record has been observed and a person's tastes established at least in part, those data can then be used to predict the type of books or CDs a customer would be interested in. It is also possible to predict the likelihood of a new purchase being prompted by a mail promotion or offer, as well as the size of the likely order. Table 12.8 summarizes the types of data used in direct marketing.

The trouble with behavioral (transactions) data is that the database quickly gets very large. Various summary measures are used to capture the key characteristics of a customer's transactions, such as the *RFM* measures of *R* (recency, or the length of time since the last purchase), *F* (the frequency of purchase during a period), and *M* (the value of purchases over a period). Other databases beyond customer transactions are also relevant to both

TABLE 12.8   TYPES OF EXPLANATORY DATA USED TO PREDICT RESPONSE

Object	Type of data	Significance	Accessibility	Variability
Customer	Demographic, lifestyle, sociographic	Low	External	High
Behavior	Transaction records, Web-browsing log file	High	Internal, accumulating	High
Product	Size, color, price	Low	Internal	Low
Solicitation	Design style	Low	Internal	Low

Source: Bose and Chen (2009).

future purchasing behavior and whether a customer will "churn"—that is, change supplier. Here, customer satisfaction with the reliability of the service can affect the probability of churning, and companies often collect survey data on this measure. (Customer satisfaction is particularly relevant to telephone companies, Internet providers, insurance companies, etc.) What has proved even more relevant is the customer's satisfaction *after* a complaint or problem such as an interruption of service or a car accident.

In most of the applications we have described thus far, the dependent variable is categorical (0 or 1). The decision made by the credit supplier is to agree an application or to reject it on the basis of the probability that the potential customer will default. In analyzing a consumer's propensity to churn, the aim is to classify customers into those who are loyal and those who are likely to switch. In direct marketing, the objective is to identify potential customers. We will use the methods of Chapter 10 to classify, for example, a loan applicant. Our aim here is to show how the models we have introduced can be used in practice to forecast individual credit behavior. (Thomas, 2009, offers a detailed review of the topic, including an examination of the evaluation of such models, expanding on our discussion in Section 10.1.1.)

12.5.1 Comparing Models

In this example, we show how the different methods of predictive classification (developed in Chapter 10) can be used. This case study in comparing models (taken with thanks to SAS as a case study in its data-mining software package, Enterprise Miner) has the objective of identifying likely defaulters for applicants for home equity credit. The full database consists of 5960 observations with 12 predictor variables, defined in Table 12.9. The target variable, *BAD*, is whether the applicant has defaulted on the loan, a 0/1 categorical variable.

TABLE 12.9   PREDICTING LOAN DEFAULT: EXPLANATORY (INPUT)
VARIABLES AND VARIABLE TYPE

Name	Description	Model Role	Measurement	Type
BAD	= 1 if the applicant defaulted on loan, = 0 if paid up	Target	Binary	Number
Loan	Amount of loan request	Input	Interval	Number
Mortdue	Amount due on existing mortgage	Input	Interval	Number
Value	Value of current property DebtCon=debt consolidation	Input	Interval	Number
Reason	HomeImp = Home improvement	Input	Binary	Character
Job		Input	Nominal	Character
YOJ	Years in present job	Input	Interval	Number
Derog	Number of derogatory reports	Input	Interval	Number
Delinq	Number of delinquent credit lines	Input	Interval	Number
CLAGE	Age of oldest credit line in months	Input	Interval	Number
NINQ	Number of recent credit inquiries	Input	Interval	Number
CLNO	Number of credit lines	Input	Interval	Number
Debtinc	Debt-to-income ratio	Input	Interval	Number

Source: Adapted from SAS output.

The input variables include a mixture of financial credit variables (such as *Loan, Mortdue, Delinq, CLAGE, NINQ, CLNO*) and personal finance variables (*Value, Debtinc*).

Job is a nominal variable describing the job held by the applicant. Each type of job is classified by a separate dummy variable, and there are five major job categories in all. *YOJ* (years in the present job) measures job stability (to a certain extent). *Reason* is a 0/1 binary dummy variable that describes the reason given by the applicant for applying for the loan.

The data set has initially been split into an estimation (training) subset (50 percent), a validation set (30 percent), and a test set (20 percent). If the database has been collected over a number of periods, the forecaster must consider whether a time-based sample should also be considered to identify "model drift," a condition that occurs when models change over time. Model drift is a common occurrence when economic circumstances change (as when a recession is developing).

We will first use all the variables in Table 12.9 in developing and comparing three models: a logistic regression model, a neural network, and a classification tree. The first stage in understanding the issues is to carry out some exploratory analysis, including frequency analysis and graphical analysis, missing variables, correlations, and more. We've left this as an exercise for the reader (Exercise 12.18); however, we note one important result: The percentage of defaulted loans in the sample of 5960 observations is 20 percent.

Logistic Regression The model, including all the explanatory variables, was estimated automatically on the 50% training set giving the results shown in Table 12.10. Missing values were replaced with their mean value (see Section 12.5.2).

With this model, each observation (in the training, validation, or test data sets) generates a prediction of whether the loan will prove good or bad. Each prediction whose probability is greater than 50 percent is categorized as bad and each prediction whose probability is less than 50 percent is categorized as good. For example, 53 observations fell above the

TABLE 12.10 LOGISTIC REGRESSION MODEL: POINT ESTIMATES AND ODDS RATIO ESTIMATES

Effect	Point Estimate	P-value	Odds Ratio
Intercept:BAD=1	−2.276	0.000	0.103
CLAGE	−0.005	0.000	0.995
CLNO	−0.023	0.000	0.977
DEBTINC	0.057	0.000	1.058
DELINQ	0.818	0.000	2.266
DEROG	0.545	0.000	1.724
JOB MGR	0.014	0.924	1.014
JOB OFFICE	−0.652	0.000	0.521
JOB OTHER	−0.126	0.260	0.882
JOB PROFEXE	−0.171	0.214	0.843
JOB SALES	0.832	0.010	2.297
LOAN	0.000	0.000	1.000
MORTDUE	0.000	0.002	1.000
NINQ	0.223	0.000	1.250
REASON DEBTCON	−0.065	0.284	0.937
VALUE	0.000	0.000	1.000
YOJ	−0.016	0.053	0.984

Note: The dependent variable is BAD (equal to 1 if applicant defaulted on the loan, 0 if no default).

Source: Data shown is from file Loans.xlsx. The table is available in SAS and SPSS formats also. The SAS database from which this was taken was originally named SAMPS10.HMEQ and is used with permission of SAS.

FIGURE 12.14   LOGISTIC REGRESSION: ROC CURVE FOR VALIDATION SAMPLE

Data: Loans.xlsx or Loans.SAS7bdat; adapted from SAS output.

50 percent cutoff, of which 40 turned out to be correct predictions of bad performance. Using alternative cutoffs generates the ROC curve as shown in Figure 12.14. Selected results are shown in Table 12.11.

Neural Network Models   We first carry out some exploration of the number of hidden nodes to include in a network with one hidden layer. We consider 1, 3, and 5 nodes, with the results shown in Table 12.11. The comparable ROC curve shows little difference between the three alternatives on the test and validation data. The results suggest little or no benefit from increasing the number of nodes beyond 1.

We have chosen to use a 50 percent cutoff that classifies the top 50 percent of scores as defaulters (bad). SAS automatically produces a similar table, but it is based on classifying *all* cases with an estimated score of 0.50 or more (interpretable as the probability of default) as "bads." This approach usually leads to a substantially smaller overall number of mis-classified cases because most of the observations from which the model was constructed are "goods." However, the target suffers a higher level of misclassification.

TABLE 12.11   MISCLASSIFICATION RATES FOR TRAINING, VALIDATION, AND TEST DATA USING VARIOUS CLASSIFICATION METHODS
(Missing values replaced for logistic and neural networks)

Description	Training: Misclassification Rate	Validation: Misclassification Rate	Test: Misclassification Rate
Logistic (50% cutoff)	0.361	0.383	0.378
Neural net: 1 hidden node	0.363	0.380	0.378
Neural net: 3 hidden nodes	0.353	0.368	0.383
Neural net: 5 hidden nodes	0.345	0.380	0.383
Classification tree	0.359	0.361	0.352

Data: Loans.xlsx or Loans.SAS7bdat

FIGURE 12.15   DECIDING ON THE NUMBER OF LEAVES TO INCLUDE

Data: Loans.xlsx or Loans.SAS7bdat

Classification Trees   In Chapter 10, we introduced Chi-squared Automatic Interaction Detection (CHAID) as an SPSS method for predicting categorical data such as the bad loans of the previous example. SAS has its own method of developing a classification tree (although it can be used to emulate CHAID and other variants of classification trees, such as CART). The results from all these different methods are similar, and no method has been shown to consistently outperform (or underperform) the others. We now add SAS's tree method to our predictive armory; the method delivers the following classes of likely defaulters on the training set:

a. Low *DEBTINC*, high *VALUE* (17 out of 20 falling into this category correctly predicted as defaulters)

b. High *DEBTINC*, low *DELINQ*, low *CLAGE* (239 out of 335 correctly predicted)

c. High *DEBTINC*, high *DELINQ* (91 out of 94 correctly predicted)

Figure 12.15 offers the analyst an insight into how many leaves to include by showing how the misclassification rate changes with the number included. (The misclassification rate used is that calculated by SAS Enterprise Miner, in contrast to Table 12.11.) Of course, on the training data set the rate always improves as the number of leaves (and the model's complexity) increases. But the same relationship does not hold on the validation data set, so a number between 5 and 7 seems appropriate here. (The misclassification rate shown is based on classifying those with a score of 0.5 or more as bad.)

Using a model with 7 leaves gives an overall misclassification rate for the training data based on 984 observations of good classified as bad plus 85 observations of bad classified as good = (984 + 85)/2980 = 35.9 percent. The overall misclassification rate for the validation data is also 35.9 percent.

12.5.2   Building Customer Relationship Management Models

In the last few sections, we have shown how three different methods of predictive classification can be used on the same problem. We now bring all these methods together to demonstrate their practical application, but before the methods can deliver their best results, the data need to be preprocessed. Crone, Lessmann, and Stahlbock (2006) have shown preprocessing to be important in examining the relative performance of different methods. Key issues include the choice of sample, missing observations, and the treatment of continuous and ordered data.

Data Preprocessing

i. *Choosing the sample data*: For most applications in customer relationship marketing, the analysis focuses on a relatively small number of individuals in a much larger population. For example, the percentage of people (or firms) who respond to a direct mail promotion is around 1 percent, and the percentage of people who default on a loan is less than 10 percent. The forecaster's aims are usually focused on improving the identification of individuals falling into these target groups. The reason is that they are, respectively, more valuable and more costly to the organization than the larger population of nonrespondents and nondefaulters. However, for some applications which use a method that is particularly computationally intensive, taking a very large sample is expensive or difficult. How large should the sample be? The answer depends in part on the composition of the population being modeled and, in particular, the percentage of people in the target class.

The standard approach to determining the database to employ is first to split the data at random into an estimation data set, a validation set, and a test data set (as we discussed in Chapter 10). However, this procedure would naturally lead to subsamples that are approximately representative of the two groups; consequently, just a small number would fall into the target group. Two alternatives spring to mind (for a fixed sample size): We can randomly oversample the target class or randomly undersample the majority class. Crone *et al.* (2006) have shown that oversampling produces better results for a number of classification methods. Therefore, we should increase the number of instances of the minority class of interest so that it is approximately the same size as the majority class (e.g., with 500 in the majority class and 50 in the minority class, we should include each member of the target tenfold). Once that decision has been made, the choice of overall sample size depends on the method being employed (and other preprocessing choices).

For example, classification trees are more sensitive to sample size than is logistic regression. Critically, methods improve with increasing sample size; even with large samples, the improvements are potentially valuable.

Figure 12.16 compares ROC curves for the 20–80 percent sample of the data used in training and validation. Two sets of comparisons are shown: models in which the data set has been enhanced by replacing missing observations and models in which the "bads" have been oversampled to increase the sensitivity of the model. The figure shows strong effects from including missing observations and some weaker benefits from oversampling. For any given level of the probability of rejecting a good loan applicant (1 − specificity), there is a higher sensitivity (of correctly identifying a bad applicant) when the target is oversampled, as here.

We can also compare the results on the test data set by using different cutoffs of 10 percent, 25 percent, and 40 percent, as shown in Table 12.12. (Note that this comparison can be made only on the raw test data because, where oversampling is used as opposed to random sampling, the training and validation data sets are not identical.)

The oversample and random sample both use 5960 observations. In the former case, 50 percent of the observations are bad, chosen by replicating the target bad observations in order to increase the sample size from 361 to 931.

As can easily be seen from Figure 12.16 and Table 12.12, using an oversampling scheme aids the identification of the target quite substantially.

ii. *Coding variables*: Many of the predictor variables in predictive classification problems are categorical (they describe a category that a customer or case belongs to, e.g. a geographical area or an occupation) or ordinal (e.g., education level). In the example examined, there are many interval-level data, such as the amount of the loan that has been requested. The advantage of recoding interval data into ordinal (dummy variable) categories is that any nonlinear effects can be easily incorporated.

FIGURE 12.16   ROC CURVE: VALIDATION SAMPLE COMPARING
OVERSAMPLING AND RANDOM SAMPLING WITH AND
WITHOUT REPLACEMENT OF MISSING VALUES
(*The oversampling scheme replicated the number of bad
applicants to make the two sample sizes equal.*)

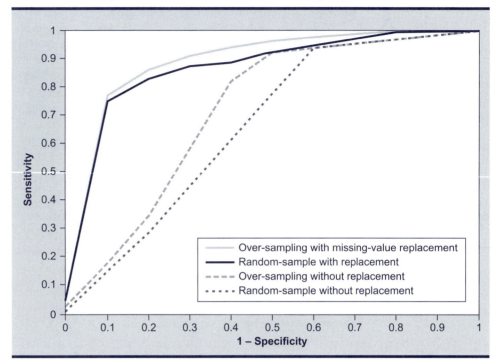

Data: Loans.xlsx, adapted from SAS output

TABLE 12.12   A COMPARISON OF MISCLASSIFICATION RATES FROM
OVERSAMPLING AND FROM REPLACEMENT OF MISSING
OBSERVATIONS: LOGISTIC REGRESSION

Cutoff Probability		**10% Cutoff**		**20% Cutoff**		**40% Cutoff**	
		%Bad	%Good	%Bad	%Good	%Bad	%Good
Random sample	Raw	2.1%	88.0%	4.6%	76.1%	11.0%	52.8%
	Replace	1.3%	87.7%	3.4%	75.8%	10.1%	52.6%
Over sample	Raw	1.3 %	87.7%	3.8%	75.9%	10.1%	52.6%
	Replace	0.8%	87.6%	2.5%	75.6%	5.9%	51.5%
Sample size		237	955				

The header "Misclassification Rate" spans the 10%, 20%, and 40% Cutoff columns.

Data: Loans.xlsx, based on the Validation Sample

Discussion Question   *Why does coding an interval variable such as age or income potentially benefit predictive classification, and what are the possible problems?*

For example, in the example of computer ownership discussed in Chapter 10, *Age* and *Income* are both interval data, although in the data file they have been assigned to categories

(8 for age, 5 for income), which in turn can be converted into dummy variables. Although we might expect computer ownership to increase linearly with *Income*, *Age* might have quite a different effect, with older and younger people perhaps less likely to be owners.

In the credit application example, there is no evidence of nonlinear effects in the explanatory variables (see Exercise 12.14).

iii. *Replacing missing values*: In a credit application data set such as this one, there are often many missing values for particular variables. Here, the length of the oldest credit line (i.e., the length of time the customer has held a mortgage or a loan, *CLAGE*) has many missing observations. There are numerous methods for replacing missing observations. For categorical data, a missing value can be replaced, for example, by the most common value or, more specifically, the most common value with the same target value. An interval-valued observation with a value missing is often replaced by the average value or the median value. Whatever the methods used (and different methods may lead to different models), it is important to replace the missing observations, because doing so can lead to a different model. A dummy variable has been added to identify those applications for which the missing value has been replaced (i.e., *M_Value* = 1 if the value of the attribute is unknown and is 0 otherwise). In the credit application data set, if logistic regression is used, these missing-value indicators prove significant and improve the misclassification rates, as shown in Table 12.12. Figure 12.16 demonstrates that the results of including both oversampling and replacement are more pronounced for higher levels of the sensitivity (i.e., where the model is capturing a greater percentage of the target variable).

Replacing the missing values and adding a missing-value indicator also changes the variables that need to be included in the model. Here, the number of recent credit inquiries in the logistic model becomes insignificant.

12.5.3   Appraising Models of Individual Behavior

We have considered a number of methods for forecasting individual behavior. No single method is consistently best. The results depend on such features as the number of observations, the characteristics of the sample (in particular, the target variable), and the number of explanatory variables. As a consequence, forecasters will usually consider a number of methods and compare the results. Some software does this relatively easily, but beware: Often the comparisons are not exactly as you would wish, and one method does not compare in detail exactly with another. Figure 12.17, taken from SAS's Enterprise Miner, illustrates the process of comparing models.

The first stage shown in Figure 12.17 is to partition the data into estimation (training), validation, and test data sets (*Data Partition*). Distribution Explorer allows the analyst to carry out some exploratory data analysis. Missing values are replaced in the *Replacement* stage. A variety of methods are then considered. Here, logistic regression is used (in the top application with *Variable* selection, which aims to cut down and simplify the variables to be considered by the *Regression* node). A classification tree (*Tree*) application is also included, as are two alternative *Neural Networks* (one with and one without variable selection). These are all then compared through an Assessment procedure. The last stage is to take the computer code from the final model so that it can be used in subsequent appraisals of different samples. This is done here through the command *Score* associated with the logistic node, but it can be written in any language, including Excel. The results of comparing the results from the methods are shown graphically in Figure 12.18, using the ROC curve and in Table 12.13. The partition employed is 50 percent training, 30 percent validation, and 20 percent test, with no rebalancing of the sample (despite rebalancing being best practice). In addition, various misclassification matrices for different cutoffs would also be analyzed. As we see, for almost all sensitivities, the classification

FIGURE 12.17 AN EXPLORATORY DATA-MINING PROCESS

Source: Taken from SAS Enterprise Miner.

FIGURE 12.18 A COMPARISON OF THREE DATA-MINING METHODS: ROC CURVES

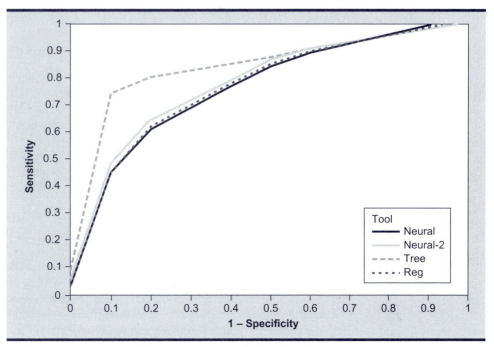

Source: Adapted from SAS output, based on the Test Data Set.

TABLE 12.13   MISCLASSIFICATION RATES FOR ALL METHODS SHOWN IN
FIGURE 12.17 (*0.5 Probability Cutoff*)

Tool	Name	Misclassification Rate		
		Training Set	**Validation Set**	**Test Set**
Logistic regression	All var	0.361	0.383	0.378
Logistic regression	Varselect	0.376	0.386	0.390
Neural network	All var	0.363	0.380	0.378
Neural network	Varselect	0.378	0.386	0.382
Tree	All var	0.359	0.359	0.352

Source: Adapted from SAS.

tree approach proved best on the validation data set and was quite substantially better on the test data set, as measured by the misclassification rate.

In short, forecasting individual behavior is a rich topic that includes many types of forecasting problems. It poses many challenges to the forecaster, from the choice of software (see Appendix C, which is located on the text companion site) to the need to come to grips with a variety of difficult techniques, all of which offer a wide variety of options that affect performance. The following box summarizes the key stages in the process:

The Process of Developing a Predictive Classification Model

1. Use as many observations as are available and computationally tractable.
2. Segment the data into estimation (training), validation, and test subsets.
3. Examine the distribution of the variables.
4. Replace missing and outlying observations.
5. Develop an oversampling scheme to ensure equal samples of the target and nontarget subpopulations.
6. Choose a variety of plausible methods.
7. Use a procedure for eliminating insignificant variables.
8. Compare performance on relevant criteria and cutoff values.
9. Evaluate performance comparatively on the test data.

There is no easy route through this complexity other than to check the effects of all these options. We've highlighted a few of the most important ones—for example, balanced sampling, replacement of outliers, and transforming interval data into groups of ordinal (dummy) variables. These problems associated with choosing a model can be resolved only through careful assessment of the results, using criteria such as the cutoff or profit-and-loss assessments (see Section 10.1.1). However, whether the application is in direct marketing, attempting to identify target consumers; in credit assessment; or in modeling consumer choice, there are major gains to be made by careful modeling.

 ## 12.6 Macroeconomic Forecasting

Macroeconomic (econometric) forecasting is one of the most important application areas of forecasting, although the forecasts are usually produced by economists rather than business forecasters. Before we look at the need for macroeconomic forecasts at an organizational level, we briefly discuss forecasting from a national government perspective. First, we should recognize that much macroeconometric modeling is focused upon trying to understand features of the economy, rather than making pure forecasts. That is, such models are used for "what-if" forecasting to develop policy options, because the policies chosen will have a material effect upon future outcomes.

Revisiting the earlier parts of this chapter, we see that it still makes sense to develop a national-level FSS, although this will now typically be stocked with series from government sources. Because policy decisions are the main motivation, the models used will be causal so that the effects of, say, a change in interest rates on unemployment can be followed through for several months and compared with a no-change scenario. In fact, many of the government models that form the basis of official government forecasts in the United States, the European Union, and elsewhere are based on a large, complex system of equations with many output variables affected by many other exogenous (i.e., external to the system) and policy variables. Fortunately, the available database of macroeconomic series is huge, even though the drivers that influence such aggregate variables as national unemployment or *GDP* are many. Even countries as self-sufficient as the United States are affected by exchange rate movements and growth in the world economy, particularly in countries such as China and India. In Europe, the interrelationships among the major economies mean that causal forecasting models would theoretically include many variables from a range of countries. However, a standard alternative approach to such a complex set of interrelationships is to use smaller VAR models, extended to include exogenous variables such as world trade. One early example was developed by Litterman (1986). It consisted of seven equations, for annual growth rates of real gross national product (*GNP*), *Inflation, Unemployment*, logged levels of the *Money Supply*, logged levels of gross private domestic *Investment*, a commercial *Interest Rate*, and the change in *Business Inventories*. Six lags were included in the *VAR* system, which was then estimated on quarterly data. As McNees (1986) and Litterman discuss, the performance of this simple model turned out to be comparable to that of much larger systems. However, Fildes and Stekler (2002) argue that the empirical evidence does not support any particular approach and, in fact, the range of forecasts produced by the different models and different modeling groups often fails to encompass the actual outcome. An all-too-worrying example has been the economic and financial crisis of 2007–2012. The ad hoc rules of accuracy according to which both U.S. inflation and real *GDP* growth could be forecast with an *MAE* of around 1 percent have all too conclusively been broken.

One particular macroeconomic forecasting problem has attracted considerable attention over the years: that of predicting turning points (business cycles) in the economy. The key variable watched is real *GDP* (or *GNP*), with both governments and businesses having considerable interest in whether an expansion or a recession is coming to an end. Some of the earliest work on forecasting dealt with business cycles and the prediction of turning points. Lahiri and Moore's (1991) book covers a range of approaches, starting with the use of leading indicators, where a future turning point in an index of leading variables (such as stock prices) is claimed to predict a turning point in *GDP* in the real economy. From its earliest beginnings as a qualitative approach, such business cycle analysis uses many of the techniques we have described in this book. Logistic regression can be used to predict the probability of a turning point (moving from positive to negative growth or vice versa). The predictors used include a wide range of leading economic variables (i.e., they are lagged variables in the logistic function). But are such methods successful? As yet, a solution to the problem of predicting economic turning points—in particular, the onset of recessions—has eluded us, leaving organizations to cope as best they can with the unexpected changes in the economy.

Many government series are available on a monthly basis (some, such as *GDP*, only quarterly), but there is also a publication lag of several weeks. Thus, a considerable amount of economic activity may take place between the latest available figures and the present time, making adjustment by informed judgment valuable if not essential. As at the company level, the process of making adjustments enables policy makers to take ownership of the forecasts.

That said, it is also often the case that political considerations may obfuscate the differences between forecasts and targets. (See Stekler, 2007, for a discussion of the process governments go through in macroeconomic forecasting.)

As with marketing promotions, government tax cuts or other stimuli can be evaluated after the fact by using standard regression methods with indicator variables, but forecasting the impact of future policy changes can, at best, be done only to the extent that the data series contain past examples of similar policy changes.

Considerable research has gone into improving the accuracy of macro forecasts (see Fildes and Stekler, 2002), ranging from using better and more timely data to employing increasingly complex econometric modeling. Overall, there is little evidence of improvement in the last 20 years for such key variables as *GDP* and *Inflation*, variables that often affect a firm's profitability. Frequently, the forecasts obtained from these models do not outperform simple extrapolative alternatives. In fact, the principles of forecasting we laid down in earlier chapters apply equally to macroeconomic forecasting.

Turning now to the organizational forecaster's objective of producing more disaggregate forecasts, we find that macroeconomic variables are often needed as explanatory variables in econometric models at the more disaggregate level required. For example, the air passenger demand models of Section 12.4.5, which are relevant to airline and airport planners, were based on macro variables of world trade and national disposable income. Similarly, a regional government forecaster would wish to link regional forecasts to national changes. We do not recommend that the forecaster make her own macro forecasts. Instead, public and private sources are available to deliver the forecasts necessary to support the needs of an organization. For example, the organization Consensus Economics (*www.consensuseconomics.com*), which works on one of our favorite principles of combining, will deliver as accurate a forecast as any other for a wide range of variables and many countries (see Exercise 12.18).

Discussion Question *Why do you think that macroeconomic forecasting is often no more accurate than a naïve extrapolative model when one is looking more than 12 months out? Why do you think that most macro forecasters failed to forecast the "Great Recession" that started in 2007?*

 ## 12.7 Other Applications

The range of application areas for the forecasting methods considered in this book is extensive. We have focused on what are perhaps the organizationally most important topics of operations and marketing. However, before an organization can forecast its financial needs, it must produce cost forecasts, including the costs of raw materials, parts, and labor. Although the methods we have introduced in the earlier chapters all apply to these problems, specialist sources are available to help determine appropriate methods and explanatory variables (i.e., those which have worked in practice). For example, in forecasting production costs, one important influence is the increasing efficiency of the production process. This feature is often captured by including cumulative production in the cost forecasting model.

Within a particular industry setting, there are many specialist issues focusing on which variables to include and how they should be measured. Areas that have seen much research include telecommunications forecasting (see Fildes and Kumar, 2002), electricity demand forecasting (see the Special *International Journal of Forecasting* Issue on Energy Forecasting, Taylor and Espasa, 2008), and sports forecasting (see, e.g., Williams and Stekler, 2010 and Stekler, Sendor, and Verlander, 2010). Likewise, financial forecasting and commodity price and agricultural forecasting are specialist areas with their own concerns. A useful summary of some of the issues in financial forecasting is given by Timmermann and Granger (2004). A key issue in forecasting financial variables and commodity and agricultural prices is whether the market is efficient (i.e., whether the current price is the best predictor of future prices; see Section 10.6.1) or whether any inefficiencies can be capitalized on. Labys (2006) examines commodities, while Allen (1994) provides a succinct and accessible survey of agricultural forecasting. Generally, however, application areas have not developed method-specific approaches; rather, it is the features of the data that determine whether causal, extrapolative, or judgmental methods are applied and in what mix.

One final area worth remarking on is where heterogeneous individual behavior over time must be modeled to produce a forecast. For example, in governments everywhere, there is a need to model the tax take (from income tax, state sales tax, etc.) and social security payments (such as unemployment benefit or pension payments). One approach to this problem is through *microsimulation models* (Merz, 1991; Mitton, Shuterland, and Weeks, 2000) or, more generally, where individuals interact, *agent-based models*. Such models differ substantially from the statistical models we have discussed and are often focused on policy or planning issues rather than the forecasts themselves. Perhaps the most well known example occurs in climate forecasting, in which the models are vast, consisting of many thousands of equations. The models are parameterized, often by experiments off-line; that is to say, they are not statistically estimated, but other evidence, such as physical laws (in climate) or market research experiments (in consumer behavior), is used to decide on the parameters to specify the model completely. An example of the use of these models in the telecommunications area is described in Fildes and Kumar (2002). In general, however, such models have rarely been validated in the way we have recommended in this book: by comparing their performance with that of some established benchmark. (See Fildes and Kourentzes, 2011, for an example applied to climate models.)

Principles

Evaluation *(see Armstrong, 2001b,c; also, Armstrong's (2001a) summary Sections 12 and 13)*

[12.1] Compare the current (or proposed) method against established benchmarks. Typical benchmarks are the random walk or a similar naïve method, as well as a suitable smoothing method, such as damped trend smoothing.

[12.2] Specify the forecasting task.

[12.3] Use error measures that are appropriate for the problem. Use a variety of error measures that are suitable for comparing accuracy across a number of time series. For intermittent demand, use the costs of achieving a desired service level.

[12.4] Base comparisons on as large a sample of time series, forecast origins, and out-of-sample forecasts as possible. Comparisons based on a small sample of forecasts are often misleading.

[12.5] Combine forecasts from methods that differ substantially.

[12.6] Use formal procedures to combine forecasts. Don't rely on informal weighting schemes.

[12.7] Use equal weights, removing the extreme forecasts from the average. Although it's a bit counterintuitive, equal-weighting schemes that exclude only extreme forecasts seem to offer the most consistent performance.

[12.8] Combine models where there is substantial uncertainty. In general, models are oversimplifications, and a combination can help to avoid bias.

Forecasting Support Systems (see Sanders, 2001, and Armstrong's (2001a) summary, Section 11)

[12.9] Structure the judgmental adjustments. Adjustments are made for any number of reasons, although promotional effects are the most important in demand forecasting. The different components should be identified separately and documented.

[12.10] Compare the system forecast with the adjusted forecast. Records should be kept of the system forecast and the final adjusted forecast and should be used to calculate the errors made and to evaluate any biases in the two sets of forecasts.

[12.11] Base the system forecast on regular periods, not on periods during which promotions are run and not on unusual periods. If promotional periods are run and are included in the calculation, they will bias the system forecasts upward unless appropriate adjustments are made.

[12.12] Use well-tested forecasting software. Commercial software cannot automatically be assumed to be well designed and validated. With new software, results should be compared with some standard benchmarks and the software tuned to produce optimal forecasts.

Operations and Marketing Product Hierarchies

[12.13] When forecasting product hierarchies, use a bottom-up approach for disaggregated data. For levels between the top and bottom, a combined approach has recently proved more effective. Information that is often available at the different levels of the product hierarchy is useful when forecasting at other levels.

New Product Diffusion Models (see Meade and Islam, 2001)

[12.14] No single diffusion model is best for all adoption processes. A variety of curves can model the adoption process. We have discussed the Bass (logistic) curve and the Gompertz curve here. It therefore makes sense to consider alternative curves in choosing the best one for the particular problem under consideration.

[12.15] Use simpler diffusion models. These models produce better forecasts than more complex models on the limited data that are typically available.

[12.16] Short-term forecasting ability is helpful in deciding whether a diffusion model is useful. Although the aim of new product forecasting is to produce accurate long term forecasts, a model's short-term accuracy offers valuable information as to its usefulness.

[12.17] Use nonlinear least squares to estimate models. Consider how the error term should be specified in the model.

Market Potential. In estimating market potential with no historical data intentions studies (Morwitz, 2001) and conjoint choice models and its variants (Wittink and Bergestuen, 2001) offer guidance.

[12.18] When estimating market potential, identify an appropriate sample of respondents for an intentions or choice-based conjoint study.

[12.19] Identify a meaningful set of attributes that are potentially important in a choice model of market potential. The chosen attributes should be distinct from each other.

[12.20] Estimate market potential with intentions data that have been modified to take into account possible biases from the respondents.

[12.21] Question respondents in as realistic a choice context as possible. Simulated environments provide respondents with information that is useful in making more realistic choices.

[12.22] Combine approaches with others, such as using analogous products.

Market Response Models *(see Brodie, Danaher, Kumar, and Leeflang, 2001)*

[12.23] Use disaggregated data. Aggregated data make identifying marketing effects difficult because of the heterogeneity in the different market segments.

[12.24] Use a regression model for longer term forecasting.

[12.25] When the sample is of medium size, use a regression model only when the current effects of the market drivers are strong, but always use a regression model for large samples.

[12.26] Use brand-specific parameters to model a competitive market.

Forecasting Individual Behavior *(this topic is not discussed directly in Armstrong (2001a), but many principles carry over)*

[12.27] Consider a variety of methods.

[12.28] Use the largest sample size possible, given the data and computer constraints, but partition into estimation and test samples whenever possible. Often, an unnecessarily limited (but large) sample is used, rather than using all the available observations that leave the model building computationally tractable. Research has shown that including as many observations as possible produces gains.

[12.29] Aim for an understandable model. Models will frequently be rejected by users if their logic cannot be understood.

[12.30] Replace missing data, and use indicator variables to tag the replacement.

[12.31] Balance the sample of the target class with the available nontarget data. Cases of interest (e.g., poor credit risks) will often be relatively rare, so the sample of targeted cases should be oversampled to match the nontarget cases. The cutoff point for classifying the target must reflect the balance of the two categories.

[12.32] In the assessment of the different methods, use criteria that reflect the profit and loss in the problem.

Other Applications

[12.33] Don't try to produce your own macro forecasts. The services that provide macro forecasts—in particular, those which provide a summary of the forecasts produced by a diversity of forecasting groups, are as accurate as you can hope for.

[12.34] In forecasting applications, use the methods, models, and principles laid down in this text. Make sure that you understand the specific factors which are important in the particular application.

Summary

The purpose of forecasting is not just to develop models in isolation, but also to use them effectively in organizational applications. After first examining the key question of how methods should be evaluated, we considered how organizations structure their forecasting information. We found that it is often done through expensive forecasting support systems. We introduced a wide range of applications that affects most organizations, from governments to small suppliers—in particular, (1) forecasting to support operations and (2) market forecasting. Within the broad heading of market forecasting, the area of trying to understand

and forecast individual consumer behavior has gained increasing prominence. New techniques are being applied, with the potential for substantial benefits.

In the final sections of the chapter, we touched on a whole range of additional applications. Although we were unable to discuss them in detail, such topics as sports forecasting and corporate earnings forecasting (by advisors offering advice to investors) have spawned major industries. The expert forecaster will be able to apply the methods of this book in these new contexts, but knowing the difference between a penalty in soccer (English football) and a penalty in American football will always remain important. The moral of this discussion is that the expert forecaster will know the range of techniques to be applied, but will also understand the data and the relationships specific to the application area.

Exercises

Evaluating Forecasting Methods; Forecasting Support Systems and Forecasting for Operations.

12.1 With the spreadsheet *Combine.xlsx*, calculate the *MAPE* and *MdAPE* obtained from using optimal weights, rather than equal weights, for the three combinations of two methods.
    a. Generalize this approach to calculate the error statistics for all three methods.
    b. Does including a constant term in the regression improve the error statistics?
    c. What are the implications for choosing the weights on the basis of the whole sample of data rather than a subsample of the first 12 periods?

12.2 Earnings forecasting is one of the most important applications of forecasting and is a major industry in that the forecasts are used by investors to decide which stock they should hold. Using the file *Earnings.xlsx*, which shows the forecasts for five companies over three years, calculate combined forecasts for each year, examining the benefits of combining 3 forecast sources, 5 sources, 10 sources, and, finally, all the sources. Are there any benefits from eliminating extreme forecasts from the calculation? [*Source:* Institutional Brokers Estimate System (I/B/E/S), a service of Thomson Reuters. The data have been provided as part of a broad academic program to encourage research into earnings expectations.]

12.3 Using a forecasting support system with which you are familiar, appraise its strengths and weaknesses compared with Excel in building a forecasting system to analyze and forecast 10 products (i) with 10 years of monthly data and (ii) falling into two product groups based on 2 years of weekly data. The short report should be suitable to be presented to a non-technical senior IT manager. [*Hint:* You can download a trial version of a commercial system to make the comparison more relevant.]

12.4 Use the promotions sales data in *Promote1.xlsx* to estimate the promotional effects and forecast 12 periods ahead, taking into account the forthcoming promotions. The start of each promotional period is shown in the database. Does it matter (i.e., does it affect the profitability of the promotion) if you take the promotion as affecting four weeks of sales rather than five or six?

12.5*In a two-period promotional model, the baseline sales model is of the form

$$B_t = \alpha + \lambda S_{t-1} + \varepsilon_t$$

and

$$S_t = B_t + \beta_0 D_{1t} + \beta_1 D_{2t},$$

where lagged sales affects promotions. B_t represents the baseline sales and $D_{1t} = 1$ if t is in the first period of the promotion, while $D_{2t} = 1$ if t is in the second period of the promotion. Show that the effect of the promotion is β_0 in the first period of the promotion and $\beta_1 + \lambda\beta_0$ in the second period.

12.6 With the data set *Bullwhip.xlsx*, use exponential smoothing to calculate the forecasting accuracy of the retailer's and the manufacturer's forecasts. Does knowledge of the retailer's sales improve the accuracy of the manufacturer's forecasts?

12.7 For the data in *Lost_sales.xlsx*, estimate the demand data for the out-of-stock observations.

12.8 For the data in *Intermittent.xlsx*, use first Croston's method and then simple exponential smoothing to calculate one-step-ahead forecasts. Does the choice of smoothing parameter have any impact on the results? Is the choice of error measure important in making the calculation? If being out of stock is very expensive, does this affect how you appraise the different methods?

Market Forecasting

12.9 What variables might you include in a forecasting model of
   i. the monthly demand for ice cream?
   ii. annual traffic fatalities?
   iii. the total U.S. market for netbooks over the next five years?
   iv. the daily energy demand in a region, partitioned by source?
   v. the probability of an individual defaulting on a credit card payment?
   vi. hourly calls into a credit card call center over the next week?

12.10 Download data on U.S. consumption, and then estimate various trend curve models. Select the curve that you regard as likely to provide the best forecast for consumption in 2020. Give reasons for your choice. Compare your analysis with that of Granger and Jeon (2007).

12.11 Using the data set *Telecoms.xlsx*, which contains data on fixed-line, mobile, and broadband communications for four European countries (the United Kingdom, Germany, Italy, and France), develop trend curve models for data up to 2007 and forecasts to 2012.
   a. Among Gompertz, logistic, and linear benchmark models, which do you prefer for forecasting? Give reasons for your choice.
   b. Is there any evidence of substitution between the different communications media?

12.12 Using the airline passenger data in *Air_passenger.xlsx*, estimate the passenger flows for the UK–Canada airline route for the years 1961–2000, considering all the relevant variables, including the world trade variable. Produce forecasts for 2001 and 2002. Include a dummy variable for 2001 and 2002, and estimate the effects of the September 11 terrorist attack.

12.13 The data file *Promote2.xlsx* includes sales and price data on eight competing products for 399 weeks. The file also contains promotional information. (A full description is included in it.) Using the data in *Promote2.xlsx*, estimate the effects of the promotions, including any competitive effects, and produce 1–5-week-ahead rolling forecasts for the periods 120–140 and 201–220. Is there any evidence of instability in the model? How does this model compare with alternative extrapolative models with regard to periods with and without promotions?

12.14 Evaluate the Divakar *et al*. (2005) study, focusing on the following questions:
   a. Do the models for volume and price include the key variables you would consider?
   b. What other aspects of the market would you wish to be informed about?
   c. Is the evaluation carried out in ways you find useful?
   d. Write an executive summary of the results, arguing why the model should be implemented.

Forecasting Individual Behavior

12.15 Using the data set *Loans.xlsx* and a linear regression model of the bad loans that incorporates the predictor variables *CLAGE, DEBTINC, NLINQ*, and *DELINQ*, develop an ROC operating curve. Compare this curve with the curves obtained by each of the three methods used in Section 12.5. Which method do you prefer and why? Does the inclusion of *JOBS* lead to any improvement in predictability?

TABLE 12.14   INTERNET PARTICIPATION RATES AS PERCENTAGES OF THE
CORRESPONDING AGE COHORT (SAMPLE ESTIMATES)

Month and Year	Age Group			
	18–29	30–49	50–64	65 plus
Sep 2005	16	12	7	5
May 2008	67	25	11	7
Nov 2008	73	36	16	4
Apr 2009	76	48	25	13
Dec 2009	83	58	36	22
May 2010	86	61	47	26

Source: Pew Research Center

12.16 Using the data set *Loans.xlsx*, develop a model that predicts the target variable bad loans.
   a. Carry out an exploratory analysis of the loans data, identifying any interesting features that may affect your subsequent model building.
   b. Set up suitable dummy variables to describe the variables *Job* and *Delinq*.
   c. Using stepwise and backward regression, decide on a subset of potentially important explanatory variables.
   d. Using the chosen subset of variables, follow the procedure set out in Section 12.5.3 and compare the methods of predictive classification with the results shown in the section.
   e. Does the sample size matter in developing the predictive model and estimating the misclassification rates on the test data?
   f. Using the data set *Loans.xlsx*, estimate whether there are any nonlinear effects of *MORTDUE* and *DEBTINC* on the probability of defaulting.

12.17 It is well known that younger people have become Internet users more rapidly than older segments of the population. Use the data in Table 12.14 to develop forecasts for each age group for 2020.

12.18 Download macroforecasts from *www.consensuseconomics.com*, and calculate the accuracy of the consensus forecast for the two years of data that are available. (You may have to estimate the actual value for the current year.) Include a number of macrovariables in this evaluation. How do the consensus forecasts compare against forecasts by the best forecasting provider, the average provider, and the worst provider? [*Hint:* You will have to decide how to rank the individual macroforecasting providers.]

Minicases

Minicase 12.1 Call Center Planning

InsurCo's call center performance was part of Ms. Chen's new responsibilities for operations. Accuracy, she knew, was important. Staff were usually scheduled for the next week (five days), and the operations director (to whom Ms. Chen reported) regarded service performance as very important. In emergencies, extra staff could be brought in for the next day. Although not a technical expert, Ms. Chen knew that the basic approach of the forecasting group had been to use Excel-based simple exponential smoothing in calculating the forecasts. If marketing information was available which suggested that something out of the ordinary was expected to happen, the statistical forecasts were adjusted. There was no set procedure laid down. On top of that, a standard seasonal adjustment was incorporated into the forecasts.

But Ms. Chen had looked at the past 40 days' (8 weeks') worth of data and could see that there was a problem. When questioned, the principal forecaster confirmed that his team used the system forecast and then tried to take into account any unexpected business drivers that affected call center activity. For example, the figures on mailings applied to just one day but often seemed to carry over to the next for the obvious reason that deliveries did not automatically occur the next day as planned. Ms. Chen thought that daily seasonality might be an issue, particularly after a weekend. (The data start on a Monday in period 1.) The standard seasonal adjustment seemed inadequate to account for the observed seasonality.

The previous operations manager (an accountant by training) had laid down the law that the forecasts had to be within 10 percent accuracy. Whatever that might mean, the net result was that one of the better trained junior staff members resigned, arguing that it just wasn't possible: Too many other factors affected the results. In particular, mailings were a problem not least because the data were rarely made available, and the marketing people (when they bothered to talk to you) argued that the type of mail promotion also had an effect.

The data can be found in the data set *Call_center.xlsx*.

1. What forecast horizon(s) are relevant for making the comparisons? What is an appropriate error measure?
2. How accurate were the department's forecasts? How did they compare with the automatic system forecast? Are the department's system forecasts more accurate than random-walk forecasts?
3. Could a standard extrapolative method such as exponential smoothing do any better?
4. Additional data were usually available to the forecasting team. The team used these data judgmentally. The periods affected by a mail promotion were labeled 1. Develop a regression model that explains the calls. Calculate prediction intervals for these forecasts, and calculate the forecast errors. Is the model more accurate than your best exponential smoothing model?
5. How can seasonality be incorporated into the forecast?
6. What suggestions would you make for possible changes in the operational forecasting system?

Minicase 12.2 Costume Jewelry

A company that markets costume jewelry has three main product lines: bracelets, necklaces, and pins. Within each line there are several groups, and within each group a number of distinct items. The details are shown in Table 12.15.[3] Organized by calendar year, the series run from Year 1, week 5, to Year 3, week 24.

The company wishes to develop a hierarchical forecasting system by product line so that forecasts of sales of each item aggregate up to the forecasts at the group level, in turn for each product line.

a. Examine different top-down and bottom-up approaches to forecasting, using at least 30 percent of the observations as a hold-out sample. Compare the accuracy of the two approaches, considering forecasting horizons of 1 week ahead and 4 weeks ahead, and cumulative sales 1–13 weeks ahead.
b. If the jewelry data relate to a manufacturer, which do you regard as the relevant lead time(s) to focus on and why? If the data relate to a distributor, does that change your conclusions?
c. How would you identify subgroups of items that appear to have similar demand patterns?

---

[3] These data form a subset of data on the products sold by an actual costume jewelry company. We are grateful to Dr. Hans Levenbach for providing the data.

TABLE 12.15 INFORMATION FOR COSTUME JEWELRY MANUFACTURER

Product Line	Product Group	Number of Items
Bracelets	B1	5
	B2	5
Necklaces	N1	6
	N2	7
	N3	5
	N4	2
Pins	P1	4
	P2	6

Data: Jewelry.xlsx.

References

Allen, P. G. (1994). Economic forecasting in agriculture. *International Journal of Forecasting*, 10, 81–135.

Armstrong, J. S. (ed.). (2001a). *Principles of Forecasting: A Handbook for Researchers and Practitioners.* Boston and Dordrecht: Kluwer.

Armstrong, J. S. (2001b). Combining forecasts. In J. S. Armstrong (ed.), *Principles of Forecasting: A Handbook for Researchers and Practitioners.* Boston and Dordrecht: Kluwer, pp. 417–439.

Armstrong, J. S. (2001c). Evaluating forecasting methods. In J. S. Armstrong (ed.), *Principles of Forecasting: A Handbook for Researchers and Practitioners.* Boston and Dordrecht: Kluwer, pp. 443–472.

Athanasopoulos, G., Ahmed, R. A., and Hyndman, R. J. (2009). Hierarchical forecasts for Australian domestic tourism. *International Journal of Forecasting*, 25, 146–166.

Bass, F. M. (1969). A new product growth model for consumer durables. *Management Science (A)*, 15, 215–227.

Berry, M. J. R., and Linoff, G. S. (2004). *Data Mining Techniques for Marketing, Sales and Customer Support.* New York: Wiley.

Bose, I., and Chen, X. (2009). Quantitative models for direct marketing: A review from systems perspective. *European Journal of Operational Research*, 195, 1–16.

Brodie, R., Danaher, P. J., Kumar, V., and Leeflang, P. S. H. (2001). Econometric models for forecasting market share. In J. S. Armstrong (ed.), *Principles of Forecasting: A Handbook for Researchers and Practitioners.* Boston and Dordrecht: Kluwer, pp. 597-611.

Clemen, R. T. (1989). Combining forecasts: A review and annotated bibliography. *International Journal of Forecasting*, 5, 559–583.

Crone, S. F., Lessmann, S., and Stahlbock, R. (2006). The impact of preprocessing on data mining: An evaluation of classifier sensitivity in direct marketing. *European Journal of Operational Research*, 173, 781–800.

de Jong, G., Fox, J., Pieters, M., Daly, A. J., and Smith, R. (2004). A comparison of car ownership models. *Transport Reviews*, 24, 379–408.

Divakar, S., Ratchford, B. T., and Shankar, V. (2005). CHAN4CAST: A multichannel, multiregion sales forecasting model and decision support system for consumer packaged goods. *Marketing Science*, 24, 334–350.

Duncan, G. T., Gorr, W., and Szczypula, J. (2001). Forecasting analagous time series. In J. S. Armstrong (ed.), *Principles of Forecasting: A Handbook for Researchers and Practitioners*. Boston and Dordrecht: Kluwer, pp. 195–213.

Fader, P. S., and Hardie, B. G. S. (2001). Forecasting trial sales of new consumer packaged goods. In J. S. Armstrong (ed.), *Principles of Forecasting: A Handbook for Researchers and Practitioners*. Boston and Dordrecht: Kluwer, pp. 613–630.

Fildes, R., and Goodwin, P. (2007). Against your better judgment? How organizations can improve their use of management judgment in forecasting. *Interfaces*, 37, 570–576.

Fildes, R., Goodwin, P., and Lawrence, M. (2006). The design features of forecasting support systems and their effectiveness. *Decision Support Systems*, 42, 351–361.

Fildes, R., Goodwin, P., Lawrence, M., and Nikolopoulos, K. (2009). Effective forecasting and judgmental adjustments: An empirical evaluation and strategies for improvement in supply-chain planning. *International Journal of Forecasting*, 25, 3–23.

Fildes, R., Hibon, M., Makridakis, S., and Meade, N. (1998). Generalising about univariate forecasting methods: Further empirical evidence. *International Journal of Forecasting*, 14, 339–358.

Fildes, R. & Kourentzes, N. (2011). Validation and forecasting accuracy in models of climate change. *International Journal of Forecasting,* 27, 968–995.

Fildes, R., and Kumar, V. (2002). Telecommunications demand forecasting: A review. *International Journal of Forecasting*, 18, 489–522.

Fildes, R., Nikolopoulos, K., Crone, S. F., and Syntetos, A. A. (2008). Forecasting and operational research: A review. *Journal of the Operational Research Society*, 59, 1150–1172.

Fildes, R., and Stekler, H. (2002). The state of macroeconomic forecasting. *Journal of Macroeconomics*, 24, 435–468.

Fildes, R., Wei, Y., and Ismail, S. (2011). Evaluating the forecasting performance of econometric models of air passenger traffic flows using multiple error measures. *International Journal of Forecasting*, 27, 902–922.

Galbraith, C. S., and Merrill, G. B. (1996). The politics of forecasting: Managing the truth. *California Management Review*, 38, 29–43.

Goodwin, P., Dyussekeneva, K., and Meeran, S. (2011). The use of analogies in forecasting the annual sales of new electronics products. *IMA Journal of Management Mathematics*, in press [as of Spring 2012].

Granger, C. W. J., and Jeon, Y. (2007). Long-term forecasting and evaluation. *International Journal of Forecasting*, 23, 539–551.

Gustafsson, A., Herrmann, A., and Huber, F. (2001) *Conjoint Measurement: Methods and Applications.* (2nd ed.), Berlin and New York: Springer.

Hanssens, D. M., Parsons, L. J., and Schultz, R. L. (2001). *Market Response Models: Econometric and Time Series Analysis,* 2nd ed. Boston and Dordrecht: Kluwer.

Jose, V. R. R., and Winkler, R. L. (2008). Simple robust averages of forecasts: Some empirical results. *International Journal of Forecasting*, 24, 163–169.

Kahn, K. B. (2002). An exploratory investigation of new product forecasting practices. *Journal of Product Innovation Management*, 19, 133–143.

Koehler, A. B., Snyder, R. D., Ord, J. K., and Beaumont, A. (2012) *Forecasting compositional time series with exponential smoothing methods.* Working paper, Monash University.

Labys, W. C. (2006). *Modeling and Forecasting Primary Commodity Prices*. Aldershot, Hampshire, UK: Ashgate Publishing.

Lahiri, K., and Moore, G. H. (eds.). (1991). *Leading Economic Indicators: New Approaches and Forecasting Record.* Cambridge, UK: Cambridge University Press.

Lau, H.-S., and Hing-Ling Lau, A. (1996). Estimating the demand distributions of single-period items having frequent stockouts. *European Journal of Operational Research*, 92, 254–265.

Lee, H. L., Padmanabhan, V., and Whang, S. (1997). The bullwhip effect in supply chains. *Sloan Management Review*, 38, 93–102.

Lee, W. Y., Goodwin, P., Fildes, R., Nikolopoulos, K., and Lawrence, M. (2007). Providing support for the use of analogies in demand forecasting tasks. *International Journal of Forecasting*, 23, 377–390.

Leonard, M. (2007). Forecasting short sesaonl time series using aggregate and analagous series. *Foresight*, 6, 16–20.

Lilien, G. L., and Rangaswamy, A. (2004). *Marketing Engineering: Computer-Assisted Marketing Analysis and Planning*, revised 2nd ed. Victoria, B.C.: Trafford Publishing.

Lilien, G. L., Rangaswamy, A., and Van den Bulte, C. (2000). Diffusion models: Managerial applications and software. In V. Mahajan, E. Muller, and Y. Wind (eds.), *New-Product Diffusion Models*. Boston and Dordrecht: Kluwer.

Litterman, R. B. (1986). Forecasting with Bayesian vector autoregressions: 5 years of experience. *Journal of Business and Economic Statistics*, 4, 25–38.

Lynn, G. S., Schnaars, S. P., and Skov, R. B. (1999). Survey of new product forecasting practices in industrial high technology and low technology businesses. *Industrial Marketing Management*, 28, 565–571.

Makridakis, S., Andersen, A., Carbone, R., Fildes, R., Hibon, M., Lewandowski, R., Newton, J., Parzen, E., and Winkler, R. (1982). The accuracy of extrapolation (time-series) methods: Results of a forecasting competition. *Journal of Forecasting*, 1, 111–153.

Makridakis, S., and Hibon, M. (1979). Accuracy of forecasting: Empirical investigation. *Journal of the Royal Statistical Society Series A—Statistics in Society*, 142, 97–145.

Makridakis, S,. and Hibon, M. (2000). The M-3 competition: Results, conclusions and implications. *International Journal of Forecasting*, 16, 451–476.

Marder, E. (1999). The assumptions of choice modelling: Conjoint analysis and SUMM. *Canadian Journal of Marketing Research*, 18, 1–12.

McCullough, B. D. (2000). Is it safe to assume that software is accurate? *International Journal of Forecasting*, 16, 349–357.

McNees, S. K. (1986). Forecasting accuracy of alternative techniques: A comparison of U.S. macroeconomic forecasts. *Journal of Business & Economic Statistics*, 4, 5–15.

Meade, N., and Islam, T. (2001). Forecasting the diffusion of innovations: Implications for time-series extrapolation. In J. S. Armstrong (ed.), *Principles of Forecasting: A Handbook for Researchers and Practitioners*. Boston and Dordrecht: Kluwer.

Merz, J. (1991). Microsimulation: A survey of principles, developments and applications. *International Journal of Forecasting*, 7, 77–104.

Mitton, L., Shuterland, H., and Weeks, M. (2000). *Microsimulation Modelling for Policy Analysis: Challenges and Innovations*. Cambridge, UK: Cambridge University Press.

Montgomery, A. L. (2005). The implementation challenge of pricing decision support systems for retail managers. *Applied Stochastic Models in Business and Industry*, 21, 367–378.

Morwitz, V. G. (2001). Methods for forecasting with intentions data. In J. S. Armstrong (ed.), *Principles of Forecasting: A Handbook for Researchers and Practitioners*. Boston and Dordrecht: Kluwer, pp. 33–56.

Natter, M., Reutterer, T., Mild, A., and Taudes, A. (2007). An assortmentwide decision-support system for dynamic pricing and promotion planning in DIY retailing. *Marketing Science*, 26, 576–583.

Newbold, P., and Granger, C. W. J. (1974). Experience with forecasting univariate time series and the combintion of forecasts. *Journal of the Royal Statistical Society, series A*, 137, 131–164.

Olafsson, S., Li, X., and Wu, S. (2008). Operations research and data mining. *European Journal of Operational Research*, 187, 1429–1448.

Ord, J. K. (1988). Future developments in forecasting: The time series connexion. *International Journal of Forecasting*, 4, 389–402.

Qian, L., and Soopramanien, D. (2011). Heterogeneous consumer preferences for alternative fuel cars in China. *Transportation Research Part D: Transport and Environment*, 16, 607–613.

Sanders, N. R. (2001). Judgmental adjustments of statistical forecasts. In J. S. Armstrong (ed.), *Principles of Forecasting: A Handbook for Researchers and Practitioners*. Boston and Dordrecht: Kluwer, pp. 405–416.

Sanders, N. R., and Manrodt, K. B. (2003). Forecasting software in practice: Use, satisfaction, and performance. *Interfaces*, 33, 90–93.

Snyder, R. D., Ord, J. K., and Beaumont, A. (2012). Forecasting the intermittent demand for slow-moving inventories: A modeling approach. *International Journal of Forecasting*, 28, 485–496.

Song, H., and Li, G. (2008). Tourism demand modelling and forecasting: A review of recent research. *Tourism Management*, 29, 203–220.

Stekler, H. O. (2007). The future of macroeconomic forecasting: Understanding the forecasting process. *International Journal of Forecasting*, 23, 237–248.

Stekler, H. O., Sendor, D., and Verlander, R. (2010). Issues in sports forecasting. *International Journal of Forecasting*, 26, 606–621.

Syntetos, A. A., and Boylan, J. E. (2006). On the stock control performance of intermittent demand estimators. *International Journal of Production Economics*, 103, 36–47.

Syntetos, A. A., Boylan, J. E., and Teunter, R. (2011). Classification for forecasting and inventory. *Foresight*, 20, 12–17.

Taylor, J. W., and Espasa, A. (2008). Energy forecasting. *International Journal of Forecasting*, 24, 561–565.

Thomas, L. C. (2009). *Consumer Credit Models: Pricing, Profit and Portfolio*. Oxford, UK: Oxford University Press.

Timmermann, A., and Granger, C. W. J. (2004). Efficient market hypothesis and forecasting. *International Journal of Forecasting*, 20, 15–27.

Williams, D. (2007). Seasonality: Shrinkage procedures for small samples. *Foresight*, 6, 21–23.

Williams, L. V., and Stekler, H. O. (2010). Sports forecasting. *International Journal of Forecasting*, 26, 445–447.

Wind, Y., and Green, P. E. (2004) *Marketing Research and Modelling: Progress and Prospects*. New York: Springer.

Wittink, D. R. and Bergestuen, T. (2001). Forecasting with conjoint analysis. In J. S. Armstrong (ed.), *Principles of Forecasting: A Handbook for Researchers and Practitioners*. Boston and Dordrecht: Kluwer, pp. 147–170.

CHAPTER 13

Forecasting in Practice

CONTENTS

In theory there is no difference between theory and practice. In practice there is.

—Yogi Berra

Introduction

In this final chapter, we focus on the practical issues that may face forecasters in carrying out their job. The book has so far concentrated on the many methods that can be applied to forecasting problems. But what do forecasters in organizations actually do to earn their living? And what do they need to do well? In the first section of the chapter, we look at the process forecasters go through in producing their forecasts. The process depends crucially on the nature of the problem and the data that can be used. These two factors together should lead the forecaster to consider a range of techniques. But often, this selection search is more limited, for good reasons and for bad. To explore why that might be, we first employ the many surveys of forecasting practice to examine the techniques actually used. We then present a *forecasting method selection tree* to aid in developing a short list of approaches the forecaster can adopt. Finally, in Section 13.1.4, we discuss the issue of monitoring and evaluating forecast errors, part of the ongoing process that forecasters need to implement for many, if not all, forecasting problems.

Forecasters do not work in an organizational vacuum. Far from it—they are subject to many political pressures that may affect both the process and the accuracy of their forecasts. In fact, in extreme cases, the politics of forecasting may be more important than any technical questions of accuracy. In Section 13.2, we discuss how forecasters fit into an organizational setting and the pressures they face in carrying out their job successfully.

Section 13.3 discusses two related topics: the uncertainty that remains, even after the most careful forecasting process has been carried out, and how to respond to that uncertainty. In Section 13.4, we return to what, for most practicing forecasters, is the key issue: how to improve forecasting in their organizations. Better forecasting methods are only a part of it. The chapter concludes with a final set of principles for effective forecasting.

The Process of Forecasting

In Chapter 1, we introduced PHIVE (*P*urpose, forecast *H*orizon, *I*nformation, *V*alue, and *E*valuation) as a set of concepts to help understand the key elements of any forecasting problem. These elements in turn define the process adopted by the forecaster to satisfy particular organizational requirements. If this all sounds a bit abstract, let's think about a fast-moving consumer goods manufacturer selling to major supermarkets as well as to independent small retailers. What is the purpose of forecasting for this company, and, as a consequence, what variables does such an organization need to forecast? The answer to this question is a long one, and many of the variables will never be considered by the organizational forecaster. But the first purpose must be to estimate demand and the production costs associated with meeting customer service expectations and company financial requirements. The company will also need a marketing plan, to decide on its promotional and advertising expenditures, but, in addition, to consider such aspects as the desirability and effects of possible new products (see Figure 12.8). These two different forecasting tasks should be distinguished. In the first, an ongoing activity is needed to forecast demand and costs on a weekly or monthly basis. The second task requires a one-time analysis to understand and predict the success and side effects of a new product launch. Which of these two alternatives is under consideration helps to define the different tasks, as we now explain.

Discussion Question *What are the important purposes behind the forecasting activities of (a) an electricity supplier and (b) a city police force?*

13.1.1 The Forecasting Task

How does a forecaster go about the process of forecasting, and what tasks are undertaken? The first task is concerned with the definition of the problem. This is rarely straightforward: One of us (RF) has twice had the experience of being asked to improve an organization's forecasting (for a manufacturer of trucks and a manufacturer of wall coverings), only to discover that the forecasts of demand being produced were not at the appropriate level of detail. So, first, we need to establish precisely what needs to be forecast.

Carrying out this task requires a discussion with the clients and users of the forecasts to establish exactly what is needed, including the time horizon (PH in our notation from Chapter 1) and the constraints under which the forecasts have to be produced. These constraints include the resources available, such as the skill level of the forecaster and colleagues, the time required to produce the forecast, and the data and computer software available to support the task.

Figure 13.1 describes the process undergone in producing the final forecasts to be used elsewhere in the organization. What exactly the forecasting problem is first needs to be agreed on by the various organizational stakeholders, including those who rely on the forecasts in making their plans and decisions. This step always needs to be gone through for a one-time forecasting problem, but is usually bypassed with operational forecasting problems (as discussed in Chapter 12) once the process is established. Two steps are then gone through in parallel: data gathering and establishing the organizational assumptions from which the forecast is derived. The two are harnessed in tandem in that the assumptions will include market drivers, such as the product's distribution, the marketing activities to be undertaken, and the proposed price. Equally, past data are needed on the market drivers if their impact is to be estimated.

FIGURE 13.1   THE FORECASTING PROCESS: A TASK-ANALYTIC PERSPECTIVE

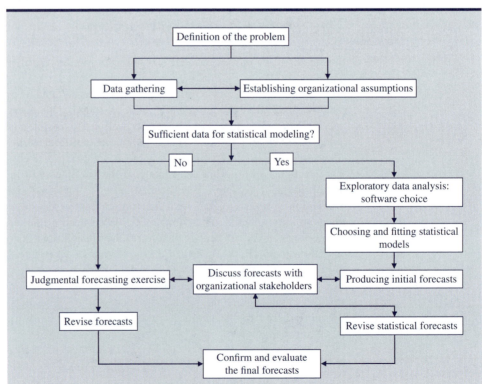

© Cengage Learning 2013.

For one-off forecasting problems, data collection can be a laborious step (even through the Internet) in which the casual omission of a key variable (such as competitive activity) can lead to major forecasting errors. For those problems for which forecasts are made regularly, the core data should be readily available through the forecasting support system (FSS; see Section 12.2)—but it often isn't! For the moment, we'll suppose that the FSS has collated all the data available for the forecaster to use. If the database is sufficiently rich for a quantitative forecasting method to be developed, the next step is to carry out some exploratory data analysis (see Chapter 2). Where there is little to build on, the forecaster has to rely on a judgmental method of forecasting (see Chapter 11).

With a rich enough database, either an extrapolative method of forecasting or a causal model can be developed. In Chapter 9, we discussed the iterative procedure of modeling and testing the results against the data, particularly the hold-out sample. The outcome is an operational model that can be used to produce forecasts. These forecasts may include not only the market drivers or economic assumptions that will determine the actual outcomes, but also various policy decisions. Equally, though, they may not: If the method adopted is an extrapolative forecasting method (such as one of those described in Chapters 3–5), it *cannot* include such factors as novel promotions or market changes. Also, it is unlikely to include all the holidays that affect sales; moving holidays such as Easter are particularly problematic, although some forecasting systems have adjustment procedures to allow for these events (e.g., Census X-12, described briefly in Section 4.5). The forecaster, whether managing a judgmental process or a statistical method, therefore needs to consider modifying the forecast to produce a final forecast that attempts to capture these missing effects.

It is at this stage of the forecasting process that the interactions between forecasters and users are particularly important. Users must try to identify the key factors that should be incorporated into the forecasting process, and forecasters must explain to users what is (and what is not) captured by the model. This interactive process will often be iterative, with adjustments made after discussions with colleagues around the organization. Such processes can be extremely time consuming and costly, even when the Internet is used as the forum for discussion. Still, these interactions are often necessary to get the organization's stakeholders to buy into the final forecasts, for they may need to inject what they see as key pieces of information they think are relevant to the expected outcomes. When the need for such interactions is recognized and scheduled into the forecasting process, the end result is often both an overall saving in time and better results.

An additional factor to consider is what these initial forecasts, either individually or in the aggregate, imply for other parts of the organization—in particular, the organization's financial objectives (usually as exemplified by the budget). Also, if the forecasts are to be accepted, they will need to reflect the understanding that managers have of the activity. For example, a sales forecast in a drug company needs to reflect marketing's understanding of the product life cycle. The result is that senior staff may well exert their influence, leading to adjustments to the initial forecasts. These adjustments are discussed further in Section 13.2.3.

The final step in Figure 13.1, often ignored, is the evaluation of the final forecasts and the monitoring of the ongoing results. When the forecasting problem is repetitive, the standard measures we laid out in Section 2.7 will be adequate to evaluate performance. When forecasts are judgmental and lead to one-time planning decisions, the track records of individual participants can sometimes be monitored over time and feedback provided to enhance the participants' own understanding of their performance. The accumulating picture of forecast errors and the reasons behind them should lead to organizational learning. Where appropriate, these reviews should include evaluations of both the statistical forecasts and the final adjusted forecast to determine whether the adjustments lead to substantive improvements.

Discussion Question *How would you provide feedback to senior managers with respect to their forecasts of major one-off events?*

13.1.2 **Forecasting Method Selection in Practice**

In earlier chapters, we presented a large number of forecasting methods. Some of them are very simple to use with readily available commercial software (e.g., exponential smoothing). but others, such as time series neural networks are much more complex (requiring non-standard and often very expensive software). What methods do forecasters use in practice—and are they the methods we would recommend? Table 13.1 shows the results of three surveys, carried out to deliver compatible results over a time span of more than 20 years. The column headed "PS" describes the results of the most recent survey, carried out in 2006 by McCarthy, Davis, Golicic, & Mentzer. Winklhofer, Diamantopoulos, & Witt (1996) gives broader coverage, but all the surveys tell similar stories:

- Judgmental methods are used more often than quantitative methods.
- Extrapolative methods are preferred to causal methods (although there is a degree of ambiguity in the surveys—for example, whether regression has been used "causally" or to estimate a time trend).
- Simple methods are preferred to complex methods.

A similar picture emerges if we examine forecasters' familiarity with the different techniques, although, in making the comparison, we occasionally see examples of a technique, such as Box–Jenkins (ARIMA), that is well known to respondents but not much used.

Although such surveys are valuable in giving some insight into forecasters' choice of different methods, they don't offer an explanation of the underlying reasons beyond familiarity: Of course people will often take the easy way out by selecting the method that is most familiar to them and easiest to adopt. But the surveys suffer from many other weaknesses if they are to be employed as benchmarks for an organization to use in deciding which methods to consider.

TABLE 13.1 FORECASTING TECHNIQUES, RANKED IN ORDER OF FREQUENCY OF USE, BY FORECAST HORIZON

Technique	Short Horizon ≤3 Months M&C	M&K	PS	Mid Horizon 4 Months–2 Years M&C	M&K	PS	Long Horizon >2 Years M&C	M&K	PS
Qualitative									
Jury of executive opinion	1	5	na	1	2	1	1	1	1
Sales force composite	1	5	2	2	2	3	8	4	3
Customer expectations	3	3	1	5	8	4	4	7	na
Quantitative									
Moving average	4	1	6	6	6	7	10	9	na
Straight-line projection	8	3	6	8	9	8	6	10	6
Exponential smoothing	4	2	3	7	1	2	9	6	5
Regression	7	5	3	2	4	6	2	2	2
Trend-line analysis	6	8	3	4	5	5	3	3	4
Simulation	11	12	na	10	13	10	6	8	na
Life cycle analysis	12	12	6	12	10	11	5	5	na
Decomposition	9	8	na	9	7	8	10	10	na
Box–Jenkins time series	10	8	na	11	11	11	11	12	na
Expert systems	nm	12	na	nm	13	11	nm	11	6
Neural networks	nm	8	na	nm	12	11	nm	13	na

Notes: M&C, Mentzer and Cox (1984), sample size = 160; M&K, Mentzer and Kahn (1995), sample size = 186; PS, present study, sample size = 86; nm, not measured in the study; na, not applicable (no respondents indicated use of the technique for that time horizon).

Source: Taken from McCarthy *et al.*, 2006.

Discussion Question *(a) Before you accept the results of the preceding surveys at their face value, what else do you want to know?*

(b) If you wished to use survey evidence as guidance on best practice in order to help appraise your own forecasting effort, what further information would you wish to collect?

Figure 13.2 presents an explanation of some of the factors that influence how organizations select their forecasting approach.

FIGURE 13.2   FACTORS AFFECTING THE USE OF DIFFERENT FORECASTING METHODOLOGIES

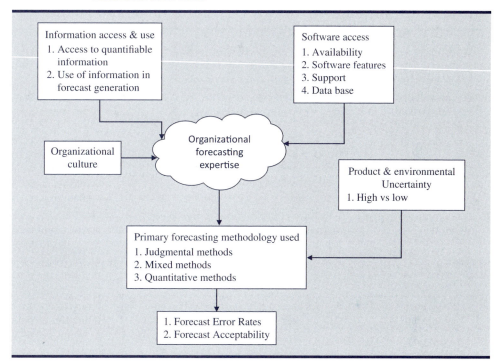

Source: Adapted from Sanders and Manrodt, 2003.

Sanders and Manrodt (2003) conducted a survey of 2340 heads of marketing of U.S. companies (with 240 usable replies) to test elements of the model presented in Figure 13.2. The key results they identified were the importance of the product market and the perceived uncertainty in the environment, but also uncertainty in the product market. Where there was high uncertainty with rapid changes in the products and the competitive position, quantitative methods were used less frequently. Others have examined additional factors, such as the effects of organizational culture on the adoption and use of various management techniques.

An important rationale for an organization's choice of forecasting approach, which Fildes and Hastings (1994) also identified, was the lack of relevant data. In addition, the organizational culture may not be conducive to using quantitative methods. In such an organization, be it public or private, forecasting is more of a political issue, a topic we will return to in Section 13.2.3. The culture itself affects two other elements: the availability of software and relevant data, and whether the organization has set up an effective process for forecasting, including employing the necessary expertise. If an organization is antagonistic to scientific management, then spreadsheet analysis and an ad hoc process of collecting opinions might prove adequate, if inefficient. But the key thing to note about Figure 13.2 is that the consequences of these choices affect both the forecast error rate and the acceptability of the final forecast to users within the organization.

13.1.3   Forecasting Method Selection: Which Methods Work Best Under What Circumstances?

All the methods we have described in this book have their merits. It is a question of which method proves best depending on the circumstances and the forecasting problem. Again, PHIVE captures the features we must consider in the choice: What are the *p*roblem, the forecast *h*orizon, and the available *i*nformation, and, crucially, what *v*alue is there to improving the forecast accuracy (*e*valuation)? Table 13.2 gives our personal evaluation of the different methods.

TABLE 13.2   ADVANTAGES AND DISADVANTAGES OF DIFFERENT FORECASTING METHODS

Method	Advantages	Disadvantages
Judgmental (see Chapter 11)		
J1 Individual experts (subjective)	Can be inexpensive; flexible, can forecast anything; anybody can do it.	Accuracy is suspect (Principles 6.3 and 6.4, Armstrong, 2001), although perhaps the quality of judgments can be improved by various forms of feedback; skills are embodied in the person rather than the organization; subject to all problems of human judgment. Hogarth and Makridakis (1981) provides a still-current survey.
J2 Committee/informal survey	Brings different perspectives to bear on the problem and has the advantages listed for J1.	One loudmouth can dominate, and this person might not be the best forecaster; no one wants to disagree with the boss; more expensive than using an individual expert; problems in selecting participants and organizing a meeting.
J3 Sales Force Composite	Includes different opinions based on detailed knowledge of the product or region. The aggregation aims to remove individual biases.	Motivation to produce accurate forecasts is limited. Each individual is subject to the problems of J1. Takes a long time and can be expensive. Tendency to link such forecasts to sales force performance measures, thereby biasing the results.
J4 Delphi	Has the advantages of the committee or the individual expert forecaster but attempts, through anonymity, to eliminate effects of authority and group domination seen in J3. Can be carried out asynchronously, thereby reducing the time and effort involved; research evidence on both how to carry out an effective Delphi and improvements in accuracy is available in Rowe and Wright (2001).	No necessary convergence to agreed-upon forecast; reluctance to take part in more than one round; consensus does not necessarily imply accuracy, and the true expert might well not be heard.
J5 Intentions Surveys	Effective for shorter term forecasting of new products and services, and has the advantage of reflecting potential consumers' beliefs as to their future courses of action.	Expensive—and although respondents appear to give helpful answers, circumstances in the marketplace change, thereby affecting longer term forecasts. Results need to be *de-biased* by comparing past intentions surveys with actual results. A survey may say more about people's current attitudes and expectations than about future activities. (See Morwitz, 2001.)

TABLE 13.2   (CONTINUED)

Method	Advantages	Disadvantages
Extrapolative Methods		
E1 Global Trend (Chapter 12)	Easy to learn, to use, and to understand. Can readily be programmed on a spreadsheet. Fits in with the idea of a product life cycle. In various application areas, such as telecoms, has been proved useful. See Meade and Islam (2006) for a recent review.	Almost too easy to use and therefore encourages thoughtlessness; particularly in long term forecasting: Why should a curve depending only on time provide a suitable description of the distant future?
E2 Decomposition (Chapter 4)	Incorporates trend, seasonal, and cyclical factors in an intuitively plausible model.	Limited statistical rationale; not ideally suited to forecasting, and suffers from the same problems as trend curves.
E3 Exponential smoothing (Chapters 3–5)	Easy to computerize for large number of products; very cheap to operate; easy to set up monitoring schemes; easily understood; good performance in forecasting competitions. Widely used, particularly for short-term operational forecasting. Can be extended to give the modeler considerable flexibility.	Misses turning points. Many different variants, so a *selection method* is needed. Often ineffectively programmed and therefore careful attention needs to be given to its implementation, particularly the choice of smoothing parameters. Prediction intervals are likely to be miscalculated (Gardner, 2006).
E4 Box–Jenkins or ARIMA (Chapter 6)	The choice of parameterizations is wide, allowing user to identify much more subtle patterns in data than with previous methods; offers philosophy of modeling based on principle of parsimony: The simpler the model the better it is, so long as it passes range of suitable diagnostic checks.	Complex and difficult to understand, but effective automatic versions are now available in many software packages; models can become too elaborate and incorporate patterns that do not carry over into future periods.
E5 Neural Networks (Chapter 10)	Very flexible through its nonlinear formulation and a theoretical proof that neural networks can approximate a wide range of relationships.	Complex with no standard software implementations. Software is often very expensive. Surveys and evaluations of early evidence are given by Zhang *et al.* (1998) and Adya and Collopy (1998), highlighting the weakness in the research evidence.
Causal (structural)		
C1 Single-equation regression (Chapters 7–10)	Sufficiently reliable models typically outperform alternatives (Allen and Fildes, 2001); are ideal in that they answer the question, "How does the company influence sales?"; can be used for control to establish policies (such as pricing) as well as in forecasting. Intuitive interpretation of parameters.	Models are difficult to develop, requiring expert staff and large amounts of data that organizations often fail to collect; also, there is a problem in forecasting exogenous drivers (see Ashley, 1983; 1988).
C2 VAR Models (Chapter 10)	Many economic systems do not naturally fall into the format of the single-equation model. Instead, the distinction between the dependent variables and the explanatory variables (e.g., sales and advertising) is unclear. VAR models overcome the problem of specifying the causality by modeling each of the system's variables as a lagged function of the remainder. Truly exogenous variables may also be included.	Can handle only a few variables and lags; otherwise the number of parameters becomes excessive. Large data requirements; statistically complex; requires expertise and is even more time consuming to develop than regression. Methods for simplification of the initial general lag scheme are needed. Estimation of a general lag structure is problematic, although Bayesian methods seem to work well.

(Continued)

TABLE 13.2   (CONTINUED)

Method	Advantages	Disadvantages
	The VAR approach has proved effective in forecasting compared with alternatives such as simultaneous system models (in which two or more variables are jointly, rather than sequentially, determined as in a VAR).	
C3 Simulation (Brief discussion in Sections 12.6 and 13.3)	A simulation model aims to represent the processes that lead to changes in the focus variable. Hence, they are usually disaggregated models (compared with other causal methods). An extreme example is the global circulation models used in forecasting climate (Fildes and Kourentzes, 2011). The models themselves can be intuitive, depending on their level of detail. Properly implemented, they can offer the decision maker substantial help and have high face validity; can be designed to be simple to use and understand; and can solve the "right" problem in focusing on policy options. With their high levels of disaggregation, it is possible to look at changes in policy where there is no history. Easy-to-use software is available.	Very expensive; often has large data requirements, although also has the flexibility to incorporate judgmental estimates; no clear rationale behind construction and level of aggregation used in modeling; requires careful validation, which is often difficult to do in modeling the effects of new policies. Other, more aggregated causal models (such as C1 and C2) can be used as a basis for simulations, especially for what-if policy simulations.

© Cengage Learning 2013.

Often, the choice of method is determined by the availability of data, as we discussed in the previous section. With no directly relevant data, quantitative methods cannot be used straightforwardly. Figure 13.3 presents a decision tree that captures the choices. To avoid making the figure overly complicated, we include only the separate branches for judgmental and quantitative methods. Combinations of the two, however, as in Figure 13.1, should always be considered as a possibility. (See *www.forecastingprinciples.com* for a much more complete selection tree.)

With insufficient objective data available, two branches occur; where the task is repetitive with feedback (and learning), unaided judgment works. But this is unusual. A second split is based on whether alternative policies need to be considered. Where the answer is "no," a number of methods rely on collecting data from experts (a sales force or an expert survey) or potential consumers (surveys asking whether people intend to purchase a product or service). Prediction markets take a radically different approach to obtaining a collective judgment of the likelihood of future events. There is little evidence of the respective merits of these alternative approaches, although Graefe and Armstrong (2011) suggest that Delphi is more accurate. Where alternative policies need to be considered, role-playing can be used to take into account these policies, as well as potential conflicts between actors in the situation; the aim is to understand the consequences of the different policies. The advantage arises because participants live out their assigned roles in the role-play, adopting the values and perspectives of those they represent and thereby leading to a closer simulation of their interactions. Scenarios, not a forecasting technique itself, but often a compound of many approaches, are also designed to take into account different policy options. Scenarios offer a methodology for working through alternative futures, usually based on group or expert judgments. They can

FIGURE 13.3   FORECASTING METHOD SELECTION TREE

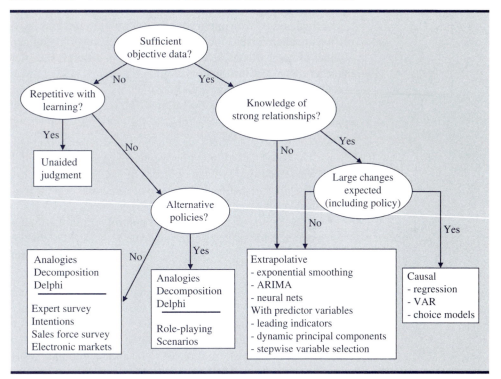

© Cengage Learning 2013.

therefore be used to examine the effects of alternative policies or even to predict what policies will be adopted. However, there is little evidence of the effectiveness of this approach compared with alternatives.

Some approaches work whether or not there are different policies to consider: analogies, making a forecast based on similarity with previous situations, decomposition of the problem into components, and Delphi, to collect and combine a variety of different expert views. All these methods were covered in Chapter 11.

Looking now at the right side of Figure 13.3, we see that when we have good objective data to use, we ask the question whether we believe that there are strong relationships between the economic or market drivers we expect to continue into the future. Also, are large changes expected in the drivers? If the answer to either question is *no*, little will be gained by developing a causal model. In fact, as Allen and Fildes (2001) summarize the evidence, the overall benefits of using a causal model are, on average, slight. Only in those situations where there is good knowledge of the causal drivers and we expect the relationships to remain constant into the future can a causal model be expected to deliver more accurate forecasts. Despite this cautionary note, for many business situations, which are driven by promotions, weather, and holidays, there is very good reason to expect success (and because of the nature of academic research, the evidence on the benefits in such problems is probably underestimated).

Where there are predictor variables that collectively have substantial impact but whose individual effects are insubstantial or largely unknown, various methods can be used to include their effects. With cross-sectional data-mining approaches (including logistic regression), automatic variable selection techniques are used effectively. (See Section 9.4 and the use of such techniques in predicting computer ownership in Chapter 10.) Similar methods may be used to improve on the accuracy of time series forecasts, but here there are typically fewer observations. As a consequence, methods of combining many weakly predictive variables in time series have been developed—most recently, so-called dynamic factor models (Stock and Watson, 2002). The basic idea is that of combining a large number of predictor variables into a smaller number of factors, which are then used in regression-type models, but the methods are beyond the scope of this text.

The final comparison applies to those common situations in which judgment and extrapolation are alternatives. Too many organizations rely on judgment (see Table 13.1). From a number of comparisons, it seems clear that, in general, statistical methods will beat judgment whenever the information available is shared. (See Lawrence, Goodwin, O'Connor, and Onkal, 2006, for a survey.) Statistical methods are also cheaper to operationalize on a large scale, as is found in operations. The reasons for this heavy reliance on judgmental approaches are as follows:

- The false belief that judgment provides more accurate forecasts.
- The belief that the quantitative model cannot capture all the complexity required for the forecasting problem whereas the judgmental forecast can.
- The need to justify the position of forecaster (e.g., if the model-based forecasts are sufficient, why do we employ a forecaster?).
- The exercise of ownership and control within the forecasting problem (e.g., if the demand forecaster can change the forecast, the change influences the product's availability, so, by adjusting the forecast, the forecaster controls the outcome to some extent).

However, we know from our discussion of combining in Section 12.1.2 that, generally, where we have two sets of alternative, preferably independently formulated forecasts, we usually do better by combining them. So, when a quantitative forecast is produced first and the forecaster is provided with information not already included in the model-based forecasts, she should adjust the forecast to take the additional information into account. Only when the statistical forecast has been sufficiently refined should the results be presented to decision makers, along with a clear picture of the underlying assumptions behind the model-based forecast. The decision makers can then make further (hopefully, appropriate) adjustments. As we mentioned before, such a process will usually lead to improved accuracy, although *both* statistical and final forecasts should be evaluated. Fildes and Goodwin (2007) explain in more detail how judgment can be improved in these circumstances.

EXAMPLE 13.1 ■ Forecasts of quarterly earnings

Forecasts based upon statistical models of quarterly earnings (often, ARIMA-based forecasts) appear to be as accurate as those made by analysts at the same point in time—that is, just after the latest earnings announcement (Brown, 1993). However, as time passes until the next announcement, no new inputs are available for the statistical model. Still, the informed analyst can build upon the statistical analysis in light of new information that emerges about the company, thereby improving upon the statistical forecast. ■

A harder task we might set for ourselves is to select the most accurate of a collection of methods, using the forecasting competition approach we described in Section 11.1.1. Of course, although carrying out a competition is sometimes a practical route forward to identifying the most accurate method, the competition must relate to the task in hand (e.g., forecasting information about all SKUs in a given sales category). Unless it is possible to consider a large number of data series and forecast origins, there is likely to remain a lot of randomness; even then, relative performance may change over time. Here again, combining is often preferable, although good software will allow the forecaster to make comparisons across individual methods and combinations to determine the best choice (see on-line Appendix C). Some available software attempts to carry out a competition automatically at each forecast origin. This approach, however, may lead to unstable forecasts, over reactive to noise, because the method chosen shifts from period to period.

Discussion Question   *Why might a selection approach in which each period selects the method that most recently performed best lead to poor performance? To improved performance?*

Discussion Question *Putting yourself in the "shoes" of a national construction company, how would you establish a framework for forecasting for the next three months of a macroeconomic variable such as monthly housing starts? How would you go about forecasting regional housing starts in a part of the country where you operate?*

13.1.4   Forecast Evaluation and Monitoring

Throughout the book, we have emphasized the need to partition the sample, whenever possible, into estimation and hold-out samples. The reason is primarily to provide a basis for model selection. When a forecasting system is already in place, the same design may be used for evaluation purposes. That is, we identify the set of time series of interest and generate corresponding forecasts over the hold-out period. The forecast performance may be measured by using the criteria first developed in Section 2.7, along with assessments of how well the prediction intervals cover the outcomes (e.g., does the 90 percent interval actually capture about 90 percent of the outcomes?). That assessment measures the statistical performance of the forecasting system and may then be used to improve it by identifying features that were previously overlooked (e.g., increases in electronic book sales that have an impact on the demand for regular books).

The second component of evaluation might be defined as *user satisfaction*: Do the forecasts provide the user with sufficiently accurate information? For example, if the forecasts are used to set safety stock levels, how much does the uncertainty in demand cost the company and how much would be saved if forecasts could be improved? That is, we examine the potential value of improvements to the forecasting system. If we are willing to accept the current forecasting system, we still need to monitor its performance over time to ensure that changing conditions do not render our approach ineffective. This need requires some form of statistical process control. The original ideas on control charts are due to Walter Shewhart. His primary focus was on manufacturing processes, where production conditions might be expected to be stable over time if and when the process is in control. Typically, a small sample was taken and the process was deemed to be out of control if the sample mean was more than three standard deviations from the underlying process mean. The time between sets of readings was sufficient to ensure that successive sample means were independent and identically distributed. We now explore how to make use of these ideas for monitoring forecast performance when the observations will be *dependent*.

Alwan and Roberts (1988) recognized the need to allow for time dependence and developed a monitoring process based upon ARIMA processes, but it is equally applicable to state-space models or any other forecasting scheme for which we can generate a predictive distribution. Alwan and Roberts also saw that it was necessary to monitor both the forecasts and the unexplained variation. They constructed charts for these two components, which they refer to as follows:

- *Common Cause Chart (CCC):* the fitted values generated by the time series model;
- *Special (or Assignable) Cause Chart (SCC):* the plot of residuals, which may be treated as a Shewhart chart when the errors are independent and identically distributed.

Alwan and Roberts (1988) urged consideration of both charts. The SCC enables the investigator to identify outliers in the usual way (as we've discussed in Section 9.7), whereas the CCC allows recognition of a potentially unacceptable trend, *even when the process is in a state of statistical control.* That is, we seek to understand the common causes leading to autocorrelated behavior, with a view to improving the process by some form of intervention. Alwan and Roberts (1995) review a number of published studies and show how the failure to allow for temporal dependence can lead to misleading conclusions.

A further point needs to be made when we consider monitoring social and economic processes. In order to calibrate the charts, we must assume either that the process is in statistical control during the calibration period or that outliers have been successfully identified and adjusted. This outlier modification step must be approached with care; typically, the parameter estimates may not change dramatically, but the residual variance may diminish considerably, thereby narrowing the control limits. If we are overly zealous in removing outliers, we may induce a "Chicken Little" effect with too many false scares whereby excessive numbers of out-of-control signals are generated in later periods.

EXAMPLE 13.2 ■ Monitoring a forecast

Let us examine the SES forecasts for the WFJ sales data introduced in Chapter 2 (in *WFJ_sales.xlsx*). We may readily determine the control limits for the SCC by using the residual variance from the estimation sample, and we plot the residuals from successive one-step-ahead forecasts. Figure 13.4 shows the SCC chart for the WFJ sales series, based upon the SES forecasts and using observations 1–40 as the estimation sample. We obtain $\alpha = 0.71$ and $RMSE = 2671$, and we plot the Z-scores for each forecast error. The unusual (out-of-control) values around the Christmas holiday periods (weeks 52–54) are clearly identified.

The CCC for the same period is shown in Figure 13.5. From this plot, the steady buildup and subsequent drop-off in sales are evident. Taken together, the two diagrams show the unusual behavior in weeks 52–54, but they also show that sales are much as expected in other time periods. If management does not like the outcomes, at least it has a clear picture of what is going on.

When the series is stationary, we may establish control limits for the CCC. However, in forecasting applications, the series being examined is often nonstationary and, consequently, does not possess a long-term mean or standard deviation. If we difference the series sufficiently to induce stationarity (Section 6.4), limits may be established for the CCC of the differenced series. ■

Discussion Question   *When the series is nonstationary, why is it not possible to use the CCC to construct a classical control chart with a fixed mean?*

FIGURE 13.4   SPECIAL CAUSE CHART FOR WFJ SALES, BASED UPON ONE-STEP-AHEAD FORECASTS (*for periods 41–62*)

Data shown is from file WFJ_sales.xlsx.

FIGURE 13.5 COMMON CAUSE CHART FOR WFJ SALES, BASED UPON
ONE-STEP-AHEAD FORECASTS (*for periods 41–62*)

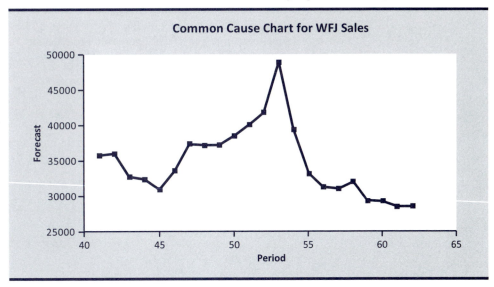

Data: WFJ_sales.xlsx.

As we have shown, the SCC and CCC plots are suitable for periodic reviews of forecast performance, but the issues are somewhat different if we are checking forecasts one period ahead for what could be a large number of products. In those circumstances, we work cross-sectionally. That is, we generate the Z-scores for the latest time period for each product and then plot them on a control chart. The process is illustrated in Figure 13.6. We consider 29 costume jewelry products (all bracelets) and use SES with $\alpha = 0.3$ to generate the

FIGURE 13.6 CROSS-SECTIONAL SCC PLOTS FOR 29 JEWELRY PRODUCTS:
(*for week 40: Z-40, and week 48: Z-48*)

Data shown is from file Jewelry_monitoring.xlsx.

one-step-ahead forecasts for each product. The plot shows the Z-scores, by product, for Week 40 (when sales were fairly quiet) and Week 48 (when the Christmas rush was beginning). The plot for Week 40 indicates relatively slow sales, whereas Week 48 exhibits sales above forecast levels for all products. Only product 13 for Week 48 lies outside the control limits. Now let's define the composite Z-score across m products as

$$Z_C = \frac{(Z_1 + Z_2 + \cdots + Z_m)}{m^{1/2}}.$$

Here, the composite Z-score yields $Z_C = -3.06$ for Week 40 and $Z_C = 10.34$ for Week 48 (Christmas is coming!).

The following box summarizes the key lessons when monitoring forecast errors.

To Successfully Monitor Forecasts:

- Compare forecasts that are outside appropriate chosen control limits.
- Check to make sure that the system is in control over the product groups.
- Adjust the control limits to ensure that only a manageable number of products have to be examined in more detail.
- Identify possible out-of-control causes.

13.1.5   A–B–C Analysis

Many forecasting organizations face the problem of forecasting and monitoring the errors arising for hundreds, if not thousands, of products. It is impossible to pay attention to all of the products equally. What is required is a way of focusing on the series that are important to the business. A standard approach is to segment the products into three classes: class A for the 20 percent or so of products that require individual attention, class B for the 30 percent of products for which an automatic monitoring scheme such as that described in the previous section would alert us to any persistent problems, and class C for the 50 percent remaining for which the forecaster looks at the errors only in response to an alert from elsewhere in the organization (e.g., an out-of-stock problem may be generating complaints). Of course, the exact proportions will always be open to debate, and what determines the importance rankings anyway? It should not be just sales volume (i.e., the highest selling products are the A products); other factors, such as profitability, may also need to be considered.

Discussion Question   *What additional factors might prove important in deciding those products (or time series) to put into class A, the category of important products?*

But such characteristics as sales volume and overall impact on profit tell only part of the story. After all, if the forecasts of a product are always 100 percent accurate, there is no reason to monitor error. The size of the error is therefore also relevant in deciding which products fall into the various classes. Consequently, we can divide the products into further subdivisions, labeled X–Y–Z, with those series with the smallest errors (as measured by *MAPE, MAE/Mean,* or *MASE*) placed in class X, those with what we consider medium sizes of errors in class Y, and those with the largest errors in class Z. Thus, the series where the greatest harm may occur is in AZ, the class of important series with large average forecasting errors.

Typically, commercial software allows the user to categorize the time series in the FSS. In addition to the A–B–C characterizations, new products or products being dropped may be separately labeled.

EXAMPLE 13.3 ■ An A–B–C analysis

Let us use the data set *Jewelry.xlsx* to identify products that require special attention. We can first divide up the series (using mean sales) to produce the box plot shown in Figure 13.7, a

FIGURE 13.7   BOX PLOT OF FORECAST ERROR (MEASURED BY MAE/MEAN)
FOR A–B–C CLASSES OF PRODUCTS

Data shown is from file Jewelry.xlsx.

diagram of forecast error (measured by *MAE/Mean*) compared with mean sales (based on three groups). Group A is defined as the top 20 percent of sales, B as the next 30 percent, and C as the remainder. Exponential smoothing was used to produce the forecasts.

Unusually, the products in class A are showing a higher level of relative error compared with the other, lower sales categories, perhaps because the products in class A have been highly promoted.

By breaking the error measure into three equal classes, we can simplify the figure further to see that we need to focus on the AZ group: products that experience large forecast errors and that are important to the business.

Table 13.3 shows that a number of series will require careful monitoring, with 51 falling into the AZ class. This is an unusually high number, because larger volume products are

TABLE 13.3   JEWELRY PRODUCTS BROKEN DOWN INTO THE NINE A–B–C, X–Y–Z CLASSES

Class	Error Class	X			Y			Z		
		n	Mean	MAE/Mean	n	Mean	MAE/Mean	n	Mean	MAE/Mean
A	69	5	160.2	1.129	13	159.2	1.933	51	217.1	4.134
B	103	37	98.5	0.984	50	105.5	1.803	16	111.2	3.160
C	173	131	52.9	0.670	40	67.9	1.790	2	57.9	3.734

X (50 percent) is the class with the smallest errors,
Y (30 percent) is the class with the medium-size errors, and
Z (20 percent) is the class with the largest errors (with 345 products, there are 345 * 20% = 69 products in class Z).

Similarly,
A (20 percent) is the class with the largest sales volume,
B (30 percent) is the class with a medium-size sales volume, and
C (50 percent) is the class with the smallest sales volume.

Each cell contains the number of products (*n*), the mean sales (*M*), and the mean absolute error divided by mean sales (*MAE/Mean*)

Data: Jewelry.xlsx.

usually easier to forecast. Sixteen products fall into class BZ. Most of the rest are either relatively unimportant or exhibit only low forecast errors.   ■

 ## The Organization of Forecasting

Forecasting takes place in many parts of an organization, private or public. In government, forecasts are needed not just for the economy as a whole, but in particular for the many services the government provides and at various levels of geographical and administrative disaggregation. For example, we may need to forecast such operational activities as the number of people in jail, the number passing through the court system, the number of telephone calls received, the cash required to keep the whole system running—the list is endless. In a manufacturing or retailing company, as we discussed in Chapter 12, a wide range of forecasts also is required, in both marketing and production/operations as well as in support of longer term strategic planning. For many working in such organizations, their role will require them to forecast (at the very least as part of the budgeting process), but their primary responsibility won't be the production of accurate forecasts. For others, however, this requirement will be written into their job specification and they will be evaluated on their forecasting performance. What do we know about such professional forecasters and how they perform? And what are those aspects of the job where there is most potential for improvement?

Discussion Question   *What do you see as the ideal educational background for a forecaster?*

13.2.1 The Forecaster

Broken down into its bare bones, the forecaster's job can be seen as taking in information and transforming it into the *final forecast*. This transformation process is heavily dependent on the input information. But the availability of this input information depends on the position the forecaster occupies within the organization. Figure 13.8 attempts to summarize a research project that examined the forecasting activity in a large multinational corporation with activities that ranged from manufacturing pharmaceuticals to producing paints and explosives (Fildes and Hastings, 1994). Each division included forecasters. In some divisions the forecasters talked to staff handling the marketing or sales function, while in other divisions the forecasters were closer to production and operations. The task these forecasters faced typically included the production of both medium- and long-term forecasts of demand. Elsewhere in some of the divisions, more short-term, focused forecasting took place. Here, we see the forecaster sitting somewhere among planning, operations, and sales/marketing or even finance. Alternatively, forecasting may be a separate function linked to management services.

  The information the forecaster receives on a regular basis will usually depend on his organizational location. In an ideal situation, the forecaster will be in receipt of sales information (at a geographical area or account level), but will also know the marketing plans and targets that are in place, such as the promotional schedule or sales-force activity. Competition may also be important, at both local and higher levels. A hierarchy of information is potentially available (see Section 12.2). But operational planning is also important, not least where there are capacity constraints that may limit product availability. In addition, there is the need to reconcile volume forecasts with financial forecasts (and budgets)—producing a unified set of forecast numbers across the organization, with money forecasts consistent with sales forecasts.

FIGURE 13.8   THE MARKET FORECASTER IN THE ORGANIZATION:
INFORMATION FLOWS

Source: Adapted from Fildes and Hastings (1994).

Discussion Question   *Why do many organizations (or business units) aspire to a unified set of forecast numbers that are used across the whole organization? Why is this aspiration often difficult to achieve? What are the arguments against relying on such a unified set?*

Figure 13.8 shows the ideal situation in which the forecaster is in receipt of all the information necessary to support the forecasting process. Of course, a similar picture could be drawn for the government forecaster or the financial forecaster. But in real situations, not all the links operate effectively (e.g., the forecaster may not know anything at all about the operational constraints on supply). Alternatively, marketing plans may be unavailable, either because of poorly drawn lines of responsibility or an inadequate FSS. It is the forecaster's responsibility, if only because of the need for self-preservation, to ensure that the necessary information is made available (see Minicase 13.1). In fact, in the case of the organization shown in Figure 13.8, lack of information beyond the sales history was common. Other researchers have also provided survey evidence from audits of organizational forecasting processes; for example, Moon *et al.* (2003) identified the lack of integrated systems and databases as a key element undermining forecasting performance.

One aspect of the forecaster's location and relationships with others in the organization is particularly important: the relationship with those who use the final forecasts and to the decisions made as a consequence. Without an effective link between the two, the forecasting activity cannot add organizational value.

Discussion Question   *Why is the organizational location of the forecaster potentially important to carrying out the job effectively?*

A useful discussion concerning the placement of the forecasting function within an organization is provided by Smith and Clark (2011). The issue they focus on is how to minimize bias in which forecasters in sales seem motivated toward optimism and those in finance toward less optimistic scenarios or even pessimism. An independent forecasting function is always a possibility, but that runs the risk of leaving the forecaster isolated, without access to the reliable flow of information needed for good forecasting.

13.2.2 The Links to the Forecast User

In many organizations, the forecaster's job is quite separate from that of the user, who will often be making decisions based on the forecast. For example, a retail demand forecast at the SKU level will be turned into an order to the supplier on the basis of the inventory on hand. Or forecasts for incoming phone calls into a call center will be turned into a staff schedule for the next month. The inventory control manager, the scheduler, the purchasing manager, the financial manager, and the account manager are usually not the forecaster. They all have different requirements of the forecasts, with different motivations. We don't in fact know much about the relationship. Anecdotally, forecasters come in for a lot of criticism for "getting it wrong," and often users will modify the final forecasts to take into account some particular aspect of the problem they believe has been inadequately dealt with. The users and their bosses have to believe the forecaster is adding value.

The Forecaster's Job

Your job as a forecaster is at risk:

- If the user of your forecasts ignores them or modifies them for unaccountable reasons.
- If the decisions made by the user do not depend on the forecasts you produce.

In an interesting (though dated) survey, Wheelwright and Clarke (1976) asked dyads composed of forecaster and user about their perceptions of each other. We give the flavor of their results in Table 13.4.

The table shows how users and forecasters differ in their perceptions; a large score indicates a major difference between the two groups. The conclusion that leaps out from the table is that neither group believes that the other has any understanding of forecasting; in particular,

TABLE 13.4 DIFFERENCES IN RATINGS BETWEEN USERS' AND FORECASTERS' VIEWS OF EACH OTHER

	Difference between Users and Forecasters, %
Forecaster's Ability	
• Understand sophisticated forecasting techniques	1%
• Understand management problems	−25%
• Produce cost-effective forecasts	−33%
• Identify best techniques	−56%
• Provide results in the time frame required	−38%
User's Ability	
• Understand essentials of forecasting	27%

The measure used for each criterion is [(% users rating the ability as good or excellent − % forecasters rating the ability as good or excellent) ÷ (% forecasters rating the ability as good or excellent)] * 100.

Source: Adapted from Wheelwright and Clarke, 1976.

users don't believe that forecasters understand the problems that need to be addressed. Only on one dimension do they agree: Forecasters apparently "understand sophisticated techniques". It sounds, however, as if there is no belief on the users' part that sophistication brings success! In fact, more recent studies, such as the survey by McCarthy *et al.* (2006), do not support this view of the technical knowledge forecasters may have: Most forecasters in organizations seem to know little about the advances in techniques that we have witnessed over the past 30 years and that are described in this book. Although we don't know much about the educational background of forecasters, there's plenty of anecdotal evidence to suggest that many, if not most, forecasters have no training in forecasting at all!

Despite the limited evidence, there are some hard lessons to be drawn here. Forecasters need to understand their users' requirements and also to explain effectively to those who employ them the value that accurate forecasts add to the business. They also need to explain the importance of a business having independent forecasters who are not caught up in organizational politics, for the reasons we explain in the next section.

Discussion Question *How would you organize the forecasting function within an organization to ensure both independence of the forecasters and good interactions with users?*

13.2.3 The Politics of Forecasting

Discussion Question *Long-term climate forecasts have embroiled climate scientists, economists, and politicians in a major argument as to the accuracy of forecasts of global warming. Why do you think this forecast is such a political issue? Can you think of any forecasts in an organizational or government setting that might prove almost as controversial?*

Research on forecasting practice has shown that forecasts are often influenced by political considerations. For evidence from government, see Deschamps (2004); from the private sector focusing primarily on financial forecasts, see Galbraith and Merrill (1996). When we examine more disaggregated short-term forecasts, the evidence we find is more circumstantial, but forecasts at the SKU level prove to be biased and, more importantly, adjustments to statistical forecasts are most often biased upward and prove overinflated (Fildes *et al.*, 2009). Similarly, forecasts of the completion and costs of information systems projects are also often biased upward (see Table 1 in Halkjelsvik, T. & Jørgensen, 2012), as they also are in new-product forecasting (Tyebjee, 1987). Likewise, many capital projects produce inflated projections of return on investment. Although there are explanations other than political influences, it seems to be that in many circumstances there is organizational pressure to produce "good news"; forecasts are just too optimistic.

Discussion Question *What other explanations can you think of to explain why capital projects in both government and the private sector tend to be optimistically biased?*

In a U.S. organizational survey of the politics of forecasting, Galbraith and Merrill (1996) found that adjustments due to political reasons were widespread (with around 50 percent of forecasts adjusted to more favorable levels) by senior management. Table 13.5 gives a full picture of why adjustments were made. Overall, the aim of these senior managerial adjustments was to inflate the outcome toward a more favorable figure (Factors 1–3 in the table). The results contrast with those set forth in Fildes and Goodwin (2007), which enumerates the reasons that *forecasters* made adjustments to the statistical forecast. Here, the reasons were much more innocuous and boiled down to incorporating the additional information available to the forecasters beyond the information incorporated into the time series history.

TABLE 13.5   TYPES OF FORECASTING BEHAVIOR

Question	Percent of Respondents Reporting High Frequency of Behavior*
FACTOR 1. Management Requests Staff Revisions	
1. After reviewing the sales/revenue forecasts, senior management request staff to adjust revenue projections to a more favorable level.	45.1
2. After reviewing cost projections, senior management request staff to adjust cost projections to a more favorable level.	51.6
3. After reviewing pro-forma profit/loss, senior management request staff to generate revised pro-formas that are more favorable.	41.3
FACTOR 2. Management Makes Own Revisions	
4. Senior management personally revise staff's cost projections to reflect a more favorable level.	30.0
5. Senior management personally revise staff's revenue/sales forecasts to reflect a more favorable level.	23.3
FACTOR 3. Management Requests "Backcasts"	
6. Senior management predetermines an "appropriate" sales/revenue level then requests staff to generate forecasts to support this level.	41.9
7. Senior management predetermines an "appropriate" cost level then requests staff to generate cost projections to support this level.	35.5
8. Senior management predetermines an "appropriate" future financial position, then requests staff to generate pro-formas to support this decision.	36.7
FACTOR 4. Use of Incorrect Techniques and Assumptions	
9. Wrong assumptions (such as industry or economic growth) are purposely used in forecasts or models.	12.9
10. Wrong assumptions (such as industry or economic growth) are accidentally used in forecasts or models.	19.4
11. Insufficient resources are provided for the forecasting modeling effort.	35.5
12. Qualitative assessments are made when there are appropriate quantitative techniques that could also be used.	32.4
FACTOR 5. Management Ignores Models/Forecasts	
13. Staff's forecasts are simply discounted by senior management as being "unimportant."	16.1
14. Staff's forecasts are simply discounted by senior management as probably being "inaccurate."	6.6
FACTOR 6. Withholding of Information	
15. Divisions/departments withhold useful data from other departments.	25.8
16. Divisions/departments provide misleading data to other departments.	12.9
FACTOR 7. Model/Forecast Mis-specification	
17. Computer models are constructed that are purposely mis-specified or don't accurately reflect reality.	6.7
18. Politically sensitive variables are purposely excluded from the computer model.	20.0
19. Computer models are constructed to have a bias, to the advantage of certain departments, projects, or activities.	13.3

*Percent reported is a combination of three responses: constant, almost always, and often.

Source: Results of a survey by Galbraith and Merrill (1996).

FIGURE 13.9 REPORTED EFFECTS OF FORECASTING AND MODELING POLITICS

Source: Galbraith and Merrill, 1996.

Why did managers make such adjustments? There were a variety of reasons given, but the most important was to gain control of additional internal resources.

Discussion Question *Why does an optimistic forecast lead to additional resources?*

Now, of course, such adjustments, if appropriate, could prove beneficial, but as Figure 13.9 shows, this is not the case. In general, the political adjustments degraded the accuracy of the forecasts. They also damaged strategic decisions and investment decisions, and had an adverse impact upon forecasters' morale. These patterns of chronic mis-estimation are particularly obvious in cost estimates for public works projects. Notorious examples include the Sydney Opera House, which cost 15 times more than was originally projected. More recently, when Boston's "Big Dig" tunnel construction project was completed, the project was 275 percent over budget. Arguably, both of these projects and others like them proved worthwhile in the end.

How can we provide more effective forecasts without risking the loss of approval? Flyvbjerg (2008 and several earlier papers) has recommended the use of *reference class forecasting*. In essence, the forecast is calibrated against the final outcomes of similar, already completed projects and is an example of forecasting using analogies, as discussed in Section 11.2.5. Providing such information may improve both forecasting processes and decision making.

More generally, various authors, including Galbraith and Merrill (1996) and Deschamps (2005), have discussed how to avoid the worst aspects of political forecasting—in particular, pervasive bias. The following are some of their suggestions:

- Forecasters need better training in forecasting and modeling techniques. Remember, most forecasters are not trained in forecasting!
- Guidelines need to be established for how the forecasting process should be carried out. Changes to the forecasters' forecasts should be made *only if* new

evidence is brought to bear on the forecast. Such changes need to be documented (as they should be in making adjustments to statistical models in operations; see Section 12.2.1).

- Make the assumptions behind the forecast explicit.
- Aim for a consensus forecast that balances the various political interests and stands a good chance of achieving user acceptance.
- Identify bias by monitoring accuracy.
- Assign responsibility to the forecasters for their errors. Do not permit users to modify the final forecasts without accepting responsibility.

But politics are an inevitable part of the forecasting process and include information sharing, arriving at assumptions and policies, and the user group's acceptance of the forecast to use it operationally in planning and decision making.

Forecast errors remain inevitable in forecasting, even with the best process in the world. In the next section, we revisit the evaluation of forecasting in an organizational setting and touch briefly on coping with the residual unavoidable uncertainty.

Discussion Question *What, if any, potentially positive effects derive from politically motivated adjustments to the forecasts?*

13.3 Dealing with Uncertainty

Through most of the book's earlier chapters, the primary focus has been on point forecasts, with one major exception: the volatility modeling in Section 6.10, where we pointed out that uncertainty is of interest in its own right, because it drives much financial decision making. But this is also true for many other areas of application. Not only do we need a point forecast, but as we have stressed repeatedly, we need to indicate the range of possible future outcomes, for example, by estimating a prediction interval. Even better, we could hope to capture the whole distribution, which is important when the errors do not follow a normal distribution. (If the errors do follow a normal distribution, then the mean and variance serve to determine the prediction interval.) But it's as important as in the volatility forecasting example of Section 6.10 to remember that these intervals and distributions are themselves forecasts of *future* uncertainty. Figure 13.10 gives an example of a fan chart, which is produced by a number of central banks to capture their forecasts of uncertainty. The forecast origin is the second quarter of 2010, and the different shadings show varying degrees of uncertainty around the point forecasts as the forecast horizon lengthens.

Each color band in Figure 13.10 has the same probability of including the actual value. However, it is important to recognize that unlikely events do happen and the darker parts of the fan will not always capture the outcomes. By the end of the first quarter of 2011, the *CPI* in the UK was already over 4 percent, very much inside the lighter, less likely shaded area.

More generally, we might be able to predict the full error distribution, shown in Figure 13.11. Even when the histogram looks symmetrical, the distribution may have heavy tails, as shown in the probability plot, so we would underestimate the possibility of large errors. Part of the problem in the 2008–2012 financial crisis was the erroneous assumption that errors were approximately normal, so risks were systematically underestimated.

Discussion Question *Identify some instances in which the extremes of the forecast error distribution are likely to have a particularly high impact, and explain why.*

FIGURE 13.10   THE FORECAST UNCERTAINTY AROUND THE BANK OF
ENGLAND'S INFLATION FORECASTS FROM 2010 TO 2012
(FAN CHART PUBLISHED NOVEMBER 2010)

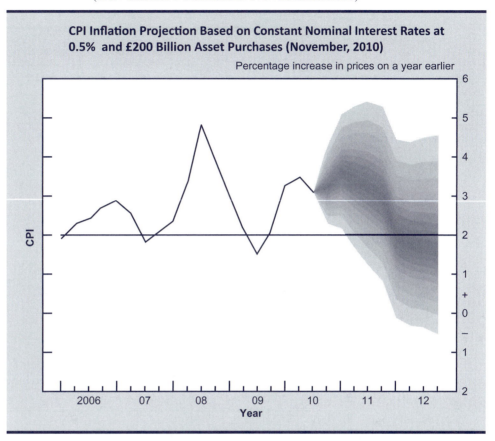

(The fan is expected to include 90 percent of outcomes. The probability of an inflation outcome
falling into each similarly colored band is 10 percent, although not falling equally on the upside
and downside because of the skewed probabilities).

Source: www.bankofengland.co.uk/publications/inflationreport/2010.htm. Reproduced with
permission.

When we have an explicit statistical model, we are usually able to use past data and the
model's residuals to generate an estimate of the distribution. For example, if we can assume
that the distribution is normal, then the output of a regression model includes an estimate
of the standard deviation of the residuals (see Chapter 8), which is used to construct
prediction intervals. Alternatively, where many past out-of-sample errors have been collected, it is better to use these to estimate the empirical error distribution (see Section 2.8).
But both approaches make a strong assumption that is common and almost unavoidable in
all forecasting: Past errors are predictive of future errors. Nonetheless, that wasn't how the
fan chart of Figure 13.10 was constructed. Although the errors the Bank of England had
made in the past were certainly influential, the fan chart itself also takes into account the
current opinions of the Bank's forecasters as to future uncertainty. In 2010, these opinions
reflected the extremely uncertain global financial environment. Thus, for major forecasts,
a combination of statistical and judgmental information will typically provide improved
estimates of the error distribution.

FIGURE 13.11 DISTRIBUTION AND PROBABILITY PLOT OF DAILY RETURNS FOR THE DOW JONES INDEX (*From January 2, 2001–September 30, 2005; n = 1200. A normal distribution is superimposed for comparison*)

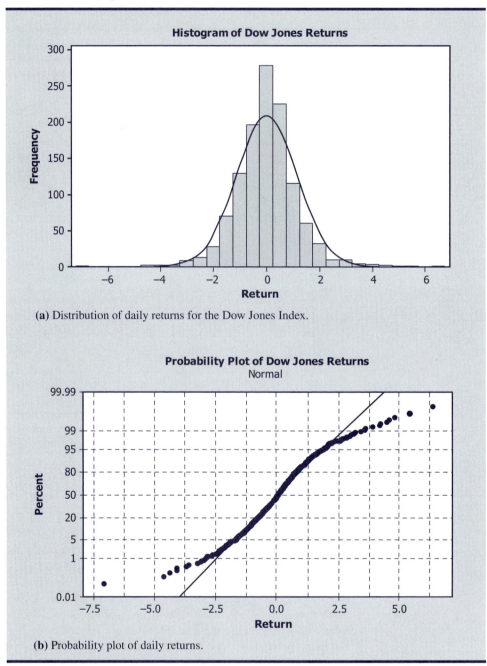

(a) Distribution of daily returns for the Dow Jones Index.

(b) Probability plot of daily returns.

Data shown is from file Dow_Jones.xlsx.

13.3.1 **Simulating Uncertainty**

In any forecasting exercise, errors arise from a multitude of sources. We have examined some of these sources in Section 8.6, but we now need to develop a more extended list. Consider an underlying model of a dependent variable Y (or a set of such variables)

$$Y_{t+k} = f_t(Y_{t+k-1}, X_{t+k}, \varepsilon_{t+k} | \boldsymbol{\beta}), \tag{13.1}$$

where f_t is an function that may be time dependent and nonlinear but is often assumed to be constant and linear, X_t represents exogenous (explanatory) variables defined outside the economic system, and ε_t are random error terms. Both Y and X may be vectors; that is, multiple variables may be involved in the forecasting exercise. $\boldsymbol{\beta}$ is a vector of unknown parameters that are estimated from past data. Errors in producing k-periods-ahead forecasts for period $t + k$ based on information available only up to time t arise from the following possible sources:

1. Estimation errors in estimating $\boldsymbol{\beta}$
2. Randomness
3. Errors in forecasting X_{t+k}
4. Errors in forecasting Y_{t+k-1}, $k > 1$ and any further lags in the model
5. Misspecification of the function f, including omitted variables and structural change
6. Data errors
7. Calculation errors.

The formulas of Section 8.6 cover only the first two sources of error, so we need to consider methods that incorporate at least sources 3 and 4 as well. Some progress may be made by the use of additional lags, as in Section 7.7.4, or, more generally, by means of the VAR models of Section 10.5, but complex systems may be beyond tractable analysis and we must turn to simulation methods.

The forecast function and associated error distribution can be estimated by the simulation approach shown in Figure 13.12.

FIGURE 13.12   FLOW CHART FOR SIMULATING A PREDICTIVE DISTRIBUTION

The idea behind this process is that N random draws are made from the distributions characterizing our uncertain knowledge of X and ε. Using the known function f and an estimate of β, the process generates a pseudo-observation on Y. By iterating through $k = 1, 2, \ldots$ to the forecast horizon K, we generate these pseudo-observations for the next K periods. This procedure is then repeated N times (where N is large) to generate a probability distribution of possible outcomes. The output from the simulation provides an estimate of the predictive distribution of the forecasts and the forecast errors. The predictive distribution can then be used to generate prediction intervals or for other purposes, such as setting safety stocks.

Perhaps the most serious problem is the failure to take into account the uncertainty in β, which our earlier analyses have assumed to be fixed. To gain insight into the uncertainty arising from the fact that we have estimated β, we can use our newly estimated equation to calculate the predicted values (for periods $t + 1$ to $t + K$) based on simulated Xs, which, when joined with the simulated errors, gives a new set of pseudo Y values. For the first t periods, the pseudo Ys are based on observed Xs while for the K periods ahead forecasts simulated Xs are used. With the newly simulated Y's, we can then estimate another β, and a corresponding set of Y's, both predicted and forecast. By repeatedly generating a pseudosample, we can derive a probability distribution for β, and the corresponding predictive distribution that now takes into account the uncertainties in X, ε, and β. An alternative is to assume a distribution for β, based on its estimated mean and variance, but this is difficult when there are more than one or two parameters unless we assume that these prior distributions are independent. This approach is explored in the next section.

13.3.2 Understanding the Impact of Uncertainty and Forecast Errors

Forecasting does not exist in an organizational vacuum. This observation is the very heart of this chapter. It affects many aspects of an organization's performance, from the service levels experienced by customers, its effects on cash flow and profitability, to the very survival of the organization. Similar examples occur in the not-for-profit and government sectors. An organization invests its resources in forecasting because the impact of "getting it wrong" hits the bottom-line deliverables. (Think less profit or poorer service.) In order to decide between different courses of action, the impact of both the point forecast and the forecast error should be taken into account.

Discussion Question *In the U.S. federal court system (in the UK, the Crown Court), what do you think are the important types of forecast error and how are these likely to affect the system's performance?*

EXAMPLE 13.4 ■ Cash-flow simulation study

As an illustration, Figure 13.13 shows a simple flow chart that links cash with predicted revenues and costs, which in turn depend on demand. (We assume that there is a capacity constraint of 1200 units, so demand is not always equivalent to sales.)

Here, price influences demand to generate sales (so long as the volume is within the capacity to supply it). In turn, revenue is produced, and once costs (made up of fixed and variable costs) are subtracted from revenue, the result is the corresponding cash—that is,

$$Cash = Price * Sales - (Fixed\,Cost + Unit\,Cost * Sales).$$

Although the primary variable we wish to forecast is demand, we will also be at least as interested in the cash projections. These in turn may be used to generate an appraisal of an investment project that would service the demand and generate both fixed and variable costs. To make the whole example more realistic, we could consider two alternative investment decisions, the more expensive of which would generate lower unit costs with the second, cheaper alternative leading to higher costs in later periods. The problem then is which of the uncertain factors have the greatest effect on *Cash* and how should we set the price.

FIGURE 13.13 A SIMPLE MODEL OF CASH AS IT IS AFFECTED BY DEMAND
AND COSTS

© Cengage Learning 2013.

Let us suppose the demand function is

$$\ln(D_t) = \beta_0 + \lambda\ln(D_{t-1}) + \beta_1\ln(P_t) + \varepsilon_t. \qquad (13.2)$$

That is to say, there is an effect of price on demand (we would expect β_1 to be negative) and a carry-over effect from the previous period's demand (we would expect λ to be positive). To complete the picture, we assume a production capacity of 1200 units.

In any appraisal of investment alternatives that affect capacity, including marketing decisions, we would assess the results over a period of time. A standard method to ensure the comparability of cash flows from projects of different length is to use net present value (*NPV*), calculated as

$$NPV = \sum_{j=0}^{12} \frac{Cash_j}{(1 + r)^j}. \qquad (13.3)$$

This equation discounts future cash flows by the discount rate r, with the rationale that cash available now is worth more to us than future cash flows. (After all, if we have cash on hand, we could invest it and gain the interest at the very least.)

In our example, we have chosen to look at the cash flows over a 12-month period following the initial month ($j = 0$). Of course, for major investment decisions, the calculation needs to cover a number of years.

As a baseline, we can assume a constant demand of 1000 units, a capacity constraint of 1200, and a discount rate r of 1 percent per month to calculate the *NPV*. The result of the *NPV* calculation equals $120,100.

We next assume that the parameters in equation (13.2) are known exactly, with $\lambda = 0.2$, $\beta_1 = -0.5$ (characteristic of a price-inelastic product), a mean level of demand of 1000 (which determines $\beta_0 = 7.0247$), and random fluctuations in demand (The error term, ε_t is normally distributed with zero mean and standard deviation 0.25.) The cost parameters we have assumed are also shown in Table 13.6. Each simulation of random

TABLE 13.6   ASSUMPTIONS REGARDING THE CALCULATION OF PROFIT IN EXAMPLE 13.4

Model Parameters	Mean Demand	Price Elasticity, β_1	Carry-over λ	Standard Error, σ	Unit Costs, ϕ	Fixed Cost	Discount Factor	Price
Assumed distribution	Fixed	Beta	Uniform	ChiSquare	Uniform	Fixed	Fixed	Fixed
Mean Value	1000	−0.5	0.2	0.25	10	200	1%	20
Range	n.a.	0 to −3.0	0 to 1	0 to ∞	8 to 12	n.a.	n.a.	n.a.

Data shown is from file Profit.xlsx.

demand leads to a new estimate of *NPV*. The results of running 10,000 simulations of demand are shown in Figure 13.14. This results in an average *NPV* of $118,193, less than the constant demand estimate of $120,100 because, for periods of high demand, the capacity constraint means that sales are lost. (In fact, the average demand over these simulation runs is 1020, from equation (13.1).)

Figure 13.14 shows the variation possible in *NPV* as the sequence of random demands changes with 90 percent of runs falling within the interval from $105, 000 to $130,000. But of course, the estimated *NPV* is even more uncertain than the figure suggests; it is based on our chosen parameter estimates. The parameters for the demand function might be estimated from past data with the use of either regression or judgment, based on our knowledge of the market, and these estimates are uncertain. So how might we take this uncertainty into account?

FIGURE 13.14   THE SIMULATED DISTRIBUTION OF THE NET PRESENT VALUE AS IT DEPENDS ON DEMAND UNCERTAINTY
(*See also Exercise 13.4*)

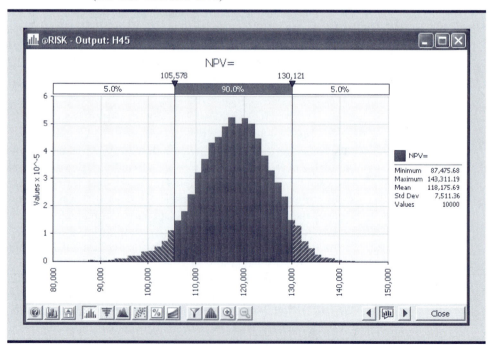

Source: Reproduced with permission from Palisade Corporation.

FIGURE 13.15   DISTRIBUTIONS AVAILABLE FOR SIMULATING UNCERTAINTY IN KEY MODEL PARAMETERS

Source: Reproduced with permission from Palisade Corporation.

One easy-to-use route is through simulating uncertainty, as we described earlier. But first we have to decide on suitable probability distributions to describe our uncertainty. Figure 13.15 shows the range of probability distributions, both discrete and continuous (more precisely, probability density functions for continuous distributions), that are available in one of the well-established commercial packages, @Risk.

First let us examine the effects of uncertainty in the error variance. We choose the Chisq(uare) distribution, which is specified with just one parameter, again with a mean of .25, but with a range from 0 to ∞. (Of course, the larger values are extremely unlikely.) We contrast the two results (the first with fixed error variance and the second with uncertain variance) in Figure 13.16. The uncertainty in the standard deviation of demand has little effect on the overall mean *NPV* but considerably increases the 10 percent to 90 percent range.

But of course, there are other key uncertainties we may wish to take into account. Some parameters might be quite well understood (or even known perfectly). Let's assume that the fixed cost is constant, as shown in Table 13.6. However, we are uncertain as to the price elasticity, believing it to lie between 0 and −1.5 on the basis of earlier research; also, we believe the lagged effect to be between 0 and 1 with a mean value of 0.5. We've assumed a beta distribution for the elasticity (see Fig. 13.15) and a uniform distribution for the lag parameter to capture our understanding. Other assumptions are as shown in Table 13.6. Of course, the analyst will not *know* the shape of the distribution, but typically the results are insensitive to the choice unless they are very different alternatives.

The final stage in the analysis is to pull all these uncertainties together to provide a summary of the effects on the *NPV*. @Risk also provides various charts that summarize which of the uncertainties is the most important in affecting the final value. One approach is to examine the sensitivity of the *NPV* to changes in parameters through a scattergram of *NPV* versus the parameter in question (say, price elasticity) where the other parameters are taken as fixed. Figure 13.17 compares the results from the uncertainty in the price elasticity with that from the carry-over effect.

Comparing the two scattergrams, we see that there is little difference from uncertainty in the two parameters (carry-over and price elasticity) on the variation in *NPV* (with a similar standard deviation of around 8800). The *NPV* distribution is also similar, with a comparable range.

FIGURE 13.16   THE SIMULATED DISTRIBUTION OF NPV AS IT IS AFFECTED
BY UNCERTAINTY IN THE ERROR VARIANCE

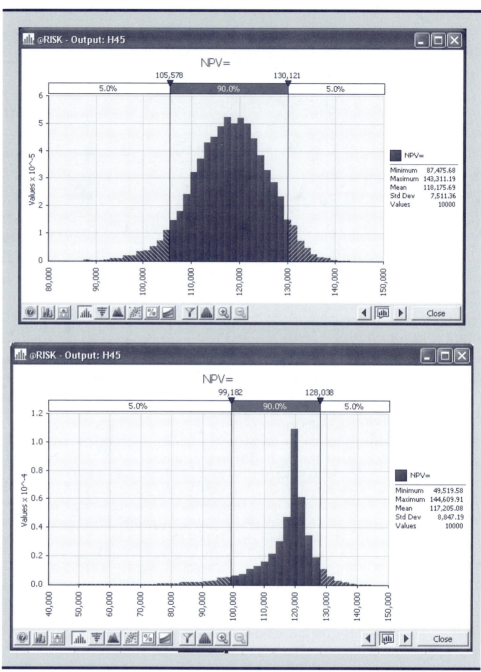

Source: Reproduced with permission from Palisade Corporation.

The scattergrams show the relationship between a selected output variable and an uncertain parameter in the model and are calculated with other parameters in the model fixed at their base level. This approach neglects the possibility of a correlation between the uncertain parameters. For example, if elasticity was high, perhaps unit costs would also have a higher mean due to the higher costs of meeting the increased fluctuations in demand. These simulation models (and software) can also incorporate this feature of the problem.

FIGURE 13.17   SCATTERGRAMS OF *NPV* VERSUS UNCERTAINTY IN MODEL
PARAMETERS

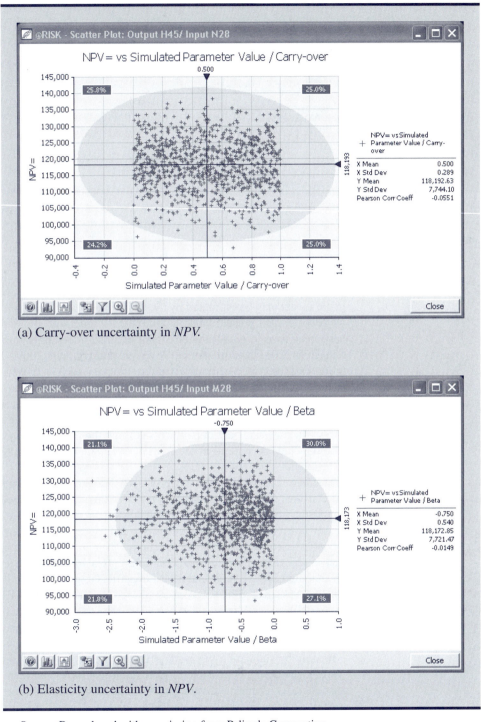

(a) Carry-over uncertainty in *NPV*.

(b) Elasticity uncertainty in *NPV*.

Source: Reproduced with permission from Palisade Corporation.

An alternative to scattergrams is to use a tornado diagram, which attempts to explain the variation in *NPV* (or another simulated output) by changes in the various parameter values on the basis of a regression model. A tornado diagram can be constructed from the input and output of the simulation runs. Each run has a set of input parameters (e.g., carry-over λ, elasticity β_1, unit costs) characterizing the distributions, and these inputs then lead to a corresponding output, here *NPV*. The regression model is of the form $NPV = f(\beta_1, \lambda, \phi)$, where the model could include interaction effects between the parameters (e.g., a term $\lambda\phi$ in the regression model).   ■

Discussion Question   *In a final examination on a business forecasting course, how many additional points out of 100 would you expect to gain from six additional hours of study? What distribution would you use to describe your uncertainty?*

Discussion Question   *In the airline industry, revenue management is used to fill the planes and get the best financial return from a flight. Discuss how you might model a two-price-class flight in which the cheaper tickets are not refundable, and what uncertainties arise around the cash the flight generates?*

Simulation models that aim to capture the key interactions in complex systems are also used as forecasting models, as we have shown in Example 13.4. Although the parameters in the model may be estimated by the techniques of earlier chapters, the dependent variable we focus on, net present value, is estimated through the simulation model. Such methods have been used to model the effects of demand uncertainty in manufacturing (Fildes and Kingsman, 2011) and in services (Sanders and Graman, 2009). But they can also be used to forecast the effects of complex policy changes such as those arising in government. For example, changes in a government's health care policy (such as Medicare) lead to individual decisions with consequences for the hospital system and government finances. The simulation model would then be based on demographic knowledge of potential patients, their likely illnesses, and patient pathways through the health-care system. The output variables would include such items as the costs of treatment and the average time for a patient's stay in hospital.

The final example in this brief overview of simulation models for forecasting is modeling climate, a topic we touched on in Section 12.7. Climate models (developed in research institutes around the world) are based on physical flows of air, water, CO_2, etc., over time through a world broken down into geographical cubes over land and sea. The flows obey physical laws, so the model is based on mathematical equations. The aim is to predict meteorological phenomena, such as temperature, rainfall, and ocean currents, across the globe and how they are affected by greenhouse gas (CO_2) concentrations. In particular, the press and politicians pay considerable attention to such headline forecasts as the predicted increase in global average temperature over the next 100 years. More detailed local forecasts are also produced by these global circulation models, and such forecasts can affect localized planning decisions. Similar simulation models are used in the short term, for day-to-day weather forecasting.

In sum, by simulating the system (be it a business process, a government policy, or the world's climate), it is possible to generate forecasts, estimate their uncertainty, and evaluate policies. The models themselves need not be statistically based, although they will often include components that rely on the methods we have described here in this book. Their validation is subject to all the forecast accuracy concerns we have discussed; therefore, the principles we have laid out hold equally for these simulation models as they do for their statistical or naïve alternatives. For an example in climate modeling of how these two approaches can usefully be compared and combined to produce better understanding and improved forecast accuracy, see Fildes and Kourentzes (2011).

13.3.3   **Scenarios as a Means for Understanding Uncertainty**

Sometimes, particularly in longer term strategic decision making, there are many components of uncertainty. They interact in complicated ways, and it would be difficult, if not impossible, to lay out the complete system of social, economic, and market interactions in a form like that shown in Figure 13.13. To deal with this type of messy or so-called *wicked problem*, scenarios have been developed. The idea of a scenario as a consistent story was introduced in Section 11.5. Such stories get increasingly complex as the time scales we need to consider lengthen and there are more and more decision points and greater environmental uncertainty. Although, in our organization, we will have control over some of these decisions and their outcomes, other actors in the system we are analyzing will in turn respond to our decisions in essentially unpredictable ways. More and more branches sprout and develop, potentially overwhelming the possibility of considering every alternative. Instead, we may choose to consider a limited number of these scenarios, which consist of a mixture of our organizational decisions, decisions by other actors (such as competitors or governments), and environmental events. Section 11.5 discussed how a limited number of scenarios should be selected from the large number of possibilities.

Because scenarios have no probabilistic interpretation, they cannot be used to provide a probabilistic summary of key variables, as in the risk analysis we described in the previous section. However, they can be used to furnish the key inputs into a broad-brush model of an organization—a model that examines the robustness of different decisions, as shown in Figure 13.18. Here, two scenarios have been developed and the organizational policies that best fit the particular environmental and competitive futures they embody have been translated into a set of outcomes. (Note that these outcomes should aim to represent equilibrium states rather than capturing transitory fluctuations.) Of course, three or more scenarios could be considered along with any number of organizational policies.

FIGURE 13.18   USING SCENARIOS TO IDENTIFY ROBUST POLICIES

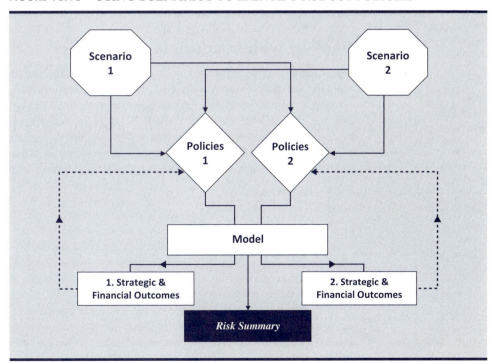

But perhaps the organization adopts policy 1 while scenario 2 (or something like it) develops—or vice versa. The *Risk Summary* aims to capture what would be lost in such circumstances. A robust policy in the face of the complex uncertainties captured by the scenarios is the a policy in which the loss in both financial terms and strategic position is small when the policy is tested over all the scenarios. In general, of course such a policy would always lose out compared with the policy chosen to fit a particular scenario (such as policy 1 for Scenario 1 in Figure 13.18).

Scenarios and Risk

A *risk summary* compares the loss from alternative policies arising from different future scenarios.

A *robust policy* is a policy in which the likely loss is small over a wide range of scenarios (relative to the policy that would have been selected if the future was known with certainty—the *perfect information* policy).

Discussion Question or Group Project   *In early 2011, oil prices moved up sharply but did not quite reach the height they had reached in 2008. Taking the role of analyst for GM or Nissan, state what you see as the major sources of uncertainty in maintaining and improving profitability over the next five years. Develop two scenarios that capture some of these key uncertainties. Who would you wish to participate in a professional scenario development activity for a car manufacturer?*

In sum, multiple scenarios offer an approach to capturing the uncertainty inherent in complex (often longer term) environmental, political, technological, and demographic developments. Such scenarios aim to capture the interactive effects of key drivers that affect the problem being analyzed. But they are unable to offer a probabilistic summary of possible outcomes. Instead, they are best used to identify applicable policies that are robust to as wide a range as possible of alternative futures as well as any outstanding major risks.

13.3.4 Dealing with Irreducible Uncertainty

Uncertainty costs organizations money, and it can even threaten their very existence. Unfortunately, we can't do away with it. In the previous sections, we examined ways we could estimate uncertainty and develop policies that are optimal or, at the very least, robust while lowering the risk level. However, sometimes protecting ourselves from extreme outcomes can be prohibitively expensive. Or, alternatively a risk activity might not be core to our business and we might not wish to develop the expertise necessary to protect ourselves (exchange-rate transactions being just such an example). Three approaches should be considered:

- *Insurance*
- *Portfolio procedures*
- *Organizational flexibility.*

Insurance: In most circumstances, there is always a residual risk whereby we accept the consequences of a particularly unlikely event (e.g., high demand leading to an out-of-stock result). However, covering the residual uncertainty and riding out the consequences may sometimes be regarded as too dangerous. Instead, the risk is reduced by transferring most of the consequences of a disaster to an insurance company. The effect, of course, is a reduced return, because insurance policies always cost money. The insurance company operates by averaging over a set of similar risky investments (see *Portfolio Procedures*, to follow), only some of which will lead to a claim.

A variant of the same notion consists of using futures markets or forward contracting to purchase an option now in order to purchase a fixed amount at a fixed price in the future. For example, raw materials (and foreign currency) can be purchased through futures markets so that the amount to be paid for a future need is known now. In marketing, long-term contracts can be made with large purchasers, even when futures markets do not exist. Although all of these devices cost money, they do meet the aim of reducing uncertainty.

A subtler variation of this idea has been described by Quinn (1989) as *logical incrementalism*. Simply put, it is the recommendation that where outcomes may prove costly and uncertainty is high, only those decisions are contemplated that are viable over a wide range of possible futures—the robustness analysis we discussed in the previous section. For example, in planning a power station, the decision regarding which fuel to use may be postponed, with plans based on either coal or oil as the power source. Designing the power station to operate with both fuel sources is another alternative. Though costly, such duplications overcome the very high uncertainty in fuel price forecasts. As the forecasting (and planning) lead time decreases, uncertainty is also decreased and more definite choices can be made. Decisions here are sequential rather than executed only once. The cost derives from the alternative courses of action being kept open for a longer period than they would if the decision had been made once and for all. Such an approach also demands sophisticated planning.

Portfolio Procedures: It has long been known that if two alternative investments can be found with similar returns but with outcomes negatively or only slightly positively correlated, a portfolio investment in both decreases the risk level, leaving the return unchanged. The same idea can be used in examining whether diversification (of products or businesses) can lead to decreased risk. In effect, the forecaster needs to forecast not just the returns from different projects but their interrelationships as well. The problem remains one of identifying alternative investments that are not strongly positively correlated with your own. The difficulties associated with the portfolio approach do not negate the usefulness of seeking out countercyclical investments. The financial crisis of 2008–2012 was partially caused by the failure to recognize that asset returns had stronger positive correlations than was historically the case.

Organizational Flexibility: The time horizon of a forecast is made up of a number of distinct components: the time to gain information (the *information lead time*), the time to plan and execute a course of action (the *planning lead time*), and the time during which the action reaps its consequences (the *action lead time*). The first two of these are under the control of the organization. By increasing the speed at which internal information is made available and by increasing the organization's responsiveness to a problem, the need to forecast is minimized. Modern manufacturing has tried hard to cut lead times and improve flexibility, although outsourcing supply to distant countries such as China (for cost reasons) has had the opposite effect, increasing the need for forecasting. For research-based organizations such as pharmaceutical firms, organizational flexibility is only of limited help, in that the action lead time associated with patents is very long.

Discussion Question *Energy prices are expected to increase substantially over the next 20 years or longer. What are the major risks to U.S. (alternatively, German) energy supplies, and what approaches should the government consider to mitigate the risk? How should household consumers living in upstate New York (alternatively, southern England) mitigate their risk?*

In the end, in most organizational settings, none of these risk-controlling concepts overcomes the need to forecast; mostly they aim to lessen the risk of the endeavor without costing too much. Without accepting some degree of risk, there is usually little reward, so we turn now to how organizations should go about improving their forecasting performance.

13.4 # Improving Forecasting

The ultimate purpose of this book is to improve an organization's forecasting activities. This purpose includes as a primary objective making the forecasts more accurate through the approaches we have summarized in Section 13.1. But there are many additional issues to consider before improvements can be implemented within an organization, and there are many barriers to improvement to be overcome. Fildes and Hastings (1994) asked forecasters two key questions in their survey of company forecasters: What barriers did they see to improving forecasting (in their organization)? and what were their priorities for making such improvements? Tables 13.7 and 13.8 address these two points. Table 13.7 shows the respondents' level of agreement (agree, neutral, disagree) with the various statements given in column 1. For example, for statement 1, the typical response was to agree, with 72 percent of respondents falling into that class.

One important issue to note is the concern the respondents (all industry forecasters) had with their lack of training! The results are illustrative only of a particular organization at a point in time. But, linked to various current pieces of evidence, they support the view that at the heart of any improvements lies a forecast support system (which is available in principle but not in practice) that can deliver data together with easy-to-use techniques that combine judgment with statistical methods (Fildes and Hastings, 1994, Table 7). The use of a forecasting audit approach led to much the same set of priorities (Moon *et al.*, 2003). In the respondents' terminology, what is needed is improved functional integration (across marketing, finance, and operations), improved approaches (better methods of forecasting beyond the naïve ones), and better systems, as indicated in Table 13.8.

But there remain some major barriers to implementing improved approaches and systems, not to mention the perennial organizational problem of better functional integration.

TABLE 13.7   BARRIERS TO ADOPTING FORMAL FORECASTING METHODS: RESPONDENTS' ATTITUDES

Statement	Qualitative Response in Median Class	Response in Median Class
1. I do not have sufficient training in the use of formalized forecasting.	Agree	72%
2. The data available for forecasting are limited in detail or history.	Disagree	63%
3. No suitable database currently exists that is directly usable.	Disagree	63%
4. Judgmental techniques are more accurate than quantitative ones in my business.	Agree	56%
5. I tried formal techniques, but they failed to produce more accurate results	Neutral	53%
6. There is no help available to provide assistance in generating forecasts.	Neutral	44%
7. I am satisfied with the standard (or results) obtained by my existing methods.	Disagree	38%
8. I do not have sufficient time and/or resources to develop formal techniques.	Agree	38%

Source: Fildes and Hastings, 1994.

TABLE 13.8   POSSIBLE ACTIONS CONTRIBUTING TO IMPROVED
FORECASTING: PERCENTAGE OF RESPONDENTS
SCORING THE ACTION AS BENEFICIAL

Action	Percent Agreeing
Developing consistent data	83%
Increased software support	70%
Improved techniques or methods	66%
Improved databases	61%
Routine forecasting	48%
Improved communications with users	35%

Source: Fildes and Hastings, 1994.

Barriers to innovation, particularly in the context of information systems, have been a major research area, so we can draw on the findings. Also, some authors have paid particular attention to improving forecasting practice (Schultz, 1984, 1992).

Since we have identified the fact that new systems and better integrated databases across functional areas are priorities, we can refer to the work of Rogers (1995) and his many successors. In most companies, there are already systems (and forecasting support systems of a sort) in place. So, compatibility with existing practices (and systems) is one factor affecting the potential for improvement. The ability to test out a new forecasting process in a part of the organizational forecasting activity lessens the risk. The ability to communicate the essence of a new system and its complexity, both in learning to use it and in everyday operation, prove important. And crucially, there is the ability to demonstrate the value of the new systems and processes to deliver improved decision making.

But this list alone has often proved insufficient. We still rely on senior management to start the process of change: There needs to be an understanding at the top of the organization that improvements can be achieved. It seems to us that senior managers may be all too aware of the inadequacies of their forecasting systems but do not appreciate the fact that improvements are possible. Sometimes, however, the dissatisfaction is transformed into action by environmental events outside the forecasting activity. A common example is a situation in which changes in the information systems area, such as the implementation of a new enterprise resources planning (ERP) system, necessitate reconsideration of the FSS as well. The final point, communication, is concerned more with the success of the implementation; that success will depend on continuing support from senior management, but also on their relationship with the designers of the new system and on the implementation strategy that is pursued so that the organization's forecasters get the most from the new system.

Implementing Improvements in Forecasting

Implementing improved forecasting processes and systems requires that the new system:

- Be compatible with existing practices if possible.
- Has its risk managed by incremental adoption. Ideally, the system can be introduced sequentially in the organization.
- Be comprehensible, with its features easily communicated to those who will use it.
- Add demonstrable value above the current system.

13.5 Principles for Improving Forecasting

The rationale for the principles that follow has been established in the course of this chapter, so we do not elaborate further upon the supporting arguments.

[13.1] When planning a forecasting activity, work through the PHIVE stages (*Purpose*, forecast *Horizon*, *Information*, *Value*, and *Evaluation*) to establish an appropriate framework.

[13.2] Where quantitative methods are a practical alternative to judgmental approaches, use the quantitative approach.

[13.3] Where there is additional information available to the forecaster, adjust the quantitative forecast to take this information into account.

[13.4] Evaluate the performance of both quantitative forecasts and the finally adjusted forecast to determine both forecast quality and the effectiveness of the adjustments.

[13.5] Where there is a range of plausible forecasts, consider the use of a combined method to produce the final forecast.

[13.6] For an ongoing forecasting problem, monitor forecast errors in the important class-A series.

[13.7] Establish a base of operations for the forecasting team that enables it both to produce forecasts free of political pressure and to communicate effectively with decision makers and forecast users in other functional areas.

[13.8] As a forecaster, make sure that your organizational links are reliable in supplying you with key pieces of information. Also, make sure those who use your forecasts are aware of their value. A key issue for forecasters is how well connected they are to other parts of the organization. In particular, the boss of the forecasting unit needs to be made aware of the value of improved forecasting.

[13.9] Identify key risks through simulation or scenario analysis.

[13.10] Identify robust strategies for high-risk problems.

[13.11] Consider adopting insurance, portfolio approaches, and organizational flexibility in situations of high risk.

[13.12] Identify the barriers to improving forecasting practice when working in an organizational setting. Key barriers include lack of consistent data, poorly designed and implemented software, and lack of adequate training for the forecasting staff. Employ trained forecasters (or develop suitable training programs based on the information presented in this book!).

Summary

The focus of this book is on forecasting methods and the principles that lead to their effective application. However, the book would be incomplete without a discussion of forecasting practice and why organizational practice is often far removed from the idealized view frequently presented in more mathematical textbooks. In Section 13.1, we discussed the process most forecasters go through to produce their forecasts, from gathering relevant data to the last step of evaluating the final forecast. A crucial step in the journey is the selection of the appropriate forecasting method from the array of possible approaches we described in earlier chapters. Surveys show that organizational practice is too reliant on unstructured judgment. In Section 13.1, we discussed the methods forecasters in fact use and we summarized the strengths and weaknesses of those methods to aid in selection. The principle to remember is that different methods are appropriate in different applications. Often, the only route is through careful evaluation followed by monitoring forecast errors, the final topic of the section.

Section 13.2 took us further into the organizational issues surrounding forecasting—in particular, the biases that can result from political pressures and the importance of linking forecasting accuracy to the value of the forecasts to the decision maker.

Despite the advances in forecasting methodology over the past 30 years, residual uncertainty remains high for many important forecasting problems, so methods are needed to understand the consequences of uncertainty and develop policies to mitigate the worst effects of those consequences. Simulating the effects of uncertainty and developing robust strategies in the light of a range of scenarios was proposed. But that still leaves the case where risk remains high and better forecasting doesn't offer a way out. Here, various organizational strategies, including insurance, may be helpful. The chapter concluded with a discussion of how organizationally-based forecasting can be improved in practice. After all, the best methods in the world will never prove sufficient if people in organizations fail to put them to work.

Exercises

13.1 Putting yourself in the shoes of a new manager in charge of a call center forecasting activity, how would you establish a framework for forecasting incoming calls for the next eight weeks?

13.2 We developed several models for Netflix sales in Chapter 3. Use these fitted models to establish SCC and CCC charts for each model, and evaluate model performance in each case.

13.3 Monitoring and, if necessary, adjusting the forecast for a product in CleanCare, a producer of cleaning products, takes an hour of management time. Using the data set *Manufact.xlsx*, which contains monthly data on the initial statistical forecasts, the final management-adjusted forecasts, and the actual outcomes, devise an A–B–C, X–Y–Z categorization that, on average, would take no more a week (35 hours) of a forecaster's time to monitor.

13.4 Using the model and data in *Profit.xlsx* and risk analysis software, evaluate two different policies: (i) a policy wherein the price is decreased 10 percent if demand in the previous period is below 950 and increased by 10 percent if demand is above 1050 and (ii) a policy of an increased capacity of an additional 100 units, which is bought at an additional unit cost of $5. If the carry-over effect lies between 0.5 and 0.9, does that affect your views of these different policies?

13.5 Using the model in *Profit.xlsx*, comment on the comparative sensitivity of the *NPV* to the uncertain parameters. Make a reasonable assumption as to the uncertainty around the unit cost. Does this assumption affect our choice between a fixed price of $20 and policy (i) in Exercise 13.4?

Minicase 13.1 The Management of Call-Center Forecasting

In CreditBank, a new manager has recently been put in charge of the call center's forecasting support function. She is an accountant by background, and forecasting is just one part of her managerial responsibilities. However, there is pressure from senior management to improve accuracy. The new manager made some preliminary inquiries which suggested that the accuracy level for the core business of forecasting incoming account inquiries as measured by *MAPE* a week ahead was 22 percent. Her view from looking at cross-industry benchmarking studies was that 10 percent was a more satisfactory level, and she was confident that her manager would find that percentage acceptable. So she gave the forecasting group a month in which to improve its performance. Within the group, Mark A. had the responsibility of forecasting these calls, which was done with an industry standard package (based on exponential smoothing and weekly profiles of calls). The accuracy figure was calculated automatically from within the software. Data on the calls are given in the data set *Credit_call.xlsx*. What would you recommend that Mark A. do?

References

Adya, M., and Collopy, F. (1998). How effective are neural networks at forecasting and prediction? A review and evaluation. *Journal of Forecasting,* 17, 481–495.

Allen, P. G. and Fildes, R. (2001). Econometric forecasting. In J. S. Armstrong (ed.), *Principles of Forecasting: A Handbook for Researchers and Practitioners.* Boston and Dordrecht: Kluwer, pp. 303–362.

Alwan, L. C., and Roberts, H. V. (1988). Time-series modeling for statistical process control. *Journal of Business and Economic Statistics*, 6, 87–95.

Alwan, L. C., and Roberts, H. V. (1995). The problem of misplaced control limits. *Applied Statistics*, 44, 269–278.

Armstrong, J. S. (2001). Standards and practices in forecasting. In J. S. Armstrong (ed.), *Principles of Forecasting: A Handbook for Researchers and Practitioners.* Boston and Dordrecht: Kluwer.

Ashley, R. (1983). On the usefulness of macroeconomic forecasts as inputs to forecasting models. *Journal of Forecasting*, 2, 211–223.

Ashley, R. (1988). On the relative worth of recent macroeconomic forecasts. *International Journal of Forecasting*, 4, 363–376.

Brown, L. D. (1993). Earnings forecasting research: Its implications for capital markets research. *International Journal of Forecasting*, 9, 295–320.

Deschamps, E. (2004). The impact of institutional change on forecast accuracy: A case study of budget forecasting in Washington state. *International Journal of Forecasting*, 20, 647–657.

Deschamps, E. (2005). Six steps to overcome bias in the forecast process. *Foresight: The International Journal of Applied Forecasting*, 2, 5–11.

Fildes, R., and Goodwin, P. (2007). Against your better judgment? How organizations can improve their use of management judgment in forecasting. *Interfaces*, 37, 570–576.

Fildes, R., Goodwin, P., Lawrence, M., and Nikolopoulos, K. (2009). Effective forecasting and judgmental adjustments: An empirical evaluation and strategies for improvement in supply-chain planning. *International Journal of Forecasting*, 25, 3–23.

Fildes, R., and Hastings, R. (1994). The organization and improvement of market forecasting. *Journal of the Operational Research Society*, 45, 1–16.

Fildes, R., and Kingsman, B. (2011). Incorporating demand uncertainty and forecast error in supply chain planning models. *Journal of the Operational Research Society*, 62, 483–500.

Fildes, R., and Kourentzes, N. (2011). Validation and forecasting accuracy in models of climate change. *International Journal of Forecasting*, 27, 968–995.

Flyvbjerg, B, (2008). Curbing optimism bias and strategic misrepresentation in planning: Reference class forecasting in practice. *European Planning Studies*, 16, 3–21.

Galbraith, C. S., and Merrill, G. B. (1996). The politics of forecasting: Managing the truth. *California Management Review*, 38, 29–43.

Gardner, E. S., Jr. (2006). Exponential smoothing: The state of the art—Part II. *International Journal of Forecasting*, 22, 637–666.

Graefe, A., and Armstrong, J. S. (2011). Comparing face-to-face meetings, nominal groups, Delphi and prediction markets on an estimation task. *International Journal of Forecasting*, 27, 183–195.

Halkjelsvik, T., and Jørgensen, M. (2012). From origami to software development: A review of studies on judgment-based predictions of performance time. *Psychological Bulletin*, 138, 238–271.

Hogarth, R. M., and Makridakis, S. (1981). Forecasting and planning: An evaluation. *Management Science*, 27, 115–138.

Lawrence, M., Goodwin, P., O'Connor, M., and Onkal, D. (2006). Judgmental forecasting: A review of progress over the last 25 years. *International Journal of Forecasting*, 22, 493–518.

McCarthy, T. M., Davis, D. F., Golicic, S. L., and Mentzer, J. T. (2006). The evolution of sales forecasting management: A 20-year longitudinal study of forecasting practices. *Journal of Forecasting*, 25, 303–324.

Meade, N., and Islam, T. (2006). Modelling and forecasting the diffusion of innovation: A 25-year review. *International Journal of Forecasting*, 22, 519–545.

Moon, M. A., Mentzer, J. T., and Smith, C. D. (2003). Conducting a sales forecasting audit. *International Journal of Forecasting*, 19, 5–25.

Morwitz, V. G. (2001). Methods for forecasting with intentions data. In J. S. Armstrong (ed.), *Principles of Forecasting: A Handbook for Researchers and Practitioners*. Boston and Dordrecht: Kluwer, pp. 33–56.

Quinn, J. B. (1989). Strategic change: Logical incrementalism (reprint). *Sloan Management Review*, 30 (4), 45–60.

Rogers, E. M. 1995. *Diffusion of Innovations*. New York: Free Press.

Rowe, G., and Wright, G. (2001). Expert opinion in forecasting: The role of the Delphi technique. In J. S. Armstrong (ed.), *Principles of Forecasting: A Handbook for Researchers and Practitioners*. Boston and Dordrecht: Kluwer, pp. 125–144.

Sanders, N. R. and Graman, G. A. (2009). Quantifying costs of forecast errors: A case study of the warehouse environment. *Omega—International Journal of Management Science*, 37 (1), 116–125.

Sanders, N. R. and Manrodt, K. B. (2003). Forecasting software in practice: Use, satisfaction, and performance. *Interfaces*, 33, 90–93.

Schultz, R. L. (1984). The implementation of forecasting models. *Journal of Forecasting*, 3, 43–55.

Schultz, R. L. (1992). Fundamental-aspects of forecasting in organizations. *International Journal of Forecasting*, 7, 409–411.

Smith, J., and Clark, S. (2011). Who should own the business forecasting function? *Foresight: The International Journal of Applied Forecasting*, 20, 4–9.

Stock, J. H., and Watson, M. W. (2002). Forecasting using principal components from a large number of predictors. *Journal of the American Statistical Association*, 97, 1167–1179.

Tyebjee, T. T. (1987). Behavioral biases in new product forecasting. *International Journal of Forecasting*, 3, 393–404.

Wheelwright, S. C., and Clarke, D. G. (1976). Corporate forecasting: Promise and reality. *Harvard Business Review*, 54 (6), 40–64, 198.

Winklhofer, H., Diamantopoulos, A., and Witt, S. F. (1996). Forecasting practice: A review of the empirical literature and an agenda for future research. *International Journal of Forecasting*, 12, 193–221.

Zhang, G., Patuwo, B. E., and Hu, M. Y. (1998). Forecasting with artificial neural networks: The state of the art. *International Journal of Forecasting*, 14, 35–62.

Name Index

n denotes a footnote.

Subject Index